Data Management:

Databases and Organizations

Data Management:

Databases and Organizations

Third edition

Richard T. Watson
Department of MIS
Terry College of Business
The University of Georgia

John Wiley & Sons, Inc.

Acquisitions Editor	Beth L. Golub
Marketing Manager	Jessica Garcia
Assistant Editor	Cynthia Snyder
Senior Production Editor	Christine Cervoni
Photo Editor	Sarah Wright
Design Director	Madelyn Lesure
Cover Image	©Sean Ellis/Stone

This book was set in 10/12 Garamond by Richard and Ned Watson and printed and bound by Malloy Lithographing. Brady Palmer printed the cover.

This book was printed on acid-free paper. ∞

To order books or for customer service call
1-800-CALL-WILEY (225-5945)

ISBN 0-471-41845-5

Printed in the United States of America

10 9 8 7 6 5 4 3

To Clare

Preface

This is not your traditional database textbook. It differs in three fundamental ways.

First, it is deeper than most database books in its coverage of data modeling and SQL. The market seeks graduates who have these fundamental skills. Time and again, students who have completed my data management class have told me how these skills have been invaluable in their first job. The intention is to place great emphasis on the core skills of data management. The consequence is that there is a better match between the skills students develop and market needs. This means that students find this text highly relevant.

Second, the treatment of data modeling and SQL is intertwined because my database teaching experience indicates that students more readily understand the intent of data modeling when they grasp the long-term goal—querying a well-designed relational database. The double helix, upward, intertwined, spiraling of data modeling and SQL is a unique pedagogical feature. Classroom testing indicates it is a superior method of teaching compared to handling data modeling and SQL separately. Students quickly understand the reason for data modeling and appreciate why it is a valuable skill. Also, rapid exposure to SQL means students gain hands-on experience that much sooner.

Third, the book is broader than most database books. Databases are one component of an expansive organizational memory. Information systems professionals need to develop a wide perspective of data management if they are to comprehend fully the organizational role of information technology. Thus the book includes coverage of groupware (e.g., Lotus Notes), imaging systems, and the Web.

In essence, the book is deeper where it matters, data modeling and SQL, and broader to give students a managerial outlook.

Information is a key resource for modern organizations. It is a critical input to managerial tasks. Because managers need high-quality information to manage change in a turbulent, global environment, many organizations have established systems for storing and retrieving data, the raw material of information. These storage and retrieval systems are an organization's memory. The organization relies on them, just as individuals rely on their personal memory, to continue as a going concern.

The central concern of information systems management is to design, build, and maintain information delivery systems. Information systems management needs to discover its organization's information requirements so that it can design systems to serve these needs. It must merge a system's design and information technology to build an application that provides the organization with data in a timely manner, appropriate format, and at a convenient location. Furthermore, it must manage applications so they evolve to meet changing needs, continue to operate under adverse conditions, and are protected from unauthorized access.

An information delivery system has two components: data and processes. This book focuses on data, which is customarily thought of as a database. I deliberately set out to extend this horizon, however, by including all forms of organizational data stores because I believe students need to understand the role of data management that is aligned with current practice. In my view, data management is the design and maintenance of computer-based organizational memory. Thus, you will find a section devoted to data management technologies such as groupware and imaging systems.

The decision to start the book with a managerial perspective arises from the belief that successful information systems practice is based on matching managerial needs, social system constraints, and technical opportunities. I want readers to appreciate the *big picture* before they become immersed in the intricacies of data modeling and SQL. In line with this perspective, business stories are used to support and enhance the text. Many of these vignettes serve double duty because they also alert students to current economic trends such as the globalization of business and the growth of the service sector. To provide an international flavor, I selected organizational stories from a variety of nations. The broad, international, managerial approach is one of several innovative pedagogical features in a data management text.

The first chapter introduces the case study, *The Expeditioner*, which is used in most subsequent chapters to introduce the key themes discussed. Often it sets the scene for the ensuing material by presenting a common business problem. I hope the case study also injects a little humor.

The second section of the book provides in-depth coverage of data modeling and SQL. Data modeling is the foundation of database quality. A solid grounding in data modeling principles and extensive practice are necessary for successful database design. In addition, this book exposes students to the full power of SQL.

I intend this book to be a long-term investment for students. There are useful reference sections for data modeling and SQL. The data modeling section details the standard structures and their relational mappings. The SQL section contains an extensive list of queries that serves as a basis for developing other SQL queries. The purpose of these sections is to facilitate *pattern matching*. For example, a student with an SQL query that is similar to a previous problem can rapidly search the SQL reference section to find the closest match. The student can then use the model answer as a guide to formulating the SQL query for the problem at hand. These reference sections are another unique teaching feature that will serve students well during the course and in their subsequent careers.

Although I set out to cast data management in a new light, I have not ignored the traditional core of a database course. Section 3 presents database architectures and their implementation. Coverage includes data storage technologies, data and file structures, client/server models, distributed database, and object-oriented models. Naturally, this section reflects a managerial perspective and discusses the trade-offs for the various options facing the data manager.

In keeping with the organizational memory theme introduced in Chapter 1, Section 4 covers other information technologies including organizational intelligence technologies (data warehousing, OLAP, and data mining), the Web, and XML.

The final section examines the management of organizational data stores. The outstanding features of this section are the rigorous treatment of data integrity and data administration.

A student completing this text will

- have a broad, managerial perspective of an organization's need for a memory;
- be able to design and create a relational database;
- be able to formulate complex SQL queries;
- have a sound understanding of database architectures and their managerial implications;
- be familiar with the full range of information technologies available for organizational memory;
- understand the fundamentals of data administration;
- know about data management developments and their organizational implications.

My purpose is to create a data management text that is innovative, relevant, and lively. I trust that you will enjoy reading this book and learn a great deal about managing data in today's organization.

Supplements

Accompanying this book are an instructors' manual[1] and an extensive Web site[2] that provides

- overhead slides in PowerPoint format;
- all relational tables in the book in electronic format;
- answers to many of the exercises;
- additional exercises;
- revisions;
- links to useful Web sites.

Acknowledgments

The support of Beth Golub at John Wiley & Sons was much appreciated. I thank my son, Ned, for help with the typesetting and my wife, Clare, for indexing the book.

---

1. Instructors should contact the author <rwatson@terry.uga.edu> for the instructors' manual.
2. www.wiley.com/college/watson

I would like to thank my reviewers for their many excellent suggestions and ideas for improving the quality of the content and presentation of this book:

Michael Barrett	University of Alberta, Canada
John E. Boggess	Purdue University
John Bradley	East Carolina University
Traci Carte	University of Oklahoma
Patrick Michael Doran	Hawaii Pacific University
Mohammad Dadashzadeh	Wichita State University
George Federman	Santa Barbara City College
Colin Freeman	University of New South Wales, Australia
Lisa Friedrichsen	Keller Graduate School of Management
Mary Gebelt	Florida Atlantic University
Barbara Haley	University of Virginia
Herman P. Hoplin	Syracuse University
Mark Hwang	Central Michigan University
Lakshmi Iyer	University of Dayton
David Kemp	University of Melbourne, Australia
Someswar Kesh	Central Missouri State University
Constance A. Knapp	Pace University
Chris F. Kemerer	University of Pittsburgh
Shaoyi Liao	City University of Hong Kong, Hong Kong
Thomas Lucy-Bouler	Auburn University
Ronald Maier	University of Regensburg, Germany
Maggie McClintock	Mississippi University for Women
Scott McIntyre	University of Colorado
Anthony F. Norcio	University of Maryland
Bruce Rollier	University of Baltimore
Thomas E. Sandman	California State University—Sacramento
Avanti Sethi	Wichita State University
Liao Shaoyi	City University of Hong Kong, Hong Kong
Ramesh Subramanian	University of Alaska, Anchorage
Ramesh Venkataraman	Indiana University
Linda Volonino	Canisius College
Charles J. Wertz	Buffalo State College

I thank Tore Ørvik of Agder College, Norway, for his major contribution to the chapter on object-oriented database. His experience and knowledge of the object-oriented approach were most valuable.

My mate and colleague, Bob Bostrom of The University of Georgia, provided many insights and suggestions and contributed extensively to two chapters. His extremely thorough review of the first edition added considerable value. I am very grateful for his many contributions to this project.

Richard T. Watson

Brief Table of Contents

Table of Contents

Section 1

The Managerial Perspective

People only see what they are prepared to see.
Emerson, *Journals*, 1863

Organizations are accumulating vast volumes of data because of the implementation of technology (e.g., bar codes and scanners) that makes it easier and cheaper to collect data. The world's data are estimated to be doubling every 20 months, and many large companies now routinely manage terabytes (10^{12} bytes) of data. Data management has become a key function for many organizations.

The first section prepares you to see the role of data and information in an organization. The managerial perspective on data management concentrates on why organizations design and maintain data management systems, or organizational memories. Chapter 1 examines this topic by detailing the components of organizational memory and then discussing some of its common problems. The intention is to make you aware of the scope of data management and its many facets. Chapter 2 discusses the relationship between information and organizational goals. Again, a very broad outlook is adopted in order to provide a sweeping perspective on the relationship of information to organizational change.

At this point, we want to give you some *maps* for understanding the territory you will explore. Since the territory is possibly very new, these maps initially may be hard to read, and so you may need to read them several times before you understand the terrain you are about to enter.

The first map (see Figure S1-1) is based on the Newell-Simon model[1] of the human information processing system, which shows that humans receive input, process it, and produce output. The processing is done by a processor, which is linked to a memory divided into data and processes. The processor retrieves both data and processes from memory.

To understand this model, consider a person receiving a message to telephone a close friend. The message is input to the human information processing system. The person re-

1. Newell, A., and H.A. Simon. 1972. *Human problem solving*. Englewood Cliffs, NJ: Prentice-Hall.

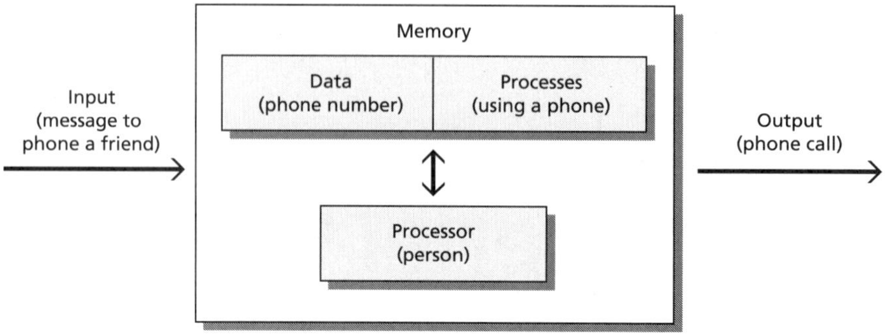

Figure S1-1. The Newell-Simon model of human information processing

trieves the friend's telephone number from memory and also retrieves the process, or instructions, for making a telephone call (e.g., pick up hand piece, press numbers, and so on). The person then makes the phone call, the processing of the input message. The phone call is the output. Sometimes these processes are so well ingrained in our memory that we never think about retrieving them, we just do it automatically.

Human information processing systems are easily overloaded. Our memory is limited, and our ability to process data is restricted; thus we use a variety of external tools to extend and augment our capacities. A telephone book is an example of external data memory. A recipe, a description of the process for preparing food, is an example of external process memory. Calculators and computers are examples of external processors we use to augment our limited processing capacity.

The original model of human information processing can be extended to include external memory, for storing data and processes, and external processors, for executing processes (see Figure S1-2).

This model of augmented human information processing translates directly to an organizational setting. Organizations collect inputs from the environment: market research, customer complaints, and competitor actions. They process these data and produce outputs: sales campaigns, new products, price changes, and so on. Figure S1-3 gives an example of how an organization might process data. As a result of some market research (input), a marketing analyst (an internal processor) retrieves sales data (data) and does a sale forecast (process). The analyst also requests a marketing consultant (an external processor) to analyze (process) some demographic data (data) before deciding to launch a new promotion (output).

An organization's memory comes in a variety of forms, as you will see in Chapter 1. This memory also can be divided into data and processes. The data part may contain information about customers. The process portion may store details of how to handle a customer order. Organizations use a variety of processors to handle data, including people and com-

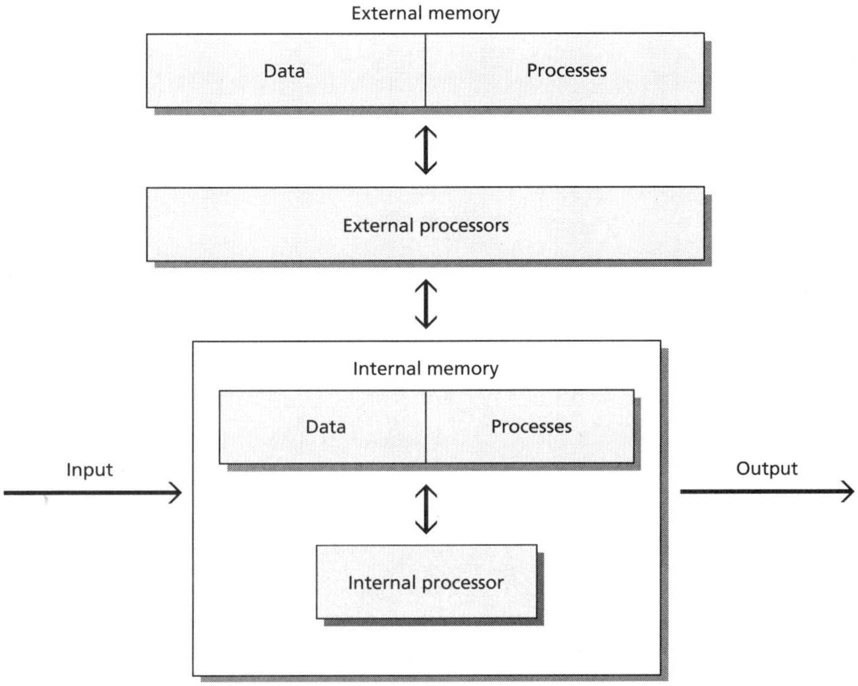

Figure S1-2. An augmented human information processing model

puters. Organizations also rely on external sources to extend their information processing capacity. For example, a business may use a specialist credit agency to check a customer's creditworthiness, or an engineering firm may buy time on a university's supercomputer for structural analysis of a bridge. Viewed this way, the augmented human information processing model becomes an organizational information processing system.

This book focuses on the data side of organizational memory. While it is primarily concerned with data stored within the organization, there is also coverage of data in external memory. The process side of organizational memory is typically covered in a systems analysis and design course.

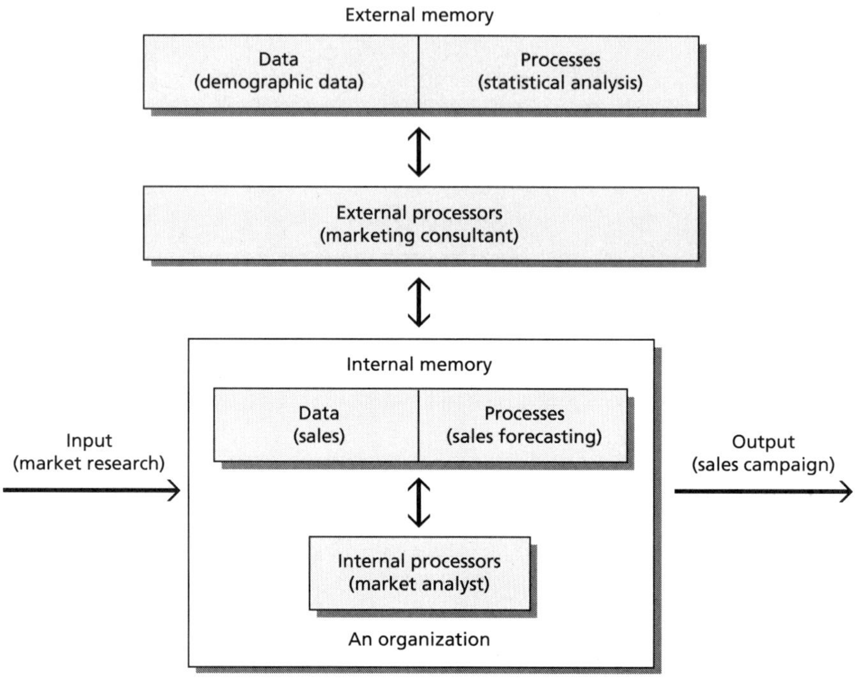

Figure S1-3. An organizational information processing model

1

Managing Data

All the value of this company is in its people. If you burned down all our plants, and we just kept our people and our information files, we should soon be as strong as ever.

Thomas Watson, Jr., former chairman of IBM[1]

Learning objectives

Students completing this chapter will

- understand the key concepts of data management;
- recognize that there are many components of an organization's memory;
- understand the problems with existing data management systems;
- realize that successful data management requires an integrated understanding of organizational behavior and information technology.

Introduction

Imagine what would happen to the bank that forgot who owed it money or the magazine that lost the names and addresses of its subscribers. Both would soon be in serious difficulty, if not out of business. Organizations have data management systems to record the myriad of details necessary for transacting business and making informed decisions. Societies and organizations have always recorded data. In some cases, the system is as simple as carving a notch in a stick to keep a tally, or as intricate as modern database technology. A memory system can be as personal as a to-do list or as public as a library.

The management of organizational data, generally known as **data management**, requires skills in designing, using, and managing the memory systems of modern organizations. It requires multiple perspectives. Data managers need to see the organization as a social system and to understand data management technology. The integration of these views, the sociotechnical perspective, is a prerequisite for successful data management.

---

1. As reported in Quinn, J. B. 1992. *Intelligent enterprise: A knowledge and service based paradigm for industry.* New York, NY: Free Press. p. 244.

Individuals also need to manage data. You undoubtedly are more familiar with individual memory management systems. They provide a convenient way of introducing some of the key concepts of data management.

Individual data management

As humans, we are well aware of our limited capacity to remember many things. The brain, our internal memory, can get overloaded with too much detail, and its memory decays with time. We store a few things internally: home and work telephone numbers, where we last parked our car, and faces of people we have met recently. We use external memory to keep track of those many things we know we should remember. External memory comes in a variety of forms.

We carry calendars to remind us of meetings and project deadlines. We have address books to record the addresses and phone numbers of those we contact frequently. We use to-do lists to remind us of the things we must do today or this week. The interesting thing about these aides-mémoire is that each has a unique way of storing data and supporting its rapid retrieval.

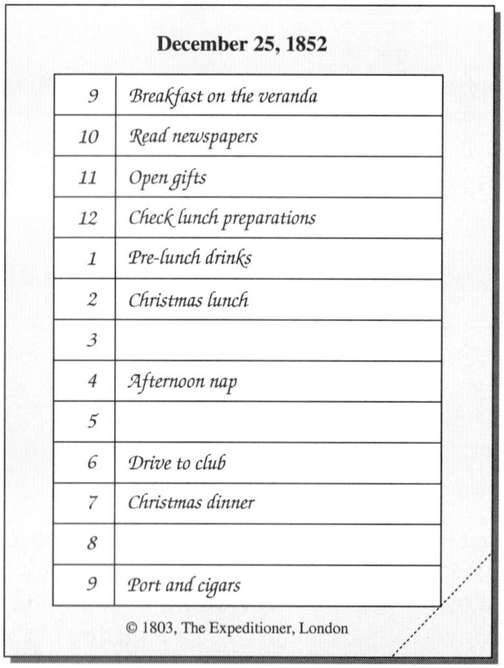

Figure 1-1. A calendar

Calendars (see Figure 1-1) come in many shapes and forms, but they are all based on the same organizing principle. A set amount of space is allocated for each day of the year, and the spaces are organized in date order, which supports rapid retrieval of any date. Some calendars have added features to speed up access. A bookmark can be used to mark the current date. Perforated tear-offs on the bottom right corner of the right-hand pages are often used to assist rapid location of current data.

Address books (see Figure 1-2) also have a standard format. They typically contain preprinted spaces for storing address details (e.g., name, street, city, zip, and phone). Another common feature is the use of alphabetic tabs to separate the sections. For example, if we are searching for Jack London, we first locate the L tab to find the appropriate set of pages on which to check more closely.

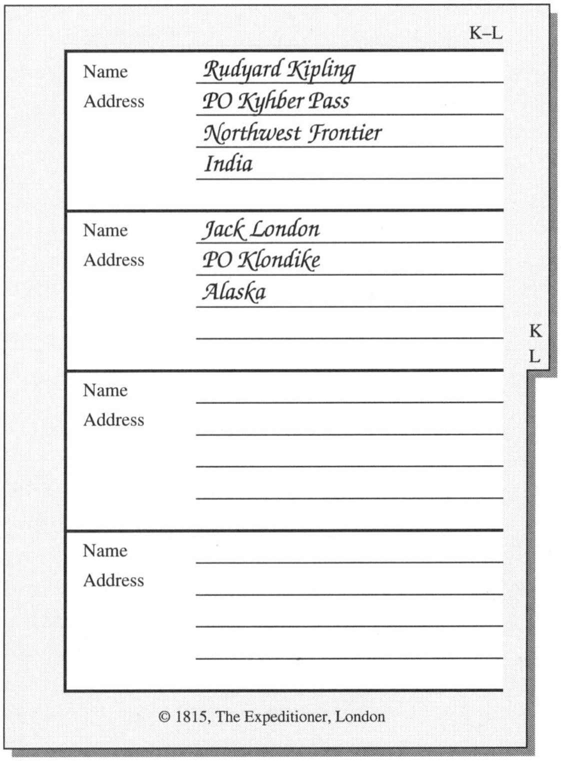

Figure 1-2. An address book

The structure of to-do lists (see Figure 1-3) tends to be fairly standard. They are often pads with ruled lines and a small left-hand margin. The idea is to write each item to be done on the right side of the page. The left side is used to check (✔) or mark those tasks that have been completed. The beauty of the check method is that you can quickly scan the left side to identify tasks yet uncompleted.

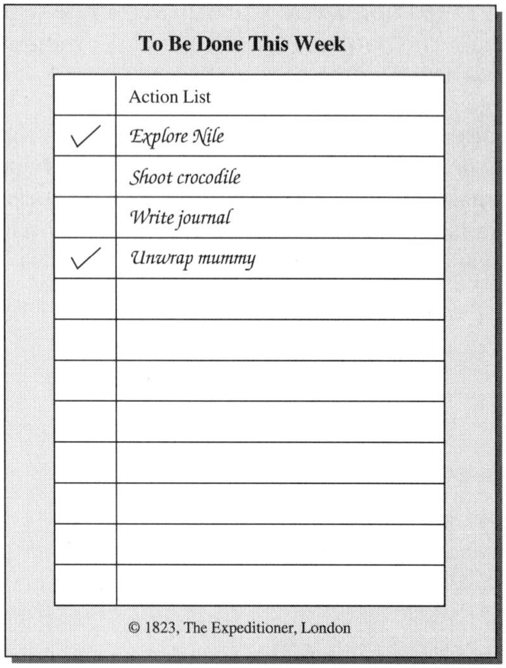

Figure 1-3. A to-do list

Many people use some form of the individual memory systems just described. They are frequently marketed as time management systems in business magazines. Stationery stores devote considerable space to them. Some of these systems are conveniently packaged into wallets containing a calendar, address book, to-do list pad, and other forms for individual memory support. Packaging figures prominently in the buyer's decision making because the buyer has to make a trade-off between the portability of pocket size and the spaciousness of desk size. Portability means reduced space for storing data. A spacious desk edition allows detailed record keeping but lacks the convenience of being easily portable.

These three examples of individual memory systems illustrate some features common to all data management systems:

- There is a storage medium. Data are written on paper in each of these examples.
- There is a structure for storing data. For instance, the address directory has labeled spaces for entering pertinent data.
- The storage device is organized for rapid data entry and retrieval. A calendar is in date sequence so that the data space for any date can be found quickly.
- The selection of a data management system frequently requires a trade-off decision. In this example, the trade-off is portability versus spaciousness.

There are differences between internal and external memories. Our internal memory is small, fast, and convenient (our brain is always with us — well, most of the time). External memory is large, slow, and not as convenient. The two systems are interconnected. We rely on our internal memory to access external memory. We need to remember that appointments are stored in a calendar. Our internal memory and our brain's processing skills manage the use of external memories. Again, we see some trade-offs. Ideally, we would like to store everything in our fast and convenient internal memory, but its limited capacity means that we are forced to use the larger, slower external memory for many items.

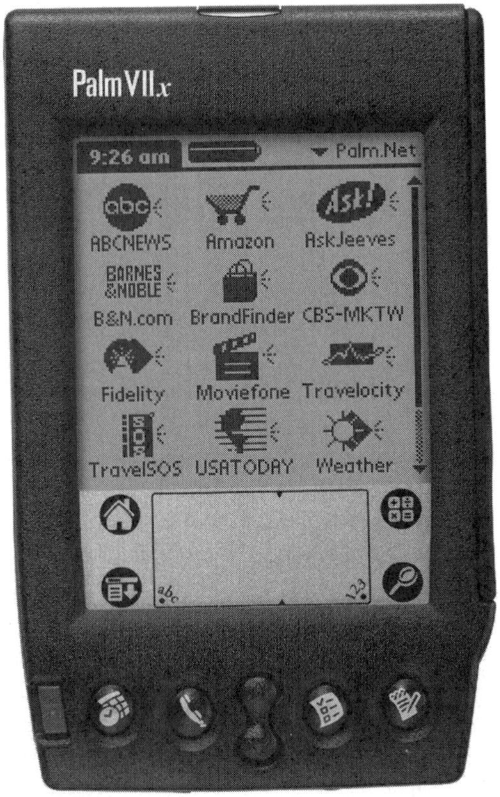

A personal digital assistant (an electronic individual memory system)

Organizational data management

Organizations, like people, need to remember many things. If you look around any office, you will see examples of the apparatus of organizational memory: people, filing cabinets, policy manuals, planning boards, and computers. The same principles found in individual memory systems apply to an organization's data management systems.

There is a storage medium. In the case of computers, the storage medium varies. Small files might be stored on a floppy disk and large, archival files on an optical disk. In Chapter 11, we discuss electronic storage media in more detail.

A table is a common structure for storing data. For example, if we want to store details of customers, we can set up a table with each row containing individual details of a customer and each column containing data on a particular feature (e.g., customer code).

Storage devices are organized for rapid data entry and retrieval. Time is the manager's enemy: too many things to be done in too little time. Because customers expect rapid responses to their questions and quick processing of their transactions, rapid data access is a key goal of nearly all data management systems. Rapid access always comes at a price, however. Fast access memories cost more, so there is nearly always a trade-off between access speed and cost.

As you will see, selecting *how* and *where* to store organizational data frequently involves a trade-off. Data managers need to know and understand what the trade-offs entail. They must know the key questions to ask when evaluating trade-offs.

When we move from individual to organizational memory, some other factors come into play. To understand these factors, we need to review the different types of information systems. The automation of routine business transactions was the earliest application of information technology to business. A **transaction processing system** (TPS) handles common business tasks such as accounting, inventory, purchasing, and sales. The realization that the data collected by these systems could be sorted, summarized, and rearranged gave birth to the notion of a **management information system** (MIS). Furthermore, it was recognized that when internal data captured by a TPS is combined with appropriate external data, the raw material was available for a **decision support system** (DSS) or **executive information system** (EIS). Recently, **on-line analytic processing** (OLAP) and **data mining** have emerged as advanced data analysis techniques for data captured by business transactions and gathered from other sources (these systems are covered in detail in Chapter 14). The purpose of each of these systems is described in Table 1-1, and their interrelationship can be understood by examining the information systems cycle.

Table 1-1: Types of information systems

Type of information system	System's purpose
Transaction processing system TPS	Collects and stores data from routine transactions
Management information system MIS	Converts data from a TPS into information for planning, controlling, and managing an organization
Decision support system DSS	Supports managerial decision making by providing models for processing and analyzing data
Executive information system EIS	Provides senior management with information necessary to monitor organizational performance and develop and implement strategies
On-line analytical processing OLAP	Presents a multidimensional, logical view of data
Data mining	Uses statistical analysis and artificial intelligence techniques to identify hidden relationships in data

The information systems cycle

The various systems and technologies found in an organization are linked in a cycle (see Figure 1-4). The routine ongoing business of the organization is processed by TPSs, the systems that handle the present. Data collected by TPSs are stored in databases, a record of the past, the history of the organization and its interaction with buyers, suppliers, and others with whom it conducts business. These data are converted into information by analysts using a variety of software (e.g., a DSS). The common feature of these technologies is that they are used by the organization to prepare for the future (e.g, sales in Finland have expanded, so we will build a new service center in Helsinki). The business systems created to prepare for the future determine the transactions the company will process and the data collected. And the process continues. The entire cycle is driven by people using technology (e.g., sales personnel using POS terminals, data administrators designing databases, and business analysts using data mining to fashion new marketing systems).

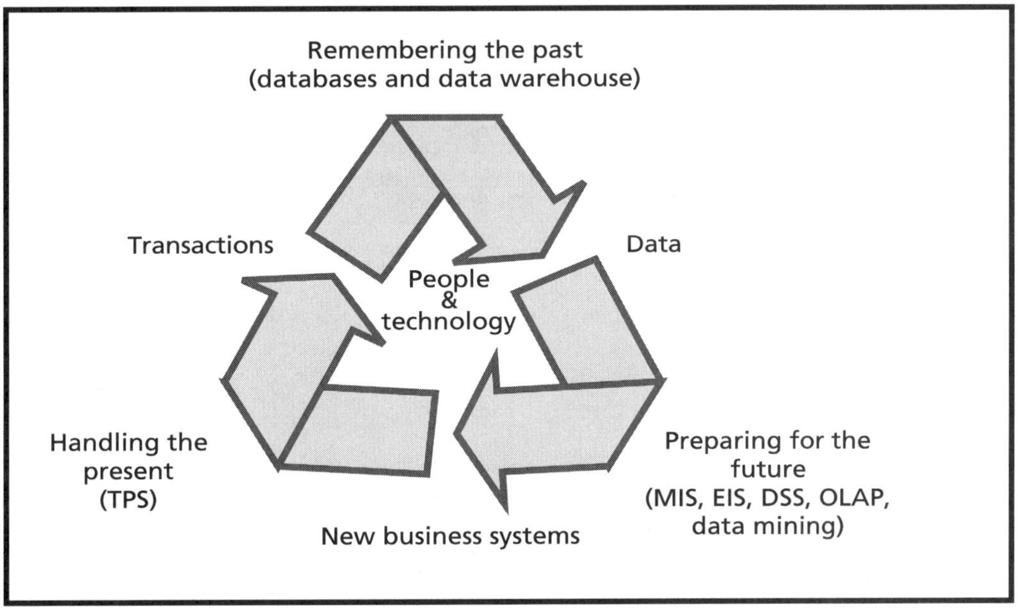

Figure 1-4. The information systems cycle

Decision making, or preparing for the future, is the central activity of modern organizations.[2] Today's organizations are busy turning out goods, services, and decisions. Knowledge and information workers, 55 percent of the U.S. labor force, produce 60 percent of the GNP.[3] Many of these people are decision makers. Their success, and their organization's success, depend on the quality of their decisions.

2. Huber, G. P., and R. R. McDaniel. 1986. The decision-making paradigm of organizational design. *Management Science* 32 (5):572–589.
3. Laudon, K. C., and J. P. Laudon. 1998. *Management Information Systems: New approaches to organization and technology*. 5th ed. Upper Saddle River, NJ: Prentice-Hall. p. 552.

Industrial society was a producer of goods, and the hallmark of success was product quality. Japanese manufacturers convincingly demonstrated that focusing on product quality was the key to market leadership and profitability. The methods and the philosophy of quality gurus, such as Deming, have been internationally recognized and adopted by many providers of goods and services. As we make the transition from an industrial society to one based on knowledge and services, the key determinant of success is likely to shift from product quality to decision quality. In the turbulent environment of global business, successful organizations will be those able to make high-quality decisions quickly.

Attributes of data

Once we realize the critical importance of data to organizations, we can recognize some desirable attributes of data (see Table 1-2).

Table 1-2: Desirable attributes of data

Shareable	Readily accessed by more than one person at a time
Transportable	Easily moved to a decision maker
Secure	Protected from destruction and unauthorized use
Accurate	Reliable, precise records
Timely	Current and up-to-date
Relevant	Appropriate to the decision

Shareable

Organizations contain many decision makers. There are occasions when more than one person will require access to the same data at the same time. For example, in a large bank it would not be uncommon for two customer representatives simultaneously to want data on the latest rate for a three-year certificate of deposit.

Organizations use a wide variety of approaches to handle the need for shareability. The success of these methods depends very much on the volatility of the data, the rate at which they change. Low-volatility data are often printed, bound, and distributed as a book. This way, each potential user has a copy. Telephone books and policy manuals are examples of low-volatility organizational memories. As data become more volatile, shareability becomes more of a problem. For instance, consider a restaurant. The permanent menu is printed, today's special might be displayed on a blackboard, and the waiter tells you what is no longer available.

Transportable

Data should be transportable from its storage location to the decision maker. Technologies that transport data have a long history. Homing pigeons were used to relay messages by the Egyptians and Persians 3,000 years ago. The telephone revolutionized business and social life because it rapidly transmitted voice data. Fax machines have accelerated organizational correspondence because they transport both text and visual data. Computers have changed the nature of many aspects of business because they enable the transport of text, visual, and voice data.

Today, transportability is more than just getting data to a decision maker's desk. It means getting product availability data to a salesperson in a client's office or advising a delivery driver, en route, of address details for an urgent parcel pickup. The general notion is that decision makers should have access to relevant data whenever and wherever required, although most organizations are a long way from reaching this target.

Secure

In a post industrial society, data are a highly valuable resource. As we have already learned, data support day-to-day business transactions and decision making. Because the forgetful organization will soon be out of business, organizations are very vigilant in protecting their data. There are a number of actions that organizations take to protect data against loss, sabotage, and theft. A common approach is to duplicate data and store the copy, or copies, at other locations. This technique is popular for data stored in computer systems. Access to data is often restricted through the use of physical barriers (e.g., a vault) or electronic barriers (e.g., a password). Another approach, which is becoming popular with knowledge workers, is a noncompetitive contract. For example, some software companies legally restrain computer programmers from working for a competitor for two years after they leave, hoping to prevent the transfer of valuable data, in the form of the programmer's knowledge of software, to competitors.

Accurate

You probably remember students who excelled in exams because of their good memory. Similarly, organizations with an accurate memory will do better than their less precise competitors. Organizations need to remember many details accurately. For example, an airline needs accurate data to predict the demand for each of the many flights it flies in a year. The quality of decision making will drop dramatically if managers use a data management system riddled with errors.

Polluted data threatens a firm's profitability. One study[4] suggests that missing, wrong, and otherwise bad data cost U.S. firms billions of dollars annually. The consequences of bad data include improper billing, cost overruns, delivery delays, and product recalls. In 1990, a major New York securities firm lost more than $200 million because of a data entry error in a risk management system. Because data accuracy is so critical, organizations need to be watchful when capturing data, the point at which data accuracy is most vulnerable.

Timely

The value of data is often determined by their age. You can fantasize about how rich you would be if you knew tomorrow's stock prices. Although decision makers are most interested in current data, the required currency of data can vary with the task. Operational

4. Knight, B. 1992.The data pollution problem. *Computerworld*, 81, 83.

managers often want real-time data. They want to tap the pulse of the production line so that they can react quickly to machine breakdowns or quality slippages. In contrast, strategic planners might be content with data that are months old because they are more concerned with detecting long-term trends.

Relevant

Organizations must maintain data that are relevant to transaction processing and decision making. When processing a credit card application, the most relevant data might be the customer's credit history, current employment status, and income level. Hair color would be irrelevant. When assessing the success of a new product line, a marketing manager probably wants an aggregate report of sales by marketing region. A voluminous report detailing every sale would be irrelevant. Data are relevant when they pertain directly to the decision and are aggregated appropriately.

Relevance is a key concern in designing a data management system. Users have to decide what should be stored because it is pertinent now or could have future relevance. Of course, identifying data that might be relevant in the future is difficult, and there is a tendency to accumulate too much. Relevance is also an important consideration when extracting and processing data from a data management system. Provided the pertinent data are available, then query languages can be used to aggregate data appropriately.

In the final years of the twentieth century, organizations started to move much of their data, both high and low volatility, to the Web. This move has increased shareability, timeliness, and availability, and has lowered the cost of distributing data.

In summary, a data management system for maintaining an organization's memory supports transaction processing, remembering the past, and decision making. Its contents must be shareable, secure, and accurate. Ideally, users of a data management system must be able to get timely and relevant data when and where required. A major challenge for data management professionals is to create data management systems that meet these criteria. Unfortunately, many existing systems fail in this regard, though we can understand some of the reasons why by reviewing the components of existing organizational memory systems.

Components of organizational memory

An organization's memory[5] resides on a variety of media in a variety of ways. It is in people, standard operating procedures, roles, organizational culture, physical storage equipment, and electronic devices. It is scattered around the organization, a jigsaw designed by Salvador Dali.[6] The pieces don't fit together, they sometimes overlap, there are gaps, and there are no edge pieces to define the boundaries. Organizations struggle to design

5. For an advanced treatment of organizational memories, see Walsh, James P., and Gerardo Rivera Ungson. 1991. Organizational memory. *Academy of Management Review* 16 (1):57–91.
6. The Spanish painter Salvador Dali (1904 - 1989) was a leader of surrealism with a declared ambition to *systemize confusion*.

structures and use data management technology to link some of the pieces. To understand the complexity of this wicked puzzle, we need to examine some of the pieces (see Figure 1-5). Data managers have a particular need to understand the different forms of organizational memory because their activities often influence a number of the components.

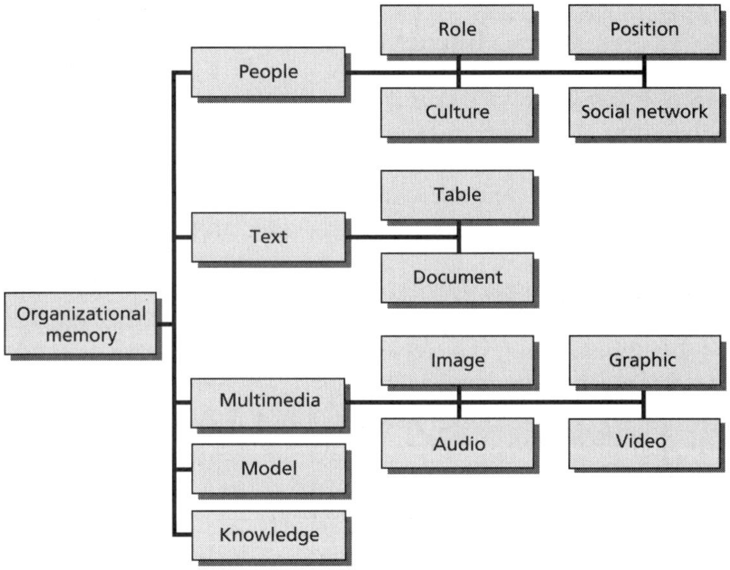

Figure 1-5. Components of organizational memory

People

People are the linchpin of an organization's memory. They recall previous decisions and business actions. They create, maintain, evolve, and use data management systems. They are the major component of an organization's memory because they know how to use all the other components. People extract data from the various components of organizational memory to provide as complete a picture of a situation as possible.

Each person in an organization has a **role** and a **position** in the hierarchy. Role and position are both devices for remembering how the organization functions and how to process data. By labeling people (e.g., Chief Information Officer) and placing their names on an organizational chart, the organization creates another form of organizational memory.

Organizational culture is the shared beliefs, values, attitudes, and norms that influence the behavior and expectations of each person in an organization. A long-lived, stable memory system, culture determines acceptable behavior and influences decision making.

People develop skills for doing their particular job and learning what to do, how to do it, and who can help them get things done. For example, they might discover someone in employee benefits who can handle personnel problems or a contact in a computer company who can answer questions promptly. These **social networks**, which often take years to develop, are used to make things happen and to learn about the business environment. Despite their high value, they are rarely documented, at least not beyond an address book or Rolodex, and are typically lost when a person leaves an organization.

Office chitchat is informal learning

Researchers report that informal learning occurs in more than a dozen ways, including teamwork, observation, and meetings, and plays a significant role in how individuals learn how to do their jobs. The findings have "profound implications on corporate culture, worker satisfaction, productivity, and improving the rate of innovation," according to Monica Aring, co-director of the research project.

The study, completed in January 1998, was based on in-depth research involving more than 1,000 employees at seven companies in seven states. "At the companies studied," Aring said, "researchers found that informal learning was widespread and served to fulfill most learning needs, perhaps as much as 70 percent. In general, we noted that informal learning was highly relevant to employee needs and involved knowledge and skills that were attainable and immediately applicable," she said. The research results are particularly relevant to companies coping with rapidly changing technology because they illustrate the role of informal learning.

While formal on-the-job training and informal learning augment each other, they are distinct. With formal training, the process of learning is determined by the company. The researchers found that with informal learning, it is not. Job skills often come from a combination of formal and informal training. Skills such as critical thinking, learning to provide constructive feedback, working as a team member, and understanding company goals are typically learned informally.

The researchers identified 13 work-related activities during which most informal learning occurs. These include teamwork, meetings, customer interactions, mentoring, and office chitchat.

Source: http://pogo.edc.org/CWD/press.htm

Conversations are an important method for knowledge workers to create, modify, and share organizational memory, and a way to build relationships and social networks. Discussions with customers are a key device for learning how to improve an organization's products and services and learning about competitors. The *conversational company* can detect change faster and react more rapidly. The telephone, fax, e-mail, coffee machine, cocktail hour, and cafeteria are all devices for promoting conversation and creating networks. Some firms deliberately create structures for supporting conversations and to make the people component of organizational memory more effective.

Standard operating procedures exist for many organizational tasks. Processing a credit application, selecting a marketing trainee, and preparing a departmental budget are typical procedures that are clearly defined by many organizations. They are described in procedure manuals, computer programs, and job specifications. They are the way an organization remembers to perform routine activities.

Successful people learn how to use organizational memory. They learn what data are stored where, how to retrieve them, and how to put them together. In promoting a new product, a salesperson might send the prospect a package containing some brochures and a copy of a product review in a trade journal, and supply the phone number and e-mail address of the firm's technical expert for that product. People's recall of how to use organizational memory is the core component of organizational memory. Academics call this **metamemory**; people in business call it *learning the ropes*. New employees spend a great deal of time building their metamemory so that they can use organizational memory effectively. Without this knowledge, organizational memory would have little value.

Tables

A table is a common form of storing organizational data. Table 1-3 shows a price list in tabular form. Often, the first row defines the meaning of data in subsequent rows.

Table 1-3: A price list

Product	Price
Pocket knife–Nile	4.50
Compass	10.00
Geo-positioning system	500.00
Map measure	4.90

A table is a general form that describes a variety of other structures used to store data. Computer-based files are tables or can be transformed into tables; the same is true for general ledgers, worksheets, and spreadsheets. Accounting systems make frequent use of tables. Card files can be readily transformed into tables. Each card becomes one row, and each data value on the card (e.g., the item's name) becomes a column (see Figure 1-6). As you will discover in the next section, the table is the central structure of the relational database model.

Data stored in tables typically have certain characteristics:

- Data in one column are of the same type. For example, each cell of the column headed price contains a number. (Of course, the exception is the first row of each column, which contains the title of the column.)
- Data are limited by the width of available space. Usually each item is less than 20 characters and rarely more than 50.

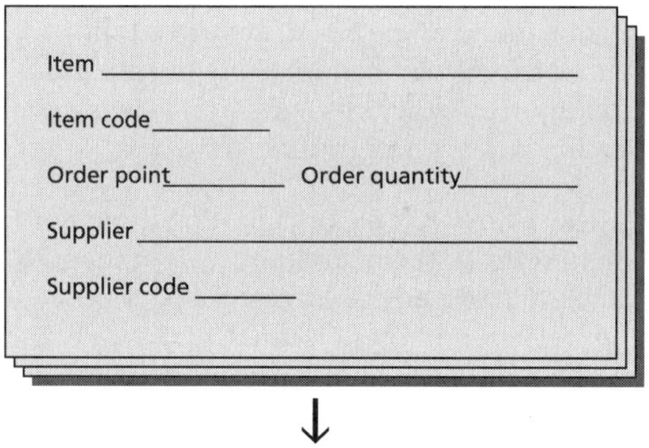

Item	Item code	Order point	Order quantity	Supplier	Supplier code
...	...	...	...	...	...

Figure 1-6. Transforming a card file to table format

Rapid searching is one of the prime advantages of a table. For example, if the price list is sorted by product name, you can quickly find the price of any product.

Tables are a common form of storing organizational data because their structure is readily understood. People learn to read and build tables in the early years of their schooling. Also, a great deal of the data organizations want to remember can be stored in tabular form. As you will see, tables are the building blocks of a relational database system.

Documents

The document, of which reports, manuals, brochures, and memos are examples, is a common medium for storing organizational data. Although documents may be subdivided into chapters, sections, paragraphs, and sentences, they lack the regularity and discipline of a table. Each row of a table has the same number of columns, but each paragraph of a document does not have the same number of sentences.

Most documents are now stored electronically. Because of the widespread use of word processing, text files are a common means of storing documents. Typically, such files are read sequentially like a book. Although there is support for limited searching of the text, such as finding the next occurrence of a specified text string, text files are usually processed linearly.

Hypertext. the familiar linking technology of the Web, supports nonlinear document processing. A hypertext document has built-in linkages between sections of text that permit the reader to jump quickly from one part to another. As a result, readers can find data they require more rapidly.

Although hypertext is certainly more user-friendly than a flat, sequential text file, it takes time and expertise to establish the links between the various parts of the text. Someone familiar with the topic has to decide what should be linked and then establish these links. While it takes the author more time to prepare a document this way, the payoff is the speed at which readers of the document can find what they want.

Multimedia

The introduction of the Web has spurred interests in storing multimedia objects, such as sound and video clips. Automotive company Web sites have video clips of cars, music outlets provide sound clips of new releases, and clothing companies have on-line catalogs displaying photos of their latest products. Maintaining a Web site, because of the many multimedia objects that some sites contain, has become a significant data management problem for some organizations (see Chapter 15 for an in-depth coverage of this topic). Consider the different types of data that CNN has to store to provide a timely, informative, and engaging Web site.

Images

Images are visual data: photographs and sketches. Image banks are maintained for several reasons. First, images are widely used for identification and security. Police departments keep fingerprints and mug shots. Second, images are used as evidence. Highly valuable items such as paintings and jewelry often are photographed for insurance records. Third, images are used for advertising and promotional campaigns, and organizations need to maintain records of material used in these ventures. Image archiving and retrieval are essential for mail order companies, which often produce several photo-laden catalogs every year. Fourth, some organizations specialize in selling images and maintain extensive libraries of clip art and photographs.

Graphics

Maps and engineering drawings are examples of electronically stored graphics. An organization might maintain a map of sales territories and customers. Manufacturers have extensive libraries of engineering drawings that define the products they produce. Graphics often contain a high level of detail. An engineering drawing will define the dimensions of all parts and may refer to other drawings for finer detail about any component of a subassembly.

A graphic differs from an image in that it contains explicitly embedded data. Consider the difference between an engineering plan for a widget and a photograph of the same item. An engineering plan shows dimensional data and may describe the composition of the various components. The embedded data are used to manufacture the widget. A photograph of a widget does not have embedded data and contains insufficient data to manufacture the product. An industrial spy will receive far more for an engineering plan than for a photograph of a widget.

Geographic information systems (GIS) are specialized graphical storage systems for geographic data. The underlying structure of a GIS is a map on which data are displayed. A power company can use a GIS to store and display data about its power grid and the location of transformers. Using a pointing device, such as a mouse, an engineer can click on a transformer's location to display a window of data about the transformer (e.g., type, capacity, installation date, and repair history). GISs have found widespread use in governments and organizations that have geographically dispersed resources.

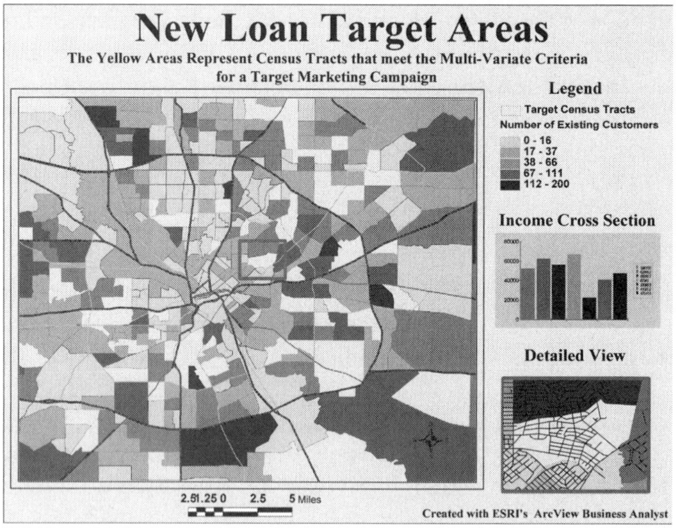

A geographic information system (GIS)

Audio

CD customers usually prefer to hear a sample of a CD prior to purchase. Music producers, such as Sony, enable prospective purchasers to hear audio clips of new CDs. National Public Radio (NPR) stores some of its special broadcasts in an archive that is accessible via the Web.

Some firms conduct a great deal of their business by phone. In many cases, it is important to maintain a record of the conversation between the customer and the firm's representative. The Royal Hong Kong Jockey Club, which covers horse racing gambling in Hong Kong, records all conversations between its operators and customers. Phone calls are stored on a highly specialized voice recorder, which records the time of the call and other data necessary for rapid retrieval. In the case of a customer dispute, an operator can play back the original conversation.

Video

A video clip can give a potential customer additional detail that cannot be readily conveyed by text or a still image. Consequently, some auto companies now use video and virtual reality to promote their cars. Visit the Honda Web site and view a video clip of the Accord or rotate an image to view the car from all angles.

Models

Organizations build mathematical models to describe their business. These models, usually placed in the broader category of DSS, are then used to analyze existing problems and forecast future business conditions. A mathematical model can often produce substantial benefits to the organization.

Knowledge

Organizations build systems to capture the knowledge of their experienced decision makers and problem solvers. This expertise is typically represented as a set of rules, semantic nets, and frames in a knowledge base, another form of organizational memory.

Decisions

Decision making is the central activity of modern organizations. Very few organizations, however, have a formal system for recording decisions. Most keep the minutes of meetings, but these are often very brief and record only a meeting's outcome. Because they do not record details such as the objectives, criteria, assumptions, and alternatives that were considered prior to making a decision, there is no formal audit trail for decision making. As a result, most organizations rely on humans to remember the circumstances and details of prior decisions.

Specialized memories

Because of the particular nature of their business, some organizations maintain memories rarely found elsewhere. Perfume companies, for instance, maintain a library of scents, and paint manufacturers and dye makers catalog colors.[7]

External memories

Organizations are not limited to their own memory stores. There are firms whose business is to store data for resale to other organizations. Such businesses have existed for many years and are growing as the importance of data in a postindustrial society expands. Lawyers, using Mead Data Central's LEXIS, can access the laws and court decisions of all 50 American states and the U.S. federal government. Similar legal data services exist in many other nations. There is a range of other services that provide news, financial, business, scientific, and medical data.

---

7. For a fascinating story of one man's highly specialized memory, read Langewiesche, W. 2000. The million-dollar nose. *The Atlantic Monthly* 286 (6), http://www.theatlantic.com/issues/2000/12/langewiesche.htm.

First change the organization

Charlie Feld is an IT firefighter. He parachutes into a firm to become its CIO for two or three years to sort out major IT problems. He has spent time as acting CIO at large firms such as Delta Air Lines, Burlington Northern and Santa Fe Railway Company, and Westinghouse.

Mr. Feld does more than fix technology. His main task is to create the right organization for the new IT system. Unless you do that, he says, "the inertia of an organization makes you end up with just another ugly IT animal."

McKinsey & Co. believes both software vendors and their customers could save themselves a lot of money by paying more attention to the organizational aspects of introducing new technology. In a study of a clothing retailer's investment in supply-chain software, McKinsey found that the program yielded savings of $15 million a year, but that another $55 million of potential savings was left on the table because the firm did not make changes in its organizational structure, business processes, and incentives.

Source: Anonymous. 2001. Even the best software won't work without organizational change. *The Economist*, Apr. 12, http://www.economist.com/displayStory.cfm?Story_ID=568313.

Problems with data management systems

Successful management of data is a critical skill for nearly every organization. Yet, few have gained completed mastery, and there are a variety of problems that typically afflict data management in most firms (see Table 1-4).

Table 1-4: Problems with organizational data management systems

Redundancy	Same data stored in different systems
Lack of data control	Data are poorly managed
Poor interface	Difficult to access data
Delays	There are frequently long delays to requests for data
Lack of reality	Data management systems do not reflect the complexity of the real world
Lack of data integration	Data are dispersed across different systems

Redundancy

In many cases, data management systems have grown haphazardly. As a result, it is often the situation that the same data are stored in several different memories. The classic example is a customer's address, which might be stored in the sales reporting system, accounts receivable system, and the salesperson's telephone book. The danger is that when the customer changes address, the amendment is not recorded in all systems. Data redundancy causes additional work because the same item must be entered several times. Redundancy causes confusion when what is supposedly the same item has different values.

Lack of data control

Allied with the redundancy problem is poor data control. Although data are an important organizational resource, they frequently do not receive the same degree of management attention as other important organizational resources such as people and money. Organizations have a personnel department to manage human resources and a treasury to handle cash. The MIS department looks after data captured by the computer systems they operate, but there are many other data stores scattered around the organization. Data are stored everywhere in the organization (e.g., on personal computers and in departmental filing systems), but there is a general lack of data management. This is particularly surprising since many pundits claim that data are a key competitive resource.

Poor interface

Too frequently, potential users of data management systems have been deterred by an unfriendly interface. The computer dialogue for accessing a data store is sometimes difficult to remember for the occasional user. People become frustrated and give up because their queries are rejected and error messages are unintelligible. Fortunately, the widespread adoption of the Web browser as the interface to many applications has alleviated the problem to some degree.

Long delays in responding to data requests

Globalization and technology have accelerated the pace of business in the last decade. Managers must make more decisions more rapidly. They cannot afford to wait for programmers to write special-purpose programs to retrieve data and format reports. They expect their questions to be answered rapidly, often within a day and sometimes more quickly. Managers, or their support personnel, need query languages that provide rapid access to the data they need in a format that they want.

Unable to answer questions about the real world

Organizational data stores must reflect the reality and complexity of the real world. Consider a typical bank customer who might have a personal checking account, mortgage account, credit card account, and some certificates of deposit. When a customer requests an overdraft extension, the bank officer needs full details of the customer's relationship with the bank in order to make an informed decision. If customer data are scattered across unrelated data stores, then these data are not easily found and in some cases important data might be overlooked. The request for full customer details is reasonable and realistic, and the bank officer should expect to be able to enter a single, simple query to obtain it. Unfortunately, this is not always the case, because data management systems do not always reflect reality.

In this example, the reality is that the personal checking, mortgage, and credit card accounts, and certificates of deposit all belong to one customer. If the bank's data management system does not record this relationship, then it does not mimic reality. This makes it impossible to retrieve a single customer's data with a single, simple query.

Many organizations have highly fragmented memories. Systems, developed piecemeal over decades, are incompatible. It can cost considerable time and resources to overcome systems incompatibilities to build integrated systems that fully support business needs.

A data management system must meet the decision-making needs of managers, who must be able to request both routine and ad hoc reports. In order to do so effectively, a data management system must reflect the complexity of the real world. If it does not store required organizational data or record a real world relationship between data elements, then many managerial queries cannot be answered quickly and efficiently.

Lack of data integration

There is a general lack of data integration in most organizations. Data are not only dispersed in different forms of organizational memory (e.g., files and image stores), but even within the one storage format there is often a lack of integration. For example, many organizations maintain file systems that are not integrated. Appropriate files in the accounting system may not be linked to the production system.

This lack of integration will be a continuing problem for most organizations for two important reasons. First, early computer systems were not integrated, because of the limitations of available technology. Organizations created simple file systems to support a particular function. Many of these systems are still in use. Second, integration is a long-term goal. As new systems are developed and old ones rewritten, and with the switch to newer database technology, organizations can evolve integrated systems. It would be too costly and disruptive to try to solve the data integration problem in one step.

Many data management problems can be solved with present technology. Data modeling and relational database technology, topics covered in Section 2, help overcome many of the current problems. In addition, object-oriented database systems (see Chapter 13) promise to address some data management problems not handled well by relational technology.

A brief history of data management systems

Data management is not a new problem. It is an old problem that has become more significant, important, and critical because of the emergence of data as a critical resource for effective performance in the modern economy. Organizations have always needed to manage their data so they could remember a wide variety of facts necessary to conduct business. The recent history of data managements systems is depicted in Figure 1-7.

File systems were the earliest form of computer-based data management. Limited by the sequential nature of magnetic tape technology, it was very difficult to integrate data from different files. The advent of magnetic disk technology[8] in the mid-1950s stimulated development of integrated file systems, and hierarchical database management system (DBMS)

8. IBM created the first disk drive in 1956.The price per megabyte was $10,000, and the 5M drive was the size of two refrigerators. In 2001, the price per gigabyte was below $10.

emerged in the 1960s, followed some years later by the network DBMS. Until the mid-1990s, the hierarchical DBMS, mainly in the form of IBM's DL/I product, was the predominant technology for managing data. It has now been replaced by the relational DBMS, a concept first discussed by Codd in an academic paper in 1970 but not commercially available until the mid-1970s. In the late 1980s, the notion of an object-oriented DBMS, primed by the ideas of object-oriented programming, emerged as a solution to situations not handled well by the relational DBMS.

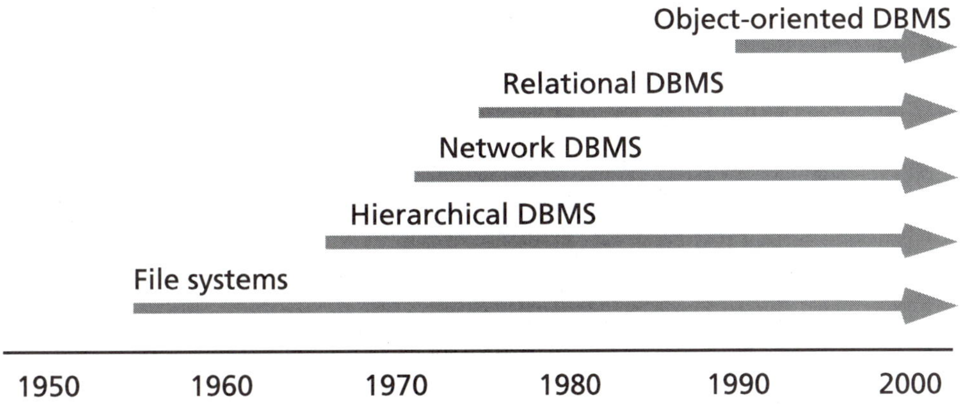

Figure 1-7. Data management systems timeline

This book concentrates on the relational model, currently the most widely used data management system, and Section 2 is devoted to the development of the necessary skills for designing and using a relational database.

Data, information, and knowledge

Often the terms *data* and *information* are used interchangeably, but they are distinctly different. **Data** are raw, unsummarized, and unanalyzed facts. **Information** is data that have been processed into a meaningful form.

A list of a supermarket's daily receipts is data, but it is not information, because it is too detailed to be very useful. Summarizing the data to give daily departmental totals is information because the store manager can use the report to monitor store performance. The same report would be data for a regional manager because again it is too detailed for meaningful decision making at the regional level. Information for a regional manager may be a weekly report of sales by department for each supermarket.

Data are always data, but one person's information can be another person's data. Information that is meaningful to one person can be too detailed for another person. A manager's notion of information can change quickly, however. If a problem is identified, a manager might request finer levels of detail to diagnose the problem's cause. Thus what was previously data suddenly becomes information because it helps solve the problem. When the problem is solved, the information reverts to data. There is a need for information systems that let managers customize the processing of data so that they always get information. As their needs change, they need to be able to adjust the detail of the reports they receive.

Knowledge is the capacity to use information. The education and experience that managers accumulate provide them with the expertise to make sense of the information they receive. Knowledge means that managers can interpret information and use it in decision making. In addition, knowledge is the capacity to recognize what information would be useful for making decisions. For example, a sales manager knows that requesting a report of profitability by product line is useful when she has to decide whether to employ a new product manager. Thus, when a new information system is delivered, managers need to be taught what information the system can deliver and what that information means.

The relationship between data, information, and knowledge is depicted in Figure 1-8. A knowledgeable person requests information to support decision making. As a result, data are converted into information. Personal knowledge is then applied to interpret the requested information and reach a conclusion. Of course, the cycle could be repeated several times if more information is needed before a decision can be made. Notice how knowledge is essential for grasping what information to request and interpreting that information in terms of the required decision.

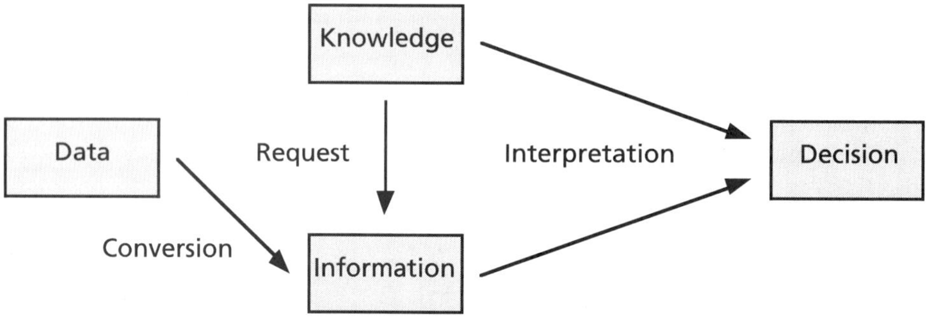

Figure 1-8. The relationship between data, information, and knowledge

The challenge

A major challenge facing organizations is to make effective use of the data stored in their diverse data management systems. This challenge exists because these various systems are not integrated and many potential users not only lack the training to access the systems but often are unaware that they exist. Before data managers can begin to address this problem, however, they must understand how organizational memories are used. In particular, they need to understand the relationship between information and managerial decision making.

Alice Lindsay was enjoying the luxuries of first-class travel. It was quite a change from being an undergraduate student of business. She was enjoying her filet mignon and glass of chardonnay. Good riddance to pizzas, hamburgers, and subs! Hello to fine food and gourmet restaurants. With her newly found wealth, she could travel in style and enjoy the very best restaurants. Alice, or Lady Alice to be more precise, had recently inherited a title, a valuable portfolio of stocks, and The Expeditioner. Her good fortune had coincided with the completion of her business degree. Now, instead of looking for a job, the job had found her: she was now chairman and managing director of The Expeditioner.

The Expeditioner is in a nineteenth-century building in Explorer's Lane, opposite Kensington Gardens and just a stone's throw from the Royal Geographical Society. Founded in the Middle Ages, The Expeditioner has a long history of equipping explorers, adventurers, and travelers. Its initial success was due to its development of a light, flexible chain mail armor. It did very well during the Middle Ages, when highway robbery was a growth business and travelers sought protection from the arrows and slings aimed at their fortunes. The branch office at the entrance to Sherwood Forest had done exceptionally well, thanks to passing wealthy clientele. The resident company wit, one Ned Thomas, often claims that "the Expeditioner was the first mail order company."

The Expeditioner's customers included the famous and the legendary. Orders from Marco Polo, Columbus, Magellan, Cook, and Livingston can be found in the ledgers. The most long-lived customer is a Mr. Walker,[9] who for several hundred years has had a standing yearly order of one roll of purple, premium-quality, non-rip, jungle twill. The Expeditioner's hats are very popular with a Mr. I. Jones, an American.

The nineteenth century was one long boom for The Expeditioner, the supplier de rigueur for the guardians of the European colonies. Branch offices were opened in Bombay, Sydney, Cape Town, and Singapore. For a generous fee, cad and renowned adventurer Harry Flashman[10] assiduously promoted The Expeditioner's wares on his many trips. As a result, orders poured in from the four corners of the globe. The Expeditioner's catalog was found in polite society and clubs throughout the British Empire.

The founder of The Expeditioner was a venturesome Scot who sought his fortune in London. Carefully guarding the family business, The Expeditioner's proprietors were inclined to be closefisted and invested their massive profits wisely. Because of their close contacts with many explorers, they made some very canny investments in mining ventures in dis-

9. For Ghost Who Walks.
10. See the *Flashman* stories by George MacDonald Fraser.

tant lands. As a result, when business contracted during the twentieth century, the investment portfolio kept the company solvent. Traditionally, ownership of the firm was inherited by the eldest child. When the most recent owner, a bachelor, died, the firm's lawyers spent months on genealogical research to identify the legal heir.

Alice had vivid memories of the day when Mr. Mainwaring phoned her to request an appointment. Like most students, she was never home, and the message was left on her answering machine. She remembered listening to it several times because she was intrigued by both the unusual accent and the message. It sounded something like, "Good afternoon, Lady Alice, I am Nigel Mannering of Chumli, Crepiny, Marchbanks, and Sinjun. If you would like to hear news to your advantage, please contact me."

Two days later, Alice met with Nigel. This also had been most memorable. The opening conversation had been confusing. He started with the very same formal introduction, "Good afternoon, Lady Alice, I am Nigel Mannering of Chumli, Crepiny, Marchbanks, and Sinjun. I am pleased to meet you," and handed Alice his card. Alice quickly inspected the card, which read, "Nigel Mainwaring, LL. B., Cholmondeley, Crespigny, Majoribanks, and St. John," but he had said nothing like that. She thought, "What planet is this guy from?"

It took fifteen minutes for Alice to discover that British English was not quite the same as American English. She quickly learned—or should that be "learnt?"—that many proper English names have a traditional pronunciation not easily inferred from the spelling.[11] Once this names problem had been sorted out, Nigel told Alice of her good fortune. She was the new owner of The Expeditioner. She also inherited the title that had been conferred on a previous owner by a grateful monarch who had been equipped by The Expeditioner for traveling in the Australian outback. She was now entitled to be called "Lady Alice of Bullamakanka." Nigel was in a bit of a rush. He left Alice with a first-class ticket to London and an attaché case of folders, and with an effusive "Jolly good show," disappeared.

Summary

Organizations must maintain a memory to process transactions and make decisions. Organizational data should be shareable, transportable, secure, and accurate, and provide timely, relevant data. The essential components are people (the most important), text, multimedia data, models, and knowledge. A wide variety of technologies can be used to manage data. External memories enlarge the range of data available to an organization. Data management systems often have some major shortcomings: redundancy, poor data control, poor interfaces, long lead times for query resolution, an inability to supply answers for questions posed by managers, and poor data integration. Data are raw facts; information is data processed into a meaningful form. Knowledge is the capacity to use information.

11. For further insights into this interesting feature of British English, see an appendix in the *Concise Oxford Dictionary.*

Key terms and concepts

Data
Data base management system (DBMS)
Data management
Data management system
Data mining
Data security
Decision making
Decision quality
Decision support system (DSS)
Documents
Executive information system (EIS)
External memory
Geographic information system (GIS)
Graphics
Hypertext
Images
Internal memory
Knowledge
Management information system (MIS)
On-line analytical processing (OLAP)
Organizational culture
Organizational memory
Shareable data
Social networks
Standard operating procedures
Storage device
Storage medium
Storage structure
Tables
Transaction processing
Transaction processing system (TPS)
Voice data

References and additional readings

Drucker, P. F. 1991. The new productivity challenge. *Harvard Business Review* 69 (6):45–53.

Schenk, D. 1997. *Data smog: surviving the information glut*. New York, NY: HarperCollins.

Exercises

1. What are the major differences between internal and external memory?
2. What is the difference between the things you remember and the things you write down?
3. What features are common to most individual memory systems?
4. What do you think organizations did before filing cabinets were invented?
5. Discuss the memory systems you use. How do they improve your performance? What are the shortcomings of your existing systems? How can you improve them?
6. Describe the most "organized" person you know. Why is that person so organized? Why haven't you adopted some of the same methods? Why do you think people differ in the extent to which they are organized?
7. Think about the last time you enrolled in a class. What data do you think were recorded for this transaction?
8. What roles do people play in organizational memory?
9. What do you think is the most important attribute of organizational memory? Justify your answer.
10. What is the difference between transaction processing and decision making?
11. When are data relevant?
12. Give some examples of specialized memories.
13. How can you measure the quality of a decision?

14. What is organizational culture? Can you name some organizations that have a distinctive culture?
15. What is hypertext? How does it differ from linear text? Why might hypertext be useful in an organizational memory system?
16. What is imaging? What are the characteristics of applications well suited for imaging?
17. What is an external memory? Why do organizations use external memories instead of building internal memories?
18. What is the common name used to refer to systems that help organizations remember knowledge?
19. What is a DSS? What is its role in organizational memory?
20. What are the major shortcomings of many data management systems? Which do you think is the most significant shortcoming?
21. What is the relationship between data, information, and knowledge?
22. Consider the following questions about The Expeditioner:
    a. What sort of data management systems would you expect to find at The Expeditioner?
    b. For each type of data management system that you identify, discuss it using the themes of shareable, transportable, security, accuracy, timeliness, and relevance.
    c. An organization's culture is the set of key values, beliefs, understandings, and norms that its members share. Discuss your ideas of the likely organizational culture of The Expeditioner.
    d. How difficult will it be to change the organizational culture of The Expeditioner? Do you anticipate that Alice will have problems making changes to the firm? If so, why?
23. Using the Web, find some stories about firms using data management systems. You might enter keywords such as "database" and "imaging" and access the Web sites of publications such as *Computerworld* and *PCWeek*. Identify the purpose of the system. How does the system improve organizational performance? What are the attributes of the technology that make it useful? Describe any trade-offs the organization might have made. Identify other organizations in which the same technology might be applied.
24. Make a list of the organizational memory systems identified in this chapter. Interview several people working in organizations. Ask them to indicate which organizational memory systems they use. Ask which system is most important and why. Write up your findings and your conclusion.
25. What is a personal digital assistant (PDA)? How do people use them? What do you think will happen with these products over the next few years?

2

Information

Effective information management must begin by thinking about how people use information — not with how people use machines.

Thomas Davenport[1]

Learning objectives

Students completing this chapter will

- understand the importance of information to society and organizations;
- be able to describe the various roles of information in organizational change;
- be able to distinguish between soft and hard information;
- know how managers use information;
- be able to describe the characteristics of common information delivery systems;
- distinguish the different types of knowledge.

Introduction

There are two key characteristics of the beginning of the twenty-first century: high velocity global change and the emerging power of information organizations. Rapid changes in international relations, the globalization of business, the redrawing of political boundaries, the demise of many dictatorships, and the creation of massive trading blocs are major forces contributing to global change. Organizations are undergoing large-scale restructuring as they attempt to reposition themselves to survive the threats and exploit the opportunities presented by this change.

In the last few years, some very powerful and highly profitable information-based organizations have emerged. Microsoft and Bill Gates are to the information age what Standard Oil and John Rockefeller were to the industrial era.[2] Chip maker Intel's dominance of the microprocessor market parallels General Motors' leadership of the auto industry 40 years

---

1. Davenport, T. H. 1994. Saving IT's soul: Human-centered information management. *Harvard Business Review* 72 (2):119–131.
2. Cook, W. J. 1993. The new Rockefeller. *U.S. News & World Report* 114 (6):64–67.

ago. CNN has become the world's news service. These examples demonstrate that information has become a foundation for organizational growth. We can obtain further insights into the value of information by considering the role of information in civilization.

A historical perspective

Three distinct phases of civilization have been identified and recently a possible fourth phase has been suggested. Agriculture, the first phase, arose around 3000 B.C.E. It prospered through the use of iron and tools. Output was recorded in units such as the bushel, a unit of volume often used for measuring the amount of grain harvested from a field. The pioneering cultures of the agricultural phase were China and Egypt. The industrial revolution, the second phase, commenced in the United Kingdom in the eighteenth century. Its success was based on harnessing energy, initially in the form of the steam engine and later as the internal combustion engine. The third phase, information society, was pioneered by the United States, where it emerged in the late twentieth century. The integrated circuit, the driving force of this society, is the basis of computer and communication technologies that manipulate and transport data. The key word in the information society is *data*. It is predicted that the twenty-first century will witness the development of a society based on creation. The key word of this civilization will be *idea*. The technology will be *idea engineering* and productivity will be measured in terms of *creative output*.[3] The form of this technology will become clearer as the new phase emerges.

An early writing system

A constant across all of these eras is organizational memory, or in its larger form, social memory. Writing and paper manufacturing developed about the same time as agricultural

3. Murakami, T., and T. Nishiwaki. 1991. *Strategy for creation*. Cambridge, UK: Woodhead Publishing.

societies. Limited writing systems developed about 30,000 years ago. Full writing systems, which have evolved in the last 5,000 years, made possible the technological transfer that enabled humanity to move from hunting and gathering to farming. Writing enables the creation of a permanent record of knowledge, and information can accumulate from one generation to the next. Before writing, knowledge was confined by the limits of human memory.

Writing is a means of encoding information. There is also a need for a technology that can store this information for extended periods and support transport of written information. The storage medium advanced from clay tablets (4000 B.C.E.) through papyrus (3500 B.C.E.) and parchment (2000 B.C.E) to paper (100 C.E.). Written knowledge gained great impetus from Gutenberg, whose achievement was a printing system involving movable metal type, ink, paper, and press. In less than 50 years, printing technology diffused throughout most of Europe. In the last century, a range of new storage media appeared (e.g., photographic, magnetic, and optical).

Organizational memories emerged with the development of large organizations such as governments, armies, churches, and trading companies. The growth of organizations during the industrial revolution saw a massive increase in the number and size of organizational memories. This growth continued throughout the twentieth century.

The Web has demonstrated that we now live in a borderless world. There is a free flow of information, investment, and industry across borders. Customers ignore national boundaries to buy products and services. For instance, teenagers in Switzerland buy CDs from U.S.-based Web sites. Highly talented people with much sought after skills find it easy to move between countries. In the borderless information age, the old ways of creating have been displaced by intelligence, marketing, global reach, and education (see Table 2-1). Excelling in the management of data, information, and knowledge has become a prerequisite to corporate and national wealth.

Table 2-1: Wealth creation

The old	The new
Military power	Intelligence
Natural resources	Marketing
Population	Global reach
Industry	Education

This brief history shows the increasing importance of information to civilization. It demonstrates how advancement was facilitated by the discovery of means for recording and disseminating information. In our society, organizations are the predominant keepers and transmitters of information.

Information characteristics

Three useful concepts for describing information are hardness, richness, and class. **Information hardness** is a subjective measure of the accuracy and reliability of an item of information. **Information richness** describes the concept that information can be *rich* or *lean* depending on the information delivery medium. **Information class** groups types of information by their key features.

Information hardness

In 1812, the Austrian mineralogist Friedrich Mohs proposed a scale of hardness, in order of increasing relative hardness, based on 10 relatively common minerals. Each mineral can scratch those with a similar or lower number, but cannot scratch higher numbered minerals.

Table 2-2: An information hardness scale

Minerals	Scale	Data
Talc	1	Unidentified source—rumors, gossip, and hearsay
Gypsum	2	Identified non-expert source—opinions, feelings, ideas
Calcite	3	Identified expert source—predictions, speculations, forecasts, estimates
Fluorite	4	Unsworn testimony—explanations, justifications, assessments, interpretations
Apatite	5	Sworn testimony—explanations, justifications, assessments, interpretations
Orthoclass	6	Budgets, formal plans
Quartz	7	News reports, non-financial data, industry statistics, survey data
Topaz	8	Unaudited financial statements, government statistics
Corundum	9	Audited financial statements
Diamond	10	Stock exchange and commodity market data

A similar approach can be used to describe information (see Table 2-2).[4] Market information, such as the current price of gold, is the hardest because it is measured extremely accurately. There is no ambiguity, and its measurement is highly reliable. In contrast, the softest information, which comes from unidentified sources, is rife with uncertainty.

Audited financial statements are in the corundum zone. They are measured according to standard rules, generally accepted accounting principles which are promulgated by national accounting societies. External auditors monitor application of these standards although there is generally some leeway in their application and sometimes multiple standards for the same item. The use of different accounting principles can lead to different profit and loss statements. As a result, the information in audited financial statements has some degree of uncertainty.

4. This scale is an extension of work by colleagues at the University of Georgia.

A lifetime of information—every day

It is estimated that a single weekday issue of the *New York Times* contains more information than the average person in seventeenth-century England came across in a lifetime. Information, once rare, is now abundant and overflowing.

Roszak, T. 1986. *The cult of information: The folklore of computers and the true art of thinking*. New York, NY: Pantheon. p. 32.

There are degrees of hardness within accounting systems. The hardest data are counts, such as units sold or customers served. These are primary measures of organizational performance. Secondary measures, such as dollar sales and market share, are derived from counts. Managers vary in their preference for primary and secondary measures. Operational managers opt for counts for measuring productivity because they are uncontaminated by price changes and currency fluctuations. Senior managers, because their focus is on financial performance, select secondary measures.

The scratch test provides a convenient and reliable method of assessing the hardness of a mineral. Unfortunately, there is no scratch test for information. Managers must rely on their judgment to assess information hardness.

Although managers want hard information, there are many cases when it is not available. They compensate by seeking information from several different sources. Although this approach introduces redundancy, this is precisely what the manager seeks. Consistent information from different sources is reassuring.

Information richness

Information can be described as rich or lean. Information is richest when delivered face-to-face. Conversation permits immediate feedback for verification of meaning. You can always stop the other speaker and ask, "What do you mean?" Face-to-face information delivery is rich because you see the speaker's body language, hear the tone of voice, and natural language is used. A numeric document is the leanest form of information. There is no opportunity for questions, no additional information from body movements and vocal tone. The information richness of some communication media is shown in Table 2-3.

Table 2-3: Information richness and communication media[a]

Richest				Leanest
Face-to-face	Telephone	Personal documents (letters and memos)	Impersonal written documents	Numeric documents

a. Daft, R. L., and R. H. Lengel. 1986. Organizational information requirements, media richness, and structural design. *Management Science* 32 (5):554–571.

Managers seek rich information when they are trying to resolve equivocality. Equivocality means ambiguity. It means that managers cannot make sense of a situation because they arrive at multiple, conflicting interpretations of the information. An example of an equivocal situation is a class assignment where some of the instructions are missing and others are contradictory (of course, this example is an extremely rare event).

Equivocal situations cannot be resolved by collecting more information because managers are uncertain about what questions to ask and often a clear answer is not possible. Managers reduce equivocality by sharing their interpretations of the available information and reaching a collective understanding of what the information means. By exchanging opinions and recalling their experiences, they try to make sense of an ambiguous situation.

Many of the situations that managers face each day involve a high degree of equivocality. Formal organizational memories, such as databases, are not much help because the information they provide is lean. Managers rely far more on talking with colleagues and using informal organizational memories such as social networks.

Data management is almost exclusively concerned with administering the formal information systems that deliver lean information. Although this is their proper role, data managers must realize that they can deliver only a portion of the data required by decision makers.

Information classes

Information can be grouped into four classes: content, form, behavior, and action (see Table 2-4). Until recently, most organizational information fell into the first category.

Table 2-4: Information classes

Class	Description
Content	Quantity, location, and types of items
Form	Shape and composition of an object
Behavior	Simulation of a physical object
Action	Creation of action (e.g., industrial robots)

Content information records details about quantity, location, and types of items. It tends to be historical in nature and is traditionally the class of information collected and stored by organizations. The content information of a car would describe its model number, color, price, options, horsepower, and so forth. Hundreds of bytes of data may be required to fully record the content information of a car. Typically, content data are captured by a TPS.

Form information describes the shape and composition of an object. For example, the form information of a car would define the dimensions and composition of every component in the car. Millions of bytes of data are needed to store the form of a car. CAD/CAM systems are used to create and store form information.

Behavior information is used to predict the behavior of a physical object using simulation techniques, which typically require form information as input. Massive numbers of calculations per second are required to simulate behavior. For example, simulating the flight of a new aircraft design may require trillions of computations. Behavior information is often presented visually because the vast volume of data generated cannot be easily processed by humans in other formats.

Action information enables the instantaneous creation of sophisticated action. Industrial robots take action information and manufacture parts, weld car bodies, or transport items. Antilock brakes are an example of action information in use.

Information and organizational change

Organizations are goal-directed. They undergo continual change as they use their resources, people, technology, and financial assets to reach some future desired outcome. Goals are often clearly stated, such as to make a profit of $100 million, win a football championship, or decrease the government deficit by 25 percent in five years. Goals are often not easily achieved, however, and organizations continually seek information that supports goal attainment. The information they seek falls into three categories: goal setting, gap, and change (see Figure 2-1).

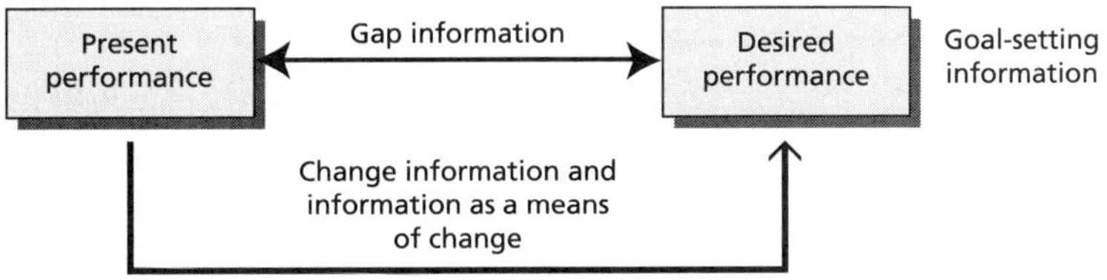

Figure 2-1. Organizational information categories

The emergence of an information society also means that information provides dual possibilities for change. Information is used to plan change and information is a medium for change.

Goal-setting information

Organizations set goals or levels of desired performance. Managers need information to establish goals that are challenging but realistic. A common approach is to take the previous goal and stretch it. For example, a company that had a 15 percent return on investment (ROI) might set the new goal at 17 percent ROI. This technique is known as "anchoring and adjusting." Prior performance is used as a basis for setting the new performance standards. The problem with anchoring and adjusting is that it promotes incremental improvement rather than radical change because internal information is used to set performance standards.

Planning is a common approach to goal setting for many enterprises. Recently, some organizations have turned to external information and are using benchmarking as a source of information for goal setting.

Planning

Planning is an important task for senior managers. To set the direction for the company, they need information about consumers' potential demands, and social, economic, technical, and political conditions. They use this information to determine the opportunities and threats facing the organization, thus permitting them to take advantage of opportunities and avoid threats.

Most of the information for long-term planning comes from sources external to the company. There are think tanks that analyze trends and publish reports on future conditions. Journal articles and books can be important sources of information about future events. There also will be a demand for some internal information. Major planning decisions, such as building a new plant, will be based on an analysis of internal data (use of existing capacity) and external data (projected customer demand).

Benchmarking

Benchmarking establishes goals based on best industry practices. It is founded on the Japanese concept of *dantotsu*, striving to be the *best of the best*. Benchmarking is externally directed. Information is sought on those companies, regardless of industry, which demonstrate outstanding performance in the areas to be benchmarked. Their methods are studied, documented, and used to set goals and redesign existing practices for superior performance.

Other forms of external information, such as demographic trends, economic forecasts, and competitors' actions can be used in goal setting. External information is valuable because it can force an organization to go beyond incremental goal setting.

Organizations need information to identify feasible, motivating, and challenging goals. Once these goals have been established, organizations need information on the extent to which these goals have been attained.

Gap information

Because goals are meant to be challenging, there is often a gap between actual and desired performance. Organizations use a number of mechanisms to detect a gap and gain some idea of its size. Problem identification and scorekeeping are two principal methods of providing gap information.

Problem identification

Business conditions are continually changing because of competitors' actions, trends in consumer demand, and government action. Often these changes are reflected in a gap between expectations and present performance. This gap is known as a problem.

To identify problems, managers use exception reports which are generated only when conditions vary from the established standard. Once a potential problem has been identified, managers collect additional information to confirm that a problem really exists. Problem identification information can also be delivered by printed report or computer screen. Once alerted, the information delivery system needs to shift into high gear. Managers will request rapid delivery of ad hoc reports from a variety of sources. The ideal organizational memory system can adapt smoothly to deliver appropriate information quickly.

Scorekeeping

Keeping track of the *score* provides gap information. Managers ask many questions: How many items did we make yesterday? What were the sales last week? Has our market share increased in the last year? They establish measurement systems to track variables that indicate whether organizational performance is on target. Keeping score is important; managers need to measure in order to manage. Also, measurement lets people know what is important. Once a manager starts to measure something, subordinates surmise that this variable must be important and pay more attention to the factors that influence it.

New systems bridge brick-and-mortar and Web shopping

Many retailers are bridging the real and virtual worlds by providing interactive shopping tools. Found's ICaM (Integrated Clicks and Mortar) solution uses a keyfob-sized scanner that allows consumers to capture up to 150 bar codes while in stores. Product information later can be output to a mall kiosk or a company's Web site.

Also planned is an integrated listing, registry, and personal catalog system called ClixList, which allows customers to scan products and then upload them to a Web-based personal registry for later purchase. The service already has been through two pilots—fastfrog.com and yoursherpa.com. Fastfrog.com provided a scanner to teens for scanning items they wanted to purchase at shopping malls. The items were added to "wish lists" on a personalized Web site, that could be e-mailed to parents or friends. The adult version, yoursherpa.com, uses Palm handhelds to allow consumers to scan items at many stores and then pick them up from one location in the mall or have them delivered to the home for an additional fee.

This technology helps merge the real-world experience of mall shopping with the virtual world of e-commerce.

Source: Portnoy, S. 2001. E-commerce in hand. *Computer Reseller News*, Feb 5 (931):41.

There are many aspects of the score that a manager can measure. The overwhelming variety of potentially available information is illustrated by the sales output information that a sales manager could track (see Table 2-5). Sales input information (e.g., number of service calls) can also be measured, and there is qualitative information to be considered. Because of time constraints, most managers are forced to limit their attention to 10 or fewer key variables singled out by the critical success factors (CSF) method.[5] Scorekeeping information is usually fairly stable, and the delivery system could be a printed report or a computer screen.

Table 2-5: Sales output tracking information

Orders:	Number of current customers
	Average order size
	Batting average (orders to calls)
Sales volume:	Dollar sales volume
	Unit sales volume
	By customer type
	By product category
	Translated to market share
	Quota achieved
Margins:	Gross margin
	Net profit
	By customer type
	By product
Customers:	Number of new accounts
	Number of lost accounts
	Percentage of accounts sold
	Number of accounts overdue
	Dollar value of receivables
	Collections of receivables

Change information

Once a gap has been detected, managers take action to close it. Change information helps them determine which actions might successfully close the gap. Accurate change information is very valuable because it enables managers to predict the outcome of various actions with some certainty. Unfortunately, change information is usually not very precise, and there are many variables that can influence the effect of any planned change. Nevertheless, organizations spend a great deal of time collecting information to support problem solving and planning.

5. Rockart, J. F. 1982. The changing role of the information systems executive: A critical success factors perspective. *Sloan Management Review* 24 (1):3–13.

Problem Solution

Managers collect information to support problem solution. Once a problem has been identified, a manager seeks to find its cause. A decrease in sales could be the result of competitors introducing a new product, an economic downturn, an ineffective advertising campaign, or many other reasons. Data can be collected to test each of these possible causes. Additional data are usually required to support analysis of each alternative. For example, if the sales decrease has been caused by an economic downturn, the manager might use a decision support system to analyze the effect of a price decrease or a range of promotional activities.

Information as a means of change

The emergence of an information society means that information can be used as a means of changing an organization's performance. Corporations are creating information-based products and services, adding information to products, and using information to enhance existing performance or gain a competitive advantage. Further insights into the use of information as a change agent are gained by examining marketing, customer service, and empowerment.

Marketing

Marketing is a key strategy for changing organizational performance by increasing sales. Information has become an important component in marketing. Airlines and retailers have established frequent flyer and buyer programs to encourage customer loyalty and gain more information about customers. These systems are heavily dependent on database technology because of the massive volume of data that must be stored. Indeed, without database technology, some marketing strategies could never be implemented.

Database technology offers the opportunity to change the very nature of communications with customers. Broadcast media have been the traditional approach to communication. Advertisements are aired on television or radio or placed in newspapers or magazines. Database technology can be used to address customers directly. No longer just a mailing list, today's database is a memory of customer relationships, a record of every message and response between the firm and a customer. Some companies keep track of customers' preferences and customize advertisements to their needs. Leading catalog retailers now send customers only those catalogs for which they estimate there is a high probability of a purchase. For example, a customer with a history of buying jazz CDs is sent a catalog of jazz recordings instead of one featuring classical music.

The Web has significantly enhanced the value of database technology. Many firms now use a combination of a Web site and a DBMS to market products and service customers. Because this topic is so important, Chapter 15 provides extensive coverage of Web data management.

Customer Service

Customer service is a key competitive issue for nearly every organization. Many American business leaders rank customer service as their most important goal for organizational success. Many of the developed economies are service economies. In the United States, services account for approximately 75 percent of the gross national product and 9 out of 10 new jobs. Many companies now fight for customers by offering superior customer service. Information is frequently a key to this improved service.

In services, execution is everything. The interaction with the customer has been described as the moment of truth when the customer discovers whether the organization's promises are real. Some organizations are almost obsessive in their attention to customers.

Empowerment

Empowerment has attracted considerable attention in the business press because many high performing businesses use empowerment. In general terms, empowerment means giving employees greater freedom to make decisions. More precisely, it is sharing with frontline employees[6]

- information about the organization's performance;
- rewards based on the organization's performance;
- knowledge and information that enables employees to understand and contribute to organizational performance;
- power to make decisions that influence organizational direction and performance.

Notice that information features prominently in the process. A critical component is giving employees access to the information they need to perform their tasks with a high degree of independence and discretion. Information is empowerment. An important task for data managers is to develop and install systems that give employees ready access to the organization's memory. By linking employees to organizational memory, data managers play a pivotal role in empowering people.

Organizations believe that empowerment contributes to organizational performance by increasing the quality of products and services. Together, empowerment and information are mechanisms of planned change.

Information and managerial work

Managers are a key device for implementing organizational change. Because they frequently use data management systems in their normal activities as a source of information about change and as a means of implementing change, it is crucial for data management systems designers to understand how managers work. Failure to take account of manage-

6. Bowen, D. E., and E. E Lawler III. 1992. The empowerment of service workers: What, why, how, and when. *Sloan Management Review* 33 (3):31-39.

rial behavior can result in a technically sound, but rarely used, system because it does not fit the social system.

Studies over several decades reveal a very consistent pattern:[7] managerial work is very fragmented. Managers spend an average of 10 minutes on any task, and their day is organized into brief periods of concentrated attention to a variety of tasks. They work unrelentingly and are frequently interrupted by unexpected disturbances. Managers are action oriented and rely on intuition and judgment far more than contemplative analysis of information.

Executives strongly prefer oral communication. They spend a great deal of time conversing directly or by telephone. Managers use interpersonal communication to establish networks, which they later use as a source of information and a way to make things happen. The continual flow of verbal information helps them make sense of events and lets them feel the organizational pulse.

Managers rarely use formal reporting systems. They do not spend their time analyzing computer reports or querying databases but resort to formal reports to confirm evidence should interpersonal communications suggest there is a problem. Even when managers are provided with a purpose-built, ultra-friendly EIS, their behavior changes very little. They may access a few screens during the day, but oral communication is still their preferred method of data gathering and dissemination.

Managers' information requirements

Managers have certain requirements of the information they receive. These expectations should shape a data management system's content and how data are processed.

Managers expect to receive information that is useful for their current task under existing business conditions. Unfortunately, managerial tasks can change rapidly. The interlinked, global, economic environment is highly turbulent. Since managers' expectations are not stable, the information delivery system must be sufficiently flexible to meet changing requirements.

Managers' demand for information varies with their perception of its hardness; they require only one source that scores 10 on the information hardness scale. The Nikkei Index at the close of today's market is the same whether you read it in the *Asian Wall Street Journal, The Western Australian*, or hear it on CNN. As perceived hardness decreases, managers demand more information (see Figure 2-2), hoping that more information will resolve uncertainty and lead to an accurate assessment of a situation. When the reliability of a source is questionable, managers seek confirmation from other sources. If a number of different sources provide consistent information, a manager gains confidence in its accuracy.

---

7. Mintzberg, H. 1973. *The nature of managerial work*. New York, NY: Harper & Row and Kotter, J. P. 1982. *The general managers.* New York, NY: Free Press.

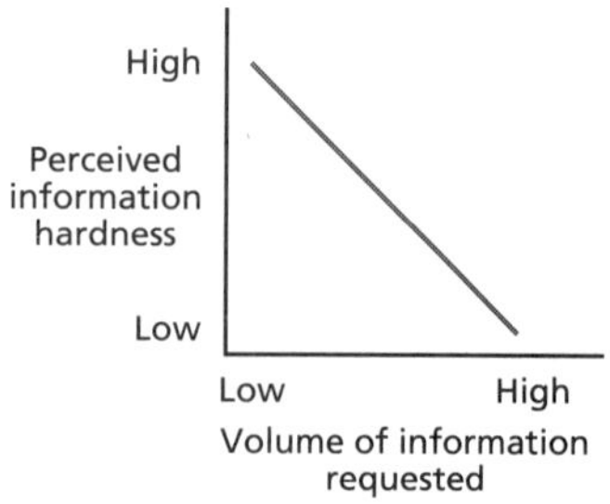

Figure 2-2. Relationship of perceived information hardness to volume of information requested

It is not unusual, therefore, to have a manager seek information from a database report, a conversation with a subordinate, and a contact in another organization. If she gets essentially the same information from each source, she has the confirmation she seeks. This means each data management system should be designed to minimize redundancy, but different components of organizational memory can supply overlapping information.

Managers' needs for information vary accordingly with responsibilities

Operational managers need detailed, short-term information to deal with well-defined problems in areas such as sales, service, and production. This information comes almost exclusively from internal sources that report recent performance in the managers' area. A sales manager may get weekly reports of sales by each person under that person's supervision.

As managers move up the organizational hierarchy, their information needs both expand and contract. They become responsible for a wider range of activities and are charged with planning the future of the organization, which requires information from external sources on long-term economic, demographic, political, and social trends. Despite this long-term focus, top level managers also monitor short-term, operational performance. In this instance, they need less detail and more summary and exception reports on a small number of key indicators. To avoid information overload as new layers of information needs are added, the level of detail on the old layers naturally must decline, as illustrated in Figure 2-3.

Information satisficing

Because managers face making many decisions in a short period, most do not have the time or resources to collect and interpret all the information they need to make the best decision. Consequently, they are often forced to satisfice.[8] They accept the first satisfacto-

8. Simon, H. A. 1976. *Administrative behavior: A study of decision-making processes in administrative organization*. 3rd ed. New York, NY: Free Press.

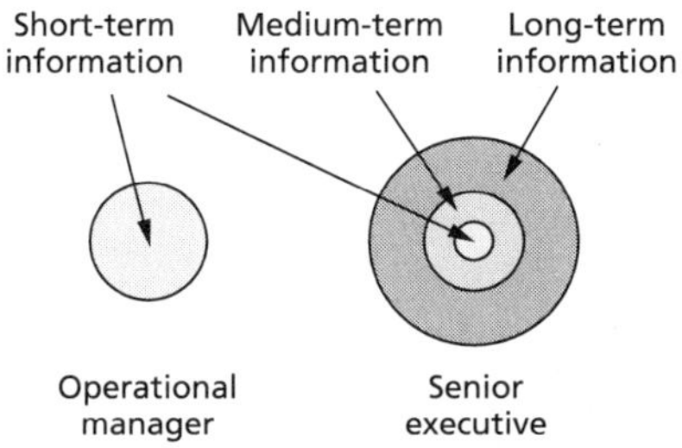

Figure 2-3. Management level and information need

ry decision they discover. They also satisfice in their information search, collecting only enough information to make a satisfactory decision.

Ultimately, information satisficing leads to lower quality decision making. But if information technology can be used to accelerate delivery and processing of the right information, then managers should be able to move from selecting the first satisfactory decision to selecting the best of several satisfactory decisions.

Information delivery systems

Most organizations have a variety of delivery systems to provide information to managers. Developed over many years, these systems are being integrated to give managers better access to information. There are two aspects to information delivery. First, there is a need for software that accesses an organizational memory, extracts the required data, and formats it for presentation. We can use the categories of organizational memories introduced in Chapter 1 to describe the software side of information delivery systems (see Table 2-6). The second aspect of delivery is the hardware that gets information from a computer to the manager. We will briefly discuss information delivery systems at this point.

Software

Software is used to move data to and from organizational memory. There is usually tight coupling between software and the format of an organizational memory. For example, a relational database management system can access tables but not decision-support models. This tight coupling is particularly frustrating for managers who often want integrated information from several organizational memories. For example, a sales manager might expect a monthly report to include details of recent sales (from a relational database) to be combined with customer comments (from e-mail messages to a customer service system). A quick glance at Table 2-6 shows that there are many different information delivery systems. We will discuss each of these briefly to illustrate the lack of integration of organizational memories.

Table 2-6: Information delivery systems software

Organizational memory	Delivery systems
People	Conversation E-mail Meeting Report Groupware
Files	Management information system (MIS)
Documents	Web browser E-mail attachment
Images	Imaging processing system (IPS)
Graphics	Computer aided design (CAD) Geographic information system (GIS)
Voice	Voice mail Voice recording system
Mathematical model	Decision support system (DSS)
Knowledge	Expert system (ES)
Decisions	Conversation E-mail Meeting Report Groupware

Verbal exchange

Conversations, meetings, and oral reporting are commonly used methods of information delivery. Indeed, managers show a strong preference for verbal exchange as a method for gathering information. This is not surprising because we are accustomed to oral information. This is the way we learned for thousands of years as a preliterate culture. Only recently have we learned to make decisions using spreadsheets and computer reports.

Voice mail

Voice mail is useful for people who are frequently away from their offices because it supports asynchronous communication; the two parties to the conversation are not simultaneously connected by a communication line. Voice mail systems also can store many prerecorded messages that can be selectively replayed using the keypad of a Touch-Tone phone. Organizations use this feature to support standard customer queries.

Electronic mail

E-mail is increasingly becoming an important system of information delivery. It too supports asynchronous messaging, and it is less costly than voice mail for communication. Many documents are exchanged as attachments to e-mail.

Written report

Formal, written reports have a long history in organizations. Before electronic communication, they were the main form of information delivery for most firms. They still have a role in organizations because they are an effective method of integrating information of varying hardness and from a variety of organizational memories. For example, a report can contain text, tables, graphics, and images.

Written reports are often supplemented by a verbal presentation of the key points in the report. Such a presentation enhances the information delivered because the audience has an opportunity to ask questions and get an immediate response.

Meeting

Because managers spend between 30 and 80 percent of their time in meetings, these become a key source of information.

Groupware

Since meetings occupy so much managerial time and in many cases are poorly planned and managed, organizations are looking for improvements. Groupware is a general term applied to a range of software systems designed to improve some aspect of group work. For example, Lotus Notes is used to accelerate the exchange of information for a wide variety of business tasks (e.g., expense reporting). Groupware is excellent for tapping soft information and the informal side of organizational memory.

Management information system

Management information systems are a common method of delivering information from data management systems. Information can be delivered on paper or via a terminal. A preplanned query is often used to extract the data. Managers who have developed some skills in using a query language might create their own custom reports as the interface to file-based memory becomes friendlier and query languages become more powerful and easier to use.

Preplanned reports often contain too much or too detailed information because they are written in anticipation of a manager's needs. Customized reports do not have these shortcomings, but they are more expensive and time consuming for programmers to write.

Web

Word processing, desk-top publishing, or HTML editors are used for preparing documents that are disseminated via placing them on a Web server. Documents can be readily shared and accessed.

Image processing system

An image processing system (IPS) captures data using a scanner, which digitizes an image. Images in the form of letters, reports, illustrations, and graphics always have been an important type of organizational memory. An IPS permits these forms of information to be captured electronically and disseminated.

Computer-aided design

Computer-aided design (CAD) is used extensively to create graphics. For example, engineers use CAD in product design and architects use it for building design. These plans are a part of organizational memory for designers and manufacturers.

Geographic information system

A geographic information system (GIS) stores graphical data about a geographic region. Many cities use a GIS to record details of roads, utilities, and services. This graphical information is another form of organizational memory. Again, special purpose software is required to access and present the information stored in this memory.

Decision support system

A decision support system (DSS) is frequently a computer-based mathematical model of a problem. DSS software, available in a range of packages, permits the model and data to be retrieved and executed. The user can often change the values of model parameters to investigate various solutions.

Expert system

An expert system (ES) has the captured knowledge of someone who is particularly skillful at solving a certain type of problem. It is convenient to think of an ES as a set of rules. An ES is typically used interactively as it asks the decision maker questions and uses the responses to determine the action to recommend.

Hardware

There are a number of ways to use hardware to deliver information. In the early days of computing, the approach was not delivery but collection. The user went to the machine to execute a program and collect the output. This approach was soon supplemented by hand delivery of computer-produced reports. Regular computer tasks were scheduled, and the output delivered using internal and external mail systems.

The next advance was to connect remote terminals, printers, and other devices to a host computer (e.g., a mainframe or minicomputer); this architecture is known as host/terminal. Using this approach, data are processed on the host computer and delivered electronically to the client's terminal or printer. This approach was dominant in the 1980s.

The development of personal computers, however, meant that users could do some of their processing at their desk, although they soon realized that much of the data they needed were located on mainframes or minicomputers. As a result, two new technologies were developed: local area networks (LANs) and client/server.

LANs can connect together collections of personal computers, which can then be connected to mainframes or minicomputers. When these systems were first introduced, personal computers were frequently relegated to the role of a terminal on a mainframe network. There was minimal use of the processing capacity of the personal computer; most processing occurred on the host.

Client/server technology was introduced to take advantage of the low-cost computing power of microcomputers. Client/server systems maintain data on the server — any form of fast computer with large secondary storage capacity — and deliver data to the client. Processing of data to information occurs on the client machine. Currently, the client/server approach is commonly implemented using a Web browser as the client.

Information integration

You can think of organizational memory as a vast, disorganized data dump. A fundamental problem for most organizations is that their memory is fragmented across a wide variety of formats and technologies. Too frequently, there is a one-to-one correspondence between an organizational memory for a particular functional area and the software delivery system. For example, sales information is delivered by the sales system, production information by the production system, and customer correspondence by an image processing system. Of course, this is not a very desirable situation because managers want all the information they need, regardless of its source or format, preferably on one screen or at least on as few screens as possible.

A response to providing access to the disorganized data dump has been the development of software, such as an EIS or Web application, that integrates information from a variety of delivery systems. This situation is shown in Figure 2-4. An important task of this software is to integrate and present information from multiple organizational memories. Recently, some organizations have created vast integrated data stores, data warehouses, that are organized repositories of organizational data (see Chapter 14 for more details).

Information integration software is really a dirty (and not necessarily very quick) fix for a very critical need. The real requirement is to integrate organizational memory so that digital data (tables, images, graphics, and voice) can be stored together. The ideal situation is shown in Figure 2-5: the entire organizational memory is accessed as a single unit[9] via one information delivery system that meets all the client's requirements.

There is a long-term trend of data integration. Early information systems were based on independent files. As these systems were rewritten, database technology was used to in-

9. Physically it might be multiple systems, but it appears to be one logical system.

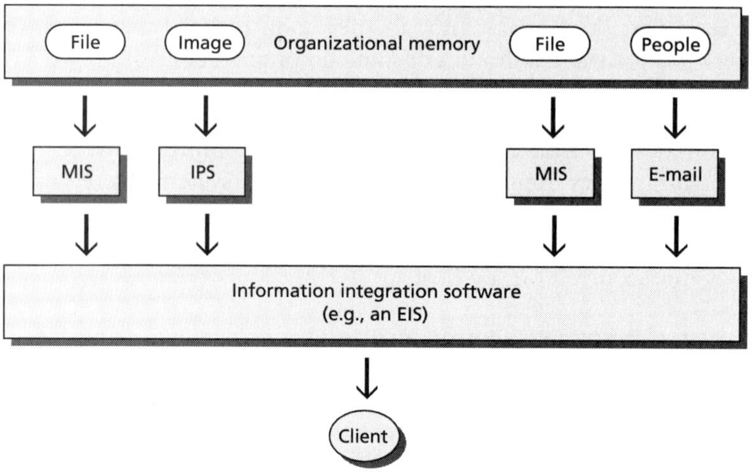

Figure 2-4. Information integration—the present situation

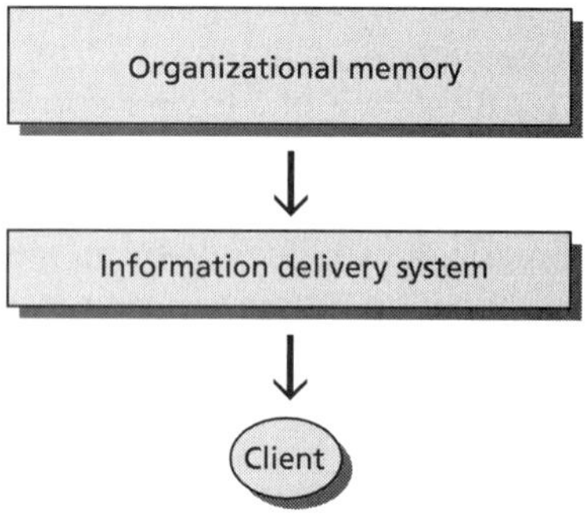

Figure 2-5. The ideal organizational memory and information delivery system

tegrate independent files into databases. The next level of integration is to get all forms of data together. For example, the customer database might contain file data (e.g., customer name and address) and image data (e.g., correspondence from the customer, photograph of an accident scene).

Knowledge

The performance of many organizations is determined more by their intellectual capabilities and knowledge than their physical assets. A nation's wealth is increasingly a result of the knowledge and skills of its citizens, rather than its natural resources and industrial plant. Currently, about 85 percent of all jobs in America and 80 percent of those in Europe are knowledge-based.[10]

10. This section is based on Quinn, B. J., P. Anderson, and S. Finkelstein. 1996. Leveraging intellect. *Academy of Management Executive* 10 (3):7–27.

An organization's knowledge, in order of increasing importance, is:

- cognitive knowledge (know what)
- advanced skills (know how)
- system understanding and trained intuition (know why)
- self-motivated creativity (care why).

This text illustrates the different types of knowledge. You develop cognitive knowledge in Section 3, when you learn about data architectures and implementations. For example, ***knowing what*** storage devices can be used for archival data is cognitive knowledge. Section 2, which covers data modeling and SQL, develops advanced skills because, upon completion of that section, you will ***know how*** to model data and write SQL queries. The first two chapters are designed to expand your understanding of the influence of organizational memory on organizational performance. You need to ***know why*** you should learn data management skills. Managers know when and why to apply technology, whereas technicians know what to apply and how to apply it. Finally, you are probably an MIS major, and your coursework is inculcating the values and norms of the MIS profession so that you *care why* problems are solved using information technology.

Organizations tend to spend more on developing cognitive skills than they do on fostering creativity (see Figure 2-6). This is, unfortunately, the wrong priority. Returns are likely to be much greater when higher level knowledge skills are developed. Well-managed organizations place more attention on creating ***know why*** and ***care why*** skills because they recognize that knowledge is a key competitive weapon. Furthermore, these firms have learned that knowledge grows, often exponentially, when shared. Knowledge is like a communication network, whose potential benefit grows exponentially as the nodes within the network grow arithmetically. When knowledge is shared within the organization, or with customers and suppliers, it multiplies as each person receiving knowledge imparts it to someone else in the organization or with one of the business' partners.

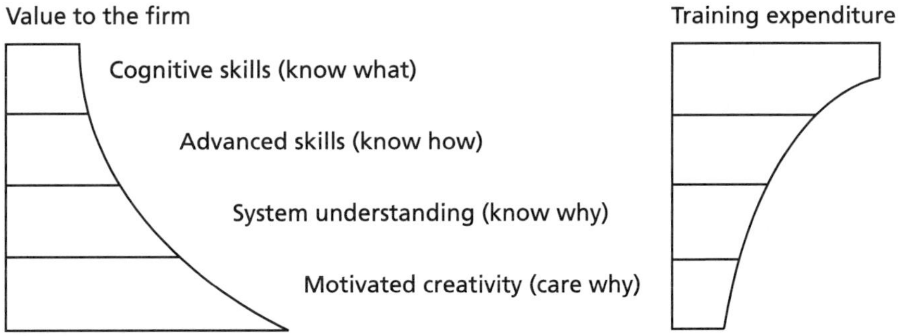

Figure 2-6. Skills values vs. training expenditures (source: Quinn et al., 1996)

There are two types of knowledge: explicit and tacit. **Explicit knowledge** is codified and transferable. This textbook is an example of explicit knowledge. Knowledge about how to design databases has been formalized and communicated with the intention of transferring it to you, the reader. **Tacit knowledge** is personal knowledge, experience, and judgment that is difficult to codify. It is more difficult to transfer tacit knowledge because it resides in people's minds. Usually, the transfer of tacit knowledge requires the sharing of experiences. In learning to model data, the subject of the next section, you will quickly learn how to represent an entity because this knowledge is made explicit. However, you will find it much harder to model data because this skill comes with practice. Ideally, you should develop several models under the guidance of an experienced modeler, such as your instructor, who can pass on his or her tacit knowledge.

Summary

Information has become a key foundation for organizational growth. The information society is founded on computer and communications technology. The accumulation of knowledge requires a capacity to encode and share information. Hard information is very exact. Soft information is extremely imprecise. Rich information exchange occurs in face-to-face conversation. Numeric reports are an example of lean information. Organizations use information to set goals, determine the gap between goals and achievements, determine actions to reach goals, and create new products and services to enhance organizational performance. Managers depend more on informal communication systems than on formal reporting systems. They expect to receive information that meets their current, everchanging needs. Operational managers need short-term information. Senior executives require mainly long-term information but still have a need for both short- and medium-term information. When managers face time constraints, they collect only enough information to make a satisfactory decision. Most organizations have a wide variety of poorly integrated information delivery systems.Organizational memory should be integrated to provide managers with one interface to an organization's information stores.

Key terms and concepts

Advanced skills (know how)
Benchmarking
Change information
Cognitive knowledge (know what)
Empowerment
Explicit knowledge
Gap information
Global change
Goal-setting information
Information as a means of change
Information delivery systems
Information hardness
Information integration
Information organization
Information requirements
Information richness
Information satisficing
Information society
Knowledge
Managerial work
Organizational change
Phases of civilization
Self-motivated creativity (care why)
Social memory
System understanding (know why)
Tacit knowledge

References and additional readings

Bessen, J. 1993. Riding the marketing information wave. *Harvard Business Review* 71 (5):150–160.

Blattberg, R. C., and J. Deighton. 1991. Interactive marketing: Exploiting the age of addressability. *Sloan Management Review* 33 (1):5-14.

Davenport, T. H. 1994. Saving IT's soul: Human-centered information management. *Harvard Business Review* 72 (2):119–131.

Eccles, R. G. 1991. The performance measurement manifesto. *Harvard Business Review* 69 (1):131–137.

Evans, P. B., and T. S. Wurster. 1997. Strategy and the new economics of information. *Harvard Business Review* 75 (5):71–82.

Nonaka, I., and H. Takeuchi. 1995. *The knowledge-creating company: How Japanese companies create the dynamics of innovation*. New York, NY: Oxford University Press.

Ohmae, K. 1990. *The borderless world*. New York, NY: HarperCollins.

Quinn, J. B. 1992. The intelligent enterprise: A new paradigm. *Academy of Management Executive* 6 (4):48–63.

Quinn, B. J., P. Anderson, and S. Finkelstein. 1996. Leveraging intellect. *Academy of Management Executive* 10 (3):7–27.

Exercises

1. What is different about the 1990s compared to the 1980s?
2. Why are Intel and Microsoft growing so rapidly?
3. Why are paper and writing systems important?
4. What is the difference between soft and hard information?
5. What is the difference between rich and lean information exchange?
6. What are three major types of information connected with organizational change?
7. What is benchmarking? When might a business use benchmarking?
8. What is gap information?
9. Give some examples of how information is used as a means of change.
10. What sort of information do senior managers want?
11. Describe the differences between the way managers handle hard and soft information.
12. What is information satisficing?
13. Describe an incident where you used information satisficing.
14. Give some examples of common information delivery systems.
15. Who uses an EIS?
16. What is a GIS? Who might use a GIS?
17. What is groupware?
18. Why is information integration a problem?
19. Select two public companies listed on the stock exchange in your country. One of these should be an information-based organization (e.g., Microsoft) and the other an industrial era company (e.g., Ford). Compare the PE ratios, assets, revenues, and number of employees. What do you observe? What does this mean?

20. How "hard" is an exam grade?
21. Could you develop a test for the hardness of a piece of information?
22. Is it worth storing very soft information in formal organizational memory? If not, where might you draw the line?
23. If you had just failed your database exam, would you use rich or lean media to tell a parent or spouse about the result?
24. Interview a businessperson to determine his/her firm's critical success factors (CSFs). Remember, a CSF is something the firm must do right to be successful. Generally a firm has about seven CSFs. For the firm's top three CSFs, identify the information that will measure whether the CSF is being achieved.
25. If you were managing a fast-food store, what information would you want to track store performance? Classify this information as short-, medium-, or long-term information.
26. Interview a manager. Identify the information that person uses to manage the company. Classify this information as short-, medium-, or long-term information. Comment on your findings.
27. Why is organizational memory like a data warehouse? What needs to be done to make good use of this data warehouse?
28. What information are you collecting to help determine your career or find a job? What problems are you having collecting this information? Is the information mainly hard or soft?
29. What type of knowledge should you gain in a university class?
30. What type of knowledge is likely to make you most valuable?

Case Questions

Imagine you are the new owner of The Expeditioner (see page 26).

1. What information would you request to determine the present performance of the organization?
2. What information would help you to establish goals for The Expeditioner? What goals would you set?
3. What information would you want to help you assist you in changing The Expeditioner?
4. How could you use information to achieve your goals?

Section 2

Data Modeling and SQL

It is a capital mistake to theorize before one has data.
Sir Arthur Conan Doyle, Scandal in Bohemia, *The Adventures of Sherlock Holmes*, 1891

The application backlog, a large number of requests for new information systems, has been a recurring problem in many organizations for decades. The demand for new information systems and the need to maintain existing systems have usually outstripped available information systems skills. The application backlog, unfortunately, is not a new problem. In the 1970s, Codd laid out a plan for improving programmer productivity and accelerating systems development by improving the management of data. Codd's **relational model**, designed to solve many of the shortcomings of earlier systems, is currently the most popular database model.

This section develops two key skills, data modeling and query formation, that are required to take advantage of the relational model. We concentrate on the design and use of relational databases. This very abrupt change in focus is part of our plan to give you a dual understanding of data management. Section 1 is the managerial perspective, and this section covers technical skills development. Competent data managers are able to accommodate both views and apply whichever perspective (or some blend of the two) is appropriate for particular circumstances.

In Chapter 1, many forms of organizational memory were identified, but in this section we focus on files and their components. Thus, only the files branch of organizational memory is detailed in Figure S2-1. A collection of related files is a **database**. Describing the collection of files as related means that it has a common purpose (e.g., data about students). Sometimes files are also called tables, and there are synonyms for some other terms. (Figure S2-1 shows the alternative names in parentheses.) Files contain **records** (or rows). Each record contains the data for one instance of the data the file stores. For example, if the file stores data about a student, each record will contain data about a single student. Records have **fields** (or columns) that store the fine detail of each instance (e.g., student's first name, last name, and date of birth). Fields are composed of **characters** (a, b, c,..., 1, 2, 3,..., %, $, #, etc.). A byte, a unit of storage sufficient to store a single character, consists of a string of eight contiguous **bits** or binary digits.

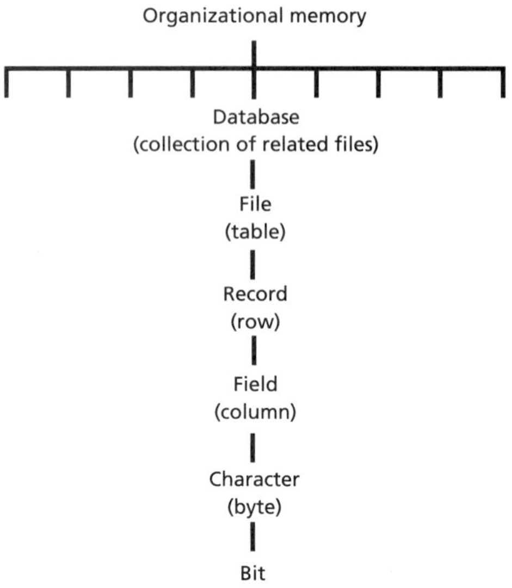

Figure S2-1. Data management hierarchy

The data management hierarchy stimulates three database design questions:

- ❖ What collection of files should the database contain?
- ❖ How are these files related?
- ❖ What fields should each record in the file contain?

The first objective of this section is to describe data modeling, a technique for answering the first two questions. Data modeling helps you to understand the structure and meaning of data, which is necessary before a database can be created. Once a database has been designed, built, and loaded with data, the aim is to deploy it to satisfy management's requests for information. Thus, the second objective is to teach you to query a relational database. The learning of modeling and querying will be intertwined, making it easier to grasp the intent of database design and to understand why data modeling is so critical to making a database an effective tool for managerial decision making.

Chapter 3 covers modeling a single entity and querying a single table database. This is the simplest database that can be created. As you will soon discover, a **data model** is a graphical description of the components of a database. One of these components is an entity, some feature of the real world about which data must be stored. This section also introduces the notions of a **data definition language** (DDL), which is used to describe a database, and a **data manipulation language** (DML), which is used to maintain and query a database. Subsequent chapters in this section cover advanced data modeling concepts and querying capabilities.

3

The Single Entity

I want to be alone.
Attributed to Greta Garbo

Learning objectives

Students completing this chapter will be able to

- ❖ model a single entity;
- ❖ define a single database;
- ❖ write queries for a single table database.

Alice pulled another folder out of the seemingly endless collection supplied by Mr. Mainwaring, the lawyer from Cholmondeley, Crespigny, Majoribanks, and St. John. She had certainly made one decision—to find a lawyer called Smith or Brown. It was most disconcerting to be unable to remember how to pronounce the man's name. The folder, boldly titled "Shares," contained a single sheet of paper on which was listed the names of 10 companies and the number of shares held in each company. Alice thought, "This is just a mass of data. What I really need to know is how much each of these shares is worth and its annual dividend." She forcefully pressed the call button to summon the attendant for a copy of the *Financial Times*.

The relational model

The relational model, introduced by Codd in 1970, is the most popular technology for managing large collections of data. At this point, the major concepts of the relational model are introduced. Extensive coverage of the relational model is left until Chapter 9, by which time you will have sufficient practical experience to appreciate fully its usefulness, value, and elegance.

A **relation**, similar to the mathematical concept of a set, is a two-dimensional table arranged in rows and columns. This is a very familiar idea. You have been using tables for many years. A **relational database** is a collection of relations, where a relation is a mathematical term for a table. The rows of a table store details of one observation, instance, or case of an item about which facts are retained: for example, one row for details of a particular student. All the rows in a table store data about the same type of item. Thus, a database might have one table for student data and another table for class data. Similarly, each column in the table contains the same type of data. For example, the first column might record a student's identification number (in the U.S., this is often a social security number). A key database design question is to decide what to store in each table. What should the rows and columns contain?

In a relational database, each row must be uniquely identified. There must be a **primary key**, such as student identifier, so that a particular row can be designated. The use of unique identifiers is very common. Telephone numbers and e-mail addresses are examples of unique identifiers in common use. Selection of the primary key, or unique identifier, is another key issue of database design.

The tables in a relational database are *connected* or *related* by means of the data in the tables. You will learn, in the next chapter, that this connection is through a pair of values—a primary key and a foreign key. Consider a table of airlines serving a city. When examining this table, you may not recognize the code of an airline, so you then go to another table to find the name of the airline. For example, if you inspect Table 3-1, you find that AM is an international airline serving Atlanta.

Table 3-1: International airlines serving Atlanta

Airlines
AM
JL
KX
LM
MA
OS
RG
SN
SR
LH
LY

If you don't know which airline has the abbreviation AM, then you need to look at the table of airline codes (Table 3-2) to discover that AeroMexico, with code AM, serves Atlanta.

The two tables are *related* by airline code. Later, you will discover which is the primary key and which is the foreign key.

Table 3-2: A partial list of airline codes

Code	Airline
AA	American Airlines
AC	Air Canada
AD	Lone Star Airlines
AE	Mandarin Airlines
AF	Air France
AG	Interprovincial Airlines
AI	Air India
AM	AeroMexico
AQ	Aloha Airlines

When designing the relational model, Codd provided commands for processing multiple records at a time. His intention was to increase the productivity of programmers by moving beyond the record-at-a-time processing that is found in most programming languages. Consequently, the relational model supports set processing (multiple records-at-a-time), which is most frequently implemented as **Structured Query Language (SQL)**.

When writing applications for earlier data management systems, programmers usually had to consider the physical features (e.g., the track size) of the storage device. This made programming more complex and also often meant that when data were moved from one storage device to another, software modification was necessary. The relational model separates the logical design of a database and its physical storage. This notion of **data independence** simplifies data modeling and database programming. In this section, we focus on logical database design, and now that you have had a brief introduction to the relational model, you are ready to learn data modeling.

Getting started

As with most construction projects, building a relational database must be preceded by a design phase. Data modeling, our design technique, is a method for creating a plan or blueprint of a database. The data model must accurately mirror real-world relationships if it is to support processing business transactions and managerial decision making.

Rather than getting bogged down with a *theory first, application later* approach to database design and use, we will start with application. We will get back to theory when you have some experience in data modeling and database querying. After all, you did not learn to talk by first studying sentence formation; you just started by learning and using simple words. We start with the simplest data model, a single entity, and the simplest database, a single table (see for example Table 3-3).

Table 3-3: Share data

Firm's code	Firm's name	Price	Quantity	Dividend	PE ratio
FC	Freedonia Copper	27.50	10,529	1.84	16
PT	Patagonian Tea	55.25	12,635	2.50	10
AR	Abyssinian Ruby	31.82	22,010	1.32	13
SLG	Sri Lankan Gold	50.37	32,868	2.68	16
ILZ	Indian Lead & Zinc	37.75	6,390	3.00	12
BE	Burmese Elephant	.07	154,713	0.01	3
BS	Bolivian Sheep	12.75	231,678	1.78	11
NG	Nigerian Geese	35.00	12,323	1.68	10
CS	Canadian Sugar	52.78	4,716	2.50	15
ROF	Royal Ostrich Farms	33.75	1,234,923	3.00	6

Modeling a single entity database

The simplest database contains information about one entity, which is some real-world thing. Some entities are physical — CUSTOMER,[1] ORDER, and STUDENT; others are conceptual — WORK ASSIGNMENT and AUTHORSHIP. We represent an entity by a rectangle: Figure 3-1 shows a representation of the entity SHARE.[2] The name of the entity is shown in singular form in uppercase in the top part of the rectangle.

Figure 3-1. The entity SHARE

An entity has characteristics or attributes. An **attribute** is a discrete element of data; it is not usually broken down into smaller components. Attributes describe an entity and contain the entity's data we want to store. Some attributes of the entity SHARE are *identification code, firm name, price, quantity owned, dividend,* and *price-to-earnings ratio.*[3] Attributes are shown below the entity's name (Figure 3-2). Notice that we refer to *share price*, rather than *price*, to avoid confusion if there should be another entity with an attribute called *price*. Attribute names must be carefully selected so that they are self-explan-

1. The convention in this book is to use uppercase for an entity's name.
2. SHARE could also be known as STOCK, EQUITY, or SECURITY.
3. Attributes are shown in italics within the text.

atory and unique. For example, ***share dividend*** is easily recognized as belonging to the entity SHARE.

Figure 3-2. The entity SHARE and its attributes

An **instance** is a particular occurrence of an entity (e.g., the facts for Freedonia Copper). To avoid confusion, each instance of an entity needs to be uniquely identified. Consider the case of customer billing. In most cases, a request to bill Smith $100 cannot be accurately processed because a firm typically has many customers called Smith. If a firm has carefully controlled procedures for ensuring that each customer has a unique means of identification, then a request to bill customer number 1789 $100 can be accurately processed. An attribute or collection of attributes that uniquely identify an instance of an entity is called an identifier. The identifier for the entity SHARE is *share code*, a unique identifier assigned by the stock exchange.

There may be several attributes, or combinations of attributes, that are feasible identifiers for an instance of an entity. Attributes that are identifiers are prefixed by an asterisk. Figure 3-3 shows an example of a representation of an entity, its attributes, and identifier.

Figure 3-3. The entity SHARE is uniquely identified by share code

In summary, entities are things in the environment about which we wish to store information. Attributes describe an entity. An entity must have a unique identifier.

Data modeling

The modeling language used in this text is designed to record the essential details of a data model. The number of modeling symbols to learn is small, and they preserve all the fundamental concepts of data modeling. Since data modeling often occurs in a variety of settings, the symbols used have been selected so that they can be quickly drawn using pencil-and-paper, whiteboard, or a general-purpose drawing program (such as that built into PowerPoint). This also means that models can be quickly revised as parts can be readily erased and redrawn.

The symbols are distinct and visual clutter is minimized because only the absolutely essential information is recorded. This also makes the language easy for clients to learn so they can read and amend models.

Models can be rapidly translated to a set of tables for a relational database. More importantly, since this text implements the fundamental notions of all data modeling languages, you can quickly convert to another language (see page 218).

Data modeling is a high level skill and the emphasis needs to be on learning to think like a data modeler rather than learning a modeling language. This text's goal is to get you off to a fast start.

Creating a single table database

The next stage is to translate the data model into a relational database. The translation rules are very direct:

- Each entity becomes a table;
- The entity name becomes the table name;
- Each attribute becomes a column;
- The identifier becomes the primary key.

The American National Standards Institute's (ANSI) recommended language for relational database definition and manipulation is Structured Query Language (SQL), which is both a data definition language (DDL) (used to define a database) and a data manipulation language (DML) (used to query and maintain a database). SQL is a common standard for describing and querying databases and is available with many commercial relational database products, including DB2, Oracle, and Microsoft Access.

SQL uses the CREATE statement to define a table. It is not a particularly friendly command, and most products have easier methods for defining tables (e.g., see Figure 3-4), but it is the standard. Because some relational databases restrict table and column names to eight characters, it is often necessary to abbreviate a data model's attribute names, as has been done in this example for the data shown in Table 3-3.

Defining a table

The CREATE command to establish a table called SHR[4] is:

```
CREATE TABLE SHR
   (SHRCODE        CHAR(3) NOT NULL,
   SHRFIRM         CHAR(20),
   SHRPRICE        DECIMAL(6,2),
   SHRQTY          DECIMAL(8),
   SHRDIV          DECIMAL(5,2),
   SHRPE           DECIMAL(2),
      PRIMARY KEY (SHRCODE))
```

The first line of the command names the table; subsequent lines describe each of the columns in it. The first component is the name of the column (e.g., SHRCODE). The second component is the data type (e.g., CHAR) and its length is shown in parentheses. SHRFIRM is a character field of length 20, which means it can store 20 characters, including spaces. SHRDIV stores a decimal number that can be as large as 999.99 because its total length is 5 digits and there are 2 digits to the right of the decimal point. Some examples of allowable data types are shown in Table 3-4. The third component (e.g., NOT NULL), which is optional, indicates any instance that cannot have null values. A column will have a null value when it is either unknown or not applicable. In the case of the share table, SHRCODE must be defined for each instance in the database because its purpose is to uniquely identify each row. In this example, all other attributes may be null or undefined.

The final line of the CREATE statement defines SHRCODE as the primary key, the unique identifier for SHR. When a primary key is defined, the relational database management system (RDBMS) will enforce the requirement that the primary key is unique. In other words, before any row is added to the table SHR, the RDBMS will first check that the value of SHRCODE for the new row does not already exist as a value for SHRCODE in an existing row of SHR. If an identical value exists, the RDBMS will not permit the new row to be inserted. The specification that SHRCODE is not null and is the primary key is known as the **entity integrity** rule. It simply means every row must have a unique, non-null primary key. Allowing the primary key to take a null value implies there is a row of SHR that cannot be uniquely identified. Thus, NOT NULL should always be specified for the primary key.

Table 3-4 shows some of the data types supported by IBM's relational database, DB2. Other implementations of the relational model may support some of these data types and additional ones (see Table 3-5 for the data types supported by MS Access). It is a good idea to review the available data types in your relational database system before defining your first table.

---

4. It is the usual practice to give the table the same name as the entity; however, this is not always possible. In this case, SHARE is not permissible because it is a reserved word in SQL; thus we have used SHR as the table name.

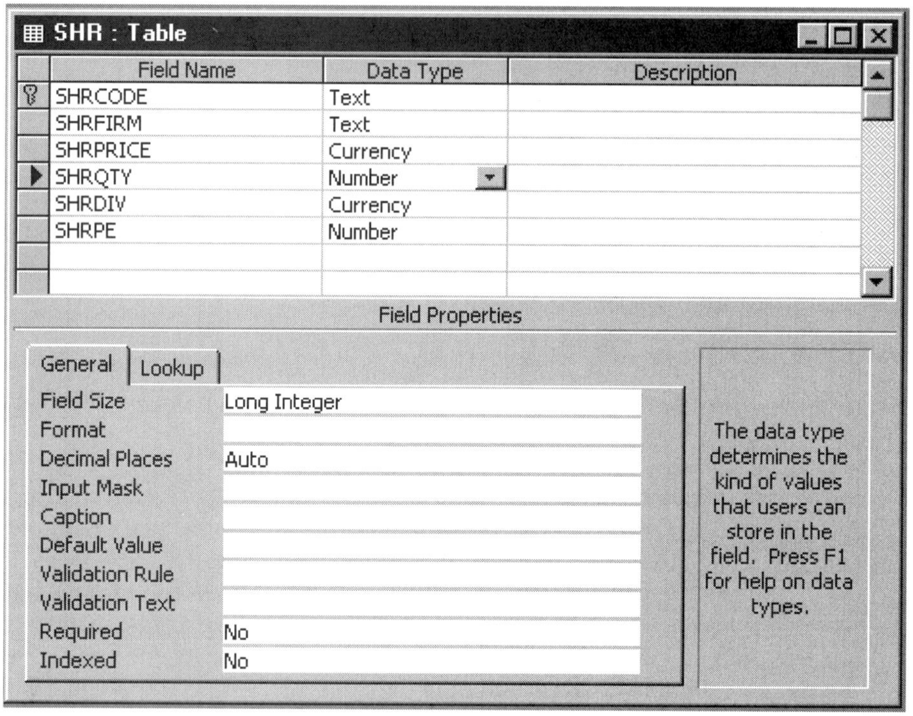

Figure 3-4. Table creation with MS Access

Table 3-4: Some allowable data types

Numeric	SMALLINT	A 15-bit signed binary value
	INTEGER	A 31-bit signed binary value
	FLOAT(*p*)	A scientific format number of *p* binary digits precision
	DECIMAL(*p*,*q*)	A packed decimal number of *p* digits total length; *q* decimal spaces to the right of the decimal point may be specified.
String	CHAR(*n*)	A fixed length character string of *n* characters
	VARCHAR(*n*)	A variable length character string of up to *n* characters
	LONG VARCHAR	A variable length character string
Date/time	DATE	Date in the form *yyyymmdd*
	TIME	Time in the form *hhmmss*
	TIMESTAMP	A combination of date and time to the nearest microsecond
Graphic	GRAPHIC(*n*)	A fixed length graphic string of *n* 16-bit bytes
	VARGRAPHIC(*n*)	A variable length graphic string of up to *n* 16-bit bytes
	LONG VARGRAPHIC	A variable length graphic string of 16-bit bytes

Table 3-5: MS Access data types

Text		A variable length character string of up to 255 characters
Memo		A variable length character string of up to 64,000 characters
Number	Byte	An 8-bit unsigned binary value
	Integer	A 15-bit signed binary value
	Long Integer	A 31-bit signed binary value
	Single	A signed number with an exponent in the range -45 to +38
	Double	A signed number with an exponent in the range -324 to +308
Date/time		A formatted date or time for the years 100 through 9999
Currency		A monetary value
AutoNumber		A unique sequential number or random number assigned by Access whenever a new record is added to a table
Yes/No		A binary field that contains one of two values (Yes/No, True/ False, or On/Off)
OLE Object		An object, such as a spreadsheet, document, graphic, sound, or other binary data
Hyperlink		A hyperlink address (e.g., a URL)

Inserting rows into a table

The rows of a table store instances of an entity. A particular shareholding, say Freedonia Copper, is an example of an instance of the entity SHARE. The SQL statement INSERT is used to add rows to a table. Although most implementations of the relational model have an easier method of row insertion, the INSERT command is defined for completeness. The following command adds one row to the table SHR:

```
INSERT INTO SHR
   (SHRCODE,SHRFIRM,SHRPRICE,SHRQTY,SHRDIV,SHRPE)
      VALUES ('FC','Freedonia Copper',27.5,10529,1.84,16)
```

There is a one-to-one correspondence between a column name in the first set of parentheses and a value in the second set of parentheses. That is, SHRCODE has the value 'FC,' SHRFIRM the value 'Freedonia Copper,' and so on. Notice that the value of a column which stores a character string (e.g., SHRFIRM) is contained within quotes.

The list of field names can be omitted when values are inserted in all fields of the table, so the preceding expression could be written

```
INSERT INTO SHR
   VALUES ('FC','Freedonia Copper',27.5,10529,1.84,16)
```

The data for the SHR table shown in Table 3-6 will be used in subsequent examples. If you have ready access to a relational database, it is a good idea to create a table and enter the data. Then you will be able to use these data to practice querying the table.

Table 3-6: SHR data

SHR					
SHRCODE	SHRFIRM	SHRPRICE	SHRQTY	SHRDIV	SHRPE
FC	Freedonia Copper	27.50	10,529	1.84	16
PT	Patagonian Tea	55.25	12,635	2.50	10
AR	Abyssinian Ruby	31.82	22,010	1.32	13
SLG	Sri Lankan Gold	50.37	32,868	2.68	16
ILZ	Indian Lead & Zinc	37.75	6,390	3.00	12
BE	Burmese Elephant	.07	154,713	0.01	3
BS	Bolivian Sheep	12.75	231,678	1.78	11
NG	Nigerian Geese	35.00	12,323	1.68	10
CS	Canadian Sugar	52.78	4,716	2.50	15
ROF	Royal Ostrich Farms	33.75	1,234,923	3.00	6

Notice that SHRCODE is underlined in the relational table to show it is a primary key. In the data model it has an asterisk prefix to indicate it is an identifier. In the relational model it becomes a primary key, a column that guarantees that each row of the table can be uniquely addressed.

Query-By-Example (QBE)[5] is the other common method for working with a relational database. QBE is easier to use than SQL because you make entries in a table rather than writing commands. There is no standard for QBE. Most implementations look similar, and once you have mastered one version it is easy to use another. We show the MS Access version of QBE because it is particularly easy to learn and MS Access is widely used. The version of QBE for Access can be used for inserting rows and querying a database. Using QBE for input is like entering data in a spreadsheet, as inspection of Figure 3-5 quickly reveals. QBE can also be used for writing queries, but more powerful queries typically require SQL. As information systems professionals must be able to write complex queries, we will focus on learning the full power of SQL.

The objective of developing a database is to make it easier to use the stored data to solve problems. Typically, a manager raises a question (e.g., How many shares have a PE ratio greater than 12?). A question or request for information, usually called a query, is then translated into a specific data manipulation or query language. The most widely used query languages for relational databases are SQL and some form of QBE. After the query has been executed, the resulting data are displayed. In the case of a relational database, the answer to a query is always a table.

There is also a query language called relational algebra, which describes a set of operations on tables. Sometimes it is useful to think of queries in terms of these operations. Also, relational algebra terms are often used for describing queries. Where appropriate we will introduce the corresponding relational algebra operation.

5. Zloof, M. M. 1975. Query by example in *Proceedings of the NCC* 44, May 1975. Zloof invented QBE.

SHR : Table

SHRCODE	SHRFIRM	SHRPRICE	SHRQTY	SHRDIV	SHRPE
AR	Abyssinian Ruby	31.82	22010	1.32	13
BE	Burmese Elephant	0.07	154713	0.01	3
BS	Bolivian Sheep	12.75	231678	1.78	11
CS	Canadian Sugar	52.78	4716	2.50	15
FC	Freedonia Copper	27.50	10529	1.84	16
ILZ	Indian Lead & Zinc	37.75	6390	3.00	12
NG	Nigerian Geese	35.00	12323	1.68	10
PT	Patagonian Tea	55.25	12635	2.50	10
ROF	Royal Ostrich Farms	33.75	1234923	3.00	6
SLG	Sri Lankan Gold	50.37	32868	2.68	16

Record: 11 of 11

Figure 3-5. Inserting rows with MS Access

Generally we use a five-phase format for describing queries:

1. A brief explanation of the query's purpose;
2. The query, prefixed by ❍ and in bold, as it might be phrased by a manager;
3. The SQL version of the query;
4. The results of the query;
5. The QBE version of the query.

The identifying stripe

Nearly every product has 13 black stripes on it somewhere. This bar code is the identifier of a manufactured item. The code has two components: a manufacturer id and product i.d. Bar codes were first established in the US as the Universal Product Code (UPC). The European version of the UPC, the European Article Number (EAN), has become an international standard and is used by 88 nations and over 500,000 companies. The existing range of codes should last until 2010. A Danish manufacturer pays an initial fee of 2,500 kronor (USD365) for the right to use the EAN, with an annual renewal fee of 1,000 kronor (USD145).

Source: Kristensen, K. 1998. Behind the bar codes. *The Copenhagen Post*, February 26, 2.

Displaying an entire table

All the data in a table can be displayed using the SELECT statement. In SQL, the *all* part is indicated by an asterisk (*).

❍ **List all data in the share table.**

```
SELECT * FROM SHR
```

SHRCODE	SHRFIRM	SHRPRICE	SHRQTY	SHRDIV	SHRPE
FC	Freedonia Copper	27.50	10529	1.84	16
PT	Patagonian Tea	55.25	12635	2.50	10
AR	Abyssinian Ruby	31.82	22010	1.32	13
SLG	Sri Lankan Gold	50.37	32868	2.68	16
ILZ	Indian Lead & Zinc	37.75	6390	3.00	12
BE	Burmese Elephant	.07	154713	0.01	3
BS	Bolivian Sheep	12.75	231678	1.78	11
NG	Nigerian Geese	35.00	12323	1.68	10
CS	Canadian Sugar	52.78	4716	2.50	15
ROF	Ruritanian Ostrich Farms	33.75	1234923	3.00	6

The QBE version of listing all rows in a table is shown in Figure 3-6.

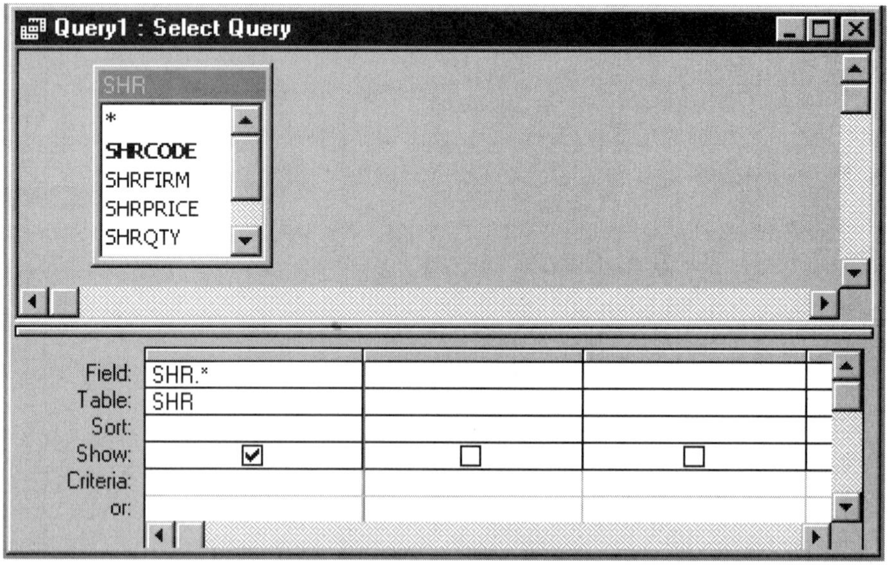

Figure 3-6. Listing all the rows in a table with MS Access

Project—choosing columns

The relational algebra operation **project** creates a new table from the columns of an existing table. Project takes a vertical slice through a table by selecting all the values in specified columns. The projection of SHR on columns SHRFIRM and SHRPE produces a new table with 10 rows and 2 columns. These columns are shaded in Table 3-7. The MS Access QBE version of project is shown in Figure 3-7.

Table 3-7: Projection of SHRFIRM and SHRPE

SHR					
SHRCODE	SHRFIRM	SHRPRICE	SHRQTY	SHRDIV	SHRPE
FC	Freedonia Copper	27.50	10,529	1.84	16
PT	Patagonian Tea	55.25	12,635	2.50	10
AR	Abyssinian Ruby	31.82	22,010	1.32	13
SLG	Sri Lankan Gold	50.37	32,868	2.68	16
ILZ	Indian Lead & Zinc	37.75	6,390	3.00	12
BE	Burmese Elephant	.07	154,713	0.01	3
BS	Bolivian Sheep	12.75	231,678	1.78	11
NG	Nigerian Geese	35.00	12,323	1.68	10
CS	Canadian Sugar	52.78	4,716	2.50	15
ROF	Ruritanian Ostrich Farms	33.75	1,234,923	3.00	6

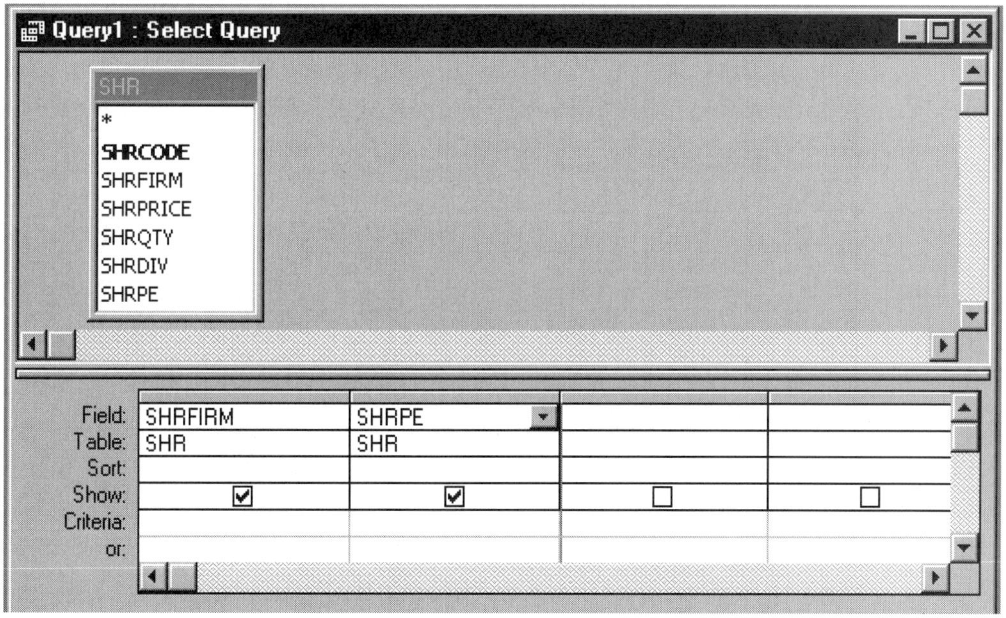

Figure 3-7. Project with MS Access

- The SQL command for project simply lists the columns to be displayed.

❍ **Report a firm's name and price-earnings ratio.**

```
SELECT SHRFIRM, SHRPE FROM SHR
```

SHRFIRM	SHRPE
Freedonia Copper	16
Patagonian Tea	10
Abyssinian Ruby	13
Sri Lankan Gold	16
Indian Lead & Zinc	12
Burmese Elephant	3
Bolivian Sheep	11
Nigerian Geese	10
Canadian Sugar	15
Royal Ostrich Farms	6

Restrict—choosing rows

The relational algebra **restrict** creates a new table from the rows of an existing table. The operation restricts the new table to those rows that satisfy a specified condition. Restrict takes all columns of an existing table but only those rows that meet the specified condition. The restriction of SHR to those rows where the PE ratio is less than 12 will give a new table with five rows and six columns. These rows are indicated by shading in Table 3-8.

Table 3-8: Restriction of SHR

SHR					
SHRCODE	SHRFIRM	SHRPRICE	SHRQTY	SHRDIV	SHRPE
FC	Freedonia Copper	27.50	10,529	1.84	16
PT	Patagonian Tea	55.25	12,635	2.50	10
AR	Abyssinian Ruby	31.82	22,010	1.32	13
SLG	Sri Lankan Gold	50.37	32,868	2.68	16
ILZ	Indian Lead & Zinc	37.75	6,390	3.00	12
BE	Burmese Elephant	.07	154,713	0.01	3
BS	Bolivian Sheep	12.75	231,678	1.78	11
NG	Nigerian Geese	35.00	12,323	1.68	10
CS	Canadian Sugar	52.78	4,716	2.50	15
ROF	Ruritanian Ostrich Farms	33.75	1,234,923	3.00	6

Restrict is implemented in SQL using the WHERE clause to specify the condition on which rows are restricted. The MS Access version of restrict is shown in Figure 3-8.

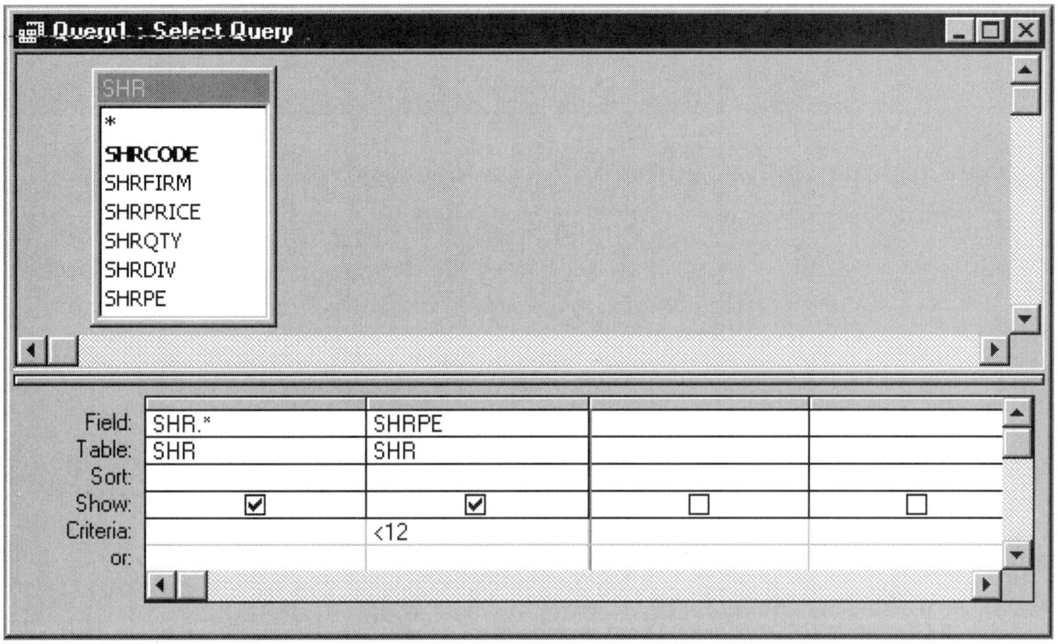

Figure 3-8. Restrict with MS Access

❍ **Get all firms with a price-earnings ratio less than 12.**

```
SELECT * FROM SHR WHERE SHRPE < 12
```

SHRCODE	SHRFIRM	SHRPRICE	SHRQTY	SHRDIV	SHRPE
PT	Patagonian Tea	55.25	12,635	2.50	10
BE	Burmese Elephant	0.07	154,713	0.01	3
BS	Bolivian Sheep	12.75	231,678	1.78	11
NG	Nigerian Geese	35.00	12,323	1.68	10
ROF	Royal Ostrich Farms	33.75	1,234,923	3.00	6

In this example, we have a *less than* condition for the WHERE clause. All permissible comparison operators are listed in Table 3-9.

Table 3-9: Comparison operators

Comparison operator	Meaning
=	Equal to
<	Less than
<=	Less than or equal to
>	Greater than
>=	Greater than or equal to
<>	Not equal to

By now, you should have a good idea of QBE principles. Because the QBE concept is implemented in different ways in RDBMSs, we will leave it to you to learn the finer details of QBE for the database you are using. We will continue to use SQL as the query language because it is the standard and is implemented to some level by nearly all RDBMSs.

Combining project and restrict—choosing rows and columns

SQL permits project and restrict to be combined. A single SQL SELECT statement can specify which columns to project and which rows to restrict.

❍ **List the firm's name, price, quantity, and dividend where the share holding is at least 100,000.**

```
SELECT SHRFIRM, SHRPRICE, SHRQTY, SHRDIV FROM SHR
   WHERE SHRQTY >= 100000
```

SHRFIRM	SHRPRICE	SHRQTY	SHRDIV
Burmese Elephant	0.07	154,713	0.01
Bolivian Sheep	12.75	231,678	1.78
Royal Ostrich Farms	33.75	1,234,923	3.00

More about WHERE

The WHERE clause can contain several conditions linked by AND or OR. A clause containing AND means all specified conditions must be true for a row to be selected. In the case of OR, at least one of the conditions must be true for a row to be selected.

❍ **Find all firms where the PE is 12 or higher and the share holding is less than 10,000.**

```
SELECT * FROM SHR
   WHERE SHRPE >= 12 AND SHRQTY < 10000
```

SHRCODE	SHRFIRM	SHRPRICE	SHRQTY	SHRDIV	SHRPE
ILZ	Indian Lead & Zinc	37.75	6390	3	12
CS	Canadian Sugar	52.78	4716	2.5	15

The power of the primary key

The purpose of a primary key is to guarantee that any row in a table can be uniquely addressed. In this example, we use SHRCODE to return a single row because SHRCODE is unique for each instance of SHR. The sought code (AR) must be specified in quotes because SHRCODE was defined as a character string when the table was created.

❍ **Report firms with code is AR.**

```
SELECT * FROM SHR WHERE SHRCODE = 'AR'
```

SHRCODE	SHRFIRM	SHRPRICE	SHRQTY	SHRDIV	SHRPE
AR	Abyssinian Ruby	31.82	22010	1.32	13

A query based on a non primary key column cannot guarantee that a single row is accessed, as the following query illustrates.

❍ **Report firms with a dividend of 2.50.**

```
SELECT * FROM SHR WHERE SHRDIV = 2.5
```

SHRCODE	SHRFIRM	SHRPRICE	SHRQTY	SHRDIV	SHRPE
PT	Patagonian Tea	55.25	12,635	2.50	10
CS	Canadian Sugar	52.78	4,716	2.50	15

The IN crowd

The keyword IN is used with a list to specify a set of values. IN is always paired with a column name. All rows for which a value in the specified column has a match in the list are selected. It is a simpler way of writing a series of OR statements.

❍ **Report data on firms with codes of FC, AR, or SLG.**

```
SELECT * FROM SHR WHERE SHRCODE IN ('FC','AR','SLG')
```

The foregoing query could have also been written as:

```
SELECT * FROM SHR
   WHERE SHRCODE = 'FC' OR SHRCODE = 'AR' OR SHRCODE = 'SLG'
```

SHRCODE	SHRFIRM	SHRPRICE	SHRQTY	SHRDIV	SHRPE
FC	Freedonia Copper	27.50	10,529	1.84	16
AR	Abyssinian Ruby	31.82	22,010	1.32	13
SLG	Sri Lankan Gold	50.37	32,868	2.68	16

The NOT IN crowd

A NOT IN list is used to report instances that do not match any of the values.

❍ **Report all firms other than those with the code CS or PT.**

```
SELECT * FROM SHR WHERE SHRCODE NOT IN ('CS','PT')
```

is equivalent to:

```
SELECT * FROM SHR WHERE SHRCODE <> 'CS' AND SHRCODE <> 'PT'
```

SHRCODE	SHRFIRM	SHRPRICE	SHRQTY	SHRDIV	SHRPE
FC	Freedonia Copper	27.50	10,529	1.84	16
AR	Abyssinian Ruby	31.82	22,010	1.32	13
SLG	Sri Lankan Gold	50.37	32,868	2.68	16
ILZ	Indian Lead & Zinc	37.75	6,390	3.00	12
BE	Burmese Elephant	0.07	154,713	0.01	3
BS	Bolivian Sheep	12.75	231,678	1.78	11
NG	Nigerian Geese	35.00	12,323	1.68	10
ROF	Royal Ostrich Farms	33.75	1,234,923	3.00	6

Ordering columns

The order of reporting columns is identical to their order in the SQL command. For instance, the query

```
SELECT SHRCODE, SHRFIRM FROM SHR WHERE SHRPE = 10
```

gives:

SHRCODE	SHRFIRM
PT	Patagonian Tea
NG	Nigerian Geese

while the query

```
SELECT SHRFIRM, SHRCODE FROM SHR WHERE SHRPE = 10
```

gives:

SHRFIRM	SHRCODE
Patagonian Tea	PT
Nigerian Geese	NG

Ordering rows

People can process an ordered report faster than an unordered one. Imagine trying to find a name in a phone book that was not sorted by last name. That's why telephone books are ordered alphabetically by last name and then within the same last name by first name. Actually, this is not true in Iceland where the telephone book is ordered alphabetically by first name. Because of Icelandic naming traditions, it is easier to search the telephone book on the basis of first name than last name.[6]

6. If an Icelandic man with the first name Ragnar has a daughter named Inga, her full name will be Inga Ragnarsdottir (literally daughter of Ragnar). If he has a son, his last name will be Ragnarsson.

In SQL, the ORDER BY clause specifies the row order in a report. The default ordering sequence is ascending (A before B, 1 before 2). Descending is specified by adding DESC after the column name.

❍ **List all firms where PE is at least 10, and order the report in descending PE. Where PE ratios are identical, list firms in alphabetical order.**

```
SELECT * FROM SHR WHERE SHRPE >= 10
   ORDER BY SHRPE DESC, SHRFIRM
```

produces:

SHRCODE	SHRFIRM	SHRPRICE	SHRQTY	SHRDIV	SHRPE
FC	Freedonia Copper	27.50	10529	1.84	16
SLG	Sri Lankan Gold	50.37	32868	2.68	16
CS	Canadian Sugar	52.78	4716	2.50	15
AR	Abyssinian Ruby	31.82	22010	1.32	13
ILZ	Indian Lead & Zinc	37.75	6390	3.00	12
BS	Bolivian Sheep	12.75	231678	1.78	11
NG	Nigerian Geese	35.00	12323	1.68	10
PT	Patagonian Tea	55.25	12635	2.50	10

Numeric versus character sorting

Numeric data in character fields (e.g., a product code) do not always sort the way you initially expect. The difference arises from the way data are stored:

- numeric fields are right justified and have leading zeros.
- character fields are left justified and have trailing spaces.

For example, the value 1066 stored in a character field of four bytes would be stored as `'1066'` and the value 45 would be stored as `'45  '`. If the column containing these data is sorted in ascending order, then `'1066'` precedes `'45  '` because `'1'` is less than `'4'`. You can avoid this problem by always storing numeric values as numeric data types (e.g., integer or decimal) or preceding numeric values with zeros when they are stored as character data. Alternatively, start numbering at 1,000 so that all values are four digits.

Derived data

One of the important principles of database design is to avoid redundancy. One form of redundancy is including a column in a table when these data can be derived from other columns. For example, we do not need a column for yield because it can be calculated by dividing dividend by price and multiplying by 100 to obtain the yield as a percentage. This means that the query language does the calculation when the value is required.

❍ **Get firm name, price, quantity, and firm yield.**

```
SELECT SHRFIRM, SHRPRICE, SHRQTY, SHRDIV/SHRPRICE*100 FROM SHR
```

SHRFIRM	SHRPRICE	SHRQTY	EXPRESSION 1
Freedonia Copper	27.50	10,529	6.69
Patagonian Tea	55.25	12,635	4.52
Abyssinian Ruby	31.82	22,010	4.15
Sri Lankan Gold	50.37	32,868	5.32
Indian Lead & Zinc	37.75	6,390	7.95
Burmese Elephant	0.07	154,713	14.29
Bolivian Sheep	12.75	231,678	13.96
Nigerian Geese	35.00	12,323	4.80
Canadian Sugar	52.78	4,716	4.74
Royal Ostrich Farms	33.75	1,234,923	8.89

Note that SQL[7] puts the results of the calculation in a column headed Expression 1. Soon you will learn how to make this heading more descriptive of the data in the column.

SQL built-in functions

SQL has built-in functions to enhance its retrieval power and handle many common queries. Four of these functions (AVG, SUM, MIN, and MAX) work very similarly. COUNT is a little different.

Count

COUNT computes the number of rows in a table. Rows are counted even if they contain null values. Count can be used with a WHERE clause to specify a condition.

❍ **How many firms are there in the portfolio?**

```
SELECT COUNT(*) AS INVESTMENTS FROM SHR
```

Investments
10

In the preceding query, the keyword **AS** is introduced to specify an **alias**, or temporary name, created for the result of the count. The statement specifies that the result of COUNT(*) is to be reported under the column heading INVESTMENTS. You can rename any column using an alias.

7. This is the case for DB2. Other systems (e.g., Oracle) may create a different column name.

❍ **How many firms have a holding greater than 50,000?**

```
SELECT COUNT(*) AS BIGHOLDINGS FROM SHR WHERE SHRQTY > 50000
```

BIGHOLDINGS
3

Average

AVG computes the average of the values in a column of numeric data. Null values in the column are not included in the calculation.

❍ **Find the average dividend.**

```
SELECT AVG(SHRDIV) FROM SHR
```

EXPRESSION 1
2.03

❍ **What is the average yield for the portfolio?**

```
SELECT AVG(SHRDIV/SHRPRICE*100) AS AVGYIELD FROM SHR
```

AVGYIELD
7.53

SUM, MIN, and MAX

SUM, MIN, and MAX differ in the statistic they calculate but are used similarly to AVG. As with AVG, null values in a column are not included in the calculation. SUM computes the sum of a column of values. MIN finds the smallest value in a column; MAX finds the largest.

Subqueries

Sometimes we need the answer to another query before we can write the query of ultimate interest. For example, to list all shares with a PE ratio greater than the portfolio average, you first must find the average PE ratio for the portfolio. You could do the query in two stages:

```
A. SELECT AVG(SHRPE) FROM SHR
B. SELECT SHRFIRM, SHRPE FROM SHR WHERE SHRPE > X
```

where *x* is the value returned from the first query.

Unfortunately, the two-stage method introduces the possibility of errors. You might forget the value returned by the first query or enter it incorrectly. It also takes longer to get the results of the query. We can solve these problems by using parentheses to indicate the first query is nested within the second one. As a result, the value returned by the inner or nested subquery, the one in parentheses, is used in the outer query. In the following example, the nested query returns 11.20, which is then automatically substituted in the outer query.

❍ **Report all firms with a PE ratio greater than the average for the portfolio.**

```
SELECT SHRFIRM, SHRPE FROM SHR
   WHERE SHRPE > (SELECT AVG(SHRPE) FROM SHR)
```

SHRFIRM	SHRPE
Freedonia Copper	16
Abyssinian Ruby	13
Sri Lankan Gold	16
Indian Lead & Zinc	12
Canadian Sugar	15

Warning: The preceding query is often mistakenly written as

```
SELECT SHRFIRM, SHRPE FROM SHR
   WHERE SHRPE > AVG(SHRPE)
```

Identity theft

Identity thieves normally operate by stealing someone's Social Security number (SSN) and then using it to apply for loans or credit cards. The Federal government, with some help from the private sector, has been making the crooks' work a lot easier.

Until quite recently, transfers of directors' corporate stock and other Securities & Exchange Commission filings listed the SSNs of corporate executives. The SEC no longer requires these SSNs to be listed, but many companies continue to do so. Fifteen companies disseminate these SEC filings; however, they cannot be forced to take the personal information off their systems.

With a written request, the Social Security Administration provides the SSNs of the deceased, who are not protected by privacy laws. Consequently, there are many Web sites selling these SSNs. Although in 1997 the Congressional Record stopped listing the SSNs of military officers who are promoted, there are sites that list and sell these numbers. Congress is considering a bill to make SSN sales unlawful.

Source: McNatt, R., and D. Blank. 2000. Not so secure as Social Security. *Business Week*, Oct 16 (3703):14.

LIKE—pattern matching

Have you ever searched a major city's phone book for someone whose last name and street address you can recall but whose first name you just cannot remember? If you are looking for a Ms. Smith in Sydney, you will spend a lot of time sequentially searching through the Smiths, looking for the matching street name. LIKE solves these types of problems when you are searching a table because it searches for a specified pattern in a nominated column. LIKE uses two symbols for specifying a search pattern:

- The percentage sign (%) is the symbol for any number of characters, or none.
- The underscore (_) is the symbol for any single character.[8]

These examples illustrate the use of LIKE.

❍ **List all firms with a name starting with 'F.'**

```
SELECT SHRFIRM FROM SHR WHERE SHRFIRM LIKE 'F%'
```

SHRFIRM
Freedonia Copper

❍ **List all firms containing 'Ruby' in their name.**

```
SELECT SHRFIRM FROM SHR WHERE SHRFIRM LIKE '%Ruby%'
```

SHRFIRM
Abyssinian Ruby

❍ **Find firms with 't' as the third letter of their name.**

```
SELECT SHRFIRM FROM SHR WHERE SHRFIRM LIKE '__t%'
```

SHRFIRM
Patagonian Tea

❍ **Find firms not containing an 's' in their name.**

This query is a little vague, even for academic work. Do you assume that it refers to the lowercase *s*, uppercase *S*, or both? In the business world, you would ask the manager who requested the data. We assume it means neither upper nor lower case.

```
SELECT SHRFIRM FROM SHR
   WHERE SHRFIRM NOT LIKE '%S%'
   AND SHRFIRM NOT LIKE '%s%'
```

8. With MS Access, use * and ? in place of % and _ , respectively.

SHRFIRM
Freedonia Copper
Patagonian Tea
Indian Lead & Zinc

DISTINCT—Eliminating Duplicate Rows

The SQL DISTINCT clause is used to eliminate duplicate rows. It can be used with the column functions or before a column name. When used with a column function, it ignores duplicate values.

❍ **Report the different values of the PE ratio.**

```
SELECT DISTINCT SHRPE FROM SHR
```

SHRPE
3
6
10
11
12
13
15
16

❍ **Find the number of different PE ratios.**

```
SELECT COUNT(DISTINCT SHRPE) AS 'Different PEs' FROM SHR
```
[9]

Different PEs
8

When used before a column name, DISTINCT prevents the selection of duplicate rows. Notice a slightly different use of the keyword AS. In this case, because the alias includes a space, the entire alias is enclosed in quotes.

DELETE—Deleting rows

Rows in a table can be deleted using the DELETE clause in an SQL statement. DELETE is typically used with a WHERE clause to specify the rows to be deleted. If there is no WHERE clause, all rows are deleted.

9. This code does not work with MS Access. Once you have learned how to create a virtual table, you will be able to write appropriate SQL for MS Access (see page 103).

❍ **Erase the data for Burmese Elephant. All the shares have been sold.**

```
DELETE FROM SHR WHERE SHRCODE = 'BE'
```

In this statement, SHRCODE is used to indicate the row to be deleted. We could have used WHERE SHRFIRM = 'Burmese Elephant' but using SHRCODE takes less typing and lessens the chance of an error.

UPDATE—Updating rows

Rows can be modified using SQL's UPDATE clause, which is used with a WHERE clause to specify the rows to be updated.

❍ **Change the share price of FC to 31.50.**

```
UPDATE SHR
   SET SHRPRICE = 31.50
   WHERE SHRCODE = 'FC'
```

❍ **Increase the total number of shares for Nigerian Geese by 10% because of the recent bonus issue.**

```
UPDATE SHR
   SET SHRQTY = SHRQTY*1.1
   WHERE SHRFIRM = 'Nigerian Geese'
```

Debriefing

Now that you have learned how to model a single entity, create a table, and specify queries, you are on the way to mastering the fundamental skills of database design, implementation, and use. Remember, planning occurs before action. A data model is a plan for a database. The action side of a database is inserting rows and running queries.

Summary

The relational database model is an effective means of representing real-world relationships. Data modeling is used to determine what data must be stored and how data are related. An entity is something in the environment. An entity has attributes, which describe it, and an identifier, which uniquely marks an instance of an entity. Every entity must have a unique identifier. A relational database consists of tables with rows and columns. A data model is readily translated to a relational database. The SQL statement CREATE is used to define a table. Rows are added to a table using INSERT. In SQL, queries are written using the SELECT statement. QBE is an alternative to SQL. Project (choosing columns) and restrict (choosing rows) are common table operations. The WHERE clause is used to specify row selection criteria. WHERE can be combined with IN and NOT IN, which specify values for a single column. The rows of a report are sorted using the ORDER BY clause. Arithmetic expressions can appear in SQL statements, and SQL has built-in functions for common arithmetic operations. A subquery is a query within a query. The LIKE clause is used for pattern matching of character strings. Duplicate rows are eliminated with the DISTINCT clause. Rows can be erased using DELETE or modified with UPDATE.

Key terms and concepts

Alias
AS
Attribute
AVG
Column
COUNT
CREATE
Data modeling
Data type
Database
DELETE
DISTINCT
Entity
Entity integrity rule
Identifier
IN
INSERT
Instance
LIKE
MAX
MIN
NOT IN
ORDER BY
Primary key
Project
Query-By-Example (QBE)
Relational database
Restrict
Row
SELECT
SQL
Subquery
SUM
Table
UPDATE
WHERE

Exercises

1. Draw data models for the following entities. In each case, make certain that you show the attributes and identifiers:
   a. Ship: A ship has a name, registration code, gross tonnage, and a year of construction. Ships are classified as cargo or passenger.
   b. Car: A car has a manufacturer, range name, and style code (e.g., a Honda Accord DX, where Honda is the manufacturer, Accord is the range, and DX is the style). A car also has a vehicle identification code, registration code, and color.
   c. Restaurant: A restaurant has an address, seating capacity, phone number, and style of food (e.g., French, Russian, Chinese).
   d. Cow: A dairy cow has a name, date of birth, breed (e.g., Holstein), and a numbered plastic ear tag.
2. Take each of the entities you have modeled, create a relational database, and insert some rows.
3. Do the following queries using SQL or QBE:
   a. List a share's name and its code.
   b. List full details for all shares with a price less than one dollar.
   c. List the name and price of all shares with a price of at least $10.
   d. Create a report showing firm name, share price, share holding, and total value of shares held. (Value of shares held is price times quantity.)
   e. List the name of all shares with a yield exceeding 5 percent.

f. Report the total dividend payment of Patagonian Tea. (The total dividend payment is dividend times quantity.)
g. Find all shares where the price is less than 20 times the dividend.
h. Find the share with the minimum yield.
i. Find the total value of all shares with a PE ratio > 10.
j. Find the share with the maximum total dividend payment.
k. Find the value of the holdings in Abyssinian Ruby and Sri Lankan Gold.
l. Find the yield of all firms except Bolivian Sheep and Canadian Sugar.
m. Find the total value of the portfolio.
n. List firm name and value in descending order of value.
o. List shares with a firm name containing 'Gold.'
p. Find shares with a code starting with 'B.'

4. Run the following queries and explain the differences in output. Write each query as a manager might state it.
   a. SELECT SHRFIRM FROM SHR WHERE SHRFIRM NOT LIKE '%s%'
   b. SELECT SHRFIRM FROM SHR WHERE SHRFIRM NOT LIKE '%S%'
   c. SELECT SHRFIRM FROM SHR WHERE SHRFIRM NOT LIKE '%s%' AND SHRFIRM NOT LIKE '%S%'
   d. SELECT SHRFIRM FROM SHR WHERE SHRFIRM NOT LIKE '%s%' OR SHRFIRM NOT LIKE '%S%'
   e. SELECT SHRFIRM FROM SHR WHERE (SHRFIRM NOT LIKE '%s%' AND SHRFIRM NOT LIKE '%S%') OR SHRFIRM LIKE 'S%'
5. A weekly newspaper, sold at supermarket checkouts, frequently reports stories of aliens visiting Earth and taking humans on short trips. Sometimes a captured human sees Elvis commanding the spaceship. Well, to keep track of all these reports, the newspaper has created the following data model.

The paper has also supplied some data for the last few sightings and asked you to create the database and add details of these aliens.
When you have created the database, answer the following queries:
   a. What's the average number of heads for an alien?
   b. Which alien has the most heads?
   c. Are there any aliens with a double *o* in their names?
   d. How many aliens are chartreuse?
   e. Report details of all aliens sorted by smell and color.

6. If you have a database system on your personal computer, create the SHR table and insert some rows. Compare the approach of standard SQL to your database system. Which was easier to use for defining a table and inserting some rows? Next, do some queries. How do the two systems compare?
7. Eduardo, a bibliophile, has a collection of several hundred books. Being a little disorganized, he has his books scattered around his den. They are piled on the floor, some are in bookcases, and others sit on top of his desk. Because he has so many books, he finds it difficult to remember what he has, and sometimes he cannot find the book he wants. Eduardo has a simple personal computer file system that is fine for a single entity or file. He has decided that he would like to list each book by author(s)' name and type of book (e.g., literature, travel, reference). Draw a data model for this problem, create a single entity table, and write some SQL queries.
   a. How do you identify each instance of a book? (It might help to look at a few books.)
   b. How should Eduardo physically organize his books to permit fast retrieval of a particular one?
   c. Are there any shortcomings with the data model you have created?
8. What is an identifier? Why does a data model have an identifier?
9. What are entities?
10. What is the entity integrity rule?

CD library case[10]

Ajay, who is a DJ in the student-operated radio station at his university, is impressed by the station's large collection of CDs but is frustrated by the time he spends searching for a particular piece of music. Recently, when preparing his weekly jazz session, he spent more than half an hour searching for a recording of Duke Ellington's "Creole Blues." An MIS major, Ajay had recently commenced a data management class. He quickly realized that a relational database, storing details of all the CDs owned by the radio station, would enable him to find quickly any piece of music.

Having just learned how to model a single entity, Ajay decided to start building a CD database. He took one of his favorite CDs, John Coltrane's "Giant Steps," and drew a model to record details of the tracks on this CD (see Figure 3-9).

Ajay pondered using *track number* as the identifier since each track on a CD is uniquely numbered, but he quickly realized that *track number* was not suitable because it uniquely identifies only those tracks on a specific CD. So, he introduced *trackid* to identify uniquely each track irrespective of the CD on which it is found.

10. This case extends your skills in data modeling and SQL. Gradually, you will design and implement a database for storing details of CDs. This case continues through to Chapter 6.

Figure 3-9. CD library V1.0

He also recorded the name of the track and its length. He had originally thought that he would record the track's length in minutes and seconds (e.g., 4:43) but soon discovered that the TIME data type of his DBMS is designed to store time of day rather than the length of time of an event. Thus, he concluded that he should store the length of a track in minutes as a decimal (i.e., 4:43 is stored as 4.72).

Table 3-10: *Giant Steps*

Trkid	Trknum	Trktitle	Trklength
1	1	Giant Steps	4.72
2	2	Cousin Mary	5.75
3	3	Countdown	2.35
4	4	Spiral	5.93
5	5	Syeeda's Song Flute	7.00
6	6	Naima	4.35
7	7	Mr. P.C.	6.95
8	8	Giant steps	3.67
9	9	Naima	4.45
10	10	Cousin Mary	5.90
11	11	Countdown	4.55
12	12	Syeeda's Song Flute	7.03

Your turn

1. Create a single table database using the data in Table 3-10.
2. Justify your choice of data type for each of the attributes.

Ajay ran a few queries on his single table database.

❍ **On what track is Giant Steps?**

```
SELECT TRKNUM, TRKTITLE FROM TRACK
   WHERE TRKTITLE = 'Giant Steps'
```

TRKNUM	TRKTITLE
1	Giant Steps
8	Giant Steps

Observe that there are two tracks with the title "Giant Steps."

❍ **Report all recordings longer than 5 minutes.**

```
SELECT TRKNUM, TRKTITLE, TRKLENGTH FROM TRACK
   WHERE TRKLENGTH > 5
```

TRKNUM	TRKTITLE	TRKLENGTH
2	Cousin Mary	5.75
4	Spiral	5.93
5	Syeeda's Song Flute	7.00
7	Mr. P.C.	6.95
10	Cousin Mary	5.90
12	Syeeda's song flute	6.03

❍ **What is the total length of recordings on the CD?**

This query makes use of the function SUM to total the length of tracks on the CD.

```
SELECT SUM(TRKLENGTH) AS SUMTRKLEN FROM TRACK
```

SUMTRKLEN
62.65

When you run the preceding query, the value reported may not be exactly 62.65. Why?

❍ **Find the longest track on the CD.**

```
SELECT TRKNUM, TRKTITLE, TRKLENGTH FROM TRACK
   WHERE TRKLENGTH = (SELECT MAX(TRKLENGTH) FROM TRACK)
```

This query follows the model described previously in this chapter. First determine the longest track (i.e., 7.03 minutes) and then find the track, or tracks, that are this length.

TRKNUM	TRKTITLE	TRKLENGTH
12	Syeeda's Song Flute	7.03

❍ **How many tracks are there on the CD?**

```
SELECT COUNT(*) AS TRACKS FROM TRACK
```

TRACKS
12

❍ **Sort the different titles on the CD by their name.**

```
SELECT DISTINCT(TRKTITLE) FROM TRACK
   ORDER BY TRKTITLE
```

TRKTITLE
Countdown
Cousin Mary
Giant Steps
Mr. P.C.
Naima
Spiral
Syeeda's Song Flute

❍ **List the shortest track containing "song" in its title.**

```
SELECT TRKNUM, TRKTITLE, TRKLENGTH FROM TRACK
   WHERE TRKTITLE LIKE '%song%'
   AND TRKLENGTH = (SELECT MIN(TRKLENGTH) FROM TRACK
      WHERE TRKTITLE LIKE '%song%')
```

The subquery determines the length of the shortest track with "song" in its title. Then any track with a length equal to the minimum and also containing "song" in its title (just in case there is another without "song" in its title that is the same length) is reported.[11]

TRKNUM	TRKTITLE	TRKLENGTH
5	Syeeda's Song Flute	7.00

❍ **Report details of tracks 1 and 5.**

```
SELECT TRKNUM, TRKTITLE, TRKLENGTH FROM TRACK
   WHERE TRKNUM IN (1,5)
```

TRKNUM	TRKTITLE	TRKLENGTH
1	Giant Steps	4.72
5	Syeeda's Song Flute	7.00

Your turn

1. Write SQL commands for the following queries:
   a. Report all tracks between 4 and 5 minutes long.
   b. On what track is "Naima"?
   c. Sort the tracks by descending length.

11. If you are using MS Access, use * in place of %.

   d. What tracks are longer than the average length of tracks on the CD?
   e. How many tracks are less than 5 minutes?
   f. What tracks start with "Cou"?

2. Add the 13 tracks from The Manhattan Transfer's *Swing* CD in the following table to the TRACK table:

Track	Title	Length
1	Stomp of King Porter	3.20
2	Sing a Study in Brown	2.85
3	Sing Moten's Swing	3.60
4	A-tisket, A-tasket	2.95
5	I Know Why	3.57
6	Sing You Sinners	2.75
7	Java Jive	2.85
8	Down South Camp Meetin'	3.25
9	Topsy	3.23
10	Clouds	7.20
11	Skyliner	3.18
12	It's Good Enough to Keep	3.18
13	Choo Choo Ch' Boogie	3.00

3. Write SQL to answer the following queries:
   a. What is the longest track on *Swing*?
   b. What tracks on *Swing* include the word Java?
4. What is the data model missing?

4

The One-to-Many Relationship

Cow of many—well milked and badly fed.
Spanish proverb

Learning objectives

Students completing this chapter will be able to

- model a one-to-many relationship between two entities;
- define a database with a one-to-many relationship;
- write queries for a database with a one-to-many relationship.

Alice sat with a self-satisfied smirk on her face. Her previous foray into her attaché case had revealed the extent of her considerable stock holdings. She was wealthy beyond her dreams. What else was there in this marvelous, magic attaché case? She rummaged further into the case and retrieved a folder labeled "Stocks—foreign." More shares!

On the inside cover of the folder was a note stating that the stocks in this folder were not listed in the United Kingdom. The folder contained three sheets of paper. Each was headed by the name of a country and followed by a list of stocks and the number of shares. The smirk became the cattiest of Cheshire grins. Alice ordered another bottle of champagne and turned to the *Financial Times* page that listed foreign stock prices. She wanted to calculate the current value of each stock and then use current exchange rates to convert the values into British currency.

Relationships

Entities are not isolated; they are related to other entities. When we move beyond the single entity, we need to identify the relationships between entities to accurately represent the real world. Once we recognize that all stocks in our case study are not listed in the United Kingdom, we need to introduce an entity called NATION. We now have two entities, STOCK[1] and NATION. Consider the relationship between them. A NATION can have many listed stocks. A stock, in this case, is listed in only one nation. There is a 1:m (one-to-many)[2] relationship between NATION and STOCK.

A 1:m relationship between two entities is depicted by a line connecting the two with a crow or chicken foot at the many end of the relationship. Figure 4-1 shows the 1:m relationship between STOCK and NATION. This can be read as: "a nation can have many stocks, but a stock belongs to only one nation." The entity NATION is identified by a *nation code* and has attributes *nation name* and *exchange rate*.

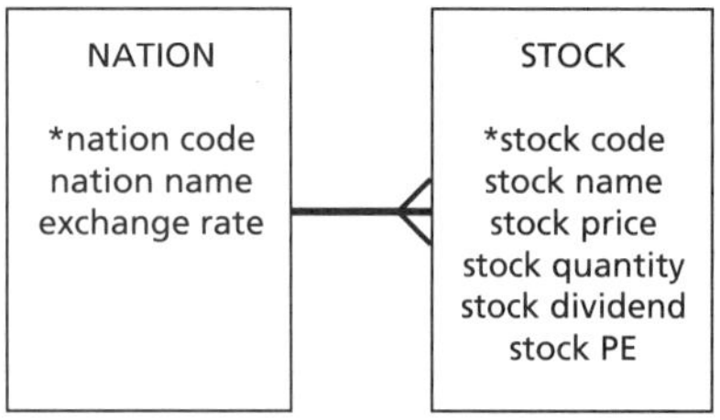

Figure 4-1. A 1:m relationship between NATION and STOCK

The 1:m relationship occurs frequently in business situations. Sometimes it occurs in a tree or hierarchical fashion. Consider a firm. It has many divisions, but a division belongs to only one firm. A division has many departments, but a department belongs to only one division. A department has many sections, but a section belongs to only one department (see Figure 4-2). We see a similar tree structure in the reporting of sales by country, region, and state.

Why did we create an additional entity?

Another approach to adding data about listing nation and exchange rate is to add two attributes to STOCK: *nation name* and *exchange rate*. At first glance, this seems a very workable solution; however, this will introduce considerable redundancy, as Table 4-1 illustrates.

---

1. Why have we changed the label to STOCK when it seems to be the same as SHR? Because, as you will see shortly, STOCK is related to another entity, whereas SHR stands alone.
2. One-to-many is the common interpretation of 1:m. You can also think of it as one-and-many because there are two relationships—STOCK is related to one NATION, and NATION is related to many STOCKs. While we believe one-and-many is more precise, we have adopted the common usage.

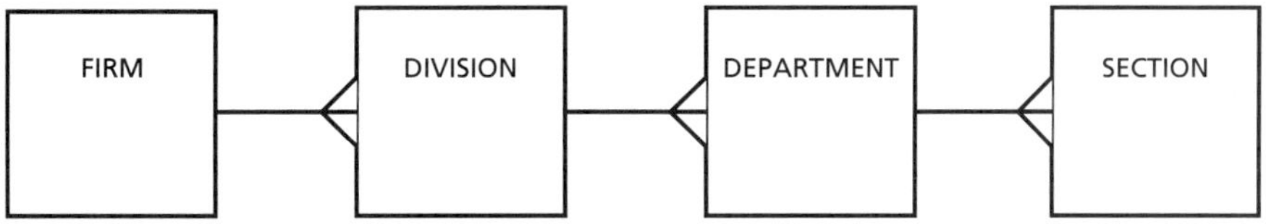

Figure 4-2. A series of 1:m relationships

Table 4-1: The table STOCK with additional columns

STOCK							
STKCODE	STKFIRM	STKPRICE	STKQTY	STKDIV	STKPE	NATNAME	EXCHRATE
FC	Freedonia Copper	27.50	10,529	1.84	16	United Kingdom	1.00
PT	Patagonian Tea	55.25	12,635	2.50	10	United Kingdom	1.00
AR	Abyssinian Ruby	31.82	22,010	1.32	13	United Kingdom	1.00
SLG	Sri Lankan Gold	50.37	32,868	2.68	16	United Kingdom	1.00
ILZ	Indian Lead &Zinc	37.75	6,390	3.00	12	United Kingdom	1.00
BE	Burmese Elephant	.07	154,713	0.01	3	United Kingdom	1.00
BS	Bolivian Sheep	12.75	231,678	1.78	11	United Kingdom	1.00
NG	Nigerian Geese	35.00	12,323	1.68	10	United Kingdom	1.00
CS	Canadian Sugar	52.78	4,716	2.50	15	United Kingdom	1.00
ROF	Royal Ostrich Farms	33.75	1,234,923	3.00	6	United Kingdom	1.00
MG	Minnesota Gold	53.87	816,122	1.00	25	USA	0.67
GP	Georgia Peach	2.35	387,333	.20	5	USA	0.67
NE	Narembeen Emu	12.34	45,619	1.00	8	Australia	0.46
QD	Queensland Diamond	6.73	89,251	.50	7	Australia	0.46
IR	Indooroopilly Ruby	15.92	56,147	.50	20	Australia	0.46
BD	Bombay Duck	25.55	167,382	1.00	12	India	0.0228

The same *nation name* and *exchange rate* pair occurs 10 times for stocks listed in the United Kingdom. Redundancy presents problems when we want to insert, delete, or update data. These problems, generally known as update anomalies, occur with these three basic operations.

Insert anomalies

We cannot insert a fact about a nation's exchange rate unless we first buy a stock that is listed in that nation. Consider the case where we want to keep a record of France's exchange rate and we have no French stocks. We cannot skirt this problem by putting in a null entry for stock details because STKCODE, the identifier, would be null, and this is not allowed. If we have a separate table for facts about a nation, then we can easily add new nations without having to buy stocks. This is particularly useful when other parts of the organization, say International Trading, also need access to exchange rates.

Delete anomalies

If we delete data about a particular stock, we might also lose a fact about exchange rates. For example, if we delete details of Bombay Duck, we also erase the Indian exchange rate.

Update anomalies

Exchange rates are volatile. Many companies need to update them every day. What happens when the Australian exchange rate changes? Every row in STOCK with NATION = "Australia" will have to be updated. In a large portfolio, many rows will be changed. There is also the danger of someone forgetting to update all the instances of the nation and exchange rate pair. As a result, there could be two exchange rates for the one nation. If exchange rate is stored in NATION, however, only one change is necessary, there is no redundancy, and there is no danger of inconsistent exchange rates.

Mastering business intelligence

Shop At Home sells collectibles and other items through its 24-hour television broadcast and companion Web site—Collectibles.com. Business intelligence systems quickly and cost-effectively supply analysts with information to make strategic business decisions. The business intelligence tools themselves range from complex query/analysis to simple reporting tools.

"We have to look at our product mix from a strategic standpoint to best achieve profitability," Lee Martin, VP of Systems Development, says. "And the only way we can find out that type of information as quickly as we need to is a business intelligence system."

The creation of these systems involves combining business knowledge and data modeling skills. Shop At Home recognizes that it is important to hire database designers and data modelers with a solid understanding of multidimensional and relational database technology.

Source: Brandel, M. 2001. Masters of business intelligence. *Computerworld*, Feb 26, http://www.computerworld.com/cwi/story/0,1199,NAV47_STO58010,00.html.

Creating a database with a 1:m relationship

As before, each entity becomes a table in a relational database, the entity name becomes the table name, each attribute becomes a column, and each identifier becomes a primary key. The 1:m relationship is mapped by adding a column to the entity at the many end of the relationship. The additional column contains the identifier of the one end of the relationship.

Consider the relationship between the entities STOCK and NATION (see Figure 4-1). The relational database (see Figure 4-3) has two tables, STOCK and NATION. STOCK has an additional column, NATCODE, which contains the identifier of NATION. If NATCODE is not stored in STOCK, then there is no way of knowing the identity of the nation where the stock is listed.

NATION		
NATCODE	**NATNAME**	**EXCHRATE**
UK	United Kingdom	1.00
USA	United States	0.67
AUS	Australia	0.46
IND	India	0.0228

STOCK						
STKCODE	**STKFIRM**	**STKPRICE**	**STKQTY**	**STKDIV**	**STKPE**	***NATCODE***
FC	Freedonia Copper	27.50	10,529	1.84	16	UK
PT	Patagonian Tea	55.25	12,635	2.50	10	UK
AR	Abyssinian Ruby	31.82	22,010	1.32	13	UK
SLG	Sri Lankan Gold	50.37	32,868	2.68	16	UK
ILZ	Indian Lead &Zinc	37.75	6,390	3.00	12	UK
BE	Burmese Elephant	.07	154,713	0.01	3	UK
BS	Bolivian Sheep	12.75	231,678	1.78	11	UK
NG	Nigerian Geese	35.00	12,323	1.68	10	UK
CS	Canadian Sugar	52.78	4,716	2.50	15	UK
ROF	Royal Ostrich Farms	33.75	1,234,923	3.00	6	UK
MG	Minnesota Gold	53.87	816,122	1.00	25	USA
GP	Georgia Peach	2.35	387,333	.20	5	USA
NE	Narembeen Emu	12.34	45,619	1.00	8	AUS
QD	Queensland Diamond	6.73	89,251	.50	7	AUS
IR	Indooroopilly Ruby	15.92	56,147	.50	20	AUS
BD	Bombay Duck	25.55	167,382	1.00	12	IND

Figure 4-3. A relational database with tables NATION and STOCK

Notice that the column name NATCODE appears in both the STOCK and NATION tables. In NATION, NATCODE is the primary key; it is unique for each instance of nation. In STOCK, NATCODE is a foreign key because it is the primary key for the table, NATION, the one end of the 1:m relationship. NATCODE is a foreign key in STOCK because it is a primary key in NATION. A matched primary key-foreign key pair is the method for recording the 1:m relationship between the two tables. This method of representing a relationship is graphically illustrated in Figure 4-3 for the two USA stocks. In the STOCK table, NATCODE is italicized to indicate that it is a foreign key. We find this method, like underlining the primary key, is a useful reminder.

Although the same name has been used for the primary key and the foreign key in this example, it is not mandatory. The two columns can have different names, and in some cases, you are forced to use different names. When possible, we find it convenient to use identical column names to help us remember that the tables are related.

The table STOCK shows that there is a total of 16 stocks, 10 listed in the United Kingdom, 2 in the United States, 3 in Australia, and 1 in India. Although a nation can have many stocks, it is not mandatory to have any. That is, in data modeling terminology, many can be zero, one, or more, but it is mandatory to have a value for NATCODE in NATION for every value of NATCODE in STOCK. This requirement, known as the **referential integrity constraint**, maintains the accuracy of a database. Its application means that every foreign key in a table has an identical primary key in that same table or another table. In this example, it means that for every value of NATCODE in STOCK, there is a corresponding entry in NATION. As a result, a primary key row must be created before its corresponding foreign key row. So, details for a NATION must be added before data about the stocks listed in that nation can be entered.

Why is the foreign key in the table at the many end of the relationship? Because each instance of STOCK is associated with exactly one instance of NATION. The rule is that a stock must be listed in one and only one nation. Thus, the foreign key field is single-valued when it is at the many end of a relationship. The foreign key is not at the one end of the relationship because each instance of NATION can be associated with more than one instance of STOCK, and this implies a multivalued foreign key. The relational model does not support multivalued fields because of the processing problems they can cause.

Using SQL, the two tables are defined in a similar manner to the way we created a single table in Chapter 3. The CREATE TABLE command is used twice, once for each table. Here are the SQL statements:

```
CREATE TABLE NATION
   (NATCODE        CHAR(3) NOT NULL,
   NATNAME         CHAR(20),
   EXCHRATE        DECIMAL(9,5),
      PRIMARY KEY(NATCODE))

CREATE TABLE STOCK
   (STKCODE        CHAR(3) NOT NULL,
   STKFIRM         CHAR(20),
   STKPRICE        DECIMAL(6,2),
   STKQTY          DECIMAL(8),
   STKDIV          DECIMAL(5,2),
   STKPE           DECIMAL(5),
   NATCODE         CHAR(3) NOT NULL,
      PRIMARY KEY(STKCODE),
      FOREIGN KEY FKNATCODE(NATCODE) REFERENCES NATION
         ON DELETE RESTRICT)
```

Notice that the definition of STOCK includes additional information to specify the foreign key and the referential integrity constraint. The FOREIGN KEY clause defines the column or columns in the table being created that comprise the foreign key. A referential integrity constraint can be named, and in this case, its name is FKNATCODE.[3] The foreign key is the column NATCODE, and it references the primary key of the table NATION. There is no need to specify the matching primary key's name because this can be derived from the definition of the table (NATION in this case) in which the primary key is found.

The ON DELETE clause specifies what processing should occur if an attempt is made to delete a row in NATION with a primary key that is a foreign key in STOCK. In this case, the ON DELETE clause specifies that it is not permissible (the meaning of RESTRICT) to delete a primary key row in NATION while a corresponding foreign key in STOCK exists. In other words, the system will not execute the delete. The user must first delete all corresponding rows in STOCK before attempting to delete the row containing the primary key.

Observe that both the primary and foreign key are defined as CHAR(3). The relational model requires that a primary key-foreign key pair have the same data type and are the same length. Later, you will learn that this means they must be defined on the same domain (page 226).

In MS Access, a 1:m relationship is represented in a similar manner to the method you have just learned. Instead of a crow's foot, an infinity sign (∞) is used to signify the many end of the relationship (see Figure 4-4). Also, note that the foreign key is shown in the many end. We omit the foreign key when data modeling because it can be inferred. In the case of MS Access, the foreign key is recorded because MS Access is a RDBMS, and what you see is an implementation of a database model.

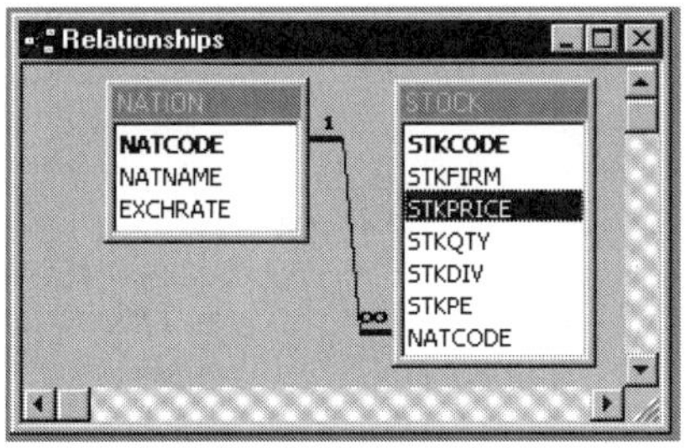

Figure 4-4. Specifying a 1:m relationship in MS Access

---

3. If a referential integrity constraint is named, then it can be turned on or off. Processing will be faster if referential integrity constraints are turned off, and this is desirable during a large database change with data that have been previously checked to ensure referential integrity is obeyed (e.g., converting from one DBMS to another).

Querying a two-table database

A two-table database offers the opportunity to learn more SQL and join, another relational algebra operation.

Join

Join creates a new table from two existing tables by matching on a column common to both tables. Often the common column is a primary key-foreign key combination: the primary key column of one table is matched with the foreign key column of another table. Join is frequently used to get the data for a query into a single row. Consider the tables NATION and STOCK. If we want to calculate the value — in British pounds — of a stock, we multiply stock price by stock quantity and then exchange rate. To find the appropriate exchange rate for a stock, get its NATCODE from STOCK and then find the exchange rate in the matching row in NATION, the one with the same value for NATCODE. For example, to calculate the value of Georgia Peach, which has NATCODE = 'US', find the row in NATION that also has NATCODE = 'US'. In this case, the stock's value is 2.35*387333*0.67 = £609,855.81.

Calculation of stock value is very easy once join is used to get the three values in one row. The SQL command for joining the two tables is:

```
SELECT * FROM STOCK, NATION
   WHERE STOCK.NATCODE = NATION.NATCODE
```

and the result is shown in Table 4-2.

Table 4-2: The join of STOCK and NATION

STKCODE	STKFIRM	STKPRICE	STKQTY	STKDIV	STKPE	NATCODE	NATCODE1	NATNAME	EXCHRATE
NE	Narembeen Emu	12.34	45619	1.00	8	AUS	AUS	Australia	0.46000
IR	Indooroopilly Ruby	15.92	56147	0.50	20	AUS	AUS	Australia	0.46000
QD	Queensland Diamond	6.73	89251	0.50	7	AUS	AUS	Australia	0.46000
BD	Bombay Duck	25.55	167382	1.00	12	IND	IND	India	0.02280
ROF	Royal Ostrich Farms	33.75	1234923	3.00	6	UK	UK	United Kingdom	1.00000
CS	Canadian Sugar	52.78	4716	2.50	15	UK	UK	United Kingdom	1.00000
FC	Freedonia Copper	27.50	10529	1.84	16	UK	UK	United Kingdom	1.00000
BS	Bolivian Sheep	12.75	231678	1.78	11	UK	UK	United Kingdom	1.00000
BE	Burmese Elephant	0.07	154713	0.01	3	UK	UK	United Kingdom	1.00000
ILZ	Indian Lead & Zinc	37.75	6390	3.00	12	UK	UK	United Kingdom	1.00000
SLG	Sri Lankan Gold	50.37	32868	2.68	16	UK	UK	United Kingdom	1.00000
AR	Abyssinian Ruby	31.82	22010	1.32	13	UK	UK	United Kingdom	1.00000
PT	Patagonian Tea	55.25	12635	2.50	10	UK	UK	United Kingdom	1.00000
NG	Nigerian Geese	35.00	12323	1.68	10	UK	UK	United Kingdom	1.00000
MG	Minnesota Gold	53.87	816122	1.00	25	US	US	United States	0.67000
GP	Georgia Peach	2.35	387333	0.20	5	US	US	United States	0.67000

There are several things to notice about the SQL command and the result:

- To avoid confusion because NATCODE is a column name in both STOCK and NATION, it needs to be qualified. Qualification means you precede a column name with its table name and separate the two by a period (e.g., NATION.NATCODE). If NATCODE is not qualified, the system will reject the query because it cannot distinguish between the two columns titled NATCODE.
- The new table has the NATCODE column replicated. It is called both NATCODE and NATCODE1. The naming convention for the replicated column varies with the RDBMS. In some, for example, the columns will be labeled STOCK.NATCODE and NATION.NATCODE.
- The SQL command specifies the names of the tables to be joined, the columns to be used for matching, and the condition for the match (equality in this case).
- The number of columns in the new table is the sum of the columns in the two tables.
- The stock value calculation is now easily specified in an SQL command because all the data are in one row.

The join operation can be streamlined to report only the columns required for decision making and also show the results of a calculation. In addition, it is useful to sort or order the report. The SQL features that you have used previously can be used with a join.

❍ **Report the value of each stockholding in UK pounds. Sort the report by nation and firm.**

```
SELECT NATNAME, STKFIRM, STKPRICE, STKQTY, EXCHRATE,
   STKPRICE*STKQTY*EXCHRATE AS STKVALUE
      FROM STOCK,NATION
         WHERE STOCK.NATCODE = NATION.NATCODE
            ORDER BY NATNAME, STKFIRM
```

NATNAME	STKFIRM	STKPRICE	STKQTY	EXCHRATE	STKVALUE
Australia	Indooroopilly Ruby	15.92	56147	0.46000	411175.71
Australia	Narembeen Emu	12.34	45619	0.46000	258951.69
Australia	Queensland Diamond	6.73	89251	0.46000	276303.25
India	Bombay Duck	25.55	167382	0.02280	97506.71
United Kingdom	Abyssinian Ruby	31.82	22010	1.00000	700358.20
United Kingdom	Bolivian Sheep	12.75	231678	1.00000	2953894.50
United Kingdom	Burmese Elephant	0.07	154713	1.00000	10829.91
United Kingdom	Canadian Sugar	52.78	4716	1.00000	248910.48
United Kingdom	Freedonia Copper	27.50	10529	1.00000	289547.50
United Kingdom	Indian Lead & Zinc	37.75	6390	1.00000	241222.50
United Kingdom	Nigerian Geese	35.00	12323	1.00000	431305.00
United Kingdom	Patagonian Tea	55.25	12635	1.00000	698083.75
United Kingdom	Royal Ostrich Farms	33.75	1234923	1.00000	41678651.25
United Kingdom	Sri Lankan Gold	50.37	32868	1.00000	1655561.16
United States	Georgia Peach	2.35	387333	0.67000	609855.81
United States	Minnesota Gold	53.87	816122	0.67000	29456209.73

Remember that during data modeling we created two entities STOCK and NATION, and defined the relationship between them. We showed that if the information was stored in one table, there could be updating problems. Now, with a join, we have combined these data. So why separate the data only to put them back together later? There are two reasons. First, we want to avoid update anomalies. Second, as you will discover, we do not join the same tables every time.

Join comes in several flavors. The matching condition can be =, <>, <=, <, >=, and >.Generally when people refer to join, however, they mean equijoin, when the matching condition is equality.

A join is readily expressed in MS Access by using the QBE facilities, as shown in Figure 4-5.

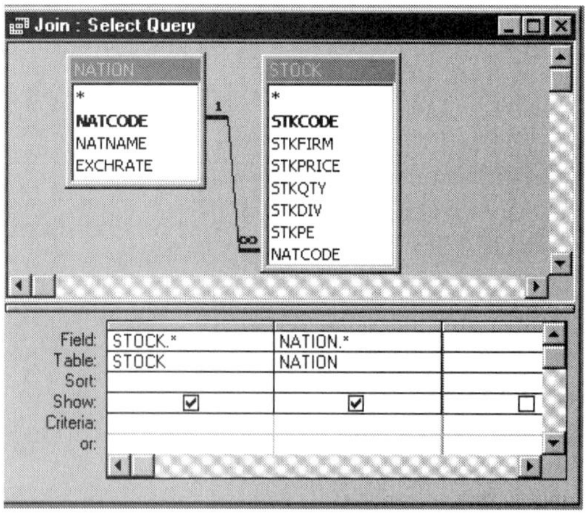

Figure 4-5. A join in MS Access

Control break reporting

The purpose of a join is to collect the necessary data for a report. When two tables in a 1:m relationship are joined, the report will contain repetitive data. If you re-examine the report from the join, you will see that NATION and EXCHRATE are often repeated because the same values apply to many stocks. A more appropriate format for the report is shown in Figure 4-6, an example of a control break report. Such reports take advantage of the fact that the values in a particular column or columns seldom change. In this case, NATNAME and EXCHRATE are often the same from one row to the next so it makes sense to report these data only when they change. The report is also easier to read. NATNAME is known as a control field. Notice that there are four groups of data because NATNAME has four different values.

Many RDBMS packages have report writing languages that make it easy to create a control break report. These languages typically support summary reporting for each group of rows having the same value for the control field(s). Remember, however, that a table must

Nation	Exchange rate			
Firm		Price	Quantity	Value
Australia	0.4600			
Indooroopilly Ruby		15.92	56,147	411,175.71
Narembeen Emu		12.34	45,619	258,951.69
Queensland Diamond		6.73	89,251	276,303.25
India	0.0228			
Bombay Duck		25.55	167,382	97,506.71
United Kingdom	1.0000			
Abyssinian Ruby		31.82	22,010	700,358.20
Bolivian Sheep		12.75	231,678	2,953,894.50
Burmese Elephant		0.07	154,713	10,829.91
Canadian Sugar		52.78	4,716	248,910.48
Freedonia Copper		27.50	10,529	289,547.50
Indian Lead & Zinc		37.75	6,390	241,222.50
Nigerian Geese		35.00	12,323	431,305.00
Patagonian Tea		55.25	12,635	698,083.75
Royal Ostrich Farms		33.75	1,234,923	41,678,651.25
Sri Lankan Gold		50.37	32,868	1,655,561.16
United States	0.6700			
Georgia Peach		2.35	387,333	609,855.81
Minnesota Gold		53.87	816,122	29,456,209.73

Figure 4-6. A control break report

be sorted on the control break field(s) before the report is created. An example of control break reporting with MS Access is shown in Figure 4-7.

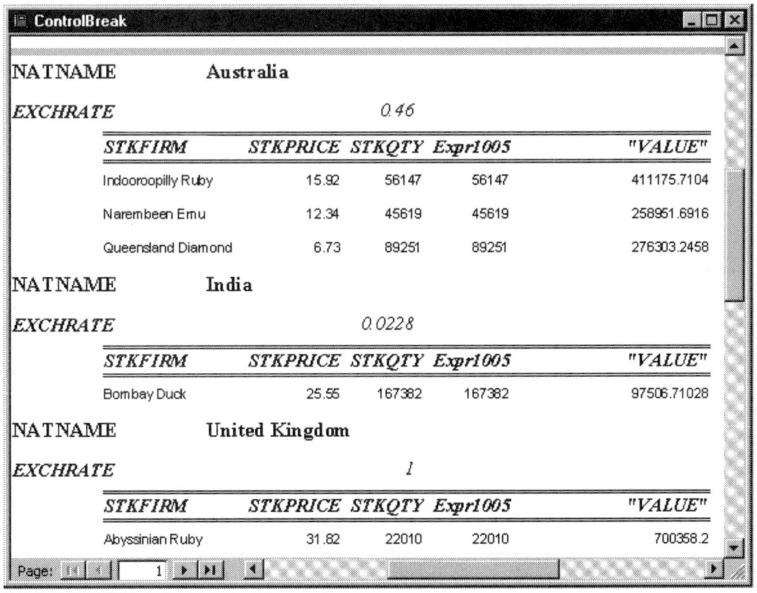

Figure 4-7. A control break report in MS Access

GROUP BY—reporting by groups

The SQL GROUP BY clause is an elementary form of control break reporting. It permits grouping of rows that have the same value for a specified column or columns, and produces one row for each different value of the grouping column(s).

❍ **Report by nation the total value of stockholdings.**

```
SELECT NATNAME, SUM(STKPRICE*STKQTY*EXCHRATE) AS STKVALUE
   FROM STOCK, NATION WHERE STOCK.NATCODE = NATION.NATCODE
      GROUP BY NATNAME
```

NATNAME	STKVALUE
Australia	946430.65
India	97506.71
United Kingdom	48908364.25
United States	30066065.54

SQL's built-in functions (COUNT, SUM, AVERAGE, MIN, and MAX) can be used with the GROUP BY clause. They are applied to a group of rows having the same value for a specified column. You can specify more than one function in the select statement. For example, we can compute total value and number of different stocks and group by nation using:

❍ **Report the number of stocks and their total value by nation.**

```
SELECT NATNAME, COUNT(*) AS 'NUMBER',
   SUM(STKPRICE*STKQTY*EXCHRATE) AS STKVALUE
      FROM STOCK, NATION WHERE STOCK.NATCODE = NATION.NATCODE
         GROUP BY NATNAME
```

In the preceding query, why is NUMBER in quotes, but not STKVALUE? NUMBER is a reserved word in some RDBMSs, and it is written within quotes so that the RDBMS does not confuse it with the reserved word.

NATNAME	NUMBER	STKVALUE
Australia	3	946430.65
India	1	97506.71
United Kingdom	10	48908364.25
United States	2	30066065.54

You can group by more than one column name; however, all column names appearing in the SELECT clause must be associated with a built-in function or be in a GROUP BY clause.

❍ **List stocks by nation and for each nation show the number of stocks for each PE ratio and the total value of those stock holdings in UK pounds.**

```
SELECT NATNAME,STKPE,COUNT(*) AS 'NUMBER',
   SUM(STKPRICE*STKQTY*EXCHRATE) AS STKVALUE
      FROM STOCK, NATION WHERE STOCK.NATCODE = NATION.NATCODE
         GROUP BY NATNAME, STKPE
```

NATNAME	STKPE	NUMBER	STKVALUE
Australia	7	1	276303.25
Australia	8	1	258951.69
Australia	20	1	411175.71
India	12	1	97506.71
United Kingdom	3	1	10829.91
United Kingdom	6	1	41678651.25
United Kingdom	10	2	1129388.75
United Kingdom	11	1	2953894.50
United Kingdom	12	1	241222.50
United Kingdom	13	1	700358.20
United Kingdom	15	1	248910.48
United Kingdom	16	2	1945108.66
United States	5	1	609855.81
United States	25	1	29456209.73

In this example, stocks are grouped by both NATNAME and STKPE. In most cases, there is only one stock for each pair of NATNAME and STKPE; however, there are two situations (United Kingdom stocks with PEs of 10 and 16) where details of multiple stocks are grouped into one report line. Examining the values in the COUNT column helps you to identify these stocks.

HAVING—the WHERE clause of groups

HAVING is the WHERE clause of GROUP BY. It restricts the number of rows considered for grouping. Used with built-in functions, HAVING is always preceded by GROUP BY and is always followed by a function (SUM, AVG, MAX, MIN, or COUNT).

❍ **Report the total value of stocks for nations with two or more listed stocks.**

```
SELECT NATNAME, SUM(STKPRICE*STKQTY*EXCHRATE) AS STKVALUE
   FROM STOCK, NATION WHERE STOCK.NATCODE = NATION.NATCODE
      GROUP BY NATNAME
         HAVING COUNT(*) >= 2
```

NATNAME	STKVALUE
Australia	946430.65
United Kingdom	48908364.25
United States	30066065.54

Subqueries

A subquery, or nested SELECT, is a SELECT nested within another SELECT. A subquery can be used to return a list of values subsequently searched with an IN clause.

❍ **Report the name of all Australian stocks.**

```
SELECT STKFIRM FROM STOCK
   WHERE NATCODE IN
      (SELECT NATCODE FROM NATION
         WHERE NATNAME = 'Australia')
```

STKFIRM
Narembeen Emu
Queensland Diamond
Indooroopilly Ruby

Conceptually, the subquery is evaluated first. It returns a list of NATCODES ('AUS') so that the query then is the same as:

```
SELECT STKFIRM FROM STOCK
   WHERE NATCODE IN ('AUS')
```

When discussing subqueries, sometimes a subquery is also called an ***inner query***. The term *outer query* is applied to the SQL preceding the inner query. In this case, the outer and inner queries are:

Outer query	`SELECT STKFIRM FROM STOCK` `WHERE NATCODE IN`
Inner query	`(SELECT NATCODE FROM NATION` `WHERE NATNAME = 'Australia')`

Note that in this case we do not have to qualify NATCODE. There is no identity crisis because NATCODE in the inner query is implicitly qualified as NATION.NATCODE and NATCODE in the outer query is understood to be STOCK.NATCODE.

This query also can be run as a join by writing:

```
SELECT STKFIRM FROM STOCK, NATION
   WHERE STOCK.NATCODE = NATION.NATCODE
   AND NATNAME = 'Australia'
```

Correlated subquery

A correlated subquery is yet another approach to solving the query:

❍ **Report the name of all Australian stocks.**

The correlated subquery approach is:

```
SELECT STKFIRM FROM STOCK
   WHERE 'Australia' IN
      (SELECT NATNAME FROM NATION
         WHERE NATION.NATCODE = STOCK.NATCODE)
```

Conceptually, think of this query as stepping through STOCK one row at a time and then executing the inner query each time. The first row has NATCODE = 'UK' so the subquery becomes

```
SELECT NATNAME FROM NATION
   WHERE NATION.NATCODE = 'UK'
```

This query returns 'United Kingdom,' and since this does not match 'Australia,' the name of the stock is not reported.

The query then proceeds to the second row of STOCK and executes the inner query again with the value of STOCK.NATCODE for the second row and so on for all rows of STOCK.

For rows 13 through 15, the inner query becomes

```
SELECT NATNAME FROM NATION
   WHERE NATION.NATCODE = 'AUS'
```

and returns 'Australia,' which matches the IN clause value. Thus, the name of the stock for these three rows is reported.

The term *correlated subquery* is used because its value depends on a variable that receives its value from an outer query (STOCK.NATCODE in this instance). A correlated subquery thus cannot be evaluated once and for all. It must be evaluated repeatedly — once for each value of the variable received from the outer query. In this respect, a correlated subquery is different from a subquery, which only needs to be evaluated once.

Views — virtual tables

You have noticed that in these examples we repeated the join and stock value calculation for each query. Ideally, we should do this once, store the result, and be able to use it with other queries. We can do so if we create a view, a virtual table. A view does not physically exist as stored data; it is an imaginary table constructed from existing tables as required. You can treat a view as if it were a table, and write SQL to query it. In MS Access, any saved query is a view.

A view contains selected columns from one or more tables. The selected columns can be renamed and rearranged. New columns based on arithmetic expressions can be created. GROUP BY can also be used to create a view. Remember, a view contains no actual data — it is a virtual table.

The following SQL command does the join and stock value calculation and saves the result as a view:

```
CREATE VIEW STKVALUE
   (NATION, FIRM, PRICE, QTY, EXCHRATE, VALUE)
      AS SELECT NATNAME, STKFIRM, STKPRICE, STKQTY, EXCHRATE,
         STKPRICE*STKQTY*EXCHRATE
            FROM STOCK, NATION
               WHERE STOCK.NATCODE = NATION.NATCODE
```

There are several things to notice about creating a view:

❖ The six names enclosed by parentheses are the column names for the view.
❖ There is a one-to-one correspondence between the names in parentheses and the names or expressions in the SELECT clause. Thus the view column named VALUE contains the result of the arithmetic expression specified in the view creation statement STKPRICE*STKQTY*EXCHRATE.

A view can be used in a query, such as:

❍ **Find stocks with a value greater than £100,000:**

```
SELECT NATION, FIRM, VALUE FROM STKVALUE WHERE VALUE > 100000
```

NATION	FIRM	VALUE
United Kingdom	Freedonia Copper	289547.50
United Kingdom	Patagonian Tea	698083.75
United Kingdom	Abyssinian Ruby	700358.20
United Kingdom	Sri Lankan Gold	1655561.16
United Kingdom	Indian Lead & Zinc	241222.50
United Kingdom	Bolivian Sheep	2953894.50
United Kingdom	Nigerian Geese	431305.00
United Kingdom	Canadian Sugar	248910.48
United Kingdom	Royal Ostrich Farms	41678651.25
United States	Minnesota Gold	29456209.73
United States	Georgia Peach	609855.80
Australia	Narembeen Emu	258951.69
Australia	Queensland Diamond	276303.24
Australia	Indooroopilly Ruby	411175.71

There are two main reasons for creating a view. First, as we have seen, query writing can be simplified. If you find that you are frequently writing the same section of code for a variety of queries, then isolate the common section and put it in a view. This means that you will usually create a view when a fact, such as stock value, is derived from other facts in the table.

The second reason is to restrict access to certain columns or rows. For example, the person who updates STOCK could be given a view that excludes STKQTY. In this case, changes in stock prices could be updated without revealing confidential information, such as the value of the stock portfolio.

Summary

Entities are related to other entities by relationships. The 1:m (one-to-many) relationship occurs frequently in data models. An additional entity is required to represent a 1:m relationship to avoid update anomalies. In a relational database, a 1:m relationship is represented by an additional column, the foreign key, in the table at the many end of the relationship. The referential integrity constraint insists that a foreign key must always exist as a primary key in some table. The foreign key constraint can be specified in a CREATE statement.

Join creates a new table from two existing tables by matching on a column common to both tables. Often the common column is a primary key-foreign key combination. The matching conditions for a join can be =, <>, <=, <, >=, and >. An equijoin describes the situation where the matching condition is equality. The GROUP BY clause is used to create an elementary control break report. The HAVING clause of GROUP BY is like the WHERE clause of SELECT. A subquery, which has a SELECT statement within another SELECT statement, causes two SELECT statements to be executed—one for the inner query and one for the outer query. A correlated subquery is executed as many times as there are rows selected by the outer query. A view is a virtual table that is created when required. Views can simplify report writing and restrict access to specified columns or rows.

Key terms and concepts

Constraint
Control break reporting
Correlated subquery
Delete anomalies
Equijoin
Foreign key
GROUP BY
HAVING
Insert anomalies
Join
One-to-many relationship
Referential integrity
Relationship
Update anomalies
Views
Virtual table

Exercises

1. Draw data models for the following situations. In each case, make certain that you show the attributes and feasible identifiers:
   a. A farmer can have many cows, but a cow belongs to only one farmer.
   b. A university has many students, and a student can attend at most one university.
   c. An aircraft can have many passengers, but a passenger can be on only one flight at a time.
   d. A nation can have many states and a state many cities.
   e. An art researcher has asked you to design a database to record details of artists

and the museums in which their paintings are displayed. For each painting, the researcher wants to know the size of the canvas, year painted, title, and style. The nationality, date of birth, and death of each artist must be recorded. For each museum, record details of its location and specialty, if it has one.

2. Report all values in British pounds:
   a. Report the value of stocks listed in Australia.
   b. Report the dividend payment of all stocks.
   c. Report the total dividend payment by nation.
   d. Create a view containing nation, firm, price, quantity, exchange rate, value, and yield.
   e. Report the average yield by nation.
   f. Report the minimum and maximum yield for each nation.
   g. Report the nations where the average yield of stocks exceeds the average yield of all stocks.
3. How would you change the queries in exercise 4-2 if you were required to report the values in American dollars, Australian dollars, or Indian rupees?
4. What is a foreign key and what role does it serve?
5. What is the referential integrity constraint? Why should it be enforced?
6. Kisha, against the advice of her friends, is simultaneously studying data management and Shakespearian drama. She thought the two subjects would be an interesting contrast. However, the classes are very demanding and often enter her midsummer dreams. Last night, she dreamed that William Shakespeare wanted her to draw a data model. He explained, before she woke up in a cold sweat, that a play had many characters but the same character never appeared in more than one play. "Methinks," he said, "the same name may have appeareth more than the once, but twas always a person of a different ilk." He then, she hazily recollects, went on to spout about the quality of data dropping like the gentle rain.
   Draw a data model to keep old Bill quiet and help Kisha get some sleep.
7. An orchestra has four broad classes of instruments (strings, woodwinds, brass, and percussion). Each class contains musicians who play different instruments. For example, the strings section of a full symphonic orchestra contains 2 harps, 16 to 18 first violins, 14 to 16 second violins, 12 violas, 10 cellos, and 8 double basses. A city has asked you to develop a database to store details of the musicians in its three orchestras. All the musicians are specialists and play only one instrument for one orchestra.
8. Answer the following queries based on the following relational database for a car dealer:
   a. What is the personid of Sheila O'Hara?
   b. List sales personnel sorted by last name and within last name, first name.
   c. List details of the sales made by Bruce Bush.
   d. List details of all sales showing the gross profit (selling price minus cost price).
   e. Report the number of cars sold of each type.
   f. What is the average selling price of cars sold by Sue Lim?
   g. Report details of all sales where the gross profit is less than the average.
   h. What was the maximum selling price of any car?

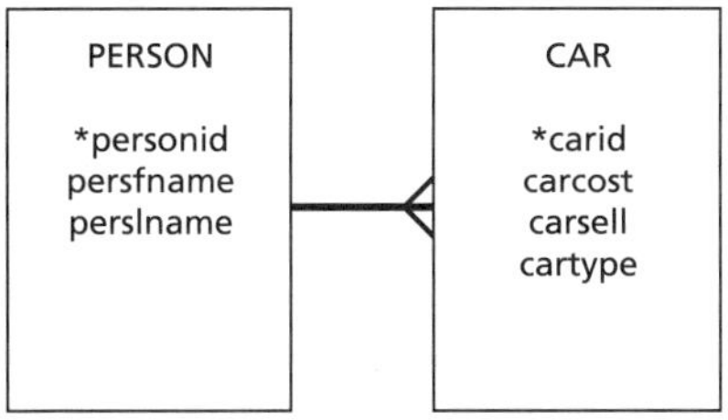

PERSON		
PERSONID	PERSFNAME	PERSLNAME

CAR				
CARID	CARCOST	CARSELL	CARTYPE	*PERSONID*

i. What is the total gross profit?
j. Report the gross profit made by each salesperson who sold at least three cars.
k. Create a view containing all the details in the CAR table and the gross profit.

9. If you have access to MS Access, solve the following query using a virtual table (a stored query in MS Access):
Find the number of different PE ratios in STOCK.
(see page 80 for the original discussion of this query)

CD library case

Ajay soon realized that a CD contains far more data that just a list of track titles and their length. Now that he had learned about the 1:m relationship, he was ready to add some more detail. He recognized that a CD contains many tracks, and a label (e.g., Atlantic) releases many CDs. He revised his data model to include these additional entities (CD and LABEL) and their relationships (see Figure 4-8).

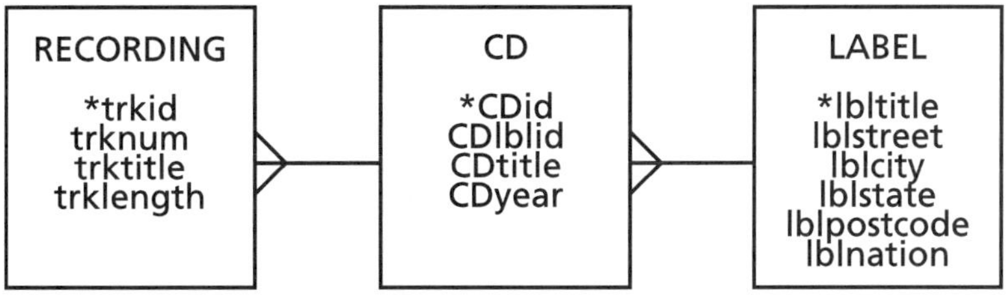

Figure 4-8. CD library V2.0

Giant Steps and *Swing* are both on the Atlantic label; the data are

lbltitle	lblstreet	lblcity	lblstate	lblpostcode	lblnation
Atlantic	75 Rockefeller Plaza	New York	NY	10019	USA

The CD data, where *lbltitle* is the foreign key, are

CDid	CDlblid	CDtitle	CDyear	*lbltitle*
1	A2 1311	Giant Steps	1960	Atlantic
2	83012-2	Swing	1977	Atlantic

The TRACK data, where *CDid* is the foreign key, are

trkid	trknum	trktitle	trklength	*CDid*
1	1	Giant Steps	4.72	1
2	2	Cousin Mary	5.75	1
3	3	Countdown	2.35	1
4	4	Spiral	5.93	1
5	5	Syeeda's Song Flute	7.00	1
6	6	Naima	4.35	1
7	7	Mr. P.C.	6.95	1
8	8	Giant Steps	3.67	1
9	9	Naima	4.45	1
10	10	Cousin Mary	5.90	1
11	11	Countdown	4.55	1
12	12	Syeeda's Song Flute	7.03	1
13	1	Stomp of King Porter	3.20	2
14	2	Sing a Study in Brown	2.85	2
15	3	Sing Moten's Swing	3.60	2
16	4	A-tisket, A-tasket	2.95	2
17	5	I Know Why	3.57	2
18	6	Sing You Sinners	2.75	2
19	7	Java Jive	2.85	2
20	8	Down South Camp Meetin'	3.25	2
21	9	Topsy	3.23	2
22	10	Clouds	7.20	2
23	11	Skyliner	3.18	2
24	12	It's Good Enough to Keep	3.18	2
25	13	Choo Choo Ch' Boogie	3.00	2

Your turn

1. Create tables to store the Label and CD data. Add a column to TRACK to store the foreign key. [4] Then, either enter the new data or download it from the Web site. Define *label* as a foreign key in CD and *CDid* as a foreign key in TRACK.

Ajay ran a few queries on his revised database.

❍ What are the tracks on *Swing*?

This query requires joining TRACK and CD because the name of a CD (*Swing* in this case) is stored on CD and track data are stored on TRACK. The foreign key of TRACK is matched to the primary key of CD (i.e. `TRACK.CDID = CD.CDID`).

```
SELECT TRKNUM, TRKTITLE, TRKLENGTH FROM TRACK, CD
   WHERE TRACK.CDID = CD.CDID
   AND CDTITLE = 'Swing'
```

trknum	trktitle	trklength
1	Stomp of King Porter	3.20
2	Sing a Study in Brown	2.85
3	Sing Moten's Swing	3.60
4	A-tisket, A-tasket	2.95
5	I Know Why	3.57
6	Sing You Sinners	2.75
7	Java Jive	2.85
8	Down South Camp Meetin'	3.25
9	Topsy	3.23
10	Clouds	7.20
11	Skyliner	3.18
12	It's Good Enough to Keep	3.18
13	Choo Choo Ch' Boogie	3.00

❍ What is the longest track on *Swing*?

Like the prior query, this one requires joining TRACK and CD. The inner query isolates the tracks on *Swing* and then selects the longest of these using the MAX function. The outer query also isolates the tracks on *Swing* and selects the track equal to the maximum length. The outer query must restrict attention to tracks on *Swing* in case there are other tracks in the TRACK table with a time equal to the value returned by the inner query.

4. Adding a column is easy in MS Access. With other systems you might have to use ALTER TABLE (see page 252).

```
SELECT TRKNUM, TRKTITLE, TRKLENGTH FROM TRACK, CD
   WHERE TRACK.CDID = CD.CDID
   AND CDTITLE = 'Swing'
   AND TRKLENGTH =
      (SELECT MAX(TRKLENGTH) FROM TRACK, CD
         WHERE TRACK.CDID = CD.CDID
         AND CDTITLE = 'Swing')
```

trknum	trktitle	trklength
10	Clouds	7.20

❍ **What are the titles of CDs containing some tracks less than 3 minutes long and on US-based labels? List details of these tracks as well.**

This is a three-table join since resolution of the query requires data from CD (*CDtitle*), TRACK (*trktitle*), and LABEL (*lblnation*).

```
SELECT CDTITLE, TRKTITLE, TRKLENGTH FROM TRACK, CD, LABEL
   WHERE TRACK.CDID = CD.CDID
   AND CD.LBLTITLE = LABEL.LBLTITLE
   AND TRKLENGTH < 3
   AND LBLNATION = 'USA'
```

CDtitle	trktitle	trklength
Giant Steps	Countdown	2.35
Swing	Sing a Study in Brown	2.85
Swing	A-tisket, A-tasket	2.95
Swing	Sing You Sinners	2.75
Swing	Java Jive	2.85

❍ **Report the number of tracks on each CD.**

This query requires GROUP BY because the number of tracks on each CD is totaled by using the aggregate function COUNT.

```
SELECT CDTITLE, COUNT(*) AS CDs FROM TRACK, CD
   WHERE TRACK.CDID = CD.CDID
      GROUP BY CDTITLE
```

CDtitle	CDs
Giant Steps	12
Swing	13

❍ **Report, in ascending order, the total length of tracks on each CD.**

This is another example of GROUP BY. In this case, the SUM function is used to accumulate track length, and ORDER BY is used for sorting in ascending order, the default sort order.

```
SELECT CDTITLE, SUM(TRKLENGTH) AS SUMTRKLEN FROM TRACK, CD
   WHERE TRACK.CDID = CD.CDID
      GROUP BY CDTITLE
      ORDER BY SUM(TRKLENGTH)
```

CDtitle	SUMTRKLEN
Swing	44.81
Giant Steps	62.65

❍ **Does any CD have more than 60 minutes of music?**

This query uses the HAVING clause to limit the CDs reported based on their total length.

```
SELECT CDTITLE, SUM(TRKLENGTH) FROM TRACK, CD
   WHERE TRACK.CDID = CD.CDID
      GROUP BY CDTITLE HAVING SUM(TRKLENGTH) > 60
```

CDtitle	EXPR1001
Giant Steps	62.65

Your Turn

1. Write SQL for the following queries:
   a. List the tracks by CD in order of track length.
   b. What is the longest track on each CD?
2. What is wrong with the current data model?
3. Could CDlblid be used as an identifier for CD?

5

The Many-to-Many Relationship

Fearful concatenation of circumstances.
Daniel Webster

Learning objectives

On completion of this chapter, you will be able to

- ❖ model a many-to-many relationship between two entities;
- ❖ define a database with a many-to-many relationship;
- ❖ write queries for a database with a many-to-many relationship.

Alice was deeply involved in uncovering the workings of her firm. She spent hours talking to the staff, wanting to know everything about the products sold. She engaged many a customer in conversation to find out why they shopped at The Expeditioner, what they were looking for, and how they thought the business could be improved. She examined all the products herself and pestered the staff to tell her who bought them, how they were used, how many were sold, who supplied them, and a host of other questions. She plowed (or should that be "ploughed") through accounting journals, sales reports, and market forecasts. She was more than a new broom; she was a giant vacuum cleaner sucking up data about the firm so that she would be prepared to manage it successfully.

Ned, the marketing manager, was a Jekyll and Hyde character. By day he was a charming, savvy, marketing executive. Walking to work in his three-piece suit, bowler hat, and furled umbrella, he was the epitome of the conservative English businessman. By night he became a computer nerd with ragged jeans; a T-shirt; thick, black-framed glasses; and unruly hair. Ned had been desperate to introduce computers to The Expeditioner for years, but he knew that he could never reveal his second nature. The other staff at The Expeditioner just would not accept such a radical change in technology. Why, they had not even switched to fountain pens until their personal stock of quill pens was finally depleted. Ned was just not prepared to face the indignant silence and contempt that would greet his mere mention of computers. It was better to continue a secret double life than admit to being a cyber punk.

But times were changing, and Ned saw the opportunity. He furtively suggested to Lady Alice that perhaps she needed a database of sales facts. Her response was instantaneous: "Yes, and do it as soon as possible." Ned was ecstatic. This was truly a wonderful woman.

The many-to-many relationship

Consider the case when items are sold. We can immediately identify two entities: SALE and ITEM. A sale can consist of many items, and an item can appear in many sales. We are not saying the same item can be sold many times, but the particular type of item (e.g., a compass) can be sold many times; thus we have a many-to-many (m:m) relationship between SALE and ITEM. When we get an m:m relationship, we create a third entity to link the entities through two 1:m relationships. Usually, it is fairly easy to name this third entity. In this case, this third entity, typically known as an **associative entity**, is called LINE ITEM. A typical sales form (see Figure 5-1 for an example) lists the items purchased by a customer. Each of the lines appearing on the order form is generally known in retailing as a line item, which links an item and a sale.

The Expeditioner					
Sale of Goods					
Sale# 123456			Date:		
	Item#	Description	Quantity	Unit price	Total
1					
2					
3					
4					
5					
6					
			Grand Total		

Figure 5-1. A sales form

The representation of this m: m relationship is shown in Figure 5-2. We say many-to-many because there are two relationships — ITEM is related to many SALEs, and SALE is related to many ITEMs. This data model can also be read as: "a sale has many line items, but a line item refers to only one sale. Similarly, an item can appear as many line items, but a line item references only one item."

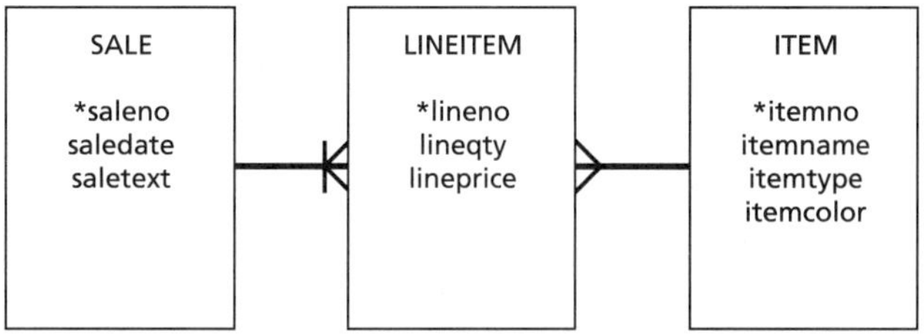

Figure 5-2. An m:m relationship

The entity SALE is identified by *saleno* and has the attributes *saledate* and *saletext* (a brief comment on the customer — soft information[1]). LINEITEM is partially identified by *lineno* and has attributes *lineqty* (the number of units sold) and *lineprice* (the unit selling price for this sale). ITEM is identified by *itemno* and has attributes *itemname*, *itemtype* (e.g., clothing, equipment, navigation aids, furniture, and so on), and *itemcolor*. LINEITEM is termed a **weak entity**[2] (see page 174) because it relies on another entity for its existence and identification.

If you look carefully at Figure 5-2, you will notice that we added a bar to the crow's foot at the many end of the 1:m relationship between SALE and LINEITEM. This bar provides information about the identifier of LINEITEM. As you know, every entity must have a unique identifier. A sales order (see Figure 5-1) is a series of lines, and *lineno* is unique only within a particular order. If we just use *lineno* as the identifier, we cannot guarantee that every instance of LINEITEM is unique. If we use *saleno* and *lineno* together, however, we have a unique identifier for every instance of LINEITEM. *Saleno* is unique for every sale, and *lineno* is unique within any sale. The bar indicates that LINEITEM's unique identifier is the concatenation of *saleno* and *lineno*.

LINEITEM is a weak or dependent entity because it relies on another entity for its existence and identification.

Why did we create a third entity?

When we have an m:m relationship, we create an associative entity to store data about the relationship. In this case, we have to store data about the items sold. We cannot store the data with SALE because a sale can be many items, and an entity only stores single-value

1. Remember, we discussed information hardness on page 34.
2. Sometimes called a dependent entity.

facts. Similarly, we cannot store data with ITEM because an item can appear in many sales. Since we cannot store data in SALE or ITEM, we must create another entity to store data about the m:m relationship.

You might find it useful to think of the m:m relationship as two 1:m relationships. An item can appear on many line item listings, and a line item entry refers to only one item. A sale has many line items, and each line item entry refers to only one sale.

Social Security number is not unique!

Two girls named Sarah Lee Ferguson were born on May 3, 1959. The U.S. government considered them one and the same and issued both the same Social Security number (SSN), a nine-digit identifier of U.S. residents. Now Sarah Lee Ferguson Boles and Sarah Lee Ferguson Johnson share the same SSN.

Mrs. Boles became aware of her SSN twin in 1987 when the Internal Revenue Service claimed there was a discrepancy in her reported income. Because SSN is widely used as an attribute or identifier in many computer systems, Mrs. Boles encountered other incidents of mistaken identity. Some of Mrs. Johnson's purchases appeared on Mrs. Boles' credit reports.

In late 1989, the Social Security Administration notified Mrs. Boles that her original number was given to her in error and she had to provide evidence of her age, identity, and citizenship to get a new number. When Mrs. Boles gets her new SSN, it is likely she will have to get a new driver's license and establish a new credit history.

AdaptedfromTwowomenshareaname,birthday,andS.S.number!*Athens[Georgia]Daily News*, January 29 1990, 7A.

Creating a relational database with an m:m relationship

As before, each entity becomes a table in a relational database, the entity name becomes the table name, each attribute becomes a column, and each identifier becomes a primary key. Remember, a 1:m relationship is mapped by adding a column to the entity of the many end of the relationship. The new column contains the identifier of the one end of the relationship.

Conversion of the foregoing data model results in the three tables shown in Table 5-1. Note the one-to-one correspondence between attributes and columns for SALE and ITEM. Observe the LINEITEM has two additional columns, SALENO and ITEMNO. Both of these columns are foreign keys in LINEITEM (remember the use of italics to signify foreign keys). Two foreign keys are required to record the two 1:m relationships. Notice in LINEITEM that SALENO is both part of the primary key and a foreign key.

The SQL commands to create the three tables are:

```
CREATE TABLE SALE
   (SALENO      INTEGER   NOT NULL,
   SALEDATE     DATE,
   SALETEXT     CHAR(50),
      PRIMARY KEY(SALENO))

CREATE TABLE ITEM
   (ITEMNO      INTEGER   NOT NULL,
   ITEMNAME     CHAR(30),
   ITEMTYPE     CHAR(1),
   ITEMCOLOR    CHAR(10),
      PRIMARY KEY(ITEMNO))

CREATE TABLE LINEITEM
   (LINENO      INTEGER   NOT NULL,
   LINEQTY      INTEGER,
   LINEPRICE    DECIMAL(7,2),
   SALENO       INTEGER   NOT NULL,
   ITEMNO       INTEGER   NOT NULL,
      PRIMARY KEY(LINENO,SALENO),
      FOREIGN KEY FKSALE(SALENO) REFERENCES SALE ON DELETE RESTRICT,
      FOREIGN KEY FKITEM(ITEMNO) REFERENCES ITEM ON DELETE RESTRICT)
```

While the SALE and ITEM tables are created in a similar fashion to previous examples, there are two things to notice about the definition of LINEITEM. First, the primary key is a composite of LINENO and SALENO. Remember, to uniquely identify an instance of LINE ITEM, you need both LINENO and SALENO. Second, there are two foreign keys because LINENO is at the many end of two 1:m relationships.

Table 5-1: Tables SALE, LINEITEM, and ITEM

SALE		
SALENO	SALEDATE	SALETEXT
1	1995-01-15	Scruffy Australian—called himself Bruce.
2	1995-01-15	Man. Rather fond of hats.
3	1995-01-15	Woman. Planning to row Atlantic—lengthwise!
4	1995-01-15	Man. Trip to New York—thinks NY is a jungle!
5	1995-01-16	Expedition leader for African safari.

LINEITEM				
LINENO	LINEQTY	LINEPRICE	*SALENO*	*ITEMNO*
1	1	4.50	1	2
1	1	25.00	2	6
2	1	20.00	2	16
3	1	25.00	2	19
4	1	2.25	2	2
1	1	500.00	3	4
2	1	2.25	3	2
1	1	500.00	4	4
2	1	65.00	4	9
3	1	60.00	4	13
4	1	75.00	4	14
5	1	10.00	4	3
6	1	2.25	4	2
1	50	36.00	5	10
2	50	40.50	5	11
3	8	153.00	5	12
4	1	60.00	5	13
5	1	0.00	5	2

ITEM			
ITEMNO	ITEMNAME	ITEMTYPE	ITEMCOLOR
1	Pocket knife–Nile	E	Brown
2	Pocket knife–Avon	E	Brown
3	Compass	N	—
4	Geo positioning system	N	—
5	Map measure	N	—
6	Hat–Polar Explorer	C	Red
7	Hat–Polar Explorer	C	White
8	Boots–snake proof	C	Green
9	Boots–snake proof	C	Black
10	Safari chair	F	Khaki
11	Hammock	F	Khaki
12	Tent–8 person	F	Khaki
13	Tent–2 person	F	Khaki
14	Safari cooking kit	E	—
15	Pith helmet	C	Khaki
16	Pith helmet	C	White
17	Map case	N	Brown
18	Sextant	N	—
19	Stetson	C	Black
20	Stetson	C	Brown

Querying an m:m relationship

A three-table join

The join operation can be easily extended from two tables to three or more merely by specifying the tables to be joined and the matching conditions. For example:

```
SELECT * FROM SALE, LINEITEM, ITEM
   WHERE SALE.SALENO = LINEITEM.SALENO
   AND ITEM.ITEMNO = LINEITEM.ITEMNO
```

Note that the three tables to be joined are listed after the FROM clause. There are two matching conditions: one for SALE and LINEITEM (SALES.SALENO = LINEITEM.SALENO) and one for ITEM and LINEITEM tables (ITEM.ITEMNO = LINEITEM.ITEMNO). The table LINEITEM is the link between the SALE and ITEM and must be referenced in both matching conditions.

You can tailor the join to be more precise and report some columns rather than all.

❍ **List the name, quantity, and value of items sold on January 16, 1995.**

```
SELECT ITEMNAME, LINEQTY, LINEPRICE, LINEQTY*LINEPRICE AS TOTAL
   FROM SALE, LINEITEM, ITEM
      WHERE LINEITEM.SALENO = SALE.SALENO
      AND ITEM.ITEMNO = LINEITEM.ITEMNO
      AND SALEDATE = '1995-01-16'
```

ITEMNAME	LINEQTY	LINEPRICE	TOTAL
Pocket knife-Avon	1	0.00	0.00
Safari chair	50	36.00	1800.00
Hammock	50	40.50	2025.00
Tent-8 person	8	153.00	1224.00
Tent-2 person	1	60.00	60.00

EXISTS—does a value exist

EXISTS is used in a WHERE clause to test whether a table contains at least one row satisfying a specified condition. It returns the value true if and only if some row satisfies the condition; otherwise it returns false. EXISTS represents the **existential quantifier** of formal logic. The best way to get a feel for EXISTS is to examine a query.

❍ **Report all clothing items for which a sale is recorded.**

```
SELECT ITEMNAME, ITEMCOLOR FROM ITEM
   WHERE ITEMTYPE = 'C'
   AND EXISTS (SELECT * FROM LINEITEM
      WHERE LINEITEM.ITEMNO = ITEM.ITEMNO)
```

ITEMNAME	ITEMCOLOR
Hat - Polar Explorer	Red
Boots - snake proof	Black
Pith helmet	White
Stetson	Black

Conceptually, we can think of this query as evaluating the subquery for each row of ITEM. The first item with ITEMTYPE = 'C', Hat - Polar Explorer (red), in ITEM has ITEMNO = 6. Thus, the query becomes

```
SELECT ITEMNAME, ITEMCOLOR FROM ITEM
   WHERE ITEMTYPE = 'C'
   AND EXISTS (SELECT * FROM LINEITEM
      WHERE LINEITEM.ITEMNO = 6)
```

Because there is at least one row in LINEITEM with ITEMNO = 6, the subquery returns *true*. The item has been sold and should be reported. The second clothing item, Hat - Polar Explorer (white), in ITEM has ITEMNO = 7. There are no rows in LINEITEM with ITEMNO = 7, so the subquery returns *false*. That item has not been sold and should not be reported.

You can also think of the query as, "Select clothing items for which a sale exists." Remember, for EXISTS to return *true*, there need be only one row for which the condition is *true*.

NOT EXISTS—select a value if it does not exist

NOT EXISTS is the negative of EXISTS. It is used in a WHERE clause to test whether all rows in a table fail to satisfy a specified condition. It returns the value *true* if there are no rows satisfying the condition; otherwise it returns *false*.

❍ **Report all clothing items that have not been sold.**

```
SELECT ITEMNAME, ITEMCOLOR FROM ITEM
   WHERE ITEMTYPE = 'C'
    AND NOT EXISTS
      (SELECT * FROM LINEITEM
         WHERE ITEM.ITEMNO = LINEITEM.ITEMNO)
```

If we consider this query as the opposite of that used to illustrate EXISTS, it seems logical to use NOT EXISTS. Conceptually, we can also think of this query as evaluating the subquery for each row of ITEM. The first item with ITEMTYPE ='C', Hat - Polar Explorer (red), in ITEM has ITEMNO= 6. Thus, the query becomes:

```
SELECT ITEMNAME, ITEMCOLOR FROM ITEM
   WHERE ITEMTYPE = 'C'
      AND NOT EXISTS
         (SELECT * FROM LINEITEM
            WHERE LINEITEM.ITEMNO = 6)
```

There is at least one row in LINEITEM with ITEMNO = 6, so the subquery returns *true*. The NOT before EXISTS then negates the *true* to give *false*; the item will not be reported because it has been sold.

The second item with ITEMTYPE ='C', Hat – Polar Explorer (white), in ITEM has ITEMNO = 7. The query becomes:

```
SELECT ITEMNAME, ITEMCOLOR FROM ITEM
   WHERE ITEMTYPE = 'C'
   AND NOT EXISTS
      (SELECT * FROM LINEITEM
         WHERE LINEITEM.ITEMNO = 7)
```

Because there are no rows in LINEITEM with ITEMNO = 7, the subquery returns *false*, and this is negated by the NOT before EXISTS to give *true*. The item has not been sold and should be reported.

ITEMNAME	ITEMCOLOR
Hat-Polar Explorer	White
Boots-snake proof	Green
Pith helmet	Khaki
Stetson	Brown

You can also think of the query as, "Select clothing items for which no sales exists." Also remember, for NOT EXISTS to return *true*, no rows should satisfy the condition.

Divide (and be conquered)

In addition to the existential quantifier that you have already encountered, formal logic has a **universal quantifier** known as *forall* which is necessary for queries such as

❍ **Find the items that have appeared in all sales.**

If a universal qualifier were supported by SQL, this query could be phrased as, "Select item names where *forall* sales there *exists* a LINEITEM row recording that this item was sold." A quick inspection of Table 5-1 shows that one item satisfies this condition (ITEMNO = 2).

While SQL does not directly support the universal qualifier, formal logic shows that *forall* can be expressed using *exists*. The query becomes, "Find items such that there does not exist a sale in which this item does not appear." The equivalent SQL expression is:

```
SELECT ITEMNO, ITEMNAME FROM ITEM
   WHERE NOT EXISTS
      (SELECT * FROM SALE
         WHERE NOT EXISTS
            (SELECT * FROM LINEITEM
               WHERE LINEITEM.ITEMNO = ITEM.ITEMNO
               AND LINEITEM.SALENO = SALE.SALENO))
```

ITEMNO	ITEMNAME
2	Pocket knife-Avon

You may be convinced that this query is correct by walking through it step by step using the data in Table 5-2 and examining the outcome of each step of the query (see Table 5-3).

Table 5-2: Condensed versions of SALE, LINEITEM, and ITEM

SALE
SALENO
1
2
3
4
5

LINEITEM		
LINENO	SALENO	ITEMNO
1	1	2
1	2	6
2	2	16
3	2	19
4	2	2
1	3	4
2	3	2
1	4	4
2	4	9
3	4	13
4	4	14
5	4	3
6	4	2
1	5	10
2	5	11
3	5	12
4	5	13
5	5	2

ITEM
ITEMNO
1
2
3
...

Step 1.

The first row of ITEM has ITEMNO=1, and the first row of SALE has SALENO = 1.

The innermost query becomes

Table 5-3: Results of the first 18 steps of the divide statement

Step	ITEMNO	SALENO	SELECT * FROM LINEITEM WHERE LINEITEM.ITEMNO = ITEM.ITEMNO AND LINEITEM.SALENO = SALE.SALENO	NOT EXISTS	SELECT * FROM SALE WHERE NOT EXISTS (SELECT * FROM LINEITEM WHERE LINEITEM.ITEMNO = ITEM.ITEMNO AND LINEITEM.SALENO =SALE.SALENO)	NOT EXISTS
1	1	1	false	true		
2	1	2	false	true		
3	1	3	false	true		
4	1	4	false	true		
5	1	5	false	true		
6					true	false
7	2	1	true	false		
8	2	2	true	false		
9	2	3	true	false		
10	2	4	true	false		
11	2	5	true	false		
12					false	true
13	3	1	false	true		
14	3	2	false	true		
15	3	3	false	true		
16	3	4	true	false		
17	3	5	false	true		
18					true	false

```
SELECT * FROM LINEITEM
   WHERE LINEITEM.ITEMNO = 1
   AND LINEITEM.SALENO = 1
```

Examination of the LINEITEM tables shows this query returns *false*, which is negated by the NOT before the innermost EXISTS to give *true*.

Step 2.

We now advance to the second row of SALE with SALENO = 2 and execute the innermost query again. This query will also return *false* which will be negated to *true*.

Steps 3-5.

The results of these and other steps are summarized in Table 5-3.

Step 6.

The subquery

```
SELECT * FROM SALE
   WHERE NOT EXISTS (...
```

has now been executed for each value of SALENO for the first value of ITEMNO and returned *true* for each row. Thus this query returns *true*, and the NOT before the EXISTS of this query changes the *true* to *false*. Since the value returned is *false*, the current value of ITEMNO is not reported.

Steps 7-11.

The results of these steps are shown in Table 5-3.

Step 12.

The subquery

```
SELECT * FROM SALE
   WHERE NOT EXISTS (...
```

has now been executed for each value of SALENO for the second value of ITEMNO and returned *false* for each row. Although this query returns *false*, the NOT before the EXISTS changes the *false* to *true*. Since the value returned is *true*, the current value of ITEMNO is reported. Item 2 appears in all sales.

It will take you some time to step through this example to understand how the double NOT EXISTS works. Once you do, you will be convinced that the query does work.

Relational algebra (Chapter 9) has the divide operation, which makes these queries easy to write. Be careful: not all queries containing the *all* are divides. With experience, you will learn to recognize and conquer divide.

To save the tedium of formulating this query from scratch, we have developed a template (see Figure 5-3) for dealing with these sorts of queries. Divide queries typically occur with m:m relationships.

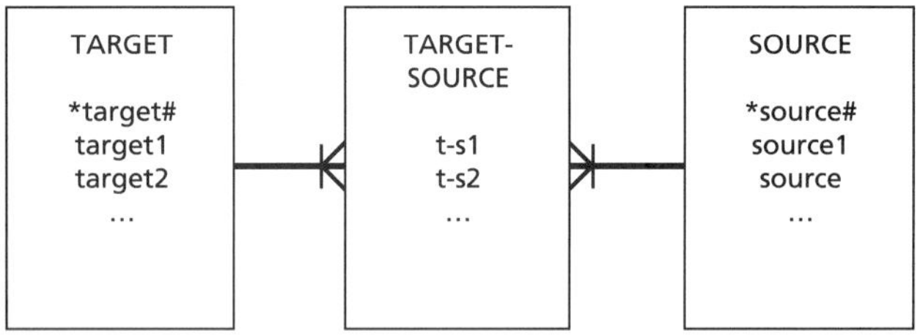

Figure 5-3. A template for divide

An appropriate generic query and template SQL command are:

- **Find the target1 that have appeared in all sources.**

```
SELECT TARGET1 FROM TARGET
   WHERE NOT EXISTS
      (SELECT * FROM SOURCE
         WHERE NOT EXISTS
            (SELECT * FROM TARGET-SOURCE
               WHERE TARGET-SOURCE.TARGET# = TARGET.TARGET#
               AND TARGET-SOURCE.SOURCE# = SOURCE.SOURCE#))
```

Beyond the great divide[3]

Divide proves troublesome to most people because of the double negative—we just don't think that way. If divide sends your neurons into knots, then try the following approach.

The query, "Find the items that have appeared in all sales" can be rephrased as "Find all the items for which the number of sales that include this item is equal to the total number of sales." This is an easier query to write than "Find items such that there does not exist a sale in which this item does not appear." The rephrased query has two parts. First, determine the total number of sales. Here we mean distinct sales (i.e., the number of rows with a distinct value for SALENO). The SQL is:

```
SELECT COUNT(DISTINCT SALENO) FROM SALE
```

Second, group the items sold by ITEMNO and ITEMNAME and use a HAVING clause with COUNT to calculate the number of sales in which the item has occurred. Forcing the count in the HAVING clause to equal the result of the first query, which becomes an inner query, results in a list of items appearing in all sales.

```
SELECT ITEM.ITEMNO, ITEM.ITEMNAME
   FROM ITEM, LINEITEM
      WHERE ITEM.ITEMNO = LINEITEM.ITEMNO
         GROUP BY ITEM.ITEMNO, ITEM.ITEMNAME
            HAVING COUNT(DISTINCT SALENO)
               = (SELECT COUNT(DISTINCT SALENO) FROM SALE)
```

Set operations

Set operators are useful for combining the values derived from two or more SQL queries. The UNION operation is equivalent to OR, and INTERSECT is equivalent to AND. Two examples demonstrate the use of the set operators.

❍ **List items that were sold on January 16, 1995 or are brown.**

Resolution of this query requires two tables: one to report items sold on January 16, 1995 and one to report the brown items. UNION (i.e., or) then combines the results of the tables including *any* rows in both tables and excluding duplicate rows.

3. Thanks to Dr. Gert Jan Hofstede of Wageningen University, The Netherlands, for pointing out this approach.

```
SELECT ITEMNAME FROM ITEM, LINEITEM, SALE
   WHERE ITEM.ITEMNO = LINEITEM.ITEMNO
   AND LINEITEM.SALENO = SALE.SALENO
   AND SALEDATE = '1995-01-16'
UNION
   SELECT ITEMNAME FROM ITEM WHERE ITEMCOLOR = 'Brown'
```

ITEMNAME
Hammock
Map case
Pocket knife-Avon
Pocket knife-Nile
Safari chair
Stetson
Tent-2 person
Tent-8 person

❍ **List items that were sold on January 16, 1995 and are brown.**

This query uses the same two tables as the previous query. In this case, INTERSECT (i.e., and) then combines the results of the tables including *only* rows in both tables and excluding duplicates.

```
SELECT ITEMNAME FROM ITEM, LINEITEM, SALE
   WHERE ITEM.ITEMNO = LINEITEM.ITEMNO
   AND LINEITEM.SALENO = SALE.SALENO
   AND SALEDATE = '1995-01-16'
INTERSECT
   SELECT ITEMNAME FROM ITEM WHERE ITEMCOLOR = 'Brown'
```

ITEMNAME
Pocket knife-Avon

Summary

There can be a many-to-many (m:m) relationship between entities, which is represented by creating an associative entity and two 1:m relationships. An associative entity stores data about an m:m relationship. The join operation can be extended from two tables to three or more tables. EXISTS tests whether a table has at least one row that meets a specified condition. NOT EXISTS tests whether all rows in a table do not satisfy a specified condition. Both EXISTS and NOT EXISTS return *true* or *false*. The relational operation divide, also known as *forall*, can be translated into a double negative. It is represented in SQL by a query containing two NOT EXISTS statements. Set operations enable the results of queries to be combined.

Key terms and concepts

Associative entity
Divide
Existential quantifier
EXISTS
INTERSECT
Many-to-many relationship
NOT EXISTS
UNION
Universal quantifier

Exercises

1. Draw data models for the following situations. In each case, think about the names you give each entity:
   a. Farmers can own cows or share cows with other farmers.
   b. A hamburger shop makes several types of hamburgers, and the same ingredient can be used with several types of hamburgers. This does not literally mean the same piece of lettuce is used many times, but lettuce is used with several types of hamburgers.
   c. A track and field meet can have many competitors, and a competitor can participate in more than one event.
   d. A patient can have many physicians, and a physician can have many patients.
   e. A student can attend more than one class, and the same class can have many students.
   f. *The Marathoner*, a monthly magazine, regularly reports the performance of professional marathon runners. It has asked you to design a database to record the details of all major marathons (e.g., Boston, London, and Paris). Professional marathon runners compete in several races each year. A race may have thousands of competitors, but only about 200 or so are professional runners, the ones *The Marathoner* tracks. For each race, the magazine reports a runner's time and finishing position and some personal details such as name, gender, and age.
2. The data model shown was designed by a golf statistician. Write SQL statements to create the corresponding relational database.

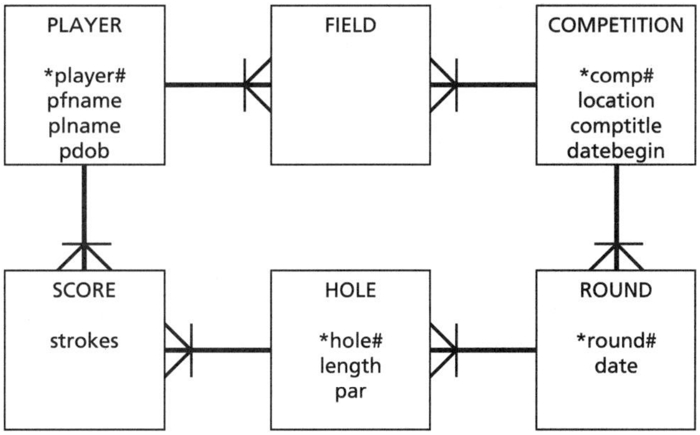

3. Write the following SQL queries for the database described in this chapter:
   a. List the names of items for which the quantity sold is greater than one.
   b. Compute the total value of sales for each item by date.
   c. Report all furniture items that have been sold.
   d. List all furniture that has not been sold.
   e. List all items that appear in sales with SALENO equal to 3 or 4.
   f. Compute the total value of each sale.
4. Write SQL statements to create a relational database described by the following data model.

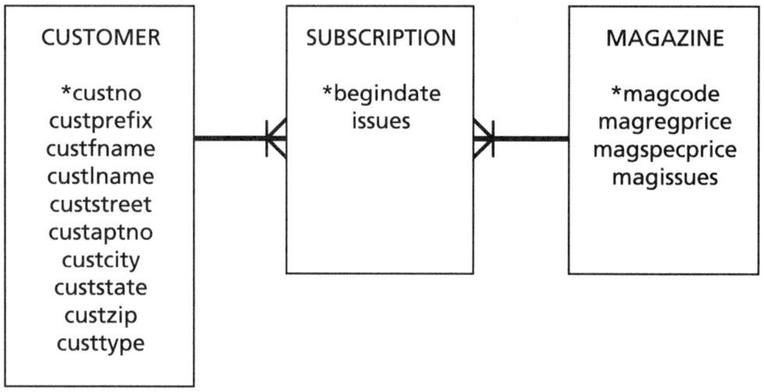

5. Why do you have to create a third entity when you have an m:m relationship?
6. What does a vertical bar on a relationship arc mean?
7. How does EXISTS differ from other clauses in an SQL statement?
8. How is the relational algebra divide statement implemented in SQL? What do you think of this approach?
9. Answer the following queries based on the described relational database.

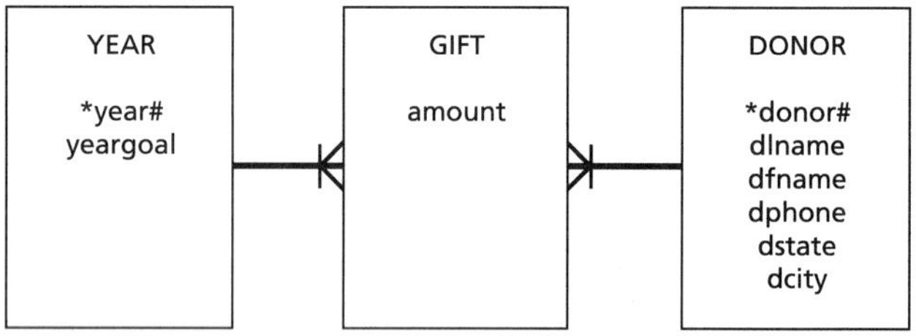

YEAR

<u>YEAR</u>	YEARGOAL

GIFT

AMOUNT	<u>*YEAR*</u>	<u>*DONORNO*</u>

DONOR

<u>DONORNO</u>	DLNAME	DFNAME	DPHONE	DSTATE	DCITY

a. List the phone numbers of donor number 106 and 125.
b. How many donors are there in the donor table?
c. How many people made donations in 1992?
d. What is the name of the person who made the largest donation in 1992?
e. What was the total amount donated in 1993?
f. List the donors who have made a donation every year.
g. List the donors who give twice the average.
h. List the total amount given by each person across all years; sort the report by the donor's name.
i. Report the total donations in 1994 by state.
j. In which years did the total donated exceed the goal for the year?

CD library case

After learning how to model m:m relationships, Ajay realized he could now model a number of situations that had bothered him. He had been puzzling over some relationships that he had recognized but was unsure how to model:

- ❖ a person can appear on many tracks, and a track can have many persons (e.g., The Manhattan Transfer, a quartet, has made many tracks);
- ❖ a person can compose many songs, and a song can have multiple composers (e.g., Rogers and Hammerstein collaborated many times with Rogers composing the music and Hammerstein writing the lyric);
- ❖ an artist can release many CDs, and a CD can feature several artists (e.g. John Coltrane, who has many CDs, has a CD, *Miles & Coltrane,* with Miles Davis).

Ajay revised his data model to include the m:m relationships he had recognized. He wrestled with what to call the entity that stored details of people. Sometimes these people are musicians; other times singers, composers, and so forth. He decided that the most general approach was to call the entity PERSON. The extended data model is shown in Figure 5-4.

In version 3.0, Ajay introduced several new entities, including COMPOSITION to record details of a composition. He initially linked COMPOSITION to TRACK with a 1:m relationship. In other words, a composition can have many tracks, but a track is of one composition. This did not seem right.

After further thought, he realized there was a missing entity—RECORDING. A composition has many recordings (e.g., multiple recordings of John Coltrane's composition "Giant Steps"), and a recording can appear as a track on different CDs (typically those whose title begins with *The Best of* ... feature tracks on earlier CDs). Also, because a recording is a performance of a composition, it is a composition that has a title, not recording or track. So, he revised version 3.0 of the data model to produce version 4.0 (see Figure 5-5).

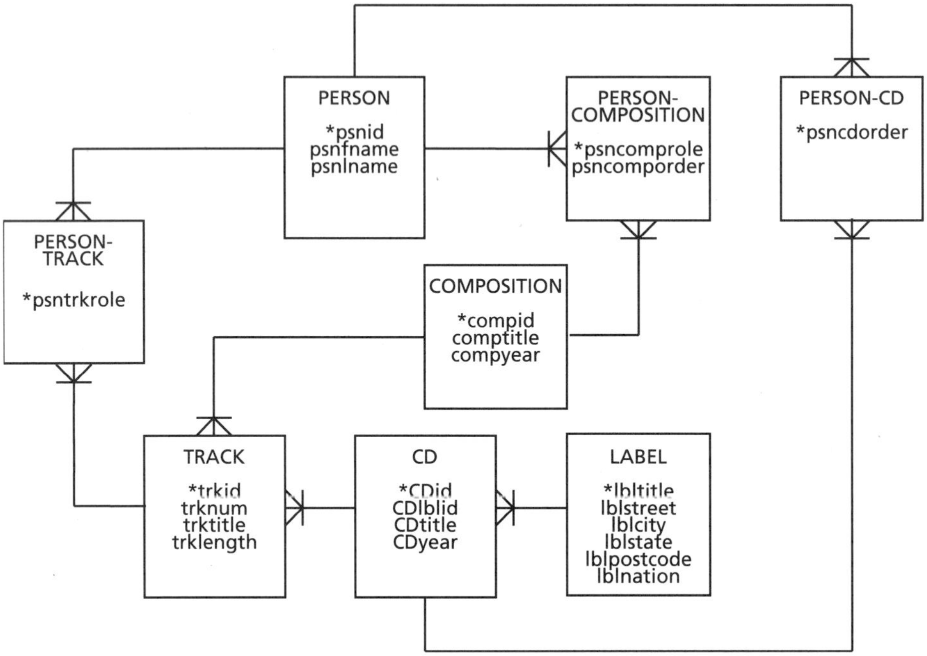

Figure 5-4. CD library V3.0

Version 4.0 of the model captures:

- the m:m between PERSON and RECORDING with the associative entity PERSON-RECORDING. The identifier for PERSON-RECORDING is a composite key (*psnid, rcdid, psnrcdrole*).The identifiers of PERSON and RECORDING are required to identify uniquely an instance of PERSON-RECORDING, which is why there are bars on the crow's feet attached to PERSON-RECORDING. Also, because a person can have multiple roles on a recording, (e.g., play the piano and sing), then *psnrcdrole* is required to uniquely identify these situations.
- the m:m between PERSON and COMPOSITION with the associative entity PERSON-COMPOSITION. The identifier is a composite key (*psnid, compid*). The attribute psncomporder is for remembering the correct sequence in those cases where there are multiple people involved in a composition. That is, the database needs to record that it is Rogers and Hammerstein, not Hammerstein and Rogers.
- the m:m between PERSON and CD with the associative entity PERSON-CD. Again the identifier is a composite key (*psnid, CDid*) of the identifiers of entities in the m:m relationship, and there is an attribute (*psncdorder*) to record the order of the people featured on the CD.
- the 1:m between RECORDING and TRACK. A recording can appear on many tracks, but a track has only one recording.
- the 1:m between CD and TRACK. A CD can have many tracks, but a track appears on only one CD. You can also think of TRACK as the name for the associative entity of

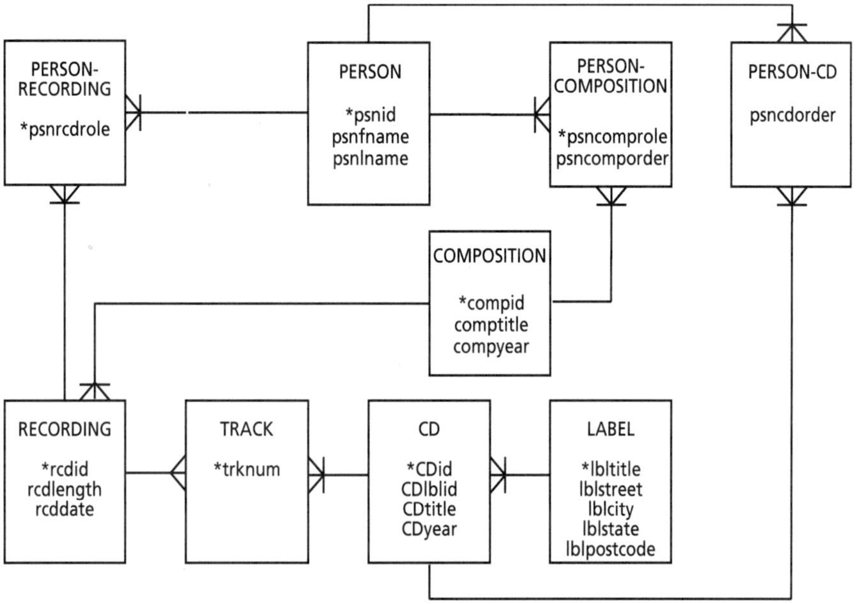

Figure 5-5. CD library V4.0

the m:m relationship between RECORDING and CD. A recording can appear on many CDs, and a CD has many recordings.

After creating the new tables, Ajay was ready to add some data. He decided first to correct the errors introduced by his initial, incorrect modeling of TRACK by inserting data for RECORDING and revising TRACK. He realized that because RECORDING contains a foreign key to record the 1:m relationship with COMPOSITION, he needed to start by entering the data for COMPOSITION.[4]

Table 5-4: The table COMPOSITION

compid	comptitle	compyear
1	Giant Steps	
2	Cousin Mary	
3	Countdown	
4	Spiral	
5	Syeeda's Song Flute	
6	Naima	
7	Mr. P.C.	
8	Stomp of King Porter	1924
9	Sing a Study in Brown	1937
10	Sing Moten's Swing	1997

4. When the text accompanying a CD does not include the year of composition, make it NULL.

Table 5-4: The table COMPOSITION (continued)

compid	comptitle	compyear
11	A-tisket, A-tasket	1938
12	I Know Why	1941
13	Sing You Sinners	1930
14	Java Jive	1940
15	Down South Camp Meetin	1997
16	Topsy	1936
17	Clouds	
18	Skyliner	1944
19	It's Good Enough to Keep	1997
20	Choo Choo Ch' Boogie	1945

Once COMPOSITION had been prepared, Ajay moved onto the RECORDING table:

Table 5-5: The table RECORDING

rcdid	compid	rcdlength	rcddate
1	1	4.72	1959-May-04
2	2	5.75	1959-May-04
3	3	2.35	1959-May-04
4	4	5.93	1959-May-04
5	5	7.00	1959-May-04
6	6	4.35	1959-Dec-02
7	7	2.95	1959-May-04
8	1	5.93	1959-Apr-01
9	6	7.00	1959-Apr-01
10	2	6.95	1959-May-04
11	3	3.67	1959-May-04
12	2	4.45	1959-May-04
13	8	3.20	
14	9	2.85	
15	10	3.60	
16	11	2.95	
17	12	3.57	
18	13	2.75	
19	14	2.85	
20	15	3.25	
21	16	3.23	
22	17	7.20	
23	18	3.18	
24	19	3.18	
25	20	3.00	

The last row of the RECORDING data indicates a recording of the composition "Choo Choo Ch' Boogie," which has compid = 20.

Next, the data for TRACK could be entered.

Table 5-6: The table TRACK

CDid	trknum	rcdid
1	1	1
1	2	2
1	3	3
1	4	4
1	5	5
1	6	6
1	7	7
1	8	1
1	9	6
1	10	2
1	11	3
1	12	5
2	1	13
2	2	14
2	3	15
2	4	16
2	5	17
2	6	18
2	7	19
2	8	20
2	9	21
2	10	22
2	11	23
2	12	24
2	13	25

The last row of the TRACK data indicates that track 13 of *Swing* (CDid = 2) is a recording of "Choo Choo Ch' Boogie" (rcdid = 25 and compid = 20).

PERSON-RECORDING stores details of the people involved in each recording. Referring to the accompanying notes for the CD *Giant Steps*, Ajay learned that the composition "Giants Steps," recorded on May 4, 1959, included the following personnel: John Coltrane on tenor sax, Tommy Flanagan on piano, Paul Chambers on bass, and Art Taylor on drums. Using the following data, he inserted four rows in the PERSON table.

Table 5-7: The table PERSON

psnid	psnfname	psnlname
1	John	Coltrane
2	Tommy	Flanagan
3	Paul	Chamber
4	Art	Taylor

Then, he linked these people to the particular recording of "Giant Steps" by entering the following data in PERSON-RECORDING.

Table 5-8: The table PERSON-RECORDING

psnid	rcdid	psncdrole
1	1	tenor sax
2	1	piano
3	1	bass
4	1	drums

Your turn

1. What data will you enter in PERSON-CD to relate John Coltrane to the *Giant Steps* CD?
2. What data will you enter in PERSON-COMPOSITION to relate John Coltrane to compositions with compid 1 through 7? You should indicate he wrote the music by entering a value of "music" for the person's role in the composition.
3. Use SQL to solve the following queries:
   a. List the tracks on *Swing*.
   b. Who composed the music for "Spiral"?
   c. Who played which instruments for the May 4, 1959 recording of "Giant Steps"?
   d. List the composers who write music and play the tenor sax.
4. What is the data model missing?

6

One-to-One and Recursive Relationships

Self-reflection is the school of wisdom.
Baltastar Gracián, *The Art of Worldly Wisdom*, 1647

Learning objectives

On completion of this chapter, you will be able to

- model one-to-one and recursive relationships;
- define a database with one-to-one and recursive relationships;
- write queries for a database with one-to-one and recursive relationships.

Alice was convinced that a database of business facts would speed up decision making. Her initial experience with the sales database had reinforced this conviction. She decided that employee data should be computerized next. When she arrived at The Expeditioner, she found the company lacked an organization chart and job descriptions for employees. One of her first tasks had been to draw an organization chart (see Figure 6-1).

She divided the firm into four departments and appointed a boss for each department. The first person listed in each department was its boss; of course, Alice was paramount.

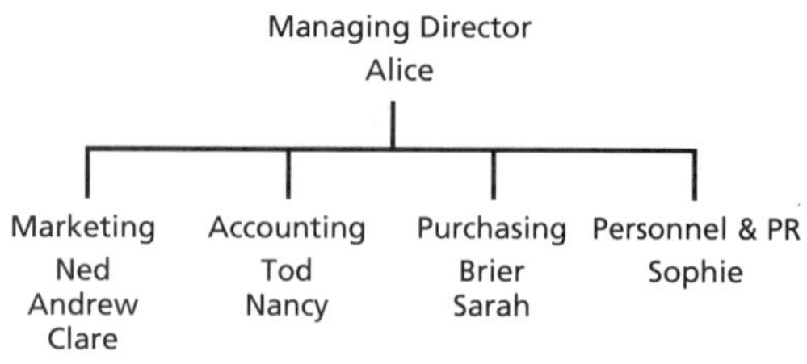

Figure 6-1. The Expeditioner's organization chart

Ned had finished the sales database, so the time was right to create an employee database. Ned seemed to be enjoying his new role, though his dress standard had slipped. Maybe Alice would have to move him out of Marketing. In fact, he sometimes reminded her of fellows who used to hang around the computer lab all day playing weird games. She wasn't quite ready to sound a "nerd alert," but it was getting close.

Modeling the one-to-one relationship

Initially, the organization chart appears to record two relationships. First, a department has one or more employees, and an employee belongs to one department. Second, a department has one boss, and a person is boss of only one department. That is, boss is a 1:1 relationship between DEPT and EMP. The data model for this situation is shown in Figure 6-2.

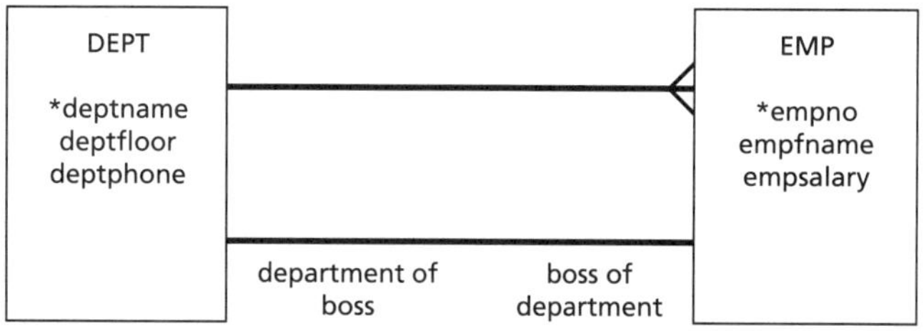

Figure 6-2. A data model illustrating a 1:1 relationship

As a general rule, the 1:1 relationship is labeled to avoid confusion because the meaning of such a relationship cannot always be inferred. This label is called a relationship descriptor. The 1:m relationship between DEPT and EMP is not labeled because its meaning is readily understood by reading the model. Use a relationship descriptor when there is more than one relationship between entities or when the meaning of the relationship is not readily inferred from the model.

If we think about this problem, we realize there is more to boss than just a department. People also have a boss. Thus, Alice is the boss of all the other employees. In this case, we are mainly interested in who directly bosses someone else. So, Alice is the direct boss of Ned, Todd, Brier, and Sophie. We need to record the person-boss relationship as well as the department-boss relationship.

The person-boss relationship is a 1:m recursive relationship because it is a relationship between employees—an employee has one boss and a boss can have many employees. The data model is shown in Figure 6-3.

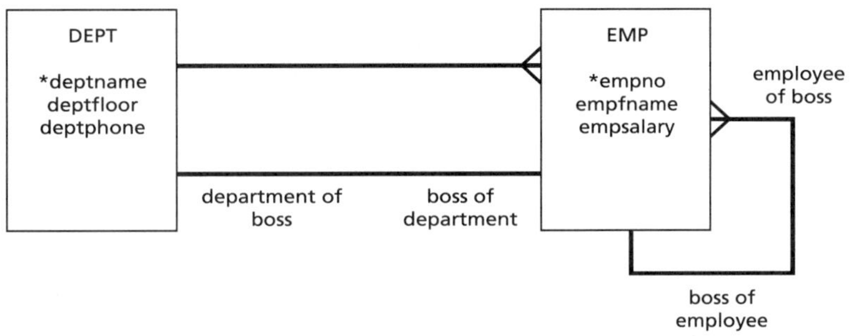

Figure 6-3. A data model illustrating a recursive1:m relationship

It is a good idea to label the recursive relationship because its meaning is often not obvious from the data model.

Mapping a one-to-one relationship

Since mapping a 1:1 relationship follows the same rules as for any other data model, the major consideration is where to place the foreign key(s). There are three alternatives:

1. Put the foreign key in DEPT.
   Doing so means that every instance of DEPT will record *empno* of the employee who is boss. Because all departments in this case have a boss, the foreign key will always be non-null.
2. Put the foreign key in EMP.
   Choosing this alternative means that every instance of EMP should record *deptname* of the department this employee bosses. Since many employees are not bosses, the foreign key will generally be null.
3. Put a foreign key in both DEPT and EMP.
   The consequence of putting a foreign key in both tables in the 1:1 relationship is the combination of points 1 and 2.

Although it does not matter where you put the foreign key, a sound approach is to select the entity that results in the fewest nulls since this tends to be less confusing to users. In this case, the simplest approach is to put the foreign key in DEPT.

Mapping a recursive relationship

A 1:m recursive relationship is mapped like a standard 1:m relationship. An additional column, for the foreign key, is created for the entity at the many end of the relationship. Of course, in this case the one and many end are the same entity, so an additional column is added to EMP. This column contains the key *empno* of the one end of the relationship. Since EMPNO is already used as a column name, a different name needs to be selected. In this case, it makes sense to call the foreign key column BOSSNO since it stores the boss's employee number.

The mapping of the data model is shown in Table 6-1. Note that *deptname* becomes a column in EMP, the many end of the 1:m relationship, and *empno* becomes a foreign key in DEPT, an end of the 1:1 relationship.

Table 6-1: The tables DEPT and EMP

DEPT			
DEPTNAME	DEPTFLOOR	DEPTPHONE	*EMPNO*
Management	5	2001	1
Marketing	1	2002	2
Accounting	4	2003	5
Purchasing	4	2004	7
Personnel & PR	1	2005	9

EMP				
EMPNO	EMPFNAME	EMPSALARY	*DEPTNAME*	*BOSSNO*
1	Alice	75000	Management	
2	Ned	45000	Marketing	1
3	Andrew	25000	Marketing	2
4	Clare	22000	Marketing	2
5	Todd	38000	Accounting	1
6	Nancy	22000	Accounting	5
7	Brier	43000	Purchasing	1
8	Sarah	56000	Purchasing	7
9	Sophie	35000	Personnel & PR	1

If you examine EMP, you will see that the boss of the employee with EMPNO = 2 (Ned) has BOSSNO = 1. You can then look up the row with EMPNO = 1 to find that Ned's boss is Alice. This "double lookup" is frequently used when manually interrogating a table that represents a recursive relationship. Soon you will discover how this is handled with SQL.

Here is the SQL to create the two tables:

```
CREATE TABLE DEPT
   (DEPTNAME        CHAR(15)      NOT NULL,
   DEPTFLOOR        SMALLINT      NOT NULL,
   DEPTPHONE        SMALLINT      NOT NULL,
   EMPNO            SMALLINT      NOT NULL,
      PRIMARY KEY(DEPTNAME))

CREATE TABLE EMP
   (EMPNO       SMALLINT NOT NULL,
   EMPFNAME     CHAR(10),
   EMPSALARY    DECIMAL(7,0),
   DEPTNAME     CHAR(15),
   BOSSNO       SMALLINT,
      PRIMARY KEY(EMPNO),
      FOREIGN KEY FKDEPT(DEPTNAME) REFERENCES DEPT
         ON DELETE RESTRICT)
```

You will notice that some of the foreign keys have not been specified in the CREATE statements. There is no foreign key definition for EMPNO in DEPT and for BOSSNO in EMP (the recursive boss relationship). Why?

First, observe that DEPTNAME is a foreign key in EMP. If we make EMPNO a foreign key in DEPT, then we have a deadly embrace. A new department cannot be added to the DEPT table until there is a boss for that department (i.e., there is a person in the EMP table with the EMPNO of the boss); however, the other constraint states that an employee cannot be added to the EMP table unless there is a department to which that person is assigned. If we have both foreign key constraints, we cannot add a new department until we have added a boss, and we cannot add a boss until we have added a department for that person. Nothing, under these circumstances, can happen if both foreign key constraints are in place. So, only one of the foreign key constraints is specified.

In the case of the recursive relationship for the entity EMPLOYEE, there is no foreign key constraint because some versions of SQL do not allow this constraint to refer to the table being created. Also, observe that the foreign key BOSSNO can be null. This caters to the situation where a person (e.g., Alice) does not have a boss. Similarly, DEPTNAME in EMP is allowed to take null values to handle the situation where a person is not assigned to a department. These two examples illustrate that each foreign key value must match a primary key value or else be null.

As this example shows, the FOREIGN KEY clause provides limited support for ensuring referential integrity. In more complex modeling situations, such as when there are multiple relationships between a pair of entities, use of a FOREIGN KEY clause may result in a deadlock. Always consider the consequences of using a FOREIGN KEY clause before applying it.

Querying a one-to-one relationship

Querying presents no special difficulties but does allow us to see additional features of SQL.

❍ **List the salary of each department's boss.**

```
SELECT EMPFNAME, DEPTNAME, EMPSALARY FROM EMP
   WHERE EMPNO IN (SELECT EMPNO FROM DEPT)
```

or

```
SELECT EMPFNAME, DEPT.DEPTNAME, EMPSALARY
   FROM EMP, DEPT WHERE
      DEPT.EMPNO = EMP.EMPNO
```

EMPFNAME	DEPTNAME	EMPSALARY
Alice	Management	75000
Ned	Marketing	45000
Todd	Accounting	38000
Brier	Purchasing	43000
Sophie	Personnel & PR	35000

Querying a recursive relationship

Handling a query for a recursive relationship is puzzling until you realize that you can join a table to itself by creating two copies of the table. In SQL, you create a temporary copy, a **table alias**, of a table by following the table's name with the alias (e.g., EMP WRK creates a temporary copy, WRK, of the permanent table EMP).[1] Table aliases are always required so that SQL can distinguish which copy of the table is being referenced. To demonstrate:

❍ **Find the salary of Nancy's boss.**

```
SELECT WRK.EMPFNAME, WRK.EMPSALARY,BOSS.EMPFNAME, BOSS.EMPSALARY
   FROM EMP WRK, EMP BOSS
      WHERE WRK.EMPFNAME = 'Nancy'
      AND WRK.BOSSNO = BOSS.EMPNO
```

Many queries are solved by getting all the data you need to answer the request in one row. In this case, the query is easy to answer once the data for Nancy and her boss are in the one row. Thus, think of this query as joining two copies of the table EMP to get the worker and her boss's data in one row. Notice that there is a suffix (WRK and BOSS) for each copy of the table to distinguish between them. It helps to use a suffix that makes sense. In this

1. In MS Access, the equivalent expression is EMP AS WRK.

case, the WRK and BOSS suffixes can be thought of as referring to the worker and boss tables, respectively. You can understand how the query works by examining Table 6-2.

Table 6-2: Joining a table with itself

EMP WRK				
EMPNO	EMPFNAME	EMPSALARY	*DEPTNAME*	*BOSSNO*
1	Alice	75000	Management	
2	Ned	45000	Marketing	1
3	Andrew	25000	Marketing	2
4	Clare	22000	Marketing	2
5	Todd	38000	Accounting	1
6	Nancy	22000	Accounting	5
7	Brier	43000	Purchasing	1
8	Sarah	56000	Purchasing	7
9	Sophie	35000	Personnel & PR	1

EMP BOSS				
EMPNO	EMPFNAME	EMPSALARY	*DEPTNAME*	*BOSSNO*
1	Alice	75000	Management	
2	Ned	45000	Marketing	1
3	Andrew	25000	Marketing	2
4	Clare	22000	Marketing	2
5	Todd	38000	Accounting	1
6	Nancy	22000	Accounting	5
7	Brier	43000	Purchasing	1
8	Sarah	56000	Purchasing	7
9	Sophie	35000	Personnel & PR	1

The first step is to find the row in WRK where the employee's name is "Nancy." This row is shaded in WRK. The BOSSNO column of this row contains 5. The second step is to join this row to the row in the BOSS table with EMPNO = 5. This row is also shaded. The result of the SQL query is

WRK.EMPFNAME	WRK.EMPSALARY	BOSS.EMPFNAME	BOSS.EMPSALARY
Nancy	22000	Todd	38000

❍ **Find the names of employees who earn more than their boss.**

```
SELECT WRK.EMPFNAME
   FROM EMP WRK, EMP BOSS
      WHERE WRK.BOSSNO = BOSS.EMPNO
      AND WRK.EMPSALARY > BOSS.EMPSALARY
```

This would be very easy if the employee and boss data were in the same row. We could simply compare the salaries of the two people. To get the data in the one row, we join by matching BOSSNO in WRK with EMPNO in BOSS. The result is as follows:

WRK					BOSS				
EMPNO	EMPFNAME	EMPSALARY	DEPTNAME	BOSSNO	EMPNO	EMPFNAME	EMPSALARY	DEPTNAME	BOSSNO
2	Ned	45000	Marketing	1	1	Alice	75000	Management	
3	Andrew	25000	Marketing	2	2	Ned	45000	Marketing	1
4	Clare	22000	Marketing	2	2	Ned	45000	Marketing	1
5	Todd	38000	Accounting	1	1	Alice	75000	Management	
6	Nancy	22000	Accounting	5	5	Todd	38000	Accounting	1
7	Brier	43000	Purchasing	1	1	Alice	75000	Management	
8	Sarah	56000	Purchasing	7	7	Brier	43000	Purchasing	1
9	Sophie	35000	Personnel & PR	1	1	Alice	75000	Management	

Now the rest of the query is very straightforward. It is easy to compare the salaries of employees and their boss. The result is as follows:

EMPFNAME
Sarah

Alice has found several histories of The Expeditioner from a variety of eras. Because many expeditions they outfitted were conducted under royal patronage, it was not uncommon for these histories to refer to British kings and queens. Alice could remember very little about British history, let alone when various kings and queens reigned. This sounded like another database problem. She would ask Ned to create a database that recorded details of each monarch. She thought it also would be useful to record details of royal succession.

Modeling a one-to-one recursive relationship

The British monarchy can be represented by a simple one entity model. A monarch has one direct successor and one direct predecessor. The sequencing of monarchs can be modeled by a **1:1 recursive relationship** shown in Figure 6-4.

Mapping a one-to-one recursive relationship

The 1:1 recursive relationship is mapped by adding two foreign keys to MONARCH: one foreign key for the succeeding and one for the preceding relationship. Since each instance of a monarch is identified by a composite key, this results in two columns being added to MONARCH for each foreign key. A portion of the resulting table is shown in Table 6-3.

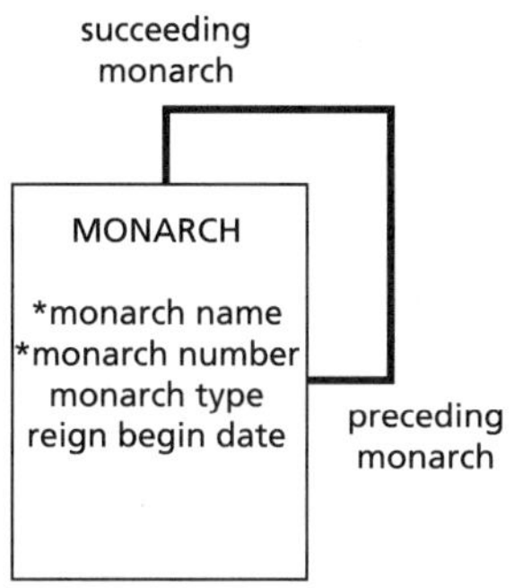

Figure 6-4. A data model illustrating a 1:1 recursive relationship

Table 6-3: The table MONARCH

MONARCH							
MONNAME	MONNUM	MONTYPE	RGNBEG	*PREMONNAME*	*PREMONNUM*	*SUCMONNAME*	*SUCMONNUM*
Victoria	I	Queen	1837/6/20	William	IV	Edward	VII
Edward	VII	King	1901/1/22	Victoria	I	George	V
George	V	King	1910/5/6	Edward	VII	Edward	VIII
Edward	VIII	King	1936/1/20	George	V	George	VI

The SQL statements to create the table are very straightforward. Notice that the primary key is a composite, and because the relationship is recursive, the two foreign key constraints cannot be defined. Also notice that the foreign keys are allowed to be null to account for the first monarch, who had no predecessor, and the latest monarch, whose successor is not yet known.

```
CREATE TABLE MONARCH
   (MONNAME     CHAR(15) NOT NULL,
   MONNUM       CHAR(5)  NOT NULL,
   MONTYPE      CHAR(5)  NOT NULL,
   RGNBEG       DATE,
   PREMONNAME   CHAR(15),
   PREMONNUM    CHAR(5),
   SUCMONNAME   CHAR(15),
   SUCMONNUM    CHAR(5),
      PRIMARY KEY(MONNAME,MONNUM))
```

Querying a one-to-one recursive relationship

Some queries on the MONARCH table demonstrate querying a 1:1 recursive relationship.

❍ **Who preceded Elizabeth II?**

```
SELECT PREMONNAME, PREMONNUM FROM MONARCH
   WHERE MONNAME = 'Elizabeth' AND MONNUM = 'II'
```

PREMONNAME	PREMONNUM
George	VI

This is simple because all the data are in one row. A more complex query is

❍ **Was Elizabeth II's predecessor a king or queen?**

```
SELECT PRE.MONTYPE FROM MONARCH CUR, MONARCH PRE
   WHERE CUR.PREMONNAME = PRE.MONNAME
   AND CUR.PREMONNUM = PRE.MONNUM
   AND CUR.MONNAME = 'Elizabeth' AND CUR.MONNUM = 'II'
```

MONTYPE
King

This is very similar to the query to find the salary of Nancy's boss. The MONARCH table is joined with itself to create a row that contains all the details to answer the query.

❍ **List the kings and queens of England in ascending order.**

```
SELECT MONTYPE, MONNAME, MONNUM, RGNBEG
   FROM MONARCH ORDER BY RGNBEG
```

MONTYPE	MONNAME	MONNUM	RGNBEG
Queen	Victoria	I	1837-06-20
King	Edward	VII	1901-01-22
King	George	V	1910-05-06
King	Edward	VIII	1936-01-20
King	George	VI	1936-12-11
Queen	Elizabeth	II	1952-02-06

This is a simple query because RGNBEG is like a ranking column. It would not be enough to store just the year in RGNBEG because two kings started their reigns in 1936; hence, the full date is required.

High Power Distance Culture and Recursive Relationships

A Brazilian insurance broker has designed a database to store information about its customers. Along with maintaining data about a customer's claims and premium payments, the database records details of a customer's personal influence and their relationship to powerful people. This database is used to differentiate the service provided to customers. Consider the following two situations.

As a result of a car accident, Maria contacts her insurance broker. On checking her database record, the broker discovers that Maria is not a major customer. However, Maria's husband, Joao, is a director of a large company and one of the broker's important customers. Furthermore, Joao is instrumental in deciding with whom his company insures. Maria is a very important customer because of her husband's influence. Consequently, the insurance broker immediately sends to the accident scene a representative authorized to negotiate an agreement with the involved parties. In addition, the account manager for Joao's firm will be notified immediately, and he will keep Joao informed of the entire process. The particular details of Maria's auto insurance policy are irrelevant. All damages will be paid irrespective of the policy because Maria is connected to a powerful person.

Elizabete, a client of the same insurance broker, has a car accident. When she contacts the insurance broker, the service representative checks the database and notes that Elizabete has a single auto insurance policy. Because neither Elizabete nor her relatives are influential, the representative advises her of the procedures for submitting a claim and asks her to come to the broker's office to sign the documents. Elizabete's claim will be examined closely to ensure that it is in line with her policy.

It is unlikely that this difference in treatment of ostensibly similar customers would be expected or accepted in Australia or the US, cultures with low power distance. Brazil is a high power distance culture. Inequities in the distribution of power are countenanced. It is accepted that powerful people are entitled to privileges.

In a low power distance culture, a database also can be used to provide differentiated treatment to a customer, but the key lies in the customer's past or potential profitability to the firm. For example, airlines reward frequent flyers with free tickets when their travel with a particular company exceeds predefined distances.

Interestingly, one of the main design problems for the Brazilian insurance broker was sorting out the many recursive relationships. As you know, people can have a wide variety of relationships to other people.

Dr. Eduardo Morgado of the State University of Sâo Paulo, Brazil provided this case.
For a comprehensive discussion of national culture, see Hofstede, G. 1991. *Culture and organizations: Software of the mind*. London, UK: McGraw-Hill.

Of course, Alice soon had another project for Ned. The Expeditioner keeps a wide range of products that are sometimes assembled into kits to make other products. For example, the animal photography kit is made up of eight items that The Expeditioner also sells separately. In addition, some kits became part of much larger kits. The animal photography kit is included as one of 45 items in the East African Safari package. All of the various items are considered products, and each has its own product code. Ned was now required to create a product database that would keep track of all the items in The Expeditioner's stock.

Modeling a many-to-many recursive relationship

The assembly of products to create other products is very common in business. Manufacturing even has a special term to describe it: a bill of materials. Data modeling is relatively simple once you realize that a product can appear as part of many other products and can be composed of many other products; that is, we have an **m:m recursive relationship** for product. As usual, we turn an m:m relationship into two 1:m relationships. Thus, we get the data model displayed in Figure 6-5.

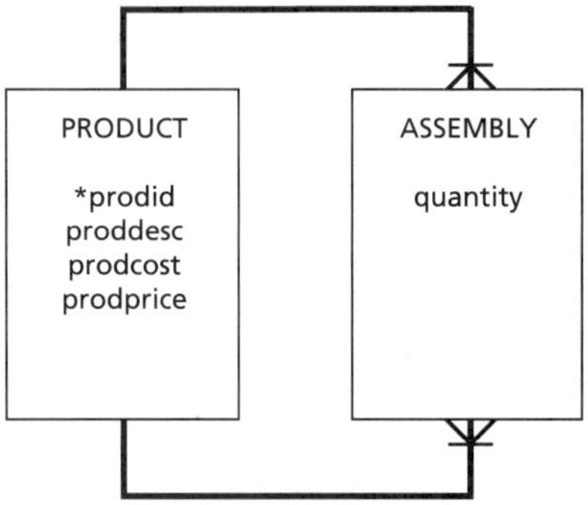

Figure 6-5. A data model illustrating a m:m relationship

Mapping a many-to-many recursive relationship

Mapping follows the same procedure described previously, producing the two tables shown in Table 6-4. The SQL statements to create the tables are shown next. Observe that ASSEMBLY has a composite key, and there are two foreign key constraints.

Table 6-4: Tables PRODUCT and ASSEMBLY

PRODUCT

PRODID	PRODDESC	PRODCOST	PRODPRICE
1000	Animal photography kit		725
101	35mm camera	150	300
102	Camera case	10	15
103	70-210 zoom lens	125	200
104	28-85 zoom lens	115	185
105	Photographer's vest	25	40
106	Lens cleaning cloth	1	1.25
107	Tripod	35	45
108	24 exp. 100ASA 35mm col neg	.85	1

ASSEMBLY

QUANTITY	*PRODID*	*SUBPRODID*
1	1000	101
1	1000	102
1	1000	103
1	1000	104
1	1000	105
2	1000	106
1	1000	107
10	1000	108

```
CREATE TABLE PRODUCT
   (PRODID      INTEGER  NOT NULL,
   PRODDESC     CHAR(30),
   PRODCOST     DECIMAL(9,2),
   PRODPRICE    DECIMAL(9,2),
      PRIMARY KEY(PRODID))

CREATE TABLE ASSEMBLY
   (QUANTITY       INTEGER  NOT NULL,
   PRODID          INTEGER,
   SUBPRODID       INTEGER,
      PRIMARY KEY(PRODID, SUBPRODID),
      FOREIGN KEY FKPROD(PRODID) REFERENCES PRODUCT
         ON DELETE RESTRICT,
      FOREIGN KEY FKSUBPROD(SUBPRODID) REFERENCES PRODUCT
         ON DELETE RESTRICT)
```

Querying a many-to-many recursive relationship

❍ **List the product id of each component of the animal photography kit.**

```
SELECT SUBPRODID FROM PRODUCT, ASSEMBLY
   WHERE PRODDESC = 'Animal photography kit'
      AND PRODUCT.PRODID = ASSEMBLY.PRODID
```

SUBPRODID
101
106
107
105
104
103
102
108

Why are the values for SUBPRODID listed in no apparent order? Remember, there is no implied ordering of rows in a table, and it is quite possible, as this example illustrates, for the rows to have what appears to be an unusual ordering. If you want to order rows, use the ORDER BY clause.

❍ **List the product description and cost of each component of the animal photography kit.**

```
SELECT PRODDESC, PRODCOST FROM PRODUCT
   WHERE PRODID IN
      (SELECT SUBPRODID FROM PRODUCT, ASSEMBLY
         WHERE PRODDESC = 'Animal photography kit'
         AND PRODUCT.PRODID = ASSEMBLY.PRODID)
```

In this case, first determine the prodid of those products in the animal photography kit (the inner query), and then report the description of these products. Alternatively, a three-way join can be done using two copies of PRODUCT.

```
SELECT B.PRODDESC, B.PRODCOST FROM PRODUCT A, ASSEMBLY, PRODUCT B
   WHERE A.PRODDESC = 'Animal photography kit'
   AND A.PRODID = ASSEMBLY.PRODID
   AND ASSEMBLY.SUBPRODID = B.PRODID
```

PRODDESC	PRODCOST
35mm camera	150.00
Camera case	10.00
70-210 zoom lens	125.00
28-85 zoom lens	115.00
Photographer’s vest	25.00
Lens cleaning cloth	1.00
Tripod	35.00
24 exp. 100ASA 35mm col neg	0.85

Summary

Relationships can be one-to-one and recursive. A recursive relationship is within a single entity rather than between entities. Recursive relationships are mapped to the relational model in the same way as other relationships. Resolution of queries involving recursive relationships often requires a table to be joined with itself. Many-to-many recursive relationships occur in business in the form of a bill of materials.

Decision Support at Lands' End

Lands' End uses direct mailing of catalogs to market clothing for adults and children. Lands' End sales for fiscal year 2000 were $1.462 billion, making the Lands' End brand one of the largest apparel brands in the United States. Printing and delivery of catalogs are expensive, and Lands' End needs to precisely target its mailing to reach the customers who are most likely to buy. Variables such as lifetime customer value, geographic location, and recent purchases can be used to determine who should receive a catalog. To assist in making such decisions, Lands' End has developed a DSS based on IBM's DB2. Prior to implementing the DSS, Lands' End staff first used data modeling to identify data items and their descriptions.

A typical business question might be: What was the return rate for the women's division, grouped by category, in our Christmas catalog? Compare this year to last year.

The SQL query is:

```
SELECT CATALOG-YEAR,
           CATALOG-DESC,
           PRODUCT-CATEGORY-DESC,
           SUM(RETURNS)/SUM(SHIPMENTS)
FROM       SHIPMENT_TBL D,
           RETURN_TBL R
WHERE      D.ORDER = R.ORDER
AND        DIVISION = WOMENS'
AND        CATALOG_YEAR IN (1992,1993)
AND        CATALOG_ID = 'XMAS'
GROUP BY   CATEGORY_YEAR
           CATALOG_DESC,
           PRODUCT_CATEGORY_DESC
```

The new DSS means that queries that would have taken hours, or sometimes days, are now satisfied in minutes. Lands' End can use its DSS to market its products more effectively.

Adapted from Bustamente, G. G., and K. Sorenson. 1994. Decision support at Lands' End—an evolution. *IBM Systems Journal* 33 (2):228–238.

Key terms and concepts

Joining a table with itself
Many-to-many recursive relationship
One-to-many recursive relationship
One-to-one recursive relationship
One-to-one relationship
Recursive relationship
Relationship descriptor

Exercises

1. Draw data models for the following two problems:
   a. (i) A dairy farmer, who is also a part-time cartoonist, has several herds of cows. He has assigned each cow to a particular herd. In each herd, the farmer has one cow that is his favorite — often that cow is featured in a cartoon.
   (ii) A few malcontents in each herd, mainly those who feel they should have appeared in the cartoon, disagree with the farmer's choice of a favorite cow, whom they disparagingly refer to as the *sacred* cow. As a result, each herd now has elected a herd leader.
   b. The originator of a pyramid marketing scheme has a system for selling ethnic jewelry. The pyramid has three levels — gold, silver, and bronze. New associates join the pyramid at the bronze level. They contribute 30 percent of the revenue of their sales of jewelry to the silver chief in charge of their clan. In turn, silver chiefs contribute 30 percent of what they receive from bronze associates to the gold master in command of their tribe. Finally, gold masters pass on 30 percent of what they receive to the originator of the scheme.
   c. The legion, the basic combat unit of the ancient Roman army, contained 3,000 to 6,000 men, consisting primarily of heavy infantry (hoplites), supported by light infantry (velites), and sometimes by cavalry. The hoplites were drawn up in three lines. The hastati (youngest men) were in the first, the principes (seasoned troops) in the second, and the triarii (oldest men) behind them, reinforced by velites. Each line was divided into 10 maniples, consisting of two centuries (60 to 80 men per century) each. Each legion had a commander, and a century was commanded by a centurion. Julius Caesar, through one of his Californian channelers, has asked you to design a database to maintain details of soldiers. Of course, Julius is a little forgetful at times, and he has not supplied the titles of the officers who command maniples, lines, and hoplites, but he expects that you can handle this lack of fine detail.
   d. A travel agency is frequently asked questions about tourist destinations. For example, customers want to know details of the climate for a particular month, the population of the city, and other geographic facts. Sometimes, they request the flying time and distance between two cities. The manager has asked you to create a database to maintain these facts.
   e. The Center for the Study of World Trade keeps track of trade treaties between nations. For each treaty, it records details of the countries signing the treaty and where and when it was signed.
   f. Design a database to store details about U.S. presidents and their terms in office. Also, record details of their date and place of birth, gender, and political party

affiliation (e.g., Caluthumpian Progress Party). You are required to record the sequence of presidents so the predecessor and successor of any president can be identified. How will you model the case of Grover Cleveland who served nonconsecutive terms as president? Is it feasible that political party affiliation may change? If so, how will you handle it?

g. The IS department of a large organization makes extensive use of software modules. New applications are built, where possible, from existing modules. Software modules can also contain other modules. The IS manager realizes that she now needs a database to keep track of which modules are used in which applications or other modules. (Hint: it is helpful to think of an application as a module.)

h. Data modeling is finally getting to you. Last night you dreamed you were asked by Noah to design a database to store data about the animals on the ark. All you can remember from Sunday school is the bit about the animals entering the ark two-by-two, so you thought you should check the real thing.

Take with you seven pairs of every kind of clean animal, a male and its mate, and two of every kind of unclean animal, a male and its mate, and also seven pair of every kind of bird, male and female. Genesis 7:2

Next time Noah disturbs your sleep, you want to be ready. So, draw a data model and make certain you record the two-by-two relationship.

2. Write SQL to answer the following queries using the DEPT and EMP tables described in this chapter:
   a. Find the departments where all the employees earn less than their boss.
   b. Find the names of employees who are in the same department as their boss (as an employee).
   c. List the departments having an average salary greater than $25,000.
   d. List the departments where the average salary of the employees of each boss is greater than $25,000.
   e. List the names and manager of the employees of the Marketing department who have a salary greater than $25,000.
   f. List the names of the employees who earn more than any employee in the Marketing department.
3. Write SQL to answer the following queries using the MONARCH table described in this chapter:
   a. Who succeeded Victoria I?
   b. How many days did Victoria I reign?
   c. How many kings are there in the table?
   d. Which monarch had the shortest reign?
4. Write SQL to answer the following queries using the PRODUCT and ASSEMBLY tables:
   a. How many different items are there in the animal photography kit?
   b. What is the most expensive item in the animal photography kit?
   c. What is the total cost of the components of the animal photography kit?
   d. Compute the total quantity of all items required to assemble 15 animal photography kits.

CD Library case

Ajay had some more time to work on this CD Library database. He picked up The Manhattan Transfer's *Swing* CD to enter its data. Very quickly he recognized the need for yet another entity if he was going to store details of the people in a group. A group can contain many people (there are four artists in The Manhattan Transfer), and also it is feasible that over time a person could be a member of multiple groups. So, there is an m:m between PERSON and GROUP. Building on his understanding of the relationship between PERSON and RECORDING and CD, Ajay realized there are two other required relationships: an m:m between GROUP and RECORDING, and between GROUP and CD. This led to yet another revision, version 5.0.

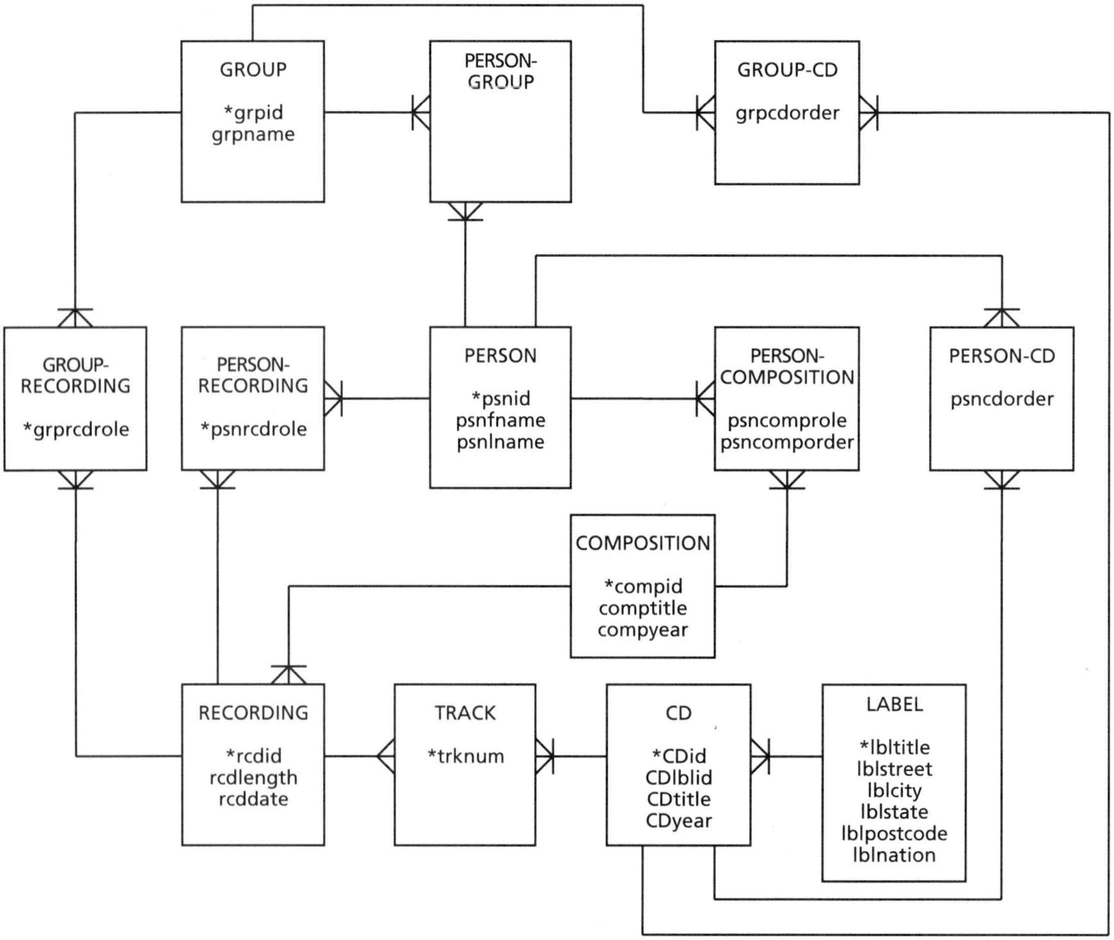

Figure 6-6. CD library V5.0

Some challenging queries

- **What CDs feature Cheryl Bentyne as an individual or member of a group?**

The challenge for this query is to recognize that a person can feature on a CD as an individual or as a member of a group. Thus, this query has two parts that are joined by UNION, which is essentially an OR. In other words, the query reports the title of any CDs that feature Cheryl Bentyne *or* any CDs that feature a group containing Cheryl Bentyne.

```
SELECT CDTITLE FROM CD, PERSON_CD, PERSON
   WHERE CD.CDID = PERSON_CD.CDID
   AND PERSON.PSNID = PERSON_CD.PSNID
   AND PSNFNAME = 'Cheryl'
   AND PSNLNAME = 'Bentyne'
UNION
SELECT CDTITLE FROM CD, GROUP_CD, [GROUP], PERSON_GROUP, PERSON
   WHERE CD.CDID = GROUP_CD.CDID
   AND GROUP_CD.GRPID = GROUP.GRPID
   AND GROUP.GRPID = PERSON_GROUP.GRPID
   AND PERSON_GROUP.PSNID = PERSON.PSNID
   AND PSNFNAME = 'Cheryl'
   AND PSNLNAME = 'Bentyne'
```

- **Report all compositions and their composers where more than one person was involved in composing the music. Make certain you report them in the correct order.**

This is another query with two parts. First, you need to find the compositions that involve more than one person. The subquery determines who those people are by using GROUP BY with HAVING to create a temporary table listing those compositions by multiple people (i.e., HAVING COUNT(*) > 1). The outer query then reports the compositions, and their respective composers, where the composition's title is in the temporary table created by the subquery. The final statement in the query gets the ordering correct.

```
SELECT COMPTITLE, PSNFNAME, PSNLNAME, PSNCOMPROLE
   FROM COMPOSITION, PERSON_COMPOSITION, PERSON
      WHERE COMPOSITION.COMPID = PERSON_COMPOSITION.COMPID
      AND PERSON_COMPOSITION.PSNID = PERSON.PSNID
      AND COMPTITLE IN
         (SELECT COMPTITLE FROM COMPOSITION, PERSON_COMPOSITION, PERSON
            WHERE COMPOSITION.COMPID = PERSON_COMPOSITION.COMPID
            AND PERSON_COMPOSITION.PSNID = PERSON.PSNID
               GROUP BY COMPTITLE HAVING COUNT(*) > 1)
         ORDER BY COMPTITLE, PSNCOMPORDER;
```

❍ **List the composers appearing on each CD.**

This query requires the joining of PERSON, PERSON-COMPOSITION, COMPOSITION, RECORDING, TRACK, and CD because data are required from PERSON (psnfname, psnlname) and CD (CDtitle). Finally, a GROUP BY is used to report the results by CD. Here is the SQL:

```
SELECT CDTITLE, PSNFNAME, PSNLNAME
   FROM PERSON, PERSON_COMPOSITION, COMPOSITION, RECORDING, TRACK, CD
      WHERE PERSON.PSNID = PERSON_COMPOSITION.PSNID
      AND PERSON_COMPOSITION.COMPID = COMPOSITION.COMPID
      AND COMPOSITION.COMPID = RECORDING.COMPID
      AND RECORDING.RCDID = TRACK.RCDID
      AND TRACK.CDID = CD.CDID
         GROUP BY CDTITLE, PSNFNAME, PSNLNAME
```

Your turn

1. The members of The Manhattan Transfer are Cheryl Bentyne, Janis Siegel, Tim Hauser, and Alan Paul. Update the database with this information, and write SQL to answer the following:
   a. Who are the members of The Manhattan Transfer?
   b. What CDs have been released by The Manhattan Transfer?
2. The group known as Asleep at the Wheel is featured on tracks 3, 4, and 7 of *Swing*. Record these data and write SQL to answer the following:
   a. What are the titles of the recordings on which Asleep at the Wheel appear?
   b. List all CDs that have any tracks featuring Asleep at the Wheel.
3. Record the following facts. The music of "Sing a Song of Brown," composed in 1937, is by Count Basie and Larry Clinton and the lyric by Jon Hendricks. "Sing Moten's Swing" features music by Buster and Benny Moten, and lyric by John Hendricks was composed in 1932. Write SQL to answer the following:
   a. For what songs has John Hendricks written the lyric?
   b. Report all compositions and their composers where more than one person was involved in composing the music. Make certain you report them in the correct order.
4. Test your SQL skills with the following:
   a. List the tracks on which Alan Paul appears as an individual or as a member of The Manhattan Transfer.
   b. List all CDs featuring a group, and also report the names of the group members.
   c. Report all tracks that feature more than one group.
5. How might you extend the data model?

7

Data Modeling

Man is a knot, a web, a mesh into which relationships are tied. Only those relationships matter.

Saint-Exupéry in *Flight to Arras*

Learning objectives

Students completing this chapter will

- ❖ be able to create a well-formed, high-fidelity data model.

Modeling

Modeling is widely used within business to learn about organizational problems and design solutions. To understand where data modeling fits within the broader context, it is useful to review the full range of modeling activities, as illustrated in Table 7-1.[1]

Table 7-1: A broad perspective on modeling

		Scope	Model	Technology
Motivation	why	Goals	Business plan	Groupware
People	who	Business units	Organization chart	System interface
Time	when	Key events	PERT chart	Scheduling
Data	what	Key entities	Data model	Relational database
Function	how	Key processes	Process model	Application software
Network	where	Locations	Logistics network	System architecture

Modeling occurs at multiple levels. At the highest level, an organization needs to determine the scope of its business by identifying the major elements of its environment, such as its goals, business units, where it operates, and critical events, entities, and processes.

1. Adapted from Zachman, J. A. 1982. Business systems planning and business information control study: A comparison. *IBM Systems Journal* 21 (1):31–53, and Bruce, T. A. 1992. *Designing quality databases with IDEF1X information models*. New York, NY: Dorset House.

At the top level, textual models are frequently used. For example, an organization might list its major goals and business processes. A map will be typically used to display where the business operates.

Once senior managers have clarified the scope of a business, models can be constructed for each of the major elements. Goals will be converted into a business plan, business units will become an organizational chart, and so on. The key models, from an MIS perspective, are the data, process, and logistics models. The required courses in most MIS programs cover these models in data management (data modeling), systems analysis and design (process modeling), and telecommunications (network modeling).

Technology, the final stage, converts models into operational systems to support the organization. Many organizations now rely extensively on e-mail and Web technology for communicating business decisions. People connect to systems through an interface, such as a Web browser. Ensuring that events occur at the right time is managed by scheduling software. This could be implemented with operating system procedures that schedule the execution of applications. In some DBMSs, triggers can be established. A **trigger** is a database procedure that is automatically executed when some event is recognized. For example, U.S. banks are required to report all deposits exceeding $10,000, and a trigger could be coded for this event.

From your MIS studies, you should know that data models are typically converted into relational databases, and process models become computer programs. The logistic network, which handles the physical flow of goods, is typically mirrored by a telecommunications network to handle the electronic flow of data that supports the physical flow (e.g., invoices and payments) and enables the flow of other communication between dispersed business units.

Thus, you can see that data modeling is one element of a comprehensive modeling activity that is often required to design business systems. When a business undergoes major change, such as a reengineering project, many dimensions can be altered and it may be appropriate to rethink many elements of the business, starting with its goals. Because such major change is very disruptive and costly, it occurs less frequently. It is more likely that data modeling is conducted as a stand-alone activity or part of process modeling to create a new business application.

Data modeling

You were introduced to the basic building blocks of data modeling in Chapters 3 through 6. Now it is time to learn how to assemble blocks to build a data model. Data modeling is a method for determining what data and relationships should be stored in the database. It is also a way of communicating a database design.

The goal of data modeling is to identify the facts that must be stored in a database. A data model is not concerned with how the data will be stored. This is the concern of those who implement the database. A data model is not concerned with how the data will be processed. This is the province of process modeling, which is generally taught in systems analysis and design courses. The goal is to create a data model that is an accurate representation of data needs and real world data relationships.

Building a data model is a partnership between a client, a representative of the eventual users of the database, and a designer. Of course, there can be a team of clients and designers. For simplicity, we assume there is one client and one designer.

Drawing a data model is an iterative process of trial and revision. A data model is a working document that will change as you learn more about the client's needs and world. Your early versions are likely to be quite different from the final product. Draw your diagrams with a pencil and keep an extra large eraser handy. Better still, use software for drawing and revising the data model.

The building blocks

The purpose of a database is to store data about things. These things can include facts (e.g., an exchange rate), plans (e.g., scheduled production of two-person tents for June), estimates (e.g., forecast of demand for geo positioning systems), and a variety of other data. A data model describes these things and their relationships with other things using four components: entity, attribute, relationship, and identifier.

Entity

The entity is the basic building block of a data model. An entity is a thing about which data should be stored, something we need to describe. Each entity in a data model has a unique name that we write in singular form. Why singular? Because we want to emphasize that an entity describes an instance of a thing. Thus, we previously used the word SHARE to define an entity because it describes each instance of a share rather than shares in general.

We have already introduced the convention that an entity is represented by a rectangle, and the name of the entity is shown in uppercase (see Figure 7-1).

Figure 7-1. The entity SHARE

A data model will typically have less than 100 entities. A database can easily contain millions of instances (rows) for any one entity (table). Imagine the number of instances in a national tax department's database.

How do you begin to identify entities? One approach is to underline any nouns in the problem description. Most nouns are possible entities, and underlining ensures that you do not overlook any potential entities. Start by selecting an entity that seems central to the problem. If you were designing a student database, you might start with the student. Once you have picked a central entity, describe it. Then move to the others.

Attribute

An attribute describes an entity. When an entity has been identified, the next step is to determine its attributes or the data that should be kept to describe the entity realistically. An attribute name is singular and unique within the data model. You may need to use a prefix to make an attribute name unique (e.g., hire date and sale date rather than just date).

Our convention is that the name of an attribute is recorded in lowercase within the entity rectangle. Figure 7-2 illustrates that SHARE has attributes share code, share name, share price, share quantity, share dividend, and share PE. Notice the frequent use of the prefix share. It is possible that other entities in the database might also have a price and quantity, so we use a prefix to create unique attribute names.

Figure 7-2. The entity SHARE with its attributes

Defining attributes generally takes considerable discussion with the client. You should include any attribute that is likely to be required for present or future decision making. But don't get carried away. Avoid storing unnecessary data. For example, to describe the entity STUDENT you usually record date of birth, but it is unlikely that you would store height. But, if you were describing an entity PATIENT, it might be necessary to record height because this is sometimes relevant to medical decision making.

An attribute has a single value, which possibly can be null. Multiple values are not allowed. If you need to store multiple values, it is a signal that you have a 1:m relationship and need to define another entity.

Relationship

Entities are related to other entities. If there were no relationships between entities, there would be no need for a data model and no need for a relational database. A simple, flat file (a single entity database) would be sufficient. A relationship is binary. It describes a linkage between two entities and is represented by an arc between them.

Because a relationship is binary, it has two relationship descriptors, one for each entity. Each relationship descriptor has a degree stating how many instances of the other entity may be related to each instance of the described entity. Consider the entities STOCK and NATION and their 1:m relationship (see Figure 7-3). We have two relationship descriptors: *stocks of nation* for NATION and *nation of stock* for STOCK. The relationship descriptor *stocks of nation* has a degree of m because a nation may have zero or more listed stocks. The relationship descriptor *nation of stock* has a degree of 1 because a stock is listed in at most one nation.

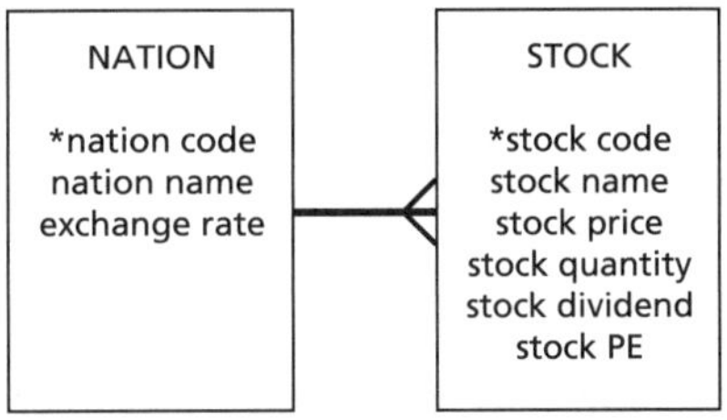

Figure 7-3. A 1:m relationship between STOCK and NATION

Because relationship descriptors frequently can be inferred, there is no need to label them; however, each additional arc between two entities must be labeled to clarify meaning. Also, it is a good idea to label 1:1 relationships because the relationship descriptors are not always obvious.

Consider the fragment in Figure 7-4. The descriptors of the 1:m relationship can be inferred as a firm has employees and employee belongs to a firm. The 1:1 relationship is clarified by labeling the arcs.

Identifier

An identifier uniquely distinguishes an instance of an entity. An identifier is one or more attributes and may include relationship descriptors. When a relationship descriptor is part of an identifier, a vertical bar is placed on the arc closest to the entity being identified. In Figure 7-5, an instance of the entity LINEITEM is identified by the composite of *lineno* and the relationship descriptor, *sale,* of LINEITEM. *Lineno* does not uniquely identify an instance of LINEITEM because it is simply a number that appears on the sales form. Thus, the identifier must include *saleno* (the identifier of SALE). So, any instance of LINEITEM is uniquely identified by the composite *saleno* and *lineno*.

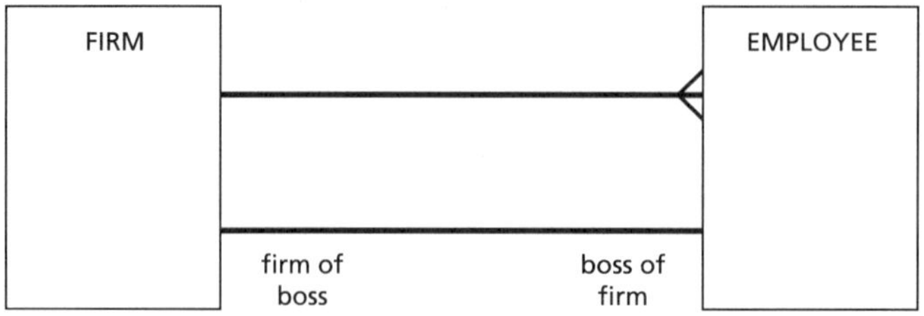

Figure 7-4. Relationship labeling

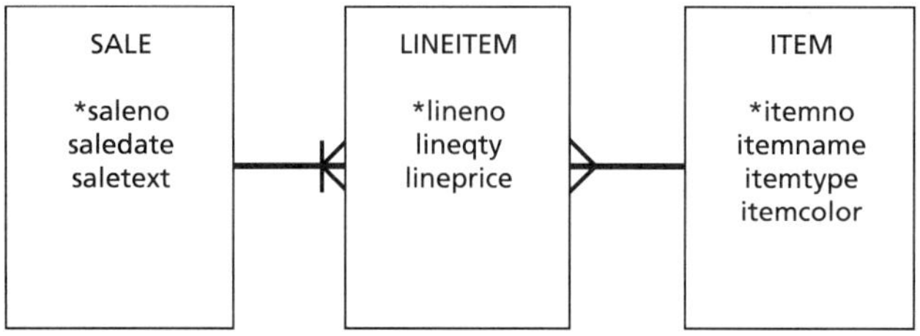

Figure 7-5. A relationship descriptor as part of the identifier

Occasionally, there will be several possible identifiers, and these are each given a different symbol. Our convention is to prefix an identifier with an asterisk (*). If there are multiple identifiers, use other symbols such as #, !, or &. Be careful: if you have too many possible identifiers, your model will look like comic book swearing. In most cases, you will have only one identifier.

No part of an identifier can be null. If this were permitted, there would be no guarantee that the other parts of the identifier were sufficiently unique to distinguish all instances in the database.

Data model quality

There are two criteria for judging the quality of a data model. It must be well-formed and have high-fidelity of image.

A well-formed data model

A well-formed data model (see Table 7-2) clearly communicates information to the client. Being well-formed means the construction rules have been obeyed. There is no ambiguity; all entities are named, and all entities have identifiers. If identifiers are missing, the client may make incorrect inferences about the data model. All relationships are recorded using the proper notation. Relationship descriptors are noted whenever there is a possibility of confusion.

> **A data model for retailing**
>
> The Association for Retail Technology Standards (ARTS) of the National Retail Federation is a retailer-driven membership organization dedicated to creating an international, barrier-free technology environment for retailers. ARTS was established in 1993 to ensure that technology works to enhance a retailer's ability to develop store level business solutions and avoid situations that limit a retailer's ability to implement change while providing industry standards designed to provide greater value at lower costs.
>
> ARTS has created a Retail Data Model, which is distributed to ARTS members via the ARTS Web site. The ARTS Data Model facilitates a high degree of plug-and-play compatibility for retail applications, which was previously difficult, or in many cases impossible, to achieve. On April 30, 2002 release 3.0 of the data model was announced.
>
> ARTS claims the model is comprehensive and applies to both food and general merchandise retailing. Also, because ARTS is an international organization, care was taken to include input from members around the world to ensure that the data model is valid on a global basis. More than 50 of the leading European retailers and their vendor partners are involved in ARTS European Consortium.
>
> Source: http://www.nrf-arts.org.

All the attributes of an entity are listed because missing attributes create two types of problems. First, it is unclear what data will be stored about each instance. Second, the data model may be missing some relationships. Attributes that can have multiple values become entities. It is only by listing all of an entity's attributes that these additional entities are recognized.

In a well-formed data model, all attribute names are meaningful and unique. The names of entities, identifiers, attributes, and relationships must be meaningful to the client because they are meant to describe the client's world. Indeed, in nearly all cases they are the client's everyday names. Take care in selecting words because they are critical to communicating meaning. The acid test for comprehension is to get the client to read the data model to other potential users. Names need to be unique to avoid confusion.

A high-fidelity image

Music lovers aspire to own a high-fidelity stereo system — one that faithfully reproduces the original performance with minimal or no distortion. A data model is a high-fidelity image when it faithfully describes the world it is supposed to represent. All relationships are recorded and are of the correct degree. There are no compromises or distortions. If the real world relationship is m: m, then so is the relationship shown in the data model. A well-formed, high-fidelity data model is complete, understandable, accurate, and syntactically correct.

Table 7-2: Characteristics of a well-formed data model

All construction rules are obeyed
No ambiguity
All entities are named
Every entity has an identifier
All relationships are represented, using the correct notation
Relationship descriptors are used to avoid misunderstanding
All attributes of each entity are listed
All attribute names are meaningful and unique

Quality improvement

A data model is an evolving representation. Each change should be an incremental improvement in quality. Occasionally, you will find a major quality problem at the data model's core and have to change the data model dramatically.

Detail and context

The quality of a data model can be determined only by understanding the context in which it will be used. Consider the data model (see Figure 7-6) used in Chapter 4 to discuss the 1:m relationship. This fragment says a nation has many stocks. But is that really what we want to represent? Stocks are listed on a stock exchange, and a nation may have several stock exchanges. For example, each Australian state's capital city has a stock exchange. Australian stocks can be listed on multiple exchanges but have a single home exchange. Furthermore, some Australian stocks are listed on the New York Stock Exchange. If this is the world we have to describe, the data model is likely to differ from that shown in Figure 7-6. Try drawing the revised data model.

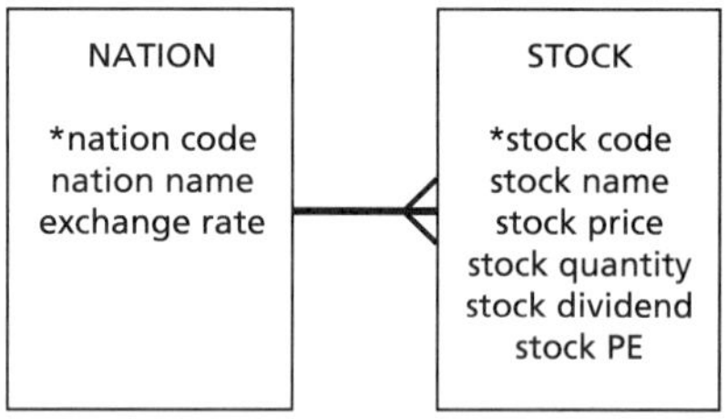

Figure 7-6. A 1:m relationship between STOCK and NATION

As you can see, the data model in Figure 7-7 is quite different from the initial data model of Figure 7-6. Which one is better? They both can be valid models; it just depends on the world you are trying to represent and possible future queries. In the first case, the purpose was to determine the value of a portfolio. There was no interest in where stocks were listed or their home exchange. So the first model has high fidelity for the described situation.

The second data model would be appropriate if the client needed to know the home exchange of stocks and their price on the various exchanges where they were listed. The second data model is an improvement on the first if it incorporates the additional facts and relationships required. If it does not, then the additional detail is not worth the extra cost.

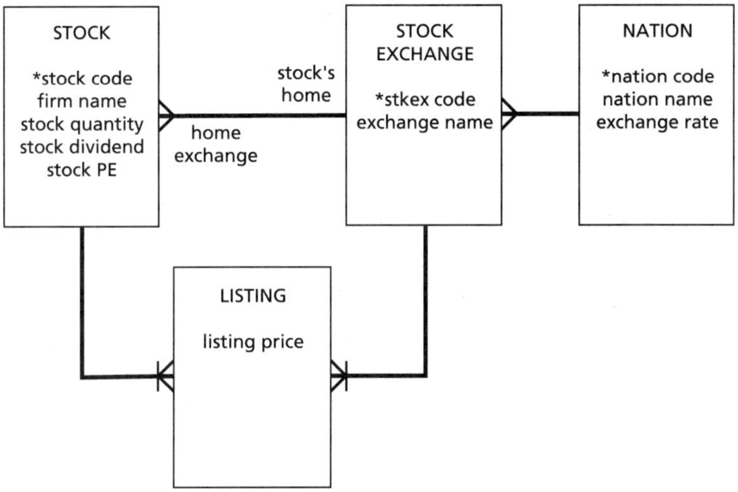

Figure 7-7. Revised NATION-STOCK data model

A lesson in pure geography

A data model must be an accurate representation of the world you want to model. The data model must account for all the exceptions — there should be no impurities. Let's say you want to establish a database to store details of the world's cities. You might start with the data model depicted in Figure 7-8.

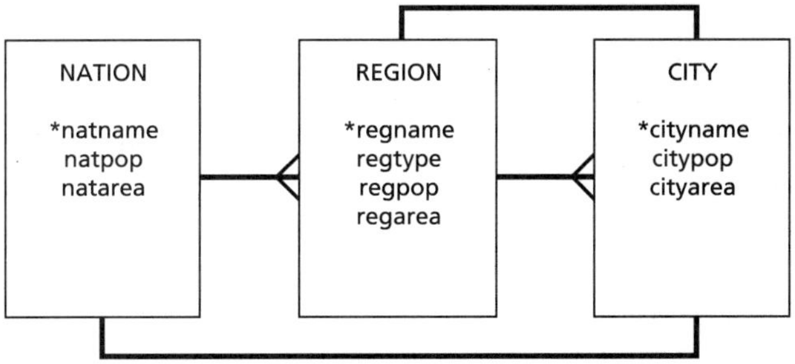

Figure 7-8. A world's cities data model

Before looking more closely at the data model, let's clarify the meaning of *regtype*. Because most countries are divided into regions that are variously called states, provinces, territories, and so forth, *regtype* indicates the type of region (e.g., state). How many errors can you find in the initial data model (see Table 7-3)?

Table 7-3: Problems and solutions for the initial world's cities data model

	Problem	**Solution**
1.	City names are not unique. There is an Athens in Greece and the U.S. has an Athens in Georgia, Alabama, Ohio, Pennsylvania, Tennessee, and Texas.	To uniquely identify a city, you need to specify its region and country. Add a vertical bar to the crow's feet between city and region, and region and nation.
2.	Region names are not necessarily unique. There used to be a Georgia in the old USSR, and there is a Georgia in the U.S. There is no guarantee that region names will always be unique.	To uniquely identify a region, you also need to know the country in which it is found. Add a vertical bar to the crow's foot between region and nation (already done to solve problem 1).
3.	There are unlabeled 1:1 arcs between city and region and city and nation. What do these mean? They are supposed to indicate that a region has a capital, and a nation has a capital.	Label the arcs (e.g., capital city of region).
4.	The assumption is that a region or nation has only one capital, but there are exceptions. South Africa has three capitals: Cape Town (legislative), Pretoria (administrative), and Bloemfontein (judicial). You only need one exception to significantly lower the fidelity of a data model.	Change the relationship between NATION and CITY to 1:m. Add an attribute *captype* to CITY to distinguish between types of capitals.
5.	Some values can be derived. National population, *natpop*, and area, *natarea*, are the sum of the regional populations, *regpop*, and areas, *regarea*, respectively. The same rule does not apply to regions and cities because not everyone lives in a city.	Remove the attributes *natpop* and *natarea* from NATION.

The revised data model is shown in Figure 7-9.

This geography lesson demonstrates how you often start with a simple model of low fidelity. Additional thinking about relationships and consideration of exceptions gradually create a high-fidelity data model.

Family matters

Families can be very complicated. It can be tricky to keep track of all those relations—maybe you need a relational database (this is the worst joke in the book; they improve after this). Before we continue, let's define a family. For the purposes of this book, and mainly to keep the examples simple, we have a very limited view of a family. A family is man

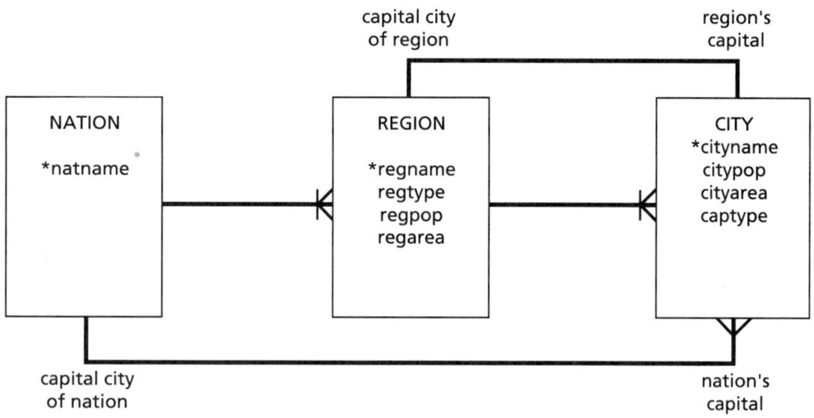

Figure 7-9. A revised world's cities data model

and woman united in marriage who may have some children. We need to be restrictive because a very liberal definition will complicate the data model. As we get into exploring marriage, we will become less restrictive. An initial fragment of the data model is shown in Figure 7-10. What do you notice about this fragment? There are several things:

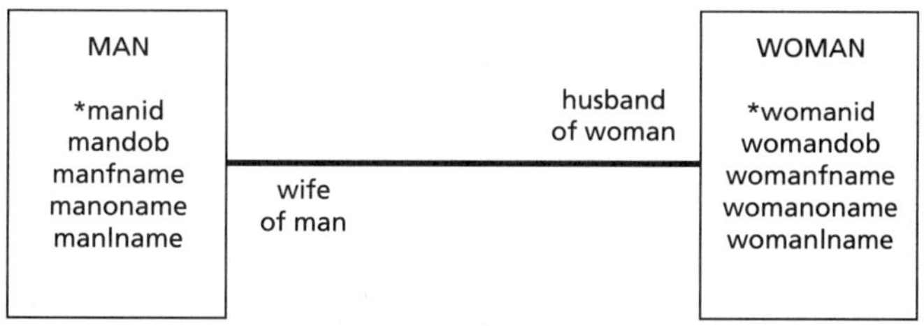

Figure 7-10. A MAN-WOMAN data model

1. There is a 1:1 relationship between man and woman. The labels indicate that this relationship is marriage, but there is no indication of the marriage date. We are left to infer that the data model records the current marriage.
2. MAN and WOMAN have the same attributes. A prefix is used to make them unique. Both have an identifier, (*...id*, in the United States this would probably be a Social Security number), date of birth (*...dob*), first name (*...fname*), other names (*...oname*), and last name (*...lname*).
3. Other names (*...oname*) looks like a multivalued attribute, which is not allowed. Should *...oname* be single or multivalue? This is a tricky decision. It depends on how these data will be used. If queries such as find all men whose other names include "Herbert" are likely, then a person's other names—kept as a separate entity

> that has 1:m relationship for MAN and WOMAN—must be established. That is, a man or woman can have one or more other names. However, if you just want to store the data for completeness and retrieve it in its entirety, then ... *oname* is fine. It is just a text string. The key question to ask is, "What is the lowest level of detail possibly required for future queries?" Also, remember that SQL's LIKE clause can be used to search for values within a text string.

The use of a prefix to distinguish attribute names in different entities suggests you should consider combining the entities. In this case, we could combine the entities MAN and WOMAN to create an entity called PERSON. Usually when entities are combined, you have to create a new attribute to distinguish between the different types. In this example, the attribute *gender* is added. We could also generalize the relationship descriptors to *spouse of person*. The revised data model appears in Figure 7-11.

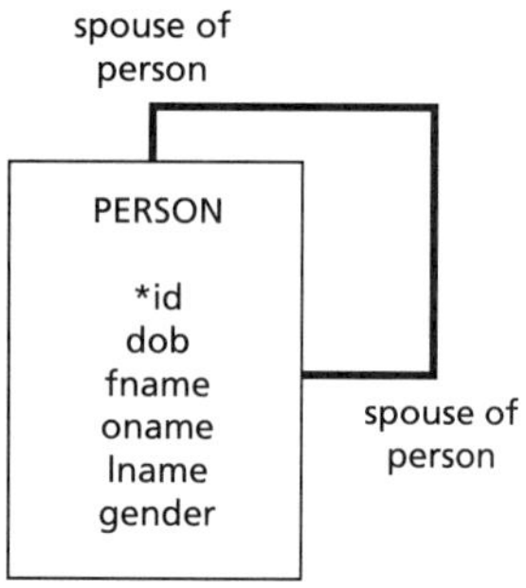

Figure 7-11. A PERSON data model

Now for a bit of marriage counseling. Marriage normally is a relationship between two people. Is that so? Well, some societies permit polygamy (one man can have many wives), and others allow polyandry (one woman can have many husbands). So marriage, if we consider all the possibilities, is an m:m relationship. Also, a person can be married more than once. To distinguish between different marriages, we really need to record the start and end date of each relationship and who was involved (see Figure 7-12).

Marriage is an m:m relationship between two persons. it has attributes *begindate* and *enddate*. An instance of marriage is uniquely identified by a composite identifier: the two *spouse of person* descriptors and *begindate*. This means any marriage is uniquely identified by the composite of two person identifiers and the beginning date of the marriage. We need *begindate* as part of the identifier because the same couple might have more than one marriage (e.g., get divorced and rewed later). Furthermore, we can safely assume that it is impossible for a couple to get married, divorced, and rewed all on the one day. *Begindate* and *enddate* can be used to determine the current state of a marriage. If *enddate* is null the marriage is current; otherwise, the couple has divorced.

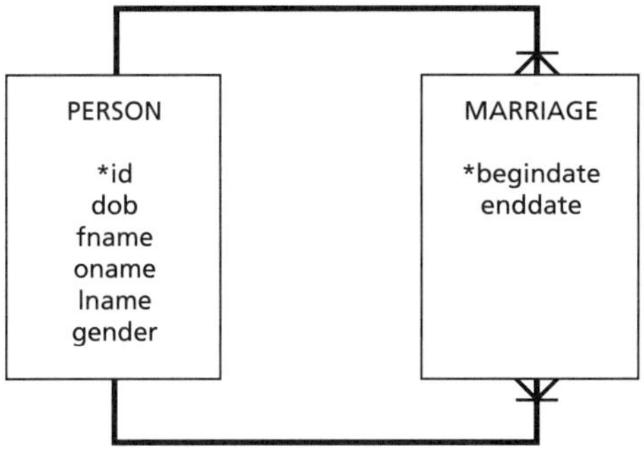

Figure 7-12. A marriage data model

This data model assumes a couple goes through some formal process to get married or divorced, and there is an official date for both of these events. What happens if they just gradually drift into cohabitation, and there is no official beginning date? Think about it. (The data model problem, that is — not cohabitation!) Many countries recognize this situation as a common-law marriage so the data model needs to recognize it. The present data model cannot handle this situation because *begindate* cannot be null —it is an identifier. Instead, a new identifier is needed, and *begindate* should become an attribute.

Two new attributes can handle a common-law marriage. *Marriageno* for marriage number can count the number of times a couple has been married to each other. In the great majority of cases, *marriageno* will be 1. *Marriagestatus* can record whether a marriage is current or ended. Now we have a data model that can also handle common-law marriages. This is also a high-quality data model in that the client does not have to remember to examine *enddate* to determine a marriage's current status. It is easier to remember to examine *marriagestatus* to check status. Also, we can allow a couple to be married, divorced, and rewed as many times as they like on the one day — which means we can now use the database in Las Vegas. The latest version of the data model is shown in Figure 7-13.

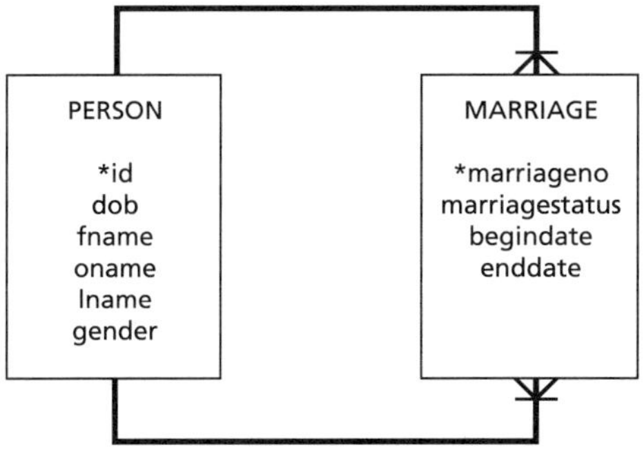

Figure 7-13. A revised marriage data model

All right, now that we have the couple successfully married, we need to start thinking about the offspring. A marriage has one or more children, but a child belongs to only one marriage. Therefore, we have a 1:m relationship between marriage and person to represent the children of a marriage (see Figure 7-14).

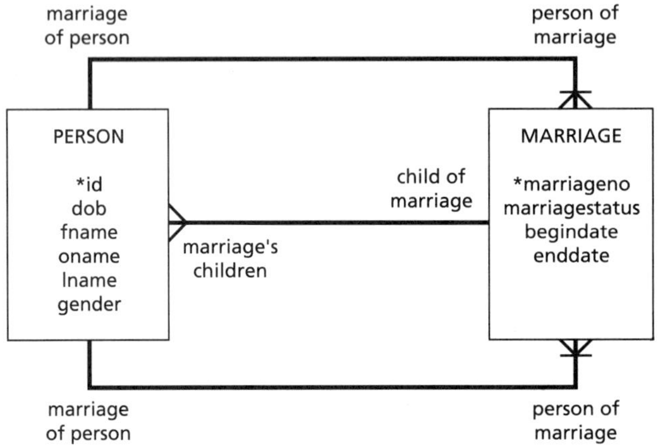

Figure 7-14. A marriage with children data model

When's a book not a book?

Sometimes we have to rethink our ideas of physical objects. Consider a data model for a library.

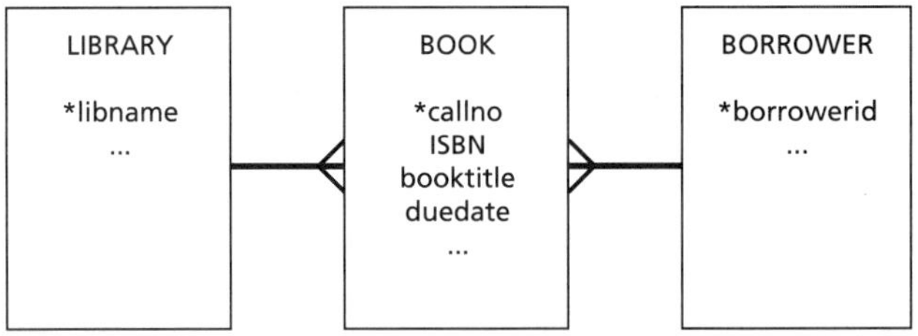

Figure 7-15. A library data model fragment

The fragment (Figure 7-15) assumes that a person borrows a book. What happens if the library has two copies of the book? Do we add an attribute to BOOK called *copy number*? No, because we would introduce redundancy by repeating the same information for each book. What you need to recognize is that in the realm of data modeling, a book is not really a physical thing but the copy is, because it is what you borrow. The revised data model fragment is illustrated in Figure 7-16.

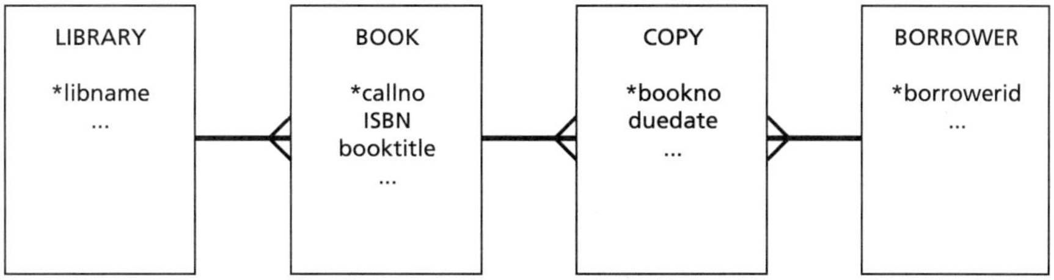

Figure 7-16. A revised library data model fragment

As you can see, a book has many copies, and a copy is of one book. A book can be identified by *callno*, which is usually a Library of Congress number or Dewey number. A copy is identified by a *bookno*. This is a unique number allocated by the library to the copy of the book. If you look in a library book, you will generally find it pasted on the inside back cover and shown in numeric and bar code format. Notice that it is called *book number* despite the fact that it really identifies a copy of a book. This is because most people, including librarians, think of the copy as a book.

The International Standard Book Number (ISBN) uniquely identifies any instance of a book (not copy). Although it sounds like a potential identifier for BOOK, it is not. ISBNs were introduced in the second half of the twentieth century, and books published before then do not have an ISBN.

A history lesson

Many organizations maintain historical data (e.g., a person's job history or a student's enrollment record). A data model can depict historical data relationships just as readily as current data relationships.

Consider the case of a employee who works for a firm that consists of divisions (e.g., production) and departments (e.g., quality control). The firm contains many departments but a department belongs to only one division. At any one time, an employee belongs to only one department. If we were modeling the current situation, the data model fragment would look like that shown in Figure 7-17.

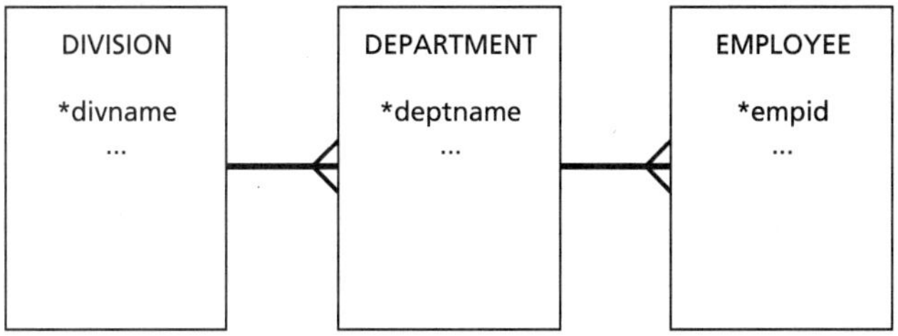

Figure 7-17. Employment history—take 1

The fragment in Figure 7-17 can be amended to keep track of the divisions and departments in which a person works. While employed with a firm, a person can work in more than one department. Since a department can have many employees, we have an m:m relationship between DEPARTMENT and EMPLOYEE. We might call the resulting associative entity POSITION (see Figure 7-18).

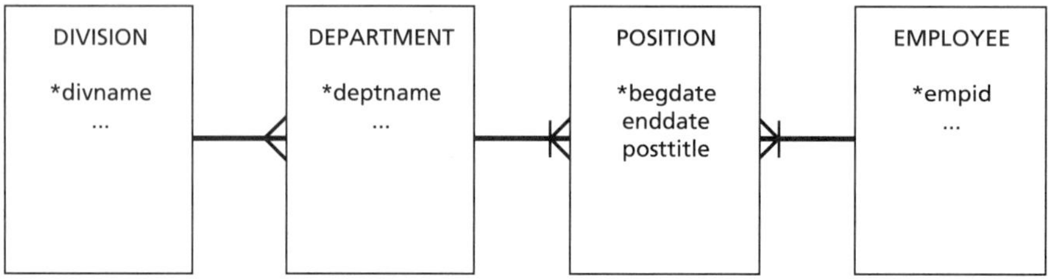

Figure 7-18. Employment history—take 2

The revised fragment records employee work history. Note that any instance of POSITION is identified by *begdate* and the relationship descriptors for EMPLOYEE and DEPARTMENT. The fragment is typical of what happens when you move from just keeping current data to recording history. A 1:m becomes an m:m relationship to record history.

People who work get paid. How do we keep track of an employee's pay data? An employee has many pay slips, but a pay slip belongs to one employee. When you look at a pay slip, you will find it contains many items: gross pay and a series of deductions for tax, medical insurance, and so on. Think of pay slip as containing many lines, analogous to a sales form. Now look at the revised data model in Figure 7-19.

Typically, an amount shown on a pay slip is identified by a short text field (e.g., gross pay). PAYSLIPLINE contains an attribute *psltype* to identify the text that should accompany an amount, but where is the text? When dealing with codes like *psltype* and their associated text, the fidelity of a data model is improved by creating a separate entity, PSLTEXT, for the code and its text (Figure 7-20).

A ménage à trois for entities[2]

Consider aircraft leasing. An aircraft broker will own many planes that over time will be leased to a variety of airlines. When a lease expires, the broker leases the plane to another airline. So, an aircraft can be leased many times, and an airline can lease many aircraft. Furthermore, there is an agent responsible for handling each deal. An agent can lease many aircraft and deal with many airlines. Over time, an airline will deal with many agents. When an agent reaches a deal with an airline to lease a particular aircraft, you have a transaction. If you analyze the aircraft leasing business, you discover there are three m:m relationships. You might think of these as three separate relationships (see Figure 7-21).

2. Also known as a ternary relationship, but its life is less interesting.

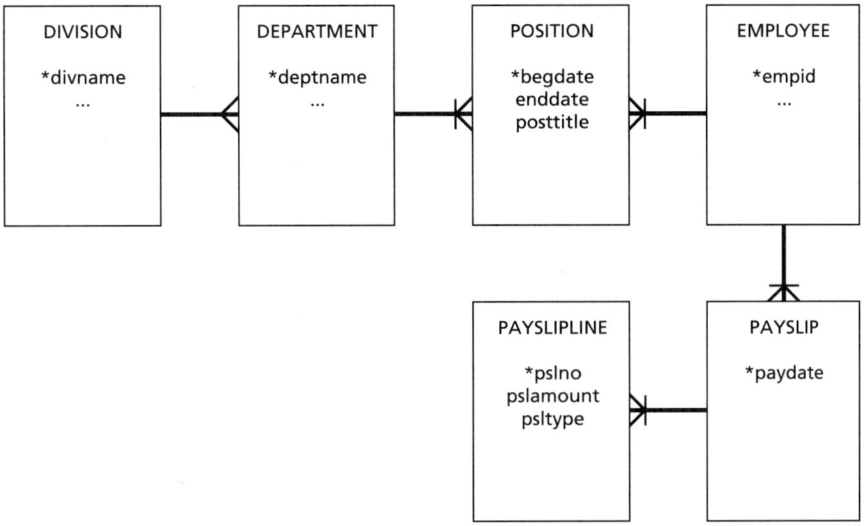

Figure 7-19. Employment history—take 3

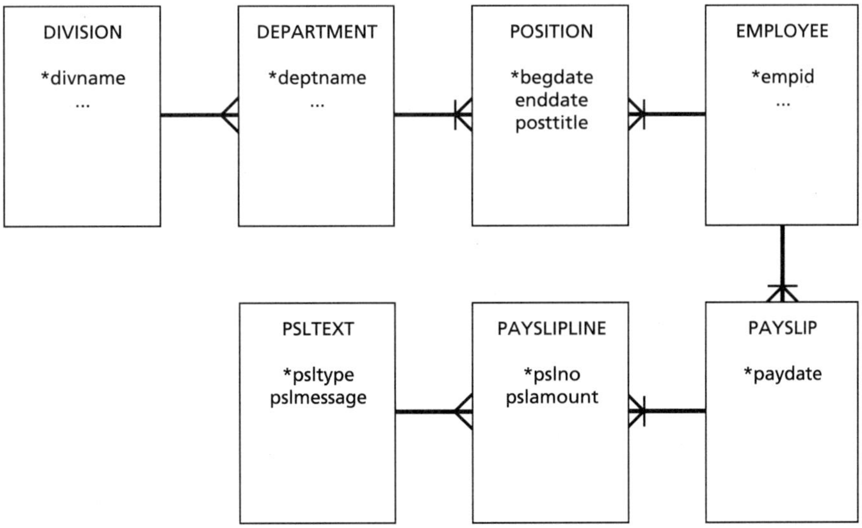

Figure 7-20. Employment history—take 4

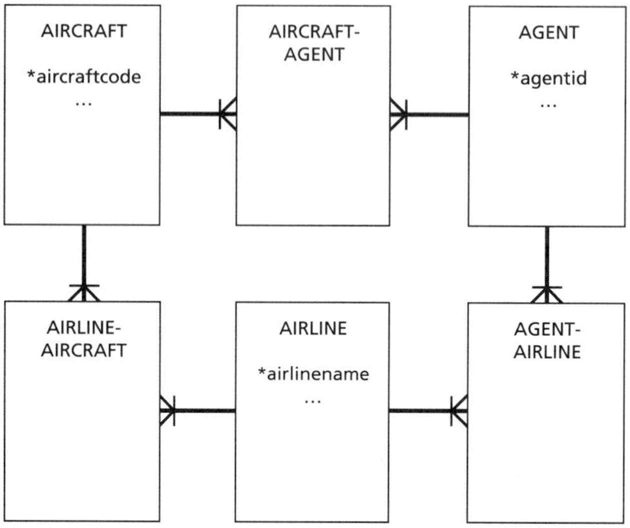

Figure 7-21. An AIRCRAFT-AIRLINE-AGENT data model

The problem with three separate m:m relationships is that it is unclear where to store data about the lease. Is it stored in AIRLINE-AIRCRAFT? If you store the information there, what do you do about recording the agent who closed the deal? After you read the fine print and do some more thinking, you discover that a lease is the association of these three entities in an m:m relationship (see Figure 7-22).

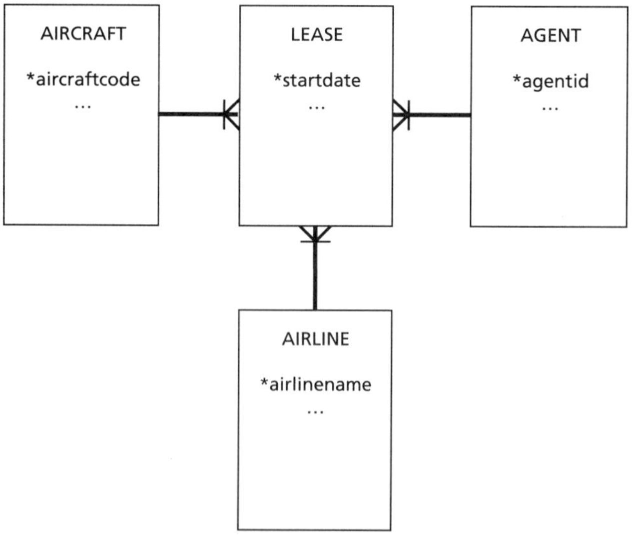

Figure 7-22. A revised AIRCRAFT-AIRLINE-AGENT data model

Project management—planning and doing

Project management involves both planned and actual data. A project is divided into a number of activities that use resources. Planning includes estimation of the resources to be consumed. When a project is being executed, managers keep track of the resources actually used in order to monitor progress and keep the project on budget. Planning data may not be as detailed as actual data and is typically fairly broad, such as an estimate of the number of hours that an activity will take. Actual data will be more detailed because they are usually collected by getting those assigned to the project to log a daily account of how they spent their time. Also, resources used on a project are allocated to a particular activity. For the purposes of this data model, we will focus only on recording time and nothing else (see Figure 7-23).

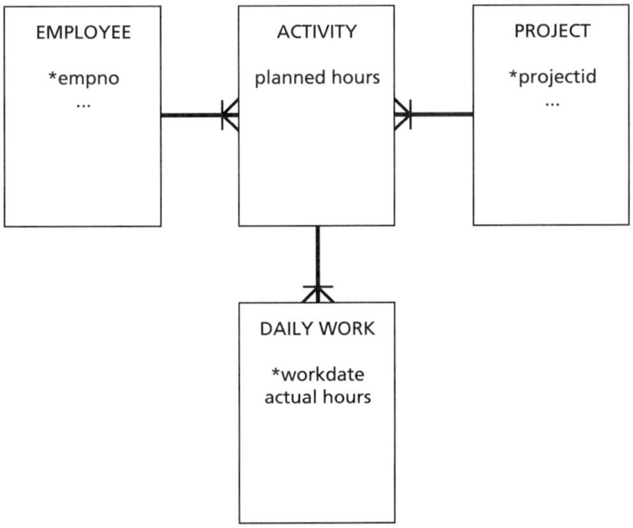

Figure 7-23. A project management data model

Notice that *planned hours* is an attribute of ACTIVITY, and *actual hours* is an attribute of DAILY WORK. The hours spent on an activity are derived by summing *actual hours* in the associated DAILY WORK entity. This is a high-fidelity data model if planning is done at the activity level and employees submit daily worksheets. Planning can be done in greater detail, however, if planners indicate how many hours of each day each employee should spend on a project. Figure 7-24 shows the revised data model fragment.

Now you see that *planned hours* and *actual hours* are both attributes of DAILY WORK. The message of this example, therefore, is not to assume that planned and actual data have the same level of detail, but do not be surprised if they do.

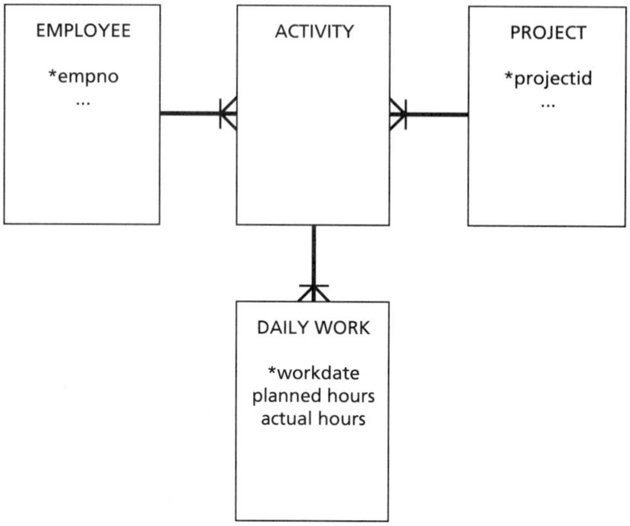

Figure 7-24. A revised project management data model

Entity types

A data model contains different kinds of entities, which are distinguished by the format of their identifiers. Labeling each of these entities by type will help you to determine what questions to ask.

Independent entity

An independent entity is often central to a data model and foremost in the client's mind. Independent entities are frequently the starting points of a data model. Remember that in the investment database, the independent entities are STOCK and NATION. Independent entities typically have clearly distinguishable names because they occur so frequently in the client's world. In addition, they usually have a single, arbitrary identifier, such as *stock code* or *nation code*.

Independent entities are often connected to other independent entities in a 1:m or m:m relationship. The data model in Figure 7-25 shows two independent entities linked in a 1:m relationship.

Weak or dependent entity

A weak entity (also known as a dependent entity) relies on another entity for its existence and identification. It is recognized by a bar on the weak entity's end of the arc (see Figure 7-26). CITY cannot exist without REGION. A CITY is uniquely identified by *cityname* and *regname*. If the composite identifier becomes unwieldy, creating an arbitrary identifier (e.g., cityno) will change the weak entity into an independent one.

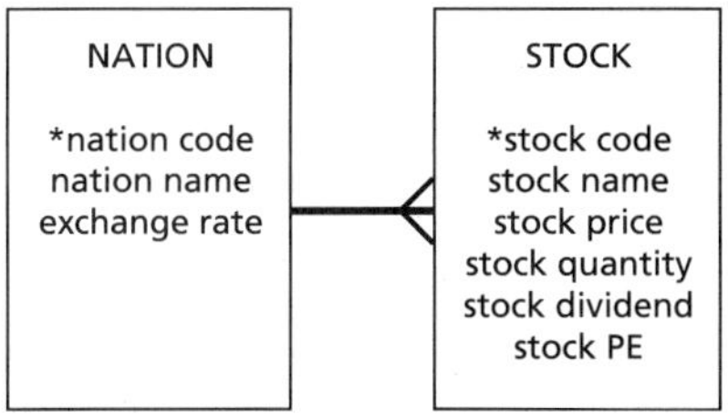

Figure 7-25. NATION and STOCK are independent entities

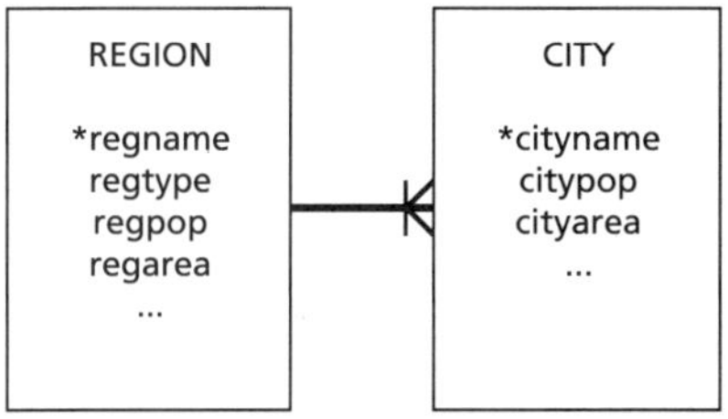

Figure 7-26. CITY is a weak entity

Associative entity[3]

Associative entities are by-products of m:m relationships. They are typically found between independent entities. Associative entities sometimes have obvious names because they occur in the real world. For instance, the associative entity for the m:m relationship between DEPARTMENT and EMPLOYEE is usually called POSITION (see Figure 7-27). If the associative entity does not have a common name, the two entity names are generally hyphenated (e.g., DEPARTMENT-EMPLOYEE). Always search for the appropriate name because it will improve the quality of the data model. Hyphenated names are a last resort.

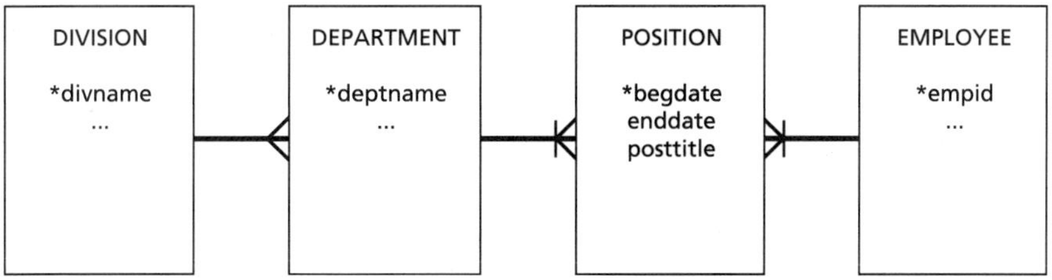

Figure 7-27. POSITION is an associative entity

3. Also known as an intersection entity in some data modeling dialects.

Associative entities can show either the current or historic relationship between two entities. If an associative entity's only identifiers are the two relationship descriptors, then it records the current relationship between the entities. If the associative entity has some time measure as a partial identifier (e.g., date or hour), then it records the history of the relationship. Whenever you find an associative entity, ask the client whether the history of the relationship should be recorded.

Creating a single, arbitrary identifier for an associative entity will change it to an independent one. This is likely to happen if the associative entity becomes central to an application. For example, if a personnel department does a lot of work with POSITION, it may find it more expedient to give it a separate identifier (e.g., *position number*).

Aggregate entity

An aggregate entity is created when several different entities have similar attributes that are distinguished by a prefix or suffix to keep their names unique. For example, because components of an address might occur in several entities (e.g., CUSTOMER and SUPPLIER), an aggregate address entity can be created to store details of all addresses. Aggregate entities usually become independent entities. In this case, we could use *address number* to uniquely identify an instance of address.

Subordinate entity

A subordinate entity stores data about an entity that can vary among instances. A subordinate entity is useful when an entity consists of mutually exclusive classes that have different descriptions. The farm animal database shown in Figure 7-28 indicates that the farmer requires different data for sheep and horses. Notice that each of the subordinate entities is identified by the relationship descriptor. You could avoid subordinate entities by placing all the attributes in ANIMAL but then you make it incumbent on the client to remember which attributes apply to horses and which to sheep. This becomes an important issue for null fields. For example, is the attribute *hay consumption* null because it does not apply to sheep, or is it null because the value is unknown?

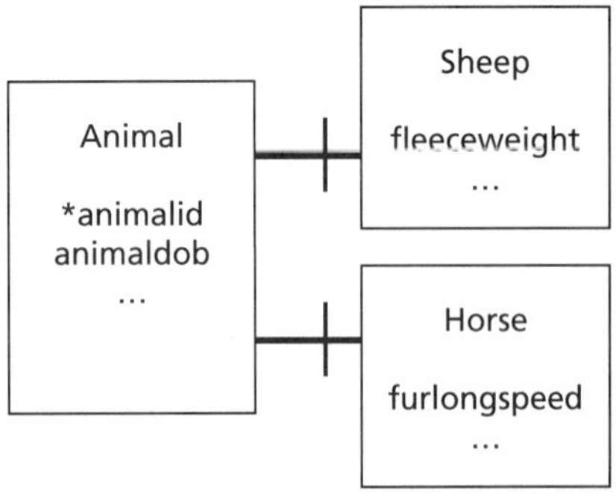

Figure 7-28. SHEEP and HORSE are subordinate entities

If a subordinate entity becomes important, it is likely to evolve to an independent entity. The framing of a problem often determines whether subordinate entities are created. Stating the problem as, "A farmer has many animals, and these animals can be horses or sheep," might lead to the creation of subordinate entities. Alternatively, saying that "a farmer has many sheep and horses" might lead to setting up sheep and horse as independent entities.

Generalization and aggregation

Generalization and aggregation are common ideas in many modeling languages, particularly object-oriented modeling languages such as the unified modeling language (UML), which is discussed further in Chapter 13.

Generalization

A generalization[4] is a relationship between a more general element and a more specific element. In Figure 7-29, the general element is ***animal***, and the specific elements are ***sheep*** and ***horse***. In other words a horse is a subtype of animal, A generalization is often called an "is-a" relationship because the subtype element ***is a*** member of the generalization.

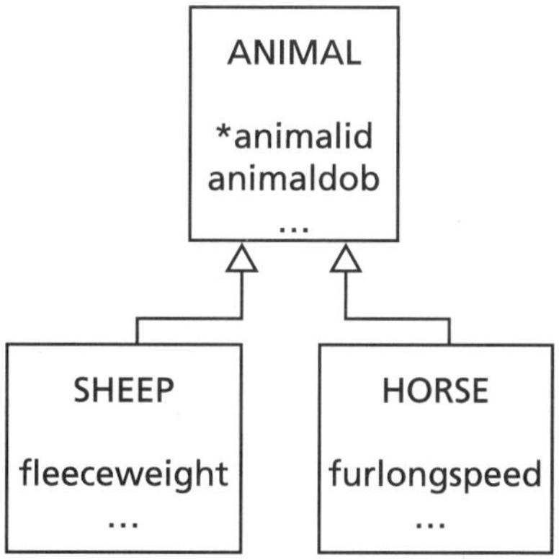

Figure 7-29. A generalization hierarchy

A generalization is directly mapped to the relational model with one table for each entity. For each of the subtype entities (i.e., SHEEP and HORSE), the primary key is that of the supertype entity (i.e., ANIMAL). You must also make this column a foreign key so that a subtype cannot be inserted without the presence of the matching supertype. A generalization is represented by a series of 1:1 relationships to weak entities (see Figure 7-28).

4. UML notation is used to represent the generalization structure.

Aggregation

Aggregation is a part-whole relationship between two entities. Common phrases used to describe an aggregation are "consists of," "contains," and "is part of." Figure 7-30 shows an aggregation where a herd consists of many cows.[5] Cows can be removed or added, but it is still a herd. An open diamond next to the whole denotes an aggregation. In data modeling terms, there is a 1:m relationship between herd and cow.

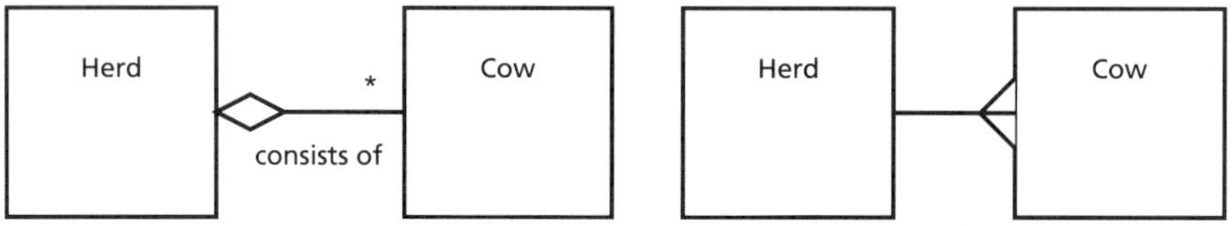

Figure 7-30. An aggregation in UML and data modeling

There are two special types of aggregation: shared and composition. With **shared aggregation**, one entity owns another entity, but other entities can own that entity as well. A sample shared aggregation is displayed in Figure 7-31, which shows that a class has many students, and a student can be a member of many classes. Students, the parts in this case, can be part of many classes. An open diamond next to the whole denotes a shared aggregation, which we represent in data modeling is an m:m relationship.

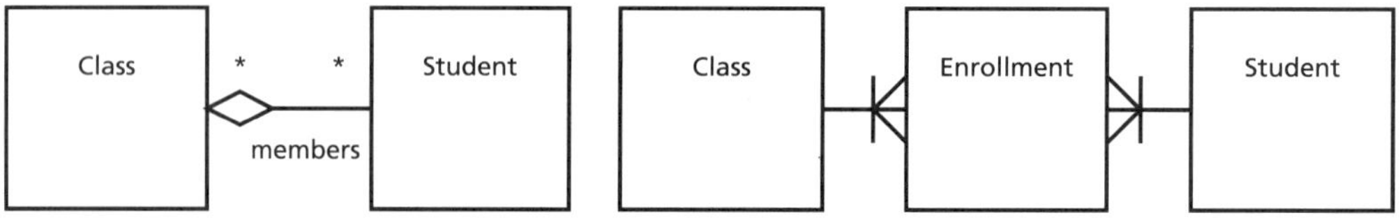

Figure 7-31. Shared aggregation in UML and data modeling

In a **composition aggregation,** one entity exclusively owns the other entity. A solid diamond at the whole end of the relationship denotes composition aggregation. The appropriate data model is a weak entity, as shown in Figure 7-32.

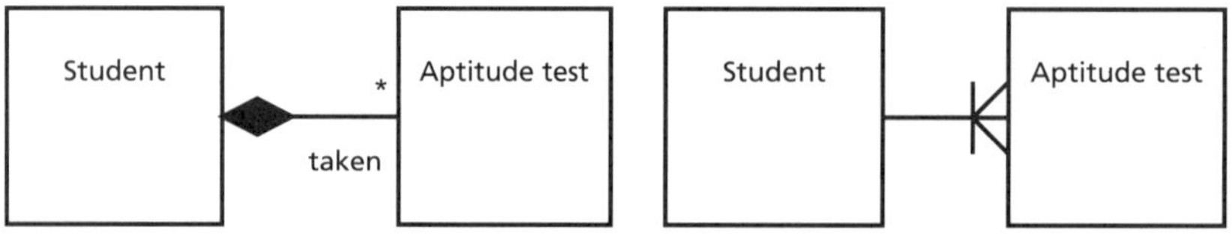

Figure 7-32. Composition aggregation in UML and data modeling

5. An asterisk (*) indicates many in UML.

Data modeling hints

A high-fidelity data model takes time to develop. The client must explain the problem fully so that the database designer can understand the client's requirements and translate them into a data model. Data modeling is like prototyping; the database designer gradually creates a model of the database as a result of interaction with the client. Some issues will frequently arise in this progressive creation, and the following hints should help you resolve many of the common problems you will encounter.

The rise and fall of a data model

Expect your data model to both expand and contract. Your initial data model will expand as you extend the boundaries of the application. You will discover some attributes will evolve into entities, and some 1:m relationships will become m:m relationships. It will grow because you will add entities, attributes, and relationships to allow for exceptions. Your data model will grow because you are representing the complexity of the real world. Do not try to constrain growth. Let the data model be as large as is necessary. As a rough rule, expect your final data model to grow to about two to three times the number of entities of your initial data model.

Expect your data model to contract as you generalize structures. Consider the abbreviated data model shown in Figure 7-33.

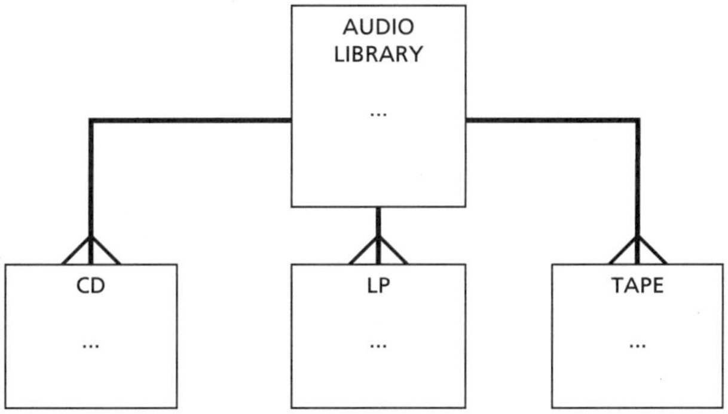

Figure 7-33. A data model that can shrink

This fragment is typical of the models produced by novice data modelers. It can be reduced by recognizing that CD, LP, and TAPE are all types of audio recordings. A more general entity, AUDIO RECORDING, could be used to represent the same data. Of course, it would need an additional attribute to distinguish the different types of audio recordings (see Figure 7-34).

As you discover new entities, your data model will grow. As you generalize, your data model will shrink.

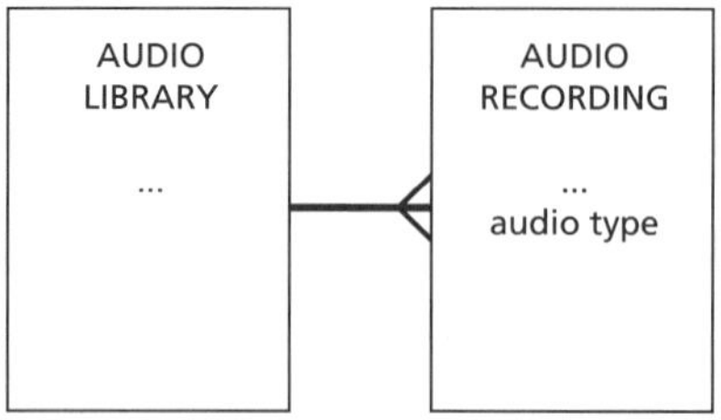

Figure 7-34. The shrunken data model

Identifier

If there is no obvious simple identifier, invent one. The simplest is a meaningless code (e.g., *person number* or *order number*). If you create an identifier, you can also guarantee its uniqueness.

Don't overwork an identifier. The worst case we have seen is a 22-character product code used by a plastics company that supposedly not only uniquely identified an item but told you its color, its manufacturing process, and type of plastic used to make it! Color, manufacturing process, and type of plastic are all attributes. This product code was unwieldy. Data entry error rates were extremely high, and very few people could remember how to decipher the code.

An identifier has to do only one thing: uniquely identify every instance of the entity. Sometimes trying to make it do double, or even triple, duty only creates more work for the client.

Position and order

There is no ordering in a data model. Entities can appear anywhere. You will usually find a central entity near the middle of the data model only because you tend to start with prominent entities (e.g., starting with STUDENT when modeling a student information system). What really matters is that you identify all relevant entities.

Attributes are in no order. You find that you will tend to list them as they are identified. For readability, it is a good idea to list some attributes sequentially. For example, first name, other names, and last name are usually together. This is not necessary, but it speeds up verification of a data model's completeness.

Instances are also assumed to have no ordering. There is no first instance, next instance, or last instance. If you must recognize a particular order, create an attribute to record the order. For example, if ranking of potential investment projects must be recorded, include an attribute (*projrank*) to store this data. This does not mean the instances will be stored in *projrank* order, but it does allow you to use the ORDER BY clause of SQL to report the projects in rank order.

If you need to store details of a precedence relationship (i.e., there is an ordering of instances and a need to know the successor and predecessor of any instance), then use a 1:1 recursive relationship. This is illustrated by the Monarch data model in Figure 7-35.

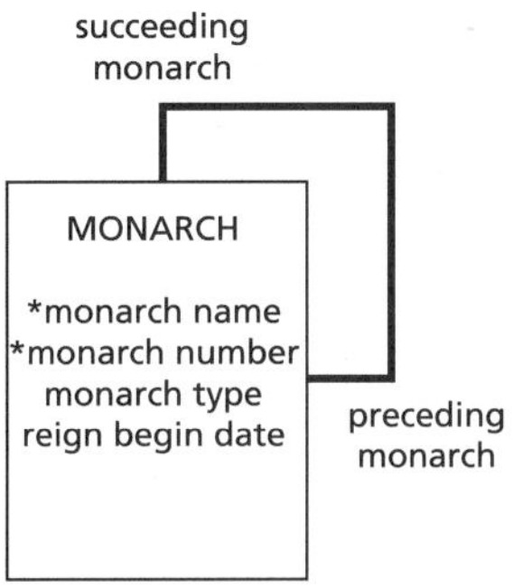

Figure 7-35. Using an attribute to record an ordering of instances

Attributes and consistency

Attributes must be consistent, retaining the same meaning for every instance. An example of an inconsistent attribute would be an attribute *stock info* that contains a stock's PE ratio or its ROI (return on investment). Another attribute, say *stock info code*, is required to decipher which meaning applies to any particular instance. The code could be "1" for PE and "2" for ROI. If one attribute determines the meaning of another, you have inconsistency. Writing SQL queries will be extremely challenging because inconsistent data increases query complexity. It is better to create separate attributes for PE and ROI.

Names and addresses

An attribute is the smallest piece of data that will conceivably form part of a query. If an attribute has segments (e.g., a person's name), determine whether these could form part of a query. If so, then make them separate attributes and reapply the query test. When you apply the query test to *person name*, you will usually decide to create three attributes: *first name*, *other name*, and *last name*.

What about titles? There are two sorts of titles: prefix titles (e.g., Mr., Mrs., Ms., and Dr.) and suffix titles (e.g., Jr. and III). These should be separate attributes, especially if you have divided name into separate attributes.

Addresses seem to cause more concern than names because they are more variant. Business addresses tend to be the most complicated, and foreign addresses add a few more twists. The data model fragment in Figure 7-36 works in most cases.

A common feature of every address is city, state, postal code, and nation. Some of these can be null. For example, Singapore does not have states. In the United States, city and

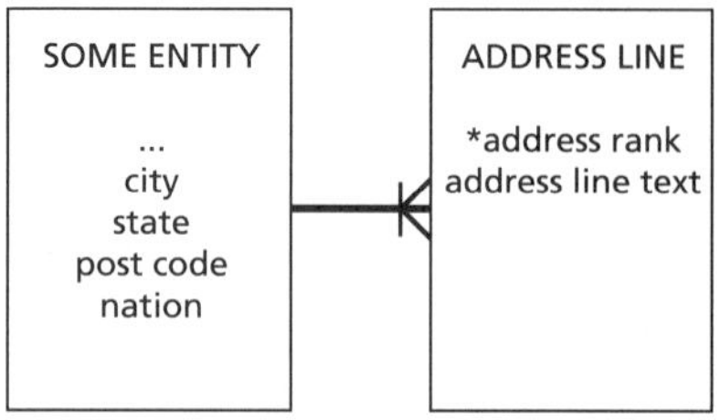

Figure 7-36. Handling addresses

state can be derived from the zip code, but this is not necessarily true for other countries. Furthermore, even if this were true for every nation, you would need a different derivation rule for each country, which could be beyond the scope of some RDBMSs. If there is a lifetime guarantee that every address in the database will be for one country, then examine the possibility of reducing redundancy by just storing *post code*.

Notice that the problem of multiple address lines is represented by a 1:m relationship. An address line is a text string that appears as one line of an address. There is often a set sequence in which these are displayed. The attribute *address rank* records this order. Any instance of ADDRESS LINE is identified by the composite of relationship descriptor and *address rank*.

How do you address students? First names may be all right for class, but it is not adequate enough for student records. Students typically have multiple addresses: a home address, a school address, and maybe a summer address. The following data model (see Figure 7-37) fragment shows how to handle this situation.

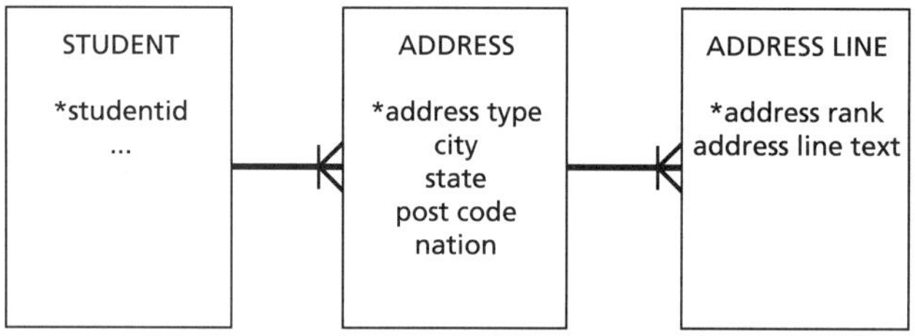

Figure 7-37. Students with multiple addresses

The identifier *address type* is used to distinguish among the different types of addresses. The same data model fragment works in situations where a business has different mailing and shipping addresses.

When data modeling, can you take a shortcut with names and addresses? It is time consuming to write out all the components of name and address for a data model. It creates clutter and does not add much fidelity. Our practical advice is to do two things. First, create a policy for all names and addresses (e.g., all names will be stored as three parts: first name, other names, last name). Second, use shorthand forms of attributes for names and address when they obey the policy. So from now on, we will use name and address as attributes with the understanding that when the database is created, the parts of these attributes will become separate columns.

Single instance entities

Do not be concerned about creating an entity with a single instance. Consider the data model fragment in Figure 7-38 which describes a single fast-food chain. Because the data model describes only one firm, the entity FIRM will have only one instance. The inclusion of this single instance entity permits facts about the firm to be maintained. Furthermore, it provides flexibility for expansion. If two fast-food chains combine, the data model needs no amendment.

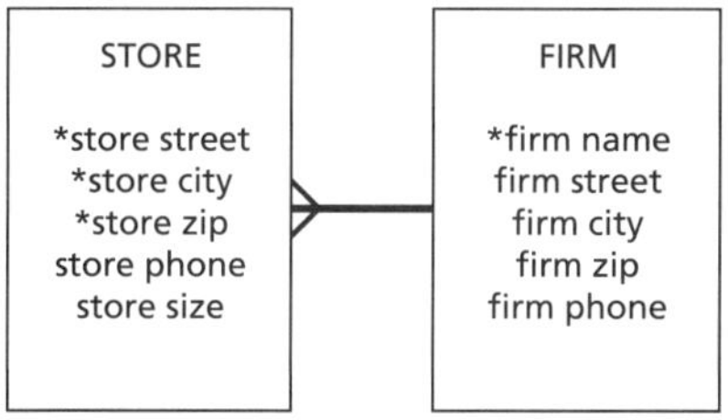

Figure 7-38. FIRM is a single instance entity

Picking words

Words are very important. They are all we have to make ourselves understood. Let the client choose the words because the data model belongs to that person and describes the client's world. If you try to impose your words on the client, you are likely to create a misunderstanding.

Synonyms

Synonyms are words that have the same meaning. For example, task, assignment, and project might all refer to the same real-world object. One of these terms, maybe the one in most common use, needs to be selected for naming the entity. Clients need to be told the official name for the entity and encouraged to adopt a single term for describing it. Alternatively, logical views of the database can be created that enable clients to use their own term. Synonyms are not a technical problem. It is a social problem of getting clients to agree on one word.

Homonyms

Homonyms are words that sound the same but have different meanings. Homonyms can create real confusion. *Sales date* is a classic example. In the aircraft manufacturing business it can have several meanings. To the salespeople, it is the day that the customer shakes hands and says, "We have a deal." For the lawyers, it is the day when the contract is signed, and for production, it is the day the customer takes delivery. In this case, the solution is reasonably obvious; redefine *sales date* to be separate terms for each area (e.g., *sales date*, *contract date*, and *delivery date* for sales, legal, and production departments, respectively).

Homonyms cause real confusion when clients do not realize that they are using the same word for different entities or attributes. Hunt down homonyms by asking lots of questions and querying a range of clients.

Exception hunting

Go hunting for exceptions. Keep asking the client questions such as

- Is it always like this?
- Would there be any situations where this could be an m:m relationship?
- Have there ever been any exceptions?
- Are things likely to change in the future?

Always probe for exceptions and look for them in the examples the client uses. Redesigning the data model to handle exceptions increases fidelity.

Relationship labeling

Relationship labeling clutters a data model. In most cases, relationship descriptors can be correctly inferred. Use labels only when there is a possibility of ambiguity.

Keeping the data model in shape

As you add to a data model, maintain fidelity. Do not add entities without also completing details of the identifier and attributes. By keeping the data model well formed, you avoid ambiguity, which frequently leads to miscommunication.

Used entities

Would you buy a used data model? Certainly, because a used data model is more likely to have higher fidelity than a brand new one. A used data model has been subjected to much scrutiny and revision and should be a more accurate representation of the real world.

Meaningful identifiers

An identifier is meaningful when some attributes of the entity can be inferred from the identifier's value (e.g., a code of B78 for an item informs a clerk that the item is black). Many data managers agree that meaningful identifiers or codes create problems. While avoiding meaningful identifiers is generally accepted as good data management practice, they are still widely used. After a short description of some examples of meaningful identifiers, this section discusses the pros and cons of meaningful identifiers.

The invoice number '98dec0001' is a meaningful identifier. The first five positions indicate in which period the invoice was generated. The last four digits of the invoice number have a meaning. The 0001 indicates it was the first invoice sent in December. In addition, email addresses, like mvdpas@bizzo.nl, have a meaning.[6]

When coding a person's gender, some systems use the codes 'm' and 'f' and others '1' and '2.' The pair (m, f) is meaningful, but (1, 2) is not and puts the onus on the user to remember the meaning. The codes 'm' and 'f' are derived from the reality that they represent. They are the first letters of the words male and female. The '1' and '2' are not abstracted from reality, and therefore they do not have a meaning. This observation is reiterated by the following quote from the International Organization for Standardization (ISO) information interchange standard for the representation of human sexes (ISO 5218):

No significance is to be placed on the fact that 'Male' is coded '1' and 'Female' is coded '2'. This standard was developed based upon predominant practices of the countries involved and does not convey any meaning of importance, ranking or any other basis that could imply discrimination.

In determining whether an identifier is meaningful, one can look at the way new values of that identifier are generated. If the creation takes place on the basis of characteristics that appear in reality, the identifier is meaningful. That is why the identifier of the invoice '98dec0002', which is the identifier assigned to the second invoice generated in December 1998, is meaningful. It is also why the email address rwatson@terry.uga.edu is meaningful.

Meaningful identifiers clearly have some advantages and disadvantages, and these are now considered. Also see the summary in Table 7-4.

Table 7-4: Advantages and disadvantages of meaningful identifiers

Advantages	Disadvantages
Recognizable and rememberable Administrative simplicity	Identifier exhaustion Reality changes Loss of meaningfulness

Advantages of meaningful identifiers

Recognizable and rememberable

People can often recognize and remember the significance of meaningful identifiers. If, for example, someone receives an email from rwatson@terry.uga.edu, this person can probably deduce the sender's name and workplace. If a manufacturer, for instance, uses the last two digits of its furniture code to indicate the color (e.g., 08 = beech), employees

6. The section is based on the work of Mark van der Pas <postmaster@markvanderpas.nl>, Information Manager, Libertel <www.libertel.nl>.

can then quickly determine the color of a packed piece of furniture. Of course, the firm could also show the color of the furniture on the label, in which case customers, who are most unlikely to know the coding scheme, can quickly determine the color of the enclosed product.

Administrative simplicity

By using meaningful identifiers, administration can be relatively easily decentralized. Administering email addresses, for instance, can be handled at the domain level. This way, one can avoid the process of synchronizing with other domains whenever a new email address is created.

A second example is the EAN[7] (European article number), the bar code on European products. Issuing EANs can be administered per country, since each country has a unique number in the EAN. When issuing a new number, a country only has to issue a code that is not yet in use in that country. The method of contacting all countries to ask whether an EAN has already been issued is time consuming and open to error. On the other hand, creating a central database of issued EAN codes is an option. If every issuer of EAN codes can access such a database, alignment among countries is created and duplicates are prevented.

Disadvantages of meaningful identifiers

Identifier exhaustion

Suppose a company with a six-digit item identifier decides to use the first three digits to uniquely specify the product group (e.g., stationary). Within this group, the remaining three digits are used to define the item (e.g., yellow lined pad). As a consequence, only one thousand items can be specified per product group. This problem remains even when some numbers in a specific product group, or even when entire product groups, are not used.

Consider the case when product group '010' is exhausted and is supplemented by the still unused product group code '940'. What seems to be a simple quick fix causes problems because a particular product group is not uniquely identified by a single identifier. Clients have to remember there is an exception.

A real world example of identifier exhaustion is a holding company that identifies its subsidiaries by using a code, where the first character is the first letter of the subsidiary's name. When the holding company acquired its seventh subsidiary, the meaningfulness of the coding system failed. The newly acquired subsidiary name started with the same letter as one of the existing subsidiaries. The system had already run out of identifiers.

---

7. UPC (universal product code) in the U.S.

When existing identifiers have to be converted because of exhaustion, printed codes on labels, packages, shelves, and catalogues will have to be redone. Recoding is an expensive process and should be avoided.

Exhaustion is not only a problem with meaningful identifiers. It can happen with non-meaningful identifiers. The problem is that meaningful identifier systems tend to exhaust sooner. To avoid identifier exhaustion and maintain meaningful identifiers, some designers increase identifier lengths (e.g., 4 digits for product group). Consequently, more disk space will be required to store the longer identifiers.

Reality changes

The second problem of meaningful identifiers is that the reality they record changes. For example, a company changes its name. The College of Business at the University of Georgia was renamed the Terry College of Business. Email addresses changed (e.g., rwatson@cba.uga.edu became rwatson@terry.uga.edu). An identifier can only remain meaningful over a long period if the meaningful part rarely or never changes.

Non-meaningful identifiers avoid reality changes. Consider the case of most telephone billing systems, which use an account id to identify a customer rather than a telephone number. This means a customer can change telephone numbers without causing any coding problems because telephone number is not the unique identifier of each customer.

A meaningful identifier can lose its meaningfulness

Consider the problems that can occur with the identifier that records both the color and the material of an article. Chipboard with a beech wood veneer is coded BW. A black product, on the other hand, is coded BL. Problems arise whenever there is an overlap between these characteristics. What happens with a product that is finished with a black veneer on beech wood? Should the code be BW or BL? And what about a black-painted product that is made out of beech wood? Maybe a new code, BB, for black beech wood is required. There will always be employees and customers who do not know the meaning of these not so meaningful identifiers and attribute the wrong meaning to them.

The solution—non-meaningful identifiers

Most people are initially inclined to try to make identifiers meaningful. There is a sense that something is lost by using a simple numeric to identify a product or customer. Nothing, however, is lost and much is gained. Non-meaningful identifiers serve their sole purpose well—to uniquely identify an entity. Attributes are used to describe the characteristics of the entity (e.g., color, type of wood). A clear distinction between the role of identifiers and attributes creates fewer data management problems now and in the future.

The seven habits of highly effective data modelers

There is often a large gap between the performance of *average* and *expert* data modelers. An insight into the characteristics that make some data modelers more skillful than others should improve your data modeling capabilities.[8]

Immerse

Find out what the client wants by immersing yourself in the task environment. Spend some time following the client around and participating in daily business. Firsthand experience of the problem will give you a greater understanding of the client's requirements. Observe, ask questions, reflect, and talk to a wide variety of people (e.g., managers, operational personnel, customers, and suppliers). The more you learn about the problem, the better equipped you are to create a high-fidelity data model.

Challenge

Challenge existing assumptions; dig out the exceptions. Test the boundaries of the data model. Try to think about the business problem from different perspectives (e.g., "How might the industry leader tackle this problem?"). Run a brainstorming session with the client to stimulate the search for breakthrough solutions.

Generalize

Reduce the number of entities whenever possible by using generalized structures (remember the Audio Library model) to simplify the data model. Simpler data models are usually easier to understand and less costly to implement. Expert data modelers can see beyond surface differences to discern the underlying similarities of seemingly different entities.

Test

Test the data model by reading it to yourself and several people intimately familiar with the problem. Test both directions of every relationship (e.g., "A farmer has many cows and a cow belongs to only one farmer"). Build a prototype so the client can experiment and learn with a concrete model. Testing is very important because it costs very little to fix a data model but a great deal to repair a system based on an incorrect data model.

Limit

Set reasonable limits to the time and scope of data modeling. Don't let the data modeling phase continue forever. Discover the boundaries early in the project and stick to these unless there are compelling reasons to extend the project. Too many projects are allowed to expand because it is easier to say *yes* than *no*. In the long run, however, you do the client a disservice by promising too much and extending the life of the project. Determine the

8. Based on Moody, D. 1996. The seven habits of highly effective data modelers. *Database programming and design* 9 (10):57–64.

core entities and attributes that will solve most of the problem, and confine the data model to this core. Keep sight of the time and budget constraints of the project.

Integrate

Step back and reflect on how your project fits with the organization's information architecture. Integrate with existing systems where feasible and avoid duplication. How does your data model fit with the corporate data model and those of other projects? Can you use part of an existing data model? A skilled data modeler has to see both the fine-grained detail of a project data model and the big picture of the corporate data resource.

Complete

Good data modelers don't leave data models ill-defined. All entities, attributes, and relationships are carefully defined, ambiguities are resolved, and exceptions handled. Because the full value of a data model is realized only when the system is complete, the data modeler should stay involved with the project until the system is implemented. The data modeler, who generally gets involved in the project from its earliest days, can provide continuity through the various phases and ensure the system solves the problem.

Summary

Data modeling is both a technique for modeling data and its relationships and a graphical representation of a database. It is also a way of communicating a database design. The goal of data modeling is to identify the facts that must be stored in a database. Building a data model is a partnership between a client, a representative of the eventual users of the database, and a designer. The building blocks of data modeling are an entity, attribute, identifier, and relationship. A well-formed data model, which means the construction rules have been obeyed, clearly communicates information to the client. A high-fidelity data model faithfully describes the world it is supposed to represent.

A data model is an evolving representation. Each change should be an incremental improvement in quality. The quality of a data model can be determined only by understanding the context in which it will be used. A data model can model historical data relationships just as readily as current ones. The five different types of entities are independent, dependent, associative, aggregate, and subordinate. Expect a data model to expand and contract. A data model has no ordering. Introduce an attribute if ordering is required. An attribute must have the same meaning for every instance. An attribute is the smallest piece of data that will conceivably form part of a query. Synonyms are words that have the same meaning; homonyms are words that sound the same but have different meanings. Identifiers should generally have no meaning. Highly effective data modelers immerse, challenge, generalize, test, limit, integrate, and complete.

Key terms and concepts

Aggregate entity
Aggregation
Associative entity
Attribute
Composite aggregation
Data model
Data model quality
Dependent entity
Determinant
Domain
Entity
Generalization
High-fidelity image
Homonym
Identifier
Independent entity
Instance
Modeling
Relationship
Relationship descriptor
Shared aggregation
Synonym
Well-formed data model

References and additional readings

Carlis, J. V. 1991. *Logical data structures*. Minneapolis, MN: University of Minnesota.

Hammer, M. 1990. Reengineering work: Don't automate, obliterate. *Harvard Business Review* 68 (4):104–112.

Wetherbe, J. C. 1991. Executive information requirements: Getting it right. *MIS Quarterly* 15 (1):51–65.

Exercises

Short answers

1. What is data modeling?
2. What is a useful technique for identifying entities in a written description of a data modeling problem?
3. When do you label arcs?
4. When is a data model well formed and when is it high fidelity?
5. How do you handle exceptions when data modeling?
6. Describe the different types of entities.
7. Why might a data model grow?
8. Why might a data model contract?
9. How do you indicate ordering of instances in a data model?
10. What is the difference between a synonym and a homonym?

Data modeling

Create a data model from the following narratives, which are sometimes intentionally incomplete. You will have to make some assumptions. Make certain you state these alongside your data model. Define the identifier(s) and attributes of each entity.

1. The president of a book wholesaler has told you that she wants information about publishers, authors, and books.

2. A university has many subject areas (e.g., MIS, Romance languages). Professors teach in only one subject area, but the same subject area can have many professors. Professors can teach many different courses in their subject area. An offering of a course (e.g., Data Management 457, French 101) is taught by only one professor at a particular time.
3. Kids'n'Vans retails minivans for a number of manufacturers. Each manufacturer offers several models of its minivan (e.g., SE, LE, GT). Each model comes with a standard set of equipment (e.g., the Acme SE comes with wheels, seats, and an engine). Minivans can have a variety of additional equipment or accessories (radio, air conditioning, automatic transmission, airbag, etc.), but not all accessories are available for all minivans (e.g., not all manufacturers offer a driver's side airbag). Some sets of accessories are sold as packages (e.g., the luxury package might include stereo, six speakers, cocktail bar, and twin overhead foxtails).
4. Steve operates a cinema chain and has given you the following information: "I have many cinemas. Each cinema can have multiple theaters. Movies are shown throughout the day starting at 11 A.M. and finishing at 1 A.M. Each movie is given a two-hour time slot. We never show a movie in more than one theater at a time, but we do shift movies among theaters because seating capacity varies. I am interested in knowing how many people, classified by adults and children, attended each showing of a movie. I vary ticket prices by movie and time slot. For instance, *Lassie Get Lost* at 11 A.M. is 50 cents for everyone but is 75 cents at 11 P.M."
5. A university gymnastics team can have as many as 10 gymnasts. The team competes many times during the season. A meet can have one or more opponents and consists of four events: vault, uneven bars, beam, and floor routine. A gymnast can participate in all or some of these events though the team is limited to five participants in any event.
6. A famous Greek shipping magnate, Stell, owns many container ships. Containers are collected at one port and delivered to another port. Customers pay a negotiated fee for the delivery of each container. Each ship has a sailing schedule that lists the ports the ship will visit over the next six months. The schedule shows the expected arrival and departure dates. The daily charge for use of each port is also recorded.
7. A medical center employs several physicians. A physician can see many patients, and a patient can be seen by many physicians though not always on the one visit. On any particular visit, a patient may be diagnosed to have one or more illnesses.
8. A telephone company offers a 10 percent discount to any customer who phones another person who is also a customer of the company. To be eligible for the discount, the pairing of the two phone numbers must be registered with the telephone company. Furthermore, for billing purposes the company records both phone numbers, start time, end time, and date of call.
9. Global Trading (GT), Inc. is a conglomerate. It buys and sells businesses frequently and has difficulty keeping track of what strategic business units (SBUs) it owns, in what nations it operates, and what markets it serves. For example, the CEO was recently surprised to find that GT owns 25 percent of Dundee's Wild Adventures, headquartered in Zaire, that has subsidiaries operating tours of Australia, Zaire, and

New York. You have been commissioned to design a database to keep track of GT's businesses. The CEO has provided you with the following information:

SBUs are headquartered in one country, not necessarily the United States. Each SBU has subsidiaries or foreign agents, depending on local legal requirements, in a number of countries. Each subsidiary or foreign agent operates in only one country but can operate in more than one market. GT uses the standard industrial code (SIC) to identify a market (e.g., newspaper publishing). The SIC is a unique four-digit code.

While foreign agents operate as separate legal entities, GT needs to know in what countries and markets they operate. On the other hand, subsidiaries are fully or partly-owned by GT, and it is important for GT to know who are the other owners of any subsidiary and what percentage of the subsidiary they own. It is not unusual for a corporation to have shares in several of GT's subsidiary companies and for several corporations to own a portion of a subsidiary. Multiple ownership can also occur at the SBU level.

10. A real estate investment company owns many shopping malls. Each mall contains many shops. To encourage rental of its shops, the company gives a negotiated discount to retailers who have shops in more than one mall. Each shop generates an income stream that can vary from month to month because rental is based on a flat rental charge and a negotiated percentage of sales revenue. Also, each shop has monthly expenses for scheduled and unscheduled maintenance. The company uses the data to compute its monthly net income per square meter for each shop and for ad hoc querying.

Reference 1

Basic Structures

Few things are harder to put up with than the annoyance of a good example.
Mark Twain, *Pudd'nhead Wilson*, 1894

Every data model is composed of the same basic structures. This is a major advantage because you can focus on a small part of a full data model without being concerned about the rest of it. As a result, translation to a relational database is very easy because you systematically translate each basic structure. This section describes each of the basic structures and shows how they are mapped to a relational database. Because the mapping is shown as a diagram and SQL CREATE statements, you will use this section frequently.

One entity

No relationships

The unrelated entity was introduced in Chapter 3. This is simply a flat file, and the mapping is very simple (see Figure R1-1). Although it is unlikely that you will have a data model with a single entity, for completeness it is included in this section.

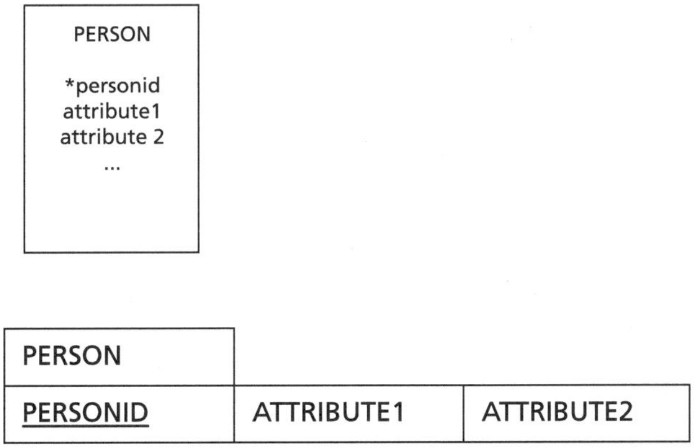

```
CREATE TABLE PERSON
   (PERSONID INTEGER NOT NULL,
   ATTRIBUTE1 … ,
   ATTRIBUTE2 … ,
   …
      PRIMARY KEY(PERSONID))
```

Figure R1-1. A single entity with no relationships

A 1:1 recursive relationship

A recursive 1:1 relationship is used to describe situations like current marriage (see Figure R1-2). A person can have zero or one current spouse. The two relationships must be labeled. Mapping to the relational database requires that the identifier of one end of the relationship become a foreign key. It does not matter which one you select. Notice that when PERSONID is used as a foreign key, it must be given an alias—in this case SPOUSE—because two columns in the same table cannot have the same name. The foreign key constraint is not defined because this constraint cannot refer to the table being created.

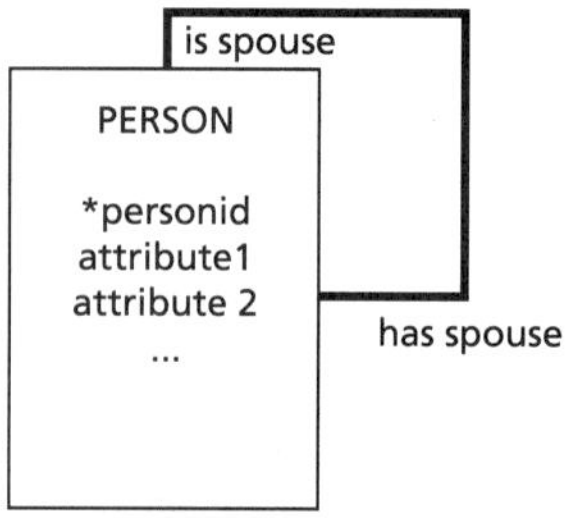

PERSON				
PERSONID	ATTRIBUTE1	ATTRIBUTE2	...	*SPOUSE*

```
CREATE TABLE PERSON
   (PERSONID INTEGER NOT NULL,
   ATTRIBUTE1 … ,
   ATTRIBUTE2 … ,
   …
   SPOUSE INTEGER,
      PRIMARY KEY(PERSONID))
```

Figure R1-2. A single entity with a 1:1 recursive relationship

A recursive 1:m relationship

A recursive 1:m relationship describes situations like fatherhood or motherhood. Figure R1-3 maps fatherhood. A father may have many biological children, but a child has only one biological father. The relationship is mapped like any other 1:m relationship. The identifier of the one end becomes a foreign key in the many end. Again, we must rename the identifier when it becomes a foreign key in the same row. Also, the foreign key constraint is not defined because it cannot refer to the table being created.

It is possible to have more than one 1:m recursive relationship. For example, details of a mother-child relationship would be represented in the same manner and result in the data model having a second 1:m recursive relationship. The mapping to the relational model would result in an additional column to contain a foreign key MOTHER, the PERSONID of the person's mother.

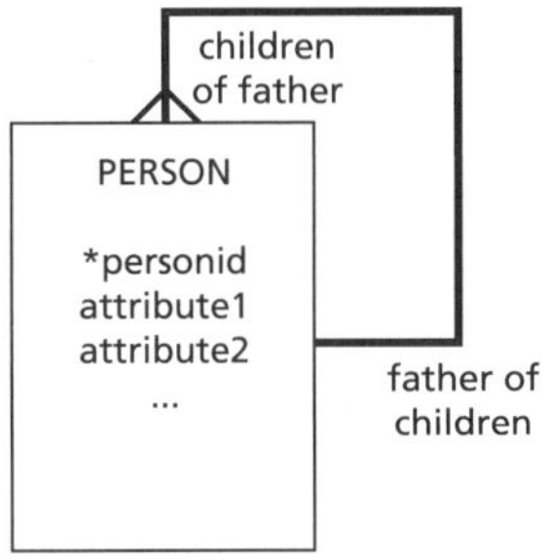

PERSON				
PERSONID	ATTRIBUTE1	ATTRIBUTE2	...	*FATHER*

```
CREATE TABLE PERSON
   (PERSONID INTEGER NOT NULL,
   ATTRIBUTE1 … ,
   ATTRIBUTE2 … ,
   …
   FATHER INTEGER,
      PRIMARY KEY(PERSONID))
```

Figure R1-3. A single entity with a 1:m recursive relationship

A recursive m:m relationship

A recursive m:m relationship can describe a situation like friendship (see Figure R1-4). A person can have many friends and be a friend to many persons. As with m:m relationships between a pair of entities, we convert this relationship to two 1:m relationships and create an associative entity.

The resulting relational table FRIENDSHIP has a composite primary key based on relational descriptors, which in effect means the two components are based on PERSONID, the primary key of PERSON. To distinguish between them, these components are called PERSONID1 and PERSONID2, so you can think of FRIENDSHIP as a pair of PERSONIDs. You will see the same pattern occurring with other m:m recursive relationships. Notice

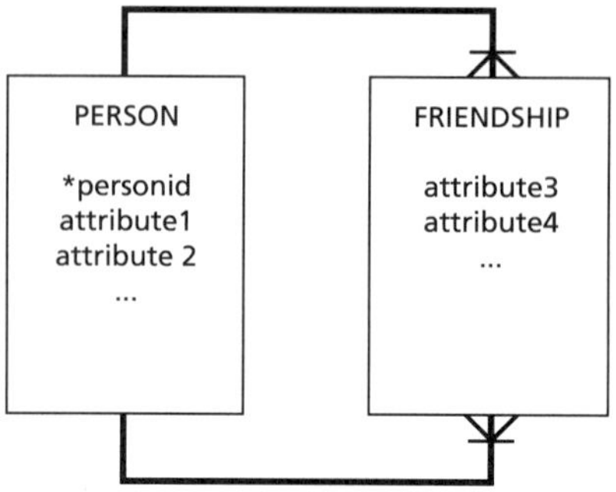

PERSON				
<u>PERSONID</u>	ATTRIBUTE1	ATTRIBUTE2	...	

FRIENDSHIP				
<u>*PERSONID1*</u>	<u>*PERSONID2*</u>	ATTRIBUTE3	ATTRIBUTE4	...

```
CREATE TABLE PERSON
   (PERSONID INTEGER NOT NULL,
   ATTRIBUTE1 … ,
   ATTRIBUTE2 … ,
   …
      PRIMARY KEY(PERSONID))

CREATE TABLE FRIENDSHIP
   (PERSONIS1 INTEGER NOT NULL,
   PERSONID2 INTEGER NOT NULL,
   ATTRIBUTE3 … ,
   ATTRIBUTE4 … ,
   …
      PRIMARY KEY(PERSONID1,PERSONID2),
      FOREIGN KEY FKFRND1(PERSONID1) REFERENCES PERSON
      FOREIGN KEY FKFRND2(PERSONID2) REFERENCES PERSON)
```

Figure R1-4. A single entity with an m:m recursive relationship

both person identifiers are independent foreign keys because they are used to map the two 1:m relationships between PERSON and FRIENDSHIP.

A single entity can have multiple m:m recursive relationships. Relationships such as enmity (not enemyship) or sibling are m:m recursive on PERSON. The approach to recording these relationships is the same as that outlined previously.

Two entities

No relationships

When there is no arc between two entities, the client has decided there is no need to record a relationship between the two entities. When you are reading the data model with the client, be sure that you check whether this assumption is correct now and for the foreseeable future. When there is no relationship between two entities, map them each as you would a single entity with no relationships.

A 1:1 relationship

A 1:1 relationship usually occurs in parallel with a 1:m relationship between two entities. It signifies some instances of an entity that have an additional role. For example, a department has many employees (the 1:m relationship), and a department has a boss (the 1:1). The data model fragment shown in Figure R1-5 represents the 1:1 relationship.

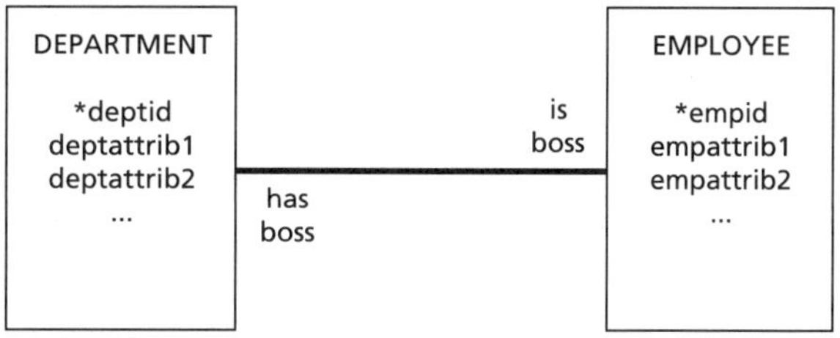

DEPARTMENT				
DEPTID	DEPTATTRIB1	DEPTATTRIB2	...	*BOSSNO*

EMPLOYEE			
EMPID	EMPATTRIB1	EMPATTRIB2	...

```
CREATE TABLE EMPLOYEE
   (EMPID INTEGER NOT NULL,
   EMPATTRIB1 … ,
   EMPATTRIB2 … ,
   …
      PRIMARY KEY(EMPID))

CREATE TABLE DEPARTMENT
   (DEPTID CHAR(3) NOT NULL,
   DEPTATTRIB1 … ,
   DEPTATTRIB2 … ,
   …
   BOSSNO INTEGER,
      PRIMARY KEY(DEPTID),
      FOREIGN KEY FKBOSS(BOSSNO) REFERENCES EMPLOYEE)
```

Figure R1-5. A 1:1 relationship between two entities

The guideline, as explained in Chapter 6, is to map the relationship to the relational model by placing the foreign key to minimize the number of instances when it will have a null value. In this case, we place the foreign key in DEPARTMENT.

A 1:m relationship

The 1:m relationship is possibly the easiest to understand and map (see Figure R1-6). The mapping to the relational model is very simple. The primary key of the one end becomes a foreign key in the many end.

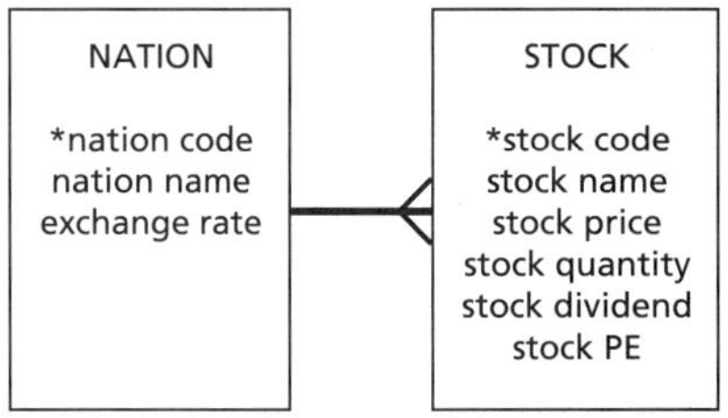

NATION		
NATCODE	NATNAME	EXCHRATE

STOCK						
STKCODE	STKFIRM	STKPRICE	STKQTY	STKDIV	STKPE	*NATCODE*

```
CREATE TABLE NATION
   (NATCODE        CHAR(3) NOT NULL,
   NATNAME         CHAR(20),
   EXCHRATE        DECIMAL(9,5),
      PRIMARY KEY(NATCODE))

CREATE TABLE STOCK
   (STKCODE        CHAR(3) NOT NULL,
   STKFIRM         CHAR(20),
   STKPRICE        DECIMAL(6,2),
   STKQTY          DECIMAL(8),
   STKDIV          DECIMAL(5,2),
   STKPE           DECIMAL(5),
   NATCODE         CHAR(3) NOT NULL,
      PRIMARY KEY(STKCODE),
      FOREIGN KEY FKNATION(NATCODE) REFERENCES NATION)
```

Figure R1-6. A 1:m relationship between two entities

An m:m relationship

An m:m relationship is transformed into two 1:m relationships. The mapping is then a two-fold application of the 1:m rule (see Figure R1-7).

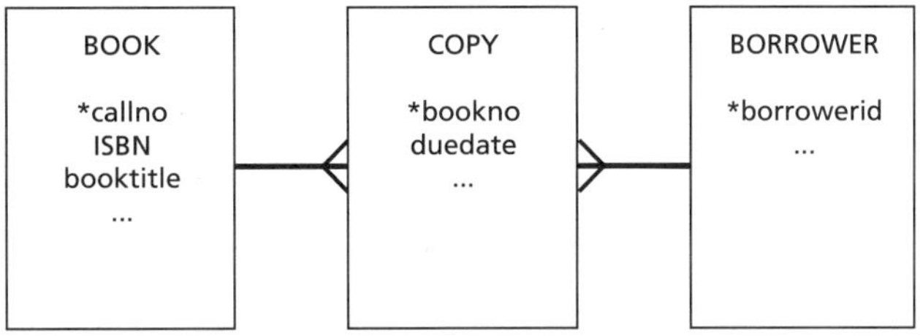

BOOK			
<u>CALLNO</u>	ISBN	BOOKTITLE	...

COPY				
<u>BOOKNO</u>	DUEDATE	...	*CALLNO*	*BORROWERID*

BORROWER	
<u>BORROWERID</u>	...

```
CREATE TABLE BOOK
   (CALLNO CHAR(12) NOT NULL,
   ISBN ... ,
   BOOKTITLE ... ,
   ...
      PRIMARY KEY(CALLNO))

CREATE TABLE BORROWER
   (BORROWERID INTEGER NOT NULL,
      ...
      PRIMARY KEY(BORROWERID))

CREATE TABLE COPY
   (BOOKNO INTEGER NOT NULL,
   DUEDATE DATE,
   ...
   CALLNO CHAR(12) NOT NULL,
   BORROWERID INTEGER,
      PRIMARY KEY(BOOKNO),
      FOREIGN KEY FKBOOK(CALLNO) REFERENCES BOOK
      FOREIGN KEY FKBORROWER(BORROWERID) REFERENCES BORROWER)
```

Figure R1-7. An m:m relationship between two entities

Notice in this example that CALLNO in COPY is specified as NOT NULL. This means every copy must have a corresponding book. BORROWERID, however, can be null because a book need not be borrowed; it can be sitting on the shelf. The BOOK and BORROWER tables must be created first because the create for COPY contains foreign key constraints that refer to BOOK and BORROWER.

Relationship descriptors as identifiers

Relationship descriptors that are used as identifiers tend to cause the most problems for novice data modelers. (A relationship descriptor is an identifier when there is a bar on an arc. The bar is almost always at the crow's foot end of a 1:m relationship.) Tables are formed by applying the following rule: the primary key of the table at the other end of the relationship becomes both a foreign key and part of the primary key in the table at the bar end. The application of this rule is shown for several common data model fragments.

A weak or dependent entity

In Figure R1-8 REGNAME is part of the primary key (because the relationship descriptor is part of the identifier) and a foreign key of CITY (because of the 1:m between REGION and CITY).

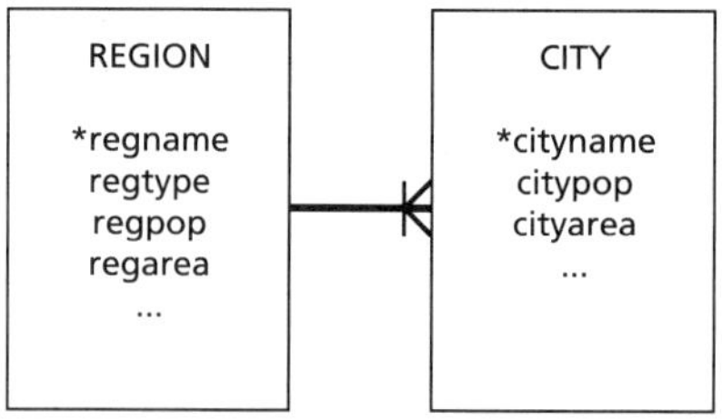

REGION				
REGNAME	REGTYPE	REGPOP	REGAREA	...

CITY				
CITYNAME	CITYPOP	CITYAREA	...	*REGNAME*

```
CREATE TABLE REGION
   (REGNAME        CHAR(20) NOT NULL,
   REGTYPE         ...,
   REGPOP          ...,
   REGPOP          ...,
   ...
      PRIMARY KEY(REGNAME))

CREATE TABLE CITY
   (CITYNAME       CHAR(20) NOT NULL,
   CITYPOP         ... ,
   CITYAREA        ... ,
   ...
   REGNAME         CHAR(20) NOT NULL,
      PRIMARY KEY(CITYNAME,REGNAME),
      FOREIGN KEY FKREGION(REGNAME) REFERENCES REGION)
```

Figure R1-8. A weak entity

An associative entity

In Figure R1-9 observe that CITYNAME and FIRMNAME are both part of the primary key (because they are relationship descriptors) and foreign keys (because of the two 1:m relationships) of STORE.

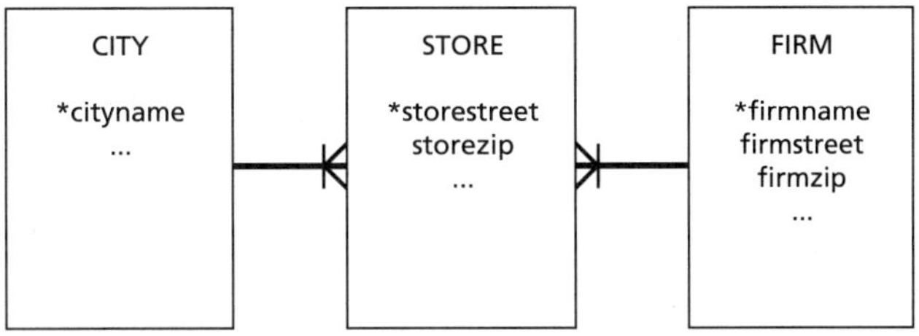

CITY	
CITYNAME	...

STORE				
STORESTREET	STOREZIP	...	*CITYNAME*	*FIRMNAME*

FIRM			
FIRMNAME	FIRMSTREET	FIRMZIP	...

```
CREATE TABLE CITY
   (CITYNAME      CHAR(20) NOT NULL,
   ...
      PRIMARY KEY(CITYNAME))

CREATE TABLE FIRM
   (FIRMNAME      CHAR(15) NOT NULL,
   FIRMSTREET     ... ,
   FIRMZIP        ... ,
   ...
      PRIMARY KEY(FIRMNAME))

CREATE TABLE STORE
   (STORESTREET CHAR(30) NOT NULL,
   STOREZIP ... ,
   ...
   CITYNAME CHAR(20) NOT NULL,
   FIRMNAME CHAR(15) NOT NULL,
      PRIMARY KEY(STORESTREET,CITYNAME,FIRMNAME),
      FOREIGN KEY FKCITY(CITYNAME) REFERENCES CITY,
      FOREIGN KEY FKFIRM(FIRMNAME) REFERENCES FIRM)
```

Figure R1-9. An associative entity

A tree structure

The interesting feature of Figure R1-10 is the primary key. Notice in Figure R1-10 that the primary key of a lower level of the tree is a composite of its identifier and the primary keys of the higher levels. The primary key of DIVISION is a composite of FIRMNAME and DIVNAME; the primary key of DEPARTMENT is a composite of FIRMNAME, DIVNAME, and DEPTNAME. Novice modelers often forget to make this translation.

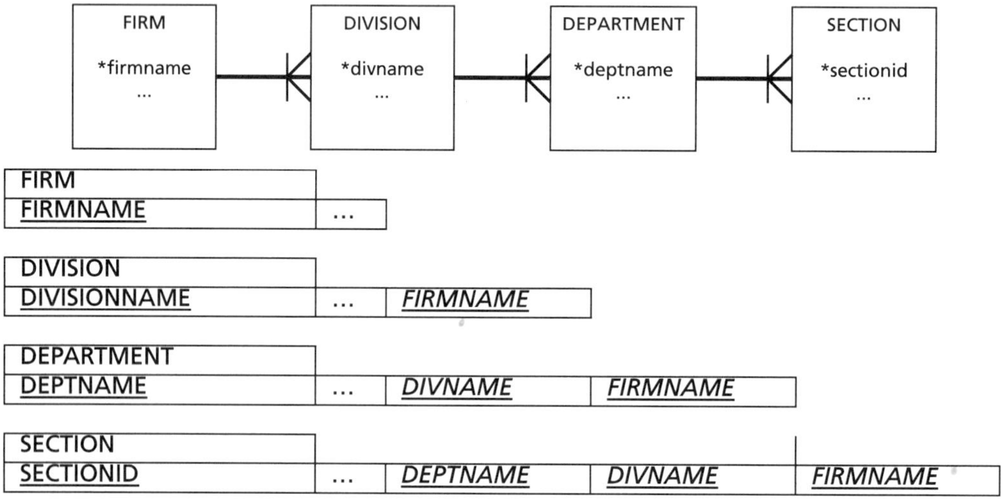


```
CREATE TABLE FIRM
    (FIRMNAME          CHAR(15) NOT NULL,
    …
        PRIMARY KEY(FIRMNAME))

CREATE TABLE DIVISION
    (DIVNAME           CHAR(15) NOT NULL,
    …
    FIRMNAME           CHAR(15) NOT NULL,
        PRIMARY KEY(FIRMNAME,DIVNAME)
        FOREIGN KEY FKFIRM(FIRMNAME) REFERENCES FIRM)

CREATE TABLE DEPARTMENT
    (DEPTNAME          CHAR(15) NOT NULL,
    … ,
    DIVNAME            CHAR(15) NOT NULL,
    FIRMNAME           CHAR(15) NOT NULL,
        PRIMARY KEY(FIRMNAME,DIVNAME,DEPTNAME)
        FOREIGN KEY FKDIVISION(FIRMNAME,DIVNAME)
            REFERENCES DIVISION)

CREATE TABLE SECTION
    (SECTIONID         CHAR(15) NOT NULL,
    … ,
    DEPTNAME           CHAR(15) NOT NULL,
    DIVNAME            CHAR(15) NOT NULL,
    FIRMNAME           CHAR(15) NOT NULL,
        PRIMARY KEY(FIRMNAME,DIVNAME,DEPTNAME,SECTIONID)
        FOREIGN KEY FKDEPARTMENT(FIRMNAME,DIVNAME,DEPTNAME)
            REFERENCES DEPARTMENT)
```

Figure R1-10. A tree structure

Exercises

Write the SQL CREATE statements for the following data models.

a.

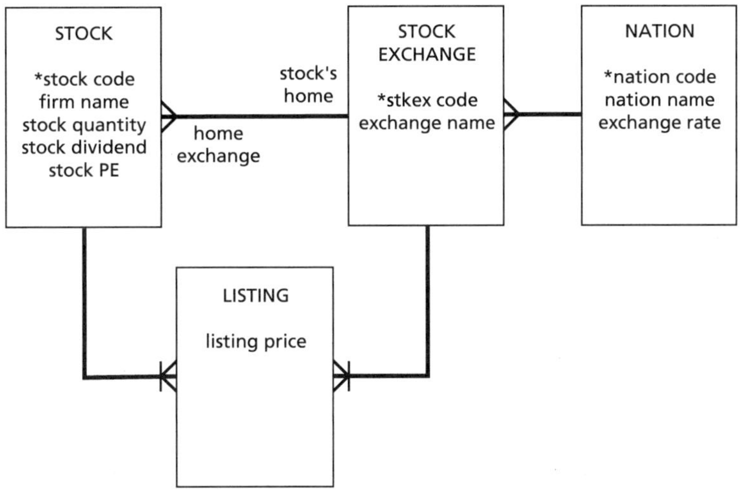

b.

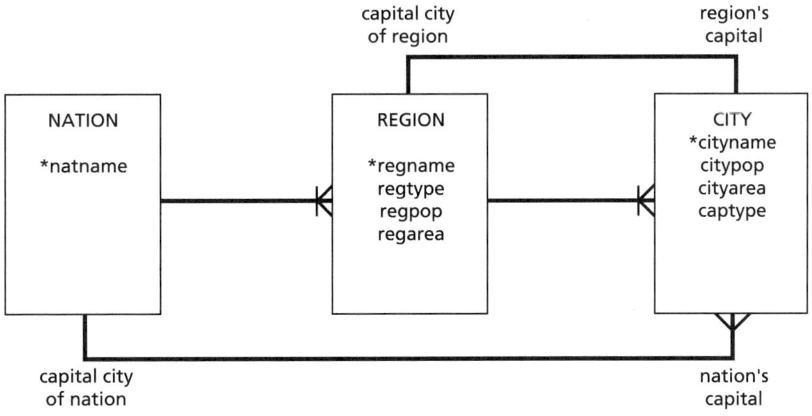

c.

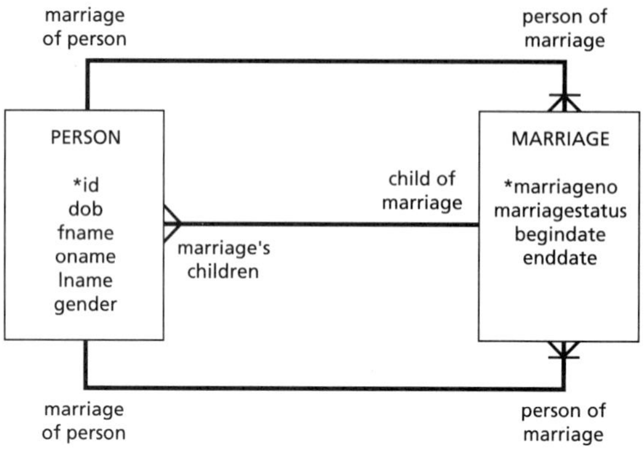
marriage
of person
person of
marriage
PERSON
*id
dob
fname
oname
lname
gender
child of
marriage
marriage's
children
MARRIAGE
*marriageno
marriagestatus
begindate
enddate
marriage
of person
person of
marriage

d.

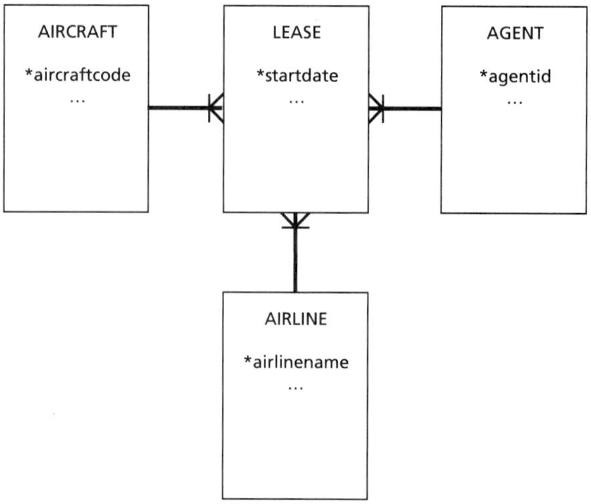
AIRCRAFT
*aircraftcode
...
LEASE
*startdate
...
AGENT
*agentid
...
AIRLINE
*airlinename
...

e.

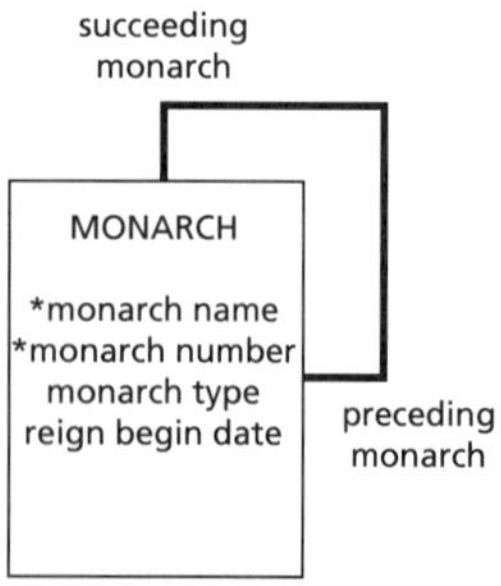
succeeding
monarch
MONARCH
*monarch name
*monarch number
monarch type
reign begin date
preceding
monarch

8

Normalization and Other Data Modeling Methods

There are many paths to the top of the mountain, but the view is always the same.
Chinese Proverb

Learning objectives

Students completing this chapter will

- ❖ understand the process of normalization;
- ❖ be able to distinguish between different normal forms;
- ❖ recognize that different data modeling approaches, while they differ in representation methods, are essentially identical.

Introduction

There are often many ways to solve a problem, and different methods frequently produce essentially the same solution. When this is the case, the goal is to find the most efficient path. We believe that data modeling, as you have learned it in the preceding chapters, is an efficient and easily learned approach to database design. There are, however, other paths to consider. One of these methods, normalization, was the initial approach to database design. It was developed as part of the theoretical foundation of the relational data model. It is useful to understand the key theoretical ideas of normalization because they advance your understanding of the relational model. Experience and research indicate, however, that normalization is more difficult to master than data modeling.

Data modeling first emerged as entity-relationship (E-R) modeling in a paper by Chen.[1] He introduced two key database design concepts:

1. Chen, P. 1976. The entity-relationship model—toward a unified view of data. *ACM Transactions on Database Systems* 1 (1):9–36.

- Identify entities and the relationships between them;
- A graphical representation improves design communication.

Chen's core concepts spawned many species of data modeling.To give you an appreciation of the variation in data modeling approaches, we briefly review Chen's E-R approach and IDEF1X, an approach used by the Department of Defense.

Normalization

Normalization is a method for increasing the quality of database design. It is also a theoretical base for defining the properties of relations. The theory gradually developed to create an understanding of the desirable properties of a relation. The goal of normalization is identical to that of data modeling—a high-fidelity design. The need for normalization seems to have arisen from the conversion of file systems into database format. Often, analysts started with the old file design and used normalization to design the new database. Now, designers are more likely to start with a clean slate and use data modeling.

Normal forms can be arrived at in several ways. The recommended approach is data modeling as experience strongly indicates people find it is an easier approach to database design. If the principles of data modeling are followed faithfully, then the outcome should be a high-fidelity model and a normalized database. In other words, if you model data correctly, you create a normalized design. Nevertheless, modeling mistakes can occur, and normalization is a useful crosscheck for ensuring the soundness of a data model. Normalization also provides a theoretical underpinning to data modeling.

Normalization gradually converts a file design into normal form by successive application of rules to move the design from first to fifth normal form. But before we look at these steps, it is useful to learn about functional dependency.[2]

Functional dependency

A **functional dependency** is a relationship between attributes in an entity. It simply means that one or more attributes determine the value of another. For example, given a stock's code you can determine its current PE ratio. In other words, PE ratio is functionally dependent on stock code. In addition, stock name, stock price, stock quantity, and stock dividend are functionally dependent on stock code. The notation for indicating that stock code functionally determines stock name is

stock code $\rightarrow$ stock name

An identifier functionally determines all the attributes in an entity. That is, if we know the value of stock code, then we can determine the value of stock name, stock price, and so on.

---

2. This section is mainly based on Kent,W. 1983.A simple guide to five normal forms in relational database theory. *Communications of the ACM* 26 (2):120–125 and Date, C. J. 1995.*An introduction to database systems*. 6th ed. Reading, MA:Addison-Wesley.

Formulae, such as yield = stock dividend/stock price*100, are a form of functional dependency. In this case, we have

(stock dividend, stock price) $\rightarrow$ yield

This is an example of **full functional dependency** because yield can be determined only from both attributes.

An attribute, or set of attributes, that fully functionally determines another attribute is called a **determinant**. Thus, stock code is a determinant because it fully functionally determines stock PE. An identifier, usually called a key when discussing normalization, is a determinant. Unlike a key, a determinant need not be unique. For example, a university could have a simple fee structure where undergraduate courses are $500 and graduate courses are $750. Thus course type $\rightarrow$ fee. Since there are many undergraduate and graduate courses, course type is not unique for all records.

There are situations where a given value determines multiple values. This **multidetermination** property is denoted as A $\rightarrow\ \rightarrow$ B and reads 'A multidetermines B.' For instance, a department multidetermines course. If you know the department, you can determine the set of courses it offers. **Multivalued dependency** means that functional dependencies are multivalued.

Functional dependency is a property of a relation's data. We cannot determine functional dependency from the names of attributes or the current values. Sometimes, examination of a relation's data will indicate that a functional dependency does not exist, but it is by understanding the relationships between data elements that we determine functional dependency.

Functional dependency is a theoretical avenue for understanding relationships between attributes. If we have two attributes, say A and B, then three possible relations are possible, as shown in Table 8-1.

Table 8-1: Functional dependencies of two attributes

Relationship	Functional dependency	Relationship
They determine each other	A $\rightarrow$ B and B $\rightarrow$ A	1:1
One determines the other	A $\rightarrow$ B	1:m
They do not determine each other	A not$\rightarrow$ B and B not$\rightarrow$ A	m:m

One-to-one attribute relationship

Consider two attributes that determine each other (A $\rightarrow$ B and B $\rightarrow$ A), for instance a country's code and its name. Using the example of Switzerland, there is a 1:1 relationship between CH and Switzerland; CH $\rightarrow$ Switzerland and Switzerland $\rightarrow$ CH. When two attributes have a 1:1 relationship, they must occur together in at least one table in a database so that their equivalence is a recorded fact.

One-to-many attribute relationship

Examine the situation where one attribute determines another (i.e., A → B), but the reverse is not true (i.e., A not→ B), as is the case with country name and its currency unit. If you know a country's name you can determine its currency, but if you know the currency unit (e.g., the dollar) you cannot always determine the country (e.g., both France and Belgium use the franc). As a result, if A and B occur in the same table, then A must be the key. In our example, country name would be the key, and currency unit would be a nonkey column.

Many-to-many attribute relationship

The final case to investigate is when neither attribute determines the other (i.e., A not→ B and B not→ A). The relationship between country name and language is m:m. For example, Belgium has two languages (French and Flemish), and French is spoken in many countries. To record the m:m relationship between these attributes, a table containing both attributes as a composite key is required. This is essentially the associative entity created during data modeling when there is an m:m relationship between entities.

As you can understand from the preceding discussion, functional dependency is an explicit form of presenting some of the ideas you gained implicitly in earlier chapters on data modeling. The next step is to delve into another theoretical concept underlying the relational model—normal forms.

Normal forms

Normal forms describe a classification of relations. Initial work by Codd identified first (1NF), second (2NF), and third normal (3NF) forms. Later researchers added Boyce-Codd (BCNF), fourth (4NF), and fifth normal (5NF) forms. Normal forms are stacked like a set of Russian dolls, with the innermost doll, 1NF, contained within all other normal forms. The hierarchy of normal forms is 5NF, 4NF, BCNF, 3NF, 2NF, and 1NF. Thus, 5NF is the outermost doll.

A new normal form, domain/key normal form (DK/NF), appeared in 1981. When a relation is in DK/NF, there are no modification anomalies. Conversely, any relation that is free of anomalies must be in DK/NF. The difficult part is discovering how to convert a relation to DK/NF.

First normal form

*A relation is in **first normal form** if and only if all columns are single-valued.* In other words, 1NF form states that all occurrences of a row must have the same number of columns. In data modeling terms, this means that an attribute must have a single value. An attribute that can have multiple values must be represented as a 1:m relationship. At a minimum, a data model will be in 1NF because all attributes of an entity are required to be single-valued.

Second normal form

Second normal form is violated when a nonkey column is dependent on a component of the primary key. This can also be stated as *a relation is in **second normal form** if and only if it is in first normal form, and all non key columns are dependent on the key.*

Consider Table 8-2. The primary key of ORDER is a composite of ITEMNO and CUSTOMERID. The problem is that CUSTOMER-CREDIT is a fact about CUSTOMERID (part of the composite key) rather than the full key (ITEMNO+CUSTOMERID), or in other words, it is not fully functionally dependent on the primary key. An insert anomaly arises when you try to add a new customer to ORDER. You cannot add a customer until that person places an order because until then you have no value for item number, and part of the primary key will be null. Clearly, this is neither an acceptable business practice nor an acceptable data management procedure.

Analyzing this problem, you realize an item can be in many orders, and a customer can order many items — an m:m relationship. By drawing the data model in Figure 8-1 you realize that CUSTOMER-CREDIT is an attribute of CUSTOMER, and you get the correct relational mapping.

Table 8-2: Second Normal Form Violation

ORDER			
ITEMNO	CUSTOMERID	QUANTITY	CUSTOMER-CREDIT
12	57	25	OK
34	679	3	POOR

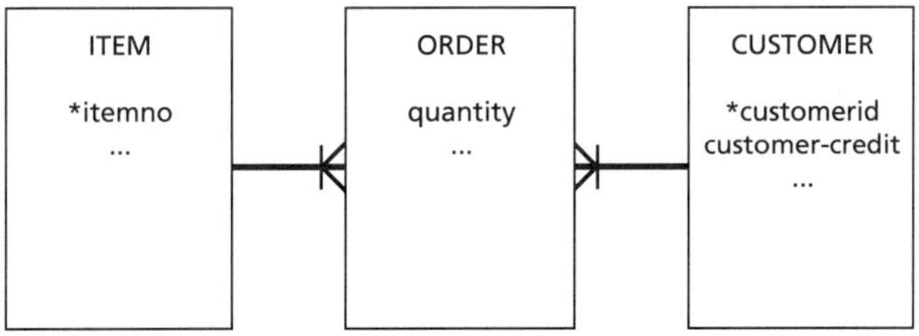

Figure 8-1. Resolving second normal form violation

Third normal form

Third normal form is violated when a nonkey column is a fact about another nonkey column. Alternatively, *a relation is in **third normal form** if and only if it is in second normal form and has no transitive dependencies.*

The problem in Table 8-3 is that EXCHANGE RATE is a fact about NATION, a nonkey field. In the language of functional dependency, EXCHANGE RATE is not fully functionally dependent on STOCK CODE, the primary key. The functional dependencies are STOCK-CODE → NATION → EXCHANGE RATE. In other words, EXCHANGE RATE is transitively[3] dependent on STOCK, since EXCHANGE RATE is dependent on NATION and NATION is dependent on STOCKCODE. The fundamental problem becomes very apparent when you try to add a new nation to the STOCK table. Until you buy at least one stock for that nation, you cannot insert it because you do not have a primary key. Similarly, if you delete MG from the STOCK table, details of the USA exchange rate are lost. There are modification anomalies.

When you think about the data relationships, you realize that a nation has many stocks and a stock belongs to only one nation. Now the data model and relational map can be created readily (see Figure 8-2).

Table 8-3: Third Normal Form Violation

STOCK		
STOCKCODE	NATION	EXCHANGE RATE
MG	USA	0.67
IR	AUS	0.46

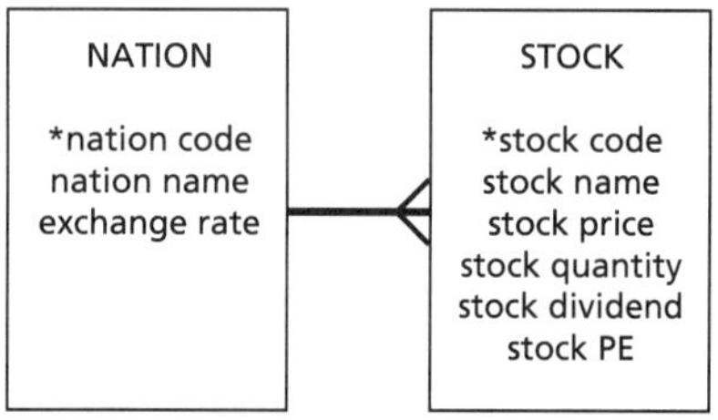

Figure 8-2. Resolving third normal form violation

Boyce-Codd Normal Form[4]

The original definition of 3NF did not cover a situation that, although rare, can occur. So **Boyce-Codd normal form**, a stronger version of 3NF, was developed. BCNF is necessary because 3NF does not cover the case when a relation

- has multiple candidate keys, where
- those candidate keys are composite, and
- the candidate keys overlap because they have at least one column in common.

3. Transitivity means that if one object bears a relation to a second object that bears the same relationship to a third object, then the first object bears this relationship to the third. For example, if $x=y$ and $y=z$, then $x=z$.
4. Based on Date, C. J. 1995. *An introduction to database systems*. 6th ed. Reading, MA: Addison-Wesley. p. 543.

Before considering an example, **candidate key** needs to be defined. Earlier we introduced the idea that an entity could have more than one unique identifier. These identifiers become candidate keys when the data model is mapped to a relational database. One of these candidates is selected as the primary key.

Consider the following case from a management consulting firm. A client can have many types of problems (e.g., finance, personnel), and the same problem type can be an issue for many clients. Consultants specialize and advise on only one problem type, but several consultants can advise on one problem type. A consultant advises a client. Furthermore, for each problem type, the client is advised by only one consultant. If you did not use data modeling, you might be tempted to create Table 8-4.

Table 8-4: Boyce-Codd normal form violation

ADVISOR		
CLIENT	PROBTYPE	CONSULTANT
Alpha	Marketing	Gomez
Alpha	Production	Raginiski

CLIENT cannot be the primary key because a client can have several problem types; however, a client is advised by only one consultant for a specific problem type, so the composite key CLIENT+PROBTYPE determines CONSULTANT. Also, because a consultant handles only one type of problem, the composite key CLIENT+CONSULTANT determines PROBTYPE. So, both of these composites are candidate keys. Either one can be selected as the primary key, and in this case, CLIENT+PROBTYPE was selected. Notice that all the previously stated conditions are satisfied — there are multiple, composite candidate keys that overlap. This means the table is 3NF, but not BCNF. This can be easily verified by considering what happens if the firm adds a new consultant. A new consultant cannot be added until there is a client — an insertion anomaly. The problem is that CONSULTANT is a determinant, CONSULTANT→ PROBTYPE, but is not a candidate key. In terms of the phrasing used earlier, the problem is that part of the key column is a fact about a nonkey column. The precise definition is ***a relation is in Boyce-Codd normal form if and only if every determinant is a candidate key.***

This problem is avoided by creating the correct data model (see Figure 8-3) and then mapping to a relational model.

Fourth normal form

Fourth normal form requires that a row should not contain two or more independent multivalued facts about an entity. This requirement is more readily understood after investigating an example.

Consider students who play sports and study subjects. One way of representing this information is shown in Table 8-5. Consider the consequence of trying to insert a student who did not play a sport. Sport would be null, and this is not permissible because part of the

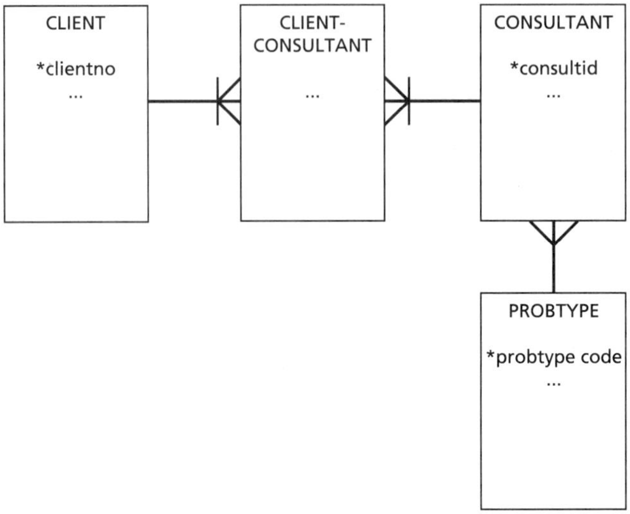

Figure 8-3. Resolving Boyce-Codd normal form violation

composite primary key would then be null — a violation of the entity integrity rule. You cannot add a new student until you know their sport and their subject. Modification anomalies are very apparent.

Table 8-5: Fourth normal form violation

STUDENT			
STUDENTID	SPORT	SUBJECT	...
50	Football	English	...
50	Football	Music	...
50	Tennis	Botany	...
50	Karate	Botany	...

This table is not in 4NF because sport and subject are independent multivalued facts about a student. There is no relationship between sport and subject. There is an indirect connection because sport and subject are associated with a student. In other words, a student can play many sports, and the same sport can be played by many students — an m:m relationship between student and sport. Similarly, there is an m:m relationship between student and subject. It makes no sense to store information about a student's sports and subjects in the same table because sport and subject are not related. The problem arises because sport and subject are multivalued dependencies of student. The solution is to convert multivalued dependencies to functional dependencies. More formally, *a relation is in **fourth normal form** if it is in Boyce-Codd normal form and all multivalued dependencies on the relation are functional dependencies.* A data model (see Figure 8-4) sorts out this problem although the correct relational mapping requires five tables.

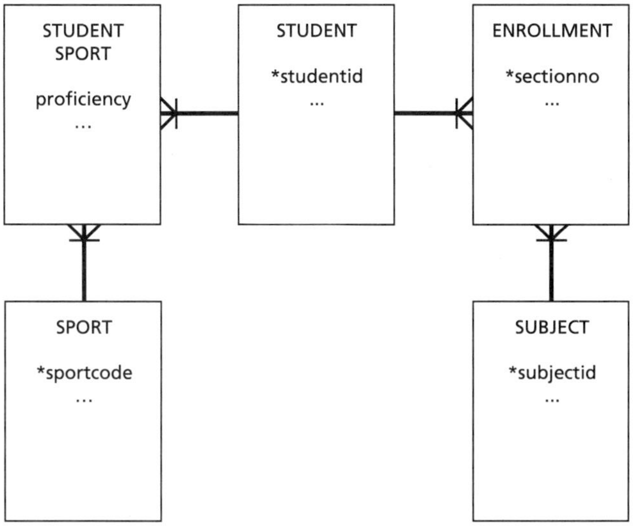

Figure 8-4. Resolving fourth normal form violation

Fifth normal form

Fifth normal form deals with the case where a table can be reconstructed from other tables. The reconstruction approach is preferred because it means less redundancy and fewer maintenance problems.

The consultants, firms, and skills problem is used to illustrate the concept of 5NF. The problem is that consultants provide skills to one or more firms and firms can use many consultants; a consultant has many skills and a skill can be used by many firms; and a firm can have a need for many skills and the same skill can be required by many firms. The data model (see Figure 8-5) for this problem has the ménage-à-trois structure introduced in Chapter 7.

The relational mapping of the three-way relationships results in four tables, with the associative entity ASSIGNMENT mapping shown in Table 8-6.

The table is in 5NF because the combination of all three columns is required to identify which consultants supply which firms with which skills. For example, we see that Tan advises IBM on database and Apple on data communications. The data in this table cannot be reconstructed from other tables.

Table 8-6 is not in 5NF if there is a rule of the following form: if a consultant has a certain skill (e.g., database) and has a contract with a firm that requires that skill (e.g., IBM), then the consultant advises that firm on that skill (i.e., he advises IBM on database). Notice that this rule means we can infer a relationship, and we no longer need the combination of the

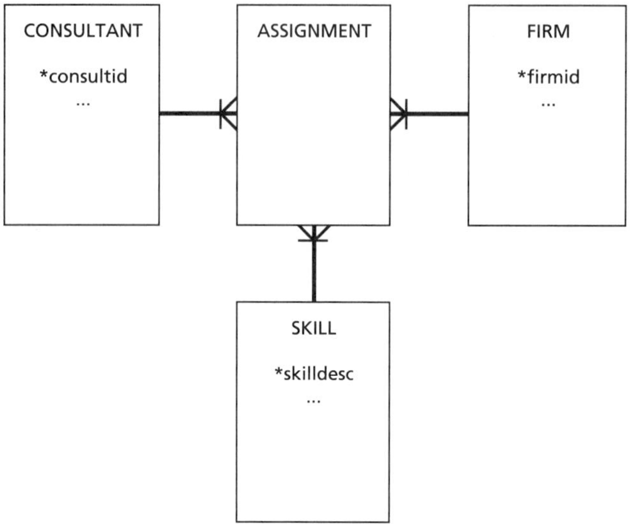

Figure 8-5. The CONSULTANT-FIRM-SKILL data model without a rule

three columns. As a result, we break the single three-entity m:m relationship into three two-entity m:m relationships. The revised data model is shown in Figure 8-6.

Table 8-6: The Relation Table ASSIGNMENT

ASSIGNMENT		
CONSULTID	FIRMID	SKILLDESC
Tan	IBM	Database
Tan	Apple	Data Comm

Further understanding of 5NF is gained by examining the relational tables resulting from these three associative entities. Notice the names given to each of the associative entities. CONTRACT records data about the firms a consultant advises; ADVISE describes the skills a consultant has; and REQUIRE stores data about the types of skills each firm requires. To help understand this problem, examine Table 8-7, Table 8-8, and Table 8-9.

Consider the results of joining CONTRACT and ADVISE, the outcome of which we call COULD ADVISE (see Table 8-10) because it lists skills the consultant could provide if the firm required them. For example, Tan has skills in database and data communications, and Tan has a contract with IBM. If IBM required database skills, Tan could handle it. We need to look at REQUIRE to determine if IBM requires advice on database; it does not.

The join of COULD ADVISE with REQUIRE gives details of a firm's skill needs that a consultant can provide. The table named CAN ADVISE (see Table 8-11) is constructed by directly joining the tables CONTRACT, ADVISE, and REQUIRE. Because we can construct CAN ADVISE from three other tables, the data are in 5NF.

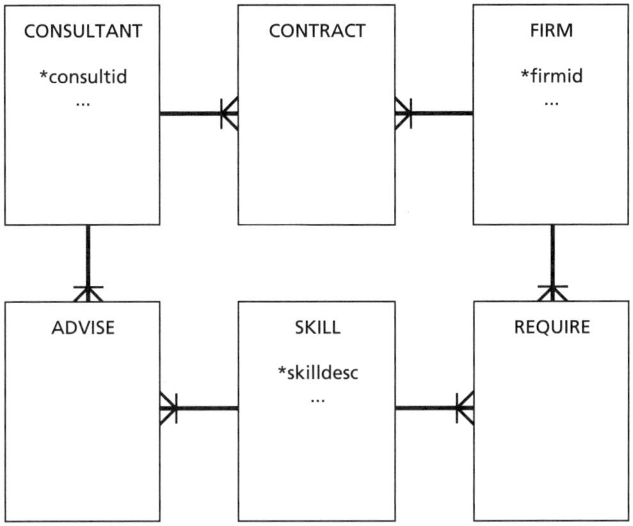

Figure 8-6. Revised data model after the introduction of the rule

Table 8-7: Relational Table CONTRACT

CONTRACT	
CONSULTID	FIRMID
Gonzales	Apple
Gonzales	IBM
Gonzales	NEC
Tan	IBM
Tan	NEC
Wood	Apple

Table 8-8: Relational Table ADVISE

ADVISE	
CONSULTID	SKILLDESC
Gonzales	Database
Gonzales	Data comm
Gonzales	Groupware
Tan	Database
Tan	Data comm
Wood	Data comm

Table 8-9: Relational Table REQUIRE

REQUIRE	
FIRMID	SKILLDESC
IBM	Data comm
IBM	Groupware
NEC	Data comm
NEC	Database
NEC	Groupware
Apple	Data comm

Table 8-10: Relational Table COULD ADVISE

COULD ADVISE		
CONSULTID	FIRMID	SKILLDESC
Gonzales	Apple	Database
Gonzales	Apple	Data comm
Gonzales	Apple	Groupware
Gonzales	IBM	Database
Gonzales	IBM	Data comm
Gonzales	IBM	Groupware
Gonzales	NEC	Database
Gonzales	NEC	Data comm
Gonzales	NEC	Groupware
Tan	IBM	Database
Tan	IBM	Data comm
Tan	NEC	Database
Tan	NEC	Data comm
Wood	Apple	Data comm

Table 8-11: Relational Table CAN ADVISE

CAN ADVISE		
CONSULTID	FIRMID	SKILLDESC
Gonzales	IBM	Data comm
Gonzales	IBM	Groupware
Gonzales	NEC	Database
Gonzales	NEC	Data comm
Gonzales	NEC	Groupware
Tan	IBM	Data comm
Tan	NEC	Database
Tan	NEC	Data comm
Wood	Apple	Data comm

Since data are stored in three separate tables, updating is easier. Consider the case where IBM requires database skills. We only need to add one row to REQUIRE to record this fact. In the case of CAN ADVISE, we would have to add two rows, one for Gonzales and one for Tan.

Now we can give 5NF a more precise definition: ***a relation is in fifth normal form** if and only if every join dependency of the relation is a consequence of the candidate keys of the relation.*

Up to this point, data modeling has enabled you to easily avoid normalization problems. Fifth normal form introduces a complication, however. How can you tell when to use a single three-way associative entity or three two-way associative entities? If there is a constraint or rule that is applied to the relationships between entities, consider the possibility of three two-way associative entities. Question the client carefully whenever you find a ménage à trois. Check to see that there are no rules or special conditions.

Domain key/normal form

The definition of DK/NF builds on three terms: key, constraint, and domain.[5] You already know a key is a unique identifier. A **constraint** is a rule governing attribute values. It must be sufficiently well-defined so that its truth can be readily evaluated. Referential integrity constraints, functional dependencies, and data validation rules are examples of constraints. A **domain** is a set of all values of the same data type (see page 226 for more detail). With the help of these terms, the concept of DK/NF is easily stated. *A relation is in domain key/normal form if and only if every constraint on the relation is a logical consequence of the domain constraints and the key constraints that apply to the relation.*

Note that DK/NF does not involve ideas of dependency; it just relies on the concepts of key, constraint, and domain. The problem with DK/NF is that while it is conceptually simple, no algorithm has been developed for converting relations to DK/NF. Hence database designers must rely on their skills to create relations that are DK/NF.

Conclusion

Normalization provides designers with a theoretical basis for understanding what they are doing when modeling data. It also alerts them to be aware of problems which they might not ordinarily detect when modeling. For example, 5NF cautions designers to investigate carefully situations (i.e., look for special rules) when their data model contains a ménage-à-trois.

5. Fagin, R. 1981. A normal form for relational databases that is based on domains and keys. *ACM Transactions of Database Systems* 6 (3):387–415.

Knowledge sharing could have avoided tire problem

The disastrous combination of Ford Explorers and Firestone tires could have been prevented if knowledge sharing between the two companies had taken place. By failing to share information, the necessary facts were not available to both Ford and Firestone for them to determine that there was a major problem.

The ironic fact is the over the past few years, Ford has developed an extremely successful knowledge sharing practice which has saved the company over $850 million. The Best Practices Replication Process involves more than 2,800 proven cost or time saving practices that are available on a company Web site to all plants.

However, with a company the size of Ford where knowledge tends to be widely dispersed, sharing all the available information both within and outside the company is a difficult task to enforce.

Source: Stewart, T. A. 2000. Knowledge worth $1.25 billion. *Fortune*, Nov 27, http://www.fortune.com/indexw.jhtml?channel=artcol.jhtml&doc_id=00000145.

Other data modeling methods

As mentioned previously, there are many species of data modeling. Here we consider two methods.

The E-R model

One of the most widely known data modeling methods is the entity-relationship model (E-R model) developed by Chen.[6] There is no standard for the E-R model, and it has been extended and modified in a number of ways.

As Figure 8-7 shows, an E-R model looks like the data models with which you are now familiar. Entities are shown by rectangles, and relationships are depicted by diamonds within which the cardinality of the relationship is indicated (e.g., there is a 1:m relationship between NATION and STOCK EXCHANGE). Cardinality can be 1:1, 1:m (conventionally shown as 1:N in E-R diagrams), and m:m (shown as M:N). Recursive relationships are also readily modeled. One important difference is that an m:m relationship is not shown as an associative entity; thus the database designer must convert this relationship to a table.

Attributes are shown as ellipses connected to the entity or relationship to which they belong (e.g., *stock name* is an attribute of STOCK). If the diagram becomes too cluttered, attributes may be listed below the entity or somewhere else on the diagram. Relationships are named, and the name is shown above or below the relationship symbol. For example, LISTING is the name of the m:m relationship between STOCK and STOCK EXCHANGE.

6. Chen, P. 1976. The entity-relationship model—toward a unified view of data. *ACM Transactions on Database Systems* 1 (1):9–36.

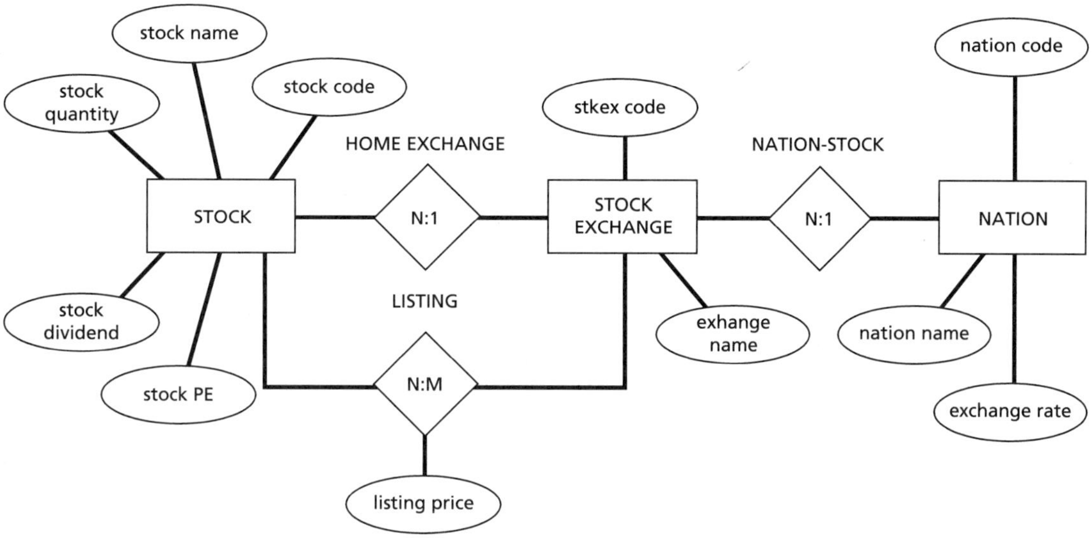

Figure 8-7. An entity-relationship (E-R) diagram

IDEF1X

IDEF1X[7] was conceived in the late 1970s and refined in the early 1980s. It is based on the work of Codd and Chen. A quick look at some of the fundamental ideas of IDEF1X will show you how similar it is to the method you have learned. Entities are represented in a similar manner, as Figure 8-8 shows.The representation is a little different (e.g., the name of the entity is outside the rectangle), but the information is the same.

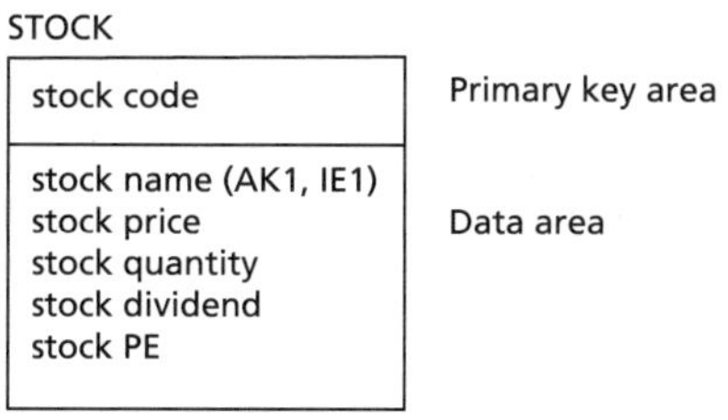

Figure 8-8. An entity

IDEF1X adds additional notation to an attribute to indicate whether it is an alternate key or inversion entry. An **alternate key** is a possible primary key (identifier) that was not se-

7. Bruce, T.A. 1992. *Designing quality databases with IDEF1X information models*. New York, NY: Dorset House.

lected as the primary key. *Stock name*, assuming it is unique, is an alternate key. An **inversion entry** indicates a likely frequent way of accessing the entity, and so it should become an index (page 322). For instance, the entity may be frequently accessed via *stock name*. Alternate keys are shown as AK1, AK2, ... and inversion entries as IE1, IE2, ... Thus, *stock name* is both an alternate key and inversion entry.

The representation of relationships is also identical, except that a dot is used rather than a crow's foot, as illustrated in Figure 8-9. Also, notice that relationships are described, whereas you learned to describe only relationships when they are not readily inferred.

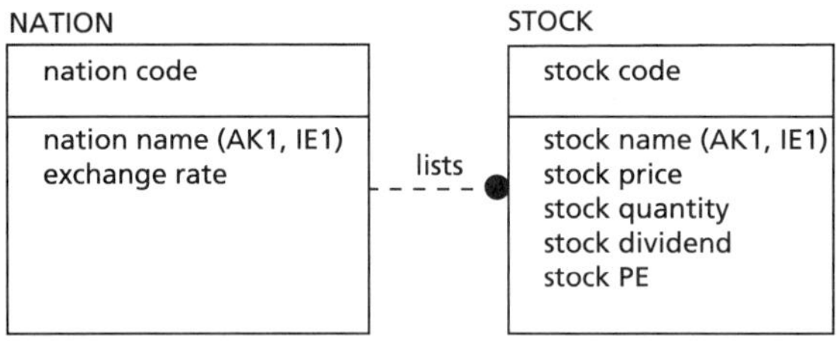

Figure 8-9. A relationship

IDEF1X also incorporates a generalization hierarchy (see page 177).

Representing relationships

The various dialects of data modeling are most distinctive in the ways in which relationships are represented (see Table 8-13). Entities are almost always shown as rectangles. Before considering how different variations of data modeling represent relationships, we need to examine two extensions that add more detail to a data model.

Mandatory and optional relationships

Some modeling languages require specifying whether a relationship is mandatory or optional. By asking the question, "Does an occurrence of this entity require an occurrence of the other entity?" you can assess whether an entity is mandatory. For example, in a relationship between a sales order and an item, it is mandatory that a sales order have a related item but optional that an item is related to a sales order because some items might not have been sold. The usual practice is to use O for optional and place it near the entity that is optional. Mandatory relationships are sometimes indicated by a short line (or bar) at right angles to the arc for the relationship between the entities.[8]

8. In the data modeling method you have learned, the bar has a different meaning.

Cardinality

Some data modeling languages are quite precise in specifying the cardinality or multiplicity of a relationship (see Table 8-12). Thus, in a 1:m relationship you might see additional information on the diagram. For example, the many end of the relationship might contain notation (such as 0,n) to indicate zero or more instances of the entity at the many end of the relationship. If an entity is optional, the minimum cardinality will be 0, and if mandatory, the minimum cardinality is 1.

Table 8-12: Cardinality options

Cardinality		Meaning
0,1	Optional	There can be zero or one occurrence of the entity relative to the other entity
0,n		There can be zero or many occurrences of the entity relative to the other entity
1,1	Mandatory	One occurrence of the entity has one occurrence relative to the other entity
1,n		One occurrence of the entity can have many occurrences relative to the other entity

The data modeling method of this text, as you now realize, has taken a broad approach to cardinality (is it 1:1 or 1:m?). We have not been concerned with greater precision (is it 0,1 or 1,1?) because the focus has been on acquiring basic data modeling skills. Once you know how to model, you can add more detail. When learning to model, too much detail and too much terminology can get in the way of mastering this difficult skill. Also, it is far easier to sketch models on a whiteboard or paper when you have less to draw. Once you switch to a data modeling tool, then adding cardinality precision is easier and appropriate.

As Table 8-13 clearly illustrates, there is a lack of consistency across various data modeling diagramming techniques, particularly for weak entities. However, you should have few problems adapting to another approach since the fundamental concepts of data modeling do not vary—only the method of representing these concepts changes.

Conclusion

The underlying concepts of different data modeling methods are very similar. They all have the same goal: improving the quality of database design. They share common concepts such as entity and relationship mapping. We have adopted an approach that is simple and effective. The method can be learned rapidly, and novice users can create high-quality models. Also, if you have learned one data modeling method, you can quickly adapt to the nuances of other methods. Interestingly, Microsoft uses a method very similar to ours in documentation of its database package, Access.

Table 8-13: Data modeling dialects

Relationship	Dialect	Diagram	Comments or alternate form
1:1	This text		
	E-R	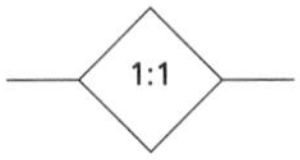	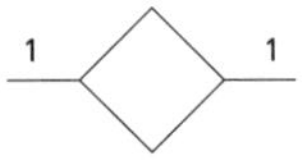
	IDEF1X	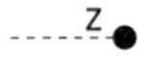	A "Z" placed beside the dot indicates a cardinality of 0 or 1.
	PowerDesigner[a]	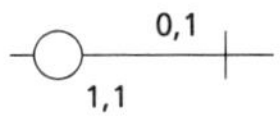	The circle indicates the left relationship is optional. The bar indicates the right relationship is mandatory.
1:m	This text	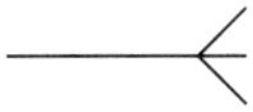	
	E-R	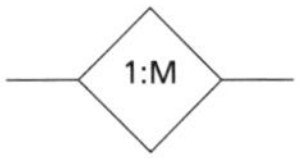	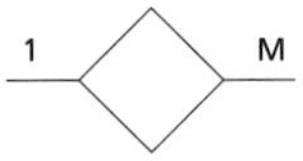
	IDEF1X		
	PowerDesigner	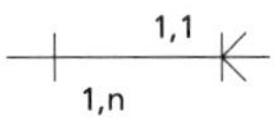	The bars indicate the relationships are mandatory.
m:m	This text		Convert to an associative entity.
	E-R		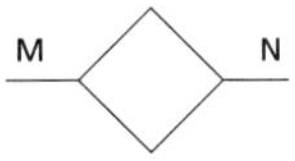
	IDEF1X		Convert to an associative entity.
	PowerDesigner		Convert to an associative entity.
weak entity (1:m)	This text		
	E-R	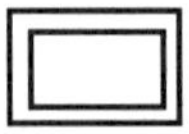	A weak entity is shown as a boxed rectangle.
	IDEF1X		A solid line indicates the entity at the dot end is weak.
	PowerDesigner	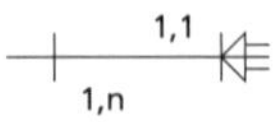	A triangle points away from the weak entity.

a. PowerDesigner (www.sybase.com/products/designtools/powerdesigner) is a data modeling tool.

Summary

Normalization gradually converts a file design into normal form by successive application of rules to move the design from first to fifth normal form. Functional dependency means that one or more attributes determine the value of another. An attribute, or set of attributes, that fully functionally determines another attribute is called a determinant. First normal form states that all occurrences of a row must have the same number of columns. Second normal form is violated when a nonkey column is a fact about a component of the prime key. Third normal form is violated when a nonkey column is a fact about another nonkey column. Boyce-Codd normal form is a stronger version of third normal form. Fourth normal form requires that a row should not contain two or more independent multivalued facts about an entity. Fifth normal form deals with the case where a table can be reconstructed from data in other tables. Fifth normal form arises when there are special rules or conditions. A high-fidelity data model will be of high normal form.

One of the most widely known methods of data modeling is the E-R model. The basic concepts of most data modeling methods are very similar: all aim to improve database design.

Key terms and concepts

Alternate key
Boyce-Codd normal form
Cardinality
Constraint
Data model
Determinant
Domain
Entity
Entity-relationship (E-R) model
Fifth normal form
First normal Form
Fourth normal form
Full functional dependency
Functional dependency
Generalization hierarchy
IDEF1X
Inversion entry
Mandatory
Many-to-many attribute relationship
Multidetermination
Multivalued dependency
Normalization
One-to-many attribute relationship
One-to-one attribute relationship
Optional
Relationship
Second normal form
Third normal form
Trigger

References and additional readings

Bruce, T. A. 1992. *Designing quality databases with IDEF1X information models*. New York, NY: Dorset House.

Chen, P. 1976. The entity-relationship model—toward a unified view of data. *ACM Transactions on Database Systems* 1 (1):9–36.

Hammer, M. 1990. Reengineering work: Don't automate, obliterate. *Harvard Business Review* 68 (4):104–112.

Kent, W. 1983. A simple guide to five normal forms in relational database theory. *Communications of the ACM* 26 (2):120-125.

Wetherbe, J. C. 1991. Executive information requirements: Getting it right. *MIS Quarterly* 15 (1):51–65.

Exercises

Short answers

1. What is normalization and what is its goal?
2. How does DK/NF differ from earlier normal forms?
3. How do E-R and IDEF1X differ from the data modeling method of this text?

Normalization and modeling

Using normalization, E-R, or IDEF1X, create data models from the following narratives, which are sometimes intentionally incomplete. You will have to make some assumptions. Make certain you state these alongside your data model. Define the identifier(s) and attributes of each entity.

1. The president of a book wholesaler has told you that she wants information about publishers, authors, and books.
2. A university has many subject areas (e.g., MIS, Romance languages). Professors teach in only one subject area, but the same subject area can have many professors. Professors can teach many different courses in their subject area. An offering of a course (e.g., Data Management 457, French 101) is taught by only one professor at a particular time.
3. Kids'n'Vans retails minivans for a number of manufacturers. Each manufacturer offers several models of its minivan (e.g., SE, LE, GT). Each model comes with a standard set of equipment (e.g., the Acme SE comes with wheels, seats, and an engine). Minivans can have a variety of additional equipment or accessories (radio, air conditioning, automatic transmission, airbag, etc.), but not all accessories are available for all minivans (e.g., not all manufacturers offer a driver's side airbag). Some sets of accessories are sold as packages (e.g., the luxury package might include stereo, six speakers, cocktail bar, and twin overhead foxtails).
4. Steve operates a cinema chain and has given you the following information:
   "I have many cinemas. Each cinema can have multiple theaters. Movies are shown throughout the day starting at 11 A.M. and finishing at 1 A.M. Each movie is given a two-hour time slot. We never show a movie in more than one theater at a time, but we do shift movies among theaters because seating capacity varies. I am interested in knowing how many people, classified by adults and children, attended each showing of a movie. I vary ticket prices by movie and time slot. For instance, *Lassie Get Lost* at 11 A.M. is 50 cents for everyone but is 75 cents at 11 P.M."
5. A telephone company offers a 10 percent discount to any customer who phones another person who is also a customer of the company. To be eligible for the discount, the pairing of the two phone numbers must be registered with the telephone company. Furthermore, for billing purposes the company records both phone numbers, start time, end time, and date of call.

9

The Relational Model

Nothing is so practical as a good theory.
K. Lewin, 1945

Learning objectives

On completion of this chapter, you will

- ❖ know the structures of the relational model;
- ❖ understand relational algebra commands;
- ❖ be able to determine whether a DBMS is completely relational.

Background

The relational model,[1] developed as a result of recognized shortcomings of hierarchical and network DBMSs, was introduced by Codd in 1970 in an article published in the *Communications of the ACM*.[2] Part of the practical value of the relational model is its strong theoretical base. As the model's major developer, Codd believed that a sound theoretical model would solve most practical problems that could potentially arise.

In another article,[3] Codd expounds the case for adopting the relational model over other database models. There is a threefold thrust to his argument. First, other database models force the application programmer to code at a low level of structural detail. As a result, application programs are more complex and take longer to write and debug. Second, no commands are provided for processing multiple records at one time. Other models do not provide the set processing capability of the relational model. The set processing feature means that queries can be more concisely expressed. Third, only the relational model,

---

1. Under the spiral approach to teaching data modeling and SQL, many aspects of the relational model were introduced earlier.This chapter consolidates and extends the earlier work to provide formal coverage of this most widely used database model.
2. Codd, E. F. 1970. A relational model for large shared data banks. *Communications of the ACM* 13 (6):377–387.
3. Codd, E. F. 1982. Relational database: A practical foundation for productivity. *Communications of the ACM* 25 (2):109–117.

through a query language such as SQL, recognizes the clients' need to make ad hoc queries. Adoption of the relational model and SQL permits an MIS department to respond far more rapidly to unanticipated requests. It can also mean that clients write and execute their own queries. Thus, Codd's assertion that the relational model is a practical tool for increasing the productivity of MIS departments is well founded.

The productivity increase arises from three of the objectives that drove Codd's research. The first objective was to provide a clearly delineated boundary between the logical and physical aspects of database management.[4] Application programmers could then be divorced from considerations of the physical representation of data. Codd labels this the **data independence objective**. The second objective was to create a simple model that was readily understood by a wide range of users and programmers. This **communicability objective** promotes effective and efficient communication between users and MIS personnel. The third objective was to increase processing capabilities from record-at-a-time to multiple records-at-a-time—the **set processing objective**. Achievement of these objectives means fewer lines of code are required to write an application program, and there is less ambiguity in client-analyst communication.

The relational model has three major components:

- data structures;
- integrity rules;
- operators used to retrieve, derive, or modify data.

Data structures

Like most theories, the relational model is based on some key structures or concepts. We need to understand these in order to understand the theory.

Domain

A **domain** is a set of values all of the same data type. For example, the domain of nation name is the set of all possible nation names. The domain of all stock prices is the set of all currency values in, say, the range $0 to $10,000,000. You can also think of a domain as all the legal values of an attribute.

In specifying a domain, you also need to think about the smallest unit of data for an attribute defined on that domain. In Chapter 7, we discussed how a candidate attribute should be examined to see if it should be segmented (e.g., we divide name into first name, other name, and last name, and maybe more). While it is unlikely that name will be a domain, it is likely that there will be a domain for first name, last name, and so on. Thus a domain contains values that are in their atomic state; they cannot be decomposed further.

The practical value of a domain is to define what comparisons are permissible. Only attributes drawn from the same domain should be compared; otherwise it is a bit like com-

4. This topic is covered in Section 3.

paring bananas and strawberries. For example, it makes no sense to compare a stock's PE ratio to its price. They do not measure the same thing; they belong to different domains. Although the domain concept is useful, it is rarely supported by relational model implementations.

Relations

A **relation** is a table of *n* columns (or attributes) and *m* rows (or tuples). Each column has a unique name, and all the values in a column are drawn from the same domain. Each row of the relation is uniquely identified. The order of columns and rows is immaterial.

The **cardinality** of a relation is its number of rows. The **degree** of a relation is the number of columns. For example, the relation NATION (see Figure 9-1) is of degree 3 and has a cardinality of 4. Because the cardinality of a relation changes every time a row is added or deleted, you can expect cardinality to change frequently. The degree changes if a column is added to a relation, but in terms of relational theory, it is considered to be a new relation. So, only a relation's cardinality changes.

Relational database

A **relational database** is a collection of relations or tables. The distinguishing feature of the relational model, when compared to the hierarchical and network models, is that there are no explicit linkages between tables. Tables are linked by common columns drawn on the same domain; thus the portfolio database (see Figure 9-1) consists of tables STOCK and NATION. The 1:m relationship between the two tables is represented by the column NATCODE that is common to both tables. Note that the two columns need not have the same name, but they must be drawn on the same domain so that comparison is possible. In the case of an m:m relationship, while a new table must be created to represent the relationship, the principle of linking tables through common columns on the same domain remains in force.

Primary key

A relation's **primary key** is its unique identifier; for example, the primary key of NATION is NATCODE. As you already know, a primary key can be a composite of several columns. The primary key guarantees that each row of a relation can be uniquely addressed. A primary key need not be indexed, though it often is.

Candidate key

In some situations, there may be several attributes—known as **candidate keys**—that are potential primary keys. NATCODE is unique in the NATION relation, for example. We also can be fairly certain that two nations will not have the same name. Therefore, NATION has multiple candidate keys: NATCODE and NATNAME.

NATION		
NATCODE	NATNAME	EXCHRATE
UK	United Kingdom	1.00
USA	United States	0.67
AUS	Australia	0.46
IND	India	0.0228

STOCK						
STKCODE	STKFIRM	STKPRICE	STKQTY	STKDIV	STKPE	*NATCODE*
FC	Freedonia Copper	27.50	10,529	1.84	16	UK
PT	Patagonian Tea	55.25	12,635	2.50	10	UK
AR	Abyssinian Ruby	31.82	22,010	1.32	13	UK
SLG	Sri Lankan Gold	50.37	32,868	2.68	16	UK
ILZ	Indian Lead &Zinc	37.75	6,390	3.00	12	UK
BE	Burmese Elephant	.07	154,713	0.01	3	UK
BS	Bolivian Sheep	12.75	231,678	1.78	11	UK
NG	Nigerian Geese	35.00	12,323	1.68	10	UK
CS	Canadian Sugar	52.78	4,716	2.50	15	UK
ROF	Royal Ostrich Farms	33.75	1,234,923	3.00	6	UK
MG	Minnesota Gold	53.87	816,122	1.00	25	USA
GP	Georgia Peach	2.35	387,333	.20	5	USA
NE	Narembeen Emu	12.34	45,619	1.00	8	AUS
QD	Queensland Diamond	6.73	89,251	.50	7	AUS
IR	Indooroopilly Ruby	15.92	56,147	.50	20	AUS
BD	Bombay Duck	25.55	167,382	1.00	12	IND

Figure 9-1. A relational database with tables NATION and STOCK

Alternate key

When there are multiple candidate keys, one is chosen as the primary key, and the remainder are known as **alternate keys**. In this case, we selected NATCODE as the primary key, and NATNAME is an alternate key.

Foreign key

The foreign key is an important concept of the relational model. It is the way relationships are represented and can be thought of as the glue that holds a set of tables together to form a relational database. A **foreign key** is an attribute (possibly composite) of a relation that is also a primary key of a relation. The foreign key and primary key may be in different relations or the same relation, but both keys should be drawn from the same domain.

Integrity rules

The integrity section of the relational model consists of two rules. The **entity integrity rule** ensures that each instance of an entity described by a relation is identifiable in some way. Its implementation means that each row in a relation can be uniquely distinguished. The rule is

No component of the primary key of a relation may be null.

Null in this case means that the component cannot be undefined or unknown; it must have a value. Notice that the rule says *component of a primary key*. This means every part of the primary key must be known; if a part cannot be defined, it implies that the particular entity it describes cannot be defined. In practical terms, it means you cannot add a nation to NATION unless you also define a value for NATCODE.

The definition of a foreign key implies that there is a corresponding primary key. The **referential integrity rule** ensures that this is the case. It states

A database must not contain any unmatched foreign key values.

Simply, this rule means that you cannot define a foreign key without first defining its matching primary key. In practical terms, it would mean you could not add a Canadian stock to the STOCK relation without first creating a row in NATION for Canada.

Notice that the concepts of foreign key and referential integrity are intertwined. There is not much sense in having foreign keys without having the referential integrity rule. Permitting a foreign key without a corresponding primary key means the relationship cannot be determined. Note that the referential integrity rule does not imply a foreign key cannot be null. There can be circumstances where a relationship does not exist for a particular instance, in which case the foreign key is null.

Manipulation languages

There are four approaches to manipulating relational tables, and you are already familiar with SQL and QBE. Less widely used manipulation languages are relational algebra and relational calculus. These languages are briefly discussed, with some attention given to relational algebra in the next section and SQL in the following chapter.

Relational algebra has a set of operations similar to traditional algebra (e.g., add and multiply) for manipulating tables. While relational algebra can be used to resolve queries, it is seldom employed because it requires you to specify what you want and how to get it. That is, you have to specify the operations on each table. This makes relational algebra more difficult to use than SQL, where the focus is on specifying what is wanted.

Relational calculus overcomes some of the shortcomings of relational algebra by concentrating on what is required. In other words, there is less need to specify how the query will operate. Relational calculus is classified as a nonprocedural language because you do not have to be overly concerned with the procedures by which a result is determined.

Unfortunately, relational calculus can be difficult to learn, and as a result language designers developed **SQL** and **QBE**, which are nonprocedural and more readily mastered. You have already gained some skills in SQL and have had some exposure to QBE. Although QBE is generally easier to use than SQL, MIS professionals need to master SQL for two reasons. First, SQL is frequently embedded in other programming languages, a feature not available with QBE. Second, it is very difficult, or impossible, to express some queries in QBE (e.g., divide). Because SQL is important, it is the focus of the next chapter.

QBE commands are translated to SQL prior to execution, and many systems allow you to view the generated SQL. This can be handy. You can use QBE to generate a portion of the SQL for a complex query and then edit the generated code to fine-tune the query.

Relational algebra

The relational model includes a set of operations (see Table 9-1), known as relational algebra, for manipulating relations. Relational algebra is a standard for judging data retrieval languages. If a retrieval language, such as SQL, can be used to express every relational algebra operator, it is said to be **relationally complete**.

Table 9-1: Relational algebra operators

Restrict	Creates a new table from specified rows of an existing table.
Project	Creates a new table from specified columns of an existing table.
Product	Creates a new table from all the possible combinations of rows of two existing tables.
Union	Creates a new table containing rows appearing in one or both tables of two existing tables.
Intersect	Creates a new table containing rows appearing in both tables of two existing tables.
Difference	Creates a new table containing rows appearing in one table but not in the other of two existing tables.
Join	Creates a new table containing all possible combinations of rows of two existing tables satisfying the join condition.
Divide	Creates a new table containing x_i such that the pair (x_i, y_i) exists in the first table for every y_i in the second table.

There are eight relational algebra operations that can be used with either one or two relations to create a new relation. The assignment operator (:=) indicates the name of the new relation. The relational algebra statement to create relation A, the union of relations B and C, is expressed as

```
A := B UNION C
```

Before we begin our discussion of each of the eight operators, note that the first two—restrict and project—operate on a single relation and the rest require two relations.

Restrict

Restrict extracts specified rows from a single relation. As the shaded rows in Figure 9-2 depict, restrict takes a horizontal slice through a relation.

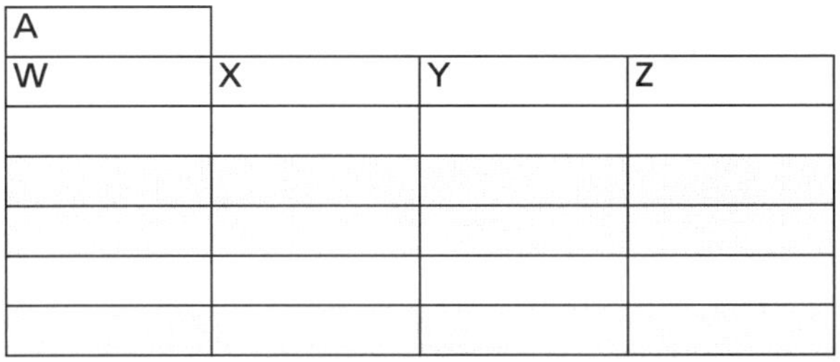

Figure 9-2. Relational operation restrict—a horizontal slice

The relational algebra command to create the new relation using restrict is

```
tablename WHERE column1 theta column2
OR
tablename WHERE column1 theta literal
```

where theta can be =, <>, >, ≥, <, or ≤.

For example, the following relational algebra command creates a new table from STOCK containing all rows with a nation code of US:

```
USSTOCK := STOCK WHERE NATCODE = 'US'
```

You will sometimes see restrict referred to as select. Nowadays, to avoid confusion with SQL's SELECT statement, restrict is the preferred term.

Project

Project extracts specified columns from a table. As Figure 9-3 shows, project takes a vertical slice through a table.

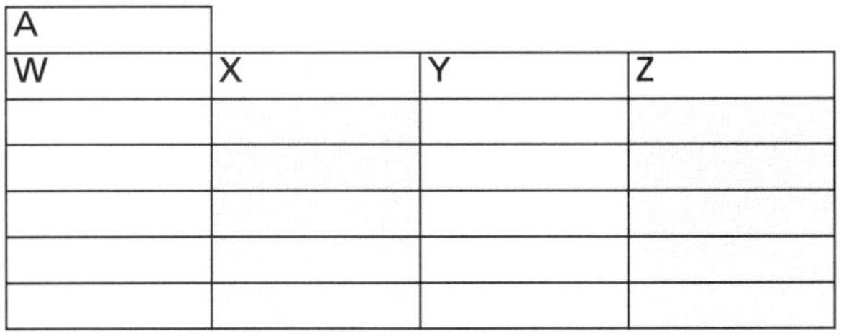

Figure 9-3. Relational operator project—a vertical slice

The relational algebra command to create the new relation using project is

```
TABLENAME [COLUMNNAME, …]
```

So, in order to create a new table from NATION that contains the nation's name and its exchange rate, for example, you would use this relational algebra command:

```
RATES := NATION[NATNAME, EXCHRATE]
```

Product

Product creates a new relation from all possible combinations of rows in two other relations. It is sometimes called TIMES or MULTIPLY. The relational command to create the product of two tables is

```
tablename1 TIMES tablename2
```

The operation of product is illustrated in Figure 9-4, which shows the result of A TIMES B.

A	
V	W
v_1	w_1
v_2	w_2
v_3	w_3

B		
X	Y	Z
x_1	y_1	z_1
x_2	y_2	z_2

A TIMES B				
V	W	X	Y	Z
v_1	w_1	x_1	y_1	z_1
v_1	w_1	x_2	y_2	z_2
v_2	w_2	x_1	y_1	z_1
v_2	w_2	x_2	y_2	z_2
v_3	w_3	x_1	y_1	z_1
v_3	w_3	x_2	y_2	z_2

Figure 9-4. Relational operator product

Union

The **union** of two relations is a new relation containing all rows appearing in one or both relations. The two relations must be **union compatible,** which means they have the same column names, in the same order, and drawn on the same domains. Duplicate rows are automatically eliminated—they must be, or the relational model is no longer satisfied. The relational command to create the union of two tables is

```
tablename1 UNION tablename2
```

Union is illustrated in Figure 9-5. Notice that corresponding columns in tables A and B have the same names. While the sum of the number of rows in relations A and B is five, the union contains four rows because one row (x_2, y_2) is common to both relations.

A	
X	Y
x_1	y_1
x_2	y_2
x_3	y_3

B	
X	Y
x_2	y_2
x_4	y_4

A UNION B	
X	Y
x_1	y_1
x_2	y_2
x_3	y_3
x_4	y_4

Figure 9-5. Relational operator product

Intersect

The **intersection of** two relations is a new relation containing all rows appearing in both relations. The two relations must be union compatible. The relational command to create the intersection of two tables is

```
tablename1 INTERSECT tablename2
```

The result of A INTERSECT B is one row, because only one row (x_2, y_2) is common to both relations A and B (see Figure 9-6)

A	
X	Y
x_1	y_1
x_2	y_2
x_3	y_3

B	
X	Y
x_2	y_2
x_4	y_4

A INTERSECT B	
X	Y
x_2	y_2

Figure 9-6. Relational operator intersect

Difference

The **difference** of two relations is a new relation containing all rows appearing in the first relation but not in the second. The two relations must be union compatible. The relational command to create the difference of two tables is

```
TABLENAME1 MINUS TABLENAME2
```

The result of A MINUS B is two rows (see Figure 9-7). Both of these rows are in relation A but not in relation B. The row containing (x_2, y_2) appears in both A and B and thus is not in A MINUS B.

A	
X	Y
x_1	y_1
x_2	y_2
x_3	y_3

B	
X	Y
x_2	y_2
x_4	y_4

A minus B	
X	Y
x_1	y_1
x_3	y_3

Figure 9-7. Relational operator difference

Join

Join creates a new relation from two relations for all combinations of rows satisfying the join condition. The general format of join is

```
tablename1 JOIN tablename2 WHERE tablename1.columnname1 theta
   tablename2.columnname2
```

where theta can be =, <>, >, ≥, <, or ≤.

Figure 9-8 illustrates A JOIN B where W=Z, which is an equijoin because theta is an equals sign. Tables A and B are matched when values in columns W and Z in each relation are equal. The matching columns should be drawn from the same domain. You can also think of join as a product followed by restrict on the resulting relation. So the join can be written

```
(A TIMES B) WHERE W THETA Z
```

Divide

Divide is the hardest relational operator to understand. Division requires that A and B have a set of attributes, in this case Y, that are common to both relations. Conceptually, A divided by B asks the question, "Is there a value in the X column of A (e.g., x_1) that has a

A	
V	W
v_1	wz_1
v_2	wz_2
v_3	wz_3

B		
X	Y	Z
x_1	y_1	wz_1
x_2	y_2	wz_3

A EQUIJOIN B				
V	W	X	Y	Z
v_1	wz_1	x_1	y_1	wz_1
v_3	wz_3	x_2	y_2	wz_3

Figure 9-8. Relational operator join

value in the Y column of A for every value of y in the Y column of B?" Look first at B, where the Y column has values y_1 and y_2. When you examine the X column of A, you find there are rows (x_1, y_1) and (x_1, y_2). That is, for x_1, there is a value in the Y column of A for every value of y in the Y column of B. Thus, the result of the division is a new relation with a single row and column containing the value x_1 (see Figure 9-9).

A	
X	Y
x_1	y_1
x_1	y_3
x_1	y_2
x_2	y_1
x_3	y_3

B
Y
y_1
y_2

A DIVIDE B
X
x_1

Figure 9-9. Relational operator divide

Querying with relational algebra

A few queries will give you a taste of how you might use relational algebra. To assist in understanding these queries, the answer is expressed, side-by-side, in both relational algebra (on the left) and SQL (on the right).

❍ **List all data in share.**

A very simple report of all columns in the table SHR.

SHR	SELECT * FROM SHR

❍ **Report a firm's name and price-earnings ratio.**

A PROJECTION of two columns from SHR.

SHR [SHRFIRM, SHRPE]	SELECT SHRFIRM, SHRPE FROM SHR

❍ **Get all shares with a price-earnings ratio less than 12.**

A RESTRICTION of SHR on column SHRPE.

SHR WHERE SHRPE < 12	SELECT * FROM SHR WHERE SHRPE < 12

❍ **List details of firms where the share holding is at least 100,000.**

A RESTRICTION and PROJECTION combined. Notice that the restriction is expressed within parentheses.

(SHR WHERE SHRQTY >= 100000) [SHRFIRM, SHRPRICE, SHRQTY, SHRDIV]	SELECT SHRFIRM, SHRPRICE, SHRQTY, SHRDIV FROM SHR WHERE SHRQTY >= 100000

❍ **Find all shares where the PE is 12 or higher and the share holding is less than 10,000.**

INTERSECT is used with two RESTRICTIONs to identify shares satisfying both conditions.

(SHR WHERE SHRPE >=12) INTERSECT (SHR WHERE SHRQTY < 10000)	SELECT * FROM SHR WHERE SHRPE >= 12 AND SHRQTY < 10000

❍ **Report all shares other than those with the code CS or PT.**

MINUS is used to subtract those shares with the specified codes. Notice the use of UNION to identify shares satisfying either condition.

SHR MINUS ((SHR WHERE SHRCODE = 'CS') UNION (SHR WHERE SHRCODE = 'PT'))	SELECT * FROM SHR WHERE SHRCODE NOT IN ('CS','PT')

❍ **Report the value of each stock holding in UK pounds.**

A JOIN of STOCK and NATION and PROJECTION of specified attributes.

❍ **Find the items that have appeared in all sales.**

(STOCK JOIN NATION
 WHERE STOCK.NATCODE =
  NATION.NATCODE)
[NATNAME, STKFIRM,
 STKPRICE, STKQTY, EXCHRATE,
 STKPRICE*STKQTY*EXCHRATE]
	SELECT NATNAME, STKFIRM,
	 STKPRICE, STKQTY, EXCHRATE,
	 STKPRICE*STKQTY*EXCHRATE
	  FROM STOCK,NATION
	   WHERE STOCK.NATCODE =
	    NATION.NATCODE

DIVIDEBY reports the ITEMNO of items appearing in all sales, and this result is then JOINed with ITEM to report the items.

((LINEITEM[ITEMNO, SALENO]
 DIVIDEBY SALE[SALENO])
  JOIN ITEM) [ITEMNO, ITEMNAME]
	SELECT ITEMNO, ITEMNAME FROM
	ITEM
	 WHERE NOT EXISTS
	  (SELECT * FROM SALE
	   WHERE NOT EXISTS
	    (SELECT * FROM LINEITEM
	     WHERE LINEITEM.ITEMNO =
	      ITEM.ITEMNO
	     AND LINEITEM.SALENO =
	      SALE.SALENO))

A primitive set of relational operations

The full set of eight relational operators is not required. As you have already seen, join can be defined in terms of product and restrict. Intersection and divide can also be defined in terms of other commands. Indeed, only five operators are required: restrict, project, product, union, and difference. These five are known as primitives because these are the minimal set of relational operators. None of the primitive operators can be defined in terms of the other operators. Table 9-2 illustrates how each primitive can be expressed as an SQL command, which implies that SQL is relationally complete.

Table 9-2: Comparison of relational algebra primitive operations and SQL

Operation	Relational algebra	SQL
Restrict	A where condition	SELECT * FROM A WHERE condition
Project	A [X]	SELECT X FROM A
Product	A times B	SELECT * FROM A, B
Union	A union B	SELECT * FROM A UNION SELECT * FROM B
Difference	A minus B	SELECT * FROM A WHERE NOT EXISTS (SELECT * FROM B WHERE A.X = B.X AND A.Y = B.Y AND …[a]

a. Essentially, where all columns of A are equal to all columns of B.

A fully relational database

The three components of a relational database system are structures (domains and relations), integrity rules (primary and foreign keys), and a manipulation language (relational algebra). A **fully relational database** system provides complete support for each of these components. Many commercial systems support SQL but do not provide support for domains or integrity rules. Such systems are not fully relational but are relationally complete.

In 1985, Codd[5] established the 12 commandments of relational database systems (see Table 9-3). In addition to providing some insights into Codd's thinking about the management of data, these rules can also be used to judge how well a database fits the relational model. The major impetus for these rules was uncertainty in the marketplace about the meaning of relational DBMS. Unfortunately, some DBMS vendors used the term *relational* somewhat freely, and this created misunderstanding about what relational database really meant. Codd's rules are a checklist for establishing the authenticity of a DBMS that claims to be relational.

Table 9-3: Codd's rules for a relational DBMS

The information rule
The guaranteed access rule
Systematic treatment of null values
Active on-line catalog of the relational model
The comprehensive data sublanguage rule
The view updating rule
High-level insert, update, and delete
Physical data independence
Logical data independence
Integrity independence
Distribution independence
The nonsubversion rule

The information rule

This rule stipulates that there is only one logical representation of data in a database. All data must appear to be stored as values in a table.

The guaranteed access rule

Every value in a database must be addressable by specifying its table name, column name, and the primary key of the row in which it is stored.

Systematic treatment of null values

There must be a distinct representation for unknown or inappropriate data.[6] This must be unique and independent of data type. The DBMS should handle null data in a systematic way. For example, a zero or a blank cannot be used to represent a null. This is one of the

5. Codd, E. F. 1985. Is your DBMS really relational? *Computerworld*, October 14, and Does your DBMS run by the rules? *Computerworld*, October 21.
6. In DB2, each column has an associated one byte field that denotes whether the column is null.

more troublesome areas because null can have several meanings (e.g., missing or inappropriate).

Active on-line catalog of the relational model

There should be an on-line catalog that describes the relational model (see page 268 for details of the system catalog). Authorized users should be able to access this catalog using the DBMS's query language (e.g., SQL).

The comprehensive data sublanguage rule

There must be a relational language that supports data definition, data manipulation, security and integrity constraints, and transaction processing operations. Furthermore, this language must support both interactive querying and application programming and be expressible in text format. SQL fits these requirements.

The view updating rule

The DBMS must be able to update any view that is theoretically updatable.

High-level insert, update, and delete

The system must support set-at-a-time operations. For example, multiple rows must be updatable with a single command.

Physical data independence

Changes to storage representation or access methods will not affect application programs. For example, application programs should remain unimpaired even if a database is moved to a different storage device or an index is created for a table.

Logical data independence

Information preserving changes to base tables will not affect application programs. For instance, no applications should be affected when a new table is added to a database.

Integrity independence

Integrity constraints should be part of a database's definition rather than embedded within application programs. It must be possible to change these constraints without affecting any existing application programs.

Distribution independence

Introduction of a distributed DBMS or redistributing existing distributed data should have no impact on existing applications (see the discussion of distributed database starting on page 365).

The nonsubversion rule

It must not be possible to use a record-at-a-time interface to subvert security or integrity constraints. You should not be able to write a COBOL program with embedded SQL commands to bypass security features.

Codd issued an additional higher-level rule, rule 0, which states that a relational DBMS must be able to manage databases entirely through its relational capacities. In other words, a DBMS is either totally relational or it is not relational.

Summary

The relational model developed as a result of recognized shortcomings of hierarchical and network DBMSs. Codd created a strong theoretical base for the relational model. Three objectives drove relational database research: data independence, communicability, and set processing. The relational model has domain structures, integrity rules, and operators used to retrieve, derive, or modify data. A domain is a set of values all of the same data type. The practical value of a domain is to define what comparisons are permissible. A relation is a table of n columns and m rows. The cardinality of a relation is its number of rows. The degree of a relation is the number of columns.

A relational database is a collection of relations. The distinguishing feature of the relational model is that there are no explicit linkages between tables. A relation's primary key is its unique identifier. When there are multiple candidates for the primary key, one is chosen as the primary key and the remainder are known as alternate keys. The foreign key is the way relationships are represented and can be thought of as the glue that binds a set of tables together to form a relational database. The purpose of the entity integrity rule is to ensure that each entity described by a relation is identifiable in some way. The referential integrity rule ensures that you cannot define a foreign key without first defining its matching primary key.

The relational model includes a set of operations, known as relational algebra, for manipulating relations. There are eight operations that can be used with either one or two relations to create a new relation. These operations are restrict, project, product, union, intersect, difference, join, and divide. Only five operators, known as primitives, are required to define all eight relational operations. An SQL statement can be translated to relational algebra and vice versa. If a retrieval language can be used to express every relational algebra operator, it is said to be relationally complete. A fully relational database system provides complete support for domains, integrity rules, and a manipulation language. Codd set forth 12 rules that can be used to judge how well a database fits the relational model. He also added rule 0—a DBMS is either totally relational or it is not relational.

Key terms and concepts

Alternate key
Candidate key
Cardinality
Catalog
Communicability objective
Data independence
Data structures
Data sublanguage rule
Degree
Difference
Distribution independence
Divide
Domain
Entity integrity
Foreign key
Fully relational database
Guaranteed access rule
Information rule
Integrity independence
Integrity rules
Intersect
Join
Logical data independence
Nonsubversion rule
Null
Operators
Physical data independence
Primary key
Product
Project
Query-by-example (QBE)
Referential integrity
Relational algebra
Relational calculus
Relational database
Relational model
Relationally complete
Relations
Restrict
Set processing objective
Union
View updating rule

References and additional readings

Bustamente, G. G., and K. Sorenson. 1994. Decision support at Lands' End—An evolution. *IBM Systems Journal* 33 (2):228-238.

Codd, E. F. 1982. Relational database: A practical foundation for productivity. *Communications of the ACM* 25 (2):109–117.

Codd, E. F. 1985. Is your DBMS really relational? *Computerworld*, October 14.

Codd, E. F. 1985. Does your DBMS run by the rules? *Computerworld*, October 21.

Codd, E. F. 1988. Fatal flaws in SQL. *Datamation*, August 15 and September 1.

Rozen, S., and D. Shasha. 1989. Using a relational system on Wall Street: The good, the bad, the ugly, and the ideal. *Communications of the ACM* 32 (8):988–994.

Exercises

1. What reasons does Codd give for adopting the relational model?
2. What are the major components of the relational model?
3. What is a domain? Why is it useful?
4. What are the meanings of cardinality and degree?
5. What is a simple relational database?
6. What is the difference between a primary key and an alternate key?
7. Why do we need an entity integrity rule and referential integrity rule?

8. What is the meaning of union compatible? Which relational operations require union compatibility?
9. What is meant by the term "a primitive set of operations?"
10. What is a fully relational database?
11. Take a microcomputer relational database package and examine how well it satisfies Codd's rules.
12. Use relational algebra to solve the following queries:

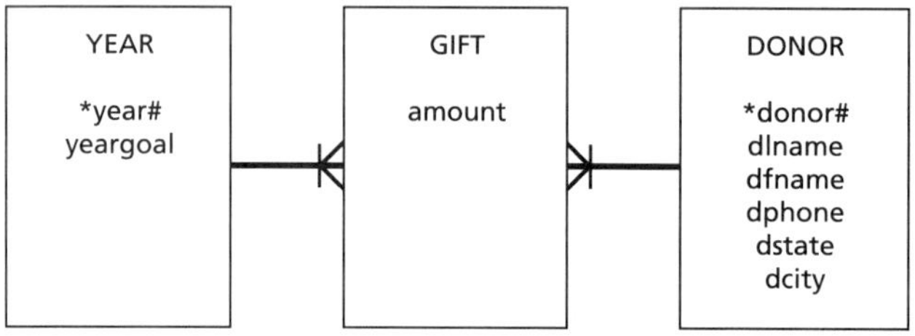

YEAR	
YEAR	YEARGOAL

GIFT		
AMOUNT	YEAR	DONORNO

DONOR					
DONORNO	DLNAME	DFNAME	DPHONE	DSTATE	DCITY

a. List all donors.
b. List the first and last names of all donors
c. List the phone numbers of donors number 106 and 125.
d. List the amount given by each donor for each year.
e. List the donors who have made a donation every year.
f. List the names of donors who live in Georgia or North Carolina.
g. List the names of donors whose last name is Watson and live in Athens, GA.

10

SQL

The questing beast.

Sir Thomas Mallory, *Le Morte D'Arthur,* 1470

Learning Objectives

Students completing this chapter will have a detailed knowledge of SQL.

Introduction

SQL is widely used as a relational database language. Both the American National Standards Institute (ANSI) and the International Organization for Standardization (ISO) have designated SQL as a standard language for relational database systems. SQL skills are essential for data management in a world that is increasingly reliant on relational technology.

SQL originated in the IBM Research Laboratory in San Jose, California. A range of IBM database management products support SQL. Versions have also been implemented by many other commercial database vendors for a wide range of operating systems. An ANSI committee, formed in 1978, has guided the definition of an SQL standard. SQL standards were released in 1986, 1989, 1992, and 1999. The most recent standard added object-oriented data management extensions to SQL.

SQL is a **complete database language**. It is used for defining a relational database, creating views, and specifying queries. In addition, it allows for rows to be inserted, updated, and deleted. In database terminology, it is both a **data definition language** (DDL) and a **data manipulation language** (DML). SQL, however, is not a complete programming language like COBOL and Java. Because SQL statements can be embedded into general purpose programming languages, SQL is often used in conjunction with such languages to create application programs. The **embedded SQL** statements handle the database processing, and the statements in the general purpose language perform the necessary tasks to complete the application.

You were introduced to SQL in Chapters 3 through 6. This chapter provides an integrated coverage of the language, pulling together the various pieces presented previously.

Data definition

One of the major advantages of relational DBMSs is that DDL statements can be executed at any time. Earlier DBMSs often require halting the entire system to perform maintenance operations such as adding a new table (actually a record type in the terminology of non-relational DBMSs) or creating an index. In many cases, this is extremely difficult to do because many systems are in use 24 hours per day. In some cases, routine maintenance is delayed until the system can be shut down for an extended period. Major holidays, such as Christmas and New Year's Day, are often used for database maintenance. Relational DBMSs greatly alleviate this problem because new tables, views, and indexes can be created without interfering with current operational use.

The DDL part of SQL encompasses statements to operate on tables, views, and indexes. Before we proceed, however, the term "base table" must be defined. A **base table** is an autonomous, named table. It is autonomous because it exists in its own right; it is physically stored within the database. In contrast, a view is not autonomous because it is derived from one or more base tables and does not exist independently. A view is a virtual table. A base table has a name by which it can be referenced. This name is chosen when the base table is generated using the CREATE statement. Short-lived temporary tables, such as those formed as the result of a query, are not named.

Keys

The concept of a key occurs several times within SQL. In general, a **key** is one or more columns identified as such in the description of a table, an index, or a referential constraint. The same column can be part of more than one key. For example, it can be part of a primary key and a foreign key. A **composite key** is an ordered set of columns of the same table. In other words, the primary key of LINEITEM is always the composite of (SALENO, LINENO) in that order. The order cannot be changed.

Comparing composite keys actually means that corresponding components of the keys are compared. Thus, application of the referential integrity rule, *the value of a foreign key must be equal to a value of the primary key,* means that each component of the foreign key must be equal to a corresponding component of a composite primary key.

So far, you have met primary and foreign keys. A **unique key** is another type of key. Its purpose is to ensure that no two values of a key are equal. This constraint is enforced by the DBMS during the execution of INSERT and UPDATE statements. A unique key is part of the index mechanism.

Indexes

Indexes are used to accelerate data access and ensure uniqueness. An **index** is an ordered set of pointers to rows of a base table. Think of an index as a table that contains two columns (see Figure 10-1). The first column contains values for the index key, and the second column contains a list of pointers or addresses of rows in the table. Since the values in the first column are ordered (i.e., in ascending or descending sequence), the index table can be searched quickly. It's like searching a phone book by a person's last name. This is easy because the telephone book is in last name sequence. In contrast, searching by phone number is extremely time consuming because the telephone book is not in this sequence. Once the required key has been found in the table, the row's address in the second column can be used to quickly retrieve the data. An index can be specified as being unique, in which case the DBMS ensures that the corresponding table does not have rows with identical index keys.[1]

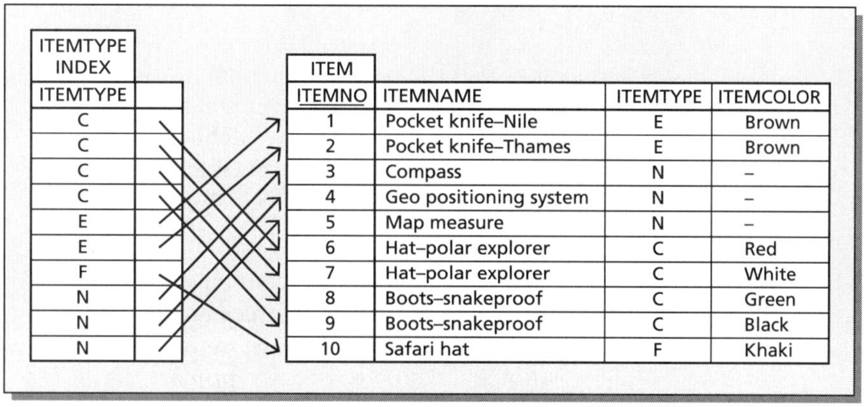

Figure 10-1. An example of an index

Notation

A short primer on notation is required before we examine SQL commands.

1. Text in uppercase is required as is.
2. Text in lowercase denotes values to be selected by the user.
3. Statements enclosed within brackets are optional.
4. An ellipsis (...) indicates that the immediate syntactic unit may be repeated optionally more than once.

Create table

CREATE TABLE is used to define a new base table either interactively or by embedding the statement in a host language. The statement specifies a table's name, provides details of its columns, and provides integrity checks. The format of the command is

```
CREATE TABLE base-table
   column-definition-block
   [primary-key-block]
   [referential-constraint-block]
   [unique-block]
```

1. Indexes are covered in depth in Chapter 11.

Column definition

The column definition block defines the columns in a table. Each column definition consists of a column name, data type, and optionally the specification that the column cannot contain null values. The general form is

```
(column-definition [, …])
```

where column-definition is of the form

```
column-name data-type [NOT NULL]
```

The NOT NULL clause specifies that the particular column must have a value whenever a new row is inserted. This clause should always be defined for a column that is a primary key or a component of a primary key. It is sometimes defined for foreign keys but not always as illustrated by the definition of the MONARCH table in Chapter 6.

Primary key definition

The primary key definition block specifies a set of column values comprising the primary key. Once a primary key is defined, the system enforces its uniqueness by checking that the primary key of any new row does not already exist in the table. A table can have only one primary key. While it is not mandatory to define a primary key, it is good practice to always define a table's primary key. The general form of the definition is

```
                           ┌    ┐
PRIMARY KEY (column-name   │ASC │ [,…])
                           │DESC│
                           └    ┘
```

The optional ASC or DESC clause specifies whether the values from this key are arranged in ascending or descending order, respectively.

Referential constraint definition

The referential constraint block defines a foreign key, which consists of one or more columns in the table that together must match a primary key (or else be null) of the specified table. A foreign key value is null when any one of the columns in the row comprising the foreign key is null. Once the foreign key constraint is defined, the DBMS will check every insert and update to ensure that the constraint is observed. The general form of the definition is

```
FOREIGN KEY constraint-name (column-name [,…])
   REFERENCES table-name
              ┌        ┐
              │RESTRICT│
   ON DELETE  │CASCADE │
              │SET NULL│
              └        ┘
```

The constraint-name definition supports naming a referential constraint. You cannot use a constraint-name more than once in the same table.

Column-name identifies the column or columns that comprise the foreign key. The data type and length of foreign key columns must match exactly the data type and length of the primary key columns.

The clause REFERENCES table-name specifies the name of the existing table that contains the primary key, which cannot be the name of the table being created.

The ON DELETE clause defines the action taken when a row is deleted from the table containing the primary key. There are three options:

1. RESTRICT prevents deletion of the primary key row until all corresponding rows in the related table, the one containing the foreign key, have been deleted. RESTRICT is the default value for this clause and also the cautious approach for preserving data integrity.
2. CASCADE causes all the corresponding rows in the related table also to be deleted.
3. SET NULLS sets the foreign key to null for all corresponding rows in the related table.

Unique definition

The unique definition block creates a unique index for the specified column or columns. A unique key is constrained so that no two of its values are equal. Columns appearing in a unique constraint must be defined as NOT NULL. The constraint is enforced by the DBMS during execution of INSERT and UPDATE statements. The general format is

```
                                       | ASC  |
UNIQUE constraint-name (column-name    |      | [,…])
                                       |DESC  |
```

The column-name clause identifies the column or columns that comprise the unique key. Also, these columns should not be the same as those of the table's primary key, which are guaranteed uniqueness by the primary key definition. The ASC and DESC options specify whether the columns of the unique key are arranged in ascending or descending order, respectively.

An example illustrates the use of CREATE TABLE.

```
CREATE TABLE STOCK
   (STKCODE     CHAR(3)NOT NULL,
   STKFIRM      CHAR(20),
   STKPRICE     DECIMAL(6,2),
   STKQTY       DECIMAL(8),
   STKDIV       DECIMAL(5,2),
   STKPE        DECIMAL(5),
```

```
    NATCODE      CHAR(3),
      PRIMARY KEY(STKCODE),
      FOREIGN KEY FKNATION(NATCODE) REFERENCES NATION
        ON DELETE RESTRICT)
```

Data types

Some of the variety of data types that can be used for a column are shown in Table 10-1. The choices are also depicted in Figure 10-2.

Table 10-1: Some allowable data types

Numeric	integer	A 31-bit signed binary value
	smallint	A 15-bit signed binary value
	float(p)	A scientific format number of *p* binary digits precision
	decimal(p,q)	A packed decimal number of *p* digits total length; *q* decimal places to the right of the decimal point may be specified
String	char(n)	A fixed length character string of *n* characters
	varchar(n)	A variable length character string up to *n* characters
	long varchar	A variable length character string
Date/time	date	Date in the form *yyyymmdd*
	time	Time in the form *hhmmss*
	timestamp	A combination of date and time to the nearest microsecond
Graphic	graphic(n)	A fixed length graphic string of *n* 16-bit bytes
	vargraphic(n)	A variable length graphic string of up to *n* 16-bit bytes
	long vargraphic	A variable length graphic string of 16-bit bytes

Smallint and integer

Most commercial computers have a 32-bit word where a word is a unit of storage. An integer can be stored in a full word or half a word. If it is stored in a full word (INTEGER), then it can be 31 binary digits in length. If half-word storage is used (SMALLINT), then it can be 15 binary digits long. In each case, one bit is used for the sign of the number. A column defined as INTEGER can store a number in the range -2^{31} to 2^{31}-1 or -2,147,483,648 to 2,147,483,647. A column defined as SMALLINT can store a number in the range -2^{15} to 2^{15}-1 or -32,768 to 32,767. Just remember that INTEGER is good for ±2 billion and SMALLINT for ±32,000.

Float

Scientists often deal with numbers that are very large (e.g., Avogadro's number is 6.02252×10^{23}) or very small (e.g., Planck's constant is 6.6262×10^{-34} joule sec). The FLOAT data type is used for storing such numbers, often referred to as floating-point numbers. A single precision floating-point number requires 32 bits and can represent numbers in the range -7.2×10^{75} to 5.4×10^{-79}, 0, 5.4×10^{-79} to 7.2×10^{75}. A double precision floating-point num-

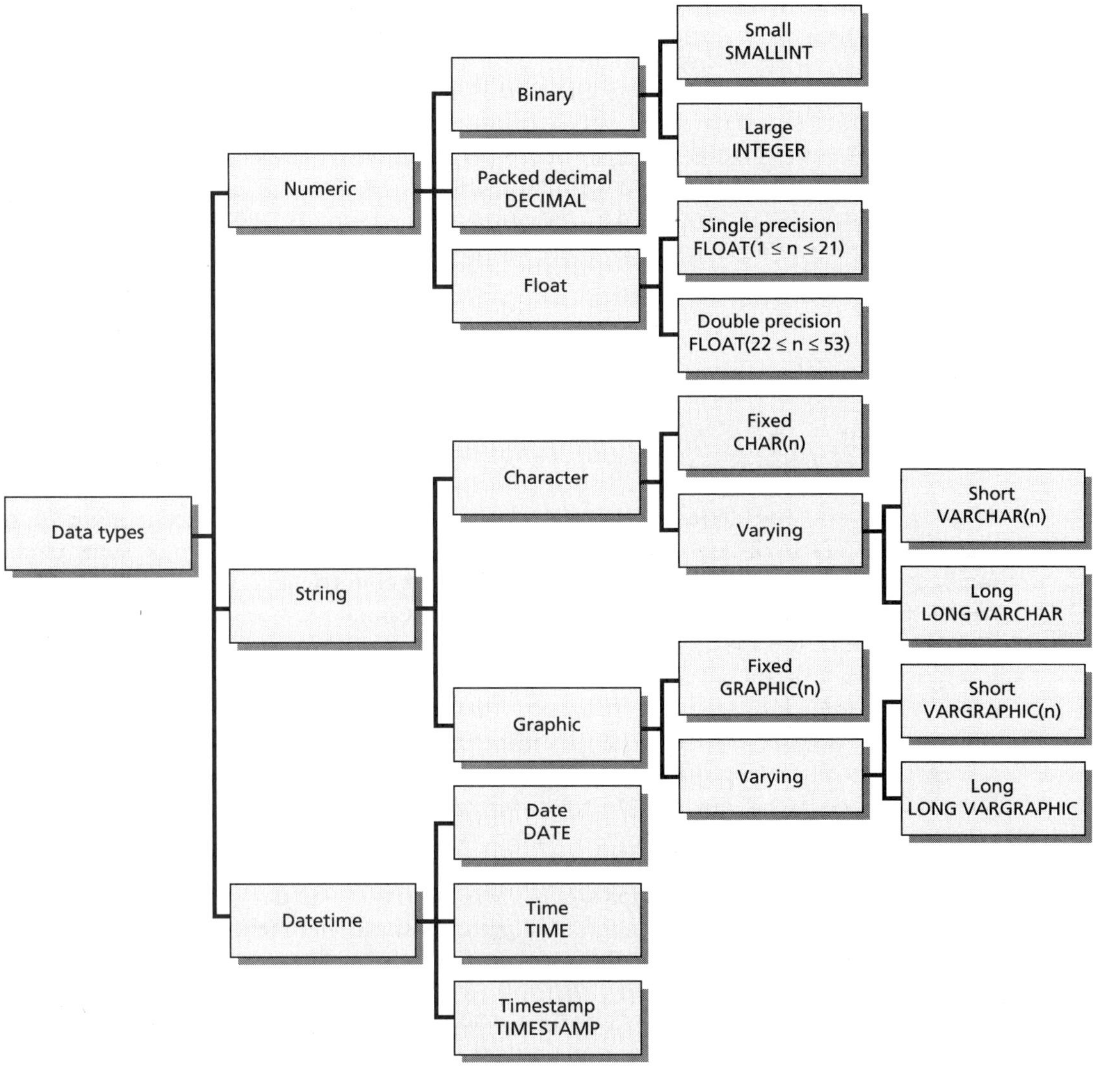

Figure 10-2. Data types

ber requires 64 bits. The range is the same as for a single precision floating-point number. The extra 32 bits are used to increase precision.

In the specification FLOAT(*n*), if *n* is between 1 and 21 inclusive, single precision floating-point is selected. If *n* is between 22 and 53 inclusive, the storage format is double precision floating-point. If *n* is not specified, double precision floating-point is assumed.

Decimal

Binary is the most convenient form of storing data from a computer's perspective. People, however, work with a decimal number system and do not want to be bothered with thinking in terms of binary numbers. The DECIMAL data type is very convenient for business applications because data storage requirements are defined in terms of the maximum number of places to the left and right of the decimal point. For example, to store the current value of an ounce of gold you would possibly use DECIMAL(6,2) as this would permit a maximum value of $9,999.99. Notice that the general form is DECIMAL(*p*,*q*) where *p* is the total number of digits in the column, and *q* is the number of digits to the right of the decimal point.

Char and varchar

Nonnumeric columns are stored as character strings. A person's family name is an example of a column that is stored as a character string. CHAR(*n*) defines a column that has a fixed length of *n* characters, where *n* can be a maximum of 255.

Family name might be defined as CHAR(20). This should be enough space to store all the characters of nearly all family names. Of course, it would be a good idea to do some checking because 20 characters might be insufficient for a country like Thailand, where family names can be quite long. It might be too much for China because Chinese family names tend to be quite short. There is a trade-off between too many and too few characters. If too few characters are defined, some family names will be truncated, and this could be offensive to some customers. If too many characters are defined, then storage is wasted because a set amount of space is allocated for each column regardless of how many characters are actually required for the column. The rightmost unused portion of a column is filled with the space character. Most database designers err on the side of making a column too long rather than too short—customers are worth more than computer memory.

Of course, there are some columns where there is no trade-off decision because all possible entries are always the same length. U.S. Social Security numbers are always nine characters.

When a column's length can vary greatly, it makes sense to define the field as VARCHAR or LONG VARCHAR. Usually, a column defined as VARCHAR consists of two parts: a header indicating the length of the character string and the character string. If a table contains a column that occasionally stores a long string of text (e.g., a message field), then defining it as VARCHAR makes sense. LONG VARCHAR can store strings up to 32,767 characters long.

Why not store all character columns as VARCHAR and save space? The answer is that there is a price for using VARCHAR. First, additional space is required for the header to indicate the length of the string. Second, additional processing time is required to handle a variable length string compared to a fixed length string. Depending on the major uses of the database, these can be important considerations.

Data compression programs are another approach to the *space wars* problem. A database can be defined with generous allowances for fixed length character columns so that important columns are not truncated. Then, a data compression program can be used to compress the file to remove the *wasted* space. Again, there is a trade-off. Data compression is slow and will increase the time it takes to answer queries. You save space at the cost of time, and save time at the cost of space. When dealing with character fields, the database designer has to decide whether time or space is more important.

Time and date

Columns that have a data type of DATE are stored as *yyyymmdd* (e.g., 1994-11-04). There are several reasons for storing data in this format. First, it is convenient for sorting in chronological order. For example, the common American way of writing dates (*mmddyy*) requires processing before chronological sorting. Second, the full form of the year should be recorded to avoid end of century problems.

For similar reasons, it makes sense to store times in the form *hhmmss* with the understanding that this is 24-hour time (also known as European time and military time). This is the format used for data type TIME.

Some applications require precise recording of events. For example, transaction processing systems typically record the time a transaction was processed by the computer. Because computer systems operate at such high speeds, the TIMESTAMP data type records date and time with microsecond accuracy. A timestamp has seven parts—year, month, day, hour, minute, second, and microsecond. Date and time are defined as previously described (i.e., *yyyymmdd* and *hhmmss*, respectively). The range of the microsecond part is 000000 to 999999.

Although times and dates are stored in a particular format, they can be reported in a variety of ways. The reporting formatting facilities that generally come with a relational DBMS usually allow tailoring of output to suit local standards. Thus for a U.S. firm, date might appear on a report in the form *mm/dd/yy*; for a European firm following the ISO standard, date would appear as *yyyy-mm-dd*.

Graphic and vargraphic

The CHARACTER data type is fine for storing characters sets such as those used in English-speaking countries, with fewer than 256 different symbols (e.g., A, 6, and *). The Chinese and Japanese languages, however, contain thousands of symbols. Chinese contains more than 50,000 distinct characters, although only 3,000-4,000 are needed for everyday communication. Providing a unique code for each of the many Chinese characters requires 16 bits, which enables representation of 65,536 different symbols (2^{16}). GRAPHIC and VARGRAPHIC data types are for storing these double-byte, 16-bit, character sets. LONG VARGRAPHIC can store a string of up to 16,834 16-bit characters.

Boolean

Boolean is a data type that can have the values true or false.[2]

BLOB

BLOB is a large-object data type that stores any kind of binary data. Binary data typically consists of a saved spreadsheet, graph, fax, satellite image, voice pattern, or any digitized data. The BLOB data type has no maximum size.

CLOB

CLOB is a large-object data type that stores any kind of text data. Text data typically consists of reports, correspondence, chapters of a manual, and contracts. The CLOB data type has no maximum size.[3]

Special registers

Some implementations of SQL have special registers for commonly required data values (e.g., today's date). Some that you might like to use are CURRENT DATE, CURRENT TIME, and CURRENT TIMESTAMP. For example:

```
INSERT INTO SALE
   (SALENO, SALEDATE, SALETEXT)
   VALUES (6, CURRENT DATE, 'Brazilian tourist')
```

Alter table

The ALTER TABLE statement has two purposes. First, it can add a single column to an existing table. Second, it can add, drop, activate, or deactivate primary and foreign keys constraints.

A base table can be altered by adding one new column, which appears to the right of existing columns. The format of the command is

```
ALTER TABLE base-table
   ADD column data-type
```

Notice that there is no optional NOT NULL clause for column-definition with ALTER TABLE. It is not allowed because the ALTER TABLE statement automatically fills the additional column with null in every case.[4] Of course, if you want to add multiple new columns, you can repeat the ALTER TABLE command. The following example illustrates the use of ALTER TABLE.

---

2. SQL3 addition.
3. SQL3 addition.
4. This may not be what happens physically, but it is a good way of visualizing why NOT NULL is an inappropriate clause

```
ALTER TABLE STOCK ADD STKRATING CHAR(3)
```

ALTER TABLE does not permit changing the width of a column, amending a column's data type, or deleting an unwanted column. It is strictly for adding a new column.

ALTER TABLE is also used to change the status of referential constraints. There are some occasions when key constraints can cause performance problems. For instance, large volumes of data will be loaded faster if referential integrity constraints are deactivated. You can deactivate constraints on a table's primary key or any of its foreign keys. Deactivation also makes the relevant tables unavailable to all users except the table's owner or someone possessing database management authority. After loading the data, referential constraints must be reactivated before they can be automatically enforced again. Activating the constraints enables the DBMS to validate the references in the data.

Drop table

A base table can be deleted at any time by using the DROP statement. The format is

```
DROP TABLE BASE-TABLE
```

The table is deleted and any views or indexes defined on the table are also deleted. Naturally, you should think carefully before dropping a table.

Create view

A view is a virtual table. It has no physical counterpart but appears to the user as if it really exists. A view is defined in terms of other tables that exist in the database. The syntax for defining a view is

```
CREATE VIEW view [column [,column] …)]
   AS subquery
```

There are several reasons for creating a view. First, a view can be used to restrict access to certain rows or columns. This is particularly important for sensitive data. An organization's PERSON table can contain both private data (e.g., annual salary) and public data (office phone number). A view consisting of public data (e.g., person's name, department, and office telephone number) might be provided to many people. Access to all columns in the table, however, might be confined to a small number of people. Here is a sample view that restricts access to a table.

```
CREATE VIEW STKLIST
   AS SELECT STKFIRM, STKPRICE FROM STOCK
```

Handling derived data is a second reason for creating a view. A column that can be computed from one or more other columns should always be defined by a view. For example, a stock's yield is computed by dividing its dividend by its price. Yield would be created by a view rather than being defined as a column in a base table.

```
CREATE VIEW STK
   (STKFIRM, STKPRICE, STKQTY, STKYIELD)
   AS SELECT STKFIRM, STKPRICE, STKQTY, STKDIV/STKPRICE*100
      FROM STOCK
```

A third reason for defining a view is to avoid writing common SQL queries. For example, there may be some joins that are frequently a part of an SQL query. Productivity can be increased by defining these joins as views. Here is an example:

```
CREATE VIEW STKVALUE
   (NATION, FIRM, PRICE, QTY, VALUE)
   AS SELECT NATNAME, STKFIRM, STKPRICE*EXCHRATE, STKQTY,
      STKPRICE*EXCHRATE*STKQTY FROM STOCK, NATION
         WHERE STOCK.NATCODE = NATION.NATCODE
```

The preceding example demonstrates how CREATE VIEW can be used to rename columns, create new columns, and involve more than one table. The view STKVALUE has five columns. The column NATION corresponds to NATNAME, FIRM to STKFIRM, and so forth. A new column, PRICE, is created by multiplying the price of the share by the exchange rate. This calculation converts all share prices from the local currency to British pounds. Also note that the query that defines the view is a join.

Data conversion is a fourth useful reason for using a view. The United States is one of the few countries that does not use the metric system, and reports for American managers often display weights and measures in pounds and feet, respectively. The database of an international company could record all measurements in metric format (e.g., weight in kilograms) and use a view to convert these measures for American reports.

When a CREATE VIEW statement is executed, the definition of the view is entered in the systems catalog, the database about the database. The subquery following AS is executed only when the view is referenced in an SQL command. For example, the following command would enable the subquery to be executed and the view created:

```
SELECT * FROM STKVALUE WHERE PRICE > 10
```

In effect, the following query is executed:

```
SELECT NATNAME, STKFIRM, STKPRICE*EXCHRATE, STKQTY,
   STKPRICE*EXCHRATE*STKQTY
      FROM STOCK, NATION
         WHERE STOCK.NATCODE = NATION.NATCODE
         AND STKPRICE*EXCHRATE > 10
```

Any table that can be defined with a SELECT statement is a potential view. Thus, it is possible to have a view that is defined by another view.

Drop view

DROP VIEW is used to delete a view from the system catalog. The syntax is:

```
DROP VIEW view
```

Remember, if a base table is dropped, all views based on that table are also dropped.

A view might be dropped because it needs to be redefined or is no longer used. It must be dropped first before a revised version of the view is created.

Create index

An index helps speed up retrieval (see Chapter 11 for a complete discussion of indexing). A column that is frequently referred to in a WHERE clause is a possible candidate for indexing. For example, if data on stocks were frequently retrieved using STKFIRM, then this column should be considered for an index. The format for CREATE INDEX is:

```
CREATE [UNIQUE] INDEX index
   ON base-table (column [order] [,column, [order]] …)
   [CLUSTER]
```

This next example illustrates use of CREATE INDEX.

```
CREATE UNIQUE INDEX STKFIRMINDX
   ON STOCK (STKFIRM)
   CLUSTER
```

In the preceding example, an index called STKFIRMINDX is created for the table STOCK. Index entries are ordered by ascending (the default order) values of STKFIRM. The optional clause UNIQUE specifies that no two rows in the base table can have the same value for STKFIRM, the indexed column. Specifying UNIQUE means that the DBMS will reject any insert or update operation that would create a duplicate value for STKFIRM. A clustering index (see Chapter 11) is denoted by the optional CLUSTER.

A composite index can be created from several columns, which is often necessary for an associative entity. The following example illustrates creation of a composite index.

```
CREATE INDEX LINEITEMINDX
   ON LINEITEM (LINENO, SALENO)
```

Drop index

Indexes can be dropped at any time by using the DROP INDEX statement. The general form of this statement is:

```
DROP INDEX index
```

For example, to drop the index called LINEITEMINDX, use the following statement:

```
DROP INDEX LINEITEMINDX
```

Data manipulation

SQL supports four DML statements—SELECT, INSERT, UPDATE, and DELETE. Each of these will be discussed in turn, with most attention focusing on SELECT because of the variety of ways in which it can be used. But first, we need to understand why we must qualify column names and temporary names.

Qualifying column names

Ambiguous references to column names are avoided by qualifying a column name with its table name, especially when the same column name is used in several tables. Clarity is maintained by prefixing the column name with the table name. The following example demonstrates qualification of the NATCODE, which appears in both STOCK and NATION.

```
SELECT * FROM STOCK, NATION
   WHERE STOCK.NATCODE = NATION.NATCODE
```

Temporary names

A table or view can be given a temporary name, or alias, that remains current for a query. Temporary names were used previously when a table was joined with itself. They were used to clearly establish unique identities for each table. The next example demonstrates how two temporary names, EMP and BOSS, were created for EMP.

```
SELECT WRK.EMPFNAME
   FROM EMP WRK, EMP BOSS
      WHERE WRK.BOSSNO = BOSS.EMPNO
```

A temporary name also can be used as a shortened form of a long table name. For example, *L* might have been used merely to avoid having to enter LINEITEM more than once. If a temporary name is specified for a table or view, any qualified reference to a column of the table or view must also use that temporary name.

Select

The SELECT statement is by far the most interesting and challenging of the four DML statements. It is interesting because it reveals a major benefit of the relational model—powerful interrogation capabilities. It is challenging because to master the power of SELECT requires considerable practice with a wide range of queries. The major varieties of SELECT are presented in this section. The SQL Playbook (page 281) reveals the full power of the command.

The general format of SELECT is

```
SELECT [DISTINCT] item(s)
   FROM table(s)
   [WHERE condition]
   [GROUP BY column(s)]
   [HAVING condition]
   [ORDER BY column(s)]
```

The simplest queries deal with a single table. Chapter 3 provides a complete coverage of single table queries; so, refer to that chapter for details. We will now consider more complex queries.

Product

Product, or more strictly Cartesian product, is a fundamental operation of relational algebra. It is rarely used by itself in a query; however, understanding its effect helps in comprehending join. The product of two tables is a new table consisting of all rows of the first table concatenated with all possible rows of the second table. An example illustrates how this is expressed in SQL.

❍ **Form the product of STOCK and NATION.**

```
SELECT * FROM STOCK, NATION
```

The new table contains 64 rows (16*4), where STOCK has 16 rows and NATION has 4 rows. It has 10 columns (7 + 3), where STOCK has 7 columns and NATION has 3 columns. The result of the operation is shown in Table 10-2. Note that each row in STOCK is concatenated with each row in NATION.

Join

Join is a very powerful and frequently used operation. Join creates a new table from two existing tables by matching on a column common to both tables. An **equijoin** is the simplest form of join; in this case, columns are matched on equality. You can think of an equijoin as first performing a product of the two tables and then doing a restrict on matching columns. Here is an example:

```
SELECT * FROM STOCK, NATION
   WHERE STOCK.NATCODE =NATION.NATCODE
```

The shaded rows in Table 10-2 shown previously indicate the result of the join.

An equijoin creates a new table that contains two identical columns. If one of these is dropped, then the remaining table is called a natural join. It can be expressed as

```
SELECT STKCODE, STKFIRM, STKPRICE, STKQTY, STKDIV, STKPE,
   STOCK.NATCODE, EXCHRATE, NATNAME
   FROM STOCK, NATION
      WHERE STOCK.NATCODE = NATION.NATCODE
```

As you now realize, join is really product with a condition clause. There is no reason why this condition needs to be restricted to equality. There could easily be another comparison operator between the two columns. This general version of join is called a theta join because theta is a variable that can take any value from the set [=, <>, >, ≥, <, ≤].

Table 10-2: Product of STOCK and NATION

STKCODE	STKFIRM	STKPRICE	STKQTY	STKDIV	STKPE	NATCODE	NATCODE1	NATNAME	EXCHRATE
FC	Freedonia Copper	27.50	10529	1.84	16	UK	UK	United Kingdom	1.00000
FC	Freedonia Copper	27.50	10529	1.84	16	UK	US	United States	0.67000
FC	Freedonia Copper	27.50	10529	1.84	16	UK	AUS	Australia	0.46000
FC	Freedonia Copper	27.50	10529	1.84	16	UK	IND	India	0.02280
PT	Patagonian Tea	55.25	12635	2.50	10	UK	UK	United Kingdom	1.00000
PT	Patagonian Tea	55.25	12635	2.50	10	UK	US	United States	0.67000
PT	Patagonian Tea	55.25	12635	2.50	10	UK	AUS	Australia	0.46000
PT	Patagonian Tea	55.25	12635	2.50	10	UK	IND	India	0.02280
AR	Abyssinian Ruby	31.82	22010	1.32	13	UK	UK	United Kingdom	1.00000
AR	Abyssinian Ruby	31.82	22010	1.32	13	UK	US	United States	0.67000
AR	Abyssinian Ruby	31.82	22010	1.32	13	UK	AUS	Australia	0.46000
AR	Abyssinian Ruby	31.82	22010	1.32	13	UK	IND	India	0.02280
SLG	Sri Lankan Gold	50.37	32868	2.68	16	UK	UK	United Kingdom	1.00000
SLG	Sri Lankan Gold	50.37	32868	2.68	16	UK	US	United States	0.67000
SLG	Sri Lankan Gold	50.37	32868	2.68	16	UK	AUS	Australia	0.46000
SLG	Sri Lankan Gold	50.37	32868	2.68	16	UK	IND	India	0.02280
ILZ	Indian Lead & Zinc	37.75	6390	3.00	12	UK	UK	United Kingdom	1.00000
ILZ	Indian Lead & Zinc	37.75	6390	3.00	12	UK	US	United States	0.67000
ILZ	Indian Lead & Zinc	37.75	6390	3.00	12	UK	AUS	Australia	0.46000
ILZ	Indian Lead & Zinc	37.75	6390	3.00	12	UK	IND	India	0.02280
BE	Burmese Elephant	0.07	154713	0.01	3	UK	UK	United Kingdom	1.00000
BE	Burmese Elephant	0.07	154713	0.01	3	UK	US	United States	0.67000
BE	Burmese Elephant	0.07	154713	0.01	3	UK	AUS	Australia	0.46000
BE	Burmese Elephant	0.07	154713	0.01	3	UK	IND	India	0.02280
BS	Bolivian Sheep	12.75	231678	1.78	11	UK	UK	United Kingdom	1.00000
BS	Bolivian Sheep	12.75	231678	1.78	11	UK	US	United States	0.67000
BS	Bolivian Sheep	12.75	231678	1.78	11	UK	AUS	Australia	0.46000
BS	Bolivian Sheep	12.75	231678	1.78	11	UK	IND	India	0.02280
NG	Nigerian Geese	35.00	12323	1.68	10	UK	UK	United Kingdom	1.00000
NG	Nigerian Geese	35.00	12323	1.68	10	UK	US	United States	0.67000
NG	Nigerian Geese	35.00	12323	1.68	10	UK	AUS	Australia	0.46000
NG	Nigerian Geese	35.00	12323	1.68	10	UK	IND	India	0.02280
CS	Canadian Sugar	52.78	4716	2.50	15	UK	UK	United Kingdom	1.00000
CS	Canadian Sugar	52.78	4716	2.50	15	UK	US	United States	0.67000
CS	Canadian Sugar	52.78	4716	2.50	15	UK	AUS	Australia	0.46000
CS	Canadian Sugar	52.78	4716	2.50	15	UK	IND	India	0.02280
ROF	Royal Ostrich Farms	33.75	1234923	3.00	6	UK	UK	United Kingdom	1.00000
ROF	Royal Ostrich Farms	33.75	1234923	3.00	6	UK	US	United States	0.67000
ROF	Royal Ostrich Farms	33.75	1234923	3.00	6	UK	AUS	Australia	0.46000
ROF	Royal Ostrich Farms	33.75	1234923	3.00	6	UK	IND	India	0.02280
MG	Minnesota Gold	53.87	816122	1.00	25	US	UK	United Kingdom	1.00000
MG	Minnesota Gold	53.87	816122	1.00	25	US	US	United States	0.67000
MG	Minnesota Gold	53.87	816122	1.00	25	US	AUS	Australia	0.46000
MG	Minnesota Gold	53.87	816122	1.00	25	US	IND	India	0.02280
GP	Georgia Peach	2.35	387333	0.20	5	US	UK	United Kingdom	1.00000
GP	Georgia Peach	2.35	387333	0.20	5	US	US	United States	0.67000
GP	Georgia Peach	2.35	387333	0.20	5	US	AUS	Australia	0.46000
GP	Georgia Peach	2.35	387333	0.20	5	US	IND	India	0.02280
NE	Narembeen Emu	12.34	45619	1.00	8	AUS	UK	United Kingdom	1.00000
NE	Narembeen Emu	12.34	45619	1.00	8	AUS	US	United States	0.67000
NE	Narembeen Emu	12.34	45619	1.00	8	AUS	AUS	Australia	0.46000
NE	Narembeen Emu	12.34	45619	1.00	8	AUS	IND	India	0.02280
QD	Queensland Diamond	6.73	89251	0.50	7	AUS	UK	United Kingdom	1.00000
QD	Queensland Diamond	6.73	89251	0.50	7	AUS	US	United States	0.67000
QD	Queensland Diamond	6.73	89251	0.50	7	AUS	AUS	Australia	0.46000
QD	Queensland Diamond	6.73	89251	0.50	7	AUS	IND	India	0.02280
IR	Indooroopilly Ruby	15.92	56147	0.50	20	AUS	UK	United Kingdom	1.00000
IR	Indooroopilly Ruby	15.92	56147	0.50	20	AUS	US	United States	0.67000
IR	Indooroopilly Ruby	15.92	56147	0.50	20	AUS	AUS	Australia	0.46000
IR	Indooroopilly Ruby	15.92	56147	0.50	20	AUS	IND	India	0.02280
BD	Bombay Duck	25.55	167382	1.00	12	IND	UK	United Kingdom	1.00000
BD	Bombay Duck	25.55	167382	1.00	12	IND	US	United States	0.67000
BD	Bombay Duck	25.55	167382	1.00	12	IND	AUS	Australia	0.46000
BD	Bombay Duck	25.55	167382	1.00	12	IND	IND	India	0.02280

A join can involve two or more tables. The extension to three tables is very direct as the following example illustrates:

```
SELECT * FROM SALE, LINEITEM, ITEM
   WHERE SALE.SALENO = LINEITEM.SALENO
   AND ITEM.ITEMNO = LINEITEM.ITEMNO
```

The three tables to be joined are listed after the FROM clause. There are two matching conditions: one to match SALE and LINEITEM (SALE.SALENO = LINEITEM.SALENO) and one to match ITEM and LINEITEM (ITEM.ITEMNO = LINEITEM.ITEMNO). The table, LINEITEM, is the link between the SALE and ITEM and must be referenced in both matching conditions.

As you discovered in Chapter 6, there are occasions when you need to join a table to itself. To do this, make two copies of the table first and give each of these copies a distinguishing name.

❍ **Find the names of employees who earn more than their boss.**

```
SELECT WRK.EMPFNAME
   FROM EMP WRK, EMP BOSS
      WHERE WRK.BOSSNO = BOSS.EMPNO
      AND WRK.EMPSALARY > BOSS.EMPSALARY
```

Simple subquery

A subquery is a query within a query. There is a SELECT statement nested inside another SELECT statement. Simple subqueries have been used extensively in Chapters 3 and 4. For reference, here is a simple subquery used in Chapter 4:

```
SELECT STKFIRM FROM STOCK
   WHERE NATCODE IN
      (SELECT NATCODE FROM NATION
         WHERE NATNAME = 'Australia')
```

Correlated subquery

A correlated subquery differs from a simple subquery in that the inner query must be evaluated more than once. Consider the following example described previously in Chapter 4:

```
SELECT STKFIRM FROM STOCK
   WHERE 'Australia' IN
      (SELECT NATNAME FROM NATION
         WHERE NATION.NATCODE = STOCK.NATCODE)
```

Aggregate functions

SQL's aggregate functions increase its retrieval power. These functions are covered in Chapter 3 and are only mentioned briefly here for completeness. The five aggregate functions are shown in Table 10-3. Nulls in the column are ignored in the case of SUM, AVG, MAX, and MIN. However, COUNT does not distinguish between null and non-null values in a column.

Table 10-3: Aggregate functions

COUNT	Counts the number of values in a column
SUM	Sums the values in a column
AVG	Determines the average of the values in a column
MAX	Determines the largest value of a column
MIN	Determines the smallest value of a column

Data, data everywhere

Aetna has 175 Tbytes of data spread across mainframe and midrange computers. Almost all of the data are located at the company's Hartford, Connecticut headquarters. Most of the information is managed by relational database technology supplied by IBM (DB2), Oracle, and Sybase.

Most of the data are health care information. Aetna has detailed records of health care providers, such as doctors, hospitals, dentists, and pharmacies. It keeps track of processed claims. The biggest concerns for Aetna are data integrity, backup, security, and system availability.

Aetna's database administrators maintain the more than 15,000 database table definitions with the ERWin data modeling tool. Manual upkeep of the table definitions became impossible years ago. While the physical management of large data stores is certainly a nontrivial effort, it is also important to manage the data from a logical perspective using data modeling tools.

Source: Nance, B. 2001. Managing tons of data. *Computerworld*, http://www.computerworld.com/rckey77/story/0,1199,NAV63_STO59819,00.html.

GROUP BY and HAVING

The GROUP BY clause is an elementary form of control break reporting and supports grouping of rows that have the same value for a specified column and produces one row for each different value of the grouping column. For example:

❍ **Report by nation the total value of stockholdings.**

```
SELECT NATNAME, SUM(STKPRICE*STKQTY*EXCHRATE)
   FROM STOCK, NATION WHERE STOCK.NATCODE = NATION.NATCODE
      GROUP BY NATNAME
```

gives:

NATNAME	SUM(EXPRESSION 1)
Australia	946430.65
India	97506.71
United Kingdom	48908364.25
United States	30066065.54

The HAVING clause is often associated with GROUP BY. It can be thought of as the WHERE clause of GROUP BY because it is used to eliminate rows for a GROUP BY condition. Both GROUP BY and HAVING are dealt with in-depth in Chapter 4, where examples demonstrate their use.

LIKE

The LIKE clause supports pattern matching to find a defined set of strings in a character column (CHAR or VARCHAR). Refer to Chapter 3 for more details.

Scalar functions

Most implementations of SQL include scalar functions that can be used in arithmetic expression, data conversion, or data extraction. Some of these functions are briefly discussed, although you will need to consult the documentation for your particular version of SQL to determine the functions it supports (see Table 10-4).

Table 10-4: Scalar functions

Char	Converts a date, time, or timestamp to a character representation.
Day	Retrieves the day portion of a date or timestamp.
Days	Converts a date or timestamp to a number of days. Useful for calculating the number of days between two dates.
Decimal	DECIMAL(*v,p,d*) reports a number *v* with precision *p* and *d* decimal place.
Float	Converts a number to floating-point representation.
Hour	Retrieves the hour portion of a time or timestamp.
Microsecond	Retrieves the microsecond portion of a time or timestamp.
Minute	Retrieves the minute portion of a time or timestamp.
Month	Retrieves the month portion of a date or timestamp.
Second	Retrieves the second portion of a time or timestamp.
Substr	Extracts a substring from a string. SUBSTR(NATNAME,1,2) gives the first two characters of a nation's name.
Year	Retrieves the year portion of a date or timestamp.

To use scalar functions, follow these examples:

```
SELECT    EMPSALARY,
          DECIMAL(EMPSALARY,9,2),
          FLOAT(EMPSALARY)
   FROM EMPLOYEE WHERE BOSSNO = 1
```

EMPSALARY	DECIMAL(EMPSALARY,EXPRESSION)	FLOAT(EMPSALARY)
45000	45000.00	4.500000000E+04
38000	38000.00	3.800000000E+04
43000	43000.00	4.300000000E+04
35000	35000.00	3.500000000E+04

❍ **How many days' sales are stored in the SALE table?**

This sounds like a simple query, but it is not. Here is one way to solve it. Can you think of any other ways?

```
SELECT DAYS(LATE.SALEDATE) - DAYS(EARLY.SALEDATE)
   FROM SALE LATE, SALE EARLY
      WHERE LATE.SALEDATE =
         (SELECT MAX(SALEDATE) FROM SALE)
      AND EARLY.SALEDATE =
         (SELECT MIN(SALEDATE) FROM SALE)
```

EXPRESSION 1
1

The preceding query is based on the idea of joining SALE with a copy of itself. The matching column from LATE is the latest sale's date (or MAX), and the matching column from EARLY is the earliest sale's date (or MIN). As a result of the join, each row of the new table has both the earliest and latest dates.

Insert

There are two formats for INSERT. The first format is used to insert a row into a table.

```
INSERT INTO TABLE [(COLUMN [,COLUMN] …)]
   VALUES (literal [,literal] …)
```

The following examples illustrate the use of INSERT:

Inserting a single record

```
INSERT INTO STOCK
   (STKCODE,STKFIRM,STKPRICE,STKQTY,STKDIV,STKPE)
   VALUES ('FC','Freedonia Copper',27.5,10529,1.84,16)
```

In this example, STKCODE is given the value 'FC', STKFIRM is 'Freedonia Copper', and so on. In general, the nth column in the table is the nth value in the list.

When the value list refers to all field names in the left-to-right order in which they appear in the table, then the columns' list can be omitted. So, it is possible to write the following:

```
INSERT INTO STOCK
   VALUES ('FC','Freedonia Copper',27.5,10529,1.84,16)
```

If some values are unknown, then the INSERT statement can omit these from the list. Undefined columns will have nulls. For example, if a new stock is to be added for which the price, dividend, and PE ratio are unknown, the following INSERT statement would be used:

```
INSERT INTO STOCK
   (STKCODE, STKFIRM, STKQTY)
   VALUES ('EE','Elysian Emeralds',0)
```

Inserting multiple records using a query

The second form of INSERT operates in conjunction with a subquery; the resulting rows then are inserted into a table. Imagine the situation where stock price information is downloaded from an information service into a table. This table could contain information about all stocks and may contain additional columns that are not required for the STOCK table. The following INSERT statement could be used:

```
INSERT INTO STOCK
   (STKCODE, STKFIRM, STKPRICE, STKDIV, STKPE)
   SELECT CODE, FIRM, PRICE, DIV, PE
   FROM DOWNLOAD WHERE CODE IN
   ('FC','PT','AR','SLG','ILZ','BE','BS','NG','CS','ROF')
```

Think of INSERT with a subquery as a way of copying a table. You can select the rows and columns of a particular table that you want to copy into an existing or new table.

Update

The UPDATE command is used to modify a table. The general format is

```
UPDATE table
   SET column = scalar expression
      [, COLUMN = SCALAR EXPRESSION] ...
   [WHERE condition]
```

Permissible scalar expressions involve columns, scalar functions (see the section on scalar functions in this chapter), or constants. No aggregate functions are allowable.

Updating a single row

UPDATE can be used to modify a single row in a table. Suppose you need to revise your data after 200,000 shares of Minnesota Gold are sold. You would code the following:

```
UPDATE STOCK
   SET STKQTY = STKQTY - 200000
   WHERE STKCODE = 'MG'
```

Updating multiple rows

Multiple rows in a table can be updated as well. Imagine the situation where several stocks change their dividend to £2.50. Then the following statement could be used:

```
UPDATE STOCK
   SET STKDIV = 2.50
   WHERE STKCODE IN ('FC','BS','NG')
```

Updating all rows

All rows in a table can be updated by simply omitting the WHERE clause. To give everyone at The Expeditioner a 5 percent raise, use

```
UPDATE EMPLOYEE
   SET EMPSALARY = EMPSALARY*1.05
```

Updating with a subquery

A subquery can also be used to specify which rows should be changed. Consider the following example. The employees in the departments on the fourth floor of The Expeditioner have won a productivity improvement bonus of 10 percent. The following SQL statement would update their salaries:

```
UPDATE EMPLOYEE
   SET EMPSALARY = EMPSALARY*1.10
   WHERE DEPTNAME IN
      (SELECT DEPTNAME FROM DEPARTMENT WHERE DEPTFLOOR = 4)
```

Delete

The DELETE statement erases one or more rows in a table. The general format is

```
DELETE FROM table
   [WHERE condition]
```

Delete a single record

If all stocks in Burmese Elephant are sold, then this row can be deleted using

```
DELETE FROM STOCK
   WHERE STKCODE = 'BE'
```

Delete multiple records

If all Australian stocks were liquidated, then the following command would delete all the relevant rows:

```
DELETE FROM STOCK
   WHERE NATCODE = 'AUS'
```

Delete all records

All records in a table can be deleted by omitting the WHERE clause. The following statement would delete all rows if the entire portfolio were sold:

```
DELETE FROM STOCK
```

This command is not the same as DROP TABLE because, although the table is empty, it still exists.

Delete with a subquery

Despite their sterling efforts in the recent productivity drive, all the employees on the fourth floor of The Expeditioner have been fired (the rumor is that they were fiddling the tea money). Their records can be deleted using:

```
DELETE FROM EMPLOYEE
   WHERE DEPTNAME IN
      (SELECT DEPTNAME FROM DEPARTMENT WHERE DEPTFLOOR = 4)
```

Nulls—much ado about missing information

Nulls are overworked in SQL because they can represent several situations. Null can represent unknown information. For example, you might add a new stock to the database, but lacking details of its latest dividend, you leave the field null. Null can be used to represent a value that is inapplicable. For instance, the EMPLOYEE table contains a null value in BOSSNO for Alice because she has no boss. The value is not unknown; it is not applicable for that field. In other cases, null might mean "no value supplied" or "value undefined." Because null can have multiple meanings, the user must infer which meaning is appropriate to the circumstances.

Do not confuse null with blank or zero, which are values. In fact, null is a marker that specifies that the value for the particular column is null. Thus, null represents no value.

Well-known database expert, Chris Date,[5] has been outspoken in his concern about the confusion caused by nulls. His advice is that nulls should be explicitly avoided by specifying NOT NULL for all columns and by using codes to make the meaning of a value clear (e.g., "U" means "unknown," "I" means "inapplicable," "N" means "not supplied").

---

5. Date, C. J. 1992. *Relational database: Writings, 1989–1991*. Reading, MA: Addison-Wesley.

Security

Data is a valuable resource for nearly every organization. Just as an organization takes measures to protect its physical assets, it also needs to safeguard electronic assets — its organizational memory, including databases. Furthermore, it often wants to limit the access of authorized users to particular parts of a database and restrict their actions to particular operations.

Two SQL features are used to administer security procedures. A view, discussed earlier in this chapter, can restrict a user's access to specified columns or rows in a table, and authorization commands can establish a user's privileges.

The authorization subsystem is based on the concept of a privilege — the authority to perform an operation. For example, a user cannot update a table unless she has been granted the appropriate update privilege. The database administrator (DBA) is king of the heap and has the highest privilege. The DBA can perform any legal operation. The creator of an object, say a base table, has full privileges for that object. Those with privilege can then use GRANT and REVOKE to extend privileges to or rescind them from other users.

Grant

The GRANT command defines a user's privileges. The general format of the statement is

```
GRANT privileges ON object TO users [WITH GRANT OPTION]
```

where "privileges" can be a list of privileges or the keyword ALL PRIVILEGES, and "users" is a list of user identifiers or the keyword PUBLIC. An "object" can be a base table or view.

The following privileges can be granted for tables and views: SELECT, UPDATE, DELETE, and INSERT.

The UPDATE privilege specifies the particular columns in a base table or view that may be updated. Some privileges apply *only* to base tables. These are ALTER and INDEX.

The following examples illustrate the use of GRANT:

❍ **Give Alice all rights to the STOCK table.**

```
GRANT ALL PRIVILEGES ON STOCK TO ALICE
```

❍ **Permit the accounting staff, Todd and Nancy, to update the price of a stock.**

```
GRANT UPDATE (STKPRICE) ON STOCK TO TODD, NANCY
```

❍ **Give all staff the privilege to select rows from ITEM.**

```
GRANT SELECT ON ITEM TO PUBLIC
```

❍ **Give Alice all rights to view STK.**

```
GRANT SELECT, UPDATE, DELETE, INSERT ON STK TO ALICE
```
[6]

The WITH GRANT OPTION

This option allows a user to transfer his privileges to another user, as this next example illustrates:

❍ **Give Ned all privileges for the ITEM table and permit him to grant any of these to other staff members who may need to work with ITEM.**

```
GRANT ALL PRIVILEGES ON ITEM TO NED WITH GRANT OPTION
```

This means that Ned can now use the GRANT command to give other staff privileges. To give Andrew permission for select and insert on ITEM, for example, Ned would enter

```
GRANT SELECT, INSERT ON ITEM TO ANDREW
```

Revoke

What GRANT granteth, **REVOKE** revoketh. Privileges are removed using the REVOKE statement. The general format of this statement is

```
REVOKE privileges ON object FROM users
```

Some examples illustrate the use of REVOKE.

❍ **Remove Sophie's ability to select from ITEM.**

```
REVOKE SELECT ON ITEM FROM SOPHIE
```

❍ **Nancy is no longer permitted to update stock prices.**

```
REVOKE UPDATE ON STOCK FROM NANCY
```
[7]

Cascading REVOKE

When a REVOKE statement removes a privilege, it can result in more than one revocation. An earlier example illustrated how Ned used his WITH GRANT OPTION right to authorize Andrew to select and insert rows on ITEM. The following REVOKE command

```
REVOKE INSERT ON ITEM FROM NED
```

automatically revokes Andrew's insert privilege.

---

6. In this case, since STK is a view, we cannot use ALL PRIVILEGES because ALL includes ALTER and INDEX privileges, which apply only to base tables and not views.
7. A revoked UPDATE privilege is not column specific.

Synonyms

The CREATE SYNONYM command is used to give a base table or view an alternative name. Synonyms can be created for users who prefer to use words with which they are familiar. For example, a column name might be called PROJECT, but some users may prefer to use the word TASK. In this case, CREATE SYNONYM customizes the system to the needs of these particular users. The command also can reduce the number of keystrokes for qualified names. Suppose you frequently access a table owned by Nostradamus containing details of predictions. By creating a synonym, you give the table a shorter name.

```
CREATE SYNONYM PREDICT FOR NOSTRADAMUS.PREDICTION
```

The query

```
SELECT * FROM PREDICT
```

is equivalent to

```
SELECT * FROM NOSTRADAMUS.PREDICTION
```

and takes fewer keystrokes.

A synonym is deleted with the DROP command, as the following example illustrates:

```
DROP SYNONYM PREDICT
```

The catalog

The catalog[8] describes a relational database. It contains the definitions of base tables, views, indexes, and so on. The catalog itself is a relational database and can be interrogated using SQL. Tables in the catalog are called system tables to distinguish them from base tables though conceptually, these tables are the same. Some important system tables are SYSCATALOG, SYSCOLUMNS, and SYSINDEXES.

SYSCATALOG contains details of all tables in the database. There is one row for each table in the database and the attributes of the rows are table name (TNAME), creator (CREATOR), number of columns (NCOLS), and other data. SYSCATALOG can be queried using SELECT on the qualified name SYSTEM.SYSCATALOG.

❍ **Find the table(s) with the most columns.**

```
SELECT TNAME FROM SYSTEM.SYSCATALOG
   WHERE NCOLS = (SELECT MAX(NCOLS) FROM SYSTEM.SYSCATALOG)
```

SYSCOLUMNS stores details about each column in the database. Each row of SYSCOLUMNS contains data such as column name (CNAME), the table in which the column ap-

8. A catalog is similar to a data dictionary, which is discussed in Chapter 18.

pears (TNAME), type of data in the column (COLTYPE), column length (LENGTH), column creator (CREATOR), and other items.

❍ **I've forgotten the length of a field in table SALE.**

```
SELECT COLNO, CNAME, COLTYPE, LENGTH FROM SYSTEM.SYSCOLUMNS
   WHERE TNAME = 'SALE' AND CREATOR = 'userid'
      ORDER BY COLNO
```

COLNO	CNAME	COLTYPE	LENGTH
1	SALENO	INTEGER	
2	SALEDATE	DATE	
3	SALETEXT	CHAR	50

Sometimes you forget parts of a table definition, such as the length of a text field. The preceding query recalls details of all the columns in a specified table. Notice that you must indicate the userid of the table's creator because others may use the same table name. For convenience, columns are reported in the same order in which they were defined.

❍ **What columns in what tables store dates?**

```
SELECT TNAME, CNAME FROM SYSTEM.SYSCOLUMNS
   WHERE COLTYPE = 'DATE'
```

SYSINDEXES contains details of indexes. There is one row for each index. The attributes of SYSINDEXES include index name (INAME), the name of table indexed (TNAME), and other data.

❍ **Find all tables that have indexes.**

```
SELECT TNAME FROM SYSTEM.SYSINDEXES
```

As you can see, querying the catalog is the same as querying a database. This is a useful feature because you can use SQL queries on the catalog to find out more about a database.

Natural language processing

Infrequent inquirers of a relational database may be reluctant to use SQL because they don't use it often enough to remain familiar with the language. While the QBE approach can make querying easier, a more natural approach is to use standard English. In this case, natural language processing (NLP) is used to convert ordinary English into SQL so the query can be passed to the relational database. The example in Table 10-5 shows the successful translation of a query to SQL. However, when *reported* was used in place of *sorted*, the natural language processor asked for clarification because it did not understand the meaning of *reported*. Thus, NLP must translate a request to SQL and request clarification where necessary. To experience NLP, visit the English Wizard.[9]

9. www.englishwizard.com

Table 10-5: An example of natural language processing

English	SQL generated for MS Access
Which movies have won best foreign film sorted by year?	`SELECT DISTINCT [Year], [Title] FROM [Awards] INNER JOIN [Movies] ON [Movies].[Movie ID] = [Awards].[Movie ID] WHERE [Category]='Best Foreign Film' and [Status]='Winner' ORDER BY [Year] ASC`

Connectivity and ODBC

Over time and because of differing needs, an organization is likely to purchase DBMS software from a variety of vendors. Also, in some situations, mergers and acquisitions can create a multivendor DBMS environment. Consequently, the SQL Access Group developed SQL call-level interface (CLI), a unified standard for remote database access. The intention of CLI is to provide programmers with a generic approach for writing software that accesses a database. With the appropriate CLI database driver, any DBMS server can provide access to client programs that use the CLI. On the server side, the DBMS CLI driver is responsible for translating the CLI call into the server's access language. On the client side, there must be a CLI driver for each database to which it connects. CLI is not a query language but a way of wrapping SQL so it can be understood by a DBMS. In 1996, CLI was adopted as an international standard and renamed X/Open CLI.

Open database connectivity (ODBC)

The de facto standard for database connectivity is **Open database connectivity** (ODBC), an extended implementation of CLI developed by Microsoft. This application programming interface (API) is cross-platform and can be used to access any DBMS or DBMS server that has an ODBC driver.This enables a software developer to build and distribute a client/server application without targeting a specific DBMS. Database drivers are then added to link the application to the client's choice of DBMS. For example, a microcomputer running under OS/2 can use ODBC to access an Oracle DBMS running on a Unix box. Major DBMS vendors (e.g., IBM, Informix, Microsoft, Oracle, and Sybase) support the ODBC API.

There is considerable support for ODBC. Application vendors like it since they do not have to write and maintain code for each DBMS; they can write one API. DBMS vendors support ODBC since they do not have to convince application vendors to support their product. For database systems managers, ODBC provides vendor and platform independence. For end-users, it provides access to corporate data from the desktop. Although the ODBC API was originally developed to provide database access from MS Windows products, many ODBC driver vendors support Linux and Mac clients.

Most vendors also have their own SQL APIs. For example, IBM's DB2 family's native protocol is ESQL/DRDA, but it also supports ODBC and X/Open CLI. The problem is that most vendors, as a means of differentiating their DBMS, have a more extensive native API protocol and also add extensions to standard ODBC. The developer who is tempted to use these extensions threatens the portability of the application.

A serious shortcoming of ODBC is that it is controlled by Microsoft, which may be tempted to move it in a direction that favors its products at the expense of those of other DBMS vendors. Another problem is that ODBC introduces greater complexity and a processing overhead because it adds two layers of software. As Figure 10-3 illustrates, a ODBC compliant application has additional layers for the ODBC API and ODBC driver. As a result, ODBC APIs can never be as fast as native APIs.

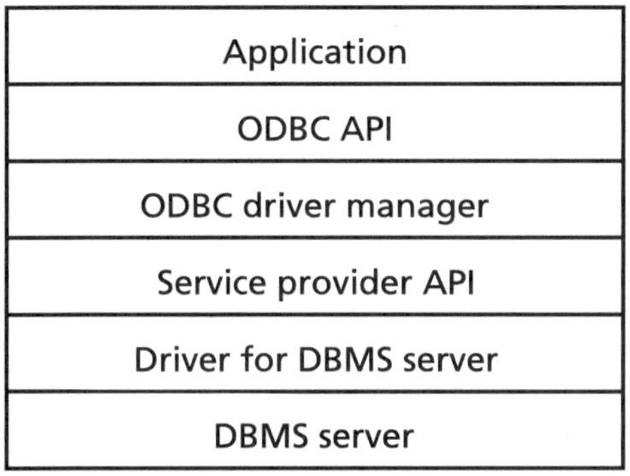

Figure 10-3. ODBC layers

Embedded SQL

SQL can be used in two modes. First, SQL is an interactive query language and database programming language. The SELECT command is used to define interactive queries; INSERT, UPDATE, and DELETE commands are used to define and maintain a database. Second, any interactive SQL statement, including both DDL and DML statements, can be embedded in an application program.

This dual-mode principle is a very useful feature. It means that programmers need learn only one database query language because the same SQL statements apply for both interactive queries and application statements. Programmers can also interactively examine SQL commands before embedding them in a program, a feature that can substantially reduce the time to write an application program.

Because SQL is not a complete programming language, however, it must be used with a traditional programming language to create applications. Common complete programming languages, such as COBOL and Java, support embedded SQL. In this case, we assume the host language is COBOL and the relational DBMS is DB2. A source program containing SQL statements must be processed by an SQL preprocessor before it is compiled. The preprocessor checks the syntax of the SQL statements, turns them into host language comments, and generates host language statements to invoke the DBMS. Portions of a sample COBOL program for DB2 follow:

```
FILE SECTION.
*****************************************************************
* Non-database files are defined here
*****************************************************************
WORKING-STORAGE SECTION.
*****************************************************************
* COBOL variables are defined here
*****************************************************************
01 VALUE              PIC S9(8)V99 COMP-3.
01 TOTAL-VALUE        PIC S9(8)V99 COMP-3.
*****************************************************************
* Define the SQL communication area
*****************************************************************
EXEC SQL INCLUDE SQLCA END-EXEC.
*****************************************************************
* Define variables used to transfer data between the
* application and DB2.
*****************************************************************
   EXEC SQL BEGIN DECLARE SECTION END-EXEC.
01 STOCK-TABLE.
   05 STOCK-CODE      PIC X(3).
   05 STOCK-FIRM      PIC X(20).
   05 STOCK-PRICE     PIC S9(4)V99 COMP-3.
   05 STOCK-QTY       PIC S9(8) COMP-3.
   05 STOCK-DIV       PIC S9(3)V99 COMP-3.
   05 STOCK-PE        PIC S99 COMP-3.
   EXEC SQL END DECLARE SECTION END-EXEC.
*****************************************************************
PROCEDURE DIVISION.
   PERFORM INITIALIZE.
   PERFORM READ-ROW
      UNTIL SQLCODE NOT = 0.
   PERFORM FINISH.
   STOP RUN.
INITIALIZE.
* Declare cursor
   EXEC SQL
    DECLARE STOCK-CURSOR CURSOR FOR
      SELECT * FROM STOCK
   END-EXEC.
* Set variables
   MOVE ZERO TO TOTAL-VALUE.
* Open the cursor
   EXEC SQL
      OPEN STOCK-CURSOR
   END-EXEC.
* Issue an initial FETCH
   EXEC SQL
      FETCH STOCK-CURSOR INTO :STOCK-TABLE
   END-EXEC.
* Check SQLCODE
   IF SQLCODE = 100
      THEN
         DISPLAY "Table is empty"
         STOP RUN
   END-IF.
READ-ROW.
* Calculate and accumulate value
   VALUE = STOCK-PRICE*STOCK-QTY.
   TOTAL-VALUE = TOTAL-VALUE + VALUE.
* Fetch the next row.
EXEC SQL
   FETCH STOCK-CURSOR INTO :STOCK-TABLE
END-EXEC.
FINISH.
   DISPLAY "Total value of stock is" TOTAL-VALUE.
   EXEC SQL
    CLOSE STOCK-CURSOR
   END-EXEC.
```

There are several things to notice about this COBOL program.

1. Every SQL statement is surrounded by the keywords EXEC SQL and END-EXEC. This enables the compiler to identify SQL statements and process them differently from COBOL statements.
2. Only one SQL statement can be included between the EXEC SQL and END-EXEC statements.
3. The DATA DIVISION describes variables that are used to pass data between the application program and DB2 and systems data shared by the application program and DB2.
4. The DECLARE SECTION defines variables that are used to transfer data between the application program and DB2.
5. The SQL table STOCK is defined in the COBOL program as STOCK-TABLE. The columns have been renamed. STKCODE is now STOCK-CODE and so on. The SQL data definitions have been converted to COBOL style. For example, CHAR(3) becomes X(3), and DECIMAL(6,2) becomes S9(4)V99 COMP-3.
6. Systems data are shared through the SQLCA (SQL communications area). SQLCA is defined by the INCLUDE SQLCA statement. SQLCA contains many data items. The most interesting is SQLCODE, which is set by DB2 after each SQL statement is executed. This code has three types of values, as shown in the accompanying table:

SQLCODE	Condition	Example
zero	Normal execution	Successful execution of SQL statement
positive	Unusual, but normal condition	End of data (SQLCODE = 100)
negative	Abnormal, unexpected condition	Insufficient file space

7. There is one difference between embedded SQL and interactive SQL statements. The difference is an INTO clause that tells DB2 the name of the variable into which to place the value(s) retrieved from the database.
8. Because it is possible for a DB2 database and application program to both define a variable with the same name, application variables in an SQL statement are distinguished by preceding them with a colon (:).

There is a fundamental difference between application programming languages, such as COBOL and SQL. COBOL processes one record at a time; SQL processes tables. Thus, an SQL statement will return a table that the COBOL application program then has to process a row or record at a time. This incompatibility is handled by defining a cursor within the application program.

Think of a cursor as a pointer that indicates the row to be processed. In the preceding example, a cursor is defined for processing the STOCK table. The DECLARE statement defines the cursor associated with a particular query.

Opening the cursor in the INITIALIZE paragraph is like opening a file; it gets the table ready for processing. The FETCH statement in the INITIALIZE paragraph retrieves the first row of the table. FETCH is like the READ statement of COBOL, which retrieves one row. A looping structure, based on the READ-ROWS paragraph, is then used to fetch subsequent rows, one at a time, until there are no more rows. Then the cursor is closed, again like a file, and the application program stops.

This brief introduction to embedded SQL is intended to give you an overview of the relationship between SQL and an application development language. Obviously, if you are to write application programs using embedded SQL, you will need considerable training in both the application language and the finer details of how it communicates with SQL.

The future of SQL

Since 1986, developers of database applications have benefited from an SQL standard, one of the most successful standardization stories in the software industry. Most current implementations of SQL follow International Standard Database Language SQL (1992). Known as SQL2, it is both a national standard for the United States and an international standard.

Although most database vendors have implemented their own proprietary extensions of SQL, standardization has kept the language consistent, and SQL code is highly portable. Standardization was relatively easy when focused on the storage and retrieval of numbers and characters. Objects have made standardization more difficult.

If SQL is to continue to thrive it needs to accommodate the major force in current systems development, object-orientation. SQL3 modifies the SQL standard to handle objects. SQLJ simplifies the interface between Java, the popular OO language, and a RDBMS.

SQL3

The **SQL3** standard, which adds object-handling extensions, is a major development. The level of change is quite substantial, and it took considerable time to reach consensus on the new standard. SQL3, which emerged as a standard in 1999, consists of 2,100 pages of definitions, syntax, and usage rules. In contrast, SQL-89 was only 150 pages.

The SQL3 standard is planned to meet three market needs:

- Better support for Java and other object-oriented languages;
- Support for multi-media extensions;
- Retention of portability by defining standards for object-oriented extensions to the relational model. Vendors have made extensions, and the strength and value of the relational model would be severely curtailed if the vendor's extensions are incompatible.

There are two major issues for SQL3. First, will vendors release products that are compatible with the standard? Some vendors have already moved ahead of the standard and added features that may not be in the standard or vary somewhat from the standard. If major vendors go their own way, then considerable cross-platform compatibility will be lost. Second, will SQL3 retain the simplicity, power, and elegance of the current SQL standard? One of the strengths of SQL is that the language is readily learned and deployed. Enhancements always have a cost because they increase complexity.

User-defined types

The SQL3 specification includes the capability to support user-defined data types (UDTs). Prior versions of SQL had predefined data types, and programmers were limited to selecting the data type and defining the length of character strings.

A UDT is used like a predefined type, but it must be set up before it can be used. In order to define a UDT, the database designer must specify 12 pieces of information. One of the basic ideas behind the object extensions is that, in addition to the normal built-in data types defined by SQL, user-defined UDTs are available. These types may be used in the same way as built-in data types. In SQL3, an UDT is defined by specifying a set of declarations of the stored attributes that represent the value of the UDT, the operations that define the equality and ordering relationships of the UDT, and the operations and derived attributes that represent the behavior of the UDT.

SQLJ

In 1997, some leading DBMS and software vendors formed a consortium to define standardization of Java development for database applications. In December 1998, the specification of SQLJ was accepted as an ANSI standard. SQLJ provides integration of SQL and Java, thus reinforcing the adoption and use of Java for enterprise data-intensive applications .

SQLJ gives Java developers a quick and easy way to use SQL directly in their Java applications without having to do database programming. This means that applications involving a very large quantity of data manipulation can be written in Java. SQLJ is a good choice for static SQL programming tasks, and many SQL applications are static in nature. SQLJ does not handle dynamic SQL actions determined at runtime by the application, in which JDBC (see page 471) must be used.

Summary

SQL, a widely used relational database language, has been adopted as a standard by ANSI and ISO. It is both a data definition language (DDL) and data manipulation language (DML). A base table is an autonomous, named table. A view is a virtual table. A key is one or more columns identified as such in the description of a table, an index, or a referential constraint. SQL supports primary, foreign, and unique keys. Indexes accelerate data access and ensure uniqueness. CREATE TABLE defines a new base table and specifies primary, foreign, and unique key constraints. Numeric, string, date, or graphic data can be stored in a column. BLOB is a new data type for multimedia databases. ALTER TABLE adds one new column to a table or changes the status of a constraint. DROP TABLE removes a table from a database. CREATE VIEW defines a view, which can be used to restrict access to data, report derived data, store commonly executed queries, and convert data. A view is created dynamically. DROP VIEW deletes a view. CREATE INDEX defines an index, and DROP INDEX deletes one.

Ambiguous references to column names are avoided by qualifying a column name with its table name. A table or view can be given a temporary name that remains current for a query. SQL has four data manipulation statements — SELECT, INSERT, UPDATE, and DELETE. INSERT adds one or more rows to a table. UPDATE modifies a table by changing one or more rows. DELETE removes one or more rows from a table. SELECT provides powerful interrogation facilities. The product of two tables is a new table consisting of all rows of the first table concatenated with all possible rows of the second table. Join creates a new table from two existing tables by matching on a column common to both tables. A subquery is a query within a query. A correlated subquery differs from a simple subquery in that the inner query is evaluated multiple times rather than once.

SQL's aggregate functions increase its retrieval power. GROUP BY supports grouping of rows that have the same value for a specified column. The LIKE clause supports pattern matching. SQL includes scalar functions that can be used in arithmetic expressions, data conversion, or data extraction. Nulls cause problems because they can represent several situations — unknown information, inapplicable information, no value supplied, or value undefined. Remember, a null is not a blank or zero. The SQL commands GRANT and REVOKE support data security. GRANT authorizes a user to perform certain SQL operations, and REVOKE removes a user's authority. The CREATE SYNONYM command can be used to give a base table or view an alternative name. SYSCATALOG, which describes a relational database, can be queried using SELECT. SQL can be used as an interactive query language and as embedded commands within an application programming language.

Natural language processing (NLP), open database connectivity (ODBC), and SQL3 are extensions to relational technology that enhance its usefulness in terms of query writing, compatibility, and handling objects, respectively. SQL3 and SQLJ are part of the trend of linking the dominant programming model, object-orientation, to the dominant data management model, relational technology.

Key terms and concepts

Abstract data type (ADT)
Aggregate functions
ALTER TABLE
ANSI
Base table
Complete database language
Complete programming language
Composite key
Connectivity
Correlated subquery
CREATE INDEX
CREATE TABLE
CREATE VIEW
Cursor
Data definition language (DDL)
Data manipulation language (DML)
Data types
DELETE
DROP INDEX
DROP TABLE
DROP VIEW
Embedded SQL
Foreign key
GRANT
GROUP BY
Index
INSERT
ISO
Join
Key
Natural language processing (NLP)
Null
Open database connectivity (ODBC)
Primary key
Product
Qualified name
Referential integrity rule
REVOKE
Scalar functions
Security
SELECT
Special registers
SQL
SQL3
SQLJ
Subquery
Synonym
SYSCATALOG
SYSCOLUMNS
SYSINDEXES
Temporary names
Unique key
UPDATE
View

References and additional readings

Date, C. J. 2000. *An introduction to database systems*. 7th ed. Reading, MA: Addison-Wesley.

Date, C. J. 1993. *A guide to the SQL Standard: A user's guide to the standard relational language SQL*. 3rd ed. Reading, MA: Addison-Wesley.

Gulutzan, P., and T. Pelzer. 1999. *SQL-99 complete, really.* Lawrence, KS: R & D Books.

Exercises

1. Why is it important that SQL was adopted as a standard by ANSI and ISO?
2. What does it mean to say "SQL is a complete database language?"
3. Is SQL a complete programming language? What are the implications of your answer?
4. List some operational advantages of a relational DBMS.
5. What is the difference between a base table and a view?
6. What is the difference between a primary key and a unique key?

7. What is the purpose of an index?
8. Consider the three choices for the ON DELETE clause associated with the foreign key constraint. What are the pros and cons of each option?
9. Specify the data type (e.g., DECIMAL(6,2)) you would use for the following columns:
   a. The selling price of a house.
   b. A telephone number with area code.
   c. Hourly temperatures in Antarctica.
   d. A numeric customer code.
   e. A credit card number.
   f. The distance between two cities.
   g. A sentence using Chinese characters.
   h. The number of kilometers from the Earth to a given star.
   i. The text of an advertisement in the classified section of a newspaper.
   j. A basketball score.
   k. The title of a CD.
   l. The X-ray of a patient.
   m. A U.S. zip code.
   n. A British or Canadian postal code.
   o. The photo of a customer.
   p. The date a person purchased a car.
   q. The time of arrival of an e-mail message.
   r. The number of full-time employees in a small business.
   s. The text of a speech.
   t. The thickness of a layer on a silicon chip.
10. How could you add two columns to an existing table? Precisely describe the steps you would take.
11. What is the difference between DROP TABLE and deleting all the rows in a table?
12. Give some reasons for creating a view.
13. When is a view created?
14. Write SQL codes to create a unique index on firm name for the SHR table defined in Chapter 3. Would it make sense to create a unique index for PE ratio in the same table?
15. What is the difference between product and join?
16. What is the difference between an equijoin and a natural join?
17. You have a choice between executing two queries that will both give the same result. One is written as a simple subquery and the other as a correlated subquery. Which one would you use and why?
18. What function would you use for the following situations?
   a. Computing the total value of a column.
   b. Finding the minimum value of a column.
   c. Counting the number of customers in the CUSTOMER table.
   d. Displaying a number with specified precision.
   e. Reporting the month part of a date.
   f. Displaying the second part of a time.

g. Retrieving the first five characters of a city's name.
h. Reporting the distance to the sun in feet.

19. A student database records a home and school term phone number for each student. Some students have a null value for school term phone number. What does this mean?
20. Write SQL statements for the following:
    a. Let Hui-Tze query and add to the NATION table.
    b. Give Lana permission to update the phone number column in the CUSTOMER table.
    c. Remove all of William's privileges.
    d. Give Chris permission to grant other users authority to select from the ADDRESS table.
    e. Create a short name for the table PINNOCHIO.FALSEHOODS.
    f. Find the name of all tables that include the word SALE.
    g. List all the tables owned by user CMS5432.
    h. What is the length of the column STREETNAME?
    i. Find all columns that have a data type of SMALLINT.
21. What are the two modes in which you can use SQL?
22. How do COBOL and SQL differ in the way they process data? How is this difference handled in an application program? What is embedded SQL?

Reference 2

SQL Playbook

Play so that you may be serious.
Anacharsis (c. 600 B.C.E.)

The power of SQL

SQL is a very powerful retrieval language, and most novices underestimate its capability. Furthermore, mastery of SQL takes considerable practice and exposure to a wide variety of problems. This reference serves the dual purpose of revealing the full power of SQL and providing an extensive set of diverse queries. To make this reference easier to use, we have named each of the queries to make them easy to remember.

Lacroix and Pirotte[1] have defined 66 queries for testing a query language's power, and their work is the foundation of this chapter. Not all their queries are included; some have been kept for the end-of-chapter exercises. Also, many of the queries have been reworded to various extents. Because these queries are more difficult than those normally used in business decision making, they provide a good test of your SQL skills. If you can answer all of them, then you are a proficient SQL programmer. The set of queries also can be used as a test package for evaluating the capability of an implementation of SQL.

You are encouraged to formulate and test your answer to a query before reading the suggested solution.[2] A *Q* has been prefixed to all entity and table names to distinguish them from entities and tables used in earlier problems. The going gets tough after the first few queries, and you can expect to spend some time formulating and testing each one, but remember, this is still considerably faster than using a conventional programming language, such as COBOL, to write the same queries.

---

1. Lacroix, M., and A. Pirotte. 1976. *Example queries in relational languages.* Brussels, M.B.L.E, Technical note no. 107.
2. The author is indebted to Dr. Mohammad Dadashzadeh of Wichita State University in Kansas, who provided valuable assistance by checking each query. Dr. Gert Jan Hofstede of Wageningen University in the Netherlands also willingly contributed some improvements. Many of their suggestions for the SQL code to answer these queries have been incorporated. All the queries have been tested with a small database. If you discover a problem with a query or a better way of expressing it, please send an e-mail message to rwatson@terry.uga.edu.

The data model accompanying Lacroix and Pirotte's queries is shown in Table R2-1. You will notice that the complexity of the real world has been reduced; a sale and a delivery are assumed to have only one item. The corresponding relational model is shown in Table R2-1, and some data that can be used to test your SQL queries appear at the end of this chapter.

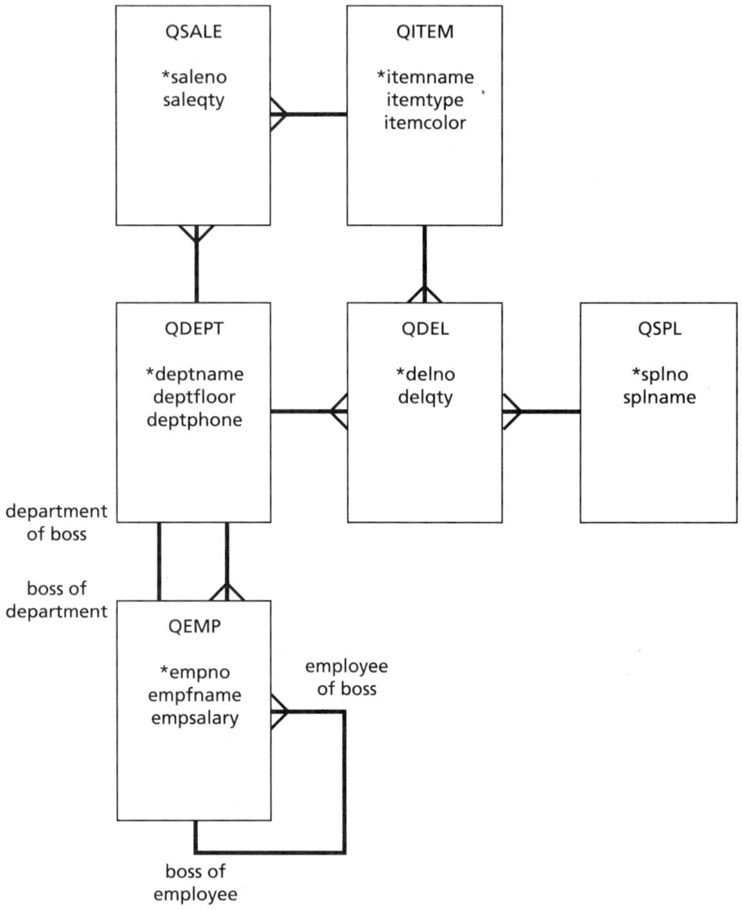

Figure R2-1. Data model

Table R2-1. Relational tables

QSALE			
<u>SALENO</u>	SALEQTY	*ITEMNAME*	*DEPTNAME*

QITEM		
<u>ITEMNAME</u>	ITEMTYPE	ITEMCOLOR

QDEL				
<u>DELNO</u>	DELQTY	*ITEMNAME*	*DEPTNAME*	*SPLNO*

QSPL	
<u>SPLNO</u>	SPLNAME

QDEPT			
<u>DEPTNAME</u>	DEPTFLOOR	DEPTPHONE	*EMPNO*

QEMP				
<u>EMPNO</u>	EMPFNAME	EMPSALARY	*DEPTNAME*	*BOSSNO*

1. A slow full toss

In cricket, a slow full toss is the easiest ball to hit. The same applies to this simple query.

❍ **Find the names of employees in the Marketing department.**

```
SELECT EMPFNAME FROM QEMP WHERE DEPTNAME = 'Marketing'
```

2. Skinning a cat

Queries often can be solved in several ways. For this query, four possible solutions are presented. Also, we indicate the resource units required to answer the query. This resource measure is supplied by SQL/VM when the query is executed.

❍ **Find the items sold by the departments on the second floor.**

2.1 Join (545 units)

```
SELECT DISTINCT ITEMNAME FROM QSALE, QDEPT
   WHERE QDEPT.DEPTNAME = QSALE.DEPTNAME
   AND DEPTFLOOR = 2
```

A join of QSALE and QDEPT is possibly the most obvious way to answer this query. In this case, it is a two-table join because ITEMNAME is a foreign key in QDEPT. If ITEMNO were the key of QITEM, a three-way join of QDEPT, QSALE, and QITEM is required.

2.2 In (8)

```
SELECT DISTINCT ITEMNAME FROM QSALE
   WHERE DEPTNAME IN
      (SELECT DEPTNAME FROM QDEPT WHERE DEPTFLOOR = 2)
```

Another simple approach is to use an IN clause. First find all the departments on the second floor, and then find a match in QSALE. The subquery returns a list of all departments on the second floor. Then use the IN clause to find a match on department name in QSALE. Notice that this is the most efficient form of the query.

2.3 Correlated subquery (7,780)

```
SELECT DISTINCT ITEMNAME FROM QSALE
   WHERE DEPTNAME IN
      (SELECT DISTINCT DEPTNAME FROM QDEPT
         WHERE QDEPT.DEPTNAME = QSALE.DEPTNAME
         AND DEPTFLOOR = 2)
```

A correlated subquery is another approach. Conceptually, you can think of this query as stepping through QSALE one row at a time. The subquery is executed for each row of QSALE, and if there is a match for the current value of QSALE.DEPTNAME, the current value of ITEMNAME is listed.

2.4 Exists (8,080)

```
SELECT DISTINCT ITEMNAME FROM QSALE
   WHERE EXISTS
      (SELECT * FROM QDEPT
         WHERE QSALE.DEPTNAME = QDEPT.DEPTNAME
         AND DEPTFLOOR = 2)
```

EXISTS works similarly to a subquery. Conceptually, think of this query as stepping through each row of QSALE and evaluating whether the existence test is true. Remember, EXISTS returns *true* if there is at least one row in the inner query for which the condition is true.

The difference between a correlated subquery and existence testing is that a correlated subquery returns either the value of a column or an empty table, while EXISTS returns either *true* or *false*. It may help to think of this version of the query as, "Select item names from sale such that there exists a department relating them to the second floor."

3. Another full toss

❍ **Find the names of items sold on floors other than the second floor.**

This straightforward query is a slight adaptation of the second. Just change the equals sign to a not equals sign.

```
SELECT DISTINCT ITEMNAME FROM QSALE, QDEPT
   WHERE QSALE.DEPTNAME = QDEPT.DEPTNAME
   AND DEPTFLOOR <> 2
```

4. Subtracting from all

❍ **Find the items sold by no department on the second floor.**

You may first think this query is the same as the preceding. However, the prior query does not exclude an item that is sold on some other floor in addition to the second floor. For example, if polo sticks are sold on both the third and second floors, they will be reported by the preceding query because they are sold on a floor other than the second floor.

The correct way to approach this is, to first get a list of all items sold on the second floor (the second query) and then subtract this result from all items sold. Clearly, the difference must be all items not sold on the second floor.

```
SELECT DISTINCT ITEMNAME FROM QSALE
   WHERE ITEMNAME NOT IN
      (SELECT DISTINCT ITEMNAME FROM QSALE, QDEPT
         WHERE QSALE.DEPTNAME = QDEPT.DEPTNAME
         AND DEPTFLOOR = 2)
```

5. Dividing

❍ **Find the items sold by all departments on the second floor.**

This is the relational algebra divide or the SQL double NOT EXISTS encountered in Chapter 5. You can think of this query as

Select items from sales such that there does not exist a department on the second floor that does not sell this item.

However, it is easier to apply the SQL template described in Chapter 5, which is

```
SELECT TARGET1 FROM TARGET
   WHERE NOT EXISTS
      (SELECT * FROM SOURCE
         WHERE NOT EXISTS
            (SELECT * FROM TARGET-SOURCE
               WHERE TARGET-SOURCE.TARGET = TARGET.TARGET
               AND TARGET-SOURCE.SOURCE = SOURCE.SOURCE))
```

The substitutions are straightforward.

TARGET1	=	ITEMNAME
TARGET	=	ITEM
SOURCE	=	QDEPT
TARGET-SOURCE	=	QSALE

Some additional code needs to be added to handle the restriction to items on the second floor. The query becomes

```
SELECT DISTINCT ITEMNAME FROM QITEM
   WHERE NOT EXISTS
      (SELECT * FROM QDEPT WHERE DEPTFLOOR =2
      AND NOT EXISTS
         (SELECT * FROM QSALE
            WHERE QSALE.ITEMNAME = QITEM.ITEMNAME
            AND QSALE.DEPTNAME = QDEPT.DEPTNAME))
```

Here is an alternative approach to formulating the problem:

Find all the items for which the number of second-floor departments that sells them is equal to the total number of departments on the second floor.

```
SELECT QSALE.ITEMNAME FROM QSALE, QDEPT
   WHERE QSALE.DEPTNAME = QDEPT.DEPTNAME
   AND QDEPT.DEPTFLOOR = 2
      GROUP BY QSALE.ITEMNAME
         HAVING COUNT(DISTINCT QDEPT.DEPTNAME) =
            (SELECT COUNT(DISTINCT DEPTNAME)
               FROM QDEPT WHERE DEPTFLOOR = 2)
```

6. At least some number

❍ **Find the items sold by at least two departments on the second floor.**

The GROUP BY and HAVING clauses make it easy for you to count the number of rows that meet some condition.

```
SELECT ITEMNAME FROM QSALE, QDEPT
   WHERE QSALE.DEPTNAME = QDEPT.DEPTNAME AND DEPTFLOOR = 2
      GROUP BY ITEMNAME
         HAVING COUNT(DISTINCT QDEPT.DEPTNAME) > 1
```

7. A friendly IN for an SQL traveler

❍ **Find the salary of Clare's manager.**

This query is readily handled with the IN clause. The inner query gets the employee number of Clare's manager, and this locates the row containing that person's salary.

```
SELECT EMPFNAME, EMPSALARY FROM QEMP
   WHERE EMPNO IN
      (SELECT BOSSNO FROM QEMP WHERE EMPFNAME = 'Clare')
```

8. Joining a table with itself

❍ **Find numbers and names of those employees who make more than their manager.**

This query is a simple play once you realize that you can conceptually create two copies of a table and join them. This type of query is discussed in more depth in Chapter 6.

```
SELECT WRK.EMPNO, WRK.EMPFNAME FROM QEMP WRK, QEMP BOSS
   WHERE WRK.BOSSNO = BOSS.EMPNO
   AND BOSS.EMPSALARY < WRK.EMPSALARY
```

9. A combination of subtract from all and a self-join

❍ **Find the departments where all the employees earn less than their manager.**

The key is to first find the departments where at least one employee earns more than or the same as the manager, and then subtract these departments from the set of all departments. Also, we exclude Management because it has no boss. What is left must be the departments where no employee earns more than the manager. This query is a combination, conceptually, of queries 4 and 8.

```
SELECT DISTINCT DEPTNAME FROM QEMP
   WHERE DEPTNAME <> 'MANAGEMENT'
   AND DEPTNAME NOT IN
      (SELECT WRK.DEPTNAME FROM QEMP WRK, QEMP BOSS
         WHERE WRK.BOSSNO = BOSS.EMPNO
         AND WRK.EMPSALARY >= BOSS.EMPSALARY)
```

10. Self-join with GROUP BY

❍ **Count the number of direct employees of each manager.**

Join the table with itself by matching employees and their managers and then group by manager's name with a count. Just in case two bosses have the same first name, employee number is included in the selection and grouping clauses.

```
SELECT BOSS.EMPNO, BOSS.EMPFNAME, COUNT(*)
   FROM QEMP WRK, QEMP BOSS
      WHERE WRK.BOSSNO = BOSS.EMPNO
         GROUP BY BOSS.EMPNO, BOSS.EMPFNAME
```

11. A self-join with two matching conditions

❍ **Find the names of employees who are in the same department as their manager (as an employee). Report the name of the employee, the department, and the boss's name.**

There is no reason why a join cannot have matching on more than one common column. Here we have two conditions: one for employee number and one for department name.

```
SELECT WRK.EMPFNAME, WRK.DEPTNAME, BOSS.EMPFNAME
   FROM QEMP WRK, QEMP BOSS
      WHERE WRK.BOSSNO = BOSS.EMPNO
      AND WRK.DEPTNAME = BOSS.DEPTNAME
```

12. Averaging with GROUP BY

❍ **List the departments having an average salary over $25,000.**

A gimme for any half-decent SQL programmer.

```
SELECT DEPTNAME, AVG(EMPSALARY) FROM QEMP
   GROUP BY DEPTNAME
      HAVING AVG(EMPSALARY) > 25000
```

13. Inner query GROUP BY and HAVING

❍ **List the departments where the average salary of the employees of each manager is more than $25,000.**

This query is more challenging than simple averaging. Note that the query implies that you should exclude the manager's salary from the calculation. An employee is the manager of a particular department if that person's employee number and the department name are in the same row in QDEPT (i.e., WRK.EMPNO = QDEPT.EMPNO AND WRK.DEPTNAME = QDEPT.DEPTNAME). Once the department manager has been excluded, then use grouping to get the employee data by department.

```
SELECT WRK.DEPTNAME, AVG(WRK.EMPSALARY)
   FROM QEMP WRK
      WHERE WRK.EMPNO NOT IN
         (SELECT QDEPT.EMPNO FROM QDEPT
            WHERE WRK.EMPNO = QDEPT.EMPNO
            AND WRK.DEPTNAME = QDEPT.DEPTNAME)
               GROUP BY WRK.DEPTNAME
                  HAVING AVG(WRK.EMPSALARY) > 25000
```

14. An IN with GROUP BY and COUNT

❍ **List the name and salary of the managers with more than two employees.**

The inner query uses grouping with counting to identify the employee numbers of managers with more than two employees. The outer query reports details of these managers.

```
SELECT EMPFNAME, EMPSALARY FROM QEMP
   WHERE EMPNO IN
      (SELECT BOSSNO FROM QEMP
         GROUP BY BOSSNO HAVING COUNT(*) > 2)
```

15. A self-join with some conditions

❍ **List the name, salary, and manager of the employees of the Marketing department who have a salary over $25,000.**

A join gets workers and bosses together in the same row, and then the various conditions are applied to restrict the rows reported.

```
SELECT WRK.EMPFNAME, WRK.EMPSALARY, BOSS.EMPFNAME
   FROM QEMP WRK, QEMP BOSS
      WHERE WRK.BOSSNO = BOSS.EMPNO
      AND WRK.DEPTNAME = 'Marketing'
      AND WRK.EMPSALARY > 25000
```

16. Making comparisons

❍ **List the names of the employees who earn more than any employee in the Marketing department.**

The first step is to determine the maximum salary of anyone in the Marketing department. Then, find anyone with a larger salary.

```
SELECT EMPFNAME, EMPSALARY FROM QEMP
   WHERE EMPSALARY >
      (SELECT MAX(EMPSALARY) FROM QEMP
         WHERE DEPTNAME = 'Marketing')
```

17. An IN with GROUP BY and SUM

❍ **Among all the departments with total salary greater than $25,000, find the departments that sell Stetsons.**

This is very similar to query 16. First, find the departments that satisfy the condition, and then select from that list any departments that sell Stetsons.

```
SELECT DISTINCT DEPTNAME FROM QSALE
   WHERE ITEMNAME = 'Stetson'
   AND DEPTNAME IN
      (SELECT DEPTNAME FROM QEMP
         GROUP BY DEPTNAME HAVING SUM(EMPSALARY) > 25000)
```

18. A double divide!

❍ **List the items delivered by every supplier that delivers all items of type N.**

SQL programmers who tackle this query without blinking an eye are superheroes. This is a genuinely true-blue, tough query because it is two divides. There is an inner divide that determines the suppliers that deliver all items of type N. The SQL for this query is

```
SELECT * FROM QSPL
   WHERE NOT EXISTS
      (SELECT * FROM QITEM WHERE ITEMTYPE = 'N'
      AND NOT EXISTS
         (SELECT * FROM QDEL
            WHERE QDEL.ITEMNAME = QITEM.ITEMNAME
            AND QDEL.SPLNO = QSPL.SPLNO))
```

Then there is an outer divide that determines which of the suppliers (returned by the inner divide) provide all these items. If we call the result of the inner query QSPN, the SQL for the outer query is

```
SELECT DISTINCT ITEMNAME FROM QDEL DEL
   WHERE NOT EXISTS
      (SELECT * FROM QSPN
         WHERE NOT EXISTS
            (SELECT * FROM QDEL
               WHERE QDEL.ITEMNAME = DEL.ITEMNAME
               AND QDEL.SPLNO = QSPN.SPLNO))
```

The complete query is

```
SELECT DISTINCT ITEMNAME FROM QDEL DEL
   WHERE NOT EXISTS
      (SELECT * FROM QSPL
         WHERE NOT EXISTS
            (SELECT * FROM QITEM WHERE ITEMTYPE = 'N'
            AND NOT EXISTS
               (SELECT * FROM QDEL
                  WHERE QDEL.ITEMNAME = QITEM.ITEMNAME
                  AND QDEL.SPLNO = QSPL.SPLNO))
         AND NOT EXISTS
            (SELECT * FROM QDEL
               WHERE QDEL.ITEMNAME = DEL.ITEMNAME
               AND QDEL.SPLNO = QSPL.SPLNO))
```

19. A slam dunk

❍ **Find the suppliers that deliver compasses.**

A simple query to recover from the double divide. It is a good idea to include supplier number since SPLNAME could possibly be non-unique.

```
SELECT DISTINCT QSPL.SPLNO, SPLNAME FROM QSPL, QDEL
   WHERE QSPL.SPLNO = QDEL.SPLNO AND ITEMNAME = 'Compass'
```

20. A 6-inch putt for a birdie

❍ **Find the suppliers that do not deliver compasses.**

This is a relatively straightforward subtract (and take one off par for a birdie).

```
SELECT SPLNO, SPLNAME FROM QSPL
   WHERE SPLNO NOT IN
      (SELECT SPLNO FROM QDEL WHERE ITEMNAME = 'Compass')
```

21. Making the count

❍ **Find the suppliers that deliver an item other than compasses.**

A simple approach is to find those suppliers that supply items other than compasses (i.e., ITEMNAME <> 'Compass') and also supply compasses (the subquery).

```
SELECT DISTINCT QDEL.SPLNO, SPLNAME FROM QSPL, QDEL
   WHERE QDEL.SPLNO = QSPL.SPLNO
   AND ITEMNAME <> 'COMPASS'
   AND QDEL.SPLNO IN
      (SELECT SPLNO FROM QDEL WHERE ITEMNAME = 'COMPASS')
```

A more general approach is to find suppliers that have delivered compasses and more than one item (i.e., COUNT(DISTINCT ITEMNAME) > 1). This means they deliver at least an item other than compasses. Note that the GROUP BY clause includes supplier number to cope with the situation where two suppliers have the same name. The DISTINCT ITEMNAME clause must be used to guard against multiple deliveries of compasses from the same supplier.

```
SELECT DISTINCT QDEL.SPLNO, SPLNAME FROM QSPL, QDEL
   WHERE QDEL.SPLNO = QSPL.SPLNO
   AND QDEL.SPLNO IN
      (SELECT SPLNO FROM QDEL WHERE ITEMNAME = 'COMPASS')
   GROUP BY QDEL.SPLNO, SPLNAME HAVING COUNT(DISTINCT ITEMNAME) > 1
```

The more general approach enables you to solve queries such as, *Find suppliers that deliver three items other than compasses by changing the HAVING clause to COUNT(DISTINCT ITEMNAME > 3).*

Unfortunately, because DISTINCT *colname* is not supported by MS Access, for that DBMS you must first create a view containing distinct SPLNO, ITEMNAME pairs and then substitute the name of the view for QDEL and drop the DISTINCT clause in the COUNT statement.

22. Minus and divide

❍ **List the departments that have not recorded a sale for all the items of type N.**

This query has two parts, an inner divide and an outer minus. The inner query finds departments that have sold all items of type N. These are then subtracted from all departments to leave only those that have not sold all items of type N.

```
SELECT DEPTNAME FROM QDEPT WHERE DEPTNAME NOT IN
   (SELECT DEPTNAME FROM QDEPT
      WHERE NOT EXISTS
         (SELECT * FROM QITEM WHERE ITEMTYPE = 'N'
         AND NOT EXISTS
            (SELECT * FROM QSALE
               WHERE QSALE.DEPTNAME = QDEPT.DEPTNAME AND
               QSALE.ITEMNAME = QITEM.ITEMNAME)))
```

23. Division with copies

❍ **List the departments that have at least one sale of all the items delivered to them.**

This is a variation on the divide concept. Normally with a divide, you have three tables representing an m:m relationship. In this case, you only have two tables, QDEL and QSALE. You can still construct the query, however, by creating two copies of QDEL (DEL1 and DEL2 in this case) and then proceeding as if you had three different tables. Also, you must match on DEPTNAME so that you get the correct (DEPTNAME, ITEMNAME) pair for comparing with QSALE.

```
SELECT DISTINCT DEPTNAME FROM QDEL DEL1
   WHERE NOT EXISTS
      (SELECT * FROM QDEL DEL2
         WHERE DEL2.DEPTNAME = DEL1.DEPTNAME
         AND NOT EXISTS
            (SELECT * FROM QSALE
               WHERE DEL2.ITEMNAME = QSALE.ITEMNAME
               AND DEL1.DEPTNAME = QSALE.DEPTNAME))
```

This query can also be written as shown next. Observe how NOT IN functions like NOT EXISTS. We will use this variation on divide with some of the upcoming queries.

```
SELECT DISTINCT DEPTNAME FROM QDEL DEL1
   WHERE NOT EXISTS
      (SELECT * FROM QDEL DEL2
         WHERE DEL2.DEPTNAME = DEL1.DEPTNAME
         AND ITEMNAME NOT IN
            (SELECT ITEMNAME FROM QSALE
               WHERE DEPTNAME = DEL1.DEPTNAME))
```

24. A difficult pairing

❍ **List the supplier-department pairs where the department sells all items delivered to it by the supplier.**

This query is yet another variation on divide. An additional complication is that you have to match the department name and item name of sales and deliveries.

```
SELECT SPLNAME, DEPTNAME FROM QDEL DEL1, QSPL
   WHERE DEL1.SPLNO = QSPL.SPLNO
   AND NOT EXISTS
      (SELECT * FROM QDEL
         WHERE QDEL.DEPTNAME = DEL1.DEPTNAME
         AND QDEL.SPLNO = DEL1.SPLNO
         AND ITEMNAME NOT IN
            (SELECT ITEMNAME FROM QSALE
               WHERE QSALE.DEPTNAME = DEL1.DEPTNAME))
```

25. Two divides and an intersection

❍ **List the items delivered to all departments by all suppliers.**

This query has three parts. First, find the items delivered by all suppliers (the first divide); then find the items delivered to all departments (the second divide). Finally, find the items that satisfy both conditions — the function of the AND connection between the two divides. The items reported must be the ones both delivered by all suppliers and delivered to all departments. The administrative departments (Management, Marketing, Personnel, Accounting, and Purchasing) should be excluded because they do not sell items.

```
SELECT ITEMNAME FROM QITEM
   WHERE NOT EXISTS
      (SELECT * FROM QSPL
         WHERE NOT EXISTS
            (SELECT * FROM QDEL
               WHERE QDEL.ITEMNAME = QITEM.ITEMNAME
               AND QDEL.SPLNO = QSPL.SPLNO))
   AND NOT EXISTS
      (SELECT * FROM QDEPT WHERE DEPTNAME
         NOT IN ('Management', 'Marketing', 'Personnel',
            'Accounting', 'Purchasing')
          AND NOT EXISTS
             (SELECT * FROM QDEL
                WHERE QDEL.ITEMNAME = QITEM.ITEMNAME
                AND QDEL.DEPTNAME = QDEPT.DEPTNAME))
```

26. A divide with a matching condition

❍ **List the items sold only by departments that sell all the items delivered to them.**

Yet another variation on divide—which is why you needed a break. There are two parts to this query. First, look for items sold by departments that sell all items delivered to them, and then make sure that no other department sells the same item.

```
SELECT DISTINCT ITEMNAME FROM QSALE SALE
   WHERE DEPTNAME IN
      (SELECT DEPTNAME FROM QDEPT DEPT1
         WHERE NOT EXISTS
            (SELECT * FROM QDEL
               WHERE QDEL.DEPTNAME = DEPT1.DEPTNAME
               AND ITEMNAME NOT IN
                  (SELECT ITEMNAME FROM QSALE
                     WHERE QSALE.DEPTNAME = DEPT1.DEPTNAME)))
   AND NOT EXISTS
      (SELECT * FROM QSALE
         WHERE ITEMNAME = SALE.ITEMNAME
         AND DEPTNAME NOT IN
            (SELECT DEPTNAME FROM QDEPT DEPT2
               WHERE NOT EXISTS
                  (SELECT * FROM QDEL
                     WHERE QDEL.DEPTNAME = DEPT2.DEPTNAME
                     AND ITEMNAME NOT IN
                        (SELECT ITEMNAME FROM QSALE
                           WHERE QSALE.DEPTNAME = DEPT2.DEPTNAME))))
```

27. Restricted divide

❍ **Who are the suppliers that deliver all the items of type N?**

A slight variation on the standard divide to restrict consideration to the type N items.

```
SELECT SPLNO, SPLNAME FROM QSPL
   WHERE NOT EXISTS
      (SELECT * FROM QITEM WHERE ITEMTYPE = 'N'
      AND NOT EXISTS
         (SELECT * FROM QDEL
            WHERE QDEL.SPLNO = QSPL.SPLNO
            AND QDEL.ITEMNAME = QITEM.ITEMNAME))
```

28. A NOT IN variation on divide

❍ **List the suppliers that deliver only the items sold by the Books department.**

This query may be rewritten as, *Select suppliers where there does not exist a delivery which does not include the items sold by the Books department*. Note the use of the IN clause to limit consideration to those suppliers that have made a delivery. Otherwise, a supplier that has never delivered an item will be reported as delivering only the items sold by the Books department.

```
SELECT SPLNAME FROM QSPL
   WHERE SPLNO IN (SELECT SPLNO FROM QDEL)
   AND NOT EXISTS
       (SELECT * FROM QDEL
          WHERE QDEL.SPLNO = QSPL.SPLNO
          AND ITEMNAME NOT IN
             (SELECT ITEMNAME FROM QSALE
                WHERE DEPTNAME = 'Books'))
```

29. All and only

❍ **List the suppliers that deliver all and only the items sold by the Equipment department.**

This is one query with three parts. The first part identifies suppliers that deliver all items sold by the Equipment department (they could also deliver other items, but these are not sold in the Equipment department). The second part identifies suppliers that deliver only items sold by the Equipment department (i.e., they do not deliver any other items). This part is similar to the previous query. The third part is the intersection of the first two queries to indicate suppliers that satisfy both conditions.

```
SELECT SPLNAME FROM QSPL
   WHERE NOT EXISTS
       (SELECT * FROM QSALE
          WHERE DEPTNAME = 'Equipment'
          AND ITEMNAME NOT IN
             (SELECT ITEMNAME FROM QDEL
                WHERE QDEL.SPLNO = QSPL.SPLNO))
                AND NOT EXISTS
                   (SELECT * FROM QDEL
                      WHERE QDEL.SPLNO = QSPL.SPLNO
                      AND ITEMNAME NOT IN
                         (SELECT ITEMNAME FROM QSALE
                            WHERE DEPTNAME = 'Equipment'))
```

30. Divide with an extra condition

❍ **List the suppliers that deliver every item of type C to the same department on the second floor.**

This is a divide in which there are three WHERE conditions in the innermost query. The extra condition handles the "same department" requirement.

```
SELECT SPLNAME FROM QSPL
   WHERE EXISTS (SELECT * FROM QDEPT
      WHERE DEPTFLOOR = 2
      AND NOT EXISTS (SELECT * FROM QITEM
         WHERE ITEMTYPE = 'C'
         AND NOT EXISTS (SELECT * FROM QDEL
            WHERE QDEL.SPLNO = QSPL.SPLNO
            AND QDEL.ITEMNAME = QITEM.ITEMNAME
            AND QDEL.DEPTNAME = QDEPT.DEPTNAME)))
```

31. At least some COUNT

❍ **List the suppliers that deliver at least two items of type N to departments.**

First, do a three-way join to get the data for deliveries, suppliers, and items. Then, group with a COUNT condition. This can be easily extended to a variety of conditions based on counts.

```
SELECT QSPL.SPLNO, SPLNAME FROM QDEL, QSPL, QITEM
   WHERE ITEMTYPE = 'N'
   AND QDEL.SPLNO = QSPL.SPLNO
   AND QDEL.ITEMNAME = QITEM.ITEMNAME
      GROUP BY QSPL.SPLNO, SPLNAME
         HAVING COUNT(DISTINCT QDEL.ITEMNAME) > 1
```

32. Double divide with a restriction

❍ **List the suppliers that deliver all the items of type B to departments on the second floor who sell all the items of type R.**

Break this query into two parts. First, create a view of departments on the second floor who sell all items of type R.

```
CREATE VIEW V32 AS
   (SELECT DEPTNAME FROM QDEPT
      WHERE DEPTFLOOR = 2
      AND NOT EXISTS (SELECT * FROM QITEM
         WHERE ITEMTYPE = 'R'
         AND NOT EXISTS (SELECT * FROM QSALE
            WHERE QSALE.ITEMNAME = QITEM.ITEMNAME
            AND QSALE.DEPTNAME = QDEPT.DEPTNAME)))
```

Second, report all the suppliers that deliver all the items of type B to the departments designated in the previously created view.

```
SELECT SPLNAME FROM QSPL
   WHERE NOT EXISTS (SELECT * FROM QITEM
      WHERE ITEMTYPE = 'B'
      AND NOT EXISTS (SELECT * FROM QDEL
         WHERE QDEL.ITEMNAME = QITEM.ITEMNAME
         AND QDEL.SPLNO = QSPL.SPLNO
         AND DEPTNAME IN (SELECT DEPTNAME FROM V32)))
```

33. Triple divide with an intersection

- **List the suppliers that deliver all the items of type B to the departments that also sell all the items of type N.**

Defeat this by dividing — *that* word again — the query into parts. First, identify the departments that sell all items of type N, and save as a view.

```
CREATE VIEW V33A AS
   (SELECT DEPTNAME FROM QDEPT
      WHERE NOT EXISTS (SELECT * FROM QITEM
         WHERE ITEMTYPE = 'N'
         AND NOT EXISTS (SELECT * FROM QSALE
            WHERE QSALE.DEPTNAME = QDEPT.DEPTNAME
            AND QSALE.ITEMNAME = QITEM.ITEMNAME)))
```

Next, select the departments to which all items of type B are delivered, and save as a view.

```
CREATE VIEW V33B AS
   (SELECT DEPTNAME FROM QDEPT
      WHERE NOT EXISTS (SELECT * FROM QITEM
         WHERE ITEMTYPE = 'B'
         AND NOT EXISTS (SELECT * FROM QDEL
            WHERE QDEL.DEPTNAME = QDEPT.DEPTNAME
            AND QDEL.ITEMNAME = QITEM.ITEMNAME)))
```

Now, find the suppliers that supply all items of type B to the departments that appear in both views.

```
SELECT SPLNAME FROM QSPL
   WHERE NOT EXISTS (SELECT * FROM QITEM
      WHERE ITEMTYPE = 'B'
      AND NOT EXISTS (SELECT * FROM QDEL
         WHERE QDEL.SPLNO = QSPL.SPLNO
         AND QDEL.ITEMNAME = QITEM.ITEMNAME
         AND EXISTS
            (SELECT * FROM V33A
               WHERE QDEL.DEPTNAME = V33A.DEPTNAME)
               AND EXISTS
                  (SELECT * FROM V33B
                     WHERE QDEL.DEPTNAME = V33B.DEPTNAME)))
```

34. An easy one COUNT

❍ **List the items delivered by exactly one supplier (i.e., list the items always delivered by the same supplier).**

A reasonably straightforward GROUP BY with an exact count.

```
SELECT ITEMNAME FROM QDEL
   GROUP BY ITEMNAME HAVING COUNT(DISTINCT SPLNO) = 1
```

35. The only one

❍ **List the supplier and the item, where the supplier is the only deliverer of some item.**

For each item delivered, check to see if there is no other delivery of this item by another supplier.

```
SELECT DISTINCT QSPL.SPLNO, SPLNAME, ITEMNAME
   FROM QSPL, QDEL DEL1
      WHERE QSPL.SPLNO = DEL1.SPLNO
      AND ITEMNAME NOT IN
         (SELECT ITEMNAME FROM QDEL
            WHERE QDEL.SPLNO <> DEL1.SPLNO)
```

36. At least some number

❍ **List the suppliers that deliver at least 10 items.**

This is an easy GROUP BY with a count condition.

```
SELECT QSPL.SPLNO, SPLNAME FROM QDEL, QSPL
   WHERE QDEL.SPLNO = QSPL.SPLNO
      GROUP BY QSPL.SPLNO, SPLNAME
         HAVING COUNT(DISTINCT QDEL.ITEMNAME) >= 10
```

37. A three-table join

❍ **For each item, give its type, the departments that sell the item, and the floor location of these departments.**

A three-table join is rather easy after all the divides.

```
SELECT QITEM.ITEMNAME, ITEMTYPE, QDEPT.DEPTNAME, DEPTFLOOR
   FROM QITEM, QSALE, QDEPT
      WHERE QSALE.ITEMNAME = QITEM.ITEMNAME
      AND QSALE.DEPTNAME = QDEPT.DEPTNAME
```

38. Using NOT IN like NOT EXISTS

❍ **List the departments for which each item delivered to the department is delivered to some other department as well.**

This is another variation on double negative logic. The query can be rewritten as, *Find departments where there is not a delivery where a supplier does not deliver the item to some other department*. In this situation, the NOT IN clause is like a NOT EXISTS.

```
SELECT DISTINCT DEPTNAME FROM QDEL DEL1
   WHERE NOT EXISTS
      (SELECT * FROM QDEL DEL2
         WHERE DEL2.DEPTNAME = DEL1.DEPTNAME
         AND ITEMNAME NOT IN
            (SELECT ITEMNAME FROM QDEL DEL3
               WHERE DEL3.DEPTNAME <> DEL1.DEPTNAME))
```

39. Minus after GROUP By

❍ **List each item delivered to at least two departments by each supplier that delivers it.**

The inner query uses grouping to identify items delivered by the same supplier to one department at most. The remaining items must be delivered by the same supplier to more than one department.

```
SELECT DISTINCT ITEMNAME FROM QDEL
   WHERE ITEMNAME NOT IN
      (SELECT ITEMNAME FROM QDEL
         GROUP BY ITEMNAME, SPLNO
            HAVING COUNT(DISTINCT DEPTNAME) < 2)
```

40. Something to all

❍ **List the items that are delivered only by the suppliers that deliver something to all the departments.**

This is a variation on query 25 with the additional requirement, handled by the innermost query, that the supplier delivers to all departments. Specifying that all departments get a delivery means that the number of departments to whom a supplier delivers (GROUP BY SPLNO HAVING COUNT (DISTINCT DEPTNAME)) must equal the number of departments that sell items (SELECT COUNT(*) FROM QDEPT WHERE DEPTNAME NOT IN ('Management', 'Marketing', 'Personnel', 'Accounting', 'Purchasing')).

```
SELECT DISTINCT ITEMNAME FROM QDEL DEL1
   WHERE NOT EXISTS
      (SELECT * FROM QDEL DEL2
         WHERE DEL2.ITEMNAME = DEL1.ITEMNAME
         AND SPLNO NOT IN
            (SELECT SPLNO FROM QDEL
               GROUP BY SPLNO HAVING COUNT(DISTINCT DEPTNAME) =
                  (SELECT COUNT(*) FROM QDEPT
                     WHERE DEPTNAME NOT IN ('Management',
                        'Marketing', 'Personnel',
                        'Accounting', 'Purchasing'))))
```

41. Intersection (AND)

❍ **List the items delivered by Nepalese Corp. and sold in the Navigation department.**

The two parts to the query — the delivery and the sale — are intersected.

```
SELECT DISTINCT ITEMNAME FROM QITEM
   WHERE ITEMNAME IN
      (SELECT ITEMNAME FROM QDEL, QSPL
         WHERE QDEL.SPLNO = QSPL.SPLNO
         AND SPLNAME = 'Nepalese Corp.')
   AND ITEMNAME IN
      (SELECT ITEMNAME FROM QSALE
         WHERE DEPTNAME = 'Navigation')
```

42. Union (OR)

❍ **List the items delivered by Nepalese Corp. or sold in the Navigation department.**

The two parts are the same as query 41, but the condition is OR rather than AND.

```
SELECT DISTINCT ITEMNAME FROM QITEM
   WHERE ITEMNAME IN
      (SELECT ITEMNAME FROM QDEL, QSPL
         WHERE QDEL.SPLNO = QSPL.SPLNO
         AND SPLNAME = 'Nepalese Corp.')
   OR ITEMNAME IN
      (SELECT ITEMNAME FROM QSALE
         WHERE DEPTNAME = 'Navigation')
```

43. Intersection/union

❍ **List the departments selling items of type E that are delivered by Nepalese Corp. and/or which are sold by the Navigation department.**

The inner query handles the and/or with OR. Remember OR can mean that the items are in both tables or one table. The outer query identifies the departments that receive the delivered items, which satisfy the inner query.

```
SELECT DISTINCT DEPTNAME FROM QSALE
   WHERE ITEMNAME IN
   (SELECT QITEM.ITEMNAME FROM QITEM, QDEL, QSPL
      WHERE QITEM.ITEMNAME = QDEL.ITEMNAME
      AND QDEL.SPLNO = QSPL.SPLNO
      AND SPLNAME = 'Nepalese Corp.'
      AND ITEMTYPE = 'E')
   OR ITEMNAME IN
      (SELECT ITEMNAME FROM QSALE
         WHERE DEPTNAME = 'Navigation')
```

44. Averaging with a condition

❍ **Find the average salary of the employees in the Clothes department.**

This is very easy, especially after conquering the divides.

```
SELECT AVG(EMPSALARY) FROM QEMP
   WHERE DEPTNAME = 'Clothes'
```

45. Averaging with grouping

❍ **Find, for each department, the average salary of the employees.**

Another straightforward averaging query.

```
SELECT DEPTNAME, AVG(EMPSALARY) FROM QEMP
   GROUP BY DEPTNAME
```

46. Average with a join, condition, and grouping

❍ **Find, for each department on the second floor, the average salary of the employees.**

A combination of several averaging queries.

```
SELECT QDEPT.DEPTNAME, AVG(EMPSALARY) FROM QEMP, QDEPT
   WHERE QEMP.DEPTNAME = QDEPT.DEPTNAME
      AND DEPTFLOOR = 2
         GROUP BY QDEPT.DEPTNAME
```

47. Averaging with multiple joins

❍ **Find, for each department that sells items of type E, the average salary of the employees.**

Four joins, a condition, and grouping — not a particularly challenging query. The multiple joins are needed to get the data required for the answer into a single row.

```
SELECT QDEPT.DEPTNAME, AVG(EMPSALARY)
   FROM QEMP, QDEPT, QSALE, QITEM
      WHERE QEMP.DEPTNAME = QDEPT.DEPTNAME
      AND QDEPT.DEPTNAME = QSALE.DEPTNAME
      AND QSALE.ITEMNAME = QITEM.ITEMNAME
      AND ITEMTYPE = 'E'
         GROUP BY QDEPT.DEPTNAME
```

48. Complex counting

❍ **What are the number of different items delivered by each supplier that delivers to all departments?**

First, determine the suppliers that deliver to each department, excluding administrative departments. The inner query handles this part of the main query. Second, count the number of different items delivered by the suppliers identified by the inner query.

```
SELECT SPLNAME, COUNT(DISTINCT ITEMNAME)
   FROM QDEL DEL1, QSPL
      WHERE DEL1.SPLNO = QSPL.SPLNO
      AND NOT EXISTS
         (SELECT * FROM QDEPT
            WHERE DEPTNAME NOT IN
               (SELECT DEPTNAME FROM QDEL
                  WHERE QDEL.SPLNO = DEL1.SPLNO)
                  AND DEPTNAME NOT IN
                     ('Management', 'Marketing', 'Personnel',
                     'Accounting', 'Purchasing'))
      GROUP BY SPLNAME
```

49. Summing with joins and conditions

❍ **Find the total number of items of type E sold by the departments on the second floor.**

Summing is very similar to averaging (see query 47).

```
SELECT SUM(SALEQTY) FROM QITEM, QSALE, QDEPT
   WHERE QITEM.ITEMNAME = QSALE.ITEMNAME
   AND QDEPT.DEPTNAME = QSALE.DEPTNAME
   AND ITEMTYPE = 'E'
   AND DEPTFLOOR = 2
```

50. Summing with joins, conditions, and grouping

❍ **Find, for each item, the total quantity sold by the departments on the second floor.**

Conceptually, this query is similar to query 47.

```
SELECT QITEM.ITEMNAME, SUM(SALEQTY) FROM QITEM, QSALE, QDEPT
   WHERE QITEM.ITEMNAME = QSALE.ITEMNAME
   AND QDEPT.DEPTNAME = QSALE.DEPTNAME
   AND DEPTFLOOR = 2
      GROUP BY QITEM.ITEMNAME
```

51. Advanced summing

❍ **List suppliers that deliver a total quantity of items of types C and N that is altogether greater than 100.**

The difficult part of this query, and it is not too difficult, is to write the condition for selecting items of type C and N. Notice that the query says C and N,[3] but don't translate this to (ITEMTYPE = 'C' AND ITEMTYPE = 'N') because an item cannot be both types simultaneously. The query means that for any delivery, the item should be type C or type N.

```
SELECT QDEL.SPLNO, SPLNAME FROM QSPL, QDEL, QITEM
   WHERE QSPL.SPLNO = QDEL.SPLNO
   AND QITEM.ITEMNAME = QDEL.ITEMNAME
   AND (ITEMTYPE = 'C' OR ITEMTYPE = 'N')
      GROUP BY QDEL.SPLNO, SPLNAME HAVING SUM(DELQTY) > 100
```

52. Comparing to the average with a join

❍ **List the employees in the Accounting department and the difference between their salaries and the average salary of the department.**

The key to solving this query is placing the average salary for Accounting employees in the same row as the department salary data. This is a two-stage process. You first need to determine the average salary of the employees in all departments and save this as a view. Then, join this view to the QEMP table matching on the Accounting department's name. Once the average departmental salary has been concatenated to each row, the query is straightforward.

```
CREATE VIEW V52(DEPTNAME, DPAVGSAL) AS
   SELECT DEPTNAME, AVG(EMPSALARY) FROM QEMP
      GROUP BY DEPTNAME

SELECT EMPFNAME, (EMPSALARY - DPAVGSAL) FROM V52, QEMP
   WHERE V52.DEPTNAME = QEMP.DEPTNAME
   AND QEMP.DEPTNAME = 'Accounting'
```

3. Aren't you glad that this isn't a bad pun about a TV network?

53. Comparing to the average with a product

❍ **List the employees in the Accounting department and the difference between their salaries and the average salary of all the departments.**

This is a slight variation on the previous query except that a join is not used to combine the data from the view with the employee table. The view is a single row and column table containing the average salary for the organization. To concatenate this row with the data for employees in the Accounting department, we use a product instead of a join. Remember, a product is specified by simply listing the names of the two tables.

```
CREATE VIEW V53(ALLAVGSAL) AS
   SELECT AVG(EMPSALARY) FROM QEMP

SELECT EMPFNAME, (EMPSALARY -ALLAVGSAL) FROM V53, QEMP
   WHERE DEPTNAME = 'Accounting'
```

54. Averaging with multiple grouping

❍ **What is, for each supplier, the average number of items per department that the supplier delivers?**

Here, the averaging is broken into two levels: department within supplier.

```
SELECT QDEL.SPLNO, SPLNAME, DEPTNAME, AVG(DELQTY)
   FROM QSPL, QDEL
      WHERE QSPL.SPLNO = QDEL.SPLNO
         GROUP BY QDEL.SPLNO, SPLNAME, DEPTNAME
```

55. More than the average with grouping

❍ **For each department, find the average salary of the employees who earn more than the average salary of the department.**

The inner query determines the average salary of each department. Look carefully at how it handles matching departments.

```
SELECT DEPTNAME, AVG(EMPSALARY) FROM QEMP OUT
      WHERE EMPSALARY > (SELECT AVG(EMPSALARY) FROM QEMP INN
         WHERE OUT.DEPTNAME = INN.DEPTNAME)
            GROUP BY DEPTNAME
```

56. The simplest average

❍ **Give the overall average of the salaries in all departments.**

This is a very simple query.

```
SELECT AVG(EMPSALARY) FROM QEMP
```

Another possible interpretation is that you have to find the total average salary after you determine the average salary for each department. To do this, you would first create a view containing the average salary for each department (see query 52) and then find the average of these average salaries.[4]

```
SELECT AVG(DPAVGSAL) FROM V52
```

57. Difference from the average

❍ **List each employee's salary, the average salary within that person's department, and the difference between the employees' salaries and the average salary of the department.**

This is a reasonably easy once you have created a view of departmental average salaries.

```
SELECT EMPFNAME, EMPSALARY,
   DPAVGSAL, (EMPSALARY - DPAVGSAL)
      FROM V52, QEMP
         WHERE V52.DEPTNAME = QEMP.DEPTNAME
```

58. Averaging with multiple joins, multiple grouping, and a condition

❍ **What is the average delivery quantity of items of type N delivered by each company who delivers them?**

This is similar to query 54.

```
SELECT QDEL.SPLNO, SPLNAME, QDEL.ITEMNAME, AVG(DELQTY)
   FROM QDEL, QSPL, QITEM
      WHERE QDEL.SPLNO = QSPL.SPLNO
      AND QDEL.ITEMNAME = QITEM.ITEMNAME
      AND ITEMTYPE = 'N'
         GROUP BY QDEL.SPLNO, SPLNAME, QDEL.ITEMNAME
```

59. Detailed averaging

❍ **What is the average delivery quantity of items of type N delivered by each supplier to each department (given that the supplier delivers items of type N to the department)?**

Now we take averaging to three levels — supplier, department, item. You can take averaging to as many levels as you like.

4. Some implementations of SQL do not permit scalar operations on views; so, you may not be able to execute this query.

```
SELECT QDEL.SPLNO, SPLNAME, DEPTNAME, QDEL.ITEMNAME, AVG(DELQTY)
   FROM QDEL, QSPL, QITEM
      WHERE QDEL.SPLNO = QSPL.SPLNO
      AND QDEL.ITEMNAME = QITEM.ITEMNAME
      AND ITEMTYPE = 'N'
         GROUP BY QDEL.SPLNO, SPLNAME, DEPTNAME, QDEL.ITEMNAME
```

60. Counting pairs

❍ **What is the number of supplier-department pairs in which the supplier delivers at least one item of type E to the department?**

First, find all the supplier-department pairs. Without DISTINCT, you would get duplicates, which would make the subsequent count wrong.

```
CREATE VIEW V60 AS
   (SELECT DISTINCT SPLNO, DEPTNAME FROM QDEL, QITEM
      WHERE QDEL.ITEMNAME = QITEM.ITEMNAME
      AND ITEMTYPE = 'E')
```

Now, it is a simple count.

```
SELECT COUNT(*) FROM V60
```

61. No Booleans

❍ **Is it true that all the departments that sell items of type C are located on the third floor? (The result can be a Boolean 1 or 0, meaning yes or no.)**

SQL cannot return *true* or *false*; it always returns a table. But you can get close to Boolean results by using counts. If we get a count of zero for the following query, there are no departments that are not on the third floor that sell items of type C.

```
SELECT COUNT(*) FROM QDEPT
   WHERE DEPTFLOOR <> 3
   AND EXISTS
      (SELECT * FROM QSALE, QITEM
         WHERE QSALE.ITEMNAME = QITEM.ITEMNAME
         AND QSALE.DEPTNAME = QDEPT.DEPTNAME
         AND ITEMTYPE = 'C')
```

Then you need to check that departments on the third floor sell items of type C. If the second query returns a non-zero value, then it is true that departments that sell items of type C are located on the third floor.

```
SELECT COUNT(*) FROM QDEPT
   WHERE DEPTFLOOR = 3
   AND EXISTS
      (SELECT * FROM QSALE, QITEM
         WHERE QSALE.ITEMNAME = QITEM.ITEMNAME
         AND QSALE.DEPTNAME = QDEPT.DEPTNAME
         AND ITEMTYPE = 'C')
```

Summary

Although SQL is a powerful retrieval language, alas, formulation of common business queries is not always trivial.

Key terms and concepts

SELECT

Exercises

Here is an opportunity to display your SQL mastery.

1. List the green items of type C.
2. Find the names of green items sold by the Recreation department.
3. Find the items not delivered to the Books department.
4. Find the departments that have never sold a geo positioning system.
5. Find the departments that have sold compasses and at least two other items.
6. Find the departments that sell at least four items.
7. Find the employees who are in a different department from their manager's department.
8. Find the employees whose salary is less than half that of their manager's.
9. Find the green items sold by no department on the second floor.
10. Find the items delivered by all suppliers.
11. Find the items delivered by at least two suppliers.
12. Find the items not delivered by Nepalese Corp.
13. Find the items sold by at least two departments.
14. Find the items delivered for which there have been no sales.
15. Find the items delivered to all departments except Administration.
16. Find the name of the highest paid employee in the Marketing department.
17. Find the names of employees who make 10 percent less than the average salary.
18. Find the names of employees with a salary greater than the minimum salary paid to a manager.
19. Find the names of suppliers that do not supply compasses or geo positioning systems.
20. Find the number of employees with a salary under $10,000.
21. Find the number of items of type A sold by the departments on the third floor.
22. Find the number of units sold of each item.
23. Find the green items delivered by all suppliers.
24. Find the supplier that delivers no more than one item.

25. Find the suppliers that deliver to all departments.
26. Find the suppliers that deliver to all the departments that also receive deliveries from supplier 102.
27. Find the suppliers that have never delivered a compass.
28. Find the type A items delivered by São Paulo Manufacturing.
29. Find, for each department, its floor and the average salary in the department.
30. If Nancy's boss has a boss, who is it?
31. List each employee and the difference between his (her) salary and the average salary of his (her) department.
32. List the departments on the second floor that contain more than one employee.
33. List the departments on the second floor.
34. List the names of employees who earn more than the average salary of employees in the Shoe department.
35. List the names of items delivered by each supplier. Arrange the report by supplier name, and within supplier name, list the items in alphabetical order.
36. List the names of managers who supervise only one person.
37. List the number of employees in each department.
38. List the green items delivered by exactly one supplier.
39. Whom does Todd manage?
40. List the departments that have not sold all green items.
41. Find the first name of Sophie's boss.
42. Find the names of employees who make less than half their manager's salary.
43. List the names of each manager and their employees arranged by manager's name and employee's name within manager.
44. Who earns the lowest salary?
45. List the names of employees who earn less than the minimum salary of the Marketing department.
46. List the items sold by every department to which all brown items have been delivered.
47. List the department and the item where the department is the only seller of that item.
48. List the brown items sold by the Books department and delivered by All Seasons.
49. Which department has the highest average salary?
50. List the supplier that delivers all and only brown items.

Data for tables

QSALE

SALENO	SALEQTY	*ITEMNAME*	*DEPTNAME*
1001	2	Boots–snakeproof	Clothes
1002	1	Pith helmet	Clothes
1003	1	Sextant	Navigation
1004	3	Hat–polar explorer	Clothes
1005	5	Pith helmet	Equipment
1006	1	Pocket knife–Nile	Clothes
1007	1	Pocket knife––Nile	Recreation
1008	1	Compass	Navigation
1009	1	Geo positioning system	Navigation
1010	5	Map measure	Navigation
1011	1	Geo positioning system	Books
1012	1	Sextant	Books
1013	3	Pocket knife–Nile	Books
1014	1	Pocket knife–Nile	Navigation
1015	1	Pocket knife–Nile	Equipment
1016	1	Sextant	Clothes
1017	1	Sextant	Equipment
1018	1	Sextant	Recreation
1019	1	Sextant	Furniture
1020	1	Pocket knife–Nile	Furniture
1021	1	Exploring in 10 Easy Lessons	Books
1022	1	How to Win Foreign Friends	Books
1023	1	Compass	Books
1024	1	Pith helmet	Books
1025	1	Elephant polo stick	Recreation
1026	1	Camel saddle	Recreation

QSPL

SPLNO	SPLNAME
101	Global Books & Maps
102	Nepalese Corp.
103	All Sports Manufacturing
104	Sweatshops Unlimited
105	All Points, Inc.
106	São Paulo Manufacturing

QITEM

ITEMNAME	ITEMTYPE	ITEMCOLOR
Boots–snakeproof	C	Green
Camel saddle	R	Brown
Compass	N	—
Elephant polo stick	R	Bamboo
Exploring in 10 Easy Lessons	B	—
Geo positioning system	N	—
Hammock	F	Khaki
Hat–polar explorer	C	White
How to Win Foreign Friends	B	—
Map case	E	Brown
Map measure	N	—
Pith helmet	C	Khaki
Pocket knife–Avon	E	Brown
Pocket knife–Nile	E	Brown
Safari chair	F	Khaki
Safari cooking kit	F	—
Sextant	N	—
Stetson	C	Black
Tent–2 person	F	Khaki
Tent–8 person	F	Khaki

QDEPT

DEPTNAME	DEPTFLOOR	DEPTPHONE	*EMPNO*
Management	5	34	1
Books	1	81	4
Clothes	2	24	4
Equipment	3	57	3
Furniture	4	14	3
Navigation	1	41	3
Recreation	2	29	4
Accounting	5	35	5
Purchasing	5	36	7
Personnel	5	37	9
Marketing	5	38	2

QDEL

DELNO	DELQTY	*ITEMNAME*	*DEPTNAME*	*SPLNO*
51	50	Pocket knife–Nile	Navigation	105
52	10	Pocket knife–Nile	Books	105
53	10	Pocket knife–Nile	Clothes	105
54	10	Pocket knife–Nile	Equipment	105
55	10	Pocket knife–Nile	Furniture	105
56	10	Pocket knife–Nile	Recreation	105
57	50	Compass	Navigation	101
58	10	Geo positioning system	Navigation	101
59	10	Map measure	Navigation	101
60	25	Map case	Navigation	101
61	2	Sextant	Navigation	101
62	1	Sextant	Equipment	105
63	20	Compass	Equipment	103
64	1	Geo positioning system	Books	103
65	15	Map measure	Navigation	103
66	1	Sextant	Books	103
67	5	Sextant	Recreation	102
68	3	Sextant	Navigation	104
69	5	Boots–snakeproof	Clothes	105
70	15	Pith helmet	Clothes	105
71	1	Pith helmet	Clothes	101
72	1	Pith helmet	Clothes	102
73	1	Pith helmet	Clothes	103
74	1	Pith helmet	Clothes	104
75	5	Pith helmet	Navigation	105
76	5	Pith helmet	Books	105
77	5	Pith helmet	Equipment	105
78	5	Pith helmet	Furniture	105
79	5	Pith helmet	Recreation	105
80	10	Pocket knife–Nile	Navigation	102
81	1	Compass	Navigation	102
82	1	Geo positioning system	Navigation	102
83	10	Map measure	Navigation	102
84	5	Map case	Navigation	102
85	5	Compass	Books	102
86	5	Pocket knife–Avon	Recreation	102
87	5	Tent–2 person	Recreation	102
88	2	Tent–8 person	Recreation	102
89	5	Exploring in 10 Easy Lessons	Navigation	102
90	5	How to Win Foreign Friends	Navigation	102
91	10	Exploring in 10 Easy Lessons	Books	102
92	10	How to Win Foreign Friends	Books	102

93	2	Exploring in 10 Easy Lessons	Recreation	102
94	2	How to Win Foreign Friends	Recreation	102
95	5	Compass	Equipment	105
96	2	Boots–snakeproof	Equipment	105
97	20	Pith helmet	Equipment	106
98	20	Pocket knife–Nile	Equipment	106
99	1	Sextant	Equipment	106
100	3	Hat–polar explorer	Clothes	105
101	3	Stetson	Clothes	105

QEMP

EMPNO	EMPFNAME	EMPSALARY	*DEPTNAME*	*BOSSNO*
1	Alice	75000	Management	
2	Ned	45000	Marketing	1
3	Andrew	25000	Marketing	2
4	Clare	22000	Marketing	2
5	Todd	38000	Accounting	1
6	Nancy	22000	Accounting	5
7	Brier	43000	Purchasing	1
8	Sarah	56000	Purchasing	7
9	Sophie	35000	Personnel	1
10	Sanjay	15000	Navigation	3
11	Rita	15000	Books	4
12	Gigi	16000	Clothes	4
13	Maggie	16000	Clothes	4
14	Paul	11000	Equipment	3
15	James	15000	Equipment	3
16	Pat	15000	Furniture	3
17	Mark	15000	Recreation	3

QDEPT

DEPTNAME	DEPTFLOOR	DEPTPHONE	*EMPNO*
Management	5	34	1
Books	1	81	4
Clothes	2	24	4
Equipment	3	57	3
Furniture	4	14	3
Navigation	1	41	3
Recreation	2	29	4
Accounting	5	35	5
Purchasing	5	36	7
Personnel	5	37	9
Marketing	5	38	2

Section 3

Database Architectures and Implementations

We shape our buildings: thereafter they shape us.
Winston Churchill, *Time*, 12 September 1960

A database architecture is a design for the storage and processing of data. Organizations strive to find an architecture that simultaneously achieves multiple goals:

1. responds to queries in a timely manner;
2. minimizes the cost of processing data;
3. minimizes the cost of storing data;
4. minimizes the cost of data delivery.

This section deals with the approaches that can be used to achieve each of these goals. We begin by tracing the development of schema architectures and conclude with a description of the ANSI/SPARC architecture.

Development of data architectures

Remember that first program you wrote? It was probably very simple—something that added two numbers and printed the result. More than likely, the two numbers to be added were *hard coded* into the program. If you wanted to add a different pair of numbers, you had to edit the program and rerun it. Most beginners' programs exemplify the situation where programs and data are not separated—also known as a no-schema architecture (see Figure S3-1). A schema is a representation of the data's structure.

As your programming skills advanced, you learned it was more efficient to separate a program and its data. Instead of hard coding data, you used variable names to represent data values, and your program read data from a file or asked the user to input values. Although you had separated the program and the data, essentially you still saw the data exactly as

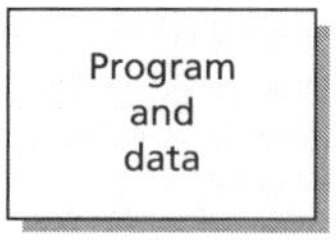

Figure S3-1. No-schema architecture

the program saw it. Your internal schemas were identical: this approach is known as a one-schema architecture (see Figure S3-2). One advantage of separating the data from a program is that the same data can be used by several different programs, or the same program can run several different sets of data.

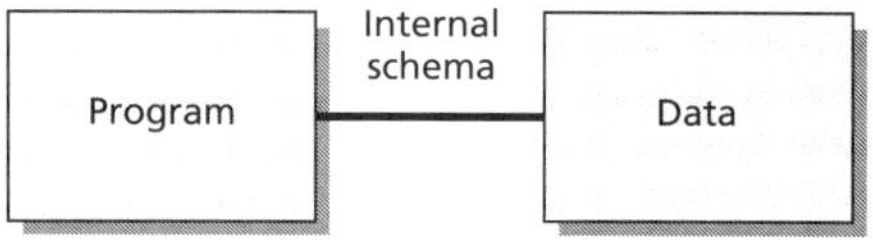

Figure S3-2. One-schema architecture

Many users, however, do not want to know how data are represented in a program or a file. They simply want a view of the data that matches their needs. As a result, the idea of an external schema emerged—charting the users' view of the data. Thus we have a two-schema architecture (see Figure S3-3) that separates the user from the data. Most word processors have a two-schema architecture; your view of the words you type is quite different from what is actually stored.

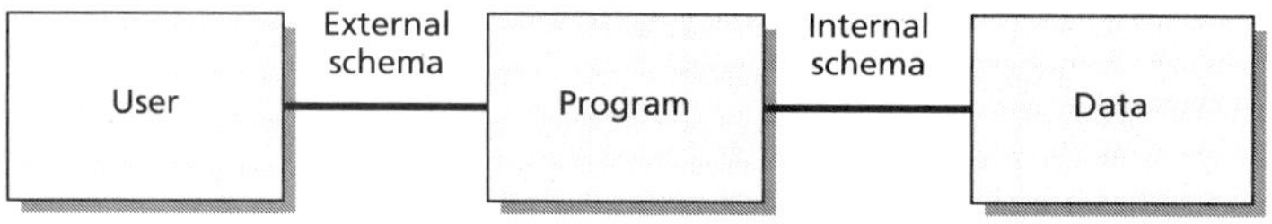

Figure S3-3. Two-schema architecture

The major shortcoming of a two-schema architecture is that every time a physical data structure is changed, programs have to be changed.[1] This problem is overcome by introducing a conceptual schema and three-level architecture to further separate a program from the data.

1. You may notice that some word processing files are not compatible across different versions of the same product. This is an example of how changing the internal schema—the data storage structures—requires the program to change. Of course, conversion programs are usually provided to bridge the gap.

ANSI/SPARC

In 1972, ANSI established a committee to examine standardization of database technology. This study group, officially known as the ANSI/X3/SPARC Study Group on Data Base Management, produced a general architecture for describing a database and its various interfaces, the only area which it concluded was suitable for standardization. Its framework for database interfaces is known as the ANSI/SPARC architecture.[2]

The ANSI/SPARC architecture consists of three schemas or levels (the word favored by the group): internal, conceptual, and external (see Figure S3-4).

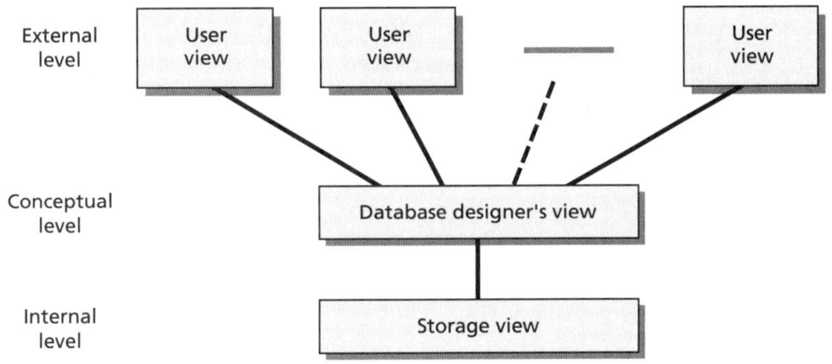

Figure S3-4. The ANSI/SPARC architecture

The External Level

The external level represents a user's view of the system. As the diagram shows, there can be many user views, and as we learned previously, multiple views can be defined for a single SQL table by using CREATE VIEW. These views can be tailored to the needs and data access privileges of any authorized user.

The Conceptual Level

The conceptual level is the database designer's view, which is completely unrestricted and includes all the files and all the fields in each file. The database designer sees everything.

The conceptual level is the mapping of the data model to the DBMS's DDL. In the case of SQL, CREATE TABLE specifies the conceptual level. Because data independence is a key goal of data administration, the selected DDL should not require any consideration of storage structure or data access mechanisms. The conceptual level may also include definitions of security and integrity level checks (e.g., GRANT and foreign key constraints).

2. Tsichritzis, D. C., and A. Klug. 1978. The ANSI/X3/SPARC DBMS framework: Report of the study group on data base management systems. *Information Systems* 3.

Ideally, this level completely describes the database without taking physical considerations into account.

The Internal Level

As the chapters in this section will discuss, the internal level—the lowest level description of a database—is concerned with the way data are stored. Although it describes attributes such as types of records stored, indexes, and record sequencing, the internal level does not deal with the device-specific attributes.

Chapter 11 covers database structure and storage alternatives. It provides the knowledge necessary to determine an appropriate data storage structure and device for a given situation. Chapter 12 addresses the fundamental questions of where to store the data and where they should be processed. An alternative to the relational data model, the object-oriented database is considered in the remaining chapter of this section.

11

Data Structure and Storage

The modern age has a false sense of superiority because it relies on the mass of knowledge that it can use, but what is important is the extent to which knowledge is organized and mastered.

Goethe, 1810

Learning objectives

Students completing this chapter will, for a given situation, be able to recommend

- a data storage structure;
- a storage device.

Every quarter, The Expeditioner's IS group measures the quality of its service. It asks users to assess whether their hardware and software are adequate for their jobs, whether IS service is reliable and responsive, and if they thought the IS staff were helpful and knowledgeable.[1] The most recent survey revealed that some users were experiencing unreasonably long delays for what were relatively simple queries. How could the IS group tune the database to reduce response time?

As though some grumpy users were not enough, Alice dumped another problem on Ned's desk. The Marketing department had

1. For more details, see Watson, R. T., L. F. Pitt, and C. B. Kavan. 1998. Information systems service quality: Lessons from two longitudinal case studies. *MIS Quarterly* 23 (1):61-79.

complained to her that the product database had been down for 30 minutes during a peak selling period. What was Ned going to do to prevent such an occurrence in the future?

Ned had just finished reading Alice's memo about the database problem when the Chief Accountant poked his head in the door. Somewhat agitated, he was waving an article from his favorite accounting journal that claimed that data stored on magnetic tape decayed with time. So what was he to do with all those financial records on magnetic tapes stored in the fireproof safe in his office? Were the magnetic bits likely to disappear tonight, tomorrow, or next week? "This business had lasted for centuries with paper ledgers. Why, you can still read the financial transactions for 1527," which he did whenever he had a few moments to spare. "But, if what I read is true, I soon won't be able to read the balance sheet from last year!"

It was just after 10 A.M. on a Monday, and Ned was faced with finding a way to improve response time, ensure that databases were continually available during business hours, and protect the long-term existence of financial records. It was going to be a long week.

Introduction

The following pages explore territory that is not normally the concern of application programmers or database users. Fortunately, the relational model keeps data structures and data access methods hidden. Nevertheless, an overview of what happens *under the hood* is part of a well-rounded education in data management.

Data structures and access methods are the province of the person responsible for physically designing the database so that it responds in a timely manner to both queries and maintenance operations. Of course, there may be installations where application programmers have such responsibilities, and in these situations you will need to know physical database design.

Data structures

An in-depth consideration of the internal level of database architecture provides an understanding of the basic structures and access mechanisms underlying database technology. As you will see, the overriding concern of the internal level is to minimize disk access. In dealing with this level, we will speak in terms of files, records, and fields rather than the relational database terms of tables, rows, and columns. We do this because the discussion extends beyond the relational model to file structures in general.

The time required to access data on a magnetic disk, the usual storage device for databases, is relatively long compared to main memory. Disk access times are measured in milliseconds (10^{-3}), and main memory access times are referred to in nanoseconds (10^{-9}). There are generally around five orders of magnitude difference between disk and main memory access— it takes about 10^5 times longer. This distinction is more meaningful if placed in everyday context; it is like asking someone a question by phone or writing them a letter. The phone response takes seconds, and the written response takes days.

For many business applications, slow disk drives are a bottleneck. The computer often must wait for a disk to retrieve data before it can continue processing a request for information. This delay means that customers are also kept waiting. Appropriate selection of data structures and data access methods can considerably reduce delays. Database designers have two options: decrease disk read/write head movement or reduce disk accesses. Before considering these options, we need a general model of database access.

Database access

A three-layer model provides a framework for thinking about minimization of data access (see Figure 11-1). This is a generic model, and a particular DBMS may implement the approach using a different number of layers. For simplicity, the discussion is based on retrieving a single record in a file, although the principles also apply to retrieval of multiple records or an entire file.

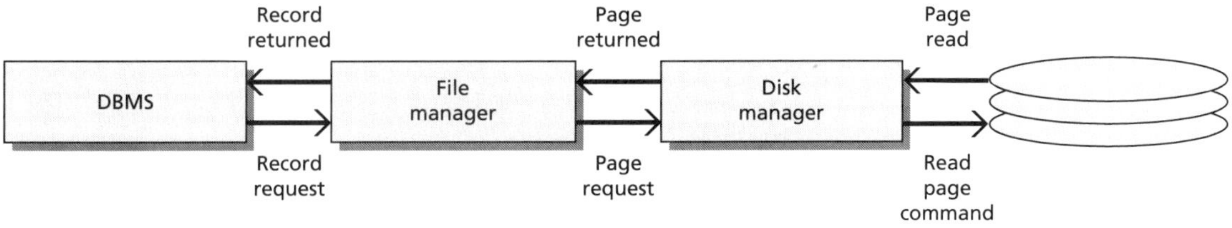

Figure 11-1. Database access layers

1. The DBMS determines which record is required and passes a request to the file manager to retrieve a particular record in a file.
2. The **file manager** converts this request into the address of the unit of storage (usually called a page) containing the specified record. A **page** is the minimum amount of storage accessed at one time and is typically around 1-4 kbytes. A page will often contain several short records (e.g., 200 bytes), but a long record (e.g., 10 kbytes) might be spread over several pages. In this example, we assume records are shorter than a page.
3. The **disk manager** determines the physical location of the page, issues the retrieval instructions, and passes the page to the file manager.
4. The file manager extracts the requested record from the page and passes it to the DBMS.

The disk manager

The disk manager is that part of the operating system responsible for physical I/O. It maintains a directory of the location of each page on the disk with all pages identified by a unique page number. The disk manager's main functions are to retrieve pages, replace pages, and keep track of free pages.

Page retrieval requires the disk manager to convert the page number to a physical address and issue the command to read the physical location. Since a page can contain multiple records, when a record is updated, the disk manager must retrieve the relevant page, update the appropriate portion containing the record, and then replace the page without changing any of the other data on it.

The disk manager thinks of the disk as a collection of uniquely numbered pages (see Figure 11-2). Some of these pages are allocated to the storage of data, and others are unused. When additional storage space is required, the disk manager allocates a page address from the set of unused page addresses. When a page becomes free because a file or some records are deleted, the disk manager moves that page's address to the unallocated set.

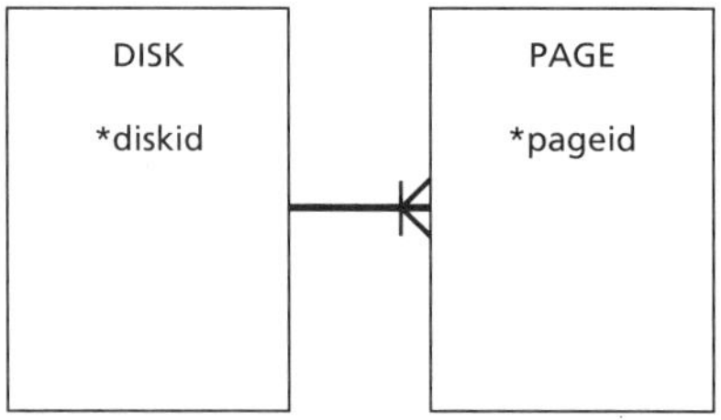

Figure 11-2. Disk manager's view of the world

The file manager

The file manager, a level above the disk manager, is concerned with the storage of files. It thinks of the disk as a set of stored files (see Figure 11-3). Each file has a unique file identifier, and each record within a file has a record identifier that is unique within that file.

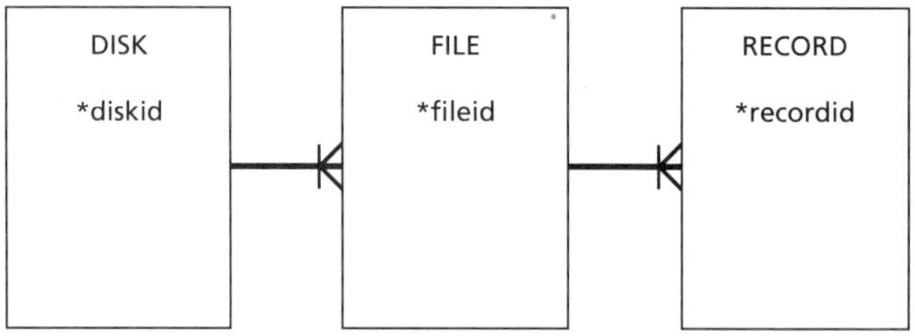

Figure 11-3. File manager's view of the world

The file manager can

- create a file,
- delete a file,
- retrieve a record from a file,
- update a record in a file,

- ❖ add a new record to a file,
- ❖ delete a record from a file.

Techniques for reducing head movement

All disk storage devices have some common features. They have one or more recording surfaces. Typically, a commercial magnetic disk drive has multiple recording surfaces, and a removable magneto-optical disk has two surfaces. Data are stored on tracks on each surface.

The key characteristics of disk storage devices that affect database access are **rotational speed** and **access arm speed**. All disks spin at high speed. The typical rotational speed of a magnetic disk is in the range 5,400 to 10,000 rpm. Reading or writing a page to disk requires moving the read/write head to the destination track and waiting for the storage address to come under the head. Because moving the head usually takes more time (e.g., about 10 msec) than waiting for the storage address to appear under it (e.g., about 5 msec), data access times can be reduced by minimizing the movement of the read/write head or rotating the disk faster. Since rotational speed is set by the disk manufacturer, minimizing read/write head movement is the only option available to database designers.

Cylinders

Head movement is curtailed by storing data that are likely to be accessed at the same time, such as records in a file, on the same track on a single surface, or on a **cylinder**, data stored on the same track on different surfaces. The advantage of cylinder storage is that all tracks can be accessed without moving the read/write head. When a cylinder is full, remaining data are stored on adjacent cylinders. Adjacent cylinders are ideal for sequential file storage because the record retrieval pattern is predefined — the first record is read, then the second, and so on.

Clustering

Cylinder storage can also be used when the record retrieval pattern has some degree of regularity to it. Consider the following familiar data model of Figure 11-4. Converting this data model to a relational database creates two tables. Conceptually, we may think of the data in each of the tables as being stored in adjacent cylinders. If, however, you frequently need to retrieve one row of NATION and all the corresponding rows of STOCK, then NATION and STOCK rows should be intermingled to minimize access time.

The term **clustering** describes the concept that records that are frequently used together should be physically close together on a disk. Some DBMSs permit the database designer to specify clustering of different files to tune the database to reduce average access times. If usage patterns change, clustering specifications should be altered. Of course, clustering should be totally transparent to application programs and users.

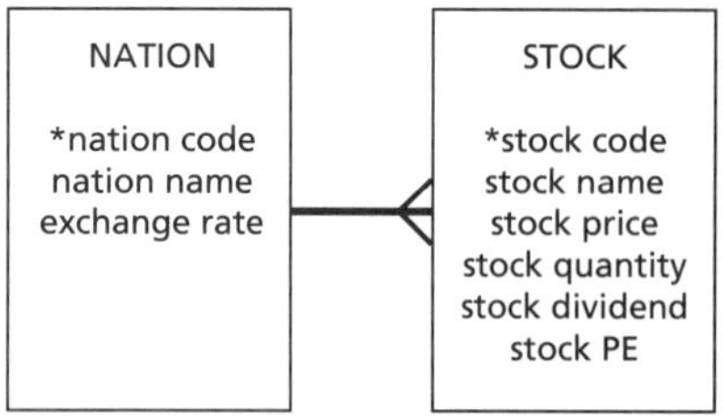

Figure 11-4. NATION and STOCK data model

Techniques for reducing disk accesses

Several techniques are used to accelerate retrieval by reducing disk accesses. The ideal situation is when the required record is obtained with a single disk access. In special circumstances, it may be possible to create a file where the primary key can convert directly to a unique disk address (e.g., the record with primary key 1 is stored at address 1001, the record with primary key 2 is stored at address 1002, and so on). If possible, this method of **direct addressing** should be used because it is the fastest form of data access; however, it is most unusual to find such a direct mapping between the primary key and a disk address. For example, it would be infeasible to use direct addressing with a student file that has a Social Security number as the primary key because so many disk addresses would be wasted. Furthermore, direct addressing can work only for the primary key. What happens if there is a need for rapid retrieval on another field?

In most cases, database designers use features such as indexing, hashing, and linked lists. **Indexing**, a flexible and commonly used method of reducing disk accesses when searching for data, centers on the creation of a compact file containing the index field and the address of its corresponding record. The **B-tree** is a particular form of index structure that is widely used as the storage structure of relational DBMSs. **Hashing** is a direct access method based on using an arithmetic function to compute a disk address from a field within a file. A **linked list** is a data structure that accelerates data access by using pointers to show relationships existing between records.

Indexing

Consider the ITEM file partially shown in Table 11-1. Let's assume that this file has 10,000 records and each record requires 1 kbyte, which is a page on the particular disk system used. Suppose a common query is to request all the items of a particular type. Such a query might be

- **Find all items of type E.**

Regardless of the number of records with ITEMTYPE='E', this query will require 10,000 disk accesses. Every record has to be retrieved and examined to determine the value of ITEMTYPE. For instance, if 20 percent of the items are of type E, then 8,000 of the disk

Table 11-1: Portion of a 10,000 Record File

<u>ITEMNO</u>	ITEMNAME	ITEMTYPE	ITEMCOLOR
1	Pocket knife—Nile	E	Brown
2	Pocket knife—Thames	E	Brown
3	Compass	N	—
4	Geo positioning system	N	—
5	Map measure	N	—
6	Hat—polar explorer	C	Red
7	Hat—polar explorer	C	White
8	Boots—snake proof	C	Green
9	Boots—snake proof	C	Black
10	Safari chair	F	Khaki

accesses are wasted because they retrieve a record that is not required. The ideal situation would be to retrieve only those 2,000 records that contain an item of type E. We get closer to this ideal situation by creating a small file containing just the value of ITEMTYPE for each record and the address of the full record. This small file is called an index. Part of the ITEMTYPE index for ITEM and the ITEM file are shown in Figure 11-5.

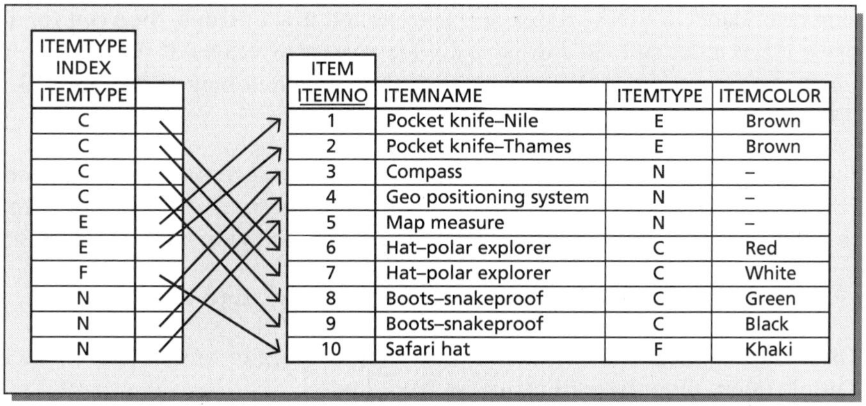

Figure 11-5. Part of the ITEMTYPE index

The ITEMTYPE index is a file. It contains 10,000 records and two fields. There is one record in the index for each record in ITEM. The first field contains a value of ITEMTYPE and the second contains a pointer, an address, to the matching record of ITEM. Notice that the index is in ITEMTYPE sequence. Storing the index in a particular order is another means of reducing disk accesses, as we will see shortly. The index is quite small. One byte is required for ITEMTYPE and four bytes for the pointer. So the total size of the index is 50 kbytes, which in this case is 50 pages of disk space.

Now consider finding all records with an item type of E. One approach is to read the entire index into memory, search it for type E items, and then use the pointers to retrieve the required records from ITEM. This method requires 2,050 disk accesses — 50 to load the index and 2,000 accesses of ITEM. Creating an index for ITEM results in substantial savings in disk accesses for this example. Here, we assume that 20 percent of the records in ITEM contained ITEMTYPE='E'. The number of disk accesses saved varies with the proportion of records meeting the query's criteria. If there are no records meeting the criteria, 9,950 disk accesses are avoided. At the other extreme, when all records meet the criteria, it takes 50 extra disk accesses to load the index.

The SQL (see page 244 for a detailed discussion of the syntax of the command) for creating the index is

```
CREATE INDEX ITEMTYPEINDX
   ON ITEM (ITEMTYPE)
```

The entire index need not be read into memory. As you will see when we discuss tree structures, we can take advantage of the index's ordering to further reduce disk accesses. Nevertheless, the clear advantage of an index is evident: it speeds up retrieval by reducing disk accesses. Like many aspects of database management, however, indexes have a drawback. Adding a record to a file without an index requires a single disk write. Adding a record to an indexed file requires at least two, and maybe more, disk writes since an entry has to be added to both the file and its index. The trade-off is between faster retrievals and slower updates. If there are many retrievals and few updates, then opt for an index, especially if the indexed field can have a wide variety of values. If the file is very volatile and updates are frequent and retrievals few, then an index may cost more disk accesses than it saves.

Indexes can be used for both sequential and direct access. Sequential access means that records are retrieved in the sequence defined by the values in the index. In our example, this means retrieving records in ITEMTYPE sequence with a range query such as

- **Find all items with a type code in the range E to K.**

Direct access means records are retrieved according to one or more specified values. A sample query requiring direct access would be

- **Find all items with a type code of E or N.**

Indexes are also handy for existence testing. Remember, the EXIST clause of SQL returns *true* or *false* and not a value. An index can be searched to check whether the indexed field takes a particular value, but there is no need to access the file because no data are returned. The following query can be answered by an index search:

- **Are there any items with a code of R?**

Multiple indexes

Multiple indexes can be created for a file. The ITEM file could have an index defined on ITEMCOLOR or any other field. Multiple indexes may be used independently, as in this query:

- **List red items.**

or jointly, with a query such as

- **Find red items of type C.**

The preceding query can be resolved by using the indexes for ITEMTYPE and ITEMCOLOR (see Figure 11-6).

ITEMTYPE INDEX

ITEMTYPE	Disk address
C	d6
C	d7
C	d8
C	d9
E	d1
E	d2
F	d10
N	d3
N	d4
N	d5

ITEMCOLOR INDEX

ITEMCOLOR	Disk address
Black	d9
Brown	d1
Brown	d2
Green	d8
Khaki	d10
Red	d6
White	d7
–	d3
–	d4
–	d5

Figure 11-6. Indexes for fields ITEMTYPE and ITEMCOLOR

Examination of the ITEMTYPE index indicates that items of type C are stored at addresses d6, d7, d8, and d9. The only red item recorded in the ITEMCOLOR index is stored at address d6, and since it is the only record satisfying the query, it is the only record that needs to be retrieved.

Multiple indexes, as you would expect, involve a trade-off. Whenever a record is added or updated, each index must also be updated. Savings in disk accesses for retrieval are exchanged for additional disk accesses in maintenance. Again, you must consider the balance between retrieval and maintenance operations.

Indexes are not restricted to a single field. It is possible to specify an index that is a combination of several fields. For instance, if item type and color queries were very common, then an index based on the concatenation of both fields could be created. As a result, such queries could be answered with a search of a single index rather than scanning two indexes as in the preceding example. The SQL for creating the combined index is

```
CREATE INDEX TYPECOLORINDX
   ON ITEM (ITEMTYPE, ITEMCOLOR)
```

Sparse indexes

Indexes are used to reduce disk accesses to accelerate retrieval. The simple model of an index introduced earlier suggests that the index contains an entry for each record of the file. If we can shrink the index to eliminate an entry for each record, we can save more disk accesses. Indeed, if we can get an index small enough, it, or key parts of it, can be retained continuously in primary memory.

There is a physical sequence to the records in a file. Records within a page are in a physical sequence, and pages on a disk are in a physical sequence. A file can also have a logical sequence, the ordering of the file on some field within a record. For instance, the ITEM file could be ordered on ITEMNO. Making the physical and logical sequences correspond is a way to save disk accesses. Remember, the ITEM file was assumed to have a record size of 1,024 bytes, the same size as a page, and one record was stored per page. If we now assume the record size is 512 bytes, then two records are stored per page. Furthermore, suppose that ITEM is physically stored in ITEMNO sequence. The index can be compressed by storing ITEMNO for the second record on each page and that page's address. The new index is shown in Figure 11-7.

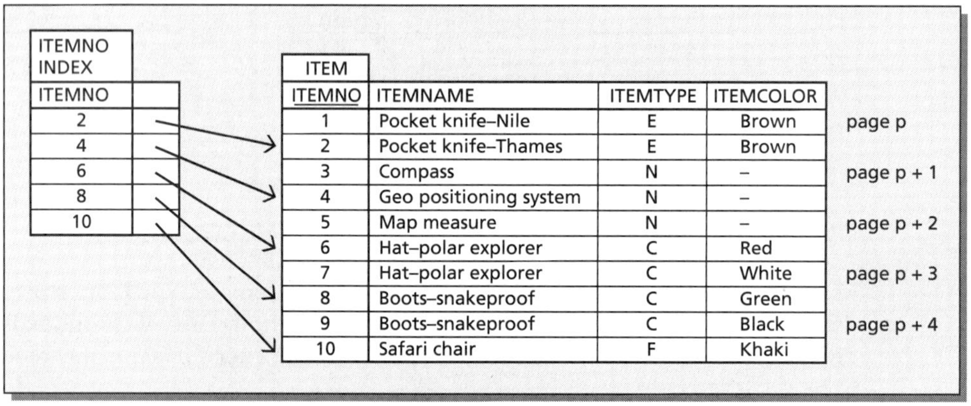

Figure 11-7. A sparse index for ITEM

Consider the process of finding the record with ITEMNO=7. First, the index is scanned to find the first value for ITEMNO that is greater than or equal to 7—the entry for ITEMNO=8. Second, the page on which this record is stored (page p+3) is loaded into memory. Third, the required record is extracted from the page.

Indexes that take advantage of the physical sequencing of a file are known as sparse or non-dense because they do not contain an entry for every value of the indexed field. (A dense index is one that contains an entry for every value of the indexed field.)

As you would expect, a sparse index has pros and cons. One major advantage is that it takes less storage space and so requires fewer disk accesses for reading. One disadvantage is that it can no longer be used for existence tests because it does not contain a value for every record in the file.

A file can have only one sparse index because it can have only one physical sequence. This field on which a sparse index is based is often called the primary key. Other indexes, which must be dense, are called secondary indexes.

In SQL, a sparse index is created using the CLUSTER option. For example, to define a sparse index on ITEM the command is

```
CREATE INDEX ITEMNOINDX
   ON ITEM (ITEMNO) CLUSTER
```

B-trees

The B-tree is a particular form of index structure that is frequently the main storage structure for relational systems. It is also the basis for IBM's VSAM (Virtual Storage Access Method), the file structure underlying DB2. A B-tree is an efficient structure for both sequential and direct accessing of a file. It consists of two parts, the sequence set and the index set.

The **sequence set** is a single-level index to the file with pointers to the records (the vertical arrows in the lower part of Figure 11-8). It can be sparse or dense, but is normally dense. Entries in the sequence set are grouped into pages, and these pages are linked together (the horizontal arrows in Figure 11-8) so that the logical ordering of the sequence set is the physical ordering of the file. Thus, the file can be processed sequentially by processing the records pointed to by the first page (records with identifiers 1, 4, and 5), the records pointed to by the next logical page (6, 19, and 20), and so on.

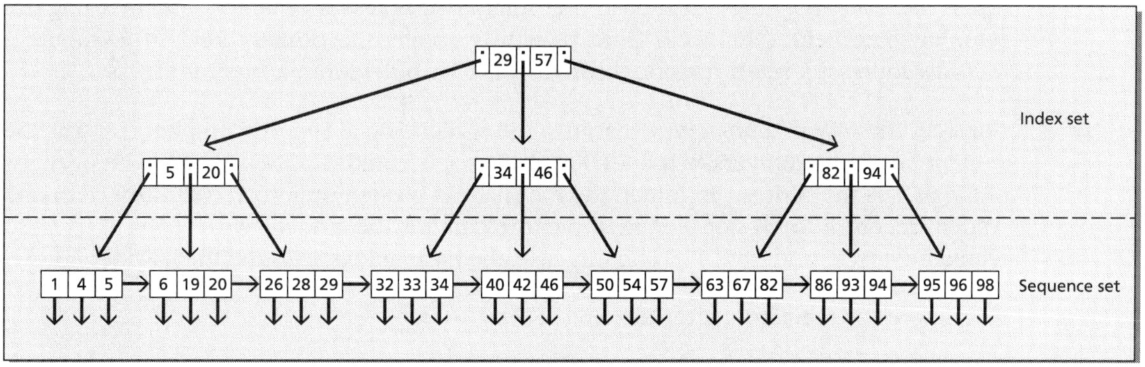

Figure 11-8. Structure of a simple B-tree

The **index set** is a tree-structured index to the sequence set. The top of the index set is a single node called the root. In this example, it contains two values (29 and 57) and three pointers. Records with an identifier less than or equal to 29 are found in the left branch, records with an identifier greater than 29 and less than or equal to 57 are found in the middle branch, and records with an identifier greater than 57 are found in the right branch. The three pointers are the page numbers of the left, middle, and right branches. The nodes at the next level have similar interpretations. The pointer to a particular record is found by moving down the tree until a node entry points to a value in the sequence set; this value can be used to retrieve the record. Thus, the index set provides direct access to the sequence set and then the data.

The index set is a B-tree. The combination of index set and sequence set is generally known as a B+ tree (**B-plus tree**). The B-tree shown in Figure 11-8 simplifies the concept in two ways. First, the number of data values and pointers for any given node is not restricted to 2 and 3, respectively. In its general form, a B-tree of order n can have at least n and no more than $2n$ data values. If it has k values, the B-tree will have $k+1$ pointers (in the example tree, nodes have two data values, k=2, and there are three, k+1=3, pointers). Second, B-trees typically have free space to permit rapid insertion of data values and possible updating of pointers when a new record is added.

As usual, there is a trade-off with B-trees. Retrieval will be fastest when each node occupies one page and is packed with data values and pointers. This lack of free space will slow down the addition of new records, however. Most implementations of B+ tree permit a specified portion of free space to be defined for both the index and sequence set.

Hashing

Hashing reduces disk accesses by allowing direct access to a file. As you know, direct accessing via an index requires at least two or more accesses. The index must be loaded and searched, and then the record retrieved. For some applications, direct accessing via an index is too slow. Hashing can reduce the number of accesses to almost one by using the value in some field (the **hash field**, which is usually the primary key) to compute a record's address. A **hash function** converts the hash field into a **hash address**.

Consider the case of a university that uses the 9-digit Social Security number (SSN) as the student key. If the university has 10,000 students, it could simply use the last four digits of the SSN as the address. In effect, the file space is broken up into 10,000 slots with one student record in each slot. For example, the data for the student with SSN 417-03-4356 would be stored at address 4356. In this case, the hash field is SSN, and the hash function is

hash address = remainder after dividing SSN by 10,000.

What about the student with SSN 532-67-4356? Unfortunately, the hashing function will give the same address because most hashing schemes cannot guarantee a unique hash address for every record. When two hash fields have the same address, they are called **synonyms**, and a collision is said to have occurred.

There are techniques for handling synonyms. Essentially, you store the colliding record in an overflow area and point to it from the hash address. Of course, more than two records can have the same hash address, which in turn creates a synonym chain. Figure 11-9 shows an example of hashing with a synonym chain. Three SSNs hash to the same address. The first record (417-03-4356) is stored at the hash address. The second record (532-67-4356) is stored in the overflow area and is connected by a pointer to the first record. The third record (891-55-4356) is also stored in the overflow area and connected by a pointer from the second record. Because each record contains the full key (SSN in this case), during retrieval the system can determine whether it has the correct record or should follow the chain to the next record.

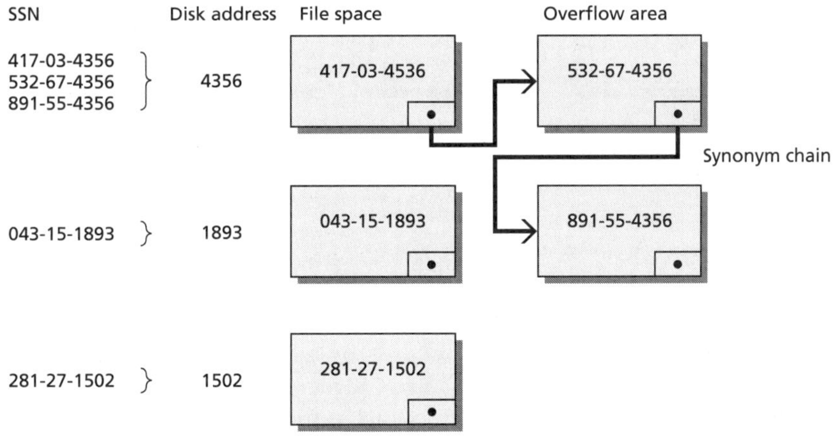

Figure 11-9. An example of hashing

If there are no synonyms, hashing gives very fast direct retrieval, taking only one disk access to retrieve a record. Even with a small percentage of synonyms, retrieval via hashing is very fast. Access time degrades, however, if there are long synonym chains.

There are a number of different approaches to defining hashing functions. The most common method is to divide by a prime and use the remainder as the address. Before adopting a particular hashing function, test several functions on a representative sample of the hash field. Compute the percentage of synonyms and the length of synonym chains for each potential hashing function and compare the results.

Of course, hashing has trade-offs. There can be only one hashing field. In contrast, a file can have many indexed fields. The file can no longer be processed sequentially because its physical sequence loses any logical meaning if the records are not in primary key sequence or sequenced on any other field.

Linked lists

A **linked list** is a useful data structure for interfile clustering. Suppose that the query, *Find all stocks of country X,* is a frequent request. Disk accesses can be reduced by storing a nation and its corresponding stocks together in a linked list (see Figure 11-10).

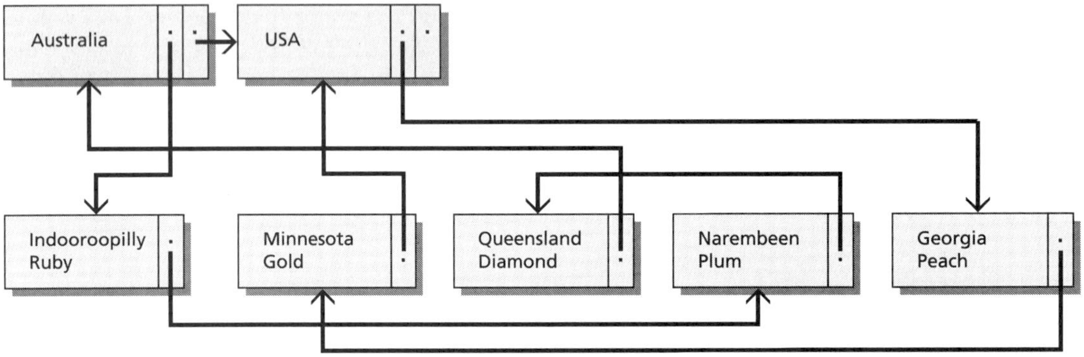

Figure 11-10. A linked list

In this example, we have two files: NATION and STOCK. Records in NATION are connected by pointers (e.g., the horizontal arrow between Australia and USA). The pointers are used to maintain the NATION file in logical sequence (by nation, in this case). Each record in NATION is linked to its STOCK records by a forward-pointing chain. The NATION record for Australia points to the first STOCK record (Indooroopilly Ruby), which points to the next (Narembeen Plum), which points to the final record in the chain (Queensland Diamond). Notice that the last record in this STOCK chain points to the STOCK record to which the chain belongs (i.e., Australia). Similarly, there is a chain for the two USA stocks. In any chain, the records are maintained in logical sequence (by firm name, in this case).

This linked list structure is also known as a parent/child structure. (The parent in this case is NATION and the child is STOCK.) Although it is a suitable structure for representing a 1:m relationship, it is possible to depict more than one parent/child relationship. For example, stocks could be grouped into classes (e.g., high, medium, and low risk). A second chain linking all stocks of the same risk class can run through the file. Interfile clustering of a nation and its corresponding stocks will speed up access; so, the record for the parent Australia and its three children should be stored on one page. Similarly, all American stocks could be clustered with the USA record and so on for all other nations.

Of course, you expect some trade-offs. What happens with a query such as, *Find the country in which Minnesota Gold is listed?* There is no quick way to find Minnesota Gold except by sequentially searching the STOCK file until the record is found and then following the chain to the parent NATION record. This could take many disk accesses. One way to circumvent this is to build an index or hashing scheme for STOCK so that any record can be found directly. Building an index for the parent, NATION, will speed up access as well.

Linked lists come in a variety of flavors. Some variations are

- There are two-way pointers, both forward and backward. These speed up deletion.
- Every child record has a parent pointer. This helps prevent chain traversal when the query is concerned with finding the parent of a particular child.

Bitmap index

A **bitmap index** uses a single bit, rather than multiple bytes, to indicate the specific value of a field. For example, instead of using three bytes to represent *red* as an item's color, the color red is represented by a single bit. The relative position of the bit within a string of bits is then mapped to a record address.

Conceptually, you can think of a bitmap as a matrix. Figure 11-11 shows a bitmap containing details of an item's color and code. An item can have three possible colors; so, three bits are required, and two bits are needed for the two codes for the item. Thus, you can see that in general *n* bits are required if a field can have *n* possible values.

Itemcode	Color			Code		Disk address
	Red	Green	Blue	A	N	
1001	0	0	1	0	1	d1
1002	1	0	0	1	0	d2
1003	1	0	0	1	0	d3
1004	0	1	0	1	0	d4

Figure 11-11. A bitmap index

When an item has a large number of values (i.e., *n* is large), the bitmap for that field will be very sparse, containing a large number of zeros. Thus, a bitmap is typically useful when the value of *n* is relatively small. When is *n* small or large? There is no simple answer; rather, database designers have to simulate alternative designs and evaluate the trade-offs.

In some situations, the bit string for a field can have multiple bits set to *on* (set to 1). A location field, for instance, may have two bits *on* to represent an item that can be found in Atlanta and New York.

The advantage of a bitmap is that it usually requires little storage. For example, we can recast the bitmap index as a conventional index (see Figure 11-12). The core of the bitmap in Figure 11-11 (i.e., the cells storing data about the color and code) requires 5 bits for each record, but the core of the traditional index requires 9 bytes or 72 bits for each record.

Itemcode	Color Char(8)	Code Char(1)	Disk address
1001	Blue	N	d1
1002	Red	A	d2
1003	Red	A	d3
1004	Green	A	d4

Figure 11-12. An index

Bitmaps have been used for some time and were a feature of some prerelational databases. Recently, some RDBMS vendors have introduced bitmaps into their products to support complex queries.

Join index

Many RDBMS queries frequently require two or more tables to be joined. Indeed, some people refer to the RDBMS as a join machine. A join index can be used to improve the execution speed of joins by creating indexes based on the matching columns of tables that are highly likely to be joined. For example, NATCODE is the common column used to join NATION and STOCK, and each of these tables can be indexed on NATCODE (see Figure 11-13).

NATION INDEX	
NATCODE	Disk address
UK	d1
USA	d2

STOCK INDEX	
NATCODE	Disk address
UK	d101
UK	d102
UK	d103
USA	d104
USA	d105

Figure 11-13. Indexes for NATCODE for the NATION and STOCK tables

A join index is a list of the disk addresses of the rows for matching columns (see Figure 11-14). All indexes, including the join index, must be updated whenever a row is inserted into or deleted from the NATION or STOCK tables. When a join of the two tables on the matching column is made, the join index is used to retrieve only those records that will be joined. This example demonstrates the advantage of a join index. If you think of a join as a product with a WHERE clause, then without a join index, 10 (2*5) rows have be retrieved, but with the join index only 5 rows are retrieved. Join indexes can also be created for joins involving several tables. As usual, there is a trade-off. Joins will be faster, but insertions and deletions will be slower because of the need to update the indexes.

JOIN INDEX	
NATION disk address	STOCK disk address
d1	d101
d1	d102
d1	d103
d2	d104
d2	d105

Figure 11-14. Join index

R-tree

Conventional DBMSs were developed to handle one-dimensional data (numbers and text strings). Nowadays, organizations also need to store multidimensional or spatial data objects (e.g., rectangles and lines). In a geographic information system (GIS), points, lines, and rectangles may be used to represent the location of retail outlets, roads, utilities, and land parcels. Such data objects are represented by sets of *x, y* or *x, y, z* coordinates. Other applications requiring the storage of spatial data include computer-aided design (CAD), robotics, and computer vision.

The B-tree, often used to store data in one-dimensional databases, can be extended to n-dimensions, where $n \geq 2$. This extension of the B-tree is called an **R-tree**. As well as storing pointers to records in the sequence set, an R-tree also stores boundary data for each object. For a two-dimensional application, the boundary data are the x and y coordinates of the lower-left and upper-right corners of the *minimum bounding* rectangle, the smallest possible rectangle enclosing the object. The index set, which contains pointers to lower-level nodes as in a B-tree, also contains data for the minimum bounding rectangle enclosing the objects referenced in the node. The data in an R-tree permits answers to such problems as, *Find all pizza stores within 5 miles of the dorm*.

How an R-tree stores data is illustrated in Figure 11-15, which depicts five two-dimensional objects labeled A, B, C, D, and E. Each object is represented by its minimum bounding rectangle (the objects could be some other form, such as a circle), Data about these objects is stored in the sequence set. The index set contains details of two intermediate rectangles, X and Y. X fully encloses A, B, and C. Y fully encloses D and E.

An example demonstrates how these data might be used to accelerate searching. Using a mouse, a person could outline a region on a map displayed on a screen. The minimum bounding rectangle for this region would then be calculated and the coordinates used to locate geographic objects falling within the minimum boundary. Because an R-tree is an index, geographic objects falling within a region can be found rapidly. In Figure 11-16, the drawn region (it has a bold border) completely covers object E. The R-tree software would determine that the required object falls within intermediate region Y, and thus take the middle node at the next level of the R-tree. Then, by examining coordinates in this node, it would determine that E is the required object.

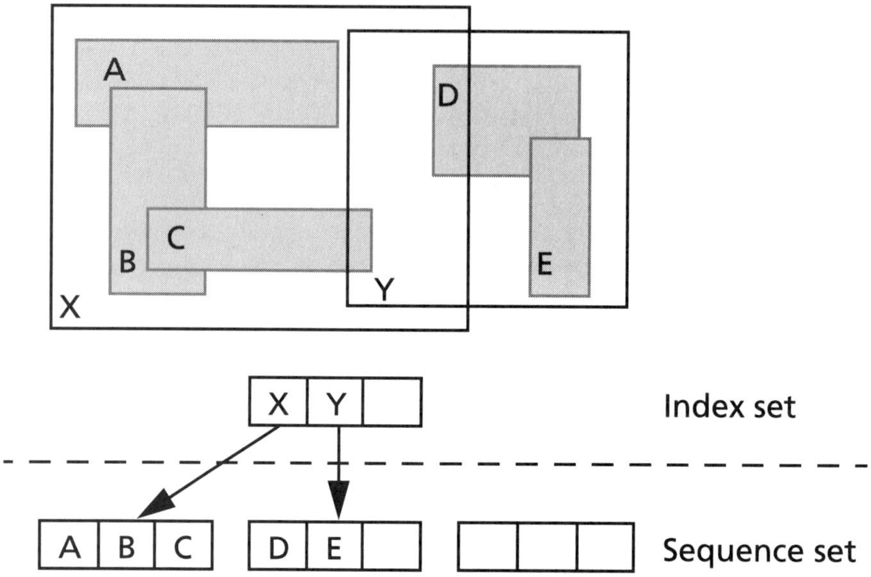

Figure 11-15. An R-tree with sample spatial data

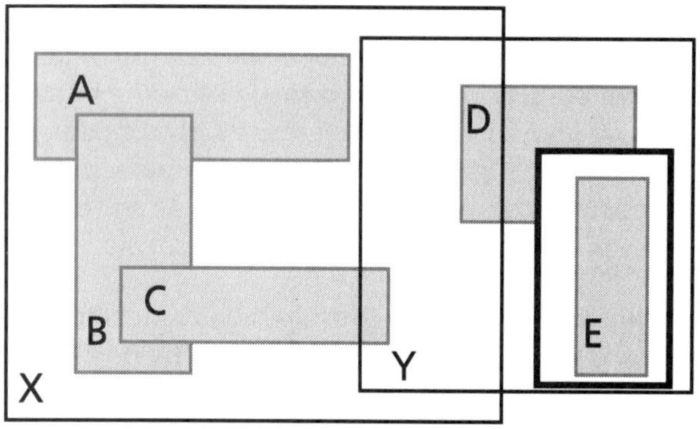

Figure 11-16. Searching an R-tree

As the preceding example illustrates, an R-tree has the same index structure as a B-tree. An R-tree stores data about n-dimensional objects in each node, whereas a B-tree stores data about a one-dimensional data type in each node. Both also store pointers to the next node in the tree (the index set) or the record (the sequence set).

Data coding standards

The successful exchange of data between two computers requires agreement on how information is coded. ASCII and Unicode are two widely used data coding standards.

ASCII

ASCII is the most common format for digital text files. In an ASCII file, each alphabetic, numeric, or special character is represented by a 7-bit code. Thus, 128 (2^7) possible characters are defined. Because most computers process data in eight-bit bytes or multiples thereof, an ASCII code usually occupies one byte.

Unicode

Unicode, officially the Unicode Worldwide Character Standard, is a system for the interchange, processing, and display of the written texts of the diverse languages of the modern world. Unicode provides a unique binary code for every character, no matter what the platform, program, or language. The Unicode standard currently contains 34,168 distinct coded characters derived from 24 supported language scripts. These characters cover the principal written languages of the world.

Unicode provides for two encoding forms: a default 16-bit form and a byte (8-bit) form called UTF-8 that has been designed for ease of use with existing ASCII-based systems. The default encoding of HTML and XML, Unicode is required for new Internet protocols. It is implemented in all modern operating systems and computer languages such as Java. Unicode is the basis of software that must function globally.

Data storage devices

Corporations double the amount of data they need to store every three to four years. So the selection of data storage devices is a key consideration for data managers. When evaluating data storage options, data managers need to consider how the device will be used:[2]

1. on-line data;
2. backup files;
3. archival storage.

Many systems require data to be on-line — continually available. Here the prime concerns are usually access speed and capacity because many firms require rapid response to large volumes of data. Backup files are required to provide security against data loss. Ideally, backup storage is high volume capacity at low cost. Archived data may need to be stored for many years; so, the archival medium should be highly reliable, with no data decay over extended periods, and low cost.

In deciding what data will be stored where, database designers need to consider a number of variables:

1. volume of data;
2. volatility of data;

2. Caveat: This section details characteristics of various devices such as storage capacity, access time, and transfer speed, but technological change can quickly date this information. Use the figures as comparative measures rather than absolute values.

3. required speed of access to data;
4. cost of data storage;
5. reliability of the data storage medium;
6. legal standing of stored data.

These design choices are discussed and considered in terms of the variables just identified.

Magnetic technology

Tens of billions are spent annually on magnetic storage devices (see Figure 11-17). Between one-third and one-half of IS hardware budgets are consumed by magnetic storage. Magnetic technology, the backbone of data storage for five decades, is based on magnetization and demagnetization of spots on a magnetic recording surface. The same spot can be magnetized and demagnetized repeatedly; so, spots can be altered many times. Magnetic recording materials may be coated on rigid platters (hard disks), flexible circular substrates (floppy disks), thin ribbons of material (magnetic tapes), or rectangular sheets (magnetic cards).

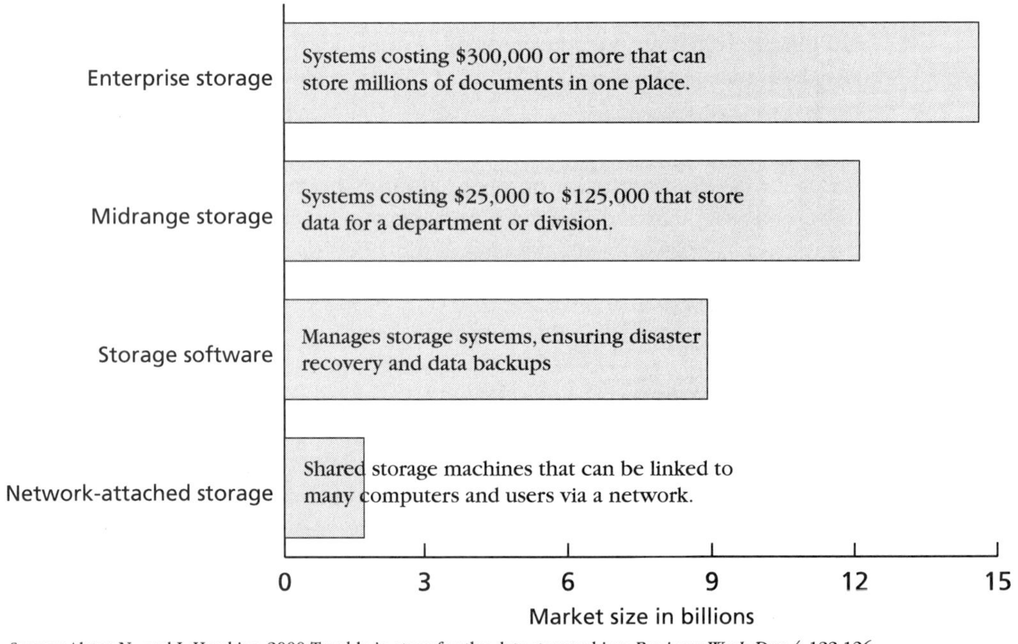

Source: Alster, N., and L. Hawkins. 2000. Trouble in store for the data-storage king. *Business Week*, Dec 4, 122,126.

Figure 11-17. The data storage market

The main advantages of magnetic technology are its relative maturity and widespread use. A major disadvantage is susceptibility to strong magnetic fields that can corrupt data stored on a disk. Another shortcoming is data storage life; magnetization decays with time.

As organizations convert paper to images, they need a very long-term, unalterable storage medium for documents that could be tabled in legal proceedings (e.g., a customer's handwritten insurance claim or a client's completed form for a mutual fund investment). Because data resident on magnetic media can be readily changed and decay with time, it is not a good medium for storing archival data or legal documents.

U.S. National Medal of Technology

The U.S. National Medal of Technology will be presented to IBM for its invention of the magnetic hard disk drive in the mid-1950s and also for its major breakthroughs in disk storage technology over that period. Over the past 20 years, the storage density of disk drives has increased more than 4,000-fold. Today, the total worldwide production of hard disk drives exceeds 170 million units each year. IBM has also played an important role in the development of magnetic tape and optical disk storage technologies.

Who would have believed that the size and capacity of those huge, expensive disk drives used during the '70s and '80s could be reduced to the matchbook-size, featherweight devices of today? IBM's first one-gigabyte disk drive was the size of a refrigerator, weighed 550 pounds (250 kg), and cost US$40,000. Today, the one-gigabyte IBM Microdrive costs less than US$500 and can hold 1,000 digitized photos, a thousand 200-page novels, or nearly 18 hours of digital music. This miniaturization has paved the way for the units uses in handheld electronic products, including digital cameras, PDAs, portable music players, and video cameras. In the future, we are likely to witness wearable computers, electronic books, global positioning system (GPS) receivers, and electronic wallets.

This award is the highest honor the U.S. president can bestow on leading innovators. It is an annual award presented to individuals, teams, or companies for the invention, development, or management of technology, as demonstrated by the introduction of new or significantly improved products, processes, or services.

Source: Anonymous. 2000. Hard disk drive inventor awarded medal. *Computing Canada*, Dec. 1, 15.

Fixed magnetic disk

A fixed magnetic disk containing one or more recording surfaces is permanently mounted in the disk drive and cannot be removed. The recording surfaces and access mechanism are assembled in a clean room and then sealed to eliminate contaminants, making the device more reliable and permitting higher recording density and transfer rates. Access time is typically between 4 and 10 ms and transfer rates can be as high as 160 Mbytes per second. Disk unit capacities range from Gbytes to Tbytes. Magnetic disk units are often called direct-access storage devices or DASD (pronounced *dasdee*).

Fixed disk is the medium of choice for most systems, from personal computers to supercomputers. It gives rapid, direct access to large volumes of data and is ideal for highly volatile files. The major disadvantage of magnetic disk is the possibility of a head crash that destroys the disk surface and data. With the read/write head of a disk just 15 millionths of an inch (40 millionths of a centimeter) above the surface of the disk, there is little margin for error. Hence, it is crucial to regularly make backup copies of hard disk files.

A disk storage unit

RAID

RAID (redundant arrays of inexpensive or independent drives) takes advantage of the economies of scale in manufacturing disks for the personal computing market. The cost of hard drives increases with their capacity and speed. RAID's idea is to use several cheaper drives whose total cost is less than one high-capacity drive. In addition to lower cost, RAID offers greater data security. All RAID levels (except level 0) can reconstruct the data on any single disk from the data stored on the remaining disks in the array in a manner that is quite transparent to the user.

RAID uses a combination of mirroring or striping to provide greater data protection. When a file is written to a mirrored array (see Figure 11-18), the disk controller writes identical copies of each record to each drive in the array. When a file is read from a mirrored array, the controller reads alternate pages simultaneously from each of the drives. It then puts these pages together in the correct sequence before delivering them to the computer. Mirroring reduces data access time by approximately the number of drives in the array because it interleaves the reading of records. During the period a conventional disk drive reads one page, a RAID system can read two or more pages (one from each drive). It is simply a case of moving from sequential to parallel retrieval of pages. Access times are halved for a two-drive array, quartered for a four-drive array, and so on.

A RAID storage unit

If a read error occurs on a particular disk, the controller can always read the required page from another drive in the array since each drive has a full copy of the file. Mirroring, which requires at least two drives, improves response time and data security; however, it does take considerably more space to store a file because multiple copies are created.

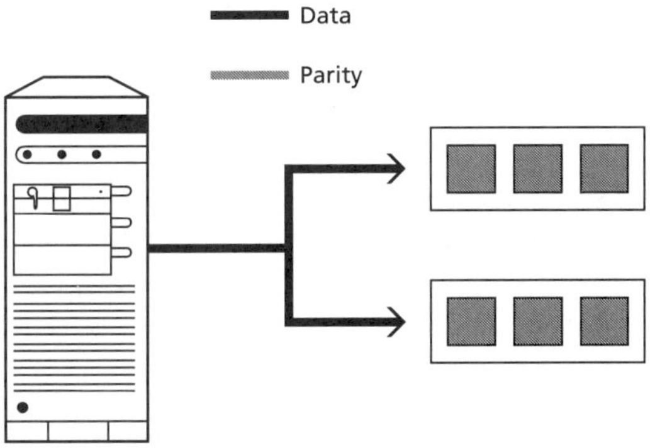

Figure 11-18. Mirroring

When a file is written to a striping array (see Figure 11-19) of three drives, for instance, one half of the file is written to the first drive and the second half to the second drive. The third drive is used for error correction. A parity bit is constructed for each corresponding pair of bits written to drives one and two, and this parity bit is written to the third drive. When a file is read by a striping array, portions are retrieved from each drive and assembled in the correct sequence by the controller. If a read error occurs, the lost bits can be reconstructed by using the parity data on the third drive. If a drive fails, it can be replaced, and the missing data restored on the new drive. Striping requires at least three drives. Normally data are written to every drive but one, and that remaining drive is used for the parity bit. Striping gives added data security without requiring considerably more storage, but it does not have the same response time increase as mirroring.

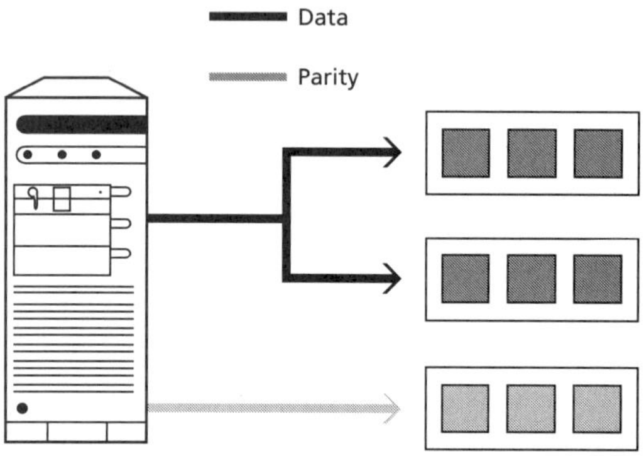

Figure 11-19. Striping

RAID subsystems are divided into six levels, labeled 0 through 5. All RAID levels, except level 0, have common features:

- There is a set of physical disk drives viewed by the operating system as a single, logical drive.
- Data are distributed across corresponding physical drives.
- Parity information is used to recover data in the event of a disk failure.

Level 0 has been in use for many years. Data are broken into blocks that are interleaved or *striped* across disks. By spreading data over multiple drives, read and write operations can occur in parallel. As a result, I/O rates are higher, which makes level 0 ideal for I/O intensive applications such as recording video. There is no additional parity information and thus no data recovery when a drive failure occurs.

Level 1 implements mirroring, as described previously. This is possibly the most popular form of RAID because of its effectiveness for critical nonstop applications, although high levels of data availability and I/O rates are counteracted by higher storage costs. Another disadvantage is that every write command must be executed twice (assuming a two-drive array), and thus level 1 is inappropriate for applications that have a high ratio of writes to reads.

Level 2 implements striping by interleaving blocks of data on each disk and maintaining parity on the check disk. This is a poor choice when an application has frequent, short random disk accesses because every disk in the array is accessed for each read operation.

However, RAID 2 provides excellent data transfer rates for large sequential data requests. It is therefore suitable for CAD/CAM and multimedia applications, which typically use large sequential files. RAID 2 is rarely used, however, because the same effect can be achieved with level 3 at lower cost.

Level 3 utilizes striping at the bit or byte level; so, only one I/O operation can be executed at a time. Compared to level 1, RAID level 3 gives lower-cost data storage at lower I/O rates and tends to be most useful for the storage of large amounts of data common with CAD/CAM and imaging applications.

Level 4 uses sector level striping; thus, only a single disk needs to be accessed for a read request. Write requests are slower, however, because there is only one parity drive.

Level 5 (see Figure 11-20), a variation of striping, reads and writes data to separate disks independently and permits simultaneous reading and writing of data. Data and parity are written on the same drive. Spreading parity data evenly across several drives avoids the bottleneck that can occur when there is only one parity drive. RAID 5 is well designed for the high I/O rates required by transaction processing systems and servers. It is the most balanced implementation of the RAID concept in terms of price, reliability, and performance. It requires less capacity than mirroring with level 1 and higher I/O rates than striping with level 3, although performance can decrease with update-intensive operations. RAID 5 is frequently found in LAN environments.

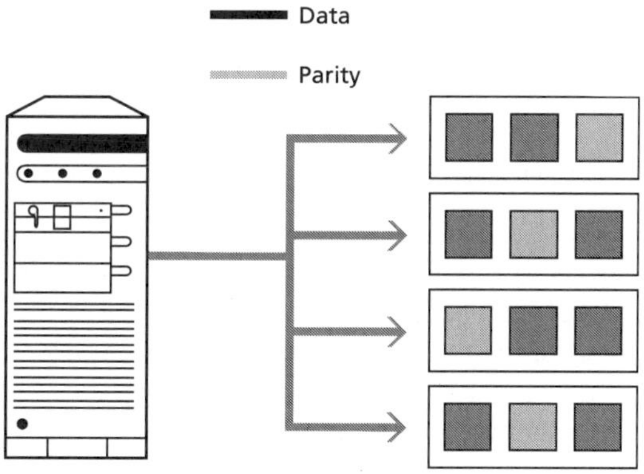

Figure 11-20. RAID level 5

RAID does have drawbacks. It often lowers systems performance in return for greater reliability and increased protection against data loss. Extra disk space is required to store redundant information. Extra disk accesses are required to access and update redundant information. You should remember that RAID is not a replacement for standard backup procedures; it is a technology for increasing the fault tolerance of critical on-line systems. Smaller RAID systems are in the 40 to 120 Gbytes range, and large systems offer terabytes.

Removable magnetic disk

A removable disk comes in two formats: single disk and disk pack. The single disk of 100 Mbytes to 5 Gbytes capacity is used with personal computers and is typically inserted, like a floppy disk, into a drive.

Disk packs consist of multiple disks mounted together on a common spindle in a stack, usually on a disk drive with retractable read/write heads. Because they are unsealed and exposed to possible contamination, storage densities and transfer rates are considerably lower than with fixed disk.

The disk's removability is its primary advantage, making it ideal for backup. For example, an organization may regularly copy its fixed disk storage to multiple disk packs. Removable disk is also useful when applications need not be continuously on-line. For instance, the monthly payroll system can be stored on a removable pack and mounted as required.

A Jaz drive with removable cartridge

Floppy disk

Floppy disks are used primarily with microcomputers. Currently the most popular format, the 3.5 inch (9 cm) disk, has a storage capacity of 1.44 Mbytes. Transfer rates are very low when compared to fixed disk. Floppies' low cost makes them ideal for storing and transporting small files and programs but because people are careless about handling or storing them, they do not score highly on reliability. A speck of dust can cause a read error.

Magnetic tape

A magnetic tape is a thin ribbon of plastic coated with ferric oxide. The once commonly used nine-track 2,400 foot (730 m) tape has a capacity of about 160 Mbytes and a data transfer rate of 2 Mbytes per second. The designation nine-track means nine bits are stored across the tape (8 bits plus one parity bit). Magnetic tape was used extensively for archiving and backup in early database systems; however, its limited capacity and sequential nature have resulted in its replacement by other media.

Magnetic tape cartridges

Tape cartridges, with a capacity measured in Gbytes and transfer rates of up to 3 Mbytes per second, have replaced magnetic tape. Easier handling is another feature favoring them over magnetic tape reels. Drives are usually less than $1,000 per unit.

Mass storage

There exists a variety of mass storage devices that automate labor-intensive tape and cartridge handling. The storage medium, with capacities of Tbytes, is typically located and mounted by a robotic arm.

Magstar 3495 tape library

Solid state storage

Solid-state storage devices connect to computers the same way regular magnetic disk drives do, but they store data on arrays of memory chips. These units are at least 10 times faster than magnetic storage but cost around $3 per Mbyte, compared to magnetic disks, which are as low as 1 cent per megabyte. Solid state is mainly used for stock-trading and video-streaming applications.

Table 11-2: A byte size table

Prefix	Size	Equivalent to
k kilo	10^3	
M mega	10^6	A 3.5 inch (9 cm) floppy disk
G giga	10^9	A symphony
T tera	10^{12}	
P peta	10^{15}	50 percent of U.S. academic libraries
E exa	10^{18}	

Optical technology

Optical technology is a more recent development than magnetic. Its advantages are high storage densities, low cost media, and direct access. Optical storage systems work by reflecting beams of laser light off a rotating disk with a minutely pitted surface. As the disk rotates, the amount of light reflected back to a sensor varies, generating a stream of ones and zeros. A tiny change in the wavelength of the laser translates into as much as a tenfold increase in the amount of information that can be stored. Currently, scientists are investigating the use of blue lasers with a shorter wavelength than the infrared or red light that is now commonly used to read optical disks. The shorter blue wavelength allows each bit of data to be stored in a smaller spot.

There are four storage media based on optical technology: CD-ROM, WORM, magneto-optical, and DVD (see Figure 11-21). All use a laser for reading and writing data but because the method of recording data differs, media are not typically interchangeable. For instance, a CD-ROM drive cannot read a magneto-optical disk.

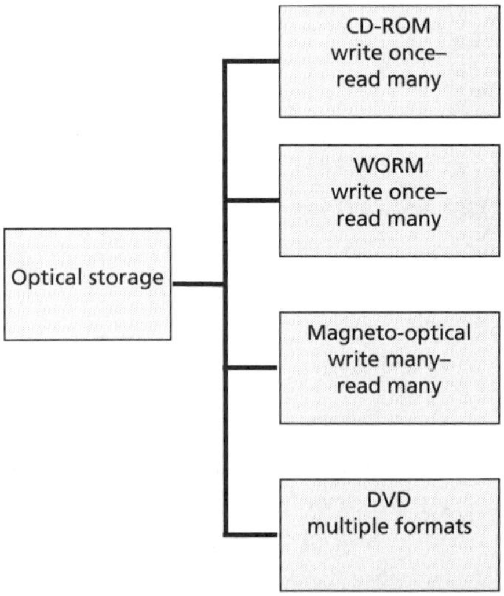

Figure 11-21. Optical storage media

Most optical disks can reliably store records for at least 10 years under prescribed conditions of humidity and temperature. Actual storage life may be in the region of 30 to 50 years. Optical technology is highly reliable because it is not susceptible to head crashes.

CD-ROM

In the early 1980s, engineers at Phillips and Sony independently recognized that compact disks (CDs) could store data as well as sound. In 1986, these two companies introduced the CD-ROM format (ROM stands for read-only memory). The storage capacity of a CD-ROM is significantly greater than a floppy diskette. Measuring approximately 5 inches (12 cm) in diameter, a CD-ROM stores some 650 Mbytes of data, whereas a typical floppy diskette of around the same physical dimensions has an upper limit of about 1 Mbyte. CD-ROM drives are relatively slow devices.

CD-ROM is a compact, robust, high capacity medium for the storage of permanent data. Initial thinking was that it would be used for storing relatively non-volatile databases, documents, directories, and other archival information. It was anticipated that major customers for these mainly text data stores would be libraries and businesses (e.g., a CD-ROM containing state-by-state details of 118 million registered voters). Indeed, this market has developed, but the major growth is in the consumer market for multimedia encyclopedias, games, and educational material. *The New Grolier Multimedia Encyclopedia,* costing less than $50, contains the text of all 21 volumes of the *Academic American Encyclopedia* and includes thousands of pictures, hundreds of maps, sound, animation, and video. CD-ROM has become the preferred medium for information distribution and multimedia applications.

Data stored on CD-ROM possibly have the highest legal standing of any of the forms discussed because once written, the data cannot be altered. Thus, it is ideal for storage of documents that potentially may be used in court.

CD-R

The CD-R (recordable) standard was defined by Philips and Sony in November 1990. CD-R writers are used to prepare discs for CD mastering, test prototype applications, and back-up systems Most newer CD-R writers support incremental packet writing, where data can be saved to a CD without finalizing a session or the CD. This means more data can be added to the CD over a period of time. The disadvantage is that the CD cannot be read in a CD-ROM player until it has been finalized.

CD-R has recently experienced a surge in popularity. There are several reasons for this growing demand. First, hardware has dropped from an original $100,000 to under $300, while CD-R media, once priced at $100 per piece, is now available for under $1.50 in quantity. Second, CD-R software is very easy to use and discs are easily written. Third, the makers of CD-R products have succeeded in perfecting the reliability and compatibility of CD-R media and CD-R drives to better than 99.7 percent.

CD-RW

In 1995 for the purpose of backing up data, Philips and Sony specified a new disc called CD-Erasable (CD-E), now known as CD-ReWritable (CD-RW). This format allows erasing and re-writing to a disc many times. CD-RW media cannot be read in some CD-ROM players that are not multiread compliant. Most of the newer CD-ROM players are multiread compliant along with second generation DVD Players. The first CD-RW writers came out in 1997 and are backward compatible with CD-R

A CD-RW drive costs about $400, and a blank CD is less than a $2 when purchased in quantity. CD-RW's main advantage is that the format can be read by the large number of CD-R drives already installed

The 650 Mbtyes storage capacity of a CD-R or CD-RW is considerably smaller than that of a DVD, but until most machines have DVD drives, CD-R and CD-RW will remain popular for information distribution.

WORM

WORM (write-once read-many) is the major storage device for images. Information once written to a blank disk cannot be altered. This is a particularly useful feature for data that must be stored for long periods. From a legal standpoint, it is important to have a storage medium that cannot be easily altered. Thus, WORM is an ideal medium for storing correspondence and legal documents.

Access time for WORM disks is around 150 to 250 ms, with data transfer rates of 256 kbytes per second. Three common disk sizes are available: 5.25 inch (13 cm), 12 inch (30 cm), and 14 inch (36 cm). The 14-inch disk can store as many as 10 Gbytes.

WORM *jukeboxes* are used to store high volumes of data. A jukebox may contain up to 2,000 WORM disks. Just like a conventional jukebox, a particular WORM disk can be loaded onto the drive, spun up to speed, and read. A WORM jukebox makes terabytes of data available in about 10 seconds.

WORM does not quite have the legal standing of CD-ROM because it is possible for a smart hacker to selectively add a document or modify an existing image. Although there are some techniques to prevent this from happening, WORM nevertheless is not as secure as CD-ROM. In the near future, DVD-R is likely to replace WORM.

Magneto-optical disk

Magneto-optical disks are a high capacity read-write medium. Drives and media come in two sizes, 3.5 inch (9 cm) and 5.25 inch (13.5 cm), and the disks can store up to 9 Gbytes. An ISO standard for both sizes makes for a free exchange of disks across same size drives of manufacturers that follow this standard.

Magneto-optical disks are a compact, high capacity, reliable, data transfer and archival storage medium. The smaller disks are suitable for personal computer storage and backup. Also, they can be used to distribute data within an organization. The 5.25-inch disks are useful for backup of databases under 9 Gbytes or the transfer of large files.

Magneto-optical technology is also very reliable since there is no possibility of a head crash, and stored data has a life of 30 years or more. At this stage, access speeds are somewhat longer than for magnetic disk.

Digital versatile disc

The most recently developed optical technology is digital versatile disc (DVD). A replacement for CD technology, DVD comes in several forms. DVD-Video and DVD-ROM are read-only versions designed respectively for storing full length movies and computer software. DVD-Audio store songs. DVD-R (recordable—write once, read many) and DVD-RAM (erasable) are designed for the computer industry. DVD-Audio more than doubles the fidelity of a standard CD and is expected to become the popular audio disk.

The same physical size as a CD-ROM, a single-sided, single-layer DVD-ROM has a storage capacity of 4.7 Gbytes, about seven times the capacity of a CD-ROM. The double-sided, double-layer version has a capacity of 17 Gbytes. DVD-R and DVD-RAM provide 3.9 Gbytes and 2.6 Gbytes, respectively, in the single-sided, single-layer format. DVD-ROM drives have transfer rates of 2.77 Mbytes/sec and access times below 100 msec. A PC DVD-ROM drive will play both audio CDs and CD-ROMs. DVD is likely to replace CD-ROM technology.

The future

Toshiba has developed technology that holds 1,000 times more data than a DVD. Based on Terabit Molecular Memory technology, the next generation disks will be able to hold 5 Tbytes of data. This technology is not likely to be introduced for another 5-7 years.

Storage-area networks

A storage-area network (SAN) is a high-speed network for connecting and sharing different kinds of storage devices, such as tape libraries and disk arrays. In the typical LAN, the storage device (usually a disk) is closely coupled to a server and communicates through a bus connection. Communication among storage devices occurs through servers and over the LAN, which can lead to network congestion.

A SAN creates a pool of storage that can be shared by multiple servers. Any server can access any storage device. A SAN supports dynamic sharing of large amounts of data, regardless of operating system or application. Generally, a SAN communicates via pipelines that consist of an interface called Fibre Channel, a high speed data connection between computer devices. Fibre Channel extends the possible distance between two connected devices. Where SCSI copper cables can extend up to 55 yards (50 m), Fibre Channels can run up to 6 miles (10 km).

SANs support disk mirroring, backup and restore, archival and retrieval of archived data, data migration from one storage device to another, and the sharing of data among different servers in a network. Typically, a SAN is part of the overall network of computing resources for an enterprise. SANs are likely to be a critical element for supporting e-commerce and applications requiring large volumes of data.

A SAN with of a couple of servers could cost between $20,000 and $30,000. A high-end SAN could cost up to 5 million depending upon the capacity and nature of the system. Thus, a SAN is part of the overall network of computing resources for an enterprise.

Long-term storage

Long-term storage of data has always been of concern to societies and organizations. Some data, such as the location of toxic-waste sites, must be stored for thousands of years. Increasingly, governments are converting their records to electronic format. Currently, about 75 percent of the U.S. government's transactions are in electronic format. Unlike paper, magnetic tapes and disks do not show degradation until it is too late to recover the data. Magnetic tapes can become so brittle that the magnetic coating separates from the backing. In addition, computer hardware and software rapidly become obsolete. The medium may be readable, but there could be no hardware to read it and no software to decode it.

Paper, it seems, is still the best medium for long-term storage (see Figure 11-22), and research is being conducted to create extra-long-life paper that can store information for hundreds of years. This paper, resistant to damage from heat, cold, and magnetism, will store data in a highly-compact format but obviously nowhere near optical disk densities.

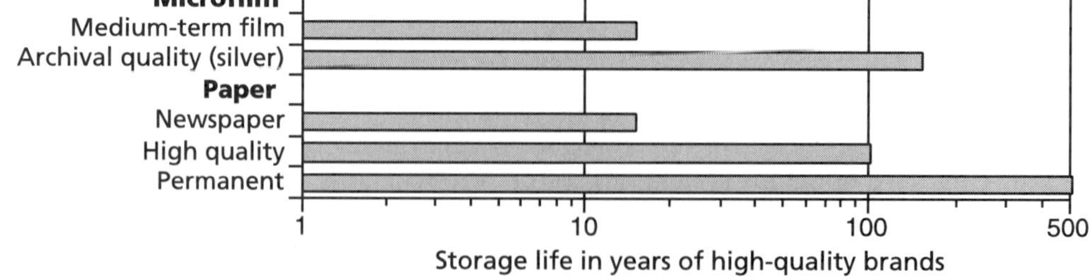

Figure 11-22. The life expectancy of various media at 20°C (68°F) and 40 percent relative humidity (source: National Media Lab)

Comparative analysis

Details of the various storage devices are summarized in Table 11-3. A simple three-star rating system has been used for each device—the more stars, the better. In regard to access speed, RAID gets more stars than floppy disk because it retrieves a stored record more quickly. Similarly, magneto-optical rates three stars because it costs less per megabyte to store data on a magneto-optical disk than a fixed disk. The scoring system is relative. The fact that a floppy disk gets a low score for reliability does not mean it is an unreliable storage medium; it simply means that it is not as reliable as other media.

Table 11-3: Relative merits of data storage devices

Device	Access speed	Volume	Volatility	Cost per megabyte	Reliability	Legal standing
Solid state	***	*	***	*	***	*
Fixed disk	***	***	***	**	**	*
RAID	***	***	***	**	***	*
Removable disk	**	**	***	**	**	*
Floppy	*	*	***	*	*	*
Tape	*	**	*	***	**	*
Cartridge	**	***	*	***	**	*
Mass Storage	**	***	*	***	**	*
SAN	***	***	***	**	***	*
CD-ROM	*	**	*	**	***	***
CD-R	*	**	*	**	***	**
CD-RW	*	**	***	**	***	*
WORM	*	***	*	***	***	**
Magneto-optical	**	***	**	***	***	*
DVD-ROM	*	***	*	***	***	***
DVD-R	*	***	*	***	***	**
DVD-RAM	*	***	**	***	***	*

Legend

Characteristic	More stars means ...
Access speed	faster access to data
Volume	more suitable for large files
Volatility	more suitable for files that change frequently
Cost per megabyte	less costly form of storage
Reliability	less susceptible to an unrecoverable read error
Legal standing	more acceptable as evidence in court

Data compression

Data compression is a method for encoding digital data so it requires less storage space and thus less network bandwidth to be transmitted. There are two basic types of compression: lossless methods, in which no data are lost when the files are restored to their original format, and lossy methods, in which some data are lost when the files are decompressed

Lossless compression

During lossless compression, the data-compression software searches for redundant or repetitive data and encodes it. For example, a string of 100 asterisks (*) can be stored more compactly by a compression system that records the repeated character (i.e., *) and the length of the repetition (i.e., 100). The same principle can be applied to a photo that contains a string of horizontal pixels of the same color. Clearly, you want to use lossless compression with text file (e.g., a business report or spreadsheet).

Lossy compression

Lossy compression is used for graphics, video, and audio files because humans are often unable to detect minor data losses in these formats. Audio files can often be compressed to 10 percent of their original file (e.g., an MP3 version of a CD recording).

Conclusion

The internal and physical aspects of database design are a key determinant of system performance. Selection of appropriate data structures can substantially curtail disk accesses and reduce response times. In making data structure decisions, the database administrator needs to weigh the pros and cons of each choice. Similarly, in selecting data storage devices, the designer needs to be aware of the trade-offs. Various devices and media have both strengths and weaknesses, and these need to be considered.

Summary

It takes considerably longer to retrieve data from a magnetic disk than from main memory. Appropriate selection of data structures and data access methods can considerably reduce delays by reducing disk accesses. The key characteristics of disk storage devices that affect database access are rotational speed and access arm speed. Access arm movement can be minimized by storing frequently used data on the same track on a single surface or on the same track on different surfaces. Records that are frequently used together should be clustered together. Intrafile clustering applies to the records within a single file. Interfile clustering applies to multiple files. The disk manager, the part of the operating system responsible for physical I/O, maintains a directory of pages. The file manager, a level above the disk manager, contains a directory of files.

Indexes are used to speed up retrieval by reducing disk accesses. An index is a file containing the value of the index field and the address of its full record. The use of indexes involves a trade-off between faster retrievals and slower updates. Indexes can be used for both sequential and direct access. A file can have multiple indexes. A sparse index does not contain an entry for every value of the indexed field. The B-tree is a particular form of index structure. It is the basis for IBM's VSAM, the file structure underlying DB2, and is an efficient structure for both sequential and direct accessing. It consists of two parts, the sequence set and the index set. Hashing is a technique for reducing disk accesses that allows direct access to a file. There can be only one hashing field. A hashed file can no longer be processed sequentially because its physical sequence has lost any logical meaning. A linked list is a useful data structure for interfile clustering. It is a suitable structure for representing a 1:m relationship. Pointers between records are used to maintain a logical sequence. Lists can have forward, backward, and parent pointers.

Systems designers have to decide what data storage devices will be used for on-line data, backup files, and archival storage. In making this decision, they must consider the volume of data, volatility of data, required speed of access to data, cost of data storage, reliability of the data storage medium, and the legal standing of the stored data. Magnetic technology, the backbone of data storage for five decades, is based on magnetization and demagnetization of spots on a magnetic recording surface. Fixed disk, removable disk, magnetic tape, floppy disk, tape cartridge, and mass storage are examples of magnetic technology. RAID uses several cheaper drives whose total cost is less than one high-capacity drive. RAID uses a combination of mirroring or striping to provide greater data protection. RAID subsystems are divided into six levels labeled 0 through 5. A storage-area network (SAN) is a high-speed network for connecting and sharing different kinds of storage devices, such as tape libraries and disk arrays.

Optical technology offers high-storage densities, low-cost medium, and direct access. CD-ROM, WORM, magneto-optical, and DVD are examples of optical technology. Optical disks can reliably store records for at least 10 years and possibly up to 30 years. Optical technology is not susceptible to head crashes.

Data compression techniques reduce the need for storage capacity and bandwidth. Lossless methods result in no data loss, whereas with lossy techniques some data are lost during compression.

Key terms and concepts

Access time
Archival file
ASCII
B-tree
Backup file
Bitmap index
CD-R
CD-ROM
CD-RW
Clustering
Conceptual schema
Cylinder
Data compression
Data storage device
Database architecture
Digital versatile disc (DVD)
Disk manager
External schema
File manager
Hash address
Hash field
Hash function
Hashing
Index
Index set
Interfile clustering
Internal schema
Intrafile clustering
Join Index
Linked list
Lossless compression
Lossy compression
Magnetic disk
Magnetic tape
Magneto-optical disk
Mass storage
Mirroring
Page
Parity
Pointer
R-tree
RAID
Sequence set
Solid state storage
Sparse index
Storage-area network (SAN)
Striping
Track
Unicode
VSAM
WORM

Exercises

1. Why is a disk drive considered a bottleneck?
2. What is the difference between a record and a page?
3. Describe the two types of delay that can occur prior to reading a record from a disk. What can be done to reduce these delays?
4. What is clustering? What is the difference between intrafile and interfile clustering?
5. Describe the differences between a file manager and a disk manager.
6. What is an index?
7. What are the advantages and disadvantages of indexing?
8. Write the SQL to create an index on the column NATCODE in the NATION table.
9. Is MP3 a lossless or lossy compression standard?
10. A Paris insurance firm keeps paper records of all policies and claims made on it. The firm now has a vault containing 100 filing cabinets full of forms. Because Paris rental costs are so high, the CEO has asked you to recommend a more compact medium for long-term storage of these documents. Because some insurance claims

are contested, she is very concerned with ensuring that documents, once stored, cannot be altered. What would you recommend and why?

11. The national weather research center of a large South American country has asked you to recommend a data storage strategy for its historical weather data. The center electronically collects hourly weather information from 2,000 sites around the country. This database must be maintained indefinitely. Periodically, weather researchers extract a portion of these data for their use. A researcher must submit a written request detailing what data are required and the purpose of the study. After review of the request, the center sets up a data file on a file server. The center's director is very concerned with cost and wants to minimize the cost of data storage. What would you recommend and why?
12. The national aviation authority in your country has asked you to recommend a data storage device for its air traffic control system. The specification states that the file is relatively small (around 500 Mbytes) and system reliability is the foremost criterion. What would you recommend and why?
13. A magazine subscription service has a toll-free number for customers who may dial the company to place orders, inquire about existing orders, or check subscription rates. All customers are uniquely identified by an 11-digit numeric code. All magazines are identified by a 2- to 4-character code. The company has approximately 10 million customers who subscribe to an average of four magazines. Subscriptions are available to 126 magazines. Draw a data model for this situation. Decide what data structures you would recommend for the storage of the data for each entity. The management of the company prides itself on its customer service and strives to answer customer queries as rapidly as possible.
14. A German consumer research company collects scanning data from supermarkets throughout central Europe. The scanned data include product code identifier, price, quantity purchased, time, date, supermarket location, and supermarket name, and in some cases where the supermarket has a frequent buyer plan, it collects a consumer identification code. It has also created a table containing details of the manufacturer of each product. The database is very large and contains nearly one Tbyte of data. The data are used by market researchers in consumer product companies. A researcher will typically request access to a slice of the database (e.g., sales of all detergents) and analyze these data for trends and patterns. The consumer research company promises rapid access to its data. Its goal is to give clients access to requested data within one to two minutes. Once clients have access to the data, they expect very rapid response to queries. What data storage and retrieval strategy would you recommend?
15. The navy of a large industrial power has many modern ships. Because of the technology and complexity of these ships, many thick, paper manuals are required to describe how to operate, maintain, and repair the many shipboard electronic and mechanical devices. In fact, because there are so many manuals, one wag suggested ships could be 10 percent smaller if they did not have to carry so much paper. What advice do you have for this navy?

16. A video producer has asked for your advice on a data storage device. She has specified that she must be able to record video at 5 to 7 Mbytes per second. What would you recommend and why?
17. A firm is planning to offer a satellite-based digital radio service to the continental US market. It will broadcast music, sports, and talk-radio programs from a library of 1.5 million digital audio files, which will be sent to a satellite uplink and then beamed to car radios equipped to accept the service. Consumers will pay $9.95 per month to access 100 channels.
    a. Assuming the average size of a digital audio file is 5Mbytes (~ 4 minutes of music), how much storage space is required?
    b. What storage technology would you recommend?
18. An airline plans to install remote diagnostic systems in its aircraft that will allow physicians on the ground to remotely monitor an ill passenger. The doctors will then be able to communicate with flight personnel on appropriate treatment. The system will send real-time electrocardiogram information, temperature (via an ear probe), blood pressure information (via a wrist cuff), blood oxygen levels, respiration rates, and other vital signs to computers at a hospital in Phoenix, Arizona. A built-in modem connected to a seat-back satellite phone will be used for data transmission. Graphical help screens will guide flight personnel through every step of the process. Since the satellite phone operates at only 2.4 kbps, what technology can be used to support this system?

12

Data Processing Architectures

The difficulty in life is the choice.
George Moore, *The Bending of the Bough,* 1900

Learning Objectives

On completion of this chapter, you will be able to

- ❖ recommend a data architecture for a given situation;
- ❖ understand the differences between two- and three-tier client/server architecture;
- ❖ discuss the fundamental principles that a hybrid architecture should satisfy;
- ❖ demonstrate the general principles of distributed database design.

On a recent transatlantic flight, Sophie, the Personnel and PR manager, had been seated next to a very charming young man who had tried to impress her with his knowledge of computing. He worked for a large systems consulting firm, and his speech was sprinkled with words like "client/server," "gooey," "host," "LAN," and "distributed database." In return, Sophie responded with some "ums," "aahs," and a sprinkling of "that's interesting." Of course, this was before the third glass of champagne. After that, he was more intent on finding out how long Sophie would be in New York and what restaurants and shows piqued her curiosity.

After an extremely pleasant week of wining, dining, and seeing the town — amid, of course, many hours of valuable work for The Expeditioner — Sophie returned to London. Now, she must ask Ned what all these weird terms meant. After all, it was difficult to carry on a conversation when you did not understand the language. That's the problem with IS, she thought, new words and technologies were always being invented. It makes it very hard for the rest of us to make sense of what's being said.

Introduction

The ANSI/SPARC architecture was developed during an earlier era of information systems. It is a product of the period when mainframe computers were dominant and personal computers were nonexistent. Now, personal computers have extended the range of architectures available for implementing the ANSI/SPARC model. The three levels of internal, conceptual, and external are still valid, but the internal level needs to be extended to include data processing in addition to data storage.

In the mainframe era, all data were stored and processed on the mainframe. The advent of personal computers on users' desks provided a choice for separating data storage and processing. In general terms, data can be stored and processed locally or remotely. Combinations of these two options provide four basic architectures (see Figure 12-1). Client/server, which is not exclusively local data processing and remote storage, is shown as overlapping adjacent quadrants.

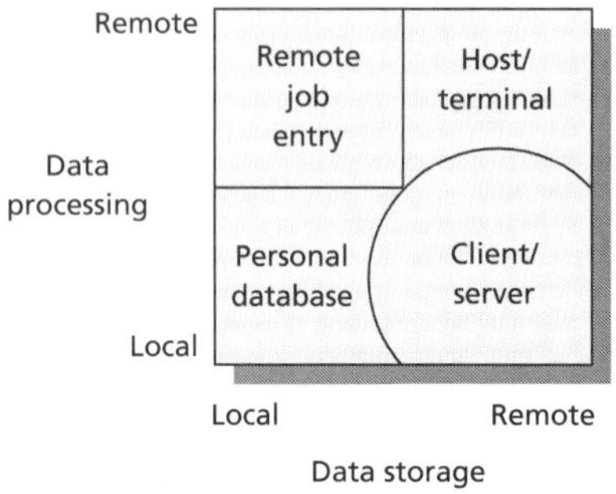

Figure 12-1. Basic architectures

Remote job entry

Remote job entry describes the situation where data are stored locally and processed remotely. Data are sent over a communication link to a remote computer for processing, and the output is returned the same way. This fairly common form of data processing is still being used today because remote job entry can overcome three shortcomings of personal computers. First, a personal computer may be too slow. Scientists and engineers need occasional access to a supercomputer for computationally intensive applications. Second, a personal computer may have insufficient main memory. Mainframe computers typically have larger amounts of main memory and can handle larger problems more easily. Third, highly specialized software is not available on the user's personal computer. For example, some statistical and mathematical modeling routines have not been ported to personal computers.

A supercomputer

Local storage is used for several reasons. First, it may be cheaper than storing on a mainframe, whose management will charge for storage space. Second, the user may be able to do some local processing and preparation of the data before sending it to the mainframe. Mainframe and supercomputing time can be expensive and, where possible, local processing is used for tasks such as data entry, validation, and reporting. Third, users may feel that local data storage is more secure for particularly sensitive data.

Personal database

Users can store and process their data locally when they have their own computers. Many personal computer database systems (e.g., MS Access and FileMaker) now permit users to develop their own applications, and there are many programs available for common applications that require database facilities.

There are a number of reasons favoring personal databases. First, the competitiveness and economies of scale of the microcomputer market make personal computers a low-cost alternative for data storage and processing. Second, users are independent of the information systems department. They have greater control and can develop their own software. The application backlog of most IS departments means that users often have a very long wait for IS department-developed systems. Third, the Windows and Macintosh operating systems make personal computers easier to use. Fourth, the size of the personal computing market has attracted many software companies, and many leading-edge applications are written for personal computers. Thus, personal computer users have an extensive choice of user-friendly software for a wide range of applications.

Of course, there is a downside to personal databases. First, there is a great danger of repetition and redundancy. The same application gets developed in a slightly different way by many users. The same data get stored on many different systems. (It is not always the same, however, because data entry errors or maintenance inconsistencies result in discrepancies across personal databases.) Second, data are not readily shared because various users are not aware of what is available or find it inconvenient to share data. Personal databases are exactly that; but much of the data may be of corporate value and should be shared. Third, data integrity procedures are often quite lax for personal databases. Users rarely make backups, databases are often not secured from unauthorized access, and data validation procedures are often ignored. Fourth, often when the user leaves the organization or moves to another role, the application and data are lost because they are not documented and the organization is unaware of their existence. Fifth, there is a danger that users get addicted to developing software and ignore their assigned work. The job of managers is to manage, not write software or build personal databases. Personal databases are clearly very important for many organizations—when used appropriately. Data that are shared require a different processing architecture.

Host/terminal

The host/terminal approach was the initial solution to making data accessible to many users. Under this architecture, data storage and processing occur at one location, typically a mainframe computer. In smaller organizational units, this might be a mini or midframe computer (e.g., an IBM AS/400). Users have terminals (also called network stations) linked to the central computer by communication lines. These terminals have minimal processing capability and are used to display data and may do some limited formatting. More recently, personal computers have been substituted for terminals, but they are usually emulating a terminal and so have the same restricted processing capabilities. Host/terminal architecture was the basis of IBM's success for many years. Its mainframe computers, terminals, communication system, and supporting software were well-suited to handling large volumes of data and high transaction processing rates.

A network computer system

A generic host/terminal architecture consists of several key components (see Figure 12-2). Requirements include the operating system, a Data Communications manager (usually abbreviated to DC manager), and Database Management System (DBMS). The DC manager handles the transfer of data between application programs and terminals. This is sometimes called a Transaction Processing (TP) monitor. For example, when a user enters a query at a terminal, the DC manager handles its transmission from the terminal to the relevant application program. Next, after some processing (e.g., validating the query), the application program passes the query to the DBMS, which retrieves the required data and returns it to the application program. The application program may then do some additional processing of the data before passing it to the DC manager for transmission to the user's terminal. As you can see from this example, mainframe-resident software does all the work.

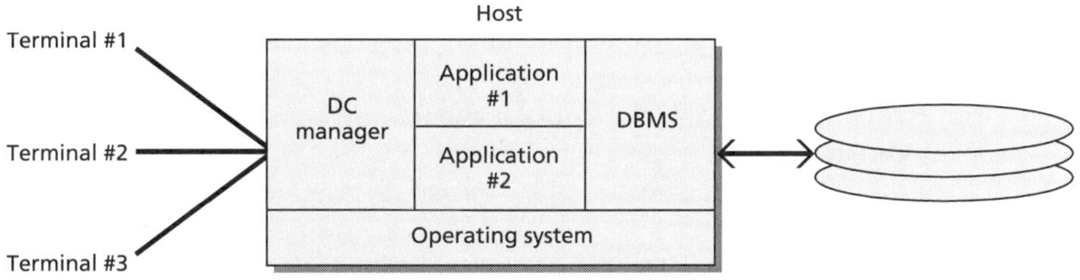

Figure 12-2. Host/terminal architecture

In a host/terminal setting, all shared resources are managed by the host. When additional processing capacity is required, the host must be upgraded or replaced. As a result, capacity changes tend to be very lumpy, and required capacity is often out of balance with actual needs.

LAN-based architectures

File/server and DBMS/server systems are variations on client/server found on a local area network (LAN). Before we delve into these architectures, however, you need a brief overview of LANs. A **LAN** connects computers and devices within the same limited geographic area (e.g., a building). High-performance communication connections enable data to be transferred on a LAN at speeds of up to 1,000 Mbits per second. A LAN enables users to share devices (e.g., laser printers), access shared files, and transfer files to others on the LAN. Its basic components include cabling to connect computers and devices, a card for each computer or device to connect it to the network, a file server for storing shared data, a network operating system (e.g., Novell's NetWare), and the computer and devices.

LAN technology is a direct result of the massive influx of personal computers into organizations. People with personal computers soon discovered they wanted to access corporate databases, share data with colleagues, and share expensive devices, such as a laser printer, within a work group.

Supercomputing Wall Street

Beowulf, a NASA project that was created in 1994, uses clustering technology to link a large number of low cost machines running Linux into a massive supercomputer. The cost savings arise from being able to parcel out complex calculations to 1,000 idle servers connected via a virtual LAN or the Internet. Although this technology is used extensively in research laboratories and universities, it has not been received favorably by companies on Wall Street due to concerns over reliability and support.

This attitude seems to be changing. J P Morgan has announced the deployment of TurboLinux's EnFuzion software in its global risk management system for fixed-income derivatives. Instead of requiring a dedicated cluster of Linux servers, EnFuzion uses a combination of machines running a mixture of operating systems, including Windows NT, Solaris, HP UX, AIX, Linux, and Tru64. This is good news for many securities firms, which typically use a mix of hardware and operating systems, many frequently sitting idle for at least 50 percent of the time while local markets are closed. This was one of the principal reasons that J P Morgan decided to adopt the EnFuzion software.

The software is being used to manage a cluster of some 50 Sun Microsystems Enterprise Server CPUs running Solaris and more than two hundred Dell workstations running Microsoft Windows NT. This system will be extended to more than a thousand cluster nodes.

Source: Webb, A. 2000. Beowulf moves from underground to trading floor. *Wall Street & Technology*, Oct., 14.

A server is a general purpose computer that provides and controls access to shareable resources such as applications, files, printers, communication lines, and databases. A server must be able to support multiple, simultaneous requests for shared resources. A server can have a single purpose (e.g., a database server and nothing else) or manage multiple shared resources (e.g., a server handles sharing of a printer and multiple files).

In a client/server environment, shared resources are often managed by several servers. Capacity increases can be very gradual as additional servers are added or some servers upgraded. Compared to a host/terminal architecture, it is far easier to keep required and actual capacity in balance.

File/server

A file/server is a LAN computer with a large disk file (see Figure 12-3). It is a central data store for the network's users. Files are kept on the file server, and processing occurs at the user's personal computer. This means that entire files are transferred on the LAN to an application running on a personal computer. For example, updating a file requires transfer of the file to the personal computer running the application, processing the update, and transferring the revised file to the file/server. Also, when a file is retrieved for update, it is locked. Other users cannot access the file until the changes have been made and the file rewritten to the server. Clearly, this approach is limited to small files and low demand. Network congestion occurs when file sizes are large, and there are multiple, active users.

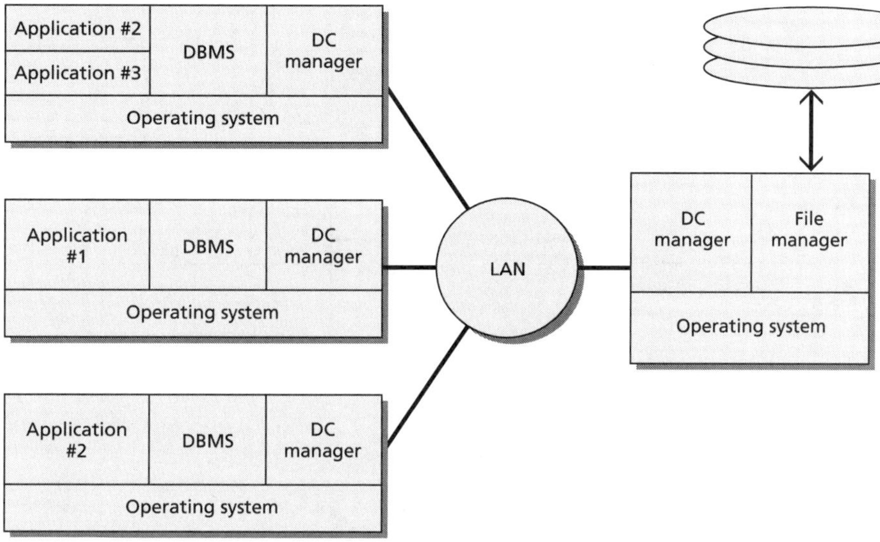

Figure 12-3. File/server architecture

File/server architecture is a relatively simple solution to data sharing on a local area network. Its shortcomings are addressed by DBMS/server architecture.

DBMS/server

Another LAN approach to client/server architecture operates a DBMS on the server, which can run on the file server or a separate computer. It does most of the DBMS processing so that only necessary records are transferred across the network, thus reducing network traffic substantially. In addition, with a DBMS/server, locking can take place at the record rather than file level (see Chapter 17 for a more detailed discussion of locking).

There are two separate programs: the DBMS/server, sometimes known as the back-end, and the client part, the front-end, which resides on the user's personal computer. The following example illustrates how the processing load can be shared in a DBMS/server environment (see Figure 12-4). When a user enters a query at a personal computer, it is handled by the resident application program, which will do local processing such as query validation. The application program then hands, for example, an SQL query to the client DC manager for transmission to the server. At the server, the server DC manager picks up the query and passes it to the DBMS, which executes the query. The result of the query is passed to the server's DC manager for transmission to the client's DC manager. The client's DC manager then passes the result to the client application program for processing. Finally, the result of the query appears on the user's personal computer.

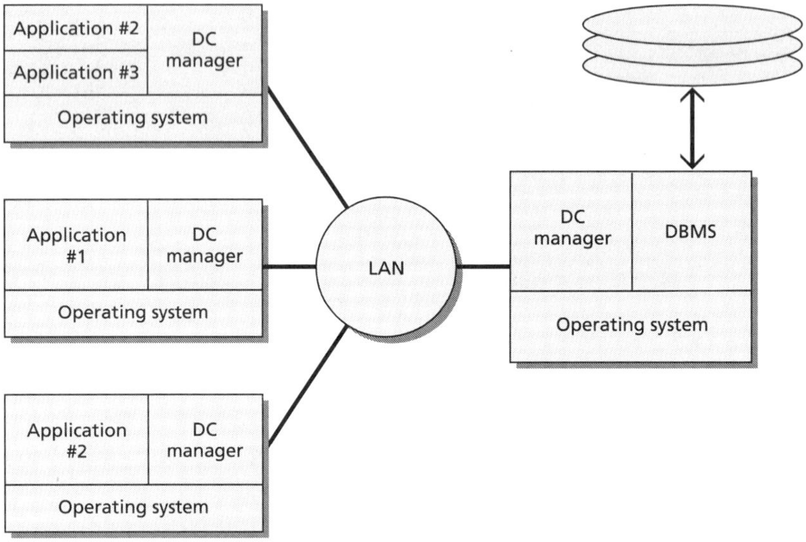

Figure 12-4. DBMS/server architecture

Client/server fundamentals

File/server and DBMS/server are examples of client/server architecture, in which two processes interact as superior and subordinate. The client process initiates requests and the server responds. The client is the dominant partner because it initiates a request. Client and server processes can run on the same computer, but generally they run on separate, linked computers. Typically, the client is a microcomputer and the server is a more powerful machine.

Client/server aims to take advantage of the lower processing cost of microcomputer technology. It is generally far cheaper to process data on a microcomputer than a mainframe. Client/server exploits this cost differential by moving processing from the mainframe to personal computers. A mainframe can be a server, but generally it is cheaper to use high-speed microcomputers as servers. Generally, processing is split between the client and the server, with most of the processing performed by the client. It is also possible that some infrequently changed data are stored locally. For example, the company logo might appear on all screens. Since a logo changes rarely, the image file containing the logo should be stored locally rather than transmitted across the network.

Most data management decisions require a trade-off. The decision to move from host/terminal architecture to client/server is no different. The costs and benefits of different architectures need to be closely investigated (see Table 12-1 for a summary).

Table 12-1: Architecture Summary

Architecture	Main use
Remote job entry	Large scale scientific or engineering work
Personal	Stand-alone, small, personal systems
Host/terminal	Large scale transaction processing
Client/server	Flexible, friendly decision support and workflow

Client/server—the second generation

The original client/server idea, as presented in the previous section, is a simple, two-tiered client/database model. Now, the client/server concept has evolved to describe a widely distributed, data-rich, cooperative environment. The second generation model embraces servers dedicated to applications, data, transaction management, systems management, and other tasks. It also extends the database side to incorporate non-relational systems, such as multidimensional databases, multimedia databases, and legacy systems. A three-tier model has emerged as the predominant incarnation of second generation client/server computing (see Figure 12-5). A major advantage of the three-tier model is that applications can be more easily created from reusable components. Applications are also more scalable.

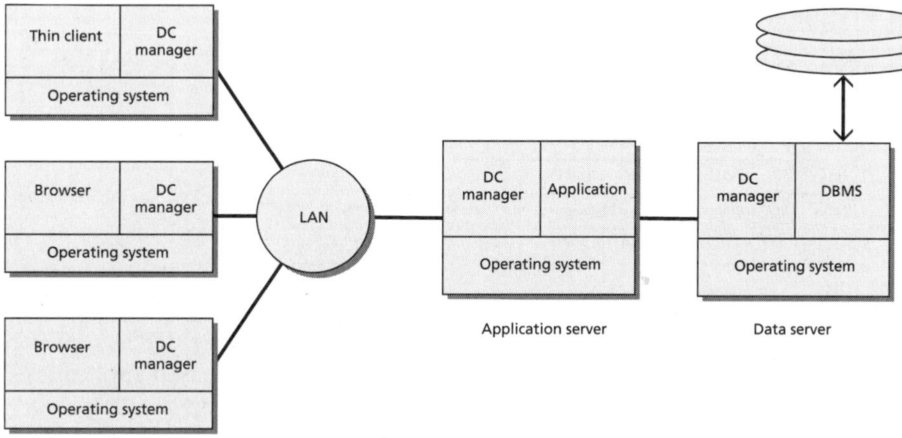

Figure 12-5. Three-tier client/server computing

The three-tier model consists of three types of systems:

- **Clients** perform presentation functions, manage the graphical user interface, and execute communication software that provides network access. In addition, the client may run code to access client-resident databases. The trend is towards the client being a browser (e.g., Netscape Communicator or Internet Explorer) or so-called thin client.
- **Application servers** are where the majority of the business and data logic are

processed. Tasks handled by an application server include providing workgroup functions, assisting in network management, and supporting messaging.

- **Data servers** provide support for relational and other DBMSs. They usually also provide backup and recovery services and transaction management control.

Under the three-tier model, the client requests a service from an application server (e.g., a Unix program), and the application server requests data from a data server (e.g., DB2 running on an IBM mainframe).

The computing environment is moving toward a complex array of clients, application servers, and data servers. An organization can spread its processing load across many servers. This enables it to more easily scale up the data processing workload. For example, if a server running several applications is overloaded, another server can be purchased and some of the workload moved to the new server.

Two-tier versus three-tier

The client in the two-tier model of client/server is also called a **fat client**, because most of the processing runs on the client side. Three-tier moves the application logic to the server, known as a **thin client** or **fat server** architecture.[1] The main differences between thin and fat clients are summarized in Table 12-2.

Table 12-2: Fat and thin clients

Type of client	Fat	Thin
Technology	LAN	Web
Application logic	Mostly on the client	Mostly on the server
Network load	Medium	Low
Data storage	Server	Server
Server intelligence	Medium	High

Two-tier is good for building departmental applications, such as decision support and groupware. However, two-tier does not scale well. Three-tier is superior for handling large-scale Internet and intranet applications. Many Web-based applications are based on the three-tier model. The client is a browser, the application is a Web server, and the data server is an RDBMS. We will investigate Web-based systems in more detail in Chapter 15.

From a data management perspective, the three-tier model provides several advantages:

- Data security is higher because the data schema is not exposed to the client but hidden in the application server.
- Performance is better because only service requests and responses are transmitted between the client and the application server. With two-tier logic, many SQL statements are sent across the network, and selected data must be downloaded to the cli-

1. Does this mean a dumb terminal is an anorexic client?

ent for analysis.

- ❖ Access to legacy data systems and heterogeneous databases is supported via gateways.
- ❖ Application software is easier to implement and maintain because it is installed on a small number of servers rather than a large number of clients.

The rise of three-tier client/server can be attributed to the benefits of adopting a component-based architecture. The goal is to build quickly scalable systems by plugging together existing components. On the client side, the Web browser is a readily available component that makes deployment of new systems very simple. When everyone in the corporation has a browser installed on their PC, rolling out a new application is just a case of e-mailing the URL to the concerned people. Under a two-tier system, software has to be installed on each PC.

On the data server side, many data management systems already exist, either in relational format or some other data model. Middle-tier server applications can make these data available to customers through a Web client. For example, UPS was able to make its parcel tracking system available via the Web because the database already existed. A middle-tier was written to connect customers using a browser to the database.

The move to client/server architecture is part of the general move toward distributing data and n-tier client/server (see Table 12-3), where there are multiple servers and databases. Thus, it is appropriate at this point to consider the topic of distributed database.

Table 12-3: Evolution of client/server computing

Architecture	Description
Two-tier	Processing is split between client PC and server, which also runs the DBMS
Three-tier	Client PC does presentation, processing is done by the server, and the DBMS is on a separate server
N-tier	Client PC does presentation. Processing and DBMS can be spread across multiple servers. A distributed resources environment.

Distributed database

Client/server architecture is concerned with minimizing processing costs by distributing processing between the server and multiple clients. Another factor in the total processing cost equation is communication. The cost of transmitting data usually increases with distance, and there can be substantial savings by locating data close to those most likely to use it. The trade-off for a distributed database is lowered communication costs versus increased complexity.

Distributed database architecture describes the situation where a database is in more than one location but still accessible as if it were centrally located. For example, a multinational organization might locate its Indonesian data in Jakarta, Japanese data in Tokyo, and Australian data in Sydney. If most queries deal with the local situation, communication costs are substantially lower than if the database were centrally located. Furthermore, since the database is still treated as one logical entity, queries that require access to different physical locations can be processed. For example, the query, "Find total sales of red hats in Australia," is likely to originate in Australia and be processed using the Sydney part of the database. A query of the form, "Find total sales of red hats," is more likely to come from a headquarter's user and is resolved by accessing each of the local databases, though the user need not be aware of where the data are stored since the database appears as a single logical entity.

A distributed database system (DDBMS) is a federation of individual DBMSs. Each site has a local DBMS and DC manager. In many respects, each site acts semi-independently. Each site also contains additional software that enables it to be part of the federation and act as a single database. It is this additional software that creates the DDBMS and enables the multiple databases to appear as one.

A DDBMS introduces a need for a data store containing details of the entire system. Information must be recorded about the structure and location of every database, table, row, column, and their possible replicas. The traditional system catalog is extended to include such information. The system catalog must also be distributed; otherwise, every request for information would have to be routed through some central point. For instance, if the systems catalog were stored in Tokyo, a query on Sydney data would first have to access the Tokyo-based catalog. This would create an expensive bottleneck.

A hybrid, distributed architecture

Any organization of a reasonable size is likely to have a mix of the data processing architectures previously described. Databases will exist on stand-alone personal computers, multiple client/server networks, distributed mainframes, and so on. Architectures continue to evolve because information technology is so dynamic. Today's best solutions for database processing can become obsolete very quickly. Yet, organizations have invested large sums in existing systems that meet their current needs and do not warrant replacement. As a result, organizations evolve a hybrid architecture — a mix of the various forms. The concern of the IS department is to patch this hybrid together so that users see it as a seamless system that readily provides needed information. In creating this ideal system, there are some underlying key concepts that should be observed. These fundamental principles (see Table 12-4) were initially stated in terms of distributed database.[2] However, they can be considered to apply broadly to the evolving, hybrid architecture that organizations must continually fashion.

Transparency

The user should not have to know where data are stored and how they are processed. The location of data, its storage format, and access method should be invisible to the user. The

2. Date, C. J. 1990. What is a distributed database system? In *Relational database writings 1985-1989*, edited by C. J. Date. Reading, MA: Addison-Wesley.

system should accept queries and resolve them expeditiously. Of course, the system should check that the user is authorized to access the requested data. Transparency is also known as **location independence**—the system can be used independent of the location of data.

Table 12-4: The fundamental principles of a hybrid architecture

Principle
Transparency
No reliance on a central site
Local autonomy
Continuous operation
Distributed query processing
Distributed transaction processing
Fragmentation independence
Replication independence
Hardware independence
Operating system independence
Network independence
DBMS independence

No reliance on a central site

Reliance on a central site for management of a hybrid architecture creates two major problems. First, because all requests are routed through the central site, bottlenecks develop during peak periods. Second, if the central site fails, the entire system fails. A controlling central site is too vulnerable, and control should be distributed throughout the system.

Local autonomy

A high degree of local autonomy avoids dependence on a central site. Data are locally owned and managed. The local site is responsible for the security, integrity, and storage of local data. There cannot be absolute local autonomy because the various sites must cooperate in order for transparency to be feasible. Cooperation always requires relinquishing some autonomy.

Continuous operation

The system must be accessible when required. Since business is increasingly global and users are geographically dispersed, the system must be continuously available. Many data centers now describe their operations as 7/24 (7 days a week and 24 hours a day).

Distributed query processing

The time taken to execute a query should be generally independent of the location from which it is submitted. Deciding the most efficient way to process the query is the system's responsibility, not the user's. For example, a Sydney user could submit the query, "Find sales of wombat coats in Japan." The system is responsible for deciding which messages and data to send between the various sites where tables are located.

Distributed transaction processing

In a hybrid system, a single transaction can require updating of multiple files at multiple sites. The system must ensure that a transaction is successfully executed for all sites. Partial updating of files will cause inconsistencies.

Fragmentation independence

Fragmentation independence means that any table can be broken into fragments and then stored in separate physical locations. For example, the sales table could be fragmented so that Indonesian data are stored in Jakarta, Japanese data in Tokyo, and so on. A fragment is any piece of a table that can be created by applying restriction and projection operations. Using join and union, fragments can be assembled to create the full table. Fragmentation is the key to a distributed database. Without fragmentation independence, data cannot be distributed.

Replication independence

Fragmentation is good when local data are mainly processed locally, but there are some applications that also frequently process remote data. For example, the New York office of an international airline may need both American (local) and European (remote) data, and its London office may need American (remote) and European (local) data. In this case, fragmentation into American and European data may not substantially reduce communication costs.

Replication means that a fragment of data can be copied and physically stored at multiple sites; thus the European fragment could be replicated and stored in New York, and the American fragment replicated and stored in London. As a result, applications in both New York and London will reduce their communication costs. Of course, the trade-off is that when a replicated fragment is updated, all copies also must be updated. Reduced communication costs are exchanged for increased update complexity.

Replication independence implies replication happens behind the scenes. The user is oblivious to replication and requires no knowledge of this activity.

There are two major approaches to replication: synchronous or asynchronous updates. **Synchronous replication** means all databases are updated at the same time. Although this is ideal, it is not a simple task and is resource intensive. **Asynchronous replication** occurs when changes made to one database are relayed to other databases within a certain period established by the database administrator. It does not provide real-time updating, but it takes fewer IS resources. Asynchronous replication is a compromise strategy for distributed DBMS replication. When real-time updating is not absolutely necessary, asynchronous replication can save scarce IS resources.

Hardware independence

A hybrid architecture should support hardware from multiple suppliers without affecting users' capacity to query files. Hardware independence is a long-term goal of many MIS managers.

Operating system independence

Operating system independence is another goal much sought by MIS executives. Ideally, the various DBMSs and applications of the hybrid system should work on a range of operating systems on a variety of hardware.

Network independence

Clearly, network independence is desired by organizations that wish to avoid the electronic shackles of being committed to any single hardware or software supplier.

DBMS independence

Independence is contagious and has been caught by the DBMS as well. Since SQL is a standard for relational databases, organizations may well be able to achieve DBMS independence. By settling on the relational model as the organizational standard, ensuring that all DBMSs installed conform to this model, and using only standard SQL, an organization may approach DBMS independence. Nevertheless, do not forget all those old systems from the pre-relational days — a legacy that must be supported in a hybrid architecture.

Organizations can gain considerable DBMS independence by using ODBC technology (see page 270). An application that uses the ODBC interface can access any ODBC-compliant DBMS. In a distributed environment, such as three-tier client/server, ODBC enables application servers to access a variety of vendors' databases on different data servers.

Conclusion

For data managers, the 12 principles just outlined are ideal goals. In the hurly-burly of everyday business, incomplete information, and an uncertain future, data managers struggle valiantly to meet clients' needs with a hybrid architecture that is an imperfect interpretation of MIS paradise. It is unlikely that these principles will ever be totally achieved. They are guidelines and something to reflect on when making the inevitable trade-offs that occur in data management.

Now that you understand the general goals of a distributed database architecture, we will consider the major aspects of the enabling technology. First, we will look at distributed data access methods and then distributed database design. In keeping with our focus on the relational model, illustrative SQL examples are used.

Distributed data access

When data are distributed across multiple locations, the data management logic must also be distributed. The various types of distributed data access methods are considered, and a banking example is used to illustrate the differences between the methods.

Remote request

A remote request occurs when an application issues a single data request to a single remote site. Consider the case of a branch bank requesting data for a specific customer from the bank's central server located in Atlanta. The SQL command specifies the name of the server (ATLSERVER), the database (BANKDB), and the name of the table (CUSTOMER).

```
SELECT * FROM ATLSERVER.BANKDB.CUSTOMER
   WHERE CUSTCODE = '12345'
```

A remote request can extract a table from the database for processing on the local database. For example, the Athens branch may download balance details of customers at the beginning of each day and handle queries locally rather than issuing a remote request. The SQL is

```
SELECT CUSTCODE, CUSTBALANCE FROM ATLSERVER.BANKDB.CUSTOMER
   WHERE CUSTBRANCH = 'Athens'
```

Remote transaction

Multiple data requests are often necessary to execute a complete business transaction. For example, to add a new customer account might require inserting a row in two tables: one row for the account and another row in the table relating a customer to the new account. A remote transaction contains multiple data requests for a single remote location. The following example illustrates how a branch bank creates a new customer account on the central server:

```
BEGIN WORK
INSERT INTO ATLSERVER.BANKDB.ACCOUNT
   (ACCNUM, ACCTYPE)
   VALUES (789, 'C')
INSERT INTO ATLSERVER.BANKDB.CUST_ACCT
   (CUSTNUM, ACCNUM)
   VALUES (123, 789)
COMMIT WORK
```

The commands BEGIN WORK and COMMIT WORK surround the SQL commands necessary to complete the transaction. The transaction is successful only if both SQL statements are successfully executed. If one of the SQL statements fails, the entire transaction fails.[3]

---

3. Chapter 17 covers transaction management in more detail.

Distributed transaction

A distributed transaction supports multiple data requests for data at multiple locations. Each request is for data on a single server. Support for distributed transactions permits a client to access tables on different servers.

Consider the case of a bank that operates in the U.S. and Norway and keeps details of employees on a server in the country in which they reside. The following example illustrates a revision of the database to record details of an employee who moves from the U.S. to Norway. The transaction copies the data for the employee from the Atlanta server to the Oslo server and then deletes the entry for that employee on the Atlanta server.

```
BEGIN WORK
INSERT INTO OSLOSERVER.BANKDB.EMPLOYEE
   (EMPCODE, EMPLNAME, …)
   SELECT EMPCODE, EMPLNAME, …
      FROM ATLSERVER.BANKDB.EMPLOYEE
         WHERE EMPCODE = 123
DELETE FROM ATLSERVER.BANKDB.EMPLOYEE
   WHERE EMPCODE = 123
COMMIT WORK
```

As in the case of the remote transaction, the transaction is successful only if both SQL statements are successfully executed.

Scrubbing data

Data cleansing software handles the complex problems of making sure addresses and other information are accurate and up-to-date and checking for duplicate records, such as multiple accounts for the same customer held under slightly different spellings. The emergence of e-commerce has highlighted the problems in data quality because data may be entered at a Web site by virtually anyone visiting the site.

The use of data-cleansing technology has been limited by the high costs, from $100,000 to $300,000 or more, plus maintenance fees of up to 20 percent per year. Also, the packages can be difficult to implement.

Catching the data errors early is vital. The deeper the inaccurate data gets into a company's system, the more it costs to fix. Most analysts agree that it is time to reassess system design to eliminate errors at the entry level. Larry English, a data-quality consultant in Brentwood, Tennessee states, "Data quality is something you design in, not something you inspect out."

Source: Faden, M. 2000. Clean up your data act. *Internetweek*, Apr 17 (809):60–62.

Distributed request

A distributed request is the most complicated form of distributed data access. It supports processing of multiple requests at multiple sites, and each request can access data on multiple sites. This means that a distributed request can handle data replicated or fragmented across multiple servers.

Let's assume the bank has had a good year and decided to give all employees a 15 percent bonus based on their annual salary and add $1,000 or 7,500 krone to their retirement account, depending on whether the employee is based in the U.S. or Norway.

```
BEGIN WORK
CREATE VIEW TEMP
   (EMPCODE, EMPFNAME, EMPLNAME, EMPSALARY)
AS
   SELECT EMPCODE, EMPFNAME, EMPLNAME, EMPSALARY
      FROM ATLSERVER.BANKDB.EMPLOYEE
   UNION
   SELECT EMPCODE, EMPFNAME, EMPLNAME, EMPSALARY
      FROM OSLOSERVER.BANKDB.EMPLOYEE
SELECT EMPCODE, EMPFNAME, EMPLNAME, EMPSALARY*.15 AS BONUS
      FROM TEMP
UPDATE ATLSERVER.BANKDB.EMPLOYEE
   SET EMPUSDRETFUND = EMPUSDRETFUND + 1000
UPDATE OSLOSERVER.BANKDB.EMPLOYEE
   SET EMPKRNRETFUND = EMPKRNRETFUND + 7500
COMMIT WORK
```

The transaction first creates a view containing all employees by doing a union (i.e., OR) on the employee tables for both locations. This view is then used to calculate the bonus. Two SQL update commands are then used to update the respective retirement fund records of the U.S. and Norwegian employees. Notice that retirement funds are recorded in U.S. dollars or Norwegian krones.

Ideally, a distributed request should not require the application to know where data are physically located. A DDBMS should not require the application to specify the name of the server. So, for example, it should be possible to write the following SQL:

```
SELECT EMPCODE, EMPFNAME, EMPLNAME, EMPSALARY*.15 AS BONUS
      FROM BANKDB.EMPLOYEE
```

It is the responsibility of the DDBMS to determine where the data are stored. In other words, the DDBMS is responsible for ensuring data location and fragmentation transparency.

Distributed database design

Designing a distributed database is a two-stage process. First, develop a data model using the principles discussed in Section 2. Second, decide how data and processing will be distributed by applying the concepts of partitioning and replication. **Partitioning** is the fragmentation of tables across servers. Tables can be fragmented horizontally, vertically, or some combination of both. **Replication** is the duplication of tables across servers.

Horizontal fragmentation

A table is split into rows when horizontally fragmented (see Figure 12-6). For example, a firm may fragment its employee table into three because it has employees in Tokyo, Sydney, and Jakarta and store the fragment on the appropriate DBMS server for each city.

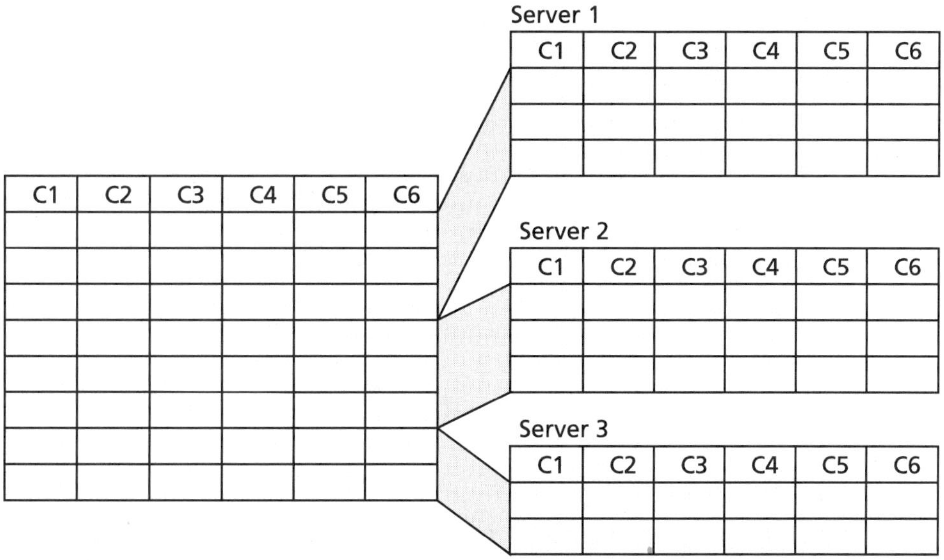

Figure 12-6. Horizontal fragmentation

Three separate employee tables would be defined. Each would have a different name (e.g., EMP-SYD) but exactly the same columns. When inserting a new employee, the SQL code would be

```
INSERT INTO TABLE EMP_SYD
   SELECT * FROM NEW_EMP
      WHERE EMP_NATION = 'Australia'

INSERT INTO TABLE EMP_TKY
   SELECT * FROM NEW_EMP
      WHERE EMP_NATION = 'Japan'
```

```
INSERT INTO TABLE EMP_JAK
   SELECT * FROM NEW_EMP
      WHERE EMP_NATION = 'Indonesia'
```

Vertical fragmentation

When vertically fragmented, a table is split into columns (see Figure 12-7). For example, a firm may fragment its employee table vertically to spread the processing load across servers. For example, there could be one server to handle address lookups and another to process payroll. In this case, the columns containing address information would be stored on one server and payroll columns on the other server. Notice that the primary key column (C1) must be stored on both servers; otherwise, the entity integrity rule is violated.

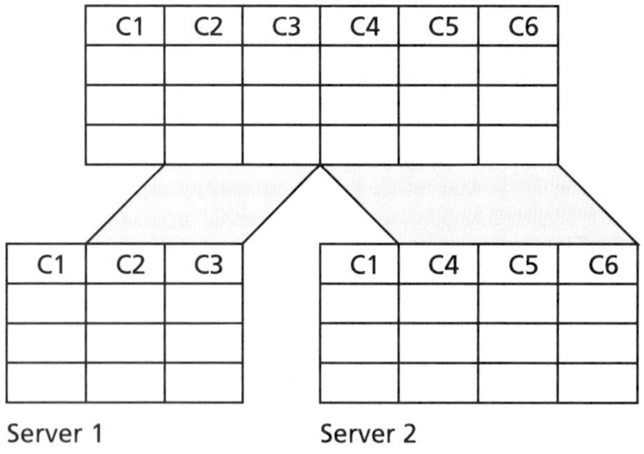

Figure 12-7. Vertical fragmentation

Hybrid fragmentation

Hybrid fragmentation is a mixture of horizontal and vertical. For example, the employee table could be first horizontally fragmented to distribute the data to where employees are located. Then some of the horizontal fragments could be vertically fragmented to split processing across servers. Thus, if Tokyo is the corporate headquarters with many employees, the Tokyo horizontal fragment of the employee database could be vertically fragmented so that separate servers could handle address and payroll processing.

Horizontal fragmentation distributes data, and thus can be used to reduce communication costs by storing data where they are most likely to be needed. Vertical fragmentation is used to distribute data across servers so that the processing load can be distributed. Hybrid fragmentation can be used to distribute both data and applications across servers.

Replication

Under replication, tables can be fully or partly replicated. **Full replication** means that tables are duplicated at each of the sites. The advantages of full replication are greater data integrity (since replication is essentially mirroring) and faster processing because it can be done locally. However, replication is expensive because of the need to synchronize inserts, updates, and deletes across the replicated tables. When one table is altered, all the replicas must also be modified. A compromise is to use **partial replication** by duplicating the indexes only. This will increase the speed of query processing. The index can be processed locally, and then the required rows retrieved from the remote database.

Conclusion

The two fundamental skills of data management, data modeling and data querying, are not changed by the development of a distributed data architecture such as client/server. Data modeling remains unchanged. A high-fidelity data model is required regardless of where data are stored and whichever architecture is selected. SQL can be used to query both local, remote, and distributed databases. Indeed, the adoption of client/server technology has seen a widespread increase in the demand for SQL skills.

Summary

Data can be stored and processed locally or remotely. Combinations of these two options provide four basic architectures: remote job entry, host/terminal, personal database, and client/server. Under remote job entry, data are sent over a communication link to a remote computer for processing, and the output is sent back. Under host/terminal architecture, data storage and processing occur at one location, typically a mainframe computer. With a personal database, users store and process their data locally. Client/server supports remote storage, and data are mainly processed locally. A LAN connects computers and devices within a limited geographic area. A server is a general purpose computer that provides and controls access to shareable resources. A file/server is a central data store for users attached to a LAN. It is a relatively simple solution to data sharing on a local area network. A DBMS/server, a server with a DBMS installed, does query processing so that only necessary records are transferred across a network. In a client/server architecture, the client process initiates requests, and the server responds. The client is thc dominant partner because it initiates a request. Client/server exploits cost savings that result from moving processing from a mainframe to less expensive minicomputers and personal computers. The key parameters to consider when comparing host/terminal with client/server are terminal versus personal computer costs, mainframe MIPS versus personal computer MIPS, and mainframe storage versus server storage.

There are two major client/server models: two-tier and three-tier, also known as thick and thin client technologies. Three-tier client server, particularly, with the advent of Web browsers (thin clients), is becoming the more dominant client/server technology.

Under distributed database architecture, a database is in more than one location but still accessible as if it were centrally located. The trade-off is lowered communication costs versus increased complexity. A hybrid architecture is a mix of data processing architectures. The concern of the IS department is to patch this hybrid together so that users see a seamless system that readily provides needed information. The fundamental principles that a hybrid architecture should satisfy are transparency, no reliance on a central site, local autonomy, continuous operation, distributed query processing, distributed transaction processing, fragmentation independence, replication independence, hardware independence, operating system independence, network independence, and DBMS independence.

There are four types of distributed data access. In order of complexity, these are remote request, remote transaction, distributed transaction, and distributed request.

Distributed database design is based on the principles of fragmentation and replication. Horizontal fragmentation splits a table by rows and reduces communication costs by placing data where they are likely to be required. Vertical fragmentation splits a table by columns and spreads the processing load across servers. Hybrid fragmentation is a combination of horizontal and vertical fragmentation. Replication is the duplication of identical tables at different sites. Partial replication involves the replication of indexes. Replication speeds up local processing at the cost of maintaining the replicas.

Key terms and concepts

Application server
Client/server
Continuous operation
Data communications manager
Data processing
Data server
Data storage
Database architecture
Database management system (DBMS)
DBMS independence
DBMS/server
Distributed data access
Distributed database
Distributed query processing
Distributed request
Distributed transaction
Distributed transaction processing
File manager
File/server
Fragmentation independence
Graphical user interface (GUI)
Hardware independence
Horizontal fragmentation
Host/terminal
Hybrid architecture
Hybrid fragmentation
Local area network (LAN)
Local autonomy
Mainframe
Network independence
Personal database
Remote job entry
Remote request
Remote transaction
Replication
Replication independence
Server
Software independence
Three-tier architecture
Transaction processing monitor
Transparency
Two-tier architecture
Vertical fragmentation
Workstation

References and additional readings

Berson, Alex. 1996. *Client/server architecture*. 2nd ed, McGraw-Hill series on computer communications. New York: McGraw-Hill.

Bobak, Angelo R. 1993. ***Distributed and multi-database systems***, Bantam professional books. New York: Bantam Books.

Morris, C. R., and C. H. Ferguson. 1993. How architecture wins technology wars. *Harvard Business Review* 71 (2):86–96.

Smith, P. 1992. *Client/server computing*. Carmal, IN: Sams.

Exercises

1. How does client/server differ from host/terminal computing?
2. How have personal computers affected data architecture decisions?
3. In what situations are you likely to use remote job entry?
4. What are the disadvantages of personal databases?
5. What are the differences between two- and three-tier client/server architecture?
6. What is a potential major problem with a file/server system?
7. Describe the difference between a file/server and a DBMS/server.
8. When is client/server likely to be a cheaper information processing solution than host/terminal?
9. What factors are likely to inhibit a company's move from host/terminal to client/server?
10. What is a firm likely to gain when it moves from a centralized to distributed database? What are the potential costs?
11. Identify some situations where you would use two-tier over three-tier client server and vice versa.
12. In terms of a hybrid architecture, what does transparency mean?
13. In terms of a hybrid architecture, what does fragmentation independence mean?
14. In terms of a hybrid architecture, what does DBMS independence mean?
15. How does ODBC support a hybrid architecture?
16. A university professor is about to develop a large simulation model for describing the global economy. The model uses data from 65 countries to simulate alternative economic policies and their possible outcomes. In terms of volume, the data requirements are quite modest, but the mathematical model is very complex, and there are many equations that must be solved for each quarter the model is run. What data processing/data storage architecture would you recommend?
17. A large retailer is about to establish a mail-order catalog division. Initially, it plans to hire 500 people to answer telephones. The system will have a few standard transactions (e.g., take an order, query the status of the order, and check inventory). It is anticipated that within two years the database will need to maintain details of two million customers and 10,000 products. What data processing/data storage architecture would you recommend?
18. A small bank has reformulated its strategy to focus on serving the wealthiest 25 percent of the population in its reasonably affluent region. Customers will have a personal banker who will offer a wide range of services. For example, a personal banker will be able to analyze an investment portfolio, organize foreign currency transfers, and book foreign travel. The bank expects to appoint 22 personal bankers

and will provide each person with extensive training in a wide range of transactions. What data processing/data storage architecture would you recommend?

19. The advertising manager of a small veterinary pharmaceutical supplier wants to track the firm's advertising in the journal and at the conference of each of the 50 U.S. state veterinary societies. Each state has one journal, which is published at most 12 times per year, and one annual conference. What data processing/data storage architecture would you recommend?
20. A multinational company has operated relatively independent organizations in 15 countries. The new CEO wants greater coordination and believes that marketing, production, and purchasing should be globally managed. As a result, the corporate IS department must work with the separate IS national departments to integrate the various national applications and databases. What are the implications for the corporate data processing and database architecture? What are the key facts you would like to know before developing an integration plan? What problems do you anticipate? What is your intuitive feeling about the key features of the new architecture?
21. Take the data model for the SQL Playbook (see page 282). Assume this company operates in three major urban areas. How might you vertically and horizontally fragment the data model to improve processing speed?

13

Object-Oriented Data Management

The goal of all inanimate objects is to resist man and ultimately to defeat him.
Russell Baker, "Observer," *The New York Times*, June 18, 1968

Learning objectives

On completion of this chapter, you will be able to

- explain the main concepts of object-orientation;
- compare and contrast the object-oriented model to the relational model;
- develop a simple object-oriented model;
- be abreast of current implementations of ODBMS.

Introduction

Information systems managers are continually searching for better ways to develop and maintain information systems. They want to deliver on time, on budget, fully functional information systems that meet clients' needs. In recent years, object orientation (OO) has attracted considerable attention because it offers the prospect of lowering systems development and maintenance costs. OO concepts are being applied to analysis, design, programming, and database. Furthermore, now that information systems have moved beyond storing only numbers and text, new applications are often required to support multimedia (video, audio, and animation), CAD/CAM, economic models, document management systems, and other complex data structures. Procedural languages and relational databases are not designed to manipulate and store these data forms, but OO programming languages (OOPLs) and object-oriented database management systems (ODBMSs) are capable of doing so.[1]

1. Tore Ørvik of Agder College (Kristiansand, Norway) was the coauthor of this chapter.

The proponents of OO[2] maintain that an ODBMS offers several advantages over current implementations of relational database technology. They assert that the shortcomings of the relational model are

1. It cannot handle complex objects, such as multimedia;
2. There is no support for general data types found in some programming languages;
3. Performance degrades when large numbers of tables must be joined to respond to a query;
4. There is a mismatch between the relational data model's set-at-a-time processing and the record-at-a-time processing of programming languages;
5. There is no support for representing and recording change, such as different versions of objects.

ODBMS technology addresses these shortcomings. We explain the concept of OO by demonstrating OO modeling and then explore the current state of ODBMS.

UML

Marching in step with the OO approach to software development is the unified modeling language (UML). Introduced in late 1997 by the Object Management Group (OMG), UML has become the common modeling language for OO software development. UML standardizes the notation for describing processes and has nine predefined diagrams (see Table 13-1). Our attention will be focused on the class diagram because of its correspondence to a data model. UML notation will be used throughout this chapter.

Table 13-1: UML predefined diagrams

Diagram	Purpose
Class	Describes the structure of a system by specifying classes and relationships
Object	Shows a number of object instances of a class
Statechart	Identifies possible states of a class or system and which events cause the state to change
Activity	Describes the activities and actions taking place in a system
Sequence	Illustrates one or several sequences of messages exchanged among objects
Collaboration	Shows collaboration among a set of objects
Use-case	Depicts the top-level relationships between actors and use-cases, which describe what a system should or does do
Component	Displays the physical structure of the code in terms of components
Deployment	Represents the physical architecture of hardware and software for a system

2. There is considerable disagreement between OO and relational adherents. This chapter tries to present a balance of the two viewpoints, but in describing the OO approach, it is often easier to present the OO proponents' perspective. Also, you need to remember that we are comparing implementations of the two concepts and not the theoretical models. For example, if the domain concept of the relational model were implemented, then some deficiencies of present relational systems would disappear.

UML in e-business

Companies model complex software applications for the same reason they hire architects to design buildings prior to starting construction. In the long run, a detailed blueprint saves time and money and produces a better system. It allows developers to consider alternatives, select the best option, work out details, and achieve agreement before anyone starts building the application. It is much less costly to change a model than it is to modify an application after it has been built. A good model documents an application's structure and simplifies future modification. This is critical when you consider that 90 percent of the costs involved in large applications occur as they are changed, extended, and otherwise maintained.

Unified modeling language (UML) is an open standards success story of the late 1990s. In three years, a dozen object-oriented modeling methodologies were replaced by UML, which is currently supported by all major software modeling tools. The Object Management Group (OMG) drove the rapid transition to UML and continues to maintain it as the world's premier open, object-oriented analysis and design standard.

UML turns out to be a key ingredient in the new model-driven development approach to software development proving so popular with e-business developers. They use UML models to drive their designs and maintain consistency.

Source: Anonymous. 2001. Building advanced applications: UML models e-business. *Softwaremag.com*, Apr/May. http://www.softwaremag.com/archive/2001apr/UMLModelsE-Biz.html.

Historical development

Although its underlying concepts have been known and used for a relatively long time, the notion of OO has only recently become commonplace and popular. The first OOPL (object-oriented programming language), SIMULA, was developed in Norway in the mid-1960s. The development of the Smalltalk language at Xerox PARC in the 1970s introduced the terms *object* and *OO* and was a major step towards popularizing OO programming. In the 1980s, several existing programming languages were extended to embrace OO. Now, languages like C++ and COBOL support OO. In addition to these languages, several pure OO languages, such as Java, were developed.

In the late 1980s, the graphical user interface (GUI), with its support for windows, icons, mouse, and pointers (WIMP), became increasingly common. OOPLs are invaluable for the development of GUI applications, which further enhanced the popularity of OO. As OO programming languages matured, OO found its way into the realms of database and systems analysis and design.

Key OO concepts

It is useful to first become familiar with some key OO concepts before examining the benefits of applying OO ideas. OO applications are created by assembling and using objects — self-contained units that can contain data — very much like entities in data modeling. An object is something in the real world. Like an entity, it can be physical (e.g., a car) or conceptual (e.g., a job). Objects also contain the necessary instructions, the algorithm, to transform data. Thus, an object contains both data and methods, which are also known as procedures, operations, or services. Objects, therefore, can be thought of as application development building blocks. For instance, an employee object may consist of textual data (such as name, address, and phone number) and multimedia data (such as a photograph, video clip, or fingerprint image) combined with methods like hire, transfer, or promote. Objects are application development building blocks.

OO modeling and data modeling have a common objective of creating a representation of a real-world information system. Consequently, they frequently deal with the same concepts but use different terminology. A comparison of some of the key concepts is shown in Table 13-2.

Table 13-2: A comparison of data modeling and OO modeling terminology

Data Modeling Term	OO Modeling Term
Entity	Object class or classes
Instance	Object
Attribute	Attribute

Data abstraction

Real-world systems are very complex, and the fundamental features of a complicated system can be difficult to extract from the mass of detail. Consequently, simplified models showing the relationships between key elements are often used to reveal the essentials. **Data abstraction** is the process of creating an abstract model to enhance understanding of reality. Data modeling (see Section 2) illustrates the use of data abstraction because a data model captures the essential elements of the relationships between entities. An organizational chart, another example of data abstraction, shows the associations between roles in an organization. A diagram of the structure of an investment portfolio is another example of data abstraction (see Figure 13-1).

The craft of data abstraction is an important skill for MIS professionals. As well as learning some common data abstraction methods, such as data modeling, you also need to develop the general skill of reducing complex systems to understandable models that can be readily drawn, described, and explained.

Object instances and classes

A database stores facts about objects, in OODMS terms, or entities, in relational terms. Each single representation is called an **object instance**. Most databases contain several

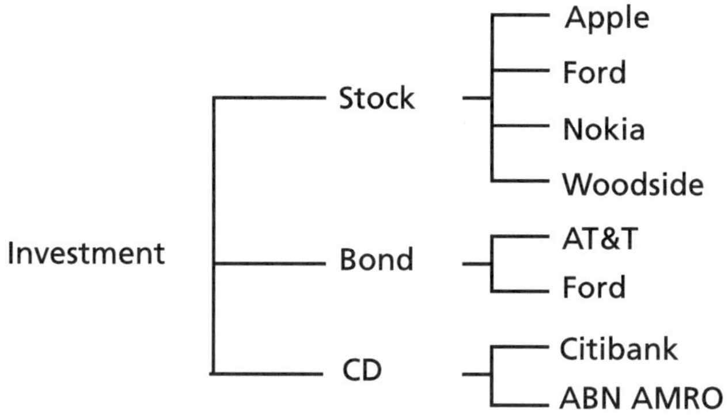

Figure 13-1. A model of an investment portfolio

objects of the same type, and these are called an **object class** or, simply, class. All the instances of the same type of object are grouped into an object class. In a grading system, for example, there will be an object class, which we will call STUDENT. Individual students are instances belonging to the student object class. In the investment portfolio model, there are object instances for each of the investments (e.g., Apple is an instance of the STOCK object class).

UML represents a class by a rectangle divided into three parts (see Figure 13-2). The upper part contains the name of the class, the attributes of the class are in the middle, and the methods appear in the lower part. Because attributes and methods may need more specification detail than can fit into the available block, each block can be visualized as an expandable window that, when fully opened, shows additional detail. This will certainly be the case if we use special purpose OO modeling software (e.g., a UML tool). In order to focus on the higher-level aspects of an OO model, however, the following examples will not always specify attributes and methods even though this additional detail is required to fully define an OO model.

The object class shown in Figure 13-2 is the familiar SHARE entity introduced in Chapter 3. Notice that as well as including the attributes in the model, there is now a method called yield for calculating the yield of a share. In the relational model, yield was determined by a calculation within a view and was not shown in the data model.

In an object model, every instance of an object has a unique identifier, the **object identification (OID)**. The OID, used to uniquely reference an instance of an object, is comparable to the table name, row name, and primary key combination that uniquely identify a value in a relational model. OIDs are generated by the system and are not related or derived from the data contained within the object. An OID remains constant for the life of an instance.

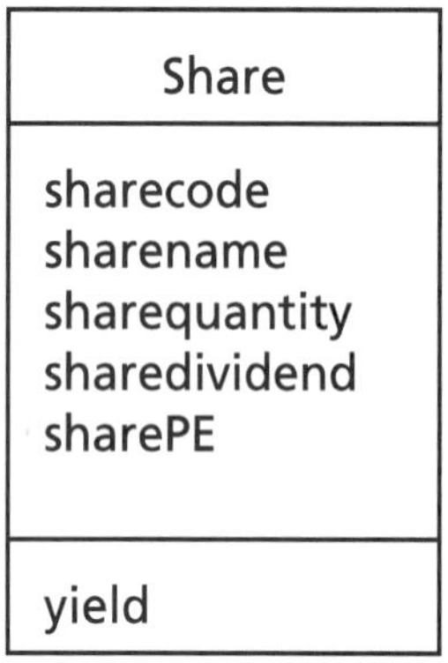

Figure 13-2. The object class Share

Encapsulation

Encapsulation means that all processing that changes the state of an object (i.e., changes the value of any of its attributes) is done within that object. Encapsulation implies that an object is shielded from interference from other objects; that is, an object cannot directly change any other objects. Encapsulation means that data and methods can be packaged together.

Message passing

Objects communicate with each other by sending and receiving messages. For example, an object may send a message to request particular data from another object. Provided a relevant method has been established for the receiving object, the requested data value is sent back to the object issuing the request. This method of communicating is usually referred to as message passing. A message can also trigger a change in the receiving object. Again, an appropriate method must be defined for the object receiving the message.

Generalization/specialization hierarchies

Classes can be specializations or generalizations of other classes. The STUDENT class, for example, may be viewed as a specialization of ACADEMIC PERSON. A superclass, in turn, might have several subclasses which, as Figure 13-3 shows, include STAFF and STUDENT. The ACADEMIC PERSON class is a generalization of the two subclasses, STUDENT and STAFF.

Inheritance

An important feature of OO is that classes in a generalization/specialization hierarchy will inherit data and methods from the superclass. The ACADEMIC PERSON class in the preceding example probably will have attributes such as person name, address, and Social Security number. These attributes will be inherited by both the STUDENT and STAFF classes. In addition, we may specify some additional attributes for the STUDENT class, such as GPA

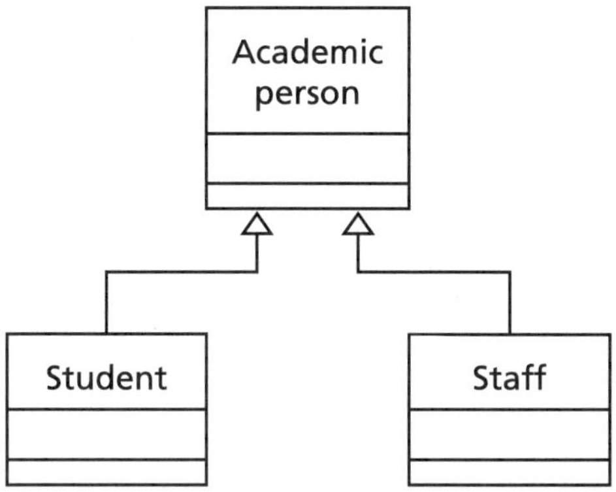

Figure 13-3. An example of a generalization/specialization hierarchy

and major, which are not relevant for the superclass. Inheritance simplifies specification and programming and is especially important for creating reusable objects.

The ideas of inheritance and generalization are conceptually similar to the independent/subordinate entities structure (see Figure 13-4) of data modeling. The independent entity, ANIMAL, contains general attributes common to all subordinate entities, which have specific attributes appropriate to the entity (e.g., fleece weight for SHEEP). Thus, you can think of SHEEP inheriting the attributes of ANIMAL, with this inheritance occurring when the two entities are joined. Of course, there are no methods explicitly associated with this data model.

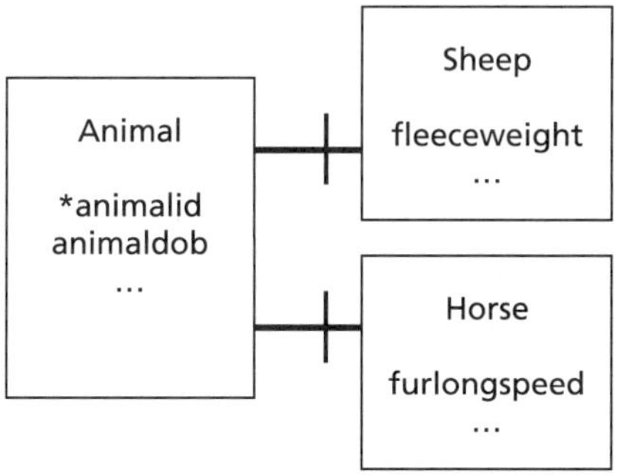

Figure 13-4. An independent/subordinate entities structure

Reuse

When building new applications with OO software tools, the programmer usually looks for existing object classes to use as building blocks. The exact required class may not be found but by creating new subclasses and using the inheritance feature, new classes can be created with little effort. For example, if you are writing a drawing program, you may avoid writing a new spelling checker by reusing the existing object class written for a word processing program. This leads to a development strategy where recognizing and exploiting similarities in classes is a major means of increasing programmer productivity.

Why OO?

Many organizations have a substantial backlog of applications because it takes significant resources to build new applications and maintain existing systems. The need to increase programmer productivity and reduce the cost of maintaining systems is the major reason for adopting the OO approach.

Productivity

The productivity of software development has not increased substantially over the years, maybe as little as a four- to seven-fold increase since the early 1960s. This is trivial compared to the massive increases in hardware throughput over the same period. As a result, many potential applications, which are economically feasible because of reduced hardware costs, are awaiting the attention of programmers. Software productivity has not kept pace with the increase in demand for new applications. Also, many of the projects in the pipeline tend to be larger and more complex than those already undertaken.

Many problems, such as WIMP-based applications, are not easily programmed using traditional, functional languages. In most cases, use of an OOPL makes programming easier and also produces more compact and efficient code. This in itself enhances productivity. More important, there is the possibility of creating reusable objects which, if this feature is exploited, can precipitate significant increases in productivity.

The potential reuse of objects has stimulated widespread interest in OO. Organizations can create or purchase libraries of objects that can become an important source of objects for new applications. Consequently, application development time and cost will be reduced because significant portions of new systems can be built using existing objects.

Maintenance

The slow growth in programmer productivity is exacerbated by the massive effort required to keep operational software systems current. Some companies spend as much as 80 percent of their potential development resources on maintenance of old systems. There are five main reasons for the maintenance problem:

1. Programming is a difficult, intellectual task and one that is prone to logic errors.
2. Determining the client's true needs is a major challenge. Too often, the specified requirements do not reflect the client's real needs, and these needs sometimes do not clearly emerge until after the first version of the software is released.
3. Additional features that could not be accommodated in the original development schedule might be needed once the system is introduced.
4. The business environment changes.
5. Hardware changes.

The first two problems are strictly maintenance, and we can alleviate them by using better programming tools and by determining requirements more precisely. Items three and four are more correctly called enhancements or extensions, and we want to handle these more speedily. The fifth item, hardware changes, we try to avoid by adhering to common architectural standards, which should result in smooth transitions when hardware is replaced.

Changing large programs is very complicated, and new errors will often be introduced in the process. Because of the tendency not to document all changes properly, the actual software and documentation become inconsistent as time passes. As developers move on to new assignments or new careers and documentation becomes outdated, it becomes increasingly complicated for maintenance programmers to get a thorough understanding of how existing programs work; therefore, it is difficult to change or correct items without introducing unwanted side effects.

To resolve the software crisis, we must build quality software faster and reduce the cost of its maintenance and enhancement. Many believe OO directly addresses several major causes of maintenance problems.

Logical and syntactical errors

OO software is constructed by creating self-contained object classes. Most objects require a small number of programming statements. As a result, a program is broken into manageable units, and the overall complexity of the software is reduced. Less complexity means fewer errors.

Errors will still occur, but changes can be made to the interior structure or processing rules of the object class without creating unforeseen changes throughout the system. Because each object is relatively independent, there is no ripple effect, which often occurs with traditional programming methods. This makes the existing code easy to understand even if documentation is sparse, or the maintenance programmer has little knowledge of the application.

Missing or incorrect specifications

Traditionally, information systems have been developed using some variation of a structured development methodology, in which the most common modeling techniques used are data flow diagramming and data modeling. OO advocates argue these techniques force clients to adopt abstract modes of thinking too remote from the way they usually think about their work, and therefore these are unsuitable for facilitating communication between the client and designer. Proponents of OO modeling claim OO alleviates this by using concepts and structuring techniques that are closer to the way people think about their work. In the everyday world, we usually think about objects like people, cars, and computers, and we also think about what these objects can do. The argument is that specifications will be more accurate because OO modeling is similar to the client's model of the world.[3]

Adding features

Methods and attributes can be easily added to existing object classes without the risk of disrupting the rest of the system. By exploiting inheritance, new classes often can be created with minimal programming effort. Thus, OO is suitable for evolutionary development in which the main features of the system are first developed, and less critical elements added as development resources become available.

Accommodating business change

In a competitive world, it is very important that information systems can be easily modified to reflect changes in the business environment. This requirement has become more apparent in recent years. The self-contained nature of the object classes and the inheritance feature of OO systems are expected to make it easier to change and expand OO-based systems than those developed using traditional methods.

Summary

As we have shown, OO can address the software crisis — slow development of new applications and expensive maintenance. Many of the claims made for adopting OO modeling, echo Codd's rationale for introducing the relational model (see Chapter 9). Data modeling and the relational model are tools for increasing programmer productivity and reducing maintenance. Codd argued for the separation of data and procedures (or methods in OO terminology) to increase productivity. The OO school claims that encapsulating both in an object will improve productivity. So who is right? We believe there is still not enough evidence to make a judgment, and there probably will be no overall advantage for either approach. OO modeling may be better suited for some applications and process modeling/data modeling for others. With research and experience, we will discover when to use each approach.

Objects and information system modeling

Modeling, as you discovered in Section 2, is a central activity of systems development. Models allow us to describe and understand information systems and to explore possible changes to such systems without interfering with or disrupting the actual system. Many different modeling techniques exist. Some deal with different aspects of information systems description (e.g., procedure modeling as compared to data modeling), and some others deal with the same aspect differently (e.g., different methods of data modeling).

Models and abstraction levels

A model is by definition an abstraction of something else. When modeling, we omit some of the features or detail we find in the real world and incorporate only those we find useful for the client's needs. For instance, there are many attributes necessary to describe a person completely (height, weight, shoe size, color of eyes), but we only select those that are pertinent to the current problem.

3. As far as we know, there is little empirical research to support these claims.

A city map is a model of some aspects of a city's streets. For the tourist, it conveys the layout of a city very concisely and effectively. It is also an abstract model of the city; many features and details are left out. Only that information which is useful for the intended purpose is depicted. As we develop software systems, we start out with quite abstract models, concentrating on understanding required functionality. As we progress, more detail is needed, and our models become more elaborate and concrete. Eventually, they become a functioning system.

The client-developer mind-frame gap

Clients frequently have problems defining what they want from an information system.[4] Even when they are reasonably certain, it is very difficult to capture all the necessary details. Modeling techniques used to capture and record details often include methods for prompting clients about their needs and ensuring that no details are overlooked. Nonetheless, if clients are not trained in data modeling techniques, their way of thinking about their information needs may not relate closely to the way the systems analysts try to model their requirements.

This communication gap between clients and systems developers is purportedly a major reason for low-quality, overdue, and over-budget projects. OO supporters assert that dealing with systems objects, which closely resemble real-life objects, is more natural than dealing with entities, relationships, and data flows. They argue that the OO approach narrows the communication gap because it uses modeling concepts and techniques that are more closely related to the clients' way of thinking.

Data and procedures

Data modeling deals with what the system needs to remember. A data model is often called static because it tends to be fairly stable and requires little change over time. This does not mean, however, that it will never change. The procedural model describes what the system needs to do and how to do it. Often referred to as the dynamic part of an information systems model, a procedural model has two main parts: processing and control.

The **processing model** records the instructions, the algorithms, for processing data. Traditionally, this has been described using data flow diagrams (DFDs) or pseudo code (a structured English description of a procedure). The **control model** deals with sequencing and timing control of processing. It also specifies any conditions that must exist in order for processing to occur.

Imagine a simple banking system with accounts for the deposit or withdrawal of money. The processing model deals with identifying and describing processes such as establishing an account, processing a withdrawal, and depositing funds; the control model defines sequencing requirements such as "a deposit cannot be made until after an account has been

4. For an excellent discussion of this problem, see Wetherbe, J. C. 1991. Executive information requirements: Getting it right. *MIS Quarterly* 15 (1):51-65.

established." State transition diagrams and entity life-history diagrams are the predominant tools for control modeling.

Statics and dynamics

In OO analysis (OOA), the terms *static* and *dynamic* assume slightly different meanings form those used in other analysis methods. The static aspects are modeled in the class diagram, which shows the potential or the capabilities of the system as opposed to what the system will actually do in a given circumstance. The model is static in the sense that it shows what the objects are capable of doing and remembering (like a data model), and these are fairly stable characteristics. In this case, static is a relative term, and both the capability for remembering and doing may change over time. Methods, the capability for doing, is possibly the more volatile. The dynamic aspect of a model deals with what the system actually does for any particular event.

Scenarios

A scenario is a typical event or sequence of events in the problem domain and the related behavior of the information system. In a simple banking system, some key scenarios are a customer making a withdrawal or a deposit and a manager requesting the day's total withdrawals and deposits. Although the same classes might be involved in the different scenarios, different data and methods will be invoked, and different messages will be transmitted. For each scenario, a subset of the potential capabilities is used and combined to yield the desired system behavior. We usually start by developing the static model, which also incorporates the main methods. We gain sufficient knowledge of all the needed methods only after a thorough analysis of all relevant scenarios.

Traditional systems have an overall control structure or main application program. There is no such parallel in OO because each scenario is associated with a sequence of actions and interactions that define system behavior in that particular context.

Static OO modeling

The basic data modeling concepts learned earlier apply to OO modeling of the static part of a system. It may help to think of object classes as entities with integrated procedural rules. Like entities, object classes can be related to other object classes. One distinction is the kinds of relationships or structures that are defined in an OO model.

Two broad types of possible relationships are depicted in an OO model: relationships between classes and relationships between individual objects. Classification or inheritance relationships are between classes; aggregation and association relationships are between individual objects. Each of these relationships will be demonstrated with an OO modeling exercise.

Finding objects and classes

Usually the initial activity in OO analysis, finding objects and classes, is, in many respects, very similar to identifying entities in data modeling. Which classes to include in a system is highly dependent on the context, the client, and the modeler. Although there is no *correct* set of classes (or entities, in the case of data modeling), the OO analyst should strive to create a high-fidelity model of the client's world. Careful questioning and looking for exceptions are key skills for an analyst. Domain area knowledge and experience also play an important role in the development of high-fidelity models.

One approach is to underline any nouns in the problem description. Most nouns are possible classes, and underlining ensures that no potential classes are overlooked. These suggestions for OO modeling also apply to data modeling. Finding entities and finding classes are similar exercises.

We will use a four-layer model of OO analysis:

- **Class and object layer** — object classes;
- **Structure layer** — structural relations between classes;
- **Attribute layer** — the attributes of each class;
- **Service layer** — the methods for each class.

Although presented sequentially, actual analysis will usually not strictly follow such a serial pattern. The sequence does suggest a main order of activities, however, because the tendency is to work in an iterative fashion rather than finishing all the activities associated with one layer before undertaking the next.

We will now explore these concepts in more depth through an example that will gradually build the layers of an OO model using UML notation.

Whither software?

Firms currently face several tricky questions. The most fundamental one is which software—meaning essentially computing intelligence—should reside in a user's computer and which on a server. The next key question is whether companies should host applications themselves or outsource them to an application service provider (ASP). Sun Microsystems argues that most software should move to the network and be accessed through browsers. Microsoft responds that there will always be a need for an "intelligent client" and a computer running Windows.

The Expeditioner has arranged many diving safaris to the Great Barrier Reef off Australia's northeast coast. The customers have been extremely pleased with these expeditions, which were handled by a local operator, Dick's Dive 'n Thrive, or DDT for short. Stories in diving magazines and word of mouth among diving devotees have generated tremendous growth for DDT. Although he is a great diver, Dick unfortunately is a poor manager. The company has been unable to handle the growth and is now in serious financial trouble. As a result, Dick has turned to one of his major customers, The Expeditioner, for help. After a thorough investigation of the business opportunities, The Expeditioner decides to take a major interest in DDT. Its management team recognizes that new business practices have to be established, especially for the rental side of DDT, which generates most of the business, and is currently losing money.

The management team concludes that existing procedures need to be automated to provide better control and information for managerial decision making, and so they hire a local systems analyst to develop and install an information system. A young lad from Townsville, Bruce "Shark" Dundee,[5] is hired. Shark has had considerable success using OO concepts and decides to create an OO model of DDT's rental business. He starts by writing a statement of the business and underlining the nouns.

Customers can rent diving equipment and boats from DDT. When a customer has seen what is available and decided what to rent, a rental agreement or contract is produced and signed.

Class and object layer

The brief description of DDT's rental business is a starting point for modeling. By underlining the nouns, we see that customer, diving equipment, contract, and boat all are prime candidates for classes (see Figure 13-5).

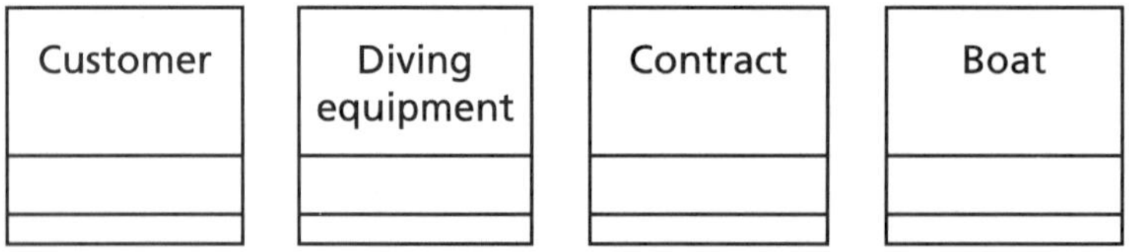

Figure 13-5. Some classes

5. Although his father is a famous crocodile hunter, Shark prefers the ocean.

Structure layer

There are two types of structures: generalization and aggregation. Each of these will be discussed in turn.

Generalization

Depending on how and with which classes we start, OO modeling can be top down or bottom up. In this example, we first look at the classes[6] BOAT and DIVING EQUIPMENT, both of which may be regarded as types of rental equipment. Thus, it is useful to establish a generalized class, which we call RENTAL EQUIPMENT. The attributes and methods established for RENTAL EQUIPMENT are inherited by the classes DIVING EQUIPMENT and BOAT. In this case, we have done bottom-up modeling (see Figure 13-6). If we had started with RENTAL EQUIPMENT, we would have done top-down modeling.

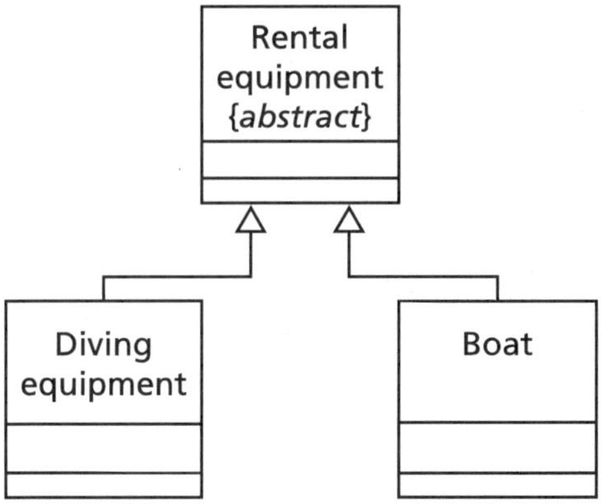

Figure 13-6. A generalization/specialization hierarchy

The RENTAL EQUIPMENT class does not contain any objects, which is why it is an *abstract* class. It serves solely as a vehicle for specifying the common attributes and methods of DIVING EQUIPMENT and BOAT.

If we look more closely at DIVING EQUIPMENT, we see that more detail may be required. DDT rents the usual diving gear such as tanks, regulators, weights, wet suits, and depth gauges, but it needs to store additional specialized information about some of this equipment. For example, diving suits are described by size, thickness, and type. Although we have not specified attributes yet, it is still necessary to think about them to determine what subclasses to create. An analyst who understands the business and the intended use of the system will soon learn the required attributes. As with data modeling, when attributes are specified, some changes in structure often occur. Thus, it makes sense to define attributes as you develop the OO model.

6. The names of classes are shown in uppercase in the text.

In this case, we recognize the need for a subclass SUIT (see Figure 13-7). Later, we might have to refine DIVING EQUIPMENT, but for now it will have only one subclass. This means that all diving equipment we rent, except diving suits, will be called DIVING EQUIPMENT, with an attribute identifying the type of rental equipment (e.g., tank, regulator, etc.). DIVING EQUIPMENT contains objects (the subclass is not abstract). In addition to the services and attributes we will later specify for it, the SUIT class will inherit all specified attributes and services from DIVING EQUIPMENT and RENTAL EQUIPMENT.

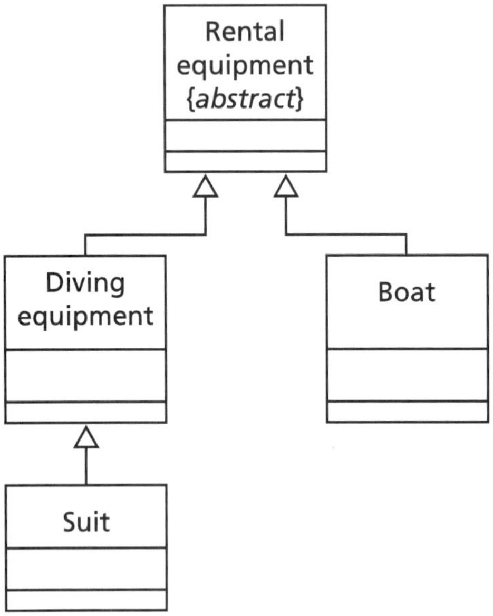

Figure 13-7. SUIT as a subclass of DIVING EQUIPMENT

We have now seen an example of generalization in which inheritance flows from the superclass to the subclass. This is sometimes referred to as an inheritance relation or an "is a kind of" relation; for instance, SUIT is a kind of DIVING EQUIPMENT. An inheritance relation is depicted by and distinguished from the other types of relationships by the open arrowheads shown in Figure 13-6 and Figure 13-7. We recommend placing the superclass above the subclasses to increase readability.

An inheritance relation is between classes, but inheritance is not like a relationship in data modeling. The inheritance relationship between SUIT and DIVING EQUIPMENT does not imply that a SUIT object (one specific suit) is linked to a corresponding DIVING EQUIPMENT object. Here, inheritance means SUIT has the same methods and attributes as DIVING EQUIPMENT and some other methods and attributes that are unique to SUIT.

Multiple inheritance

So far, generalization structures have been simple tree structures. Each subclass has one superclass from which it inherits methods and attributes. Multiple inheritance means a class can inherit attributes and methods from more than one superclass. The generalization structure then becomes more like a lattice than a tree.

Looking at DDT's customers, we see a difference (see Figure 13-8). Some customers rent boats and others rent diving equipment. If this difference is significant in DDT's context (due to different licensing and insurance requirements, for example), we could create a class for each group.

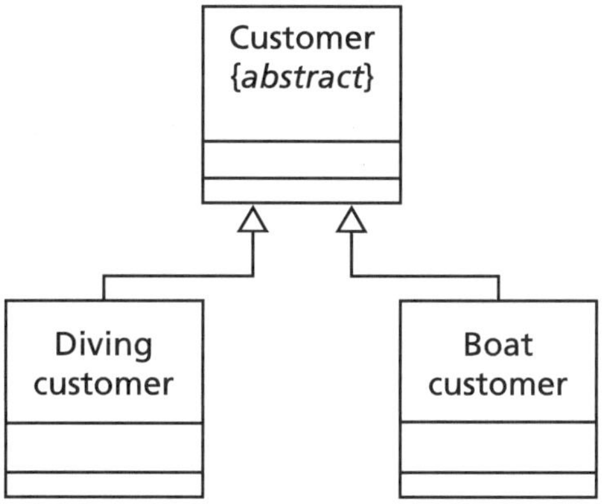

Figure 13-8. Classes of CUSTOMER

Some customers probably will be both diving customers and boat customers (see the model in Figure 13-9), so COMBINED CUSTOMER inherits methods and attributes from both DIVING CUSTOMER and BOAT CUSTOMER.

As you may anticipate, multiple inheritance can create problems when an application is executed. There may be conflicts between the inherited methods and attributes. Although there are different strategies for dealing with this problem, the issue remains unresolved. One strategy is not to support multiple inheritance, which is the approach taken by some OOPLs. From a modeling perspective, it is certainly possible to model multiple inheritance and defer considerations about conflict resolution until time for design. Some modelers recommend avoiding multiple inheritance altogether, especially if the software environment does not support it.

Aggregation

Now, let us now look more closely at the class BOAT. Some of DDT's boats are rented with a trailer and some with zero, one, or two motors. Trailers and motors always stay with the same boats. Motors are never rented without boats or taken away from the boats to which

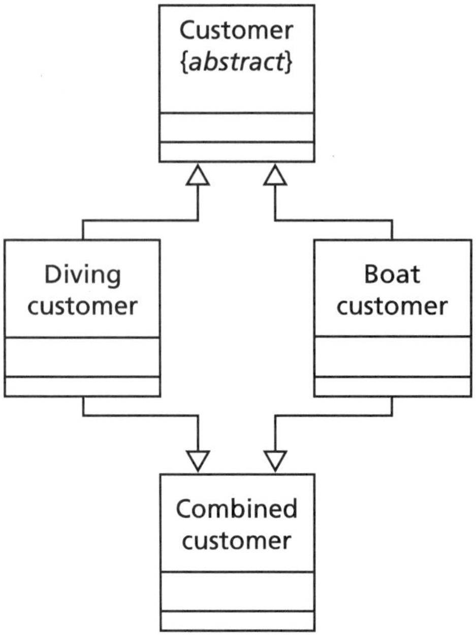

Figure 13-9. Multiple inheritance

they belong except to be serviced or replaced. We now have a BOAT ASSEMBLY which includes BOAT, TRAILER, and MOTOR classes, as shown in Figure 13-10. This is an aggregation, depicting the whole (the boat assembly) and its parts. The relationship is sometimes called a whole/part structure because a TRAILER is a *part of* BOAT ASSEMBLY. It is also sometimes called an owned relationship.

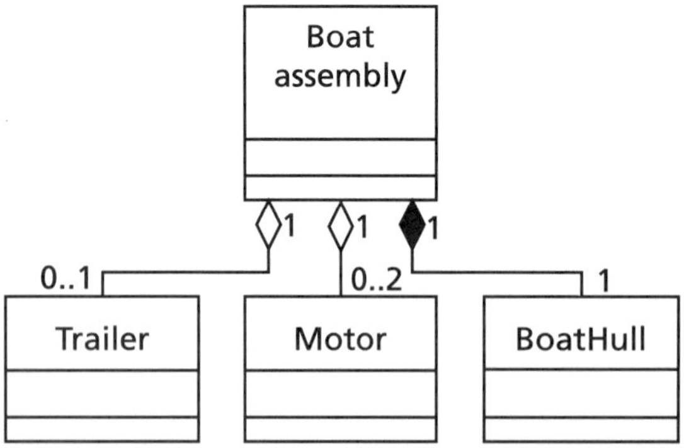

Figure 13-10. An aggregation

The **composition relationship** is distinguished from the other types of relationships by open or filled diamonds (see page 178). In this case, we have a composition aggregation between boat assembly and the boat's hull. In other words, the boat assembly exclusively owns the hull; they are inseparable. The other two aggregations are shared because a boat assembly might not always have a trailer or motor.

An OO model, like a data model, records details of the aggregation relationship. In the case of an OO model, the relationship is between objects. Since a boat assembly can have one or two motors, this must be shown on the OO model. Furthermore, a motor belongs to one and only one boat assembly at a particular time.

Read the aggregation model (Figure 13-10) as follows:

- ❖ A boat has zero or one trailers, and a trailer belongs to one boat;
- ❖ A boat has zero, one, or two motors, and a motor belongs to one boat;
- ❖ A boat has one hull, and one hull belongs to one boat.

We can now combine the completed pieces to illustrate the current state of our OO model (Figure 13-11). Observe that the model is incomplete at this stage because it does not include CUSTOMER or CONTRACT.

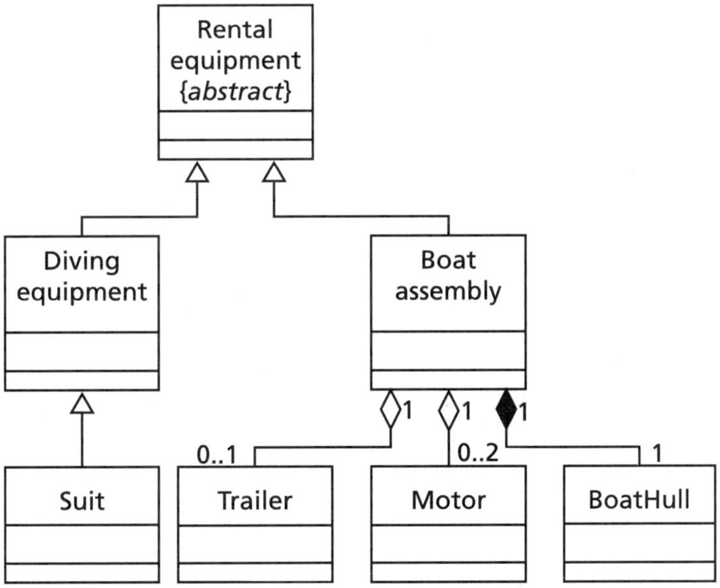

Figure 13-11. OO model—take 1

Attribute layer

The attribute layer has two purposes: specification of attributes and specification of association relationships.

Attributes

Attributes are the facts to be remembered by the object. Some OO proponents argue that the definition of attributes is not needed until physical design or implementation. We recommend that you specify attributes as you discover them. It is only by recording attributes that you really understand the nature of the object classes. As a result, you may have to revise some classes and structures to improve the fidelity of your OO model. Attribute names are listed in the middle segment in the class representation (see Figure 13-12).

Figure 13-12. Attributes of customer

As in data modeling, more information (e.g., range, length, and validation criteria) about an attribute than is provided in the model will be needed before a system can be fully described. Attribute names serve as references to more detailed descriptions that we store elsewhere, typically in a UML modeling tool database. due to space limitations, we might also want to show aggregate attributes in the model and then completely specify them elsewhere. Address, for example, is usually an aggregate of address lines, city, state, and postal code. By specifying only address in the model, we avoid cluttering it with too much detail, although we still convey an impression of what is included.

When deciding which attributes to include, the same principles that are used in data modeling apply to OO modeling. The selection of attributes is based on understanding how objects are described in the problem domain, the responsibilities they will have in the information system, and what they need to remember and do. For example, a student object is unlikely to include details of hair color. Although this is an attribute of a student, this fact probably will not be used by any object and need not be remembered by the system.

If an attribute is only relevant for some of the objects in a class, another class, a specialization, might be needed. For example, diving certificate issue date may be an attribute, but it is not relevant for customers who only rent a boat assembly. We then must differentiate between different types of customers by introducing specialized classes for diving equipment customers and boat assembly customers. To keep the model simple, attribute names are not shown in our examples except where needed for illustration purposes.

Association relationships

Association relationships, or reference relationships, depict links between occurrences of an object. Sometimes called instance connections, they are conceptually the same as relations in data modeling. For example, a specific contract or rental agreement is associated with a specific customer. A CUSTOMER can be associated with many CONTRACTs.[7] A CONTRACT is related to one and only one CUSTOMER (see Figure 13-13). A CONTRACT is also related to RENTAL EQUIPMENT because a CONTRACT describes the RENTAL EQUIPMENT rented (see Figure 13-14).

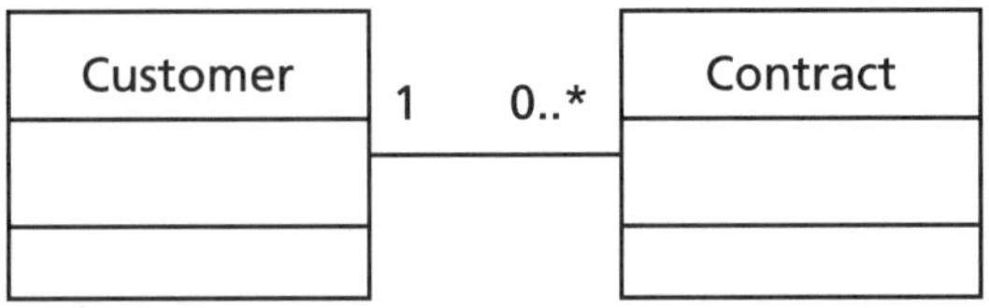

Figure 13-13. A 1:m association between CUSTOMER and CONTRACT

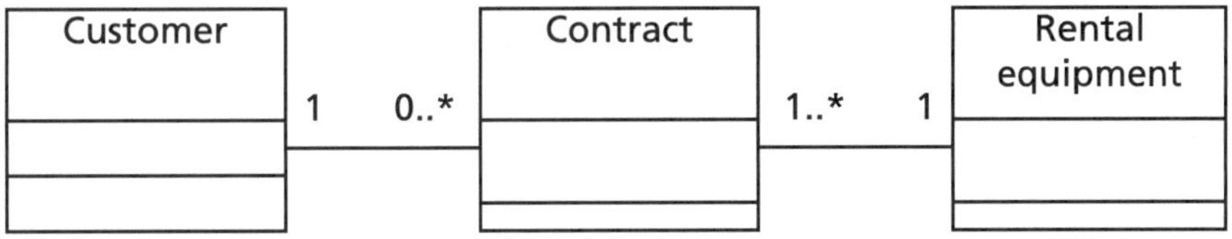

Figure 13-14. An association between CUSTOMER, CONTRACT, and RENTAL EQUIPMENT

As you can see, there is an m:m association between CUSTOMER and RENTAL EQUIPMENT objects. A customer can rent many pieces of equipment and a piece of equipment can be rented by many customers. When a customer rents equipment, a contract is created, and this typically includes many items. Because there is an m:m association between CONTRACT and RENTAL EQUIPMENT objects, the model should include another object class, CONTRACT ITEM, which is related to CONTRACT. We have shown this as an aggregation relationship because it reflects the client's thinking that an item on a contract is logically part of a contract (see Figure 13-15).

The aggregation relationship is actually a special version of the association relationship. It reflects a strong tie between objects and also resembles a fundamental way of thinking about objects in the real world: an object as part of another object. All aggregation relationships conceivably can be modeled with association relationships although some OO proponents discard the aggregation relationship altogether. By using it, we obtain a model that is less abstract and closer to the way we usually think about objects. The final version of the model, at least as far as we will go in this text, is shown in Figure 13-16.

7. UML uses an asterisk (*) to indicate many.

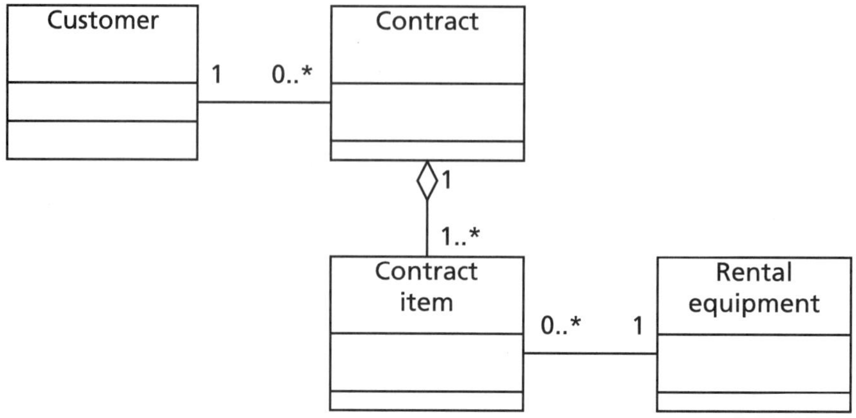

Figure 13-15. An aggregation relationship between CONTRACT and CONTRACT ITEM

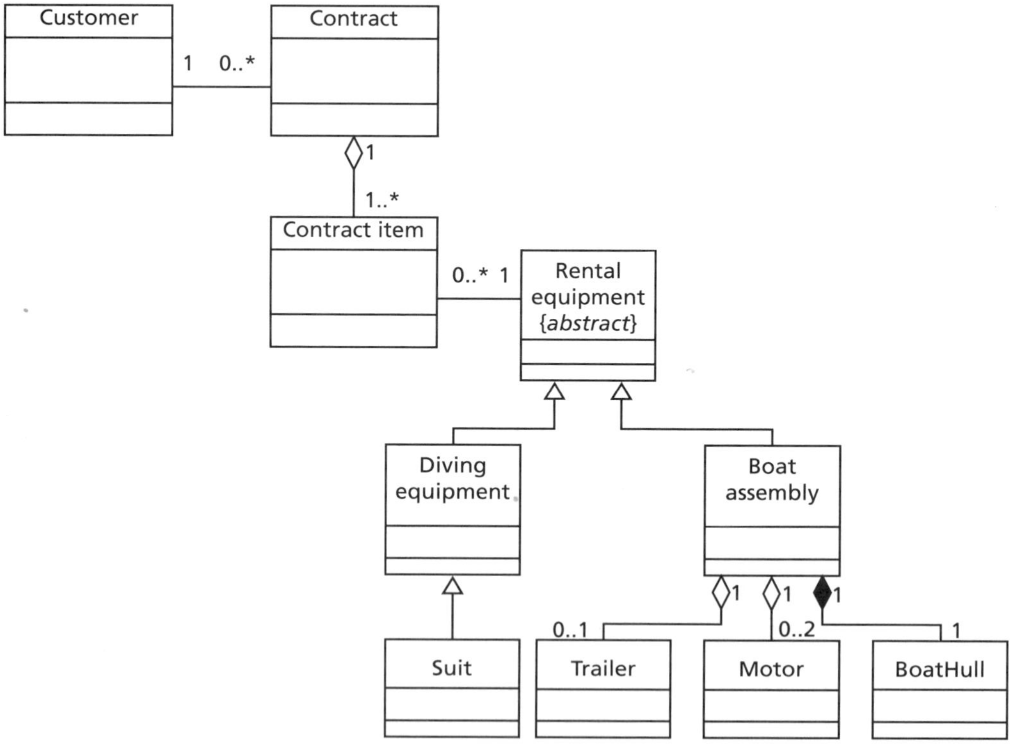

Figure 13-16. OO model—final

Service layer

The required processing for each object is specified in the service layer. Simple and complex services are distinguished. Simple services are the standard services that most objects need to be able to perform. These are usually implied as always being available and are not shown in the model. Simple services typically include create, connect, access, and release.

Complex or nonstandard services, which are shown explicitly, fall into two categories: calculate and monitor. For example, the object class CONTRACT needs to calculate a rental fee. This nonstandard service is shown in the services window (see Figure 13-17). The service name shown in the model is also a reference to a detailed specification of the rental fee calculation algorithm. The actual specification is usually deferred until the static model has stabilized after a few iterations.

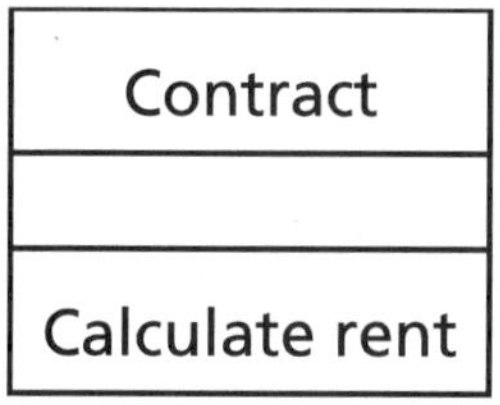

Figure 13-17. The service *Calculate rent*

This completes the first iteration of the static class and object model. You now have seen examples of the three types of relationships — inheritance, aggregation, and association, which are basic features of OO modeling.

Summary

Many concepts were introduced in the preceding discussion on OO modeling. Figure 13-18 maps the links between some key OO ideas. An object class, composed of individual occurrences of objects, has attributes and methods. Attributes are the facts an object remembers, and methods are the actions an object can perform. Associations describe the links between object occurrences. Objects can participate in two types of structures: generalization (*is a kind of*) and aggregation (*is part of*).

The OO and relational paradigms

Now that you have some understanding of the fundamental ideas of OO, it is useful to review the key differences between the object and relational paradigms, which are summarized in Table 13-3.

In practice, the relational model reigns in data management, and the OO model dominates software engineering. Thus, there is a need to know how to transform a class diagram into a relational database so that you can translate between these major paradigms.

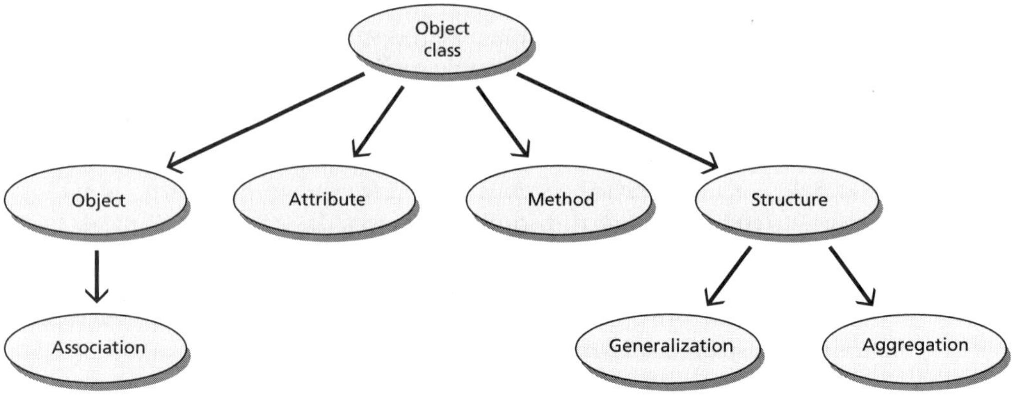

Figure 13-18. A map of OO concepts

Table 13-3: The OO and relational paradigms

OO paradigm	Relational paradigm
Based on software engineering principles of coupling,[a] cohesion,[b] and encapsulation.	Founded on the mathematical concepts of set theory.
The goal is to improve the quality of systems, and there is concern for both data and processes.	The goal is to improve data management.
To access data you traverse objects via relationships.	To access data you match primary and foreign keys.

a. Coupling is a measure of how cleanly the modules in a system are separated from one another.
b. Cohesion is the measure of the strength of functional relatedness of elements within a module.

Mapping objects to a relational database

Mapping attributes to columns

Each attribute is mapped to zero or more columns, usually one column. Non-persistent attributes, those that can be derived (e.g., the yield of a share), are not mapped. Some attributes, such as address, need to broken into their components (e.g., street, city, postal code) before mapping.

Generalization

There are three possible approaches to mapping a generalization or inheritance structure.

Vertical mapping

Each class is mapped to a separate table. The tables resulting from mapping the subclasses have the primary key of the superclass as a foreign key. This mapping is likely to be relatively slow for queries because of the frequent need to join tables corresponding to a subclass and its superclass.

Horizontal mapping

Each subclass is mapped to a different table, and the superclass is not mapped to a table.The tables resulting from mapping the subclasses have all the attributes of the corresponding class plus those inherited from the superclass. This method works well when the superclass has few attributes.

Filtered mapping

All classes are mapped to the same table. The table contains columns for all attributes in both classes with a column added to distinguish between the subclasses. This method violates normalization rules and will have many columns with a null value. It is not recommended.

Vertical mapping preserves object-oriented and relational concepts the best of the three approaches. It should be used as the default choice unless there are compelling reasons for either horizontal or filtered mapping.

Association and aggregation

From a database perspective the only difference between association and aggregation relationships is how tightly the objects are bound to each other. With aggregation anything that you do to the whole in the database you almost always need to do to the parts, whereas with association that is not the case.

Associations are mapped like their corresponding data model parallels. For example, a m:m association is mapped by creating an associative entity.

Aggregation relationships are mapped in the same manner as relationships in a data model (see page 178). Physically, an aggregation might be implemented using clustering (see page 321) or a linked list (see page 330) because the whole and parts are often retrieved together.

Persistent objects

In OO programming, objects only exist for the duration of a program's execution. If we use OO for information systems, we need to be able to store details of *persistent* objects, those that last much longer. We need a database that stores objects and has facilities for accessing and executing them. What we need is an object-oriented database management system (ODBMS).

Object-oriented database management systems

An ODBMS stores simple and complex objects. It also supports the creation of abstract data types, encapsulation, and inheritance. An ODBMS is the database extension of OO concepts. It stores data when the OO application is no longer executing. ODBMSs also are designed to work closely with OOPLs, and the linkage is tighter than that between a RDBMS and procedural languages. Because of the consistent use of OO concepts, OO applications are more suited to managing data using ODBMS rather than RDBMS technology. As you would expect, ODBMSs also manage data sharing, concurrent data access, and recovery control, which are necessary features of any database technology.

There are some fundamental differences between ODBMS and RDBMS technology. An ODBMS has pointers, like prerelational models, for quickly accessing data. Every object has a system-generated unique object identifier, which contains the address of the pointer to the data. This is a significant difference from the approach of the relational data model, where relationships are maintained by foreign keys. As a result, the system can directly access the required data. An ODBMS does not require joins.

The so-called impedance problem, the mismatch between RDBMS set-at-time processing and procedural language record-at-time processing, is cited as a shortcoming of relational technology. If you look back at the COBOL program in Chapter 10, you will see how the cursor handles the impedance problem. OOPLs and ODBMSs do not have this problem because all operations are at the record level. Of course, this also means the relational model advantage of set-at-time processing is lost. Furthermore, some procedural languages do not handle RDBMS data types and arithmetic. For example, SQL permits the definition of date as a data type and supports arithmetic on dates, but not all procedural languages support all SQL data types or may store them differently, which can cause additional work when programming. There is no mismatch between ODBMS and OOPL data types.

ODBMS standards

Information systems managers are reluctant to adopt technology that ties them to a particular vendor. They seek compatibility and standardization because it gives them greater flexibility when buying new hardware and software. Consequently, OO technology vendors have established the Object Management Group (OMG)[8] to create and promulgate standards for OO technology and object interaction. The OMG is also working on ODBMS issues. Its objective is to minimize incompatibilities across various implementations of the ODBMS idea and standardize some of the features. OMG has released an object database standard,[9] which it intends to promote as an industry standard.

---

8. http://www.odmg.org/
9. Cattell, R. G. G., D. K. Barry, M. Berler, J. Eastman, D. Jordan, C. Russel, O. Schadow, T. Stanienda, and F. Velez, eds. 2000. *The object data standard: OMG 3.0*. San Francisco: Morgan Kaufmann.

Directions

DBMS vendors are following two major directions. One approach is the pure ODBMS path and the other is a hybrid object-relational model. Most major vendors have followed the hybrid road, although one major vendor released a pure ODBMS, Jasmine, in 1997.

Computer Associates is the only major database vendor to have expressed faith in a fully object-oriented database. Previously, object databases have been marketed by smaller vendors, and they have had little impact on the dominance of relational technology. Jasmine, a joint effort of Computer Associate and Fujitsu, quickly attracted attention because of its support for rapid application development and creation of Web applications. Jasmine does not appear to have captured much market share as a DBMS, and it is now marketed as Jasmine ii, a platform for ebusiness.

Interest in ODBMS technology appears to have peaked. There is now far less on the topic in the computing popular press than two or three years ago.

J2EE

The goal of J2EE (Java 2 Enterprise Edition) is to deliver Java's write-once run anywhere promise to the server. J2EE is not a single product but a series of specifications that vendors use to build products, most notably application servers. Sun recognized the whole of Java was greater than the sum of its parts; so, it started to bundle and integrate its Java products into a coherent platform, J2EE.

J2EE provides programmers with the necessary infrastructure to create new applications. Most web applications today, particularly corporate ones, are written in Java and run on a J2EE-compliant server program such as IBM's WebSphere. What companies like is that J2EE allows them to develop highly customized applications quickly without having to start from scratch.

Features included in J2EE are Enterprise JavaBeans (EJBs); Corba; XML messaging; Java Server Pages (JSP), Java Servlets; Java Naming and Directory Interface (JNDI) to access directory services; Java Database Connectivity (JDBC); and Java Message Service (JMS) for asynchronous messaging.

Driving the adoption of J2EE is the acceptance of Java and the fact that developers know their code will work on any platform once an application server is certified as J2EE-compliant. To be certified as J2EE-compliant, an application server must pass a battery of 13,000 validation tests.

Source: Patrizio, A. 2001. Serving up Java 2 Enterprise Edition. *Informationweek.com*, Apr 23, http://www.informationweek.com/834/ooj2ee.htm.

Hybrid technology

There are two forms of hybrid technology: object-relational and extended-relational. **Object-relational** databases try to add objects on top of relational technology. These hybrids, such as Informix's Dynamic Server (with universal data option) and Oracle's Universal Data Server, are not full implementations of an object database model. For example, they do not support inheritance, which must be implemented with application code. **Extended-relational systems**, such as DB2 from IBM, add user-defined data types to their underlying relational structures.

The label **universal server** has been generally applied to extensions of the relational model. The standard universal server model (e.g., Oracle8) assumes that all data are physically stored within the database. The **extended universal server** model recognizes that there may be very good reasons for not storing all data in the DBMS. Therefore, the DBMS must also be able to efficiently access data stored in external files. Large data values (e.g., images) are stored externally, and a pointer to each image file is stored inside the database as a column value.

Hybrid systems at their core are relational data stores. Thus, object purists criticize the hybrid approach because the DBMS must decompose objects into relational tables—rows and columns—for storage and then rebuild them into objects before delivery to the user. Requests for data objects from the database must be continually assembled and disassembled. Consequently, flexibility and performance can suffer in hybrid databases. It has been estimated that one-third of hybrid database processing time is spent translating data into objects. Hybrid database implementations represent compromises to both the object database and relational models.

The release of SQL3 (see page 274) will hopefully see vendors standardize the different approaches to adding OO concepts to the relational model. Failure to get convergence will likely result in a reluctance of developers to take full advantage of the new standard.

If product performance meets a client's requirements, however, it does not matter whether the system is pure object or hybrid. What the product does is hidden and unless its architecture interferes with maintenance and enhancement, clients should be indifferent. Experience will demonstrate whether the RDBMS vendors are successful in adapting the relational model for complex-data support.

The future of ODBMS

A question that many data managers ask is, "Will ODBMS replace RDBMS in the next five years?" Based on the slowness with which the RDBMS technology was adopted, this is unlikely. RDBMS technology first appeared in 1979, and it took many years for it to replace hierarchical and network systems. Organizations have a heavy investment in relational database systems and have learned how to build and manage such systems. They are unlikely to discard this large investment quickly. Many companies still maintain pre-relational legacy systems; so, ODBMSs cannot be expected to become a dominant force in the next few years. If anything, ODBMS technology has lost momentum over the last few years and few regard it has ever being a competitor to relational technology.

There is no single database system that is *right* for all applications. Instead of generally adopting a single model, database designers need to consider the characteristics of the data, data structures, and the system's goals before deciding on which DBMS is appropriate. Clearly, applications that must handle complex objects are well-suited to ODBMS. Our prognosis is that relational systems will continue to evolve to handle new data types.

Summary

OO has attracted considerable attention because it offers the prospect of lowering systems development and maintenance costs. OO concepts are being applied to analysis, design, programming, and database. OO modeling creates a representation of a real-world information system. An ODBMS with an OOPL can overcome some of the shortcomings of relational database technology. OOPLs are invaluable for the development of GUI applications.

OO applications are created by assembling and using objects, self-contained units that can contain data. Objects also contain the necessary instructions to transform data. Encapsulation means that all processing that changes the state of an object is done within an object. Objects are individual occurrences, often corresponding to objects in the real world. Objects of the same type are called an object class. Objects communicate with each other by sending and receiving messages.

Classes can be specializations or generalizations of other classes. Classes in a generalization hierarchy will inherit data and methods from the superclass. Inheritance simplifies specification and programming and is especially important for creating reusable objects. Recognizing and exploiting similarities in classes is a major means of increasing programmer productivity.

Modeling is a central activity of systems development. A model is an abstraction of something. OO supporters argue that their approach narrows the communication gap between client and analyst because it uses modeling concepts and techniques that are more closely related to the clients' way of thinking. It is necessary to describe two aspects of an information system, data and procedures. The static part of a model shows what objects are capable of doing and remembering; the dynamic aspect deals with what the system actually does for any particular event. A scenario is a typical event or sequence of events in the problem domain and the related behavior of the information system.

Two broad types of possible relationships are shown in an OO model: relationships between classes and relationships between individual objects. Finding objects and classes is usually the initial activity in OO analysis. One approach is to underline any nouns in the problem description. A four-layer model of OO analysis includes class and object layer, structure layer, attribute layer, and service layer.

The two types of structures are generalization and aggregation. A generalization is sometimes referred to as an inheritance relation or an *is a kind of* relation. Multiple inheritance means a class can inherit attributes and methods from more than one superclass.

The attribute layer has two purposes: specification of attributes and specification of association relationships. Attributes are the facts to be remembered by the object. Association relationships depict links between actual object occurrences. They are conceptually the same as relations in data modeling. The aggregation relationship is a special version of the association relationship. The processing required for each object is specified in the service layer. Simple services are the standard services that most objects need to be able to perform. Complex or nonstandard services fall into two categories: calculate and monitor. Objects can have message connections and use relationships.

An ODBMS stores details of persistent objects; it is the database extension of OO concepts. ODBMSs have high synergy with OOPLs. ODBMSs manage data sharing, concurrent data access, and recovery control. Every object has a system-generated unique object identifier, which contains the address of the pointer to the data. All operations are at the record level. OO technology vendors have established the Object Management Group (OMG) with the goal of creating and promulgating standards for OO technology and object interaction. Relational systems are likely to continue to dominate over the next few years, especially with the release of the SQL3 standard and its embrace of OO ideas.

Key terms and concepts

Abstract class
Aggregation
Association
Attribute
Complex objects
Complex service
Composition
Dynamic model
Encapsulation
Extended-relational
Generalization
Hybrid technology
Impedance problem
Information engineering
Inheritance
Layer
Message passing
Methods
Object
Object class
Object identifier
Object Management Group (OMG)
Object relational
Object-orientation (OO)
ODBMS
OO analysis (OOA)
OO design (OOD)
OO modeling
OO programming language (OOPL)
Persistent object
Relationship
Reusable objects
Scenario
Service
Simple service
Software productivity
Specialization
Static model
Structured analysis
Subclass
Subject
Superclass
UML
Windows, icon, mouse, pointer (WIMP)

References and additional readings

Ambler, S. W. 2000. Mapping objects to relational databases: Ronin International. http://www.AmbySoft.com/mappingObjects.pdf.

Booch, G. 1991. *Object-oriented design with applications.* Redwood City, CA: Benjamin/ Cummings.

Cattell, R. G. G. 1991. Next-generation database systems. *Communications of the ACM* 34 (10):31-33.

Coad, P., and E. Yourdon. 1990. *Object-oriented analysis.* Englewood Cliffs, NJ: Prentice-Hall.

Pascal, F. 1993. Objection! *Computerworld*, 127–128, 130.

Exercises

1. What circumstances have stimulated interest in OO concepts?
2. What is encapsulation? Why is it desirable?
3. Draw a generalization/specialization hierarchy to describe audio recording media (e.g., cassette, CD, LP).
4. Draw a generalization/specialization hierarchy to describe farm animals.
5. What are the advantages of inheritance?
6. Draw a generalization/specialization hierarchy to describe transport choices (e.g., bus, car, plane, boat). What attributes are common to all object classes? What are some unique attributes of a plane?
7. What are the advantages of the OO approach?
8. How does OO reduce maintenance costs?
9. How does a data model differ from a procedural model?
10. Why do objects pass messages?
11. What is the difference between association and aggregation relationships?
12. Why is an ODBMS required?
13. How do an ODBMS and RDBMS differ in the way they handle recording relationships?
14. What are ODBMS vendors doing to increase the likelihood of the adoption of ODBMS technology?
15. What is the likely future for ODBMS and RDBMS?
16. A travel company sells two types of trips: ship cruises and bus tours. Customers fall into two categories: group and individual. Group customers belong to an affinity group (e.g., a bird watchers' club), which will book a block of tickets on a trip. Individual customers make personal bookings. Some individual customers, because of their frequent use of the travel company, are designated *gold star travelers* and receive additional benefits when traveling. Draw a class and object layer model.
17. Night-on-the-Town offers a package deal to New York tourists. For a flat fee, a person can select a Broadway play, dinner at a fancy restaurant, and jazz at a nightclub. Night-on-the-Town offers a choice in each category, and the customer selects one from each of the three categories (i.e., the customer goes to a play, eats dinner, and then listens to jazz). Draw a class and object layer model.

18. An agent can represent many bands, but a band has only one agent. A band consists of many musicians, but a musician belongs to only one band. Model this situation using association and aggregation relationships.
19. A government treasury bond provides a guaranteed stream of future payments. The date and amount of each of these payments are known. Model this relationship first, and then add to your model the information that the BOND object can use an object called NET PRESENT VALUE to calculate the current value of this stream of payments. Show relevant attributes.
20. An educational software developer has asked you to develop a database of orchestral musical instruments. An orchestra consists of four broad classes (strings, woodwinds, brass, and percussion). What data would you store for each musical instrument? How would the data describing a drum differ from a violin? Draw a class and object layer model. Consider one of the microcomputer databases with which you are familiar. How suitable would it be for this database?

Section 4

Organizational Memory Technologies

Science and technology revolutionize our lives, but memory, tradition and myth frame our response.

Arthur M. Schlesinger, Jr. "The Challenge of Change" in *New York Times Magazine*, 27 July 1986

In recent years, data management has become more critical to organizational performance. Organizations have realized that they can learn a great deal from analyzing the data they collect as part of their everyday operations. They also know that they can greatly improve marketing and customer service by using the Web to interact with customers. Of course, the Web can also be used to interact with other stakeholders such as employees, suppliers and investors. In the network economy where organizations cooperate extensively, the Internet has become a key conduit for exchanging data. However, you need more than just a high speed communication line to exchange data; you also need a standard to describe the exchanged data so that the meaning is also shared.

Organizational intelligence is the outcome of an organization's efforts to collect, store, process, and interpret data from internal and external sources. Unfortunately, many companies have inadequate organizational intelligence systems because they make limited use of the vast amounts of data collected by their transaction processing systems. They fail to use the data to support managerial decision making because they are scattered across many systems rather than centralized in one readily accessible, integrated data store. Recently, technologies have been introduced to enable organizations to create single, vast repositories of data that can be then analyzed using special purpose software. Technologies such as data warehousing, on-line analytic processing, and data mining have become increasingly important to data managers over the last few years, and these are covered in Chapter 14.

Internet technology, in particular **Web** browsers, has greatly enlarged the capability of organizations to capture, manage, and distribute organizational memory. Organizations are using the Internet, intranets, and extranets to share data with customers, employees, and business partners. Consequently, data managers now have a new domain. They must be concerned with managing the data stored on Web servers and making accessible, via a Web browser, data stored in existing organizational data stores. The Web has given data management a more central role because organizations now have a cost-effective and simply mastered means of making organizational memory available to a wide range of stakeholders. The relationship between Web and DBMS technology is the theme of Chapter 15.

XML has emerged at the beginning of this century as the standard for describing data. The emergence of this common language for data exchange adds another skill set to those that the data manager must acquire. XML will become a critical data management technology in the next few years because it is at the core of cooperation among firms. In the network economy, firms exchange high volumes of data to coordinate their activities. They need to exchange data without comprising internal operational autonomy. Firms want to cooperate while maintaining different information architectures.

As you may have surmised, the intent of this section is to broaden your understanding and knowledge of the role of data management. In our view, a data manager who focuses solely on databases is providing a poor and incomplete customer service. Data managers need to embrace the full gamut of technologies that can improve organizational performance by making better use of an organization's memory.

14

Organizational Intelligence Technologies

There are three kinds of intelligence: one kind understands things for itself, the other appreciates what others can understand, the third understands neither for itself nor through others. This first kind is excellent, the second good, and the third kind useless.

Machiavelli, *The Prince*, 1513

Learning objectives

Students completing this chapter will be able to

- ❖ select an appropriate combination of hardware and software to support organizational intelligence activities for a defined environment;
- ❖ decide whether to use verification or discovery for a given problem;
- ❖ select the appropriate data analysis technique(s) for a given situation;
- ❖ select variables to be included in a multidimensional database.

Introduction

Too many companies are *data rich* but *information poor*. They collect vast amounts of data with their transaction processing systems, but they fail to turn these data into the necessary information to support managerial decision making. Many organizations make limited use of their data because data are scattered across many systems rather than centralized in one readily accessible, integrated data store. Recently, technologies have been introduced to enable organizations to create single, vast repositories of data that can be then analyzed using special purpose software.

Organizational intelligence[1] is the outcome of an organization's efforts to collect, store, process, and interpret data from internal and external sources. The conclusions or clues gleaned from an organization's data stores enable it to identify problems or opportunities, which is the first stage of decision making.

An organizational intelligence system

Transaction processing systems (TPSs) are a core component of organizational memory and thus an important source of data. Along with relevant external information, the various TPSs are the bedrock of an organizational intelligence system. They provide the raw facts that an organization can use to learn about itself, its competitors, and the environment. A TPS can generate huge volumes of data. In the U.S., a regional telephone company may generate 200 million records per day detailing the telephone calls it has handled. The 600 million credit cards on issue in the world generate more than 100 billion transactions per year. A popular Web site can have millions of hits per day. TPSs are creating a massive torrent of data that potentially reveals to an organization a great deal about its business and its customers.

Unfortunately, many organizations are unable to exploit, either effectively or efficiently, the massive amount of data generated by TPSs. Data are typically scattered across a variety of systems (e.g., sales and production), in different database technologies (e.g., hierarchical and relational), in different operating systems (e.g., MVS and Unix), and in different locations (e.g., Atlanta and Paris). The fundamental problem is that organizational memory is highly fragmented. Consequently, organizations need a technology that can accumulate a considerable proportion of organizational memory into one readily accessible system. Making these data available to decision makers is crucial to improving organizational performance, providing first-class customer service, increasing revenues, cutting costs, and preparing for the future. For many organizations, their memory is a major untapped resource—*an underused intelligence system containing undetected key facts about customers*. To take advantage of the mass of available raw data, an organization first needs to organize these data into one logical collection and then use software to sift through this collection to extract meaning.

The **data warehouse**, a subject-oriented, integrated, time-variant, and nonvolatile set of data that supports decision making,[2] has emerged as the key device for harnessing organizational memory. *Subject* databases are designed around the essential entities of a business (e.g., customer) rather than applications (e.g., auto insurance). *Integrated* implies consistency in naming conventions, keys, relationships, encoding, and translation (e.g., gender is always coded as *m* or *f* in all relevant fields). *Time-variant* means that data are organized by various time periods (e.g., by months). Because a data warehouse is updated with a bulk upload, rather than as transactions occur, it contains *nonvolatile* data.

1. Intelligence in this case means the gathering and distribution of information and making sense of such information.
2. Inmon, W. H. 1996. *Building the data warehouse*. 2nd ed. New York, NY: Wiley. p. 33.

Data warehouses are enormous collections of data, often measured in terabytes, compiled by mass marketers, retailers, and service companies from the transactions of their millions of customers. Associated with a data warehouse are data management aids, (e.g., data extraction), analysis tools (e.g., OLAP[3]), and applications (e.g., EIS). The three aspects of the data warehouse environment shown in Figure 14-1 are discussed in detail in the following sections.

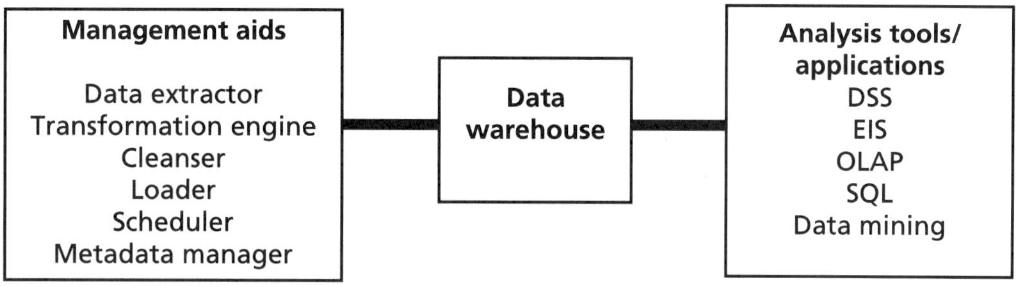

Figure 14-1. The data warehouse environment

The data warehouse

Creating and maintaining the data warehouse

A data warehouse is a snapshot of an organization at a particular time. In order to create this snapshot, data must be extracted from existing systems, transformed, cleaned, and loaded into the data warehouse. In addition, regular snapshots must be taken to maintain the usefulness of the warehouse.

Extraction

Data from the operational systems, stored in operational data stores (ODS), are the raw material of a data warehouse. Unfortunately, it is not simply a case of pulling data out of ODSs and loading them into the warehouse. Operational systems were often written many years ago at different times. There was no plan to merge these data into a single system. Each application is independent or shares little data with others. The same data may exist in different systems with different names and in different formats. The extraction of data from many different systems is time consuming and complex. Furthermore, extraction is not a one-time process. Data must be extracted from operational systems on an ongoing basis so that analysts can work with current data.

3. OLAP is discussed in detail, starting on page 423.

Transformation

Transformation is part of the data extraction process. In the warehouse, data must be standardized and follow consistent coding systems. There are several types of transformation:

- Encoding: converting to a common coding system. Gender may be coded, for instance, in a variety of ways (e.g., m/f, male/female, or M/F) in different systems. The extraction program must transform data from each application to a single coding system (e.g., m/f).
- Unit of measure: distance, volume, and weight can be recorded in varying units in different systems (e.g., centimeters and inches) and must be converted to a common system.
- Field: the same attribute may have different names in different applications (e.g., sales-date, sdate, or saledate), and a standard name must be defined.
- Date: dates are stored in a variety of ways. In Europe, the standard for date is dd/mm/yy, and in the U.S. it is mm/dd/yy, whereas the ISO standard is yyyy-mm-dd.

Cleaning

Unfortunately, some of the data collected from applications may be *dirty*—they contain errors, inconsistencies, or redundancies. There are a variety of reasons why data may need cleaning:

- The same record is stored by several departments. For instance, both Human Resources and Production have an employee record. Duplicate records must be deleted.
- Multiple records for a company as a result of an acquisition. For example, the record for Time Warner should be removed because it was acquired by AOL.
- Multiple entries for the same entity because there are no corporate data entry standards (e.g., FedEx and Federal Express both appear in different records for the same company).
- Misuse of data entry fields. For example, an address line field is used to record a second phone number.

Data cleaning starts with determining the dirtiness of the data. An analysis of a sample should indicate the extent of the problem and whether commercial data cleaning tools are required. Data cleaning is unlikely to be a one-off process. All data added to the data warehouse should be validated in order to maintain the integrity of the warehouse. Cleaning can be performed using specialized software or custom written code.

Loading

Data that have been extracted, transformed, and cleaned can be loaded into the warehouse. There are three types of data loads:

- **Archival**: Historical data (e.g., sales for the period 1980–1992) that is loaded once. Many organizations may elect not to load these data because of their low value relative to the cost of loading.

- **Current**: Data from current operational systems.
- **Ongoing**: Continual revision of the warehouse as operational data are generated. Managing the ongoing loading of data is the largest challenge for warehouse management. This loading is done either by completely reloading the data warehouse or just updating it with the changes.

Data warehouse improves BKK's customer service quality

BKK Bundesverband is a federal association of over 330 German company health insurance funds. When the government passed a law requiring all health care settlements to be processed electronically, BKK knew it had a major problem. With over 10 million policyholders, it had to process large volumes of data. Management also wanted immediate data analysis so that it could improve customer service and increase market share.

BKK installed an NCR Teradata data warehouse that provides access to two years of data. The system has one Tbyte of disk capacity and 350 Gbytes of raw data. The warehouse is updated daily.

The currency of information and data analysis tools enables BKK to provide a higher quality service than its competitors. The more than 180 users perform complex ad hoc queries and detailed decision analysis.

Source: NCR cases studies, 2001, http://www.ncr.com/repository/case_studies/cs_repository.htm.

Scheduling

Refreshing the warehouse, which can take many hours, must be scheduled as part of a data center's regular operations. Because a data warehouse supports medium- to long-term decision making, it is unlikely that it would need to be refreshed more frequently than daily. For shorter decisions, operational systems are available. Some firms may decide to schedule less frequently after comparing the cost of each load with the cost of using data that are a few days old.

Metadata

A data dictionary is a reference repository containing *metadata* (i.e., *data about data*). It includes a description of each data type, its format, coding standards (e.g., volume in liters), and the meaning of the field. For the data warehouse setting, a data dictionary is likely to include details of which operational system created the data, transformations of the data, and the frequency of extracts. Analysts need access to metadata so they can plan their analyses and learn about the contents of the data warehouse. If a data dictionary does not exist, it should be established and maintained as part of ensuring the integrity of the data warehouse.

Data warehouse technology

Selecting an appropriate data warehouse system is critical to support significant data mining or OLAP. Data analysis often requires intensive processing of large volumes of data, and large main memories are necessary for good performance. In addition, the system should be scalable so that as the demand for data analysis grows, the system can be readily upgraded. The three key building blocks of a data warehouse are the overall warehouse architecture, the server architectures, and the DBMS.

Warehouse architectures

Designing a data warehouse starts with selecting the physical and logical structure of the warehouse architecture. The fundamental physical choice is between a centralized or distributed data warehouse. A **centralized data warehouse** (see Figure 14-2) gives processing efficiency and lowers support costs.

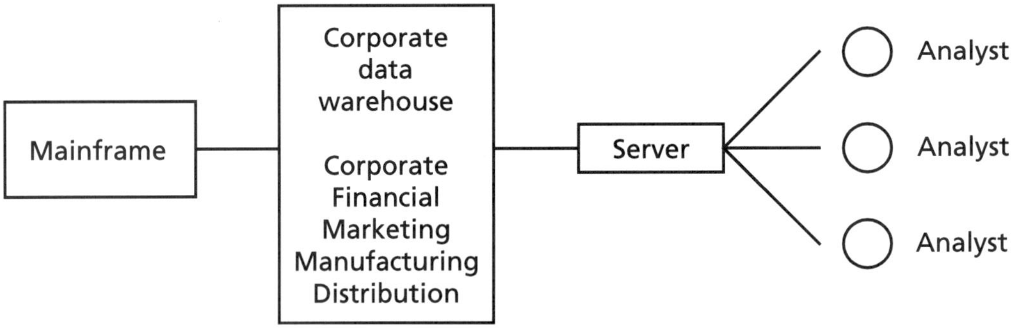

Figure 14-2. A centralized data warehouse

A distributed architecture can be either federated or tiered. With a **federated data warehouse**, data are distributed by function. For example, financial data are on one DBMS server, marketing data on a different DBMS server at the same location, and manufacturing data on a DBMS server at a different location. To the analyst, the data warehouse may appear as one logical structure, but in order to reduce response time it is physically dispersed across several related physical databases (see Figure 14-3).

A **tiered architecture** houses highly aggregated data on an analyst's workstation, with more detailed summaries on a second server, and most detailed data on a third server. The first tier handles most data requests, with the second and third tiers handling respectively fewer requests (see Figure 14-4). The workstation at the first tier is selected to handle a heavy data analyst workload, while a third tier server is chosen to handle high data volumes but a light data analysis workload. The second tier is a **data mart,** a local, single subject database. In some situations, a data mart may be stand-alone rather than linked to the corporate data warehouse.

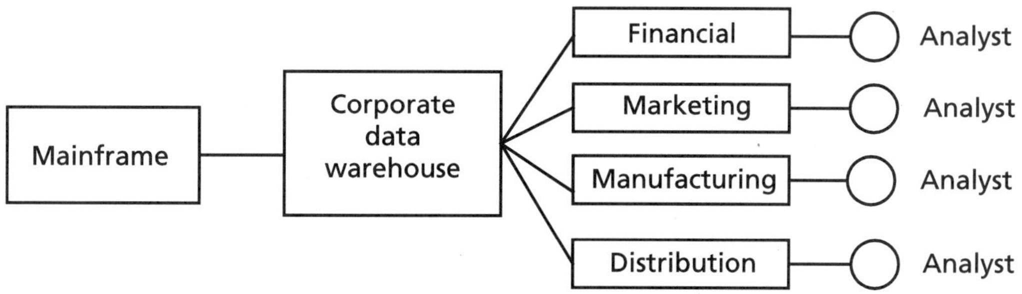

Figure 14-3. A federated data warehouse

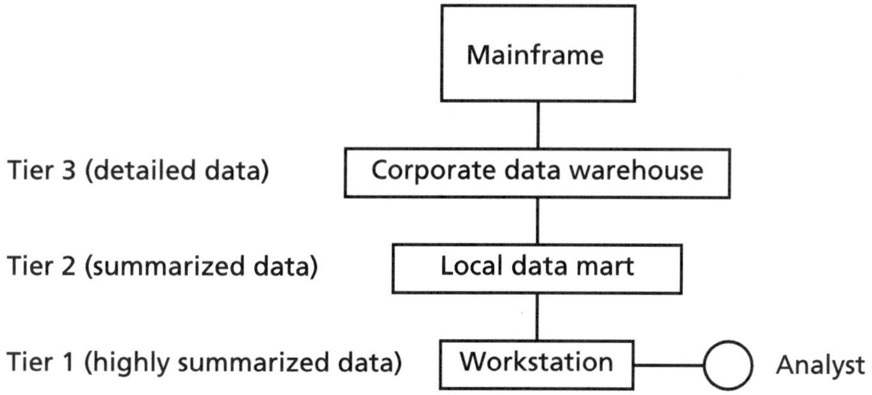

Figure 14-4. A tiered data warehouse

Server and DBMS selection

Server options

Servers hold and deliver data to analysts. The selection of the type of server is determined by an organization's need for scalability, availability of servers, and ease of management of the system. There are four options (see Figure 14-5):

- The simplest option is a single processor server, which is easy to manage but has limited processing power and scalability. Also, a single server system limits reliability because when it is unavailable, so is the warehouse.
- A symmetric multiprocessor (SMP) has multiple servers sharing memory and disks. Because processors can be added as additional processing capacity is required, an SMP is scalable. However, as processors are added, the memory bus can become con-

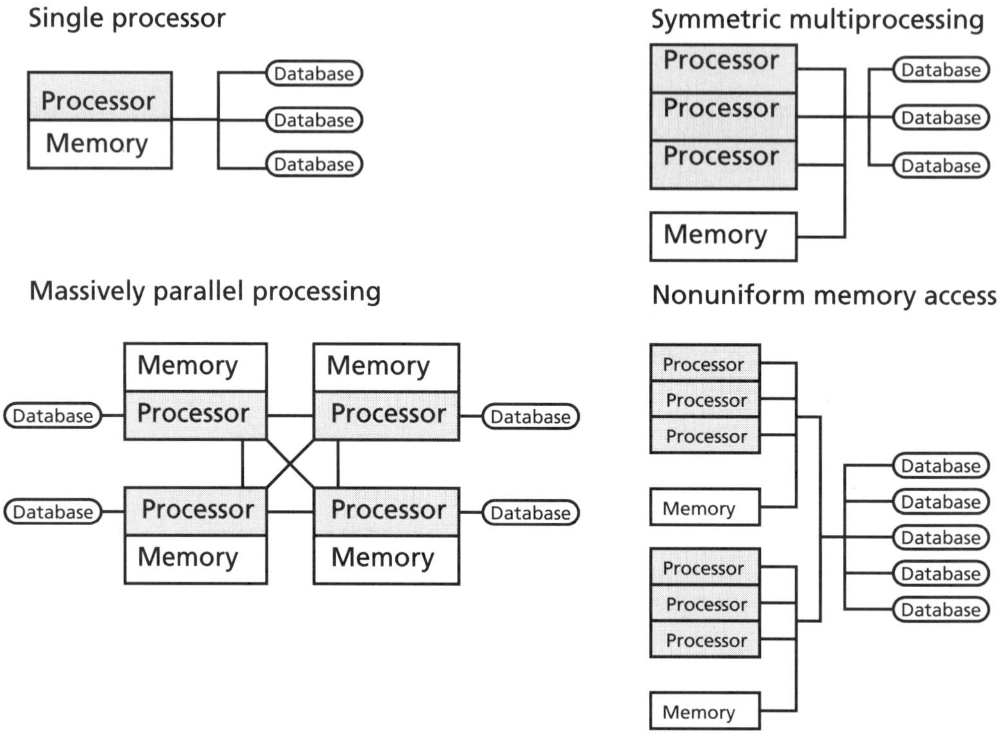

Figure 14-5. Server architectures

gested, and too many CPUs will slow performance. Although applications don't have to be specifically designed to run in this environment, the operating system must be designed for multiprocessing.

- A massively parallel processor (MPP) connects an array of processors with a high-speed, high-bandwidth link. These processors have independent memory and disks, so there is no shared memory or disk. To take advantage of parallelism, applications must be designed to work in parallel. MPP, while expensive, has the processing capacity for searching large databases using a parallel version of a DBMS.
- A nonuniform memory access (NUMA) machine joins multiple SMP nodes into a single, distributed memory pool with a single operating system. NUMA has the simplicity of operation of an SMP, and existing DBMSs and applications can be used without modification. The downside is that the operating system must be designed for NUMA, and this technology has not been widely used in commercial environments.

DBMS options

To improve responsiveness, large data warehouses often require features that are not found in a traditional RDBMS, and these features are seldom found within one type of database (see Table 14-1). **Super-relational systems** can include specialized hardware, a database machine, to accelerate retrievals. Performance of these systems is also improved by using join indexes, fully inverted index lists, or other indexing methods (see Chapter 11). Some RDBMSs use parallelism to improve performance. For example, a parallel version of a RDBMS might split a join across several processors and run the parts simultaneously.

Table 14-1: DBMS choices (Weldon, 1997)

Features/functions	Relational	Super-relational	Multidimensional (logical)	Multidimensional (physical)	Object-relational
Normalized data structures	✔	✔			✔
Abstract data types					✔
Parallelism	✔				
Multidimensional structures		✔	✔	✔	
Drill-down			✔	✔	✔
Rotation			✔	✔	✔
Data-dependent operations					✔

Analysts often want to see data from several dimensions (e.g., sales by region by product line and by division). These **multidimensional views** can be achieved by either a logical or physical **multidimensional database** (MDDB).[4] The *logical* approach uses multiple tables and pointers with a RDBMS to simulate a multidimensional structure. In the logical approach, multidimensionality is supported at a layer above the database. Providing multidimensionality at this layer is costly in terms of response performance, but there is tremendous flexibility because the underlying relational data can be tapped. The *physical* approach is based on a database technology specifically designed to support multidimensional data. In this case, multidimensionality is supported at the database layer. Consequently, physical systems respond more rapidly. However, additional implementation effort is required because the way in which clients use the database must be predetermined and data presummarized. Drill-down and rotation, features of a MDDB, are discussed in detail later in this chapter. Major RDBMS vendors are likely to integrate MDDB capabilities into their products, just as they are also integrating object management.

As you learned in Chapter 13, traditional databases lack support for video, images, documents, and other *abstract data types*. If these types of objects must be stored in a data warehouse, an ODBMS or **object-relational database** is required. These databases store and process objects and require specialized operators for handling abstract data types.

Hardware and software

The selection of a server architecture and DBMS are not independent decisions. Parallelism is generally only an option for RDBMSs, such as DB2 Parallel and Oracle Parallel, and not available for multidimensional and object-relational technologies. The data warehouse manager has to find the best fit between hardware and data management technologies that meets the organization's goals. The data warehouse decision matrix (see Table 14-2)

4. See page 424 for details on MDDB.

is a useful tool for relating the business needs to technology options. Notice that the decision is driven by the business requirements and the needs of the clients, which is what you should expect.

Table 14-2: Data warehouse decision matrix (Weldon, 1997)

For these environments ...			**Choose ...**		
Business requirements	**Client population**	**Systems support**	**Architecture**	**Server**	**DBMS**
Scope: departmental **Uses:** data analysis	Small; single location	Minimal local; average central	Consolidate; turnkey package	Single-processor or SMP	MDDB
Scope: departmental **Uses:** analysis plus informational	Large; analysis at single location; informational users dispersed	Minimal local; average central	Tiered; detail at central; summary at local	Clustered SMP for central; SP or SMP for local	RDBMS for central; MDDB for local
Scope: Enterprise **Uses:** analysis plus informational	Large; geographically dispersed	Strong central	Centralized	Clustered SMP	Object-relational Web support
Scope: departmental **Uses:** exploratory	Small; few sites	Strong central	Centralized	MPP	RDBMS with parallel support

The scope of the hardware/software decision can range from a department (e.g., a marketing data mart) to the enterprise data warehouse. The power and functionality of a data warehouse usually increase with its scope. Groups using standardized reports and predefined queries will require a simpler environment than business analysts using the data warehouse for decision support. In a highly volatile environment with many changes to the data warehouse, a RDBMS will be more efficient than a MDDB, which could require rebuilding after each change. These and other factors need to be carefully reviewed when selecting a hardware and data management combination. Once a data warehouse is established, the volume of data and number of users will grow. In addition, it is also likely that the complexity of queries will increase as clients learn to take full advantage of an integrated data store. Thus, it is important to select a system that is scalable across the dimensions of data volume, number of users, and query complexity.

The decision must embrace the entire data warehouse environment (see Figure 14-1). While considering the hardware and software combination, attention must also be paid to the tools that are used to manage the data warehouse and systems that will be used to analyze the stored data. The management tools, usually part of the data warehouse software, must be assessed for their ease of use and ability to perform the required functions. Some of the analysis software may already exist (e.g., current DSSs), and the ease of integration of the data warehouse and existing systems should be a key consideration.

Exploiting data stores

Two of the more recently developed approaches to analyzing a data store (i.e., a database or data warehouse) are data mining and OLAP. Before discussing each of these approaches, it is helpful to recognize the fundamentally different approaches that can be taken to exploiting a data store.

Verification and discovery

The **verification** approach to data analysis is driven by a hypothesis or conjecture about some relationship (e.g., customers with incomes in the range of $50,000–75,000 are more likely to buy minivans). The analyst then formulates a query to process the data to test the hypothesis. The resulting report will either support or disconfirm the theory. If the theory is disconfirmed, the analyst may continue to propose and test hypotheses until a target customer group of likely prospects for minivans is identified. Then, the minivan firm may market directly to this group because the likelihood of converting them to customers is higher than mass marketing to everyone. The verification approach is highly dependent on a persistent analyst eventually finding a useful relationship (i.e., who buys minivans?) by testing many hypotheses. OLAP, DSS, EIS, and SQL-based querying systems support the verification approach.

Data mining uses the **discovery** approach. It sifts through the data in search of frequently occurring patterns and trends to report generalizations about the data. Data mining tools operate with minimal guidance from the client. Data mining tools are designed to efficiently yield useful facts about business relationships from a large data store. The advantage of discovery is that it may uncover important relationships that no amount of conjecturing would have revealed and tested.

A useful analogy for thinking about the difference between verification and discovery (see Table 14-3) is the difference between conventional and open-pit gold mining. A conventional mine is worked by digging shafts and tunnels with the intention of intersecting the richest gold reef. Verification is like conventional mining—some parts of the gold deposit may never be examined. The company drills where it believes there will be gold. In open-pit mining, everything is excavated and processed. Discovery is similar to open-pit mining—everything is examined. Both verification and discovery are useful; it is not a case of selecting one or the other. Indeed, analysts should use both methods to gain as many insights as possible from the data.

Table 14-3: A comparison of verification and discovery queries

Verification	Discovery
What is the average sale for in-store and catalog customers?	What is the best predictor of sales?
What is the average high school GPA of students who graduate from college compared to those who do not?	What are the best predictors of college graduation?

On-line analytic processing (OLAP)

Codd, the father of the relational model, and colleagues proclaimed in 1993 that RDBMSs were never intended to provide powerful functions for data synthesis, analysis, and consolidation. This was the role of spreadsheets and special purpose applications. They argued that analysts need data analysis tools that complement RDBMS technology and put forward the concept of **OLAP**, the analysis of business operations with the intention of making timely and accurate analysis-based decisions.

Instead of rows and columns, OLAP tools provide multidimensional views of data, as well as some other differences (see Table 14-4). OLAP means fast and flexible access to large volumes of derived data whose underlying inputs may be changing continuously.

Table 14-4: Comparison of TPS and OLAP applications

TPS	OLAP
Optimized for transaction volume	Optimized for data analysis
Process a few records at a time	Process summarized data
Real-time update as transactions occur	Batch update (e.g., daily)
Based on tables	Based on hypercubes
Raw data	Aggregated data
SQL is widely used	No common query language

For instance, an OLAP tool enables an analyst to view how many widgets were shipped to each region by each quarter in 1997. If shipments to a particular region are below budget, the analyst can find out which customers in that region are ordering less than expected. The analyst may even go as far as examining the data for a particular quarter or shipment. As this example demonstrates, the idea of OLAP is to give analysts the power to view data in a variety of ways at different levels. In the process of investigating data anomalies, the analyst may discover new relationships. The operations supported by the typical OLAP tool include:

- calculations and modeling across dimensions, through hierarchies, or across members;
- trend analysis over sequential time periods;
- slicing subsets for on-screen viewing;
- drill-down to deeper levels of consolidation;
- drill-through to underlying detail data;
- rotation to new dimensional comparisons in the viewing area.

An OLAP system should give fast, flexible, shared access to analytical information. Rapid access and calculation are required if analysts are to make ad hoc queries and follow a trail of analysis. Such quick-fire analysis requires computational speed and fast access to data. It also requires powerful analytic capabilities to aggregate and order data (e.g., summarizing sales by region ordered from most to least profitable). Flexibility is another desired feature. Data should be viewable from a variety of dimensions, and a range of analyses should be supported.

Multidimensional databases

OLAP is typically used with a **multidimensional database** (MDDB), a data management system in which data are represented by a multidimensional structure. The MDDB approach is to mirror and extend some of the features found in spreadsheets by moving beyond two dimensions. These tools are built directly into the MDDB to increase the speed with which data can be retrieved and manipulated. These additional processing abilities, however, come at a cost. The dimensions of analysis must be identified prior to building the database, and changes can be costly and time consuming. In addition, MDDBs have size limitations that RDBMSs do not have and, in general, are an order of magnitude smaller than a RDBM.

MDDB technology is optimized for analysis, whereas relational technology is optimized for the high transaction volumes of a TPS. For example, SQL queries to create summaries of product sales by region, region sales by product, and so on, could involve retrieving many of the records in a marketing database and could take hours of processing. A MDDB could handle these queries in a few seconds. TPS applications tend to process a few records at a time (e.g., processing a customer order may entail one update to the customer record, two or three updates to inventory, and the creation of an order record). In contrast, OLAP applications usually deal with summarized data.[5]

A significant shortcoming of MDDBs is that vendors have very little in common. Fortunately, RDBMS vendors have standardized on SQL, and this provides a commonality that allows analysts to transfer considerable expertise from one relational system to another. This is not the case with MDDB, where each vendor has its own language. This is a barrier to the widespread adoption of MDDB technology, unless the vendors can agree on a standard, which is difficult because many of the products already exist.

The current limit of MDDB technology is approximately 10 dimensions, which can be millions to trillions of data points. At this level, response is too slow. However, as MDDB technology is implemented for multiprocessor server architectures, this current limit will be extended.

ROLAP

An alternative to a physical MDDB is a relational OLAP (or ROLAP) in which case a multidimensional model is imposed on a relational model. As we discussed earlier, this is also known as a logical MDDB. Not surprisingly, a system designed to support OLAP should be superior to trying to retrofit relational technology to a task for which it was not specifically designed.

The **star model** is used by some MDDBs to represent multidimensional data within a relational structure. The center of the star is a table storing multidimensional *facts* derived from other tables. Linked to this central table are the *dimensions* (e.g., region) using the familiar primary key/foreign key approach of the relational model. Figure 14-6 depicts a star model for an international automotive company. The advantage of the star model is that it makes use of a RDBMS, a mature technology capable of handling massive data stores

5. If you want to experience OLAP, spend some time playing with the PivotTable feature of Microsoft's Excel.

and having extensive data management features (e.g., backup and recovery). However, if the fact table is very large, performance may be slow.

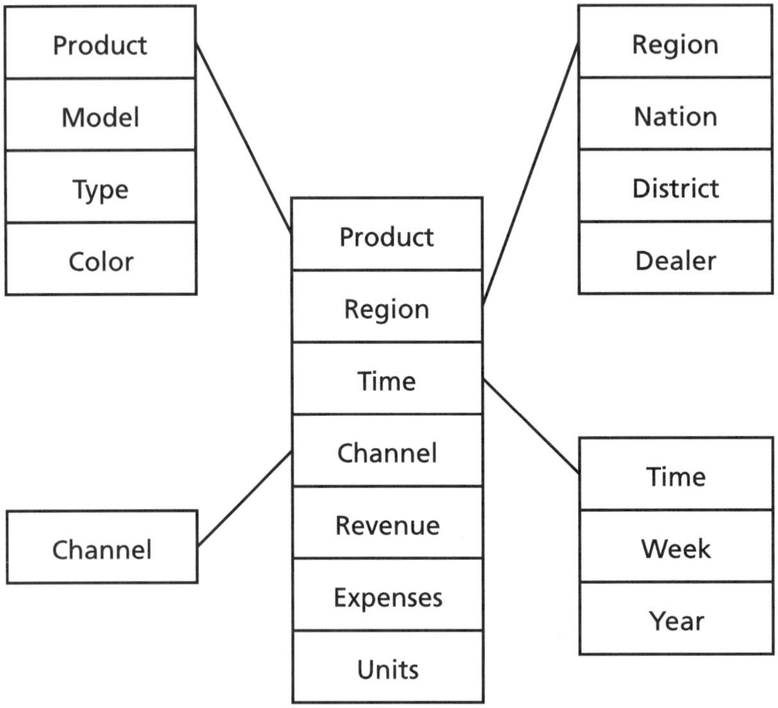

Figure 14-6. A star structure

Rotation, drill-down, and drill-through

MDDB technology supports **rotation** of data objects (e.g., changing the view of the data from by year to by region as shown in Figure 14-7) and **drill-down** (e.g., reporting the details for each nation in a selected region as shown in Figure 14-8), which is also possible with a relational system. Drill-down can slice through several layers of summary data to get to finer levels of detail. The Japanese data, for instance, could be dissected by region (e.g., Tokyo region), and if the analyst wants to go further, the Tokyo region could be analyzed by store. In some systems, an analyst can **drill-through** the summarized data to examine detail data within the organizational data store from which the MDDB summary data was extracted.

		Region			
Year	Data	Asia	Europe	North America	Grand Total
1995	Sum of Hardware	97	23	198	318
	Sum of Software	83	41	425	549
1996	Sum of Hardware	115	28	224	367
	Sum of Software	78	65	410	553
1997	Sum of Hardware	102	25	259	386
	Sum of Software	55	73	497	625
Total Sum of Hardware		314	76	681	1071
Total Sum of Software		216	179	1332	1727

		Year			
Region	Data	1995	1996	1997	Grand Total
Asia	Sum of Hardware	97	115	102	314
	Sum of Software	83	78	55	216
Europe	Sum of Hardware	23	28	25	76
	Sum of Software	41	65	73	179
North America	Sum of Hardware	198	224	259	681
	Sum of Software	425	410	497	1332
Total Sum of Hardware		318	367	386	1071
Total Sum of Software		549	553	625	1727

Figure 14-7. Rotation

The hypercube

From the analyst's perspective, a fundamental difference between MDDB and RDBMS is the representation of data. As you know from data modeling, the relational model is based on tables, and analysts must think in terms of tables when they manipulate and view data. The relational world is two-dimensional. In contrast, the **hypercube** is the fundamental representational unit of a MDDB (see Figure 14-9). Analysts can move beyond two dimensions. To envisage this change, consider the difference between the two-dimensional blueprints of a house and a three-dimensional model. The additional dimension provides greater insight into the final form of the building.

Of course, on a screen or paper only two dimensions can be shown. This problem is typically overcome by selecting an attribute of one dimension (e.g., North region) and showing the other two dimensions (i.e., product sales by year). You can think of the third dimension (i.e., region in this case) as the page dimension—each page of the screen shows one region or slice of the cube (see Figure 14-10).

Region	Sales variance
Africa	105%
Asia	57%
Europe	122%
North America	97%
Pacific	85%
South America	163%

Nation	Sales variance
China	123%
Japan	52%
India	87%
Singapore	95%

Figure 14-8. Drill-down

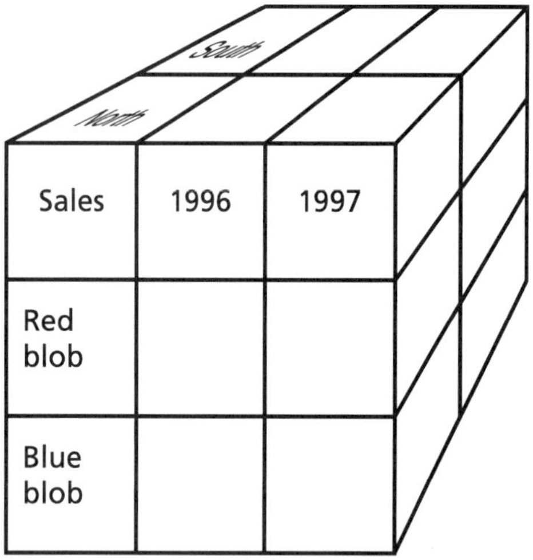

Figure 14-9. A hypercube

A hypercube can have many dimensions. Consider the case of a furniture retailer who wants to capture six dimensions of data (see Table 14-5). Although it is extremely difficult to visualize a six-dimensional hypercube, it helps to think of each cell of the cube as representing a fact (e.g., the Atlanta store sold five Mt. Airy desks in January to a business).

Page

Region: North

Columns

Sales

Rows

Year

	Red blob	Blue blob	Total
1996			
1997			
Total			

Figure 14-10. A three-dimensional hypercube display

Table 14-5: A six-dimensional hypercube

Dimension	Example
Brand	Mt. Airy
Store	Atlanta
Customer segment	Business
Product group	Desks
Period	January
Variable	Units sold

A six-dimensional hypercube can be represented by combining dimensions as shown in Figure 14-11. Brand and store are combined in the row dimension by showing the stores within a brand. The column dimension, which shows for each type of furniture the units sold and revenue, combines the product group and variable dimensions. The page, the third dimension, combines month and customer segment. Although combining dimensions enables the display of a multidimensional hypercube, it frequently has a cost. Tables can become quite large and no longer fit on one screen. As a result, the analyst is unable to see the complete picture without scrolling, and this can make the detection of patterns or anomalies more difficult.

Page

Month
Segment

Columns

Product group
Variable

Rows

Brand
Store

March	Business	Desks		Chairs	
		Units	Revenue	Units	Revenue
Carolina	Atlanta				
	Boston				
Mt. Airy	Atlanta				
	Boston				
Totals					

Figure 14-11. A six-dimensional hypercube display

The link between RDBMS and MDDB

A quick inspection of Table 14-4 (see page 424) reveals that relational and multidimensional database technologies are designed for very different circumstances. Thus, the two technologies should be considered as complementary, not competing, technologies. Appropriate data can be periodically extracted from a RDBMS, aggregated, and loaded into a MDDB. Ideally, this process is automated so that the MDDB is continuously updated. Because analysts sometimes want to drill-down to low-level aggregations and even drill-through to raw data, there must be a connection from the MDDB to the RDBMS to facilitate access to data stored in the relational system. The relationship between the two systems is illustrated in Figure 14-12.

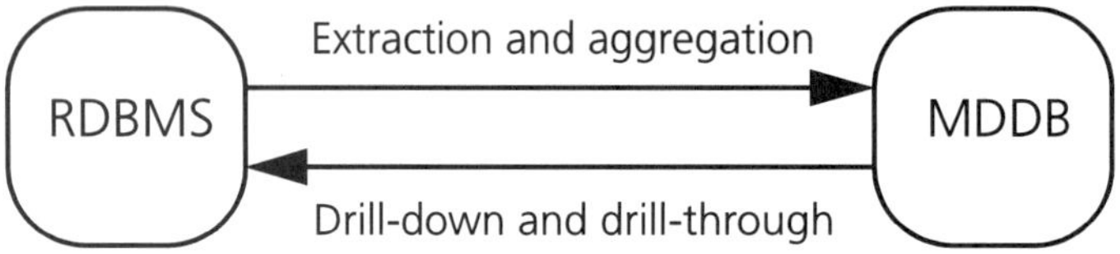

Figure 14-12. The relationship between RDBMS and MDDB

Designing a multidimensional database

The multidimensional model, based on the hypercube, requires a different design methodology from the relational model. At this stage, there is no commonly used approach, such as the entity-relationship principle of the relational model. However, the method proposed by Thomsen (1997) deserves consideration.

The starting point is to identify what must be tracked (e.g., sales for a retailer or passenger miles, cost, and revenue per passenger mile for a transportation firm). A collection of tracking variables is called a ***variable dimension***.

The next step is to consider what types of analyses will be performed on the variables dimension. In a sales system, these may include sales by store by month, comparison of this month's sales with last month's for each product, and sales by class of customer. These types of analyses cannot be conducted unless the instances of each variable have an identifying tag. That is, in this case, each sale must be tagged with time, store, product, and customer type. Each set of identifying factors is an ***identifier dimension***.

As a cross-check for identifying either type of dimension, use the five basic prompts shown in Table 14-6.

Table 14-6: Basic prompts for determining dimensions

Prompt	Example
When?	June 5, 1998
Where?	Paris
What?	Tent
How?	Catalog
Outcome?	Revenue of 6,000 FF

Variables and identifiers are the key concepts of multidimensional database design. The difference between the two is illustrated in Table 14-7. Observe that time, an identifier, follows a regular pattern, whereas sales do not. Identifiers are typically known in advance and remain constant (e.g., store name and customer type), while variables change. It is this difference that readily distinguishes between variables and identifiers. Unfortunately, when this is not the case, there is no objective method of discriminating between the two. As a result, some dimensions can be used as both identifiers and variables.

Table 14-7: A sales table

Identifier time (hour)	**Variable** sales (dollars)
10:00	523
11:00	789
12:00	1,256
13:00	4,128
14:00	2,634

There can be a situation when your intuitive notion of an identifier and variable is not initially correct. Consider a Web site that is counting the number of hits on a particular page. In this case, the identifier is a hit and time is the variable because the time of each hit is recorded (see Table 14-8).

Table 14-8: A hit table

Identifier hit	**Variable** time (hh:mm:ss)
1	9:34:45
2	9:34:57
3	9:36:12
4	9:41:56

The next design step is to consider the form of the dimensions. You will recall from statistics that there are three types of variables (dimensions in MDDB language): nominal, ordinal, and continuous. A nominal variable is an unordered category (e.g., region), an ordinal variable is an ordered category (e.g., age group), and a continuous variable has a numeric value (e.g., passenger miles). A hypercube is typically a combination of several types of dimensions. For instance, the identifier dimensions could be product and store (both nominal), and the variable dimensions could be sales and customers. A dimension's type comes into play when analyzing relationships between identifiers and variables, which are known as independent and dependent variables in statistics (see Table 14-9). The most powerful forms of analysis are available when both dimensions are continuous. Furthermore, it is always possible to recode a continuous variable into ordinal categories. As a result, wherever feasible, data should be collected as a continuous dimension.

Table 14-9: Relationship of dimension type to possible analyses

		Identifier dimension	
		Continuous	Nominal or ordinal
Variable dimension	Continuous	Regression and curve fitting *Sales by quarter*	Analysis of variance *Sales by store*
	Nominal or ordinal	Logistic regression *Customer response (yes or no) to the level of advertising*	Contingency table analysis *Number of sales by region*

This brief introduction to multidimensionality modeling has demonstrated the importance of distinguishing between types of dimensions and considering how the form of a dimension (e.g., nominal or continuous) will affect the choice of analysis tools. Because multidimensional modeling is a relatively new concept, you can expect design concepts to evolve. If you become involved in designing a MDDB, then be sure to review carefully current design concepts. In addition, it would be wise to build some prototype systems, preferably with different vendor implementations of the multidimensional concept, to enable analysts to test the usefulness of your design.

Data mining

Data mining is the search for relationships and global patterns that exist in large databases but are *hidden* in the vast amounts of data. In data mining, an analyst combines knowledge of the data with advanced *machine learning* technologies to discover *nuggets* of knowledge hidden in the data. Data mining software can find meaningful relationships that might take years to find with conventional techniques. The software is designed to sift through large collections of data and by using statistical and artificial intelligence techniques, identify hidden relationships. The mined data typically include electronic point of sales records, inventory, customer transactions, and customer records with matching demographics, usually obtained from an external source. Data mining does not require the presence of a data warehouse. An organization can mine data from its operational files or independent databases. However, data mining independent files will not uncover relationships that exist between data in different files. Data mining will usually be easier and more effective when the organization accumulates as much data as possible in a single data store, such as a data warehouse. Recent advances in processing speeds and lower storage costs have made large-scale mining of corporate data a reality.

Database marketing, a common application of data mining, is also one of the best examples of the effective use of the technology. Database marketers use data mining to develop, test, implement, measure, and modify tailored marketing programs. The intention is to use data to maintain a lifelong relationship with a customer. The database marketer wants to anticipate and fulfill the customer's needs as they emerge. For example, recognizing that a customer buys a new car every three or four years and with each purchase gets an increasingly more luxurious car, the car dealer contacts the customer during the third year of the life of the current car with a special offer on its latest luxury model.

Data mining uses

There are many applications of data mining. For example:

- ❖ Predicting the probability of default for consumer loan applications. Data mining can help lenders to substantially reduce loan losses by improving their ability to predict bad loans.
- ❖ Reducing fabrication flaws in VLSI chips. Data mining systems can sift through vast quantities of data collected during the semiconductor fabrication process to identify conditions that are causing yield problems.
- ❖ Predicting audience share for television programs. A market share prediction system allows television programming executives to arrange show schedules to maximize market share and increase advertising revenues.
- ❖ Predicting the probability that a cancer patient will respond to radiation therapy. By more accurately predicting the effectiveness of expensive medical procedures, health-care costs can be reduced without affecting quality of care.
- ❖ Predicting the probability that an offshore oil well is going to produce oil. An offshore oil well may cost $30 million. Data mining technology can increase the probability that this investment will be profitable.
- ❖ Identifying quasars from trillions of bytes of satellite data. This was one of the earliest applications of data mining systems as the technology was first applied in the scientific community.

Creating a toolbox

Fingerhut, one of the U.S.'s oldest and largest catalog publishers, with sales of nearly $1.8 billion in 2000, claims to have collected data on 30 million households. However, it has not found a complete data analysis package to meet its needs. Because different business problems require different data analysis programs, the company has been creating a "toolbox" of these applications. The most recent tool in the box is Quadstone, a data-mining solution which is being used to determine which customers should be contacted, how often, and what method works the best: catalogs and mailers, phone centers, or the Internet. The software provides workers, not just the IT managers, the capability to run analyses of model customer behavior.

In addition, Fingerhut uses software from SAS and SPSS Inc. depending on which tool is more applicable to the data. Regression techniques are used in the SAS modules to derive formulas for customer habits. Sequences of events, such as the series of steps taken during a purchase, are analyzed using SPSS. Another tool, called Knowledge-Seeker from Angoss, helps analyze customers in categories, such as urban female shoppers. Around 100 data models are used by Fingerhut to analyze customer data and behavior on a regular basis. In addition, at least 100 marketing campaigns are undertaken each year.

Source: Tillet, L. S. 2001. Data tools for Fingerhut. *Internetweek*, Mar 5 (851):19.

Data mining functions

Based on the functions they perform, five types of data mining functions exist:

Associations

An association function identifies affinities existing among the collection of items in a given set of records. These affinities or relationships can be expressed by rules such as, 72 percent of all the records that contain items A, B, and C also contain items D and E. Knowing that 85 percent of customers who buy a certain brand of wine also buy a certain type of pasta can help supermarkets improve use of shelf space and promotional offers. Discovering that fathers on the way home from work on Friday often grab a six-pack of beer after buying some diapers, enabled a supermarket to improve sales by placing beer specials next to diapers.[6]

Sequential patterns

Sequential pattern mining functions identify frequently occurring sequences from given records. For example, these functions can be used to detect the set of customers associated with certain frequent buying patterns. Data mining might discover, for example, that 32 percent of female customers within six months of ordering a red jacket also buy a gray skirt. A retailer with knowledge of this sequential pattern can then offer the red-jacket buyer a coupon or other enticement to attract the prospective gray-skirt buyer.

Classifying

Classifying divides predefined classes (e.g., types of customers) into mutually exclusive groups such that the members of each group are as *close* as possible to one another, and different groups are as *far* as possible from one another, where distance is measured with respect to specific predefined variables. The classification of groups is done before data analysis. Thus, based on sales, customers may be first categorized as *infrequent, occasional,* and *frequent.* A classifier could be used to identify those attributes, from a given set, that discriminate among the three types of customers. For example, a classifier might identify frequent customers as those with incomes above $50,000 and having two or more children. Classification functions have been used extensively in applications such as credit risk analysis, portfolio selection, health risk analysis, and image and speech recognition. Thus, when a new customer is recruited, the firm can use the classifying function to determine the customer's sales potential and accordingly tailor its market to that person.

Clustering

Whereas classifying starts with predefined categories, clustering starts with just the data and discovers the *hidden* categories. These categories are derived from the data. Clustering divides a dataset into mutually exclusive groups such that the members of each group are as *close* as possible to one another, and different groups are as *far* as possible from one

---

6. Brandel, M. 1995. Fermenting a new formula. *Computerworld.* June 1.

another, where distance is measured with respect to all available variables. The goal of clustering is to identify categories. Clustering could be used, for instance, to identify natural groupings of customers by processing all the available data on them. Examples of applications that can use clustering functions are market segmentation, discovering affinity groups, and defect analysis.

Prediction

Prediction calculates the future value of a variable. For example, it might be used to predict the revenue value of a new customer based on that person's demographic variables.

These various data mining techniques can be used together. For example, a sequence pattern analysis could identify potential customers (e.g., red jacket leads to gray skirt), and then classifying could be used to distinguish between those prospects who are converted to customers and those who are not (i.e., did not follow the sequential pattern of buying a gray skirt). This additional analysis should enable the retailer to further refine its marketing strategy to increase the conversion rate of red jacket customers to gray skirt purchasers.

Data mining technologies

Data miners use technologies that are based on statistical analysis and data visualization.

Decision trees

Tree-shaped structures can be used to represent decisions and rules for the classification of a dataset. As well as being easy to understand, tree-based models are suited to selecting important variables and are best when many of the predictors are irrelevant. For an example, see Figure 14-13.

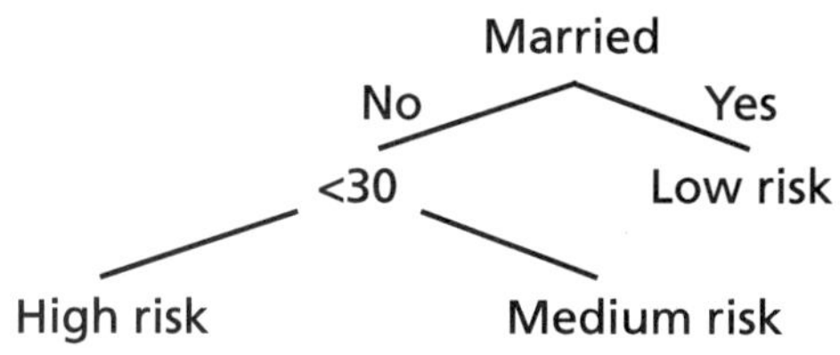

Figure 14-13. A decision tree

Genetic algorithms

Genetic algorithms are optimization techniques that use processes such as genetic combination, mutation, and natural selection in a design based on the concepts of evolution. Possible solutions for a problem compete with each other. In an evolutionary struggle of the survival of the fittest, the best solution survives the battle. Genetic algorithms are suited for optimization problems with many candidate variables (e.g., candidates for a loan).

K-nearest neighbor method

The nearest neighbor method is used for clustering and classification. In the case of clustering, the method first plots each record in n-dimensional space, where n attributes are used in the analysis. Then, it adjusts the weights for each dimension to cluster together data points with similar goal features. For instance, if the goal is to identify customers who frequently switch phone companies, the k-nearest method would adjust weights for relevant variables (such as monthly phone bill and percentage of non-U.S. calls) to cluster switching customers in the same neighborhood. Customers who did not switch would be clustered some distance apart.

Neural networks

A neural network, mimicing the neurophysiology of the human brain, can learn from examples to find patterns in data and classify data. While neural networks can be used for classification, they must first be trained to recognize patterns in a sample dataset. Once trained, a neural network can make predictions from new data. Neural networks are suited to combining information from many predictor variables and work well when many of the predictors are partially redundant. One shortcoming of a neural network is that it can be viewed as a black box with no explanation of the results provided. Often managers are reluctant to apply models they do not understand, and this can limit the applicability of neural networks.

Data visualization

Data visualization can make it possible for the analyst to gain a deeper, intuitive understanding of data. Because they present data in a visual format, visualization tools take advantage of our capability to rapidly discern visual patterns. Data mining can enable the analyst to focus attention on important patterns and trends and explore these in depth using visualization techniques. Data mining and data visualization work especially well together.

Conclusion

Data management is a rapidly evolving discipline. Where once the spotlight was clearly on TPSs and the relational model, there are now multiple centers of attention. In an information economy, the knowledge to be gleaned from data collected by routine transactions can be an important source of competitive advantage. The more an organization can learn about its customers by studying their behavior, the more likely it can provide superior products and services to retain existing customers and lure prospective buyers. As a result, data managers now have the dual responsibility of administering databases that keep the organization in business today and tomorrow. They must now master the organizational intelligence technologies described in this chapter.

The SAS data mining method

A senior statistician at SAS Institute, a large supplier of statistical analysis software, advocates a five-step process to data mining, which he calls SEMMA.

Sample:	extract a portion of the dataset for data mining. This set should be large enough to contain significant data and small enough for rapid data mining.
Explore:	search for unanticipated trends and relationships to gain insights to the data and ideas for further exploration.
Modify:	create, select, and transform variables with the intention of building a model.
Model:	specify a relationship of variables that reliably predicts a desired goal.
Assess:	evaluate the practical value of the findings and the model resulting from the data mining effort.

Source: SAS Institute. 1996. Data mining reveals the diamonds in your databases. *SAS Communications* 22(2): 15–21.

Summary

Organizations are increasingly realizing that data are a key resource. It is necessary for the daily operations of a business and its future success. Recent developments in hardware and software have given organizations the capability to accumulate and process vast collections of data using organizational intelligence technologies. Data warehouse software supports the creation and management of huge data stores. The choice of architecture, hardware, and software is critical to establishing a data warehouse. The two approaches to exploiting data are verification and discovery. DSS, EIS, and OLAP are mainly data verification methods. Data mining, a data discovery approach, uses statistical analysis techniques to discover ***hidden*** relationships. The relational model was not designed for OLAP, and the MDDB is the appropriate data store to support OLAP. MDDB design is based on recognizing variable and identifier dimensions.

Key terms and concepts

Association
Centralized data warehouse
Classifying
Cleaning
Clustering
Continuous variable
Database marketing
Data mart
Data mining
Data visualization
Data warehouse
Decision support system (DSS)
Decision tree
Discovery
Drill-down
Drill-through
Executive information system (EIS)
Extraction
Federated data warehouse
Genetic algorithm
Hypercube
Identifier dimension
Information systems cycle
K-nearest neighbor method
Loading
Management information system (MIS)
Massively parallel processor (MPP)
Metadata
Multidimensional database (MDDB)
Neural network
Nominal variable
Nonuniform memory access (NUMA)
Object-relational
On-line analytical processing (OLAP)
Operational data store (ODS)
Ordinal variable
Organizational intelligence
Prediction
Rotation
Scheduling
Sequential pattern
Star model
Super-relational system
Symmetric multiprocessor (SMP)
Tiered architecture
Transaction processing system (TPS)
Transformation
Variable dimension
Verification

References

Codd, E. F., S. B. Codd, and C. T. Salley. 1993. Beyond decision support. *Computerworld*, 87–89.

Finkelstein, R. 1995. MDD: Database reaches the next dimension. *Database Programming & Design* 8 (4):27–38.

Hurwicz, M. 1997. Take your data to the cleaners. *Byte* 22 (1):97–102.

Inmon, W. H. 1996. *Building the data warehouse*. 2nd ed. New York, NY: Wiley.

Thomsen, E. 1997. *OLAP solutions: Building multidimensional information systems*. New York, NY: Wiley.

Weldon, J. L. 1997. Warehouse cornerstones. *Byte* 22 (1):85–88.

Exercises

1. Identify data captured by a TPS at your university. Estimate how much data are generated in a year.
2. What data does your university need to support decision making? Does the data come from internal or external sources?
3. What database architecture would you recommend for your university?

4. What database architecture might be appropriate for a regional telephone company?
5. What database architecture might be appropriate for a global bank?
6. What special feature must you look for in software if you select an MPP?
7. Discuss the differences between a logical and a physical MDDB.
8. If your university were to implement a data warehouse, what examples of dirty data might you expect to find?
9. How frequently do you think a university should revise its data warehouse?
10. Write five data verification questions for a university data warehouse.
11. Write five data discovery questions for a university data warehouse.
12. Imagine you work as an analyst for a major global auto manufacturer. What techniques would you use for the following questions?
    a. How do sports car buyers differ from other customers?
    b. How should the market for trucks be segmented?
    c. Where does our major competitor have its dealers?
    d. How much money is a dealer likely to make from servicing a customer who buys a luxury car?
    e. What do people who buy midsize sedans have in common?
    f. What products do customers buy within six months of buying a new car?
    g. Who are the most likely prospects to buy a luxury car?
    h. What were last year's sales of compacts in Europe by country and quarter?
    i. We know a great deal about the sort of car a customer will buy based on demographic data (e.g., age, number of children, and type of job). What is a simple visual aid we can provide to sales personnel to help them show customers the car they are most likely to buy?
13. What impact is the Web likely to have on organizational intelligence technologies?
14. Discuss the conceptual views of a database presented by the relational, object, and multidimensional models. How do you reconcile these different views? Are they likely to cause confusion for data analysts?
15. An international airline has commissioned you to design a multidimensional database for its marketing department. Choose identifier and variable dimensions. List some of the analyses that could be performed against this database and the statistical technique that might be appropriate for them.
16. A regional telephone company needs your advice on the data it should include in its multidimensional database. It has an extensive relational database that captures details (e.g., calling and called phone numbers, time of day, cost, length of call) of every call. As well, it has access to extensive demographic data so it can allocate customers to one of 50 lifestyle categories. What data would you load into the multidimensional database? What aggregations would you use? It might help to identify initially the identifier and variable dimensions.
17. What are the possible dangers of data mining? How might you avoid these?
18. Download the file exped.dbf from the book's Web site and open it with MS Excel. This file is a sample of 1,000 sales transactions for The Expeditioner. For each sale, there is a row recording when it was sold, where it was sold, what was sold, how it

was sold, the quantity sold, and the sales revenue. Use the PivotTable Wizard (Data>PivotTable Report) to produce the following report:

Sum of REVENUE	HOW			
WHERE	Catalog	Store	Web	Grand Total
London	50,310	151,015	13,009	214,334
New York	8,712	28,060	2,351	39,123
Paris	32,166	104,083	7,054	143,303
Sydney	5,471	21,769	2,749	29,989
Tokyo	12,103	42,610	2,003	56,716
Grand Total	108,762	347,537	27,166	483,465

Continue to use the PivotTable Wizard to answer the following questions:

a. What was the value of catalog sales for London in the first quarter?
b. What percent of the total were Tokyo Web sales in the fourth quarter?
c. What percent of Sydney's annual sales were Catalog sales?
d. What was the value of catalog sales for London in January? Give details of the transactions.
e. What was the value of Camel saddle sales for Paris in 1997 by quarter?
f. How many Elephant polo sticks were sold in New York in each month of 1997?

15

The Web and Data Management

Experience is never limited, and it is never complete; it is an immense sensibility, a kind of huge spider-web of the finest silken threads suspended in the chamber of consciousness, and catching every air-borne particle in its tissue.

Henry James, *The Art of Fiction*, 1884

Learning objectives

Students completing this chapter will be able to

- ❖ design a Web site;
- ❖ understand the principles of Web site management;
- ❖ understand how a Web browser can access a database server;
- ❖ develop using PHP a Web-based interface to a relational DBMS;
- ❖ discuss the likely developments in data management technology for Web applications.

Introduction

The capability of organizations to capture, manage, and distribute organizational memory has been greatly enhanced by the development of Internet technology, in particular the use of Web browsers. Data managers now have a new domain. They must be concerned with managing the data stored on Web servers and making accessible, via a Web browser, data stored in organizational data stores.

The Web has given data management a more central role because organizations now have a cost-effective and simply mastered means of making organizational memory available to a wide range of stakeholders. For example:

- ❖ a UPS customer can track the status of her parcel;

- a Vanguard investor can check the value of his mutual funds;
- a supplier to GE can browse open contracts;
- an amateur photographer can read Kodak's advice on selecting film, composing photos, and using a flash.

As organizations are increasingly reliant on clearly communicating information to a wide variety of stakeholders, data managers must be familiar with the principles of information design, Web site management, database application development for the Web, and the use of Java as an application language.

Database problem stops trading

Charles Schwab & Co. was forced to temporarily switch its online trading Web site to a backup server for six hours because of a database problem, a move that blocked the discount broker's customers from receiving trade confirmation messages and left them unable to view their previous transaction records. Customers were instead asked to contact Schwab representatives by telephone.

The glitch at Schwab came less than three weeks after the Securities and Exchange Commission (SEC) released a report calling for brokerage firms and securities dealers to evaluate their online trading programs and try to "enhance their practices" in areas such as processing performance and security. Lori Richards, director of the SEC's Office of Compliance Inspections and Examinations, said it's becoming "ever more important for broker/dealers to ensure that their online systems are meeting the needs and expectations of investors," given the rapid growth in Internet-based trading.

Source: Trombly, M. 2001. Schwab database glitch cuts users off from some information. *Computerworld*, Feb. 13, http://www.computerworld.com/cwi/story/0,1199,NAV47_STO57675,00.html

Information presentation

Information technologies, such as a RDBMS and fast server, provide rapid access to extensive volumes of information, but just because a machine can retrieve information rapidly does not mean that humans can process it speedily. Information must be meaningfully organized for human consumption.[1]

The meaningful organization of data is termed **information architecture**.[2] Instances of information architecture are an annual report, a musical composition, or a Web site. An information architecture results from the arrangement of data elements into an interrelated system. Thus, a Web site is a cohesive assembly of pages, with each page composed of

1. This section is primarily based on Mok, C. 1966. *Designing business: multiple media, multiple disciplines*. San Jose, CA: Adobe. A beautiful, inspiring, and insightful book.
2. Information architecture is sometimes used to describe an organization's information technology collection. Here it has a broader sense, which embraces information technology architecture.

related information structures (e.g., text, hyperlinks, sounds, and images). This arrangement of information structures is known as **information design**. The thoughtful arrangement of information elements on a page is called **information arts**.

Organization models

There are seven universal models (see Table 15-1) for the organization of information. Text, audio, music, images, and video can be organized using these models. A novel is a *linear* organization, because data are organized and processed sequentially. A novel is designed to be read from cover to cover. The play-off chart for a tennis competition or the NCAA basketball tournament are instances of *hierarchical* structures even though usually turned sideways. A *web* is the underlying structure of a thesaurus, because readers can jump from one word to another, particularly with an electronic thesaurus. Timetables for airlines, trains, and buses follow a *parallel* structure. Details such as time and type of service, for any route, are listed in parallel—side by side or one under the other. Most calendars show dates in *matrix* format. All the days on which Monday occurs are shown in the same column and all the days of a week in the same row. With an electronic calendar, each cell of the matrix is active, and clicking on a cell results in the display of the details for that day. The *overlay* model is often used to show levels of detail. By turning the plastic sheets of an anatomical model, the reader peels away layers of a body. Some presenters use the overlay model to gradually reveal features on a single slide. *Spatial zoom* is seen on some Web pages. Clicking on a thumbnail of an image results in display of the object at full magnification. In the case of OLAP, drill-down is magnification.

Table 15-1: Information organization models

Type	Examples
Linear	A novel
Hierarchical	An organizational chart
Web	Thesaurus
Parallel	Airline timetable
Matrix	Calendar
Overlay	X-ray
Spatial zoom	Magnification of a thumbnail image

When designing the interface to a data collection, the designer must decide which of the information organization models is appropriate at the macro and micro level. At the macro level the designer needs to decide on the basic structure for the collection. A textbook author usually selects a linear structure for the macro level, but may use many of the other structures within this overall structure. Matrix structures (tables) are a common feature of many texts. The Web page designer has more design choices and decisions, because electronic media are inherently more flexible. Thus, a designer of a CD-ROM might settle on a hierarchical structure at the macro level, but then make extensive use of a Web organization to link sections of the text, as well as use many of the other information organization options.

The matrix format of the relational model is likely to be a fundamental feature of many information reports for managers. However, with the emergence of the Web browser as the common interface to information systems, designers now need to think about the broader structure within which tables are presented and reports accessed.

Information design

An information designer must understand how various information elements can work together to convey meaning. In the case of a Web site, this means comprehending how information elements support the design goals of a page, and how a collection of linked pages supports the design goals of a Web site. As well, the designer must decide which information organization models are appropriate for structuring data elements. For example, should a collection of images be presented using spatial zoom within a matrix structure, as a linear sequence of full-size images, or some other structure? In many cases the purpose of the project will determine the organizational structure and information elements. A price list, for example, is well suited to a matrix organization with possibly spatial zoom for additional details of any item. The information designer must always remember that the purpose is to enable people to find meaningful information quickly. The combination of purpose, organizational models, and information design creates a solution.

Navigation aids

When a Web site contains many pages, there is always the danger that visitors will get lost in a maze of pages and hyperlinks. Signs are necessary to let visitors know where they are and how to get around. Metropolitan railway systems (e.g., the London underground and Paris Métro) are good examples of navigation systems. There are large signs to tell travelers the name of the current station and maps for the various destinations. Similarly, each Web page should have signage to indicate the purpose of the current page and how to move to other pages.

The design process

The design of a Web site is a top-down process:

1. **Architecture**. The designer sketches the architecture of the site by broadly defining the content, navigation structure, and interface of the site. This means the goal of the site must be clearly described and a general idea of what is on each page identified, the navigation signage designed, and the look-and-feel of the interface delineated.
2. **Design**. The form of each section of the Web site is clarified, where a section is a collection of closely related pages. The main output of this stage is greater detail of the content, navigation, structure, and interface of each page.
3. **Information arts**. Information elements are added to each page to provide content, navigation signage, and the interface.

Many Web sites are at the heart of a hierarchical structure. Thus, a good starting point is to use the outliner in your word processor to sketch the architecture of the site, as illustrated in Figure 15-1.

Figure 15-1. Using an outliner for initial Web site design

```
Data management home page
  support
  revision
  exercises
    chapter 1
    chapter 2
    ...
    chapter 20
```

As you become more involved in design, you might create a more visual representation and also include details of the files stored on the Web site. Figure 15-2 indicates that the Web site is in the directory rwatson on the server www.negia.net. The directory is composed of several html files (e.g., index.html) and subdirectories (e.g., exercises).

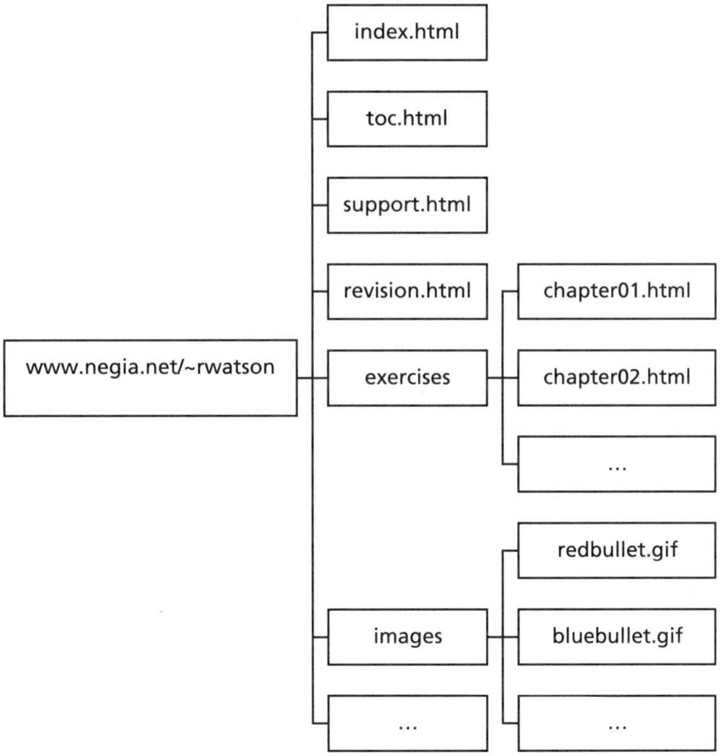

Figure 15-2. A Web site's hierarchical structure

The default entry point for a Web site is usually the file called index.html. For example, the URL for this book's supporting Web site is http://www.wiley.com/college/watson, which means the browser first accesses the server known as www.wiley.com,then the directory college/watson, and then the file index.html. It is a good idea to adopt this convention (i.e., the default entry point being index.html), because it is widely followed and requires less typing.

During design, you should also specify nonhierarchical linkages. For example, visitors might find it useful to be able to move directly from the exercises for Chapter 1 to those of Chapter 2, and so on, as illustrated by the partial Web site design of Figure 15-3. In addition to the forward links, there are backward links. A Web site management tool should support graphical design of the relationship between Web pages and automatic generation of the links between pages. This would relieve much of the tedious work of creating and maintaining a Web site.

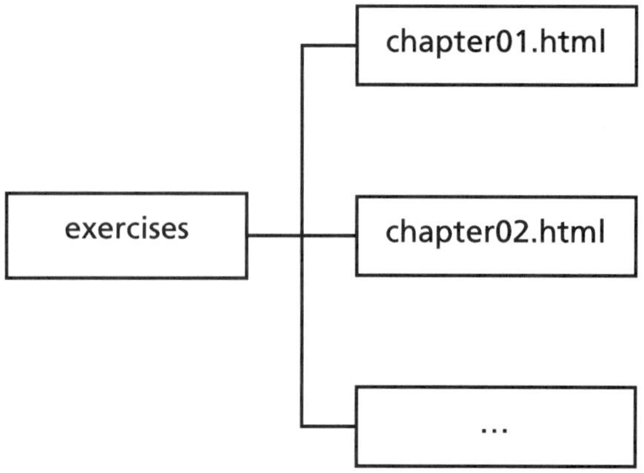

Figure 15-3. Defining linkages between Web pages

Consistency

Visitors to a Web site will find navigation easier if the site has a consistent layout and set of icons. This means a uniform design for each page, including standard navigation icons in the same place on each page. To maintain consistency, a Web site management tool should permit the specification of a common page layout for all pages in a site. This does not mean every page has exactly the same layout, but that there is an evident consistency that assists the visitor to move about the site. For instance, root-level pages may have different navigation aids from those at the second level in the Web page hierarchy, but all pages should have a very similar look and feel. A Web site management tool that supports site level or global changes (e.g., changing the image representing the left icon on all pages) simplifies maintaining consistency and is especially valuable when a site contains hundreds of pages. Style sheets, which you will learn about in Chapter 16, also support consistency.

A performance, not a system

Think of a Web site as a Broadway performance rather than a system. A Web site is designed to attract visitors and encourage them to browse the site. Traditional information systems are very utilitarian—information only and no pizzazz. Web sites are often entertaining and informative.

A firm's Web site is often the most definitive impression of a company and the main conduit for communicating with a wide range of stakeholders. The combined skills of Marketing and MIS must be effectively combined, so that a firm's Web site conveys the desired image and communicates clearly. Marketing front-end skills must be integrated with MIS back-end expertise to create the appropriate performance for each Web visitor.

This means that the front-end of a Web system—what the visitor sees—may change often, just like the window display of a retail store. Marketing personnel will want to continually revise, and sometimes completely revamp, a firm's Web pages. Unchanging marketing displays and Web sites convey the image of a static company with no new products or services. MIS is not very familiar with building and managing such systems. Traditional MIS applications change more slowly. Because a Web site is more like a performance than a system, data management is more dynamic. Thus, Web site management tools should support rapid development of a new front-end.

The back-end of a Web site is frequently an existing MIS system. For example, the UPS[3] parcel tracking system relies on a database that was created prior to the development of the Web. MIS has considerable experience managing these types of applications and traditional data management tools, such as relational technology, are applicable. Linking the back-end to the front-end will be discussed in this chapter.

Web site management

A Web site is a collection of text (HTML code) and image files (e.g., gif and jpg files) and may also include audio, video, animation, and other file types. Once an organization's Web site exceeds more than a dozen pages, a data management problem emerges, and tools for managing the site are required. Web site data-management software has different features from database technology, because the stored data have different characteristics. It is not as structured as data in a production planning system. Web site management tools typically have two components: page creation and site management.

Creating and maintaining HTML files

The Web is a client/server system in which the client is called a **browser**. The **server** contains files that are converted by the browser for display on a monitor. The file pulled from the server by the browser contains instructions written in **Hypertext Markup Language (HTML)**, a language for describing how a Web browser should display a file from a server, declaring hyperlinks, and defining multimedia objects included with a Web document.

3. www.ups.com

HTML editors, such as Adobe GoLive and Microsoft FrontPage, accelerate the creation and maintenance of Web pages. HTML editors permit you to lay out text and images in a WYSIWYG mode, as illustrated in Figure 15-4.

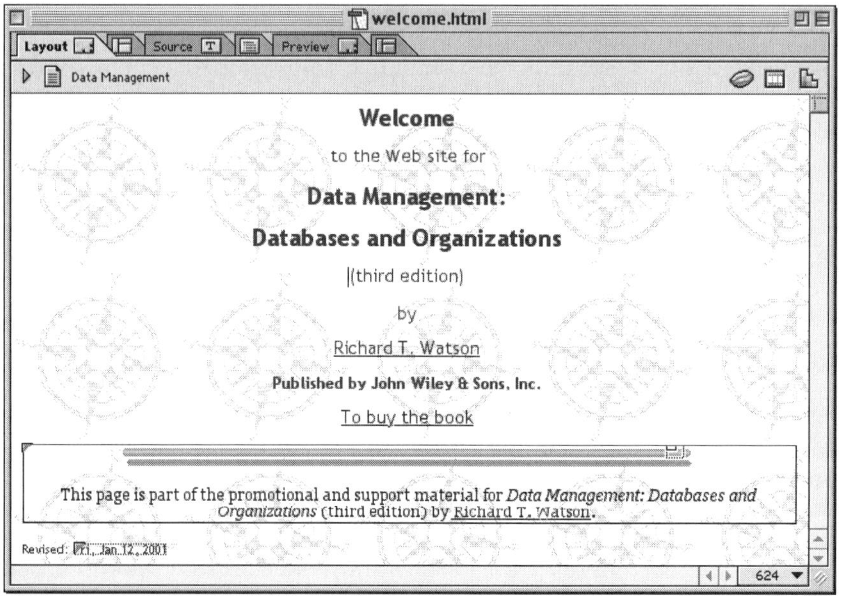

Figure 15-4. A HTML editor in WYSIWYG mode

Managing a Web site

Managing the many files and links in a Web site requires appropriate software. Although there are several alternatives available, this section focuses on Adobe GoLive. Each of its major features will be discussed.

Visual site management

Site management software will typically display the organization and layout of a Web site in a variety of ways. For example, you might want to visualize the links to and from a particular html file (see Figure 15-5), the hierarchical structure of the site, or a site's external links. These and other features of a site's structure are generally provided by Web site management software.

Automatic link changes

When you change a file name, all the files that link to it are automatically changed to reflect the file's new name. This is a very useful feature and helps to avoid the dreaded 404 message, "Error! The file you requested was not found."

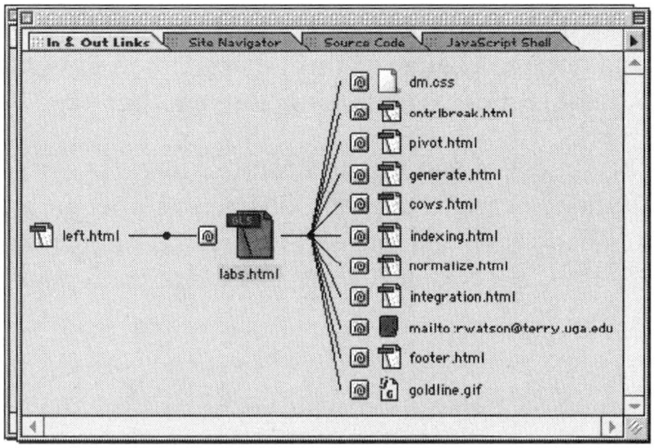

Figure 15-5. GoLive link view

Link checker

Broken links are a major source of irritation to Web visitors. That is, a visitor clicks on a link and gets the all too familiar 404 message. Detecting and repairing broken links are a data management problem, because an invalid link means a visitor cannot access data. A broken link is akin to a missing foreign key (recall the referential integrity rule).

A Web site has internal links and external links. Files within the site's root directory are internal links, those outside are external links. The link checker verifies the status of all links and reports those that are broken. The difficult task, more so for external links, is to find the link's new name if it still exists. Link checker also reports any files that are not referenced by any HTML files within the site. The link checker should be run on a regular basis to maintain the integrity of a Web site, because URLs tend to change frequently, as illustrated in Figure 15-6, where the bug icon indicates a broken link.

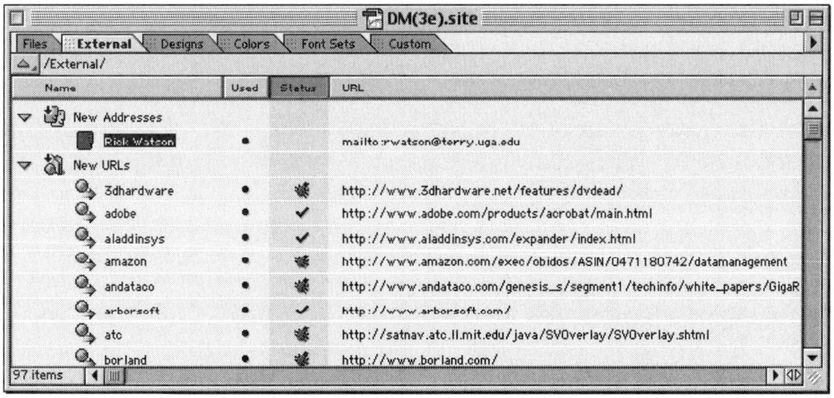

Figure 15-6. External link checking

Another goal of the broken-link issue is to ensure that other Web sites linked to your Web site remain valid. For instance, if the support site for this book were changed to www.rick-watson.nom, there would be a need to change all links that pointed to www.wiley.com/college/watson. Fortunately, finding those pages that link to another page is very easy.

Links to a particular site can be checked by using the advanced features of a search engine, such as Google. On the advanced search page of Google, you specify a page-specific search for the link www.wiley.com/college/watson. The search engine will identify all pages linked to this URL. You then need to notify the owners of each page that the URL has changed.

Web site publishing

The usual procedure is to maintain a copy of all Web site files on your personal computer and transfer these files, using FTP, to the Web server upon completion of any changes. Site management software should make uploading a site a one or two click process and should also only upload those pages that have changed.

Data management guidelines

Two simple guidelines greatly facilitate the management of Web site data.

All images in one file

Store all images (i.e., gifs and jpgs) in one file. This means you can have a single, common library of images. Usually, the image file is one level below the root directory, as shown in Figure 15-2.

Consistent naming

Some Web servers are case sensitive (e.g., they distinguish between mis/index.html and MIS/index.html). Consequently, if you spell the URL correctly, but get the case wrong, then you get the dreaded 404. To avoid this problem, many Web site developers lowercase all file names. This is a sensible convention to adopt.

Resource Description Framework

One of the major issues of Web data management is the difficulty in automating many tasks, because the Web mainly operates as a forum for human interaction. Since most Web documents are written for human consumption, the only available form of searching is to simply match words or sentences contained in documents. This is not very effective, and many found items are irrelevant.

What we need is a more precise description of what is on the Web. Then, we can move the Web from machine-readable to machine-understandable, which would greatly facilitate more efficient use of the Web.

The Resource Description Framework (RDF) is a general framework for describing any Internet resource, such as a Web site and its content. An Internet resource is defined as any resource with a Uniform Resource Identifier (URI). This includes the Uniform Resource Locators (URL) that identify entire Web sites and specific Web pages.

An RDF description can include metadata, such as the authors of the resource, date of creation or updating, the organization of the pages on a site, information that describes content in terms of audience or content rating, key words for search engine data collection, subject categories, and so forth.

An RDF makes it possible for everyone to share Web site and other descriptions more easily and for software developers to build products that can use the metadata to provide better search engines and directories, to act as intelligent agent, and to give Web users more control of what they are viewing. The RDF is an application of XML (see Chapter 16). A sample RDF is shown in Table 15-2.

Table 15-2: A sample RDF

```
<rdf:RDF xmlns:rdf="http://www.w3.org/1999/02/22-rdf-syntax-ns#"
         xmlns:dc="http://purl.org/dc/elements/1.0/">
   <rdf:Description rdf:about="http://www.wiley.com/college/watson"
      dc:creator="Richard T. Watson"
      dc:title="Data Management"
     dc:description="Support for the 3rd edition of Data Management: Databases
          and Organizations by Richard T. Watson"
      dc:date="2001-07-01" />
</rdf:RDF>
```

As a device for managing data describing Web resources, the RDF is another tool of which data managers should be aware. It is particularly relevant for those who manage Web sites. The RDF is a work in progress and is still not widely implemented.[4]

Web browser to DBMS server connectivity

The Web browser has emerged as a popular interface to database applications for several important reasons. *First*, there is a one-time installation. Once a browser has been installed, all Web-based applications are accessible. Deployment of new systems is easy and fast. Client/server systems require a new client to be installed for each application. *Second*, the Web is global, and those in remote locations can easily connect to the application. *Third*, the simple page-oriented design of Web applications makes application development relatively straightforward. *Fourth*, once people have learned how to use a browser, they acquire most of the skills for using any new application, and training costs are lower. Consequently, it is not surprising that many organizations have adopted the Web browser as the standard interface to most applications.

Web applications are **thin client** systems (see page 363 for a comparison of thin and fat clients). Converting legacy applications to thin-client Web applications is generally easier

4. For more information, see http://www.w3.org/RDF/#overview.

than converting them to fat clients, because mainframe applications expect the client to do so little. With a thin client, most of the work is done by the server, and as a result, network traffic is lower, because there is less need to exchange messages between the client and the server.

Browsers interface to a DBMS server via a three-tier architecture (see Figure 15-7). The first tier is the browser. This tier operates with any browser (e.g., Internet Explorer on a Macintosh or Netscape Navigator on Windows). The first tier may have some application logic, for instance some JavaScript to validate an input form. The Web server, the second tier, processes the bulk of the application logic, and manages security and access to the application. It also is a client to DBMS servers. It issues DBMS commands to DBMS servers, the third tier, which contain the data and referential integrity rules. The DBMS servers can be those of a variety of vendors. Briefly, the first tier handles presentation, the second processes application logic, and the third manages data.

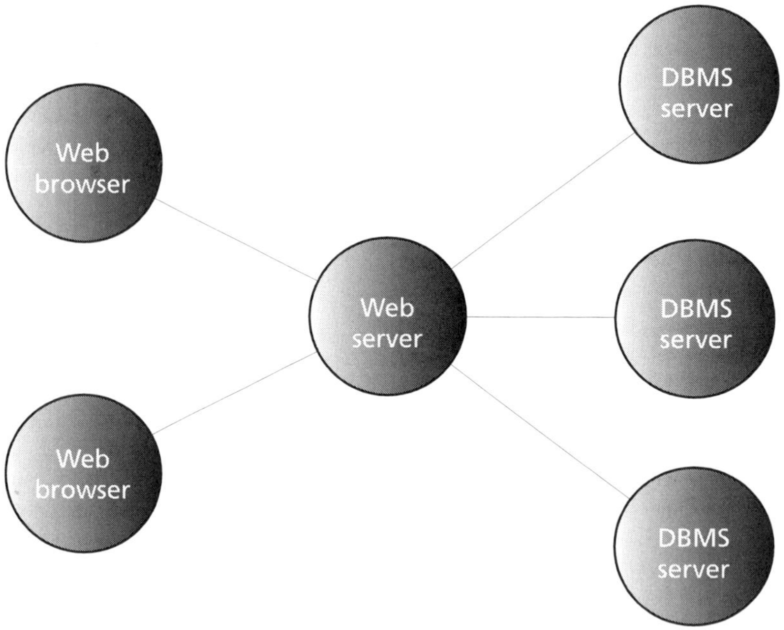

Figure 15-7. Three-tier architecture

Options

The marketplace currently provides many ways of interfacing a Web browser to a DBMS server. Nearly every DBMS vendor offers such software, and there are a variety of third-party vendors. Software developers usually prefer a vendor independent approach or a method that works on multiple platforms. In keeping with this goal, this section discusses PHP, which satisfies the multiple platforms' criterion, and Java programming language, which is vendor independent and cross-platform. The section concludes with a discussion of CORBA.

Other server-side technologies are now briefly discussed before commencing the coverage of PHP, a vendor independent server-side scripting language.

Common gateway interface (CGI)

A CGI program is a gateway between the browser request and the data required. Perl is the most popular of the many languages for CGI programming. The downside of CGI is that it does not scale well to handle high transaction volumes.

Proprietary Web server APIs

Both Microsoft and Netscape have written application programming interfaces (APIs) to support server-side processing. The major shortcoming of using this approach is that it ties the application to the particular vendor's server software.

ASP

Active server pages (ASP) combines HTML, scripting, and server-side components into a single file called an Active Server Page. Scripting can be in Jscript (Microsoft's version of JavaScript) or VBScript. ASP operates only with Microsoft's Web servers (e.g., IIS) on its operating systems (e.g., Windows NT), and thus portability is restricted.

SSJS

Netscape's competitor to ASP is server-side JavaScript (SSJS), which is based on HTML and JavaScript. Because it is limited to Netscape servers, it has the same shortcomings as ASP. Another problem is that SSJS applications must be compiled before execution.

Java Servlets and JSP

Java servlets and JavaServer pages (JSP) are based on the Java programming language. Sun's Java Servlet APIs are extensions to Java to support server-side processing by Java Servlets. A JSP combines HTML, Java code, and JavaBeans components, and thus is similar in concept to ASP and SSJS. The major problem with the Java-based approach is that Java is difficult for novice programmers to learn.

PHP

PHP, developed in 1994 by Rasmus Lerdorf to track visitors to his on-line resume, was released in 1995 as personal home page tools. Since then, PHP has been embraced by the Web community and has gained considerable acceptance among commercial sites because it is free and open source. It is an alternative to Microsoft's Active Server Page (ASP) technology. In May 2000, PHP 4.0 was released.

A PHP application consists of HTML and PHP script, which are executed by the server before sending a page of HTML code to the browser. Because PHP generates HTML, it works with any browser. In addition, PHP is platform independent and versions are available for most operating systems and Web servers, including popular ones such as Apache and IIS.

PHP server-side processing offers several important advantages, including:

- There is less network traffic, because the browser has to send fewer commands to the server.
- PHP generates HTML, so, it works with any browser.
- It is a simple interface to a DBMS.
- PHP code cannot be seen by the browser user, and thus security is high.

PHP basics

Before considering how to use PHP to access a database, let's get familiar with some of the basics.

- PHP code is embedded within an HTML page.[5]
- PHP code is surrounded by the pair of tags <?php and ?>.
- The command ***echo*** outputs a character string.

Your turn

1. Use a text editor or HTML editor to create the code in Table 15-3.
2. Load the code using FTP to your Web server account as the file simple.php.
3. Execute the code via your Web browser (e.g., http://ebiz.terry.uga.edu/~rwatson/simple.php).
4. View the source of the page displayed (for IE, use View > Source).

Table 15-3: An elementary PHP script (simple.php)

```
<html>
  <?php
    echo "PHP displays this message.";
  ?>
</html>
```

The PHP script of Table 15-3 produces the display shown in Figure 15-8.

Some more basic PHP knowledge is necessary before you can do more scripting:

- // indicates the remainder of the line is a comment.
- Multiline comments are surrounded by /* and */.

5. Basic familiarity with HTML is assumed for this section.

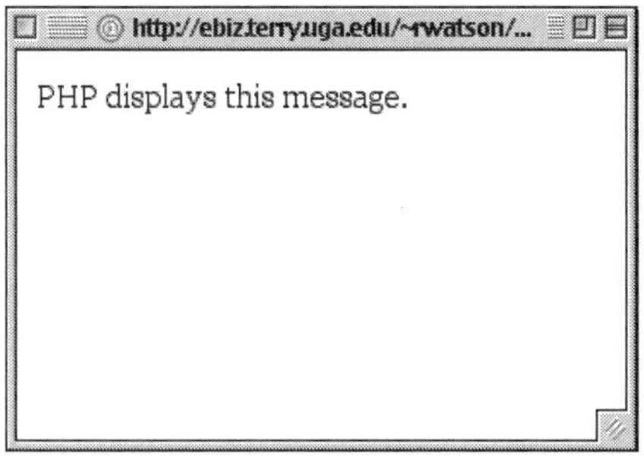

Figure 15-8. Browser display for simple.php

- All variable names start with '$' (e.g., $db_name).
- PHP is a weakly typed language, and variables need not be defined prior to their first use.

Database access with PHP

Having completed the previous example, you now know that PHP is relatively simple to code and execute. After learning a few more commands, you will be able to access a database and display the results via a Web browser. You will remember from Chapter 10 that OBDC is the defacto standard for database connectivity (see page 270), and we will focus on these commands.

A program written using OBDC commands can access any database supporting the OBDC standard. There will, however, be a performance overhead when using OBDC commands if these are not natively supported by the DBMS. Some systems (e.g., IBM's DB2) support OBDC natively and thus avoid the performance problem. Once you have learned how to apply the OBDC commands, it is an easy step to write a PHP script that is DBMS specific (e.g., Oracle or Interbase).

Making the connection

The first step for any script is to connect from the client to the database. The following code (Table 15-4) defines the data necessary to make the connection.

Table 15-4: Connecting to a database (connect.php)

```
<html>
  <?php
  // Connection data
  $db_name = "sample";
  $db_username = "rwatson";
  $db_passwd = "secret";
  $connect = odbc_pconnect($db_name,$db_username,$db_passwd);
  ?>
</html>
```

The characters strings database name, userid, and password[6] are required by ***odbc_pconnect***. The ***odbc_pconnect*** {7}[7] command returns a link identifier, $connect in this case, which is used to identify future connections during the current session.

Your turn

1. Create a file called connect.php containing the preceding code, and FTP it to your Web server account.
2. Run the code as is.
3. Make a change to $db_passwd so that it is invalid, run the code, and note the error message.

There are two types of connection commands: ***odbc_connect*** and ***odbc_pconnect.*** A connection created by ***odbc_pconnect*** is persistent and saves the overhead of creating and closing a connection when, over a short period of time, a large number of connections are made to the server. As a default, use persistent connections, especially if you are planning to do transaction processing.

Executing SQL

SQL commands are embedded within a PHP script. In the following example, the SQL code is stored in $query. The ***odbc_exec*** command sends the SQL command to the DBMS server, which returns a table into $result. The table is displayed by using ***obdc_result_all*** (see Table 15-5).

Table 15-5: Executing SQL (execsql.php)

```
1  <html>
2    <?php
3    // Connection data
4    $db_name = "sample";
5    $db_username = "rwatson";
6    $db_passwd = "secret";
7    $connect = odbc_pconnect($db_name,$db_username,$db_passwd);
8    $sql = "select * from shr";
9    echo $sql;
10   $result=odbc_exec($connect,$sql);
11   odbc_result_all($result);
12   ?>
13 </html>
```

While the preceding code can be used to execute any SQL command, it is cumbersome to use such an approach every time you want to run SQL. What we need is a PHP-based application for entering and executing SQL commands. The coding is simpler to understand if we break this application into two parts: one for entering the SQL command and the other for executing the command.

---

6. You will need to get these data from the instructor for your course.
7. In this chapter, numbers in {} refer to line numbers in the corresponding PHP script.

The command entry part is simply a form for entering an SQL command. It requires only HTML code, as illustrated in Table 15-6. The code generates the entry screen shown in Figure 15-9.

Table 15-6: SQL command entry form (sqlcmd.html)

```
1  <html>
2    <title>SQL interface</title>
3    <body bgcolor="white">
4      <form method="post" action="execsqlcmd.php">
5        Enter SQL query<br>
6        <textarea name="sqlcmd" rows="5" cols="60"></textarea><br>
7        <input type="Submit">
8      </form>
9    </body>
10 </html>
```

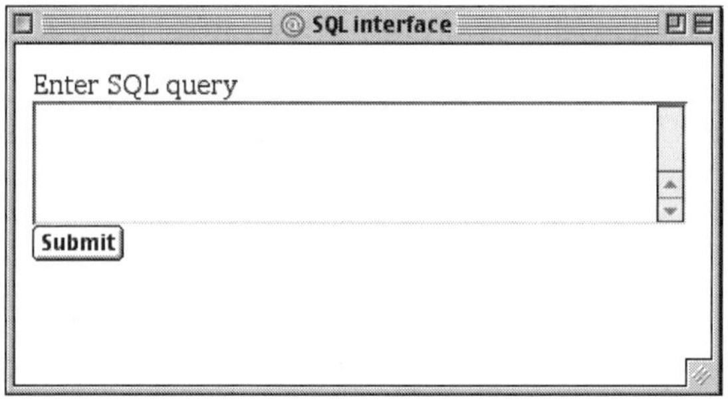

Figure 15-9. SQL command entry form

The SQL command is entered in the text box area and stored in the variable sqlcmd (the textarea name) {6}. Finally, the variable sqlcmd is passed to the application sqlexec.php (the action specification for the form) {4}, when the submit command is selected. Execution of the SQL is performed by sqlexeccmd.php (see Table 15-7).

Because quotes have significance to PHP, any quotes in entered text are preceded by a backslash (\). For example, (`select * from shr where shrcode = "FC"`) will be converted to (`select * from shr where shrcode = \"FC\"`) before passing to PHP for processing. Thus, when a PHP application receives an SQL command, the slashes must be removed before passing the SQL command to the DBMS. The ***stripslashes*** function {9}, as the name suggests, removes slashes.

A good interface will display the SQL executed command. Because HTML represents special characters in a particular way (e.g., $lt for an <), any character string destined for browser display must be converted to HTML, which is the purpose of the ***htmlspecialchars*** function {10}. In PHP, the concatenation symbol is the period (.). The "
\n" at the end for the ***echo*** function line generates a new line {10}. Finally, the form section of the application passes control to sqlcmd.html when the submit button is clicked {14}.

Table 15-7: SQL execution (execsqlcmd.php)

```
<html>
  <body bgcolor="white">
    <?php
    // Connection data
    $db_name = "sample";
    $db_username = "rwatson";
    $db_passwd = "secret";
    $connect = odbc_pconnect($db_name,$db_username,$db_passwd);
    $query=stripslashes($sqlcmd);
    echo "Query: " . htmlspecialchars($query) . "<br>\n";
    $result=odbc_exec($connect,$query);
    odbc_result_all($result);
    ?>
    <form action="sqlcmd.html">
      <input type="submit" value="New query">
    </form>
  </body>
</html>
```

Your turn

1. Create sqlcmd.html and execsqlcmd.php in your Web account.
2. Test your work by creating a table, inserting two or three rows, and querying the table.

Error handling

So far, we have ignored the possibility of any errors in the execution of SQL commands. This is a folly we need to correct now. Most PHP functions return 0 if an error is detected. Thus, you can use a conditional ***if*** statement to detect and report errors. The code in Table 15-8 shows how an ***if*** statement {11} is used to detect and report an error. Sometimes the DBMS will also report the error.

Table 15-8: Error detection (execsqlerr.php)

```
1  <html>
2    <?php
3    // Connection data
4    $db_name = "sample";
5    $db_username = "rwatson";
6    $db_passwd = "secret";
7    $connect = odbc_pconnect($db_name,$db_username,$db_passwd);
8    $sql = "select * from shr";
9    echo $sql;
10   $result=odbc_exec($connect,$sql);
11   if($result == 0) echo "SQL command error";
12   odbc_result_all($result);
13   ?>
14 </html>
```

Your turn

1. Create execsqlerr.php in your Web account.
2. Investigate and report the results produced by various errors:
   a. Table does not exist.
   b. Column does not exist.
   c. SQL syntax error.
3. How would you make the code in Table 15-8 more robust?

Bulk loading

When converting data from a file management system to a relational database system, you will want to do a bulk load. For example, you might have data in a spreadsheet that you now want to store as a database table. As you already know, you can insert rows one-at-time using `INSERT`. To do a bulk load, you write a script that reads one record at a time from the file, creates the SQL insert command for the corresponding row, and executes that command. In other words, you use a loop structure to read records and write rows until all records have been read.

The code in Table 15-9 shows the following:

- The file alien.dat is opened for reading {6}. This file is in the same directory as the PHP script.
- If there is an error with opening the file, the script is terminated {7}.
- The field delimiter is a tab, which has an ASCII code of 9 {12}.
- The loop processes records from the file until end-of-file is detected {13-26}.
- The ***fgets*** function reads a record of up to 1024 characters in length {14}. In practice, set the length to some value greater than the longest record.
- The ***split*** function breaks up the input record into its constituent fields and stores them in a list {15}.
- The insert is constructed by concatenating the various pieces together {17-23}.
- The SQL command is executed {25} and the loop continues.

Your turn

1. Get a copy of the file cntrycode.dat from the book's Web site.
2. FTP this to your Web site account.
3. Create a table called COUNTRY, which has two columns, CNTRYCODE AND CNTRYNAME. Inspect cntrycode.dat to determine the data type for each column.
4. Write a PHP script to load the table COUNTRY with the data from cntrycode.dat.
5. Query the table to verify your script has worked as intended.

Table 15-9: Bulk loading of a table (bulkload.php)

```
<?php
$db_name = "sample";
$db_username = "rwatson";
$db_passwd = "secret";
$connect = odbc_pconnect($db_name,$db_username,$db_passwd);
$file = fopen ("alien.dat", "r");
if (!$file) { // ! is NOT symbol so this tests whether $file is false
    echo "<p>Unable to open remote file.\n";
    exit;
    }
// the script assumes fields in the file are tab delimited
  $delimiter = chr(9);
while (!feof ($file)) { // read while not at end-of-file
    $record = fgets ($file, 1024); // read a record
    list($alnum,$alname,$alheads,$alcolor,$alsmell) = split($delimit-
           er,$record); // separate into fields
    $insertcmd = "insert into alien values (" // head of insert
    . $alnum . "," // a numeric column
    . "'" . $alname . "'" . "," // a character column
    . $alheads . "," // a numeric column
    . "'" . $alcolor . "'" . "," // a character column
    . "'" . $alsmell . "'" // a character column
    . ")"; // tail of insert
    echo $insertcmd . "<br>\n";
    $result=odbc_exec($connect,$insertcmd);
    }
fclose($file);
?>
```

Map collection case

The Expeditioner has added a new product line to meet the needs of its changing clientele. It now stocks a range of maps. The firm's data modeler has created a data model describing the situation (see Figure 15-10). A map has a scale (e.g., a scale of 1:1 000 000 means that 1 unit on the map is 1,000,000 units on the ground (i.e., 1 cm is 10 kms, or 1 inch is ~16 miles). There are three types of maps: road, rail, and canal.

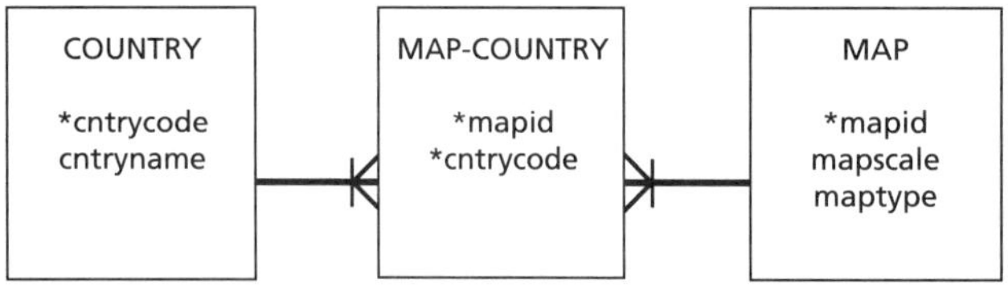

Figure 15-10. The Expeditioner's map collection data model

Data entry

Once the tables have been defined, we want to insert some records. This could be done using the scripts just created, but it would be very tedious as we would type INSERT statements for each row (e.g., `INSERT INTO MAP VALUES (1, 1000000, 'Rail'))`.

A better approach is to create a HTML data entry form, as illustrated by the code in Table 15-10, which results in the data entry screen shown in Figure 15-11.

Table 15-10: HTML for data entry (mapinsert.html)

```
1  <html>
2    <head>
3      <title>Map insert</title>
4    </head>
5    <body bgcolor="white">
6        <h2>Map data entry</h2>
7      </div>
8      <form name="MapInsert" action="mapinsert.php" method="post">
9        <p>Map identifier: <input type="text" name="mapid" size="13">
10       <p>Scale: <input type="text" name="mapscale" size="24" value="">
11             (e.g., enter 1:1000 as 1000)
12       <p>Type: <select name="maptype" size="1">
13           <option selected>Select map type</option>
14           <option value="Canal">Canal</option>
15           <option value="Rail">Rail</option>
16           <option value="Road">Road</option>
17         </select>
18       <p><input type="submit" name="submitbutton" value="Submit">
19     </form>
20   </body>
21 </html>
```

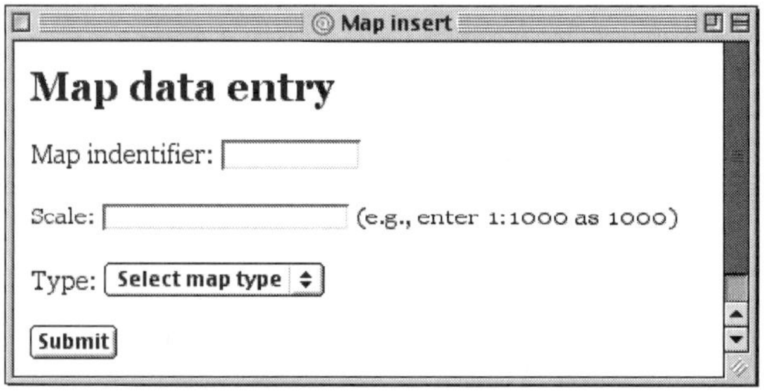

Figure 15-11. Map collection data entry form (mapinsert.html)

Inspection of the HTML code reveals that on submission of the form, control is passed to mapindb.php {8}, which is a script (see Table 15-11) to create the `INSERT` statement (for adding a row to the map database and execute the statement.

Your Turn

1. Copy from the book's supporting Web site the code in Tables 15-10 and 15-11 and FTP it into your Web account.
2. Execute mapinsert.html and experiment with data entry.
3. Query MAP to review the results of the data entry.

Table 15-11: PHP to insert a row (mapinsert.php)

```
<html>
  <body bgcolor="white">
    <?php
    // Connection data
    $db_name = "sample";
    $db_username = "rwatson";
    $db_passwd = "secret";
    $connect = odbc_pconnect($db_name,$db_username,$db_passwd);
    // create the insert statement
    $insertcmd = "insert into map values ("
      . $mapid . "," . $mapscale . "," . "'" . $maptype . "'" . ")";
    echo $insertcmd . "<br>\n";
    $result=odbc_exec($connect,$insertcmd);
    ?>
    <form action="mapinsert.html">
      <input type="submit" value="New map">
    </form>
  </body>
</html>
```

Data validation

A significant shortcoming of the code for inserting a row is that it does not validate the data entered. It assumes entry of numeric values for both mapid and mapscale and selection of a valid map type. This is a dangerous assumption, and we will need to add some code for data validation.

Data can be validated on the client- or server-side. JavaScript,[8] originally created by Netscape, is a standard language[9] well suited to client-side data validation. It is supported by the two most common browsers (i.e., Internet Explore and Netscape Navigator), so it provides considerable platform independence. If you want to learn more, you will find there are on-line tutorials[10] and textbooks readily available.

We will focus on server-side validation using PHP, because you have already learned some PHP. To introduce JavaScript would make this section doubly difficult, due to the syntactical differences between PHP and JavaScript. At this point, we will examine some code segments for data validation, and, in the next section on transaction processing, show the complete PHP script.

Numeric validation

Values that should be numeric can be validated using the ***settype*** function, which explicitly sets the data type of a variable. If the function fails to set the data type because the value entered is invalid, ***settype*** returns false. The following code (Table 15-12) illustrates how to check whether an entered value is numeric.

---

8. Microsoft's version is called JScript.
9. Approved as international standard ISO/IEC 16262 in April 1998.
10. For example, see http://wdvl.com/Authoring/JavaScript/.

Table 15-12: Numeric validation

```
settype ($mapid,integer); // sets to false if variable contains alphas
if ($mapid == false)
  echo = "Map identifier must be numeric";
```

Selection validation

When the input value can be selected from a pull down list, as in selecting the type of map, it is important to check that a value is selected. The following code (Table 15-13) demonstrates selection validation.

Table 15-13: Selection validation

```
if ($maptype == "Select map type")
  echo "No map type selected";
```

Transaction processing

Consider the map case, when you enter the details for a map it is convenient to also define the countries on the map. This means you want to insert one row in MAP, and insert as many rows as necessary in MAP-COUNTRY to record details of the number of countries represented on the map. One problem is that we don't know the maximum number of countries that any map will cover, so we need to have an open-ended approach (i.e., a loop) to entering countries on a map. One approach is to have a script (addmap.php) that captures details of the map and the name of at least one country (since all maps have at least one country), and another script (addcountry.php) that captures the other countries on the map. This second script can be used repeatedly until all countries have been entered (see Figure 15-12), at which point the transaction is committed.

When there is more than one script for an application, as in this case, we often need to share data among the scripts. In fact, for this transaction, if we have a map with four countries, we will execute addmap.php once and addcountry.php three times. Thus, in this case, we need to share data across four executed scripts during a single transaction. However, there is a problem. HTTP (the communication protocol of the Web) is connectionless, meaning that each request to a Web server is independent of all the other requests. In other words, the Web server does not remember data between requests. In PHP, the **session** commands support data sharing or remembering data between Web server requests. Variables to be remembered are identified by the ***session_register*** function (see Table 15-14), which is executed by the script that begins the session. It is useful, in the case of transaction processing, to associate a session with a transaction. Each transaction constitutes one session.

To access shared variable in subsequent scripts, you simply need to place ***session_start()*** at the beginning of the PHP script (e.g., see Table 15-22) to access the variables defined by session_register for the current session. Variables captured by the form that called the script, however, must be explicitly set using the $HTTP_POST_VARS function.

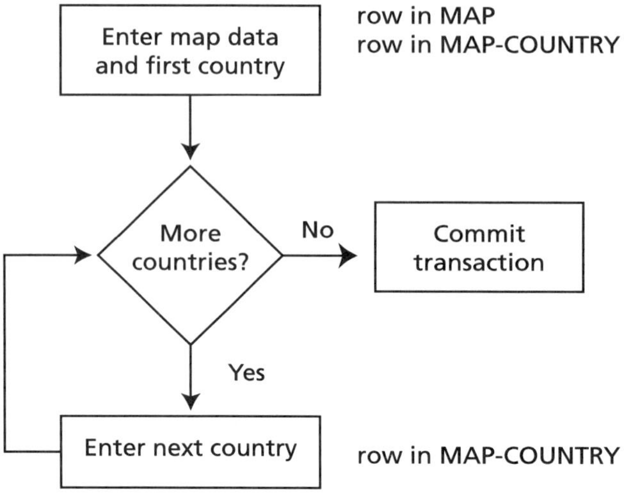

Figure 15-12. Flowchart for map and countries data capture

Table 15-14: Specifying sessions variables

```
<?php
// Set session registers
session_register("mapid");
session_register("mapscale");
session_register("maptype");
session_register("country");
session_register("cntcount");
session_register("cntrycode");
?>
```

Now we have all the pieces to put together a transaction to enter details of a map and the countries represented. The script will also do some validation (the missing pieces will be left for you to complete).

All the code for displaying forms is in a single file, common.php, which is included in each script. However, to make the explanation easier, the file is broken up into its constituent functions.

The scripter-defined mapentryform function (see Table 15-15) generates the HTML to create the form (Figure 15-13) for map data entry. The form supports three possible actions: add another country (i.e., the map covers more than one country), finish the transaction (i.e., the map has one country), or terminate the transaction (i.e., do not insert the data into the database). When any of the buttons on the form are clicked, the script addmap.php is executed.

The scripter-defined mapcntentryform function (see Table 15-16) generates the HTML to create the form (see Figure 15-14) for adding another country to the map. This form offers

Table 15-15: Function mapentryform

```
<? } ?><?php function mapentryform() { ?>
<html>
  <head>
    <title>Map Management System</title>
  </head>
  <body bgcolor="white">
  <h2>Map data entry</h2>
    <form name="mapinsert" method="post" action = "addmap.php">
      <p>Map identifier: <input type="text" name="mapid" size="12" > </p>
      <p>Scale: <input type="text" name="mapscale" size="25"> (e.g., enter
           1:1000 as 1000)</p>
      <p>Type: <select name="maptype" size="1">
          <option selected>Select map type</option>
          <option value="Canal">Canal</option>
          <option value="Rail">Rail</option>
          <option value="Road">Road</option>
        </select></p>
      <p>Country: <select name="cntrycode" size="1">
          <option selected>Select country</option>
          <option value="at">Austria</option>
          <option value="be">Belgium</option>
          <option value="fr">France</option>
          <option value="de">Germany</option>
          <option value="nl">Netherlands</option>
          <option value="ch">Switzerland</option>
        </select></p>
      <p><input type="submit" name="action" value="Add another country">
      <input type="submit" name="action" value="Finish transaction">
      <input type="submit" name="action" value="Terminate transaction"></p>
    </form>
  </body>
</html>
<? } ?>
```

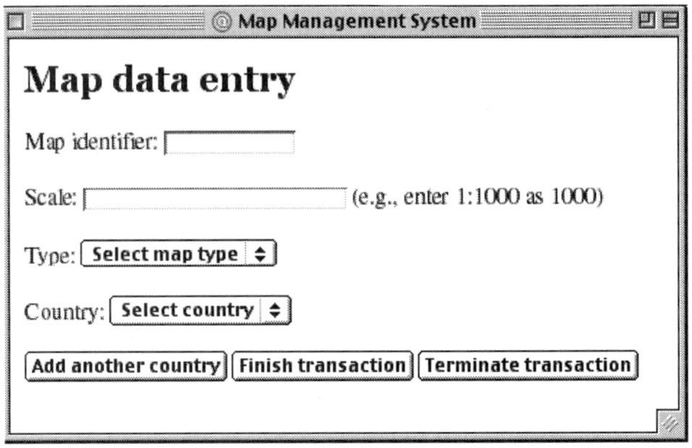

Figure 15-13. Form generated by mapentryform

the same three functions as mapentry form. When any button is selected, however, the script addcountry.php is executed.

Table 15-16: Function mapcntryentryform

```
<?php function mapcntryentryform() { ?>
<html>
  <head>
    <title>Map Management System</title>
  </head>
  <body bgcolor="white">
      <h2>Map-country relationship data entry</h2>
    <form name="cntryinsert" method="post" action = "addcountry.php">
      <p>Country: <select name="cntrycode" size="1">
          <option selected>Select country</option>
          <option value="at">Austria</option>
          <option value="be">Belgium</option>
          <option value="fr">France</option>
          <option value="de">Germany</option>
          <option value="nl">Netherlands</option>
          <option value="ch">Switzerland</option>
        </select>
      <p><input type="submit" name="action" value="Add another country">
      <input type="submit" name="action" value="Finish transaction">
       <input type="submit" name="action" value="Terminate transaction"></p>
    </form>
  </body>
</html>
<? } ?>
```

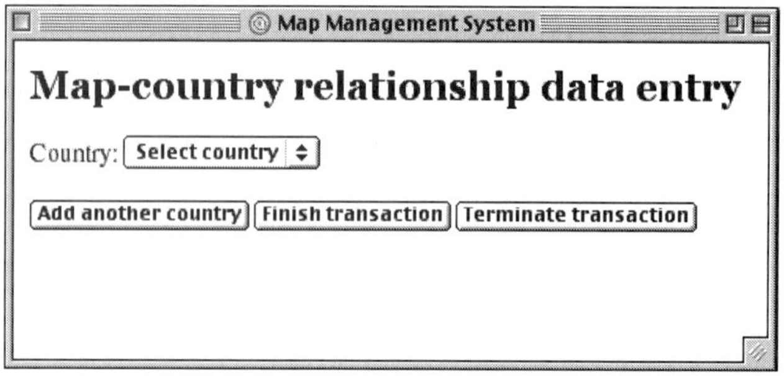

Figure 15-14. Form generated by mapcntryentryform

The functions maperror (see Table 15-17) and cntryerror (see Table 15-18) are used to report data entry errors for the map and country entry forms, respectively. When the button on these form is clicked, the designated script (i.e., mapmain.php {7} or country.php {7}) is activated.

Newmap is designed to execute mapmain.php (i.e., generate a new map entry form) when a transaction is finished or terminated.

Finally, there is a function to connect to the database. Instead of repeating the code in each script, it is simpler to create a function to execute the connection. This is also means that, if the connection parameters are changed, there is only one piece of code to change.

The three scripts for the complete transaction are described in the following sections.

Table 15-17: PHP function maperror

```
<?php function maperror() { ?>
<html>
  <head>
    <title>Map Management System</title>
  </head>
  <body bgcolor="white">
    <form name="maperror" method="post" action="mapmain.php">
    <input type="submit" name="back" value = "Return to map data entry">
    </form>
  </body>
</html>
<? } ?>
```

Table 15-18: Function cntryerror

```
<?php function countryerror() { ?>
<html>
  <head>
    <title>Map Management System</title>
  </head>
  <body bgcolor="white">
    <form name="cntryerror" method="post" action="country.php">
    <input type="submit" name="back" value = "Return to country data entry">
    </form>
  </body>
</html>
<? } ?>
```

Table 15-19: Function newmap

```
<?php function newmap() { ?>
<html>
  <head>
    <title>Map Management System</title>
  </head>
  <body bgcolor="white">
    <form name="newmap" method="post" action="mapmain.php">
    <input type="submit" name="newmap" value = "New map">
    </form>
  </body>
</html>
<? } ?>
```

Table 15-20: Function pconnect

```
<?php function pconnect() {
$db_name = "sample";
$db_username = "rwatson";
$db_passwd = "secret";
$connect = odbc_pconnect($db_name,$db_username,$db_passwd);
return $connect;
}
?>
```

Getting starting

The main program for the transaction (see Table 15-21) sets the session registers and displays the map entry form using the mapentryform function.

Table 15-21: mapmain.php

```
<?php
// Main program
// Set session registers & display map entry form
session_register("mapid");
session_register("mapscale");
session_register("maptype");
session_register("country");
session_register("cntrycount");
session_register("cntrycode");
require ("common.php");
mapentryform();
?>
```

Adding a map

The script addmap.php (Table 15-22) performs five tasks:

- turns off autocommit {9} to enable processing of a complete transaction. Otherwise rows are committed as they are inserted, which means that the inserted rows of terminated transaction cannot be reversed by a rollback;
- rollbacks the transaction if it is terminated, and initiates a new map entry {10-12}.
- Validates the entered data by checking that mapid and mapscale are numeric {16-30}. If data validation fails, error messages are display (i.e., maperror is called) {37};
- commits the transaction (i.e., write rows to the database) if the finish option is selected and the entered data are valid, and then initiate a new map entry form {40-48};
- inserts a row in mapcountry and displays the form for entering another country, if this option is selected and the entered data are valid {52-58}.

Adding another country

The script addcountry.php (see Table 15-23) performs four tasks:

- rollbacks the transaction if it is terminated, and initiates a new map entry {6-8};
- validates that a country has been selected from the pull down list. If data validation fails, error messages are display (i.e., cntryerror is called) {12-14};
- commits the transaction (i.e., write rows to the database) if the 'finish' option is selected and a country selected from the pull down list, and initiates a new map entry form {17-21};
- inserts a row in mapcountry and displays the form for entering another country, if this option is selected and the entered data are valid {25-29}.

Notice the use of $HTTP_POST_VARS to set the variable $cntrycode {4}. This code is required because $cntrycode was entered on the form that called addcountry.php.

Table 15-22: addmap.php

```php
<?php
session_start();
require ("common.php");
mapid = $HTTP_POST_VARS["mapid"];
$mapscale = $HTTP_POST_VARS["mapscale"];
$maptype = $HTTP_POST_VARS["maptype"];
$cntrycode = $HTTP_POST_VARS["cntrycode"];
$connect = pconnect();
odbc_autocommit($connect, false); // turn off autocommit
if ($action == "Terminate transaction") {
  odbc_rollback($connect); // rollback;
  newmap();
  exit();
}
else {
// first validate the data entered
  $valid = true;
  $msg1 = "";
  $msg2 = "";
// check mapid
  settype ($mapid,integer); // sets to false if variable contains alphas
  if ($mapid == false) {
  $msg1 = "Map identifier must be numeric" . "<br>\n";
  $valid = false;
  }
// check mapscale
  settype ($mapscale,integer); // sets to false if variable contains alphas
  if ($mapscale == false) {
  $msg2 = "Map scale must be numeric" . "<br>\n";
  $valid = false;
  }
}
if (!$valid) {
  echo "Map data entry error" . "<br>\n" . "<br>\n";
  echo $msg1;
  echo $msg2;
  maperror();
  }
else {
  if ($action == "Finish transaction") {
  $insertcmd = "insert into map values ("
     . $mapid . "," . $mapscale . "," . "'" . $maptype . "')";
  odbc_exec($connect,$insertcmd);
  $insertcmd = "insert into mapcountry values ("
     . $mapid . "," . "'" . $cntrycode . "')"; // insert map row
  odbc_exec($connect,$insertcmd); // insert map-country row
  odbc_commit($connect); // commit
  newmap();
  exit();
  }
  else { // map with multiple countries
  $insertcmd = "insert into map values ("
     . $mapid . "," . $mapscale . "," . "'" . $maptype . "')";
  odbc_exec($connect,$insertcmd);
  $insertcmd = "insert into mapcountry values ("
     . $mapid . "," . "'" . $cntrycode . "')"; // insert map row
  odbc_exec($connect,$insertcmd); // insert map-country row
    mapcntryentryform();
    }
}
?>
```

Table 15-23: addcountry.php

```
<?php
session_start();
require ("common.php");
$cntrycode = $HTTP_POST_VARS["cntrycode"];
$connect = pconnect();
if ($action == "Terminate transaction") {
  odbc_rollback($connect); // rollback
  newmap();
  exit();
  }
// Must be add a country so validate a country entered
if ($cntrycode == "Select country") {
  echo "No country selected" . "<br>\n";
  cntryerror();
  exit;
  }
if ($action == "Finish transaction") {
  $insertcmd = "insert into mapcountry values ("
    . $mapid . "," . "'" . $cntrycode . "')"; // insert map row
  odbc_exec($connect,$insertcmd); // insert map-country row
  odbc_commit($connect); // commit
  newmap();
  exit();
  }
else { // insert another country
  $insertcmd = "insert into mapcountry values ("
    . $mapid . "," . "'" . $cntrycode . "')";
  odbc_exec($connect,$insertcmd); // insert map-country row
  mapcntryentryform();
  exit();
  }
?>
```

Your turn

1. Copy from the book's supporting Web site the scripts for inserting a map (map.zip) and FTP these into your Web account.
2. Execute the scripts so that you are understand how they work by adding some maps and checking the results by querying the database.
3. Modify addmap.php to validate that a type of map was selected from the pull-down list.

Database application development with Java

Java is a platform-independent application development language. Its object-oriented nature makes it easy to create and maintain software and prototypes. These features make Java an attractive development language for many applications, including database systems.

Java gains independence and portability through the embedding of a Java Virtual machine in browsers and operating systems and the development of a Java OS (see Figure 15-15). Java applets, when compiled for the Java Virtual Machine, are roughly 80 percent compiled and 20 percent interpreted code. Consequently, Java applets will be slower than compiled code, but the development of Just-in-Time compilers is likely to alleviate this shortcoming.[11]

Figure 15-15. The Java options

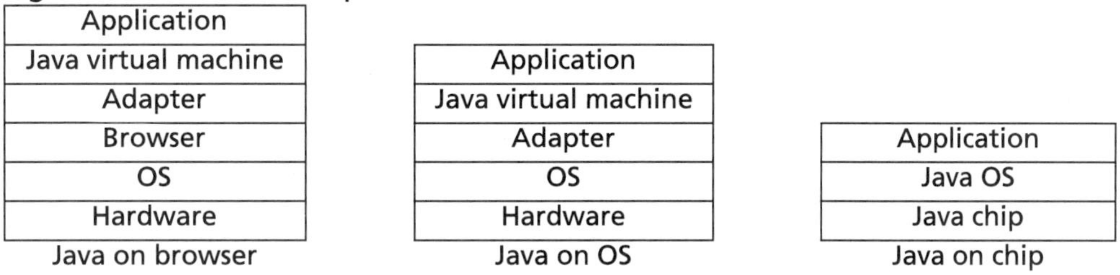

The great advantage of Java is that it provides a simple approach to the development, management, and deployment of client/server applications. It is simpler because it has the good parts of C++, a popular OO development language, but not the bad features. New applications or modifications of existing systems are easily distributed by placing them on the server. There is no need to install a new or updated client on each machine—distribution is immediate. In addition, many vendors provide support for JDBC, which is discussed in the next section.

Before discussing Java database application development, we need to briefly cover Java's three major object-oriented constructs: interface, class, and object, as illustrated in Figure 15-16. An *interface* defines fields and methods but does not contain programming statements. A *class* implements the actions that objects perform by implementing methods declared in the interface or by declaring and implementing its own methods. An *object* is a run-time instance of a class.

Java Database Connection (JDBC)

Java database connection (JDBC), a Java version of a portable SQL CLI, is modeled on ODBC (see page 270). JDBC enables programmers to write Java software that is both operating system and DBMS independent. As Figure 15-17 illustrates, JDBC provides two major services: an application programming interface (JDBC API) and a driver interface (JDBC driver manager). There are two approaches to implementing a Java driver. A *direct* driver sits on top of the DBMS's native interface. A *bridged* driver is built on top of an existing ODBC driver. Since JDBC is based on ODBC, the translation between protocols for a bridged driver should be very fast.

The JDBC core

The JDBC core, which handles 90 percent of database programming, contains seven interfaces and two classes. The purpose of each these classes is summarized in Table 15-24.

11. Applets are Java programs that run under the control of the browser.Applications are Java programs that run under the control of the OS.

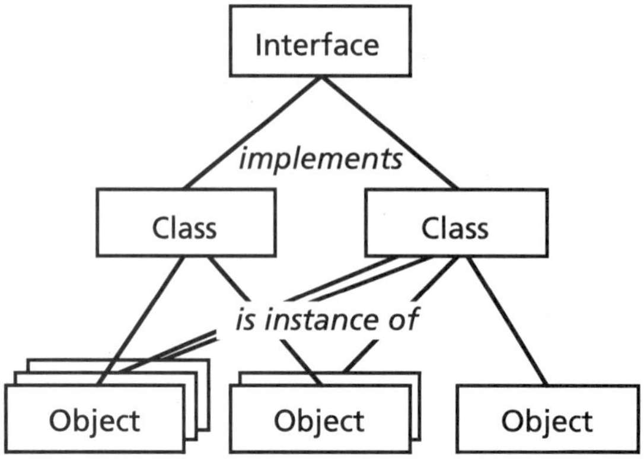

Figure 15-16. Relationship between interface, class, and object

Figure 15-17. JDBC layers

Application
JDBC API
JDBC driver manager
Service provider API
Driver for DBMS server
DBMS server

Table 15-24: JDBC core interfaces and classes

Interfaces	**Description**
Driver	Locates a driver for a specified database
Connection	Connects an application to a database
Statement	A container for an SQL statement
PreparedStatement	Precompiles an SQL statement and then use it multiple times
CallableStatement	Executes a stored procedure
ResultSet	The rows returned when a query is executed
ResultSetMetaData	The number, types, and properties of the result set
Classes	
DriverManager	Loads driver objects and creates database connections
DriverPropertyInfo	Used by specialized clients

You will need a course in Java programming before you can write database applications in Java. Nevertheless, to give you a feel for how Java and the JDBC core work, a very brief coverage of the main aspects of database application development is provided in diagrammatic format (see Figure 15-18).

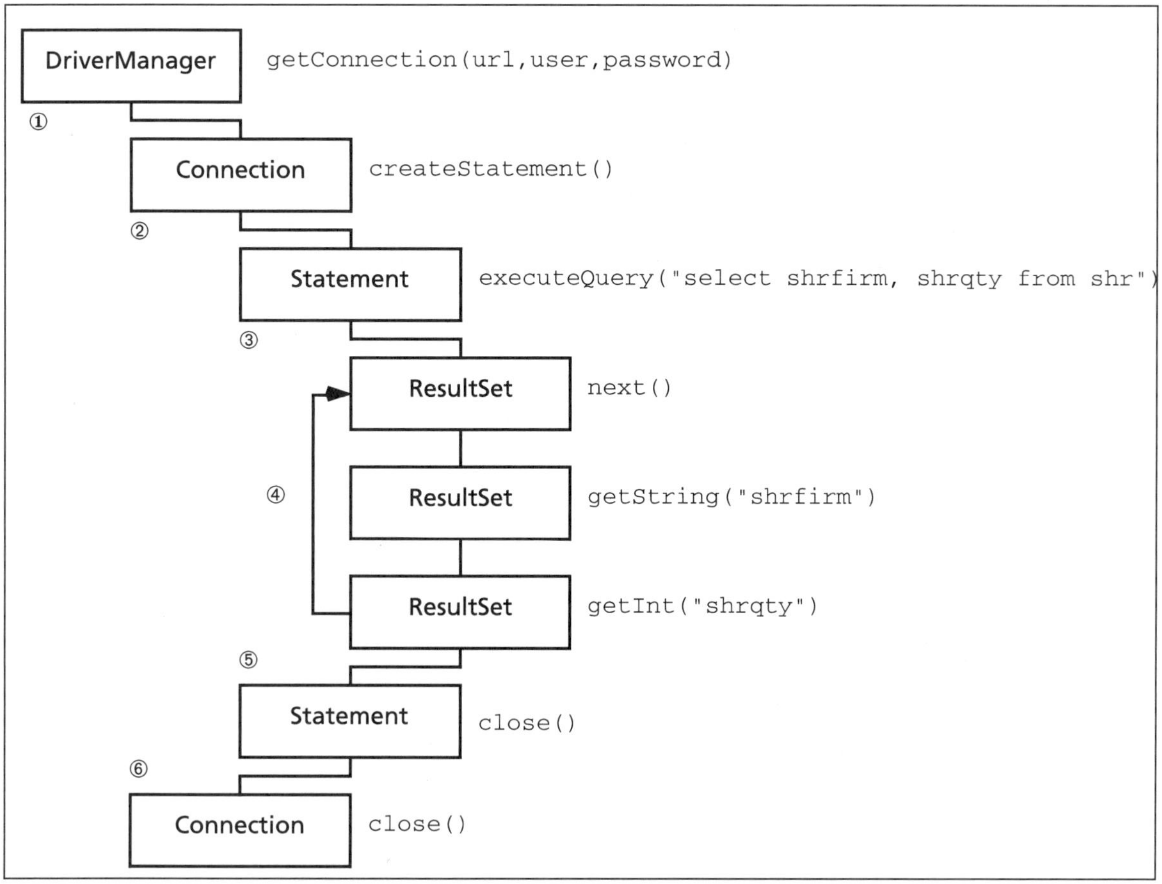

Figure 15-18. An SQL query with JDBC

The diagram indicates which interface (or class) and method are used for each step of an SQL query. For instance, the first step is to use the *getConnection* method of the Driver-Manager class to connect to the required database. The major steps in processing a SQL query are:

1. **Connect to the database.** The *getConnection* method of the DriverManger specifies the URL of the database, the user id, and password. The DriveManager locates a driver that can process the database and returns a Connection object.
2. **Get a statement object**. The *createStatement* method is invoked to produce a Statement object.
3. **Execute the query**. The SQL query is passed as a string by the *executeQuery* method of the Statement object. The results are returned in a ResultSet object.
4. **Process the table.** The rows in the table are processed a row at a time using the *next* method of the ResultSet object. Columns are retrieved one at a time using a *getFunction*, where *Function* is determined by the column's SQL data type. In the

illustrative example, *getString* and *getInt* are used to process SQL data types of character and integer, respectively.

5. **Release the Statement object**. The resources associated with the Statement object are freed using *close*.
6. **Release the Connection object**. The resources associated with the Connection object are freed using *close*.

SQLJ (see page 275) is a simpler alternative to JDBC when an application contains only static SQL. It has a higher-level programming interface. Dynamic SQL requires JDBC.

CORBA

The future for Web database applications is likely to be **Common object request broker architecture (CORBA)**—a distributed object bus designed to support global client/server systems. CORBA is an open standard developed by the Object Management Group (OMG). In 1995, OMG commenced work on the integration of Java and CORBA. The result of this work is the Object Web model, a three-tier model (see Figure 15-19).

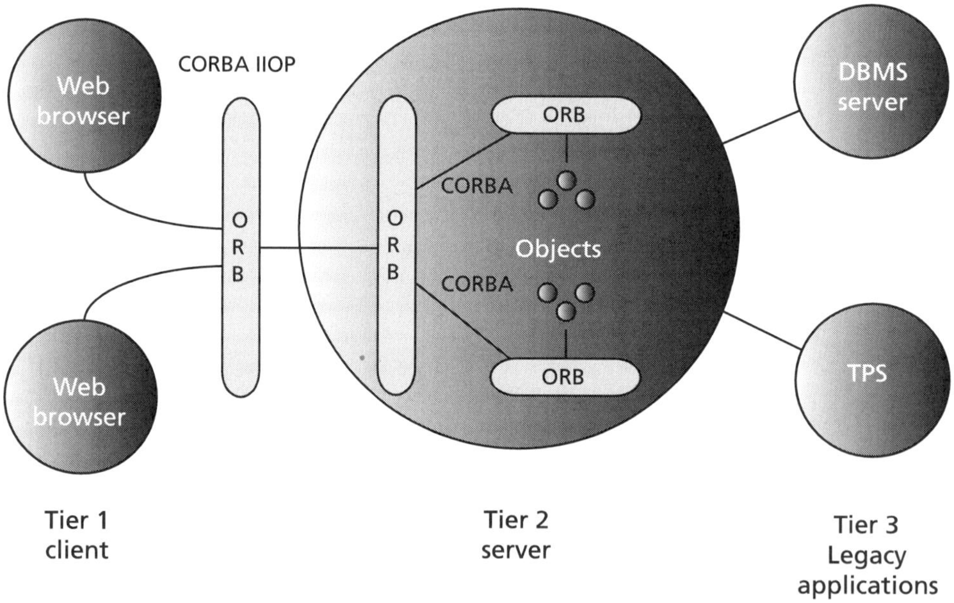

Figure 15-19. Object Web model

The browser, Java clients, and Java applets belong to the first tier. The middle tier contains the Web server and CORBA objects, which are application servers. The third tier contains anything with which a CORBA object can communicate. For example, it can talk to a DBMS or TPS. CORBA objects are the heart of the Object Web, they interact with the first and third tiers as well as communicate with any other CORBA object using a CORBA **ob-**

ject request broker (ORB). The protocol for interaction between the first and second tiers is **Internet inter-ORB protocol (IIOP)**, which is essentially TCP/IP with some CORBA-defined message capability. Effectively, CORBA objects substitute for CGI applications, and IIOP replaces HTTP. HTTP and CORBA IIOP both run over the Internet, which means that Web pages are loaded using HTTP, and CORBA is used for client/server communication. Thus, a typical interaction might be:

1. browser downloads HTML from HTTP (Web) server;
2. browser retrieves Java applet from HTTP server;
3. browser loads applet;
4. applet invokes CORBA server objects.

Java's main goal is to support distributed application development and employment, but it is not designed for client/server. CORBA provides the client/server element by facilitating a distributed object environment. CORBA lets a Java object communicate with any other object wherever it might be. Thus, the Java/CORBA combination provides a universal platform for Web applications.

The Java/CORBA combination provides several advantages over the current CGI/HTTP solution. *First*, it is faster because a client can directly invoke an object on the server. *Second*, CORBA maintains state between invocations but CGI does not. *Third*, CORBA objects can be distributed across multiple servers, giving greater scalability than a CGI, which is often a bottleneck because it cannot be distributed. *Fourth*, CORBA enables Java applets to communicate with other objects. These differences are a consequence of the approach taken to the development of each solution. CORBA was designed to enable three-tier client/server. CGI/HTTP is a work around to enable client/server on the Web.

Conclusion

The Web is giving database applications, and many other information systems, a new face—the browser. This new face brings with it a broader set of tools for presenting information. The table, the mainstay of the relational model, has been augmented by six other information organization models. Thus, database application design, with more choices for information presentation, becomes more complicated.

The technology for creating the new face, and the back-end that supports it, is in many cases still under development and often new to the market. Consequently, there is likely to be considerable change in the next few years. For example, the Java/CORBA approach previously discussed may not emerge as a widely used standard. Some other combination of programming language and distributed object Web model could become common. Web database application developers need to keep a close watch on the market place to see which way it moves. In the meantime, it is important to learn the fundamental principles of information presentation, the three-tier client, and the object Web model so these core concepts can be readily applied to a particular implementation of them.

Summary

The data on a Web site must be managed. HTML editors and Web site managers are tools to support Web site creation and management. Web site designers need to create an information architecture and apply information design and information arts skills when creating a Web site. There are seven universal models for the organization of data (linear, hierarchical, web, parallel, matrix, overlay, and spatial zoom). The Web browser, a thin-client, is becoming a standard interface to database applications. Three-tier architecture consists of a Web browser (first tier), Web server (second tier), and DBMS server (third tier). Some Web database application development approaches are CGI, proprietary APIs, active server pages (ASP), server-side JavaScript (SSJS), Java servlets and JSP, and PHP. PHP is an open source, cross-platform, server-side scripting language.

Cool ICE links databases to Web

Unisys Corp. has released software that makes it easier to keep electronic commerce sites current with data on back-end servers. Cool Internet Commerce Enabler (Cool ICE) integrates multiple, sometimes disparate, back-end database systems so that stored information can be accessed via the Web.

Scottsdale, Arizona-based Antigua Group, Inc., which designs and embroiders sports clothing, used Cool ICE to make its Web site interactive by linking it to its back-end data. Visitors can access its Web pages to get data from Antigua Group's AS/400 24 hours a day. Company officials have seen the volume of order-status calls from sales reps and customers drop from about 100 per day to virtually nothing. As a result, Antigua can grow its business without adding staff.

The Hillsborough County (FL) Sheriff's Office used the Unisys software to set up an intranet service to give criminal justice agencies access to information, such as arrest reports and arraignment lists. Agency professionals previously exchanged information by telephone, fax, and mail and even hand-delivered time-sensitive documents. Defense attorneys often had to wait until they were in court to see documents. Now, that information is posted on the intranet at 2 A.M., allowing them to better prepare for court appearances. There has been a significant reduction in calls to the sheriff's office as a result of the intranet system.

Source: Sliwa, C. 1998. Unisys middleware links databases to Web. *Computerworld*, http://www.computerworld.com/cwi/story/0,1199,NAV47_STO30346,00.html.

Key terms and concepts

Active server page (ASP)
Applet
Application
Browser
Commit
Common gateway interface (CGI)
Connectivity
Common object request broker architecture (CORBA)
Fat client
HTML editor
Hypertext markup language (HTML)
Information organization
Information arts
Information design
Internet inter-ORB protocol (IIOP)
Intranet
Java
Java database connection (JDBC)
JavaServer page (JSP)
JavaScript
Navigation aids
Object request broker (ORB)
Object Web model
Organization model
PHP
Rollback
Server
Servlet
Session
Site management
Thin client
Three-tier architecture
Transaction processing
Two-tier architecture

References

Castagnetto, J., H. Rawat, S. Schumann, C. Scollo, and D. Veliath. 1999. *Professional PHP programming*. Birmingham, UK: Wrox.

Graham, I. S. 1996. *HTML source book: a complete guide to HTML 3.0.* 2nd ed. New York, NY: Wiley.

Mok, C. 1996. *Designing business: multiple media, multiple disciplines*. San Jose, CA: Adobe.

Orfali, R., and D. Harkey. 1997. *Client/server programming with Java and CORBA*. New York, NY: Wiley.

Exercises

1. The development of a Web site requires blending the skills of MIS and graphics arts professionals. What roles should each of these professionals play in information architecture, information design, and information arts? Who is likely to play the major role in each phase?
2. Surf the Web to find examples of each of the seven universal models of information organization. Which model appears to be most commonly used?
3. Design a Web page for a Book Store.
4. Distinguish between fat and thin clients. If you were in charge of running the computer laboratories at your university, would your prefer fat or thin clients?
5. What are the advantages and disadvantages of PHP?
6. Describe the advantages and disadvantages of database application development using Java.
7. What are the differences between Java and JavaScript?
8. What are the advantages and disadvantages of CORBA?

9. Investigate Microsoft's alternatives for Web database application development. What does the industry press say about these products?
10. Write a suite of PHP scripts to maintain the database defined by the following data model:

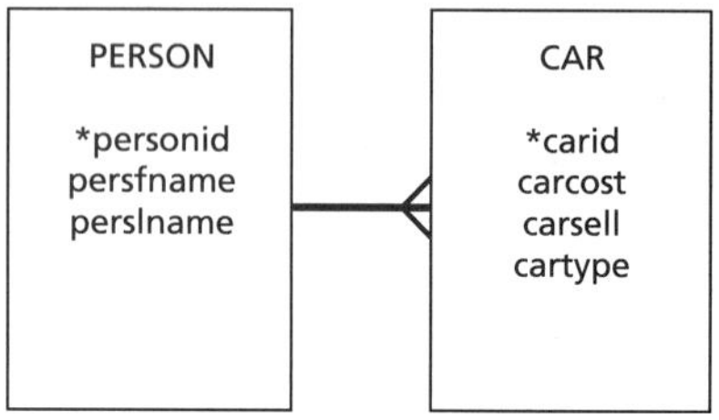

16

XML: Managing Data Exchange

Words can have no single fixed meaning. Like wayward electrons, they can spin away from their initial orbit and enter a wider magnetic field. No one owns them or has a proprietary right to dictate how they will be used.

David Lehman, *End of the Word*, 1991

Learning objectives

Students completing this chapter will be able to

- define the purpose of XML;
- create a DTD;
- code data in XML format;
- create an XML stylesheet;
- discuss data management options for XML documents.

Introduction

There are four central problems in data management: capture, storage, retrieval, and exchange. The focus for most of this book has been on storage (i.e., data modeling) and retrieval (i.e., SQL). Now it is time to consider capture and exchange. Capture has always been an important issue, and the guiding principle is to capture data once in the cheapest possible manner. Likewise, data exchange has long been an issue, but the Internet has elevated the import of this issue. Electronic data interchange (EDI), the traditional standard of data exchange for large organizations, is giving way to XML, which is likely to become the data exchange standard for all organizations, irrespective of size.

EDI

EDI, which has been used for some 20 years, describes the electronic exchange of standard business documents between firms. A structured, standardized data format is used to exchange common business documents (e.g., invoices and shipping orders) between trading partners. In contrast to the free form of e-mail messages, EDI supports the exchange of repetitive, routine business transactions. Standards mean that routine electronic transactions can be concise and precise. The main standard used in the United States and Canada is known as ANSI X.12, and the major international standard is EDIFACT. Firms following the same standard can electronically share data. Before EDI, many standard messages between partners were generated by computer, printed, and mailed to the other party, then manually entered the data into its computer. The main advantages of EDI are

- paper handling is reduced, saving time and money;
- data are exchanged in real time;
- data are keyed only once, resulting in fewer errors;
- activities are better coordinated between business partners through enhanced data sharing;
- money flows are accelerated and payments received sooner.

Despite these advantages, for most companies EDI is still the exception, not the rule. A U.S. survey in the mid-1990s reported that almost 80 percent of the information flow between firms was on paper. Paper should be the exception, not the rule. Most EDI traffic has been handled by value-added networks (VANs) or private networks. VANs add communication services to those provided by common carriers (e.g., AT&T). However, these networks are too expensive for all but the largest 100,000 of the 6 million businesses in existence today in the United States. As a result, many businesses have not been able to participate in the benefits associated with EDI. However, the Internet will enable more smaller companies to take advantage of EDI.

Internet communication costs are typically less than with traditional EDI. In addition, the Internet is a global network potentially accessible by nearly every firm. Consequently, the Internet is displacing VANs as the electronic transport path between trading partners. The simplest approach is to use the Internet as a means of replacing a VAN by using a commercially available Internet EDI package. Another approach is to reexamine the technology of data exchange, since EDI was developed in the 1960s. A result of this rethinking is XML, but before considering XML, we need to learn about SGML, the parent of XML.

SGML

It is estimated that document management consumes up to 15 percent of a typical company's revenue, nearly 25 percent of its labor costs, and anywhere between 10 and 60 percent of an office worker's time. A U.S. Navy Cruiser, for example, has 26 tons of manuals in paper format on board. Each year, the U.S. Navy generates 15 million technical manuals and 237 million drawings which cost $4 billion to maintain. The standard generalized markup language (SGML) is designed to reduce the cost and increase the efficiency of document management.

A **markup language** embeds information about the text in the text. In Table 16-1, the markup tags indicate that the text contains CD liner notes. Note also that the titles and identifiers of the mentioned CDs are explicitly identified.

Table 16-1: Markup language

```
<cdliner>This uniquely creative collaboration between Miles Davis and
Gil Evans has already resulted in two extraordinary albums—<cdti-
tle>Miles Ahead</cdtitle><cdid>CL 1041></cdid> and <cdtitle>Porgy and
Bess</cdtitle><cdid>CL 1274</cdid>.</cdliner>
```

SGML is an International Standard (ISO 8879) that defines the structure of documents. It is a vendor-independent language that supports cross system portability and publication for all media. Developed in 1986 to manage software documentation, SGML is widely accepted as the markup language for a number of information-intensive industries. SGML is the mother of both HTML and XML. Thus, SGML can generate both these markup languages. SGML provides a stable platform for managing data when technology is rapidly changing. Because SGML is software- and hardware-neutral, businesses can choose *best of breed* tools to create, manage, retrieve, and disseminate data.This stability of SGML comes from its open systems approach.

SGML has three major advantages for data management:

- ❖ **Reuse.** Information can be created once and reused over and over. By storing critical documents in SGML, firms do not need to duplicate effort when there are changes to documents. For example, a firm might store all its legal contracts in SGML.
- ❖ **Flexibility**. SGML documents can be published in any medium for a wide variety of audiences. The same document, for example, could be printed, presented on the Web in HTML, or written to a CD.
- ❖ **Revision**. SGML enhances control over revision and enables version control. When stored in an SGML database, original data are archived alongside any changes. That means you know exactly what the original document contained and what changes were made.

Electronic publishing does not require SGML. CD-ROMs and Web sites can be created without SGML. However, the use of SGML preserves textual information independent of how and when it is presented. SGML protects a firm's investment in documentation for the long term. Because it is now possible to display documentation using multiple media (e.g., Web and CD-ROM), firms have become sensitized to the need to store documents in a single, independent manner that can then be converted for display by a particular media.

SGML's power is derived from its recording of both text and the meaning of that text. A short section of SGML demonstrates clearly the features and strength of SGML (see Table 16-2). The tags surrounding a chunk of text describe its meaning and thus support presentation and retrieval. For example, the pair of tags <title> and </title> surrounding "Managing Data Exchange" indicate that it is the chapter title.

Table 16-2: SGML code

```
<chapter>
<no>16</no>
<title>XML: Managing Data Exchange</title>
<section>
<quote><emph type = "2">Words can have no single fixed meaning. Like
wayward electrons, they can spin away from their initial orbit and
enter a wider magnetic field. No one owns them or has a proprietary
right to dictate how they will be used.</emph></quote>
</section></chapter>
```

Taking this piece of SGML, it is possible, using an appropriate stylesheet, to create a print version where the title of the chapter is displayed in Times, 16 point, bold, or a HTML version where the title is displayed in red, Georgia, 14 point, italics. Furthermore, the database in which this text is stored can be searched for any chapters that contain "exchange" in their title.

Now, consider the case where the text is stored as HTML (see Table 16-3). How do you with complete certainty identify the chapter title? Do you extract all text contained by <h1> and </h1> tags. You will then retrieve "16" as a possible chapter title. What happens if there is other text displayed using <h1> and </h1> tags? The problem with HTML is that it defines presentation and not meaning. A similar problem exists for documents prepared with a word processor.

Table 16-3: HTML code

```
<html>
<body>
<h1><b>16 </b></h1>
<h1><b>XML: Managing Data Exchange</b></h1>
<p><i>Words can have no single fixed meaning. Like wayward electrons,
they can spin away from their initial orbit and enter a wider magnetic
field. No one owns them or has a proprietary right to dictate how they
will be used.</i>
</body>
</html>
```

By using embedded tags to record meaning, SGML makes a document platform independent and greatly improves the effectiveness of searching. However, before a firm can use SGML, it needs to determine what meaning is contained within its document. In other words, it needs to define a data model[1] and create a **document type definition** (DTD).

1. And you thought you had said goodbye to this beast :)

Document elements to be marked up in SGML are *mapped* to a DTD. The accuracy of an SGML mapping can then be validated using the DTD.

Fortunately, several industries have already developed DTDs for common documents. Today, DTDs have been designed for the aerospace, automotive, electronics manufacturing, publishing, software development, and telecommunications documentation sectors. For example, the publishing industry has defined ISO12083 for articles, books, and serials.[2]

There are some features of SGML that are considered to make implementation difficult, and that also limit the ability to create tools for information management and exchange. As a result, XML, a derivative of SGML, was developed.

XML

Extensible markup language (XML), a new language designed to make information self-describing, retains the core ideas of SGML. You can think of XML as SGML for electronic and mobile commerce. XML has the potential to extend the Internet beyond information delivery to many other kinds of human activity. Since the definition of XML was completed in early 1998 by the World Wide Web Consortium (W3C), this new standard has spread rapidly because it solves a critical data management problem. XML is more than a mere incremental improvement of HTML. It is a conceptual change because XML is a meta-language—a language to generate languages. XML will steadily replace HTML on many Web sites. The major differences between XML and HTML are captured in Table 16-4.

Table 16-4: XML vs. HTML

XML	HTML
Structured text	Formatted text
User-definable structure (extensible)	Predefined formats (not extensible)
Context-sensitive retrieval	Limited retrieval
Greater hypertext linking	Limited hypertext linking

HTML, an electronic-publishing language, describes how a Web browser should display text and images on a computer screen. It tells the browser nothing about the meaning of the data. For example, the browser does not know whether a piece of text represents a price, a product code, or a delivery date. Humans infer meaning from the context (e.g., Aug 8, 2001 is recognized as a date). Given the explosive growth of the Web, HTML clearly works well enough for exchanging data between computers and humans. It does not, however, work for exchanging data between computers, because computers are not smart enough to infer meaning from context.

Successful data exchange requires that the meaning of the exchanged data be readily determined by a computer. The XML solution is to embed tags in a file to describe the data (e.g., insert tags into an order that indicate attributes such as price, size, quantity, and color). A browser, or program for that matter, can then recognize this document as a cus-

2. See http://www.xmlxperts.com/12083.htm

tomer order. Consequently, it can do far more than just display the price. For example, it can convert all prices to another currency. More importantly, the data can be exchanged between computers.

XML consists of rules (see Table 16-5) that anyone can follow to create a markup language (e.g., a markup language for financial data). Hence, the eXtentsible in the XML name indicates that the language can be easily extended to include new tags. In contrast, HTML is not extensible and its set of tags is fixed, which is one of the major reasons why HTML is easy to learn.The XML rules ensure that a parser, a type of computer program, can process any extension or addition of new tags.

Table 16-5: XML rules

- Elements must have both a closing and an ending tag.
- Elements must follow a strict hierarchy with only one root element.
- Elements must not overlap other elements.
- Element names must obey XML naming conventions.
- XML is case sensitive.

Consider the credit card company that wants to send your latest statement via the Internet so you can load it into your financial program. Since this is a common problem for credit card companies and financial software authors, these industry groups have combined to create OFX, a language for the exchange of financial data across the Internet.

XML has a small number of rules. Tags almost always come in pairs, as in HTML. A pair of tags surrounds each piece of data (e.g., <price>89.12</price>) to indicate its meaning, whereas in HTML they indicate how the data are presented.Tag pairs can be nested inside one another to multiple levels, which effectively creates a tree or hierarchical structure. Because XML uses Unicode (see page 335), it enables exchange of information not only between different computer systems but also across language boundaries.

The differences between HTML and XML are captured in the following examples for each markup language. Note how HTML incorporates formatting instructions (i.e., the course code is bold), whereas XML describes the meaning of the data.

Table 16-6: Comparison of HTML and XML coding

HTML	XML
<p><b>MIST7600</b> Data Manage- ment 3 credit hours</p>	<course> <code>MIST7600</code> <title>Data Management</title> <credit>3</credit> </course>

The introduction of XML will see a shift of processing from the server to the browser. At present, most processing has to be done by the server because that is where knowledge about the data is stored. The browser knows nothing about the data and therefore can only present but not process. However, when XML is implemented, the browser can take on processing that previously had to be handled by the server.

Imagine that you are selecting a shirt from a mail-order catalog. The merchant's Web server sends you data on 20 shirts (100k of text and images) with prices in U.S. dollars. If you want to see the prices in euros, the calculation will be done by the server and the full details for the 20 shirts retransmitted (i.e., another 100k is sent from the server to the browser). However, once XML is in place, all that needs to be sent from the server to the browser is the conversion rate of dollars to euros and a Java program to compute the conversion at the browser end (see Table 16-7). In most cases, less data will be transmitted between a server and browser when XML is in place. Consequently, widespread adoption of XML will reduce network traffic.

Table 16-7: Execution of HTML and XML code

HTML	XML
Retrieve shirt data with prices in $US Retrieve shirt data with prices in euros	Retrieve shirt data with prices in $US Retrieve conversion rate of $US to euro Retrieve Java program to convert currencies Compute prices in euros

XML will also make searching more efficient and effective. At present, search engines look for matching text strings, and consequently return many links that are completely irrelevant. For instance, if you are searching for details on the Nomad MP3 player, and specify "nomad" as the sought text string, you will get links to many items that are of no interest (e.g., *The Fabulous Nomads Surf Band*). Searching will be more precise when you can specify that you are looking for a product name that includes the text "nomad." The search engine can then confine its attention to text contained with the tags <productname> and </productname>, assuming these tags are the XML standard for representing product names.

The major expected gains from the introduction of XML are

- **store once and format many ways**—data stored in XML format can be extracted and reformatted for multiple presentation styles (e.g., printed report, CD-ROM);
- **hardware and software independence**—one format for all systems;
- **capture once and exchange many times**—data are captured as close to the source as possible and never again (i.e., no rekeying);
- **accelerated targeted searching**—searches are more precise and faster because they use XML tags;
- **less network congestion**—the processing load shifts from the server to the browser.

XML language design

XML lets developers design application-specific vocabularies. To create a new language, designers must agree on three things:

Classified ads XML standard

The NAA Classified Advertising Standards Task Force of approximately 40 classified advertisers, advertising publishers, aggregators, system users, suppliers, and technology experts is designing a standard for the electronic exchange of classified ads. The standard will define a common classified advertising data structure that technology providers can use to create better tools and systems for handling these data. With standardization, advertisers, ad aggregators and publishers can simplify their workflows and more effectively provide data sought by consumers.

The task force has generated a document type description (DTD) to define XML tags and their proper usage in conjunction with this standard. The DTD has a set of elements, or fields, which describe a product being listed for sale. The use of keyword tagging and standardized ad data fields will dramatically improve searching speed and accuracy.

Source: http://www.naa.org/technology/clsstdtf/index.html

- the allowable tags;
- the rules for nesting tagged elements;
- which tagged elements can be processed.

The first two—the language's vocabulary and structure—are typically defined in a Document Type Definition (DTD). Programmers use the DTD to understand the meaning of tags so they can write software to process an XML file.

XML tags describe meaning, independent of the display medium. An XML stylesheet, another set of rules, defines how an XML file is automatically formatted for various devices. This set of rules is called a Extensible Stylesheet Language (XSL). Stylesheets allow data to be rendered in a variety of ways, such as Braille or audio for visually impaired persons.

DTD

A document type definition (DTD) is a file associated with an XML document that informs an application how to interpret markup tags. The advantage of a DTD is that it leads to standardization. Consistently named and defined tags create conformity and support organizational efficiency. They avoid the confusion and loss of time when the meaning of data is not clear.

XML does not require the creation of a DTD. If a document is well-formed, XML will interpret it correctly. A well-formed document follows XML syntax and has tags that are correctly nested. One of the strengths of XML is that browser writers have agreed to reject any XML file that is not well-formed. HTML works on some browsers and not others, so using XML should result in greater consistency across browsers. XML coders will not get away with sloppy work that creates incompatibilities.

A DTD is a very strict specification and any errors will be detected when parsing. A DTD defines

- ❖ the names and contents of all elements that are permissible in a certain document;
- ❖ how often an element may appear;
- ❖ the order in which the elements must appear;
- ❖ whether the start- or end-tag may be omitted;
- ❖ the contents of all elements (i.e., the names of the other generic identifiers that are allowed to appear inside them);
- ❖ the attributes and their default values;
- ❖ the names of the reference symbols that may be used.

DOM

The **document object model** (DOM) is the data model of an XML document. It is based on a tree (i.e., it supports 1:1 and 1:m, but not m:m relationships). A document is modeled as a hierarchical collection of nodes that have parent/child relationships. The node is the primary object and can be of different types (such as, document, element, attribute, text, processing instruction, CDATA section, and comment). Each document has a single document node which has no parent, and zero or more children that are element nodes. It is good practice to create a visual data model of the XML document and then to convert this to a DTD, which is XML's formal representation of the DOM.

At this point, an example is the best way to demonstrate XML, DTD, and DOM concepts. We will use the familiar CD problem that was introduced in Chapter 3 (see page 84). In keeping with the style of this text, we define a minimal amount of XML to get you started, and then more features are added once you have mastered the basics.

CD library case

The CD library case gradually develops, over several chapters, a data model for recording details of a CD collection, culminating in the model on page 152. Unfortunately, we cannot quickly convert this final model to an XML document model since a DOM is based on a tree model. Thus, we must start afresh.

The model, in this case, is based on the observation that a CD library has many CDs, and a CD has many tracks. This model is shown in Figure 16-1, using the now familiar data modeling symbols.

This model is then mapped into an XML DTD using the following procedure.

- ❖ Each entity becomes an element type.
- ❖ Each data model attribute[3] becomes an element type.
- ❖ The 1:m relationship is recorded as part of the mapping of the entity at the one end of the relationship.

3. XML also has the notion of an attribute, and so we need to be precise when talking about attributes.

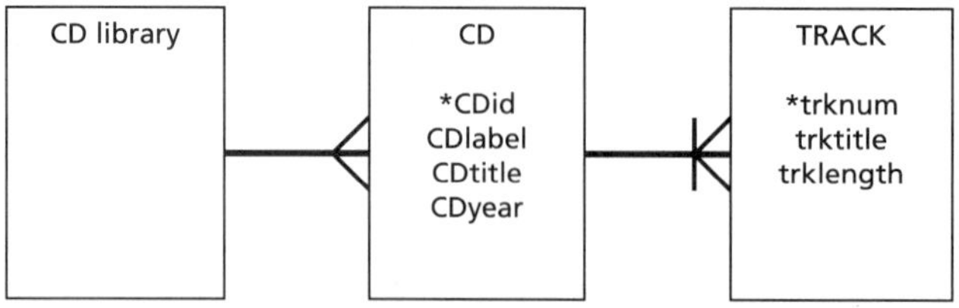

Figure 16-1. CD library tree data model

The mapping of the CD library is shown in Table 16-8. For convenience of exposition, the source code lines have been numbered, but these numbers are not part of a DTD.

Table 16-8: DTD for CD library (cdlib.dtd)

```
1 <!--DTD for CD library-->
2 <!ELEMENT cdlibrary (cd+ )>
3 <!ELEMENT cd (cdid , cdlabel , cdtitle , cdyear , track+ )>
4 <!ELEMENT cdid (#PCDATA )>
5 <!ELEMENT cdlabel (#PCDATA )>
6 <!ELEMENT cdtitle (#PCDATA )>
7 <!ELEMENT cdyear (#PCDATA )>
8 <!ELEMENT track (trknum, trktitle, trklen)>
9 <!ELEMENT trknum (#PCDATA )>
10 <!ELEMENT trktitle (#PCDATA )>
11 <!ELEMENT trklen (#PCDATA )>
```

Comments, as in line 1, are placed inside the tag pair '<!--' and '-->'.

Line 2 defines the CDLIBRARY entity as an element. In XML terms, the **cdlibrary** element contains one or more **cd** elements (i.e. there is an1:m relationship between CDLIBRARY and CD), with the plus sign (+) denoting one or more elements. Other occurrence indicator symbols are shown in Table 16-9.

Table 16-9: Occurrence indicators

Indicator	Meaning
none	exactly one occurrence (required and nonrepeatable)
?	zero or one occurrence (optional and nonrepeatable)
*	zero or more occurrences (optional and repeatable)
+	one or more occurrences (required and repeatable)

Line 3 defines the entity CD, lists its data model attributes, and the 1:m relationship between CD and TRACK. It states that a **cd** element contains one **cdid** element, one **cdlabel** element, one cdtitle element, one cdyear element, and one or more track elements. The commas between the elements specify that they must appear in the specified sequence (i.e.,cdid, then cdlabel, then cdtitle, etc.). The DTD connectors are defined in Table 16-10.

Lines 4 through 7 and 9 through 11 specify that the indicated elements can store *parsed character data* (i.e., text).

Table 16-10: Connectors

Indicator	Meaning	
,	Sequence	The elements must appear and must be in the order shown
|	Choice	One element or the other may appear
&	No sequence	The elements must appear but can be in any order

Line 8 maps the entity TRACK into the XML element **track**, which has three elements, namely **trknum**, **trktitle**, and **trklen**.

As you would expect, software has been developed to support DOM modeling. In Figure 16-2, you see Extensibility's XML Authority[4] diagram of the CD library DOM.

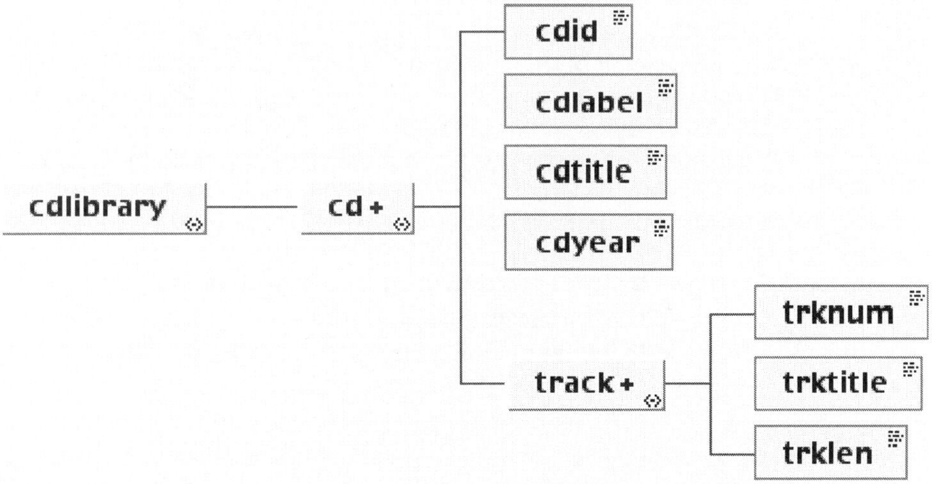

Figure 16-2. Schema as represented in XML Authority

The purpose of a DTD is to define the contents and structure of an XML file. It is also used to verify that an XML file has a valid structure and that all elements in the XML file are defined in the DTD.

We can now use the recently defined CDlibrary DTD to describe a small CD library containing the following CD.

The XML for describing the CD library is displayed in Table 16-12. There are several things to observe:

❖ All XML documents begin with an XML declaration, as in line 1.

4. See http://www.extensibility.com/. You can download a trial version that can be used 10 times.

Table 16-11: CD data

Id	A2 1325	
Label	Atlantic	
Title	Pyramid	
Year	1960	
Track	Title	Length
1	Vendome	2:30
2	Pyramid	10:46
3	It don't mean a thing	5:02
4	Django	5:23
5	How high the moon	6:15
6	Romaine	7:28

- The DOCUTYPE declaration immediately follows the XML declaration and identifies the root element of the document (i.e., cdlibrary) and the DTD[5] (i.e., cdlib.dtd).
- The body of the document starts at line 3 with the <cdlibrary> tag and ends at line line 40 with the </cdlibrary> tag.
- The definition of a single CD and its tracks is captured by lines 4 through 39. If you were to define a second CD, the definition would follow line 39.
- The first track on the CD is defined by lines 9 through 13.

As you now realize, the definition of an XML document is relatively straightforward. It is a bit tedious with all the typing of tags to surround each data element. However, there are XML editors which relieve this tedium (see www.freesitetools.com/utilities/editors/xml_editors.html for a list of free editors).

Your turn

1. Use Internet Explorer[6] to access this book's Web site, link to the XML section, and click on cdlib.xml. You will see how IE displays XML. Investigate what happens when you click minus (-) and then plus (+).
2. Save the XML code (File > Save As>) displayed by IE and paste it into a text editor or word processor. Notice that line 2 as displayed by IE might be different from that of the original XML file.
   Now, add details of the CD[7] displayed in Table 16-13 to this XML code, save it as cdlibv2.xml, and open it with IE.

5. IE5.5, the release available at the time of writing, does not validate an XML file against its DTD.
6. Netscape Navigator does not display xml files correctly for all systems.
7. The CD actually has 16 tracks, but let's settle for entering five tracks.

Table 16-12: XML for describing a CD (cdlib.xml)

```
<?xml version = "1.0"?>
<!DOCTYPE cdlibrary SYSTEM "cdlib.dtd">
<cdlibrary>
  <cd>
    <cdid>A2 1325</cdid>
    <cdlabel>Atlantic</cdlabel>
    <cdtitle>Pyramid</cdtitle>
    <cdyear>1960</cdyear>
    <track>
      <trknum>1</trknum>
      <trktitle>Vendome</trktitle>
      <trklen>2:30</trklen>
    </track>
    <track>
      <trknum>2</trknum>
      <trktitle>Pyramid</trktitle>
      <trklen>10:46</trklen>
    </track>
    <track>
      <trknum>3</trknum>
      <trktitle>It don't mean a thing</trktitle>
      <trklen>5:02</trklen>
    </track>
    <track>
      <trknum>4</trknum>
      <trktitle>Django</trktitle>
      <trklen>5:23</trklen>
    </track>
    <track>
      <trknum>5</trknum>
      <trktitle>How high the moon</trktitle>
      <trklen>6:15</trklen>
    </track>
    <track>
      <trknum>6</trknum>
      <trktitle>Romaine</trktitle>
      <trklen>7:28</trklen>
    </track>
  </cd>
</cdlibrary>
```

Table 16-13: CD data

Id	314 517 173-2	
Label	Verve	
Title	The essential Charlie Parker	
Year	1992	
Track	Title	Length
1	Now's the time	3:01
2	If I should lose you	2:46
3	Mango Mangue	2:53
4	Bloomdido	3:24
5	Star Eyes	3:28

XSL

As you now know from the prior exercise, the browser display of XML is not particularly usable. What is missing is a stylesheet that tells the browser how to display an XML file. **Extensible Stylesheet Language (XSL)** is a language for defining the rendering of an XML file. An XSL document defines the rules for presenting an XML document's data. XSL is an application of XML, and an XSL file is also an XML file.

The power of XSL is demonstrated by applying the stylesheet shown in Table 16-14 to the XML displayed in Table 16-12 to produce Figure 16-3.

Figure 16-3. Result of applying a stylesheet to CD data

To use a stylesheet with an XML file, you must add a line of code to point to the stylesheet file. In this case, you add the following:

```
<?xml-stylesheet type="text/xsl" href="cd.xsl" media="screen"?>
```

as the third line of cd.xml (i.e., it appears before <cdlibrary>). The added line of code points to cd.xsl as the stylesheet. This means when the browser loads cdstyle.xml,[8] it uses the contents of cd.xsl to determine how to render the contents of cdstyle.xml.

We now need to examine the contents of cd.xsl so you can learn some basics of creating XSL commands. You will soon notice that all XSL commands are preceded by xsl:.

- Line 1 tells the browser it is processing an XML file.
- Line 2 specifies that the file is a stylesheet.
- Line 3 tells the transformation engine to start processing at the root element of the source document (i.e., cdlibrary, in this case).

8. The cd.xml file with the additional line of code to identify the stylesheet.

Table 16-14: Stylesheet for displaying an XML file of CD data (cdlib.xsl)

```
1 <?xml version="1.0"?>
2 <xsl:stylesheet xmlns:xsl="http://www.w3.org/TR/WD-xsl">
3 <xsl:template match="/">
4 <html>
5   <title>Complete List of Songs</title>
6   <body>
7     <table border="2">
8       <tr bgcolor="khaki">
9         <th align="left">CD id</th>
10        <th align="left">Title</th>
11        <th align="left">Label</th>
12        <th align="left">Year</th>
13      </tr>
14      <tr>
15        <td align="left"><xsl:value-of select="//cdid"/></td>
16        <td align="left"><xsl:value-of select="//cdtitle"/></td>
17        <td align="left"><xsl:value-of select="//cdlabel"/>></td>
18        <td align="left"><xsl:value-of select="//cdyear"/></td>
19        </tr>
20    </table>
21    <p></p>
22    <table border="2">
23      <tr bgcolor="beige">
24        <th colspan="3">Songs</th>
25      </tr>
26        <tr bgcolor="beige">
27        <th align="left" rowspan="5">Track</th>
28        <th align="left" rowspan="5">Title</th>
29        <th align="left" rowspan="5">Length</th>
30      </tr>
31      <xsl:for-each select="cdlibrary/cd/*">
32      <tr>
33        <td align="left"><xsl:value-of select=".//trknum"/></td>
34        <td><xsl:value-of select=".//trktitle"/></td>
35        <td align="center"><xsl:value-of select=".//trklen"/></td>
36      </tr>
37      </xsl:for-each>
38    </table>
39  </body>
40 </html>
41 </xsl:template></xsl:stylesheet>
```

- Lines 7-13 are standard HTML for defining a table, and in this case defining the column headers.
- Lines 15-18 define the variables to be placed in each column using XSL commands to indicate which variables are associated with each cell. For example, <xsl:value-of select="//cdid"/> specifies selection of **cdid** for the first (i.e., leftmost) column of the table.
- Line 31 is the beginning of a loop terminated in line 37. The code creates one row for each of the multiple elements of a CD (i.e., for each of the tracks). Refer to Table 16-8 and Figure 16-2 for the DTD.

Your turn

1. Use Internet Explorer to access this book's Web site, link to the XML section, and download cdlib.xsl into a directory on your machine.
2. Edit a copy of cdlib.xml by inserting the following as the third line of cdlib.xml `<?xml-stylesheet type="text/xsl" href="cdlib.xsl" media="screen"?>`.
3. Save the file as cdlibv3.xml in the same directory as cdlib.xsl and open it with IE.
4. Make a similar change to cdlibv2.xml and open it with IE.

Converting XML

There are occasions when there is a need to convert an XML file.

- **transformation**—conversion from one XML vocabulary to another (e.g., between financial language FPML to finML);
- **manipulation**—reordering, filtering, or sorting parts of a document prior to presentation;
- **rendering in another language**—rendering the XML file using another format, such as Wireless Access Protocol (WAP).

You have already seen how XSL can be used to transform XML for rendering as HTML. The original XSL language has been split into three languages:

- XSLT for transformation and manipulation;
- XSLF for rendition;
- XPath for accessing the structure of an XML file.

For a data management course, this is as far as you need to go with learning about XSL. Just remember that you have only touched the surface. To become proficient in XML, you will need an entire course on the topic.

XML and databases

XML is more than a document processing technology. It is also a powerful tool for data management. For database developers, XML is likely to be used to facilitate middle tier data integration and schemas. Most of the current major DBMS producers are developing XML-centric extensions to their product lines.

XML documents have to be stored for the long term, because they are an important repository of organizational memory. As a data exchange language, XML is also a means of moving data between databases, which means we will need tools for exporting and importing XML.

XML documents can be stored in the same format as you would store a word processing or HTML file: you just place them in an appropriately named folder. File systems, however, have limitations that become particularly apparent when a large number of files need to be stored, as in the corporate setting.

What is needed is a database management system for storing, retrieving, and manipulating XML documents. Such a DBMS should

- be able to store a large number of documents;
- be able to store large documents;
- support access to portions of a document (e.g., the data for a single CD in a library of 20,000 CDs);
- enable concurrent access to a document but provide locking mechanisms to prevent the *lost update problem* (see page 509), which can happen when two or more people are editing the same portion of a document;
- keep track of different versions of a document;
- integrate data from other sources (e.g., insert the results of an SQL query formatted as an XML fragment into an XML document).

There are several possible solutions for XML document management: RDBMS, OODBMS, or an XML database.

RDBMS

An XML document could be stored within an RDBMS. Storing an intact XML document as a CLOB (see page 252) is a sensible strategy if the XML document contains static content that will only be updated by replacing the entire document. Examples include written text such as articles, advertisements, books, or legal contracts. These *document-centric* files[9] (e.g., articles and legal contracts) are retrieved and updated in their entirety.

For more dynamic *data-centric* XML files[10] (e.g., orders, price lists, airline schedules), the RDBMS must be extended to support the structure of the data so that portions of the document (e.g., elements) can be retrieved and updated. The object-relational extensions of most major databases provide the wherewithal to capture the structure of an XML document. For example, Oracle's XML SQL utility can store an XML document by mapping it to an object-relational format. The same utility can then retrieve the data as an XML document.

You can expect most RDBMS vendors to offer extensions for supporting storage and retrieval of both document- and data-centric XML files. Some of them are likely to release XML servers that are built on underlying relational technology.

9. Document-centric files have low structure (i.e., a few elements and mainly text).
10. Data-centric files have high structure (i.e., many elements, often repeated).

Another issue is the conversion of existing relational data to XML. Already, products are emerging, such as DB2XML.

DB2XML

Some sources estimate that more than 75 percent of current Web pages are generated from database data. These data are typically converted into HTML by a server-side script, which you learned how to write in Chapter 15. An alternative is to convert relational data to XML, and with an appropriate stylesheet, let the browser generate the presentation. This approach has the advantage of reducing the complexity of applications by separating SQL and server-side scripting code. DB2XML[11] is an example of a tool for converting relational data to XML.

DB2XML has three main functions:

- transform the results of a query into an XML document;
- generate a DTD for the XML;
- transform the XML using a stylesheet.

Your turn

1. Use your browser to access http://www.informatik.fh-wiesbaden.de/~turau/DB2XML/demo/db2xmlxslservlet.html and execute one of the demonstrations. Inspect the stylesheet and XML document.
2. Which do you think is easier to write and maintain, PHP and server-side scripting or DB2XML and stylesheets?

A DBMS is designed to store data and XML is designed for data interchange.Thus, we need tools, such as DB2XML, for converting data extracted from a database into a format that can be exchanged among organizations. However, it is not clear at this point which path data presentation should follow: SQL and server-side scripting or XML and stylesheets. As tools are developed to support both of these paths, this uncertainty should be resolved.

OODBMS

OODBMS vendors can also use their technology for storing XML documents. However, at this point most have done little more than store entire XML documents as objects. This is not surprising, as OODBMS vendors do not have the market size of RDBMS vendors and hence have less resources to invest in creating advanced XML handling features.

Some argue that the OODBMS model is a better candidate for managing XML documents than the relational model. As we learned in Chapter 13, despite some advantages, the OODBMS model has made little progress in replacing relational technology.

---

11. http://www.informatik.fh-wiesbaden.de/~turau/DB2XML/

XML database

A third approach is to build a special-purpose XML database. Tamino is an example of such an approach, and you can expect others to emerge in the near future. Because this is such a new area, this textbook can do little more than make you aware of the technology and urge you to monitor the development of XML databases.

XML in Government

The U.K.'s e-Government Interoperability Framework (e-GIF) sets out the government's technical policies and standards for achieving interoperability and information systems conformity across the public sector. It defines the essential prerequisite for linked, Web-enabled government and is a cornerstone policy in the overall e-government strategy.

The main thrust is to adopt Internet and Web standards for all government systems. The e-GIF also adopts standards that are well supported in the market place. It is a pragmatic strategy that aims to reduce cost and risk for government systems whilst aligning them to the global Internet revolution.

The government policy is to use: XML and XML schemas for data integration; UML (unified modeling language), RDF (resource description framework), and XML for data modelling and description language; XSL, DOM and XML for data presentation. XML products will be written so as to comply with the recommendations of the World Wide Web Consortium (W3C).

e-GIF is a key plank in the government's drive to get all its services online by 2005 and cut bureaucracy within the public sector. There are two main benefits the policy will bring: creating 24-hour one-stop government and banishing bureaucracy in government by moving the public sector away from traditional paper based ways of working by electronically integrating information across a range of government departments and organizations.

The government has launched the U.K. GovTalk initiative. This is a Cabinet Office led, joint government and industry forum for generating and agreeing on XML data schemas for use throughout the public sector. The GovTalk Group will manage the acceptance, publication, and any subsequent change requests for the schema. The initiative helps developers by providing information, best practice guidance, and toolkits for conversion of legacy data. It is intended to make adoption of the e-GIF policies and standards simple, attractive, and cost-effective.

Source: http://www.citu.gov.uk/egif/contents.htm

Your turn

1. Visit the Web site for Tamino[12] and review the benefits and architecture of the product.
2. Search the Tamino site or the computer press[13] to learn which companies have adopted Tamino.
3. What conclusions do you reach about the usefulness of an XML database?

Conclusion

XML is a significant technological development, and its importance and value will be increasingly apparent. It is clear that its main role will be to facilitate the exchange of data between organizations and within those organizations that do not have integrated systems. XML will achieve much of what was promised by EDI in that it will significantly lower the cost of transactions by accelerating the transfer of information from paper to electrons.

Whether XML will become dominant in data presentation and storage is undecided. There are acceptable alternatives for data presentation (e.g. server-side scripting and Java), and the superiority of XSL is not obvious. Similarly, relational technology can be successfully extended to store and process XML documents. Thus, the case for pure XML database technology is also not obvious.

New technologies inevitably generate a lot of excitement and speculation about the downfall of prior technology. XML certainly has a role in the management of organizational data. Although the size and extent of this role is unclear, it is certain that all data managers must have some knowledge of XML.

Mastery of XML is well beyond the scope of a single chapter. Indeed, it is a book length topic and more than 100 books have already been written on this relatively recent technology. It is important to remember that the prime goal of XML is to support data interchange.

Summary

Electronic data exchange has become more important with the widespread use of the Internet. EDI, which penetrated mainly the major organizations, is being replaced by XML. SGML, a precursor of XML, defines the structure of documents. SGML's value derives from its reusability, flexibility, and support for revision. XML, a derivative of SGML, is designed to support electronic commerce and overcome some of the shortcomings of SGML. XML supports data exchange by making information self-describing. It is a metalanguage be-

12. http://www.softwareag.com/tamino platform/introduction.htm
13. e.g., http://computerworld.com/

The tags on retail

The Association for Retail Technology Standards (ARTS), the standards arm of the National Retail Federation, has compiled a dictionary of XML tags. These tags are a prerequisite for exchanging business information on line in XML and are essential if B2B electronic commerce is to expand.

These tags are plain English words and not computer codes. They are used to set off and define critical data in an XML transmission. For example, a brand name in an XML document would be flanked by the tags <brand name>. By having a standard data dictionary, XML messages can be transmitted without confusion in their interpretation.

The retail industry has not had an XML data dictionary until now. Currently, there are several in the works. The Uniform Code Council is compiling one as part of its UCCnet B2B exchange and data-synchronization initiative. The National Association of Convenience Stores (NACS) is developing a data dictionary for the convenience store and petroleum retailing industries.

There are two versions of the ARTS data dictionary. The standard, public-domain version is accessible at www.nrf-arts.org/. It contains 2,298 tags for the retail industry with explanations for each tag.

Source: Anonymous. 2000. ARTS publishes XML retail data dictionary. *Chain Store Age* 76 (11):108.

cause it is a language to generate other languages (e.g., finML). It promises substantial gains for the management and distribution of data. The XML language consists of a DTD, DOM, and XSL.

A DTD defines the structure of a document and how an application should interpret XML markup tags. The DOM is a tree-based data model of an XML document. XSL is used to specify a stylesheet for displaying an XML document.

XML documents can be stored in either a RDBMS, OODBMS, or XML database. There are tools for converting relational data to XML format and vice versa. XML is a significant technological development that will facilitate the exchange of data between and within organizations.

Key terms and concepts

Connectors
Document object model (DOM)
Document type definition (DTD)
Electronic data interchange (EDI)
Extensible markup language (XML)
Extensible style language (XSL)
Hypertext markup language (HTML)
Markup language
Occurrence indicators
Standard generalized markup language (SGML)
XML database

References

Anderson, R. 2000. *Professional XML*. Birmingham, UK; Chicago: Wrox Press.

Exercises

1. A business has a telephone directory that records the first and last name, telephone number, and e-mail address of everyone working in the firm. Departments are the main organizing unit of the firm, so the telephone directory is typically displayed in department order, and shows for each department the contact phone and fax numbers and e-mail address.
   a. Create a hierarchical data model for this problem.
   b. Define the DTD.
   c. Create an XML file containing some directory data.
   d. Create an XSL file containing a stylesheet.
2. Create a DTD for your university or college's course bulletin.
3. Create a DTD for a credit card statement.
4. Take a page in a dictionary and do the following:
   a. Create a hierarchical data model for this problem.
   b. Define the DTD.
   c. Create an XML file containing some directory data.
   d. Create an XSL file containing a stylesheet.
5. Search the Web to identify an XML standard for an industry. What do you observe about the standard? How detailed is it (e.g., how many elements)? Is industry adopting the standard?

Case: A conference support system

An ideal conference support system would record all conference data (e.g., accepted articles, timetable, attendees) in SGML (standard generalized markup language) in a conference information repository. Then, using the data in the repository, reports could be generated from multiple contexts (e.g., text on a PDA, synthesized voice on cell phone, and XML on a browser). The essence of the system is captured in Figure 16-4.

The major aspects of the data management problem are that the multiple documents of the conference information repository are prepared using a variety of word processing systems (e.g., Microsoft Word and Adobe Framemaker). Furthermore, some authors use a variety of stylesheets and some use none. Consequently, the current system makes it almost

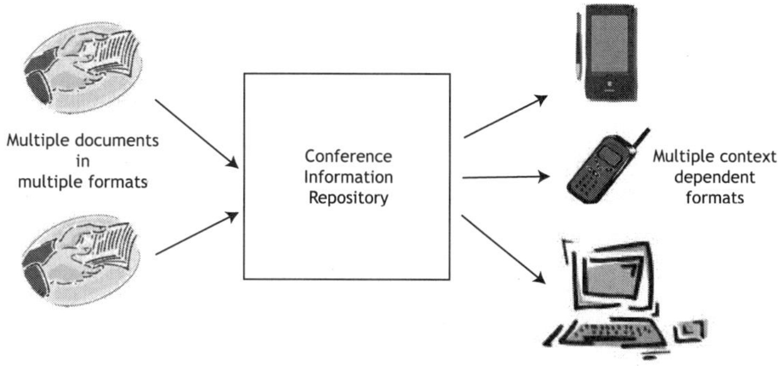

Figure 16-4. The conference support system

impossible to convert accepted articles into a standard content recording language, such as SGML or XML.

Answer the following questions:

1. What system might you implement for getting authors to create documents that can be readily converted to XML? Don't try to be too fancy as it is probably sufficient to capture heading levels as well as the body text.
2. What technology would you select for the conference information repository?
3. What technologies exist for converting XML to different devices (e.g., cell phones, PDAs)?
4. Design the XML DTD.

Section 5

Managing Organizational Memory

Everyone complains of his memory, none of his judgment.
François Duc de La Rochefoucauld "Sentences et Maximes,"
Morales No. 89 1678

As you now realize, organizational memory is an important resource requiring management. An inaccurate memory can result in bad decisions and poor customer service. Some aspects of organizational memory (e.g., chemical formulae, marketing strategy, and R&D plans) are critical to the well-being of an organization. The financial consequences can be extremely significant if these memories are lost or fall into the hands of competitors. Consequently, organizations must develop and implement procedures for maintaining data integrity. They need policies to protect the existence of data, maintain its quality, and ensure its confidentiality. Some of these procedures may be embedded in organizational memory technology and others may be performed by data management staff. Data integrity (Chapter 17) is the first issue addressed in this section.

When organizations recognize a resource as important to their long-term viability, they typically create a formal mechanism to manage it. For example, most companies have a human resources department, responsible for activities such as compensation, recruiting, training, and employee counseling. People are the major resource of nearly every company, and the human resources department manages this resource. Similarly, the finance department manages a company's financial assets.

In the information age, data—the raw material of information—need to be managed. Consequently, data administration has become a formal organizational structure in many enterprises. Data administration is the focus of Chapter 18.

17

Data Integrity

Integrity without knowledge is weak and useless, and knowledge without integrity is dangerous and dreadful.

Samuel Johnson, *Rasselas*, 1759

Learning objectives

After completing this chapter, you will

- understand the three major data integrity outcomes;
- understand the strategies for achieving each of the data integrity outcomes;
- understand the possible threats to data integrity and how to deal with them;
- understand the principles of transaction management;
- realize that successful data management requires making data available and maintaining data integrity.

The Expeditioner has become very dependent on its databases. The day-to-day operations of the company would be adversely affected if the major operational databases were lost. Indeed, The Expeditioner may not be able to survive a major data loss. Recently, there have also been a few minor problems with the quality and confidentiality of some of the databases. A part-time salesperson was discovered making a query about staff salaries. A major order was nearly lost when it was shipped to the wrong address because the complete shipping address had not been entered when the order was taken. The sales database had been off-line for 30 minutes last Monday morning because of a disk-sector read error.

The Expeditioner had spent much time and money creating an extremely effective and efficient management system. It became clear, however, that more attention needed to be paid to maintaining the system and ensuring that high-quality data were continuously available to authorized users.

Introduction

The management of data is driven by two goals: availability and integrity. **Availability** deals with making data available to whoever needs it, whenever and wherever they need it, and in a meaningful form. As illustrated in Figure 17-1, availability concerns the creation, interrogation, and update of data stores. Although most of the book, thus far, has dealt with making data available, a database is of little use to anyone unless it has integrity. Maintaining data integrity implies three goals:[1]

1. Protecting existence: data are available when needed.
2. Maintaining quality: data are accurate, complete, and current.
3. Ensuring confidentiality: data are accessed only by those authorized to do so.

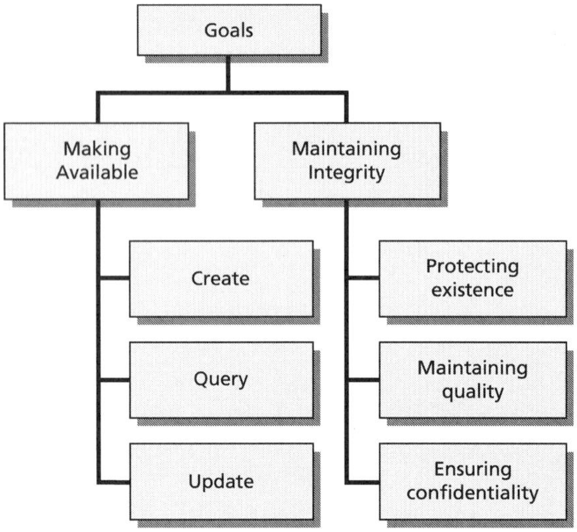

Figure 17-1. Goals of managing organizational memory

This chapter considers the three types of strategies for maintaining data integrity:

- **Legal** strategies are externally imposed laws, rules, and regulations. Privacy laws are an example.

1. To our knowledge, Everest was the first to define integrity in terms of these three goals. See Everest, G., 1986. *Database management: objectives, systems functions, and administration*. New York, NY: McGraw-Hill, .

- **Administrative** strategies are organizational policies and procedures. An example is a standard operating procedure of storing all backup files in a locked vault.
- **Technical** strategies are those incorporated in the computer system (e.g., DBMS, application program, or operating system). An example is the inclusion of validation rules (e.g., NOT NULL) in a database definition that are used to ensure data quality when a database is updated.

A **consistent database** is one in which all data integrity constraints are satisfied.

Our focus is on data stored in multiuser computer databases and technical and administrative strategies for maintaining integrity.[2] The term **database integrity** is commonly used to denote data integrity in computer system environments. More and more, organizational memories are being captured in computerized databases. From an integrity perspective, this is a very positive development. Computers offer some excellent mechanisms for controlling data integrity, but this does not eliminate the need for administrative strategies. Both administrative and technical strategies are still needed.

Who is responsible for database integrity? Some would say the data users, others the database administrator (see Chapter 18). Both groups are right; database integrity is a shared responsibility, and the way it is managed may differ across organizations. Our focus is on the tools and strategies for maintaining data integrity, regardless of who is responsible.

The strategies for achieving the three integrity outcomes are summarized in Table 17-1. We will cover the strategies for protecting existence, followed by those for maintaining integrity, and finally those used to ensure confidentiality. Before considering each of these goals, we need to examine the general issue of transaction management.

Table 17-1: Strategies for maintaining database integrity

Database integrity outcome	Strategies for achieving the outcome
Protecting existence	Isolation (preventive) Database backup and recovery (curative)
Maintaining quality	Update authorization Integrity constraints/data validation Concurrent update control
Ensuring confidentiality	Access control Encryption

Transaction management

Transaction management focuses on ensuring that transactions are correctly recorded in the database. The **transaction manager** is the element of a DBMS that processes transactions. A **transaction** is a series of actions to be taken on the database such that they must be entirely completed or aborted. A transaction is a **logical unit of work**. All its elements must be processed; otherwise, the database will be incorrect. For example, with

2. Many of the concepts presented are also applicable to noncomputerized data stores.

a credit sale of a product, the transaction consists of least two parts: an update to the inventory on hand, and an update to the customer information with the items sold in order to bill the customer later. Updating only the inventory or only the customer information would create a database without integrity or an inconsistent database.

The two critical features of a transaction management are that all transactions be processed on an **all-or-nothing** rule and that any collection of transactions is **serializable**. When a transaction manager has these two criteria; it provides **transaction atomicity**.

The all-or-nothing basis means that there are no partial transactions. When a transaction is executed, either all its changes to the database are completed or none of the changes are performed. In other words, the entire unit of work must be completed. If a transaction is terminated before it is completed, the transaction manager must undo the executed actions to restore the database to its state before the transaction commenced. Once a transaction is successfully completed, it does not need to be undone. For efficiency reasons, transactions should be no larger than necessary to ensure the integrity of the database. For example, in an accounting system, a debit and credit would be an appropriate transaction, because this is the minimum amount of work to keep the books in balance.

Serializability relates to the effect of the execution of a set of transactions. An interleaved execution schedule (i.e., the elements of different transactions are intermixed) is serializable if its outcome is equivalent to a noninterleaved (i.e., serial) schedule. Interleaved operations are often used to increase the efficiency of computing resources, so it is not unusual for the components of multiple transactions to be interleaved. Interleaved transactions cause problems when they interfere with each other, and, as a result, the correctness of the database is compromised.

The all-or-nothing rule and serializability are critical to concurrent update control and recovery after a transaction failure.

Concurrent update control

When updating a database, most users implicitly assume that their actions do not interfere with any other users' actions. If the DBMS is a single-user system, then a lack of interference is guaranteed. Most DBMSs, however, are multiuser systems, where many can be accessing a given database at the same time. When two or more transactions are allowed to update a database concurrently, the integrity of the database is threatened. For example, multiple agents selling airline tickets should not be able to sell the same seat twice. Similarly, inconsistent results can be obtained by a retrieval transaction when retrievals are being made simultaneously with updates. This gives the appearance of a loss of database integrity. We will first discuss the integrity problems caused by concurrent updates and then show how to control them to ensure database quality.

Lost update

Uncontrolled concurrent updates can result in the *lost-update* or *phantom-record* problem. To illustrate the lost-update problem, suppose two concurrent update transactions simultaneously want to update the same record in an inventory file. Both want to update the quantity on hand field (QUANTITY). Assume QUANTITY has a current value of 40. One update transaction wants to add 80 units (a delivery) to QUANTITY, while the other transaction wants to subtract 20 units (a sale).

Suppose the transactions have concurrent access to the record; that is, each transaction is able to read the record from the database before a previous transaction has been committed. This sequence is depicted in Figure 17-2. Note that the first transaction, A, has not updated the database when the second transaction, B, reads the same record. Thus, both A and B read in a value of 40 for QUANTITY. Both make their calculations, then A writes the value of 120 to disk, followed by B promptly overwriting the 120 with 20. The result is that the delivery of 80 units, transaction A, is *lost* during the update process.

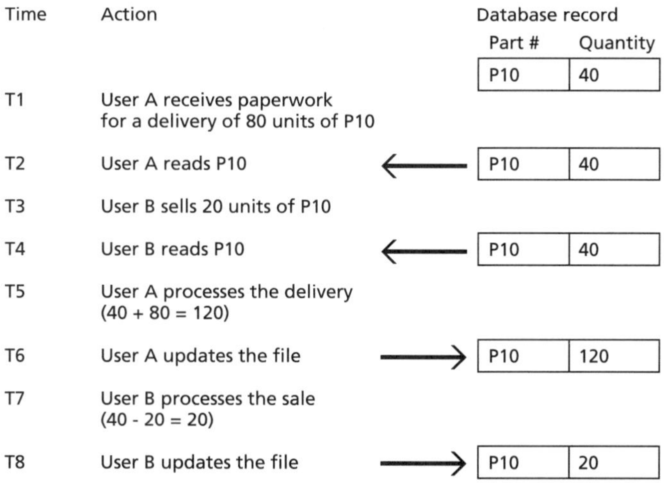

Figure 17-2. Lost update when concurrent accessing is allowed

Inconsistent retrievals occur when a transaction calculates some aggregate function (e.g., sum) over a set of data while other transactions are updating the same data. The problem is the retrieval may read some data before they are changed and other data after they are changed, thereby yielding inconsistent results.

The solution: locking

To prevent lost updates and inconsistent retrieval results, the DBMS must incorporate a resource **lock**, a basic tool of transaction management to ensure correct transaction behavior. Any data retrieved by one user with the intent of updating must be locked out or denied access by other users until the update is completed.

There are two types of locks: **Slocks** (shared or read locks) and **XLocks** (exclusive or write locks). Some key points to understand about these types of locks are

- When a transaction has a Slock on a database item, other transactions can issue Slocks on the same item, but there can be no Xlocks on that item.
- Before a transaction can read a database item, it must be granted a Slock or Xlock on that item.
- When a transaction has a Xlock on a database item, no other transaction can issue either a Slock or Xlock on that item.
- Before a transaction can write to a database item, it must be granted a Xlock on that item.

Consider the example used previously. When A accesses the record for update, the DBMS must refuse all further accesses to that record until transaction A is complete (i.e., a XLock). As Figure 17-3 shows, B's first attempt to access the record is denied until transaction A is finished. As a result, database integrity is maintained. Unless the DBMS controls concurrent access, a multiuser database environment can create both data and retrieval integrity problems.

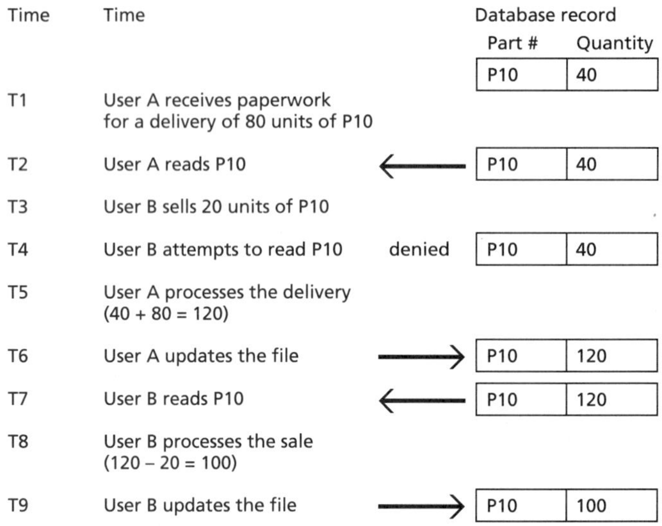

Figure 17-3. Valid update when concurrent accessing is not allowed

To administer locking procedures, a DBMS requires two pieces of information:

1. whether a particular transaction will update the database;
2. where the transaction begins and ends.

Usually, the data required by an update transaction are locked when the transaction begins and then released when the transaction is completed (i.e., committed to the database) or aborted. Locking mechanisms can operate at different levels of **locking granularity**: database, file (or table), page, record (or row), or data element. At the most precise level, a DBMS can lock individual data elements so that different update transactions can update different items in the same record concurrently. This approach increases processing overhead but provides the fewest resource conflicts. At the other end of the continuum, the DBMS can lock the entire database for each update. If there were many update transactions to process, this would be very unacceptable due to the long waiting times. Locking at the record level is the most common approach taken by commercial DBMSs.

In most situations, users are not concerned with locking, because it is handled entirely by the DBMS. But in some DBMS, choices are provided to the user. These are primarily limited to programming language interfaces.

Resource locking solves some data and retrieval integrity problems, but it may lead to another problem, referred to as **deadlock** or the **deadly embrace**. Deadlock is an impasse that occurs because two users lock certain resources, then request resources locked by the other user. Figure 17-4 illustrates a deadlock situation. Both transactions require records 1 and 2. Transaction A first accesses record 1 and locks it. Then transaction B accesses record 2 and locks it. Next, B's attempt to access record 1 is denied, so the application waits for the record to be released. Finally, A's attempt to access record 2 is denied, so the application waits for the record to be released. Thus, user A's update transaction is waiting for record 2 (locked by user B), and user B is waiting for record 1 (locked by user A). Unless the DBMS intervenes, both users will wait indefinitely.

There are two ways to resolve deadlock: prevention and resolution. **Deadlock prevention** requires users to lock in advance all records they will require. User B would have to lock both records 1 and 2 (in Figure 17-4) before processing the transaction. If these records are locked, B would have to wait.

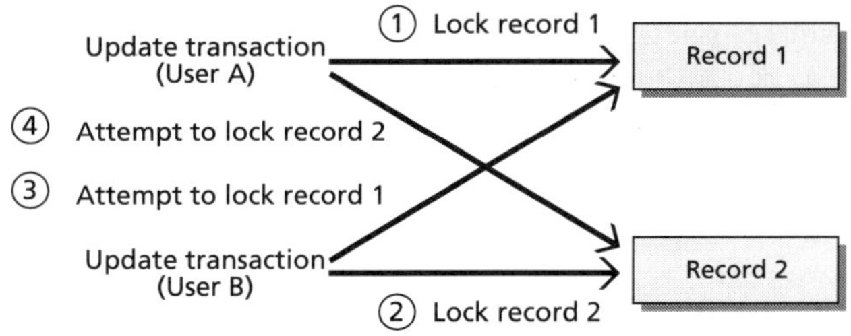

Figure 17-4. An example of deadlock

The **two-phase locking protocol** is a simple approach to preventing deadlocks. It operates on the notion that a transaction has a growing phase followed by a shrinking phase. During the growing phase, locks can be requested. The shrinking phase is initiated by a release statement, which means no additional locks can be requested. A release statement enables the programmer to signal to the DBMS the transition from requesting locks to releasing locks.

Another approach to deadlock prevention is **deadlock resolution,** whereby the DBMS detects and breaks deadlocks. The DBMS usually keeps a resource usage matrix, which instantly reflects which users (e.g., update transactions) are using which resources (e.g., records). By scanning the matrix, the DBMS can detect deadlocks as they occur. The DBMS then resolves the deadlock by backing out one of the deadlocked transactions. For example, the DBMS might release user A's lock on record 1, thus allowing user B to proceed. Any changes made by user A up to that time (e.g., updates to record 1) would be rolled back. User A's transaction would be restarted when the required resources became available.

Transaction failure and recovery

When a transaction fails, there is the danger of an inconsistent database. Transactions can fail for a variety of reasons, including

- program error (e.g., a logic error in the code);
- action by the transaction manager (e.g., resolution of a deadlock);
- self-abort (e.g., an error in the transaction data means it cannot be completed);
- system failure (e.g., an operating-system bug).

If a transaction fails for any reason, then the DBMS must be able to restore the database to a correct state. To do this, two statements are required: an **end of transaction (EOT)** and **commit**. EOT indicates the physical end of the transaction, the last statement. Commit, an explicit statement, must occur in the transaction code before the EOT statement. The only statements that should occur between Commit and EOT are database writes and lock releases.

When a transaction issues a Commit, the transaction manager checks that all the necessary write record locks for statements following the Commit have been established. If these locks are not in place, the transaction is terminated. Otherwise, the transaction is committed and it proceeds to execute the database writes and release locks. Once a transaction is committed, a system problem is the only failure to which it is susceptible.

When a transaction fails, the transaction manager must take one of two corrective actions:

- If the transactions has not been committed, the transaction manager must return the database to its state prior to the transaction. It must **rollback** the database to its most recent valid state.
- If the transaction has been committed, the transaction manager must ensure that the database is established at the correct post-transaction state. It must check that all write statements executed by the transaction and those appearing between Commit and EOT have been applied. The DBMS may have to redo some writes.

Protecting existence

One of the three database integrity outcomes is protecting the existence of the database — ensuring data are available when needed. Two strategies for protecting existence are isolation and database backup and recovery. **Isolation** is a preventive strategy that involves administrative procedures to insulate the physical database from destruction. Some mechanisms for doing this are keeping data in safe places, such as vaults or underground, having multiple installations, and security systems. For example, one organization keeps backup copies of important databases on removable magnetic disks. These are stored in a vault, that is always guarded. To gain access to the vault, employees need a badge with an encoded personal voice print. Many companies are building total backup computer centers, which contain duplicate databases and documentation for system operation. If something should happen at the main center (e.g., a flood), they can be up and running at their backup center in a few hours or even minutes in some highly critical situations. What isolation strategies do you use to protect the backup medium of your personal computer? Do you backup?

Backup and recovery

Database backup and recovery is a curative strategy to protect the existence of a physical database and to recreate or recover the data, whenever loss or destruction occurs. The possibility of loss always exists. The use of and choice among backup and recovery procedures depends upon an assessment of the risk of loss and the cost of applying recovery procedures. The procedures in this case are carried out by the computer system, usually the DBMS. Data loss and damage should be anticipated. No matter how small the probability of such events may be, there should be a detailed plan for data recovery.

There are several possible causes for data loss or damage, which can be grouped into three categories.

Storage-medium destruction

In this situation, a portion or all of the database is unreadable due to catastrophes such as power or air-conditioning failure, fire, flood, theft, sabotage, and the overwriting of disks or tapes by mistake. A more frequent cause is a disk failure. Some of the disk blocks may be unreadable due to a read or write malfunction, such as a head crash.

Abnormal termination of an update transaction

In this case, a transaction fails part way through execution, leaving the database partially updated. The database will be inconsistent because it does not accurately reflect the current state of the business. The primary causes of an abnormal termination are a transaction error or system failure. Some operation in the transaction, such as division by zero, may cause it to fail. A hardware or software failure will usually result in one or more active programs being aborted. If these programs were updating the database, integrity problems could result.

Incorrect data discovered

In this situation, an update program or transaction incorrectly updated the database. This usually happens because a logic error was not detected during program testing.

Because most organizations rely heavily on their databases, a DBMS must provide the following mechanisms for restoring a database quickly and accurately after loss or damage:

1. **backup facilities** that create duplicate copies of the database;
2. **journaling facilities** that provide backup copies or an audit trail of transactions or database changes;
3. **a recovery facility** within the DBMS to restore the database to a consistent state and restart the processing of transactions.

Before discussing each of these mechanisms in more depth, let us review the steps involved in updating a database and how backup and journaling facilities might be integrated into this process.

An overview of the database update process is captured in Figure 17-5. The process can be viewed as a series of database-state changes. The initial database, state 1, is modified by an update transaction, such as deleting customer Jones, creating a new state (state 2). State 1 reflects the state of the organization with Jones as a customer, while state 2 reflects the organization without this customer. Each update transaction changes the state of the database to reflect changes in organizational data. Periodically, the database is copied or backed up, possibly onto a different storage medium and stored in a secure location. In Figure 17-5, the backup is made when the database is in state 2.

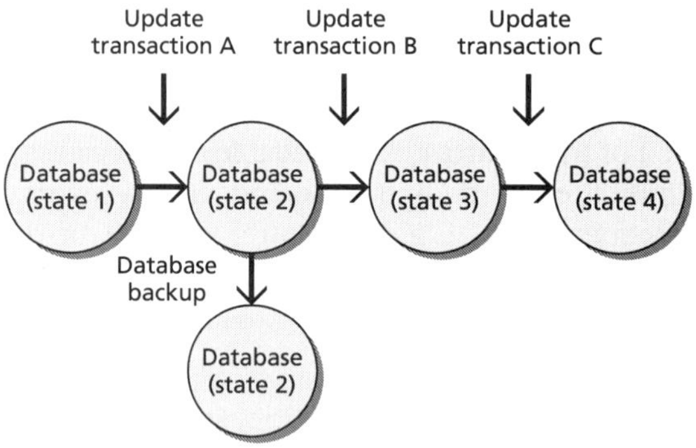

Figure 17-5. Database update procedures

A more detailed illustration of database update procedures and the incorporation of backup facilities is shown in Figure 17-6. The updating of a single record is described in the following steps.

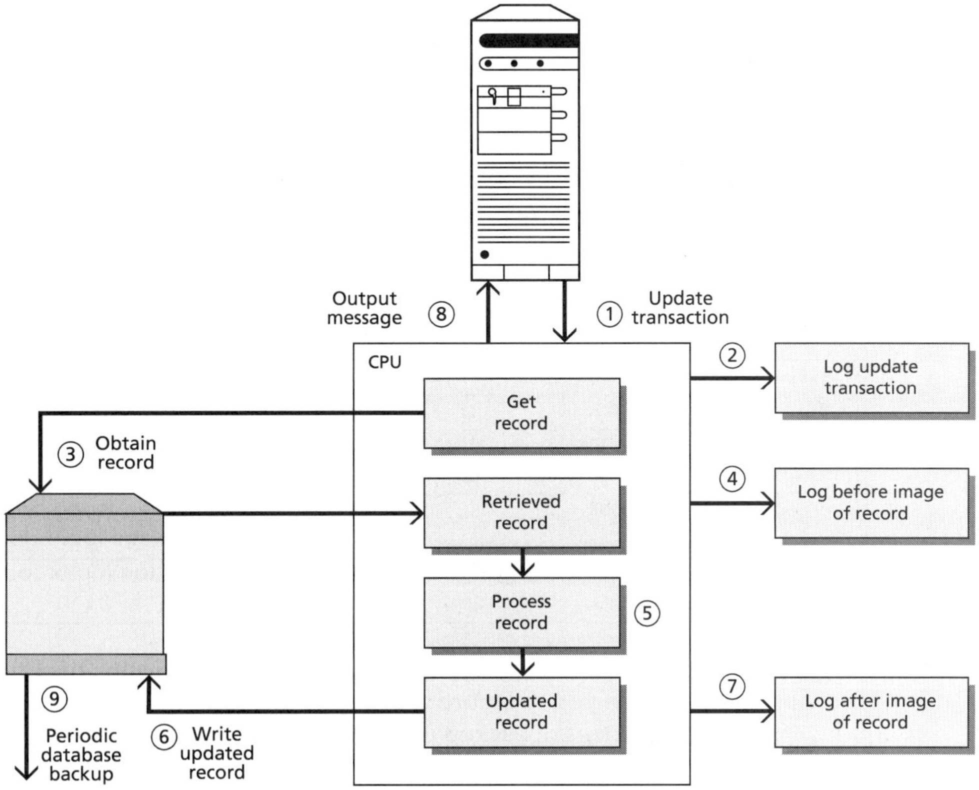

Figure 17-6. Possible procedures for a database update

1. The user submits an update transaction from a workstation.
2. The transaction is edited and validated by an application program or the DBMS. If it is valid, it is logged or stored in the transaction log or journal. A journal or log is a special database or file storing information for backup and recovery.
3. The DBMS obtains the record to be updated.
4. A copy of the retrieved record is logged to the journal file. This copy is referred to as the *before image*, because it is a copy of the database record before the transaction changes it.
5. The transaction is processed by changing the affected data items in the record.
6. The DBMS writes the updated record to the database.
7. A copy of the updated record is written to the journal. This copy is referred to as the *after image*, because it is a copy of the database record after the transaction has updated it.
8. An output message tells the user that the update has been successfully completed.
9. The database is copied periodically. This backup copy reflects all updates to the database up to the time when the copy was made. An alternate strategy to periodic

copying is to maintain multiple (usually two) complete copies of the database online and update them simultaneously. This technique, known as *mirroring*, is discussed in Chapter 11.

In order to recover from data loss or damage, it is necessary to store backup data, such as a complete copy of the database or the necessary data to restore the accuracy of a database. Preferably, backup data should be stored on another medium and kept separate from the primary database. As the description of the update process indicates, there are several options for backup data (see Table 17-2), depending on the objective of the backup procedure.

Table 17-2: Backup options

Objective	Action
Complete copy of database	Dual recording of data (mirroring)
Past states of the database (also known as database dumps)	Database backup
Changes to the database	Before-image log or journal After-image log or journal
Transactions that caused a change in the state of the database	Transaction log or journal

Data stored for backup and recovery are generally some combination of periodic database backups, transaction logs, and before and after image logs. Different recovery strategies use different combinations of backup data to recover a database.

The recovery method is highly dependent on the backup strategy. The database administrator selects a backup strategy based on a trade-off between ease of recovery from data loss or damage and the cost of performing backup operations. For example, keeping a mirror database is more expensive then keeping periodic database backups. But a mirroring strategy is useful when recovery is needed very quickly, say seconds or minutes. An airline reservations system would probably use mirroring to ensure fast and reliable recovery. In general, the cost of keeping backup data is measured in terms of interruption of database availability (e.g., time the system is out of operation when a database is being restored), storage of redundant data, and degradation of update efficiency (e.g., extra time taken in update processing to save before or after images).

Recovery strategies

The type of recovery strategy or procedure used in a given situation depends on the nature of the data loss, the type of backup data available, and the sophistication of the DBMS's recovery facilities. The following discussion outlines the four major recovery strategies: switch to a duplicate database; backward recovery or rollback; forward recovery or roll forward; and reprocessing transactions.

California blackouts

Rolling blackouts in California in January 2001 caused local companies to reevaluate their backup systems, contingency plans, and power usage to be better prepared for possible further outages. Businesses have various back-up systems to keep their most important operations in operation. Many are relying on backup generators.

AT&T's hosting centers are equipped with redundant generators and uninterruptible power supplies (UPS) capable of weathering any power outage, even if this means refueling every 48 hours. WorldCom's largest data centers are equipped with four diesel generators and at least two UPS systems. Some companies have initiated conservation measures such as turning off radios and lights. Another measure being considered is relocating employees to premises that are unaffected by the blackouts.

However, larger issues are at stake. Some high-tech companies are reassessing whether to expand operations in California. AT&T, Intel, Oracle, and other companies are indicating that California is becoming a less attractive place for business.

Source: Nelson, M. G. 2001. Power outages force mission-critical contingency plans. *Informationweek* (821):24.

The recovery procedure of switching to a duplicate database requires the maintenance of the mirror copy. The other three strategies assume a periodic dumping or backing up of the database. Periodic dumps may be made on a regular schedule, triggered automatically by the DBMS or triggered externally by personnel. The schedule may be determined by time (hourly, daily, weekly) or by event (the number of transactions since the last backup).

Switching to a duplicate database

This recovery procedure requires maintaining at least two copies of the database and updating both simultaneously. When there is a problem with one database, access is switched to the duplicate. This strategy is particularly useful when recovery must be accomplished in seconds or minutes. This procedure offers good protection against certain storage-medium destruction problems, such as disk failures, but none against events which damage or make both databases unavailable, such as a power failure or a faulty update program. This strategy entails additional costs in terms of doubling on-line storage capacity. It can also be implemented in dual computer processors where each computer updates its copy of the database. This duplexed configuration offers greater backup protection at a greater cost.

Backward recovery or rollback

Backward recovery (also called rollback or rolling back) is used to back out or undo unwanted changes to the database. For example, Figure 17-5 shows three updates (A, B, and

C) to a database. Let's say that update B terminated abnormally, leaving the database, now in state 3, inconsistent. What we need to do is return the database to state 2 by applying the before images to the database. Thus, we would rollback by changing the database to state 2 with the before images of the records updated by transaction B.

Backward recovery reverses the changes made when a transaction abnormally terminates or produces erroneous results. To illustrate the need for rollback, consider the example of a budget transfer of $1,000 between two departments.

1. The program reads the account record for Department X and subtracts $1,000 from the account balance and updates the database.
2. The program then reads the record for Department Y and adds $1,000 to the account balance, but while attempting to update the database, the program encounters a disk error and cannot write the record.

Now the database is inconsistent. Department X has been updated but Department Y has not. Thus, the transaction must be aborted and the database recovered. The DBMS would apply the before image to Department X to restore the account balance to its original value. The DBMS may then restart the transaction and make another attempt to update the database.

Forward recovery or roll forward

Forward recovery (also called roll forward or bringing forward) involves recreating a database using a prior database state. Returning to the example in Figure 17-5, suppose that state 4 of the database was destroyed and that we need to recover it. We would take the last database dump or backup (state 2) and then apply the after-image records created by update transactions B and C. This would return the database to state 4. Thus, roll forward starts with an earlier copy of the database, and by applying after images (the results of good transactions), the backup copy of database is moved forward to a later state.

Reprocessing transactions

Although similar to forward recovery, this procedure uses update transactions instead of after images. Taking the same example shown in Figure 17-5, assume the database is destroyed in state 4. We would take the last database backup (state 2) and then reprocess update transactions B and C to return the database to state 4. The main advantage of using this method is its simplicity. The DBMS does not need to create an after image journal, and there are no special restart procedures. The one major disadvantage, however, is the length of time to reprocess transactions. Depending on the frequency of database backups and the time needed to get transactions into the identical sequence as previous updates, several hours of reprocessing may be required. Processing new transactions must be delayed until the database recovery is complete.

Table 17-3 reviews the three types of data losses and the corresponding recovery strategies one could use. The major problem is to recreate a database using a backup copy, a previous state of organizational memory. Recovery is done through forward recovery, reprocessing, or switching to a duplicate database if one is available. With abnormal termination or incorrect data, the preferred strategy is backward recovery, but other procedures could be used.

Table 17-3: What to do when data loss occurs

Problem	Recovery procedures
Storage-medium destruction (database is unreadable)	* Switch to a duplicate database—this can be transparent with RAID Forward recovery Reprocess transactions
Abnormal termination of an update transaction (transaction error or system failure)	* Backward recovery Forward recovery or reprocess transactions—bring forward to the state just before termination of the transaction
Incorrect data detected (database has been incorrectly updated)	* Backward recovery Reprocess transactions (Excluding those from the update program that created the incorrect data)

* Preferred strategy

Use of recovery procedures

Usually the person doing a query or an update is not concerned with backup and recovery. Database administration personnel often implement strategies that are automatically carried out by the DBMS. ANSI has defined standards governing SQL processing of database transactions that relate to recovery. Transaction support is provided through the use of two SQL statements: COMMIT and ROLLBACK. These commands are employed when a procedural programming language such as COBOL is used to update a database. Consider the program segment in Figure 17-7, which contains the SQL commands to execute an update transaction.

The programmer wants the two update actions (statements 2 and 3) to be considered as a transaction. If both update actions are not successfully completed, the database would be inconsistent.

In the example, therefore, the programmer issues a COMMIT WORK command to the DBMS (or transaction processing portion of the DBMS), if the program completes the two updates successfully, which will commit the changes to the database and make them permanent. If anything goes wrong, however, the program issues the ROLLBACK WORK command to undo any changes made so far. The ROLLBACK WORK command works just like the backward recovery procedure previously discussed.

```
MAIN
* If an error occurs perform undo code block
1 EXEC SQL WHENEVER SQL ERROR PERFORM UNDO
* Insert a single row in table A
2 EXEC SQL INSERT
* Update a row in table B
3 EXEC SQL UPDATE
* Successful transaction, all changes are now permanent
4 EXEC SQL COMMIT WORK
5 PERFORM FINISH
UNDO
* Unsuccessful transaction, rollback the transaction
6 EXEC SQL ROLLBACK WORK
FINISH
 EXIT
```

Figure 17-7. Use of COMMIT and ROLLBACK

Maintaining quality

The second integrity goal for organizational memory is to maintain quality, which implies keeping the data accurate, complete, and current. Functions are needed within the DBMS to ensure that update actions are performed by authorized persons in accordance with stated rules or integrity constraints, and that the results are properly recorded. These functions are accomplished by update authorization, data validation using integrity constraints, and concurrent update control. Each of these functions is discussed in turn.

Update authorization

Without proper controls, update transactions can diminish the quality of a database. Unauthorized users could sabotage a database by entering erroneous values. The first step is to ensure that anyone who wants to update a database is authorized to do so. Some responsible person—usually the database owner or database administrator—must tell the DBMS who is permitted to initiate particular database operations. The DBMS must then check every transaction to ensure it is authorized. Unauthorized access of a database exposes an organization to many risks, including fraud and sabotage.

Update authorization is accomplished through the same access mechanism used to protect confidentiality. We will discuss access control more thoroughly later in this chapter. In SQL, access control is implemented through the GRANT command, which gives a user a privilege, and REVOKE, which removes a privilege. (These commands are discussed in Chapter 10.) A control mechanism may lump all update actions into a single privilege or separate them for greater control. In SQL, they are separated as follows:

- UPDATE (privilege to change field values using UPDATE. This can be column specific);
- DELETE (privilege to delete records from a table);
- INSERT (privilege to insert records into a table).

Separate privileges for each of the update commands allow tighter controls on certain update actions, such as updating a salary field or deleting records.

Data validation using integrity constraints

Once the update process has been authorized, the DBMS must ensure that a database is accurate and complete before any updates are applied. Consequently, the DBMS needs to be aware of any integrity constraints or rules that apply to the data. For example, the QDEL table in the relational database described previously (see page 281) would have constraints such as

- delivery number (DELNO) must be unique, numeric, and in the range 1-99999;
- delivered quantity (DELQTY) must be non-zero;
- item name (ITEMNAME) must appear in the QITEM table;
- supplier code (SPLNO) must appear in the QSPL table.

Once integrity constraints are specified, the DBMS must monitor or validate all insert and update operations to ensure that they do not violate any of the constraints or rules.

The key to updating data validation is a clear definition of valid and invalid data. Data validation cannot be performed without integrity constraints or rules. A person or the DBMS must know what the data should look like — valid values, tests to perform, procedures to invoke — to determine their validity. All data validation is based on a prior expression of integrity constraints.

Data validation may not always produce error-free data, however. Sometimes integrity constraints are unknown or are not well defined. In other cases, the DBMS does provide a convenient means for expressing and performing validation checks. Sometimes the costs of implementing the constraints are too high. Certain checks may take too long or require the storage and management of too much extra data. For example, to validate American state codes, you need to create a table containing the correct codes for all 50 states and Washington, D.C. This is not very expensive to establish. But what if you decided to validate all zip codes? Like most design decisions, establishing integrity constraints involves trade-offs.

Based on how integrity constraints have been defined, data validation can be performed outside the DBMS by people or within the DBMS itself. External validation is usually done by reviewing input documents before they are entered into the system and by checking system outputs to ensure that the database was updated correctly. Maintaining data quality is of paramount importance, and data validation preferably should be handled by the DBMS as much as possible, rather than by the user. The user should handle the exceptions and respond to any failed data-validation checks.

Integrity constraints are usually specified as part of the database definition supplied to the DBMS. For example, the primary key uniqueness and referential integrity constraints can be specified within the SQL CREATE statement (see Chapter 10). DBMSs generally permit some constraints to be stored as part of the database schema and are used by the DBMS to monitor all update operations and perform appropriate data validation checks. Any given database is likely to be subject to a very large number of constraints, but not all of these can be automatically enforced by the DBMS. Some will need to be handled by application programs.

The general types of constraints applied to a data item are outlined in Table 17-4. Not all of these necessarily would be supported by a DBMS, and a particular database may not use all types.

Table 17-4: Types of data items in integrity constraints

Type of Integrity constraint	Explanation	Example
TYPE	Validating a data item value against a specified data type.	Supplier number is numeric.
SIZE	Defining and validating the minimum and maximum size of a data item.	Delivery number must be at least 3 digits, and at most 5.
VALUES	Providing a list of acceptable values for a data item.	Item colors must match the list provided.
RANGE	Providing one or more ranges within which the data item must fall or must NOT fall.	Employee numbers must be in the range 1–100.
PATTERN	Providing a pattern of allowable characters that define permissible formats for data values.	Department phone number must be of the form 542-nnnn (stands for exactly four decimal digits).
PROCEDURE	Providing a procedure to be invoked to validate data items.	A delivery must have valid item-name, department, and supplier values before it can be added to the database. (Tables are checked for valid entries.)
CONDITIONAL	Providing one or more conditions to apply against data values.	If item type is 'Y', then color is null.
NOT NULL (MANDATORY)	Indicating whether the data item value is mandatory (not null) or optional. The not-null option is required for primary keys.	Employee number is mandatory.
UNIQUE	Indicating whether stored values for this data item must be unique (unique compared to other values of the item within the same table or record type). The unique option is also required for identifiers.	Supplier number is unique.

As mentioned, integrity constraints are usually specified as part of the database definition supplied to the DBMS. Table 17-5 contains some typical specifications of integrity constraints for a relational DBMS.

Table 17-5: Examples of integrity constraints

Examples	Explanation

`CREATE TABLE STOCK`
`(STKCODE CHAR(3) NOT NULL,`
`...,`
`NATCODE CHAR(3),`
`PRIMARY KEY(STKCODE),`
`FOREIGN KEY FKNATION(NATCODE)`
`REFERENCES NATION`
`ON DELETE RESRICT)`
	STKCODE must always be assigned a value of 3 or less alphanumeric characters. STKCODE must be unique because it is a primary key.
	NATCODE must be assigned a value of 3 or less alphanumeric characters. NATCODE must exist as the primary key of the table NATION.
	Do not allow the deletion of a row in NATION while there still exist rows in STOCK containing the corresponding value of NATCODE.

Data quality control does not end with the application of integrity constraints. Whenever an error or unusual situation is detected by the DBMS, some form of response is required. Response rules need to be given to the DBMS along with the integrity constraints. The responses can take many different forms such as: abort the entire program, reject entire update transaction, display a message and continue processing, and let the DBMS attempt to correct the error. The response may vary depending on the type of integrity constraint violated. If the DBMS does not allow the specification of response rules, then it must take a default action when an error is detected. For example, if alphabetic data are entered in a numeric field, most DBMSs will have a default response and message (e.g., non-numeric data entered in numeric field). In the case of application programs, an error code is passed to the program from the DBMS. The program would then use this error code to execute an error-handling procedure.

Ensuring confidentiality

Thus far, we have discussed how the first two goals of data integrity can be accomplished: data are available when needed (protecting existence); data are accurate, complete, and current (maintaining quality). This section deals with the final goal, ensuring confidentiality or data security. Two DBMS functions—access control and encryption—are the primary means of ensuring the data are accessed only by those authorized to do so. We begin by discussing an overall model of data security.

General model of data security

Figure 17-8 depicts the two functions for ensuring data confidentiality, access control and encryption. Access control consists of two basic steps — identification and authorization. Once past access control, the user is permitted to access the database. Access control is applied only to the established avenues of entry to a database. Clever people, however, may be able to circumvent the controls and gain unauthorized access. To counteract this possibility, it is often desirable to hide the meaning of stored data by encrypting them, so that it is impossible to interpret their meaning. Encrypted data are stored in a transformed or coded format that can only be decrypted and read by those with the appropriate key.

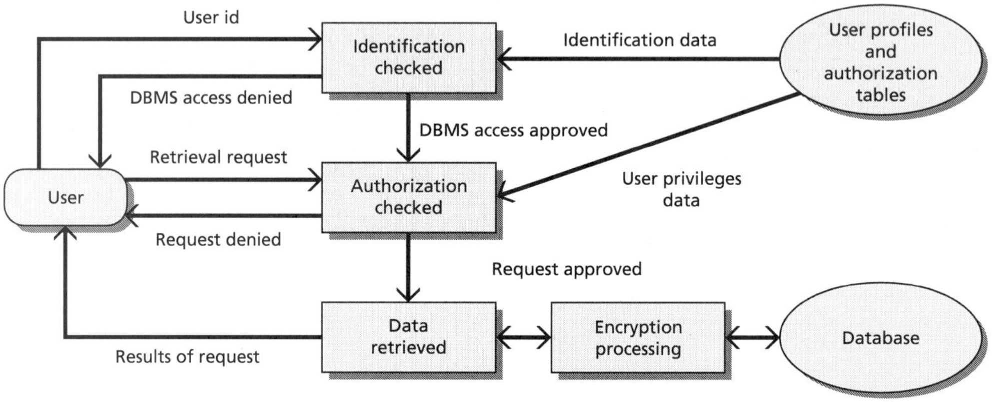

Figure 17-8. A general model of data security

Now let us walk through Figure 17-8 in detail.

- A user must be identified and provide additional information required to authenticate this identification (e.g., a userid and password). User profile information (e.g., a password or a voice print) is used to verify or authenticate a user.
- Having authenticated the user, the authorization step is initiated by a user request (retrieve or update database). The previously stored user-authorization rules (the data each user can access and the authorized actions on that data) are checked to determine if the user has the right or privilege to access the requested data. (The previously stored user privileges are created and maintained by an authorized person, database owner, or administrator.) A decision is made to permit or deny the execution of the user's request. If access is permitted, the user's transaction is processed against the database.
- Data are encrypted before storage and retrieved data decrypted before presentation.

Data access control

Data access control begins with some identification of the user or subject, an organizational entity that can access the database. Examples are individuals, departments, groups of people, transactions, terminals, and application programs. Subjects also may be combination. For example, a particular person entering a certain transaction at a particular terminal. A user identification (often called *userid*) is the first piece of data the DBMS receives from the subject. It may be a name or number. The user identification enables the DBMS to locate the corresponding entry in the stored user profiles and authorization tables (see Figure 17-8).

Taking this information, the DBMS goes through the process of authentication. The system attempts to match additional information supplied by the intended user with the information previously stored in the user profile. The system may perform multiple matches to ensure the identity of the user (see Table 17-6 for the different types). If all tests are successful, the DBMS assumes the subject is an authenticated user.

Table 17-6: Authenticating mechanisms[a]

Class	Examples
Something a person knows: **remembered information**	Name, account number, password
Something the person has: **possessed object**	Badge, plastic card, key
Something the person is: **personal characteristic**	Fingerprint, voiceprint, signature, hand size

a. Adapted from Everest, *Data management*, op. cit.

Many systems use remembered information to control access. The problem with remembered information is that it does not positively identify the user. Passwords have been the most widely used form of access control. If used correctly, they can be very effective. Unfortunately, people leave them around where others can pick them up, allowing unauthorized people to gain access to databases.

To deal with this problem, organizations are moving toward using personal characteristics and combinations of authenticating mechanisms to protect sensitive data. Collectively, these mechanisms can provide even greater security. For example, access to a large firm's very valuable marketing database requires a smart card and fingerprint, a combination of personal characteristic and a possessed object. The database can be accessed through only a few terminals in specific locations,an isolation strategy. Once the smart card test is passed, the DBMS requests entry of other remembered information—password and account number—before granting access.

Data access authorization is the process of permitting users, whose identity has been authenticated, to perform certain operations on certain data objects in a shared database. The authorization process is driven by rules incorporated into the DBMS. Authorization rules are readily shown in a table that includes subjects, objects, actions, and constraints for a given database. An example of such a table is shown in Table 17-7. Each row of the table indicates that a particular subject is authorized to take a certain action on a database object, perhaps subject to some constraint. For example, the last entry of the table indicates that Brier is authorized to delete supplier records with no restrictions.

We have already discussed subjects, but not objects, actions, and constraints. Objects are database entities protected by the DBMS. Examples are databases, views, files, records, and data items. In Table 17-7, the objects are all records. A view is another form of security. It restricts the user's access to a database. Any data not included in a view are unknown to the user. Although views promote security, several persons may share a view or unauthorized persons may gain access. Thus, a view is another object to be included in the authorization process. Typical actions on objects are shown in Table 17-7: read, insert, modify, and delete. Constraints are particular rules that apply to a subject-action-object relationship. As Table 17-7 shows, Todd (subject) can only modify (action) the type and color fields in the item record (object).

Table 17-7: Sample authorization table

Subject/Client	Action	Object	Constraint
Accounting department	Insert	Supplier record	None
Purchase department clerk	Insert	Supplier record	If quantity < 200
Purchase department supervisor	Insert	Delivery record	If quantity ≥ 200
Production department	Read	Delivery record	None
Todd	Modify	Item record	Type and color only
Order processing program	Modify	Sale record	None
Brier	Delete	Supplier record	None

Implementing authorization rules

Most contemporary DBMSs do not implement the complete authorization table shown in Table 17-7. Usually, they implement a simplified version. The most common form is an authorization table for subjects with limited applications of the constraints' column. Let us take the granting of table privileges in SQL as an example. Table privileges are needed in order to authorize subjects to perform operations on both tables and views (see Table 17-8).

Table 17-8: Authorization commands

SQL Command	Result
SELECT	permitted to retrieve data
UPDATE	permitted to change data; can be column specific
DELETE	permitted to delete records or tables
INSERT	permitted to add records or tables

The GRANT and REVOKE SQL commands discussed in Chapter 10 are used to define and delete authorization rules. Some examples:

```
GRANT SELECT ON QSPL TO VIKKI
GRANT SELECT, UPDATE (SPLNAME) ON QSPL TO HUANG
GRANT ALL PRIVILEGES ON QITEM TO VIKKI
GRANT SELECT ON QITEM TO HUANG
```

The GRANT commands have essentially created two authorization tables, one for user Huang and the other for user Vikki. These tables, shown in Table 17-9, illustrate how most current systems create authorization tables for subjects using a limited set of objects (e.g., tables) and constraints.

Table 17-9: A sample authorization table

Client	Object (table)	Action	Constraint
Vikki	QSPL	SELECT	None
Vikki	QITEM	UPDATE	None
Vikki	QITEM	INSERT	None
Vikki	QITEM	DELETE	None
Vikki	QITEM	SELECT	None
Huang	QSPL	SELECT	None
Huang	QSPL	UPDATE	SPLNAME only
Huang	QITEM	SELECT	None

Because authorization tables contain highly sensitive data, they must be protected by stringent security rules and encryption. Normally, only selected persons in data administration have authority to access and modify them.

Encryption

Encryption techniques complement access control. As Figure 17-8 illustrates, access control applies only to established avenues of access to a database. There is always the possibility that people will circumvent these controls and gain unauthorized access to a database. To counteract this possibility, encryption can be used to obscure or hide the meaning of data. Encrypted data cannot be read by an intruder, unless that person knows the method of encryption and the key. Considerable research has been devoted to developing encryption methods.

Encryption is any transformation applied to data that makes it difficult to extract meaning. Encryption transforms data to cipher text, and decryption reconstructs the original data from cipher text. To demonstrate encryption, examine the simple method shown in Table 17-10. We have used a substitution method to shift each letter to its immediate successor in the alphabet. (We assume that the *blank* appears immediately before the letter *A* and that it follows the letter *Z*.) It would be difficult for an authorized user to understand *M mbx*. But if they examine a number of words, they probably will break the code. DBMSs use far more sophisticated encryption techniques to protect sensitive data.

Table 17-10: A simple text encryption method

Original data		Cipher text
Nancy	Encryption	M mbx
M mbx	Decryption	Nancy

Data encryption standard (DES) and **public key encryption** are the most common techniques. The DES algorithm, which can be implemented in hardware or software, uses a variable 56-bit key supplied by the sender. The sender uses the algorithm to encode data in a series of complex operations. The receiver applies the same key, and the DES algorithm reverses the operations to decode the message. Using a very fast supercomputer, it is possible to try all variations of possible keys to decipher a message. Finding a secure method of distributing the secret key is another major shortcoming of DES. This problem is exacerbated by the frequent need to change keys in case there has been a security leak and the existing key is no longer secret.

Public key encryption overcomes some of the problems with DES. A public key system has private and public keys. A person's public key can be freely distributed because it is quite separate from his or her private key. To send and receive messages, communicators first need to create private and public keys and then exchange their public keys. The sender encodes a message with the intended receiver's public key, and upon receiving the message, the receiver applies her private key (see Figure 17-9). The receiver's private key, the only one that can decode the message, must be kept secret to provide secure message exchanging.

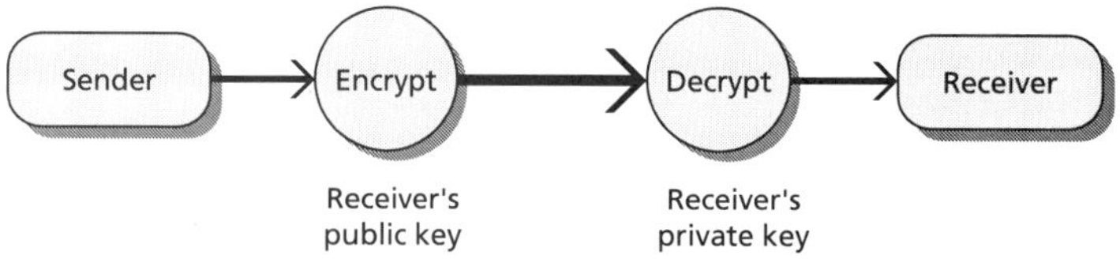

Figure 17-9. Public key encryption

In a DBMS environment, encryption techniques can be applied to transmitted data sent over communication lines to and from terminals, or between computers, and to all highly sensitive stored data in active databases or their backup versions. Some DBMS products include encryption routines that automatically encrypt sensitive data when they are stored or transmitted over communication channels. Other DBMS products provide exits that allow users to code their own encryption routines. Encrypted data may also take less storage space because they are often compressed.

Monitoring activity

Sometimes no single activity will be detected as an example of misuse of a system. However, examination of a pattern of behavior may reveal undesirable behavior (e.g., persistent attempts to log into a system with a variety of userids and passwords). Many systems now monitor all activity using **audit trail analysis**. A time- and date-stamped audit trail of all system actions (e.g., database accesses) is maintained. This audit log is dynamically analyzed to detect unusual behavior patterns and alert security personnel to possible misuse.

A form of misuse can occur when an authorized user violates privacy rules by using a series of authorized queries to gain access to private data. For example, some systems aim to protect individual privacy by restricting authorized queries to aggregate functions (e.g., average and count). Since it is impossible to do nonaggregate queries, this approach should prevent access to individual-level data, which it does at the single query level. However, multiple queries can be constructed to circumvent this restriction.

Assume we know that a professor in the MIS department is aged 40 to 50, single, and attended the University of Minnesota. Consider the results of the following set of queries.[3]

```
SELECT COUNT(*) FROM FACULTY
   WHERE DEPT = 'MIS'
   AND AGE >= 40 AND AGE <= 50
```

```
        10
```

```
SELECT COUNT(*) FROM FACULTY
   WHERE DEPT = 'MIS'
   AND AGE >= 40 AND AGE <= 50
   AND DEGREE_FROM = 'Minnesota'
```

```
         2
```

```
SELECT COUNT(*) FROM FACULTY
   WHERE DEPT = 'MIS'
   AND AGE >= 40 AND AGE <= 50
   AND DEGREE_FROM = 'Minnesota'
   AND MARITAL_STATUS = 'S'
```

```
         1
```

```
SELECT AVG(SALARY) FROM FACULTY
   WHERE DEPT = 'MIS'
   AND AGE >= 40 AND AGE <= 50
   AND DEGREE_FROM = 'Minnesota'
   AND MARITAL_STATUS = 'S'
```

```
   85,000
```

The preceding set of queries, while all at the aggregate level, enables one to deduce the salary of the professor. This is an invasion of privacy and counter to the spirit of the restriction queries to aggregate functions. An audit trail should detect such **tracker queries**, one or more authorized queries that collectively violate privacy. One approach to preventing tracker queries is to set a lower bound on the number of rows on which a query can report.

3. Adapted from Helman, P. 1994. *The science of data management.* Burr Ridge, IL: Irwin. p. 434.

Summary

The management of organizational data is driven by the joint goals of availability and integrity. Availability deals with making data available to whoever needs them, whenever and wherever they need them, and in a meaningful form. Maintaining integrity implies protecting existence, maintaining quality, and ensuring confidentiality. There are three strategies for maintaining data integrity: legal, administrative, and technical. A consistent database is one in which all data integrity constraints are satisfied. Manual systems cannot approach the degree of data integrity available in a well-designed computerized system.

In a multiuser DBMS, stored data are accessed by programs or transactions. A transaction must be entirely completed or aborted before there is any effect on the database. Transactions are processed as logical units of work to ensure data integrity. The transaction manager is responsible for ensuring that transactions are correctly recorded.

Concurrent update-control focuses on making sure updated results are correctly recorded in a database. When two or more update transactions are allowed to update a database concurrently, the integrity of the database is threatened. To prevent loss of updates and inconsistent retrieval results, a DBMS must incorporate a resource locking mechanism. The two types of locks are Slocks and Xlocks. Deadlock is an impasse that occurs because two users lock certain resources, then request resources locked by the other user. Deadlock prevention requires users to lock all records they will require at the beginning of the transaction. Deadlock resolution uses the DBMS to detect and break deadlocks.

Isolation is a preventive strategy that involves administrative procedures to insulate the physical database from destruction. Database backup and recovery is a curative strategy that protects an existing database and recreates or recovers the data whenever loss or destruction occurs. Possible causes of data loss or damage include: storage-medium destruction, abnormal termination of an update transaction, and incorrect data discovered. A DBMS needs to provide backup, journaling, and recovery facilities to restore a database to a consistent state and restart the processing of transactions. A journal or log is a special database or file that stores information for backup and recovery. A before-image is a copy of a database record before a transaction changes the record. An after-image is a copy of a database record after a transaction has updated the record.

In order to recover from data loss or damage, it is necessary to store redundant, backup data. The recovery method is highly dependent on the backup strategy. The cost of keeping backup data is measured in terms of interruption of database availability, storage of redundant data, and degradation of update efficiency. The four major recovery strategies are: switch to a duplicate database, backward recovery or rollback, forward recovery or roll forward, and reprocessing transactions. Database administration personnel often implement recovery strategies automatically carried out by the DBMS. The SQL statements COMMIT and ROLLBACK are used with a procedural programming language for implementing recovery procedures.

Maintaining quality implies keeping data accurate, complete, and current. The first step is to ensure that anyone wanting to update a database has authorization. In SQL, access control is implemented through GRANT and REVOKE. Data validation cannot be performed without integrity constraints or rules. Data validation can be performed external to the DBMS by personnel or within the DBMS based on defined integrity constraints. Because maintaining data quality is of paramount importance, it is desirable that the DBMS handle data validation rather than the user. Whenever an error or unusual situation is detected by the DBMS, some form of response is required. Response rules need to be given to the DBMS along with the integrity constraints.

Two DBMS functions, access control and encryption, are the primary mechanisms for ensuring the data are accessed only by authorized persons. Access control consists of identification and authorization. Organizations are moving toward using personal characteristics and combinations of authenticating mechanisms to identify authorized users. Data access authorization is the process of permitting users, whose identity has been authenticated, to perform certain operations on certain data objects in a shared database. Encryption is any transformation applied to data making it difficult to extract meaning. Encrypted data cannot be read by an intruder, unless that person knows the method of encryption and the key. DES and public key encryption are the most common techniques. Public key encryption attempts to overcome some of the problems with DES. In a DBMS environment, encryption techniques can be applied to transmitted data sent over communication lines to and from terminals, or between computers and stored data.

Database activity is monitored to detect patterns of activity indicating misuse of the system. An audit trail is maintained of all system actions. A tracker query is a series of aggregate function queries designed to reveal individual-level data.

It is electronically elementary, my dear Watson

Stop! Don't write that check without first considering the personal information you are divulging to a possible stranger. Does your check contain your name, address, telephone number, Social Security or driver's license number? Consider what students at the University of Alabama at Birmingham discovered about their instructor, with just his name, as part of a class project on Privacy Issues.

First, they went to the offices of the Tax Assessor and Collector at the courthouse in the county where the instructor lived. These offices provided the students with the information the government had on the properties (in this case, a house and two cars) on which he paid taxes. In fact, the offices gave them photocopies and duplicates of the tax bills and other information (e.g., location of the house, amount of mortgage, the seller, the lien holder, and the valuation and description of the properties.) This information is in the public domain and is available to anybody in the United States. Included among the documents found at the courthouse was the professor's Social Security number, which, along with his name and address, provided enough information for the students to get his credit report.

Having obtained his license tag number from the courthouse, the students then called the Department of Motor Vehicles, which proceeded to give them his entire driving record. In addition, they went to the university library and looked up his employment record. Being a state employee, the instructor's salary, rank, position, and date of employment are public information. At this point the students stopped, but could have obtained further public domain information about his marital and criminal history.

The students gathered all the information in about a week. These aspiring Sherlock Holmeses used the following two books as a guideline:

Culligan, J. J. 1993. *You, too, can find anybody: a reference manual.* Miami, FL: Hallmark.

Gunderson, T. L. 1989. *How to locate anyone anywhere without leaving home.* New York, NY: Dutton.

Electronic tracking services are readily available at low cost. For example, Find a Friend (findafriend.com) charges $20.00 to find the address of the owner of a Social Security number.

Contributed by Dr. Sanjay Singh, Department of Management, The University of Alabama. Birmingham.

Key terms and concepts

- Administrative strategies
- After image
- All-or-nothing rule
- Audit trail analysis
- Authentication
- Authorization
- Backup
- Before image
- COMMIT
- Concurrent update control
- Consistent database
- Data access control
- Data availability
- Data encryption standard (DES)
- Data quality
- Data security
- Database integrity
- Deadlock prevention
- Deadlock resolution
- Deadly embrace
- Decryption
- Encryption
- Ensuring confidentiality
- GRANT
- Integrity constraint
- Isolation
- Journal
- Legal strategies
- Locking
- Maintaining quality
- Private key
- Protecting existence
- Public key encryption
- Recovery
- Reprocessing
- REVOKE
- Roll forward
- ROLLBACK
- Rollback
- Serializability
- Slock
- Technical strategies
- Tracker query
- Transaction
- Transaction atomicity
- Transaction manager
- Two-phase locking protocol
- Validation
- Xlock

References and additional readings

Clarke, Roger A. 1988. Information technology and dataveillance. *Communications of the ACM* 31 (5):498–512.

Culnan, Mary J. 1993. "How did they get my name?": An exploratory investigation of consumer attitudes toward secondary information use. *MIS Quarterly* 17 (3):341–363.

Exercises

1. What are the three goals of maintaining organizational memory integrity?
2. What strategies are available for maintaining data integrity?
3. A large corporation needs to operate its computer systems continuously to remain viable. It currently has data centers in Miami and San Francisco. Do you have any advice for the CIO?
4. An investment company operates out of a single office in Boston. Its business is based on many years of high quality service, honesty, and reliability. The CEO is concerned that the firm has become too dependent on its computer system. If some disaster should occur and the firm's databases were lost, its reputation for

reliability would disappear overnight—and so would many of its customers in this highly competitive business. What should the firm do?

5. What mechanisms should a DBMS provide to support backup and recovery?
6. What is the difference between a *before image* and an *after image*?
7. A large organization has asked you to advise on backup and recovery procedures for its weekly, batch payroll system. They want reliable recovery at the lowest cost. What would you recommend?
8. An on-line information service operates globally and prides itself on its uptime of 99.98 percent. What sort of backup and recovery scheme is this firm likely to use? Describe some of the levels of redundancy you would expect to find.
9. The information systems manager of a small manufacturing company is considering the backup strategy for a new production planning database. The database is used every evening to create a plan for the next day's production. As long as the production plan is prepared before 6 A.M. the next day, there is no impact upon plant efficiency. The database is currently 200 Mbytes and growing about 2 percent per year. What backup strategy would you recommend and why?
10. How do backward recovery and forward recovery differ?
11. What are the advantages and disadvantages of reprocessing transactions?
12. When would you use ROLLBACK in an application program?
13. When would you use COMMIT in an application program?
14. Give three examples of data-integrity constraints.
15. What is the purpose of locking?
16. What is the likely effect on performance between locking at a row compared to locking at a page?
17. What is a deadly embrace? How can it be avoided?
18. What are three types of authenticating mechanisms?
19. Assume that you want to discover the grade point average of a fellow student. You know the following details of this person. She is a Norwegian citizen who is majoring in MIS and minoring in philosophy. Write one or more aggregate queries that should enable you to determine her GPA.
20. What is encryption?
21. What are the disadvantages of the Data encryption standard (DES)?
22. What are the advantages of public key encryption?
23. A national stock exchange requires listed companies to transmit quarterly reports to its computer center electronically. Recently, a hacker intercepted some of the transmissions and made several hundred thousands of dollars because of advance knowledge of one firm's unexpectedly high quarterly profits. How could the stock exchange reduce the likelihood of this event?

18

Data Administration

Bad administration, to be sure, can destroy good policy; but good administration can never save bad policy.

Adlai Stevenson, speech given in Los Angeles, September 11, 1952

Learning objectives

After completing this chapter, you will

- understand the importance and role of data administration;
- understand how system level data administration functions are used to successfully manage a database environment;
- understand how project level data administration activities support the development of a database system;
- understand what skills data administration requires and why it needs a balance of people, technical, and business skills to carry out its roles effectively;
- understand how computer-based tools can be used to support data administration activities;
- understand the management issues involved in initiating, staffing, and locating data administration organizationally.

The Tahiti tourist resort had been an outstanding success for The Expeditioner. Located 40 minutes from Papeete, the capital city, on a stretch of tropical forest and golden sand, the resort had soon become the favorite meeting place for The Expeditioner's board. No one objected to the long flight to French Polynesia. The destination was well worth the journey, and The Expeditioner had historic ties to that part of the South Pacific. Early visitors to Tahiti, James Cook and William Bligh, had been famous customers of The Expeditioner in the eighteenth century. Before Paul Gauguin embarked on his journey to paint scenes of Tahiti, he had purchased supplies from L'Explorateur, now the French division of The Expeditioner.

Although The Expeditioner is very successful, there are always problems for the board to address. A number of board members are very concerned by the seeming lack of control over the various database systems that are vital to the firm's profitability. Recently there had been a number of incidents that had underscored the problem. Purchasing had made several poor decisions. For example, it had ordered too many parkas for the North American stores and had to discount them heavily to sell all the stock. The problem was traced to poor data standards and policies within Sales. Personnel and Marketing had been squabbling for some time over access to the personnel database. Personnel claimed ownership of the data and was reluctant to share data with Marketing, which wanted access to some of the data to support its new incentive program. A new database project for the Travel Division had been seriously delayed when it was discovered that the Travel Division's development team was planning to implement a system incompatible with The Expeditioner's existing hardware and software.

After the usual exchange of greetings and a presentation of the monthly financial report, Alice forthrightly raised the database problem. "We all know that we depend on information technology to manage The Expeditioner," she began as she glanced at her notes on her personal digital assistant. "The Information Systems department does a great job running the computers, building new systems, and providing us with excellent service, but," she stressed, "we seem to be focusing on managing the wrong things. We should be managing what really matters: the data we need to run the business. Data errors, internecine[1] fighting over data, and project delays are costly. Our present system for managing data is fragmented. We don't have anyone or any group who manages data centrally. It is critical that we develop an action plan for the organizational management of data." Pointing to Bob, she continued, "I have invited Bob to brief us on data administration and present his proposal for solving our data management problem. It's all yours, Bob."

Introduction

In the information age, data are the lifeblood of every organization and need to be properly managed to retain their value to the organization. The importance of data as a key organizational resource has been emphasized throughout this book. Data administration is the management of organizational data stores.

Information technology permits organizations to capture, organize, and maintain a greater variety of data. These data can be hard (e.g., financial or production figures) or soft (e.g., management reports, correspondence, voice conversations, and video). If these data are to be used in the organization, they must be managed just as diligently as accounting information. Data administration is the common term applied to the task of managing orga-

1. She had certainly waited a long time to use this word, learned when studying for the university admission exam.

nizational memory. Although common, basic management principles apply to most kinds of organizational data stores, the discussion in this chapter refers primarily to databases.

A Pbytes SAN

At companies involved in oil exploration activities, IT managers sometimes have to wait weeks for the arrival of historical geologic or seismographic data that can help pinpoint prospective drilling sites. As a result, the information is often outdated.

Seitel Solution, a joint venture between IBM and Seitel Inc. which maintains a seismic database used by more than 400 petroleum companies, is expected to eventually store as much as two Pbytes of data on a massive storage-area network (SAN) that will make more than a petabyte of information available to users via the Web. The oil companies will then be able to access 20 years of seismographic charts, geographical surveys, and photos that will be stored in a connected series of data warehouses. The SAN will connect data warehouses that stretch from Houston to Colorado to Calgary, Alberta.

The SAN will be based on IBM's tape storage devices and its Shark enterprise storage system, with storage management software from IBM's Tivoli Systems Inc. subsidiary. The project could mark a turning point in SAN scalability standards, provided that the two companies are able to build the kind of network they envision.

Source: Mearian, L. 2001. IBM, Seismic data provider building petabyte plus SAN. *Computerworld.* http://www.computerworld.com/cwi/story/0,1199,NAV47_STO55577,00.html

Why manage data?

Data are constantly generated in every act and utterance of every stakeholder (employee, shareholder, customer, or supplier) in relation to the organization. Some of these data are formal and structured, such as, invoices, grade sheets, or bank withdrawals. A large amount of relatively unstructured data is generated too, such as feedback from customers. Much of the unstructured data generated in organizations, while potentially useful, are never captured and recorded.

Organizations typically begin maintaining systematic records for data most likely to impinge on their performance. Often, different departments or individuals would like to maintain records for the same data. For instance, you may have experienced completing multiple copy forms — perhaps forms with half a dozen copies. Each copy was required by a different functional group or department. The same data may be used in different ways by each department, and so each department may adopt a different system of organizing the data. Over time, an organization accumulates a great deal of redundant data, which demands considerable, needless administrative overhead for its maintenance. Inconsistencies may begin to emerge between the various forms of the same data. A department may incorrectly enter some data, which could result in embarrassment at best or a serious financial loss for the organization at worst.

When data are fragmented across several departments or individuals, and especially when there is personnel turnover, data may not be accessible when most needed. This is nearly as serious a problem as not having any data. Yet another motivation is that effective data management can greatly simplify and assist in the identification of new information system application development opportunities. Also, poor data management can result in breaches of security. Valuable information may be revealed to competitors or antagonists.

In summary, the problems arising from poor data management are

- the same data may be represented through multiple, inconsistent definitions;
- there may be inconsistencies among different representations;
- essential data may be missing from the database;
- data may be inaccurate or incomplete;
- some data may never be entered into the database and thus are effectively lost to the organization;
- there may be no way of knowing how to locate data when they are needed.

The overall goal of data administration is to prevent the occurrence of these problems by enabling users to access the data they need in the format most suitable for achieving their organizational goals and by assuring the integrity of organizational databases.

A data center

Management of the database environment

In many large organizations, there is a formal data administration function to manage corporate data. The relationship between these components is shown in Figure 18-1. Note that there are two levels of data administration, system and project, with the project level contained within the system level.

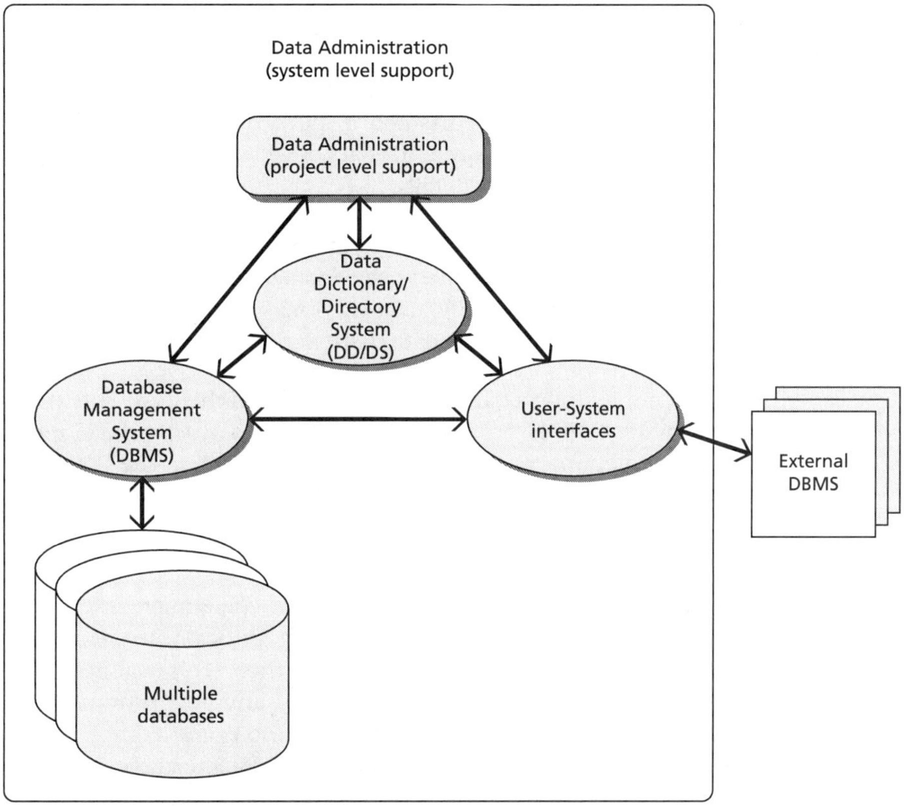

Figure 18-1. Management of the database environment

Databases

A DBMS can manage multiple databases covering different aspects of an organization's activities. When a database has multiple users, it may be designed to meet all their requirements, even though a specific user may need only a portion of the data contained within the database. For instance, a finished goods database may be accessed by production and finance, as well as marketing. It may contain costing information that is accessible by production and finance but not by marketing. It may contain pricing information that is accessible by finance and marketing but not by production.

User interface

The user interface consists of screen formats, menus, icons, and command languages that enable users to direct the system to manipulate data. Users may range from casual novices, who need to be insulated from the underlying complexity of the data, to expert application developers, who manipulate the data using programming languages or other data handling tools.

Data dictionary

A data dictionary is a reference repository containing *metadata* (i.e., *data about data*) that is stored in the database. Among other things, the data dictionary contains a list of all the databases; their component parts and detailed descriptions such as field sizes, data types, and data validation information for data entry purposes; authorized users and their access privileges; and ownership details.

A data dictionary is a map of the data in organizational data stores. It permits the data administration staff and users to document the database, design new applications, and redesign the database if necessary. The data dictionary/directory system (DD/DS), itself a DBMS, is software for managing the data dictionary.

Early DBMSs did not include a data dictionary as part of the basic software. DD/DSs were add-ons developed by DBMS vendors and third-party software developers. Given the importance of a data dictionary and the intense competition in the DBMS market, it has become common for DBMS vendors to provide an integrated DD/DS within their DBMS.

External databases

For organizations to remain competitive in a rapidly changing marketplace, access to data from external sources is becoming increasingly critical. Research and development groups need access to the latest developments in their technical fields and need to track information such as patents filed, research reports, and new product releases. Marketing departments need access to data on market conditions and competitive situations as reported in various surveys and the media in general. Financial data regarding competitors and customers are important to senior executives. Monitoring political situations may be critical to many business decisions, especially in the international business arena. Such external data are often delivered to executives via an EIS.

Extensive external data are available electronically through commercial information services such as Dow Jones News Service (financial data), Reuters (news), and LEXIS-NEXIS (legal data), or from various Web sites. Tools are available to download external data into internal databases, from which they may be accessed through the same interface as for internal data.

Data administration

Data administration is responsible for the management of data-related activities. There are two levels of data administration activities: system and project. System level functions deal with management issues applicable to the entire database environment and all databases managed within that environment. System level functions include planning, developing data standards and policies, establishing data integrity procedures, resolving data conflict issues, and managing the DBMS and data dictionary.

At the project level, data administration supports the development and use of a specific database system. Data administration project level activities include defining user requirements, developing data models, training and consulting, establishing and monitoring data integrity, monitoring database usage, and controlling database changes. Both system and project level functions will be discussed in more detail.

Data administration versus database administration

Organizational data may be managed at two different functional levels, which may be termed the system level and the project level. System level administration is broader in scope. Another pair of terms that has been used to capture this distinction is data administration and database administration. These terms, however, are confusing because of their similarity. We feel it is better to discuss data administration activities in terms of scope or level, that is system and project. Also, in keeping with our managerial perspective, we will use data administration rather than database administration.

System level administration is concerned with establishing overall policies and procedures for the management and use of data in the organization. Formulating a data strategy and specifying an information architecture for the organization are also system level data administration functions. System level responsibilities may cover both electronic and non-electronic corporate data.

Project level data administration deals more with the specifics, such as optimizing specific databases for operational efficiency, establishing and implementing database access rights, creating new databases, and monitoring database use.

In general, the system level function takes a broader perspective of the role played by data in achieving business objectives, while the project level function is more concerned with the actual mechanics of database implementation and operation. We use data administration to refer to both functional levels.

Data administration functions and roles

An **organizational function** is a related set of routine and nonrecurring organizational activities that must be performed in order to achieve some organizational objective. Accounting, marketing, and manufacturing are examples of organizational functions. A function is fulfilled by one or more individuals, each of whom is assigned a role and performs some or all of the activities required of the function. In some organizations, the accounting function is performed by an entire accounting department, which may include several roles such as accounts manager, accountant, account clerk, and secretary. Each of these roles may be occupied by one or more individuals. For instance, there may be one manager (accounts), two accountants, several account clerks, and a secretary. In a small firm, the accounting function may be performed by a single accountant.

The functions of data administration may be accomplished through multiple roles or job titles such as database administrator, database developer, database consultant, and database analyst, collectively referred to as the data administration staff. A single role could be responsible for both system and project levels of data administration, or responsibility may be distributed among several persons, depending on the size of the organization, the number of database applications, and the number of users.

In addition, data administration could be carried out entirely in a client department. For instance, a client could be the data steward responsible for managing all corporate data for some critical business-related entity or activity (e.g., a customer, a production facility, a supplier, a division, a project, or a product) regardless of the purpose for which the data are used. **Data stewards** coordinate planning of the data for which they are responsible. Tasks include data definition, quality control and improvement, security, and access authorization. The data steward role is especially important today because of the growing emphasis on customer satisfaction and cross-functional teams. Data stewardship seeks to align data management with organizational strategy.

Database levels

Databases may be maintained at several levels of use: personal, workgroup (e.g., project team or department), and organizational. The more users, the greater the complexity of both the database and its management.

Personal databases in the form of diaries, planners, and name and address books have existed for a long time. The availability of notebook computers and personal digital assistants (PDAs) has made it convenient to maintain electronic personal databases. Personal databases may not require a sophisticated DBMS. Indeed, versatile software tools known as personal information managers (PIMs) are often better suited for the task of storing personal information. PIMs are able to store both structured and unstructured personal information such as calendars and appointments; names, addresses, and contact information; to-do lists; and meeting notes and observations.

Workgroup databases cannot be as idiosyncratic because they are shared by many people. Managing them requires more planning and coordination to ensure that all users' needs are addressed, and data integrity is maintained. Organizational databases are the most complex in terms of both structure and need for administration. All databases, regardless of scope or level, require administration.

Managing a personal database is relatively simple. Typically, the user of the database is also its developer and administrator. Issues such as access rights and security are settled quite easily, perhaps by the user locking the computer when away from the desk. Managing workgroup databases is more complex. Controls almost certainly will be needed to restrict access to certain data. On the other hand, some data will need to be available to many group members. Also, responsibility for backup and recovery must be established. Small workgroups may jointly perform both system and project level data administration activities. Meetings may be a way to coordinate system level data administration activities, and project level activities may be distributed among different workgroup members. Larger groups may have a designated data administrator, who is also a group member.

Managing organizational databases is typically a full-time job requiring special skills to work with complex database environments. In large corporations, several persons may handle data administration, each carrying out different data administration activities. System level data administration activities may be carried out by a committee led by a senior IS executive (who may be a full- or part-time data administrator), while project level data administration activities may be delegated to individual data administration staff members.

System level data administration functions

System level data administration functions, which may be performed by one or more persons, are summarized in Table 18-1.

Table 18-1: System level data administration functions

Planning
Developing data standards and policies
Defining XML DTDs
Maintaining data integrity
Resolving data conflict
Managing the DBMS
Establishing and maintaining the data dictionary
Selecting hardware and software
Managing external databases
Benchmarking
Internal marketing

Planning

Because data are a strategic corporate resource, planning is perhaps the most critical data administration function. A key planning activity is creating an organization's information architecture, which includes all the major data entities and the relationships between them. It indicates which business functions and applications access which entities. An information architecture also may address issues such as how data will be transmitted and where they will be stored. Since an information architecture is an organization's overall strategy for data and applications, it should dovetail with the organization's long-term plans and objectives.

Developing data standards and policies

Whenever data are used by more than one person (for example, a workgroup or even an entire organization, there must be standards to govern their use. Data standards become especially critical in organizations using heterogeneous hardware and software environments. Why could this become a problem? For historical reasons, different departments may use different names and field sizes for the same data item. These differences can cause confusion and misunderstanding. For example, sales date may have different meanings for the legal department (e.g., the date the contract was signed) and the sales department (e.g., the date of the sales call). Furthermore, the legal department may store data in the form *yyyy-mm-dd* and the sales department as *dd-mm-yy*. Data administration's task is to develop and publish data standards so that field names are clearly defined, and a field's size and format are consistent across the enterprise.

Furthermore, some data items may be more important to certain departments or divisions. For instance, customer data are often critical to the marketing department. It is useful in such cases to appoint a data steward from the appropriate functional area as custodian for these data items.

Policies need to be established regarding who can access and manipulate which data, when, and from where. For instance, should employees using their home computer be allowed to access corporate data? If such access is permitted, then data security and risk exposure must be considered and adequate data safeguards implemented.

Defining XML DTDs

Data administration is responsible for defining document type definitions (DTDs) for data exchange within the organization and among business partners. This is a new role that will be more important in the next few years as organizations adopt XML as the data exchange standard. Data administration is also responsible for keeping abreast of industry DTD standards so that the organization is in conformance with common practice. Advanced adopters of XML may even work on defining a DTD for an industry.

Maintaining data integrity

Data must be made available when needed but only to authorized users. The data management aspects of data integrity were discussed at length in Chapter 17.

Resolving data conflict

Data administration involves the custodianship of data *owned* or originating in various organizational departments or functions, and conflicts are bound to arise at some point. For instance, one department may be concerned about a loss of security when another department is allowed access to its data. In another instance, one group may feel that another is contaminating a commonly used data pool because of inadequate data validation practices. A department may want exclusive control over a particular database because of the department's high transaction volume. Incidents like these, and many others, require management intervention and settlement through a formal or informal process of discussion and negotiation in which all parties are assured of a fair hearing. Data administration facilitates negotiation and mediates dispute resolution.

Managing the DBMS

While project level data administration is concerned more directly with the DBMS, the performance and characteristics of the DBMS ultimately impinge on the effectiveness of the system level data administration function. It is, therefore, important to monitor characteristics of the DBMS. Over a period, benchmark statistics for different projects or applications will need to be compiled. These statistics are especially useful for addressing user complaints regarding the performance of the DBMS, which may then lead to design changes, tuning of the DBMS, or additional hardware.

Database technology is rapidly advancing. For example, relational DBMSs are continually being extended, and ODBMS technology promises greater versatility and flexibility for some applications (see Chapter 13). Keeping track of developments, evaluating their benefits, and deciding on converting to new database environments are critical system level data administration functions that can have strategic implications for the corporation.

Establishing and maintaining the data dictionary

A data dictionary is a key data administration tool that provides details of data in the organizational database and how they are used (e.g., by various application programs). If modifications are planned for the database (e.g., deleting a column or changing the size of a column in a table), the data dictionary helps to determine which applications will be affected by the proposed changes.

In the early days of data administration, data dictionaries were manually maintained. The widespread need and demand for a data dictionary facility resulted in some independent vendors creating the necessary data dictionary software for a variety of commercial DBMSs. Some data dictionary systems are merely electronic versions of a manual data dictionary, in that they operate independently of the database itself. Any changes in the database are not automatically reflected in the data dictionary. Someone must remember to update the dictionary. More sophisticated data dictionary systems are closely integrated with specific database products. They are updated automatically whenever the structure of the underlying database is changed.

The initial purchase price of an automated data dictionary may be higher, but the additional cost may be worthwhile. Automated dictionaries have more safeguards against human error. Competition in the DBMS market has led to several database vendors providing integrated, automated data dictionaries along with their DBMSs.

Selecting hardware and software

Evaluating and selecting the appropriate hardware and software for an organizational database are critical responsibilities with strategic organizational implications. These are not an easy tasks due to the dynamic nature of the database industry, the continually changing variety of available hardware and software products, and the rapid pace of change within many organizations. Today's excellent choice might become tomorrow's nightmare, if, for instance, the vendor of a key database component goes out of business or ceases product development.

Selection of a query language may be an important decision. Should the firm select SQL or a proprietary query language? SQL is an industry standard, and there is likely to be a large pool of skilled programmers. On the other hand, SQL may not be ideal for the intended application, and a proprietary query language may be more suitable for the organization's needs.

Extensive experience and knowledge of the database software business and technological progress in the field are essential to making effective database hardware and software decisions. The current and future needs of the organization need to be assessed in terms of capacity as well as features. Relevant questions include the following:

- How many users will simultaneously access the database?
- Will the database need to be geographically distributed? If so, what is the degree to which the database will be replicated, and what is the nature of database replication that is supported?
- What is the maximum size of the database?
- How many transactions per second can the DBMS handle?
- What kind of support for on-line transaction processing is available?
- What are the initial and ongoing costs of using the product?
- Can the database be extended to include new data types?
- What is the extent of training required, who can provide it, and what are the associated costs?

DBMS selection should cover technical, operational, and financial considerations. An organization's selection criteria are often specified in a Request For Proposal (RFP). This document is sent to a short list of potential vendors, who are invited to respond with a software or hardware/software proposal outlining how their product or service meets each criterion in the RFP. Visits to current user sites are usually desirable to gain confirming evidence of a vendor's claims. The final decision should be based on the manner and degree to which each vendor's proposal satisfies these criteria.

Benchmarking

Benchmarking, the comparison of alternative hardware and software combinations, is an important step in the selection phase. Because benchmarking is an activity performed by many MIS units, the MIS community gains if there is one group that specializes in rigorous benchmarking of a wide range of systems. The Transaction Processing Council (TPC)[2] is the MIS profession's Consumer Union.

TPC has established benchmarks for a variety of business situations. Here we consider four benchmarks that are useful for data managers.

2. http://www.tpc.org

TPC-C

Many data managers are concerned with the efficiency of transaction processing systems. TPC-C models a complete computing environment where terminal operators execute transactions against a database. The benchmark simulates the principal transactions of an order-entry environment. These transactions include entering and delivering orders, recording payments, checking the status of orders, and monitoring the level of stock at warehouses. TPC-C is measured in transactions per minute (tpm). A benchmark provides precise information for a clearly specified hardware/software combination (e.g., a Digital AlphaServer 1200 5/533 running under UNIX 4.0D and using Sybase SQL Server 11.5 processes 7023 tpm).

TPC-H

The TPC-H (ad-hoc, decision support) benchmark describes a decision support environments where there is no prior knowledge of the queries to be executed. Given their unplanned nature, optimization of these queries cannot be built into the DBMS system, and query execution times can be very long

TPC-R

TPC-R is a business reporting and decision support benchmark. It assesses an environment where clients run a standard set of queries against a database system. Pre-knowledge of the queries is assumed, and the DBMS system can be optimized to run these standard queries very rapidly

TPC-W

Many organizations have recently developed Web sites, and TPC introduced a Web Commerce benchmark (TPC-W) in late 1998. TPC-W is designed to represent any business (e.g., a retail store, airline reservation) that markets and sells over the Web. It also represents intranet environments that use Web-based transactions for internal operations. The benchmark is designed to measure the performance of systems supporting customers browsing, ordering, and conducting transaction-oriented business activities.

Managing external databases

Providing access to external databases has increased the level of complexity of data administration, which now has the additional responsibility of identifying information services that meet existing or potential managerial needs. Data administration must determine the quality of such data and the means by which they can be channeled into the organization's existing information delivery system. Costs of data may vary among vendors. Some may charge a flat monthly or annual fee, while others may have a usage charge. Data may arrive in a variety of formats, and data administration may need to make them adhere to corporate standards. Data from different vendors and sources may need to be integrated and presented in a unified format and on common screens, perhaps including them in an EIS.

Monitoring external data sources is critical because data quality may vary over time. Data administration must determine whether user needs are continuing to be met and data quality is being maintained. If they are not, a subscription may be canceled and an alternative vendor sought. Security is another critical problem. When corporate databases are connected to external communication links, there is a threat of hackers breaking into the system and gaining unauthorized access to confidential internal data. Also, corporate data may be contaminated by spurious data or even by viruses entering the internal databases from external sources. Data administration must be cautious when incorporating external data into the database.

Training users to access external databases can also be a data administration responsibility. If using external databases is very cumbersome or time-consuming for users, the data administration staff may have to access external databases on behalf of users.

Internal marketing

Because IS applications can have a major impact on organizational performance, the IS function is becoming more proactive in initiating the development of new applications. Many users are not aware of what is possible with newly emergent technologies, and hence do not see opportunities to exploit these developments. Also, as custodian of organizational data, data administration needs to communicate its goals and responsibilities throughout the organization. People and departments need to be persuaded to share data that may be of value to other parts of the organization. There may be resistance to change when people are asked to switch to newly established data standards. In all these instances, data administration must be presented in a positive light to lessen resistance to change. Data administration needs to market internally its products and services to its customers.

Project level data administration

At the project level, data administration focuses on the detailed needs of individual users and applications. Data administration supports the development and use of a specific database system.

Systems development life cycle

Database development follows a fairly predictable sequence of steps or phases similar to the systems development life cycle for applications. This sequence is called the database development life cycle (DDLC). The database and application development life cycles together constitute the systems development life cycle (SDLC) described in Table 18-2.

Table 18-2: Systems development life cycle (SDLC)

Application Development Life Cycle (ADLC)	Database Development Life Cycle (DDLC)
Project planning	Project planning
Requirements definition	Requirements definition
Application design	Database design
Application construction	

Table 18-2: Systems development life cycle (SDLC) (continued)

Application Development Life Cycle (ADLC)	Database Development Life Cycle (DDLC)
Application testing	Database testing
Application implementation	Database implementation
Operations	Database usage
Maintenance	Database evolution

Application development involves the eight phases shown in Table 18-2. It commences with project planning which, among other things, involves determining project feasibility and allocating the necessary personnel and material resources for the project. This is followed by requirements definition, which involves considerable interaction with clients to clearly specify the system. These specifications become the basis for a conceptual application design which is then constructed, through program coding, and tested. Once the system is thoroughly tested, it is installed and user operations begin. Over time, changes may be needed to upgrade or repair the system, and this is called system maintenance.

The database development phases parallel application development. Data administration is responsible for the DDLC. Data are the focus of database development, rather than procedures or processes. Database construction is folded into the testing phase since database testing typically involves minimal effort. In systems with integrated data dictionaries, the process of constructing the data dictionary also creates the database shell (i.e., tables without data). While the sequence of phases in the cycle as presented is generally followed, there is often a number of iterations within and between steps. Data modeling is iterative, and the final database design evolves from many data modeling sessions. A previously unforeseen requirement may surface during the database design phase, and this may prompt a revision of the specifications completed in the earlier phase.

System development may proceed in three different ways.

1. The database may be developed independently of applications, following only the DDLC steps.
2. Applications may be developed for existing databases, following only the ADLC steps.
3. Application and database development may proceed in parallel, with both simultaneously stepping through the ADLC and DDLC.

Consider further each of these possibilities.

A database may be developed independently of applications. Database development may proceed independently of application development for a number of reasons. The database may be created for storing information that later may be used by an application or for ad hoc querying using a built-in query language. In another case, an existing database may undergo changes to improve efficiency or integrity. For instance, if it is found that a new query cannot be handled efficiently by the current database model (i.e., processing takes an inordinate amount of time), redesigning the database may overcome the problem. In such situations, the developer goes through the appropriate stages of the DDLC.

Application development may proceed based on an existing database. In some instances, the required database may already be in place. For instance, a personnel database may already exist to serve a set of applications, such as payroll. This database could be used as the basis for a new personnel benefits application, which must go through all the phases of the ADLC.

A new system requires both application and database development. Frequently, a new system will require creation of both a new database and applications. For instance, a computer manufacturer may start a new Web-based order sales division and wish to monitor its performance. The vice-president in charge of the division may be interested in receiving daily sales reports by product and by customer as well as a weekly moving sales trend analysis for the prior 10 weeks. This requires both the development of a new sales database as well as a new application for sales reporting. Here, the ADLC and DDLC are both used to manage development of the new system.

Another possibility is that a newly introduced DBMS may provide easy-to-use query facilities that are superior to existing applications. Here again, changing the database may trigger a corresponding change in applications.

Database development roles

Database development involves several roles, chiefly those of developer, end user, and data administrator. The roles and their responsibilities are outlined in Table 18-3.

The database developer shoulders the bulk of the responsibility for developing data models and implementing the database. This can be seen in Table 18-3, where most of the cells in the *database developer* column are labeled "Does." The database developer does project planning, requirements definition, database design, database testing, and database implementation, and in addition, is responsible for database evolution.

The client's role is to establish the goals of a specific database project, provide the database developers with access to all information needed for project development, and review and regularly scrutinize the developer's work.

The data administrator's prime responsibilities are implementing and controlling, but the person also may be required to perform activities and consult. In some situations, the database developer is not part of the data administration staff and may be located in a user department, or may be an analyst from an IS project team. In these cases, the data administrator advises the developer on organizational standards and policies as well as provides specific technical guidelines for successful construction of a database. When the database developer is part of the data administration staff, developer and data administration activities may be carried out by the same person, or by the person(s) occupying the data administration role. In all cases, the data administrator should understand the larger business context in which the database will be used and should be able to relate business needs to specific technical capabilities and requirements.

Database development life cycle (DDLC)

Previously, we discussed the various roles involved in database development and how they may be assigned to different persons. In this section, we will assume that administration and development are carried out by the data administration staff, since this is the typical situation encountered in many organizations. The activities of developer and administrator, shown in the first two columns of Table 18-3, are assumed to be performed by data administration staff.

Table 18-3: Database development roles

Database Development Phase	Database Developer	Data Administrator	Client
Project planning	Does	Consults	Provides information
Requirements definition	Does	Consults	Provides requirements
Database design	Does	Consults Data integrity	Validates data models
Database testing	System and client testing	Consults Data integrity	Testing
Database implementation	System related activities	Consults Data integrity	Client activities
Database usage	Consults	Data integrity monitoring	Uses
Database evolution	Does	Change control	Provides additional requirements

Now, let us consider data administration project level support activities in detail (see Figure 18-2). These activities are discussed in terms of the DDLC phase they support.

Database project planning

Database project planning includes establishing project goals, determining project feasibility (financial, technical, and operational), creating an implementation plan and schedule, assigning project responsibilities (including data stewards), and establishing standards. All project stakeholders including users, senior management, and developers are involved in planning. They are included for their knowledge as well as to gain their commitment to the project.

Requirements definition

During requirements definition, users and developers establish what the users' needs are and develop a mutual understanding of what the new system will deliver. Data are defined and the resulting definitions stored in the data dictionary. Requirements definition generates documentation that should serve as an unambiguous reference for database development. While in theory the users are expected to *sign-off* on the specifications and accept

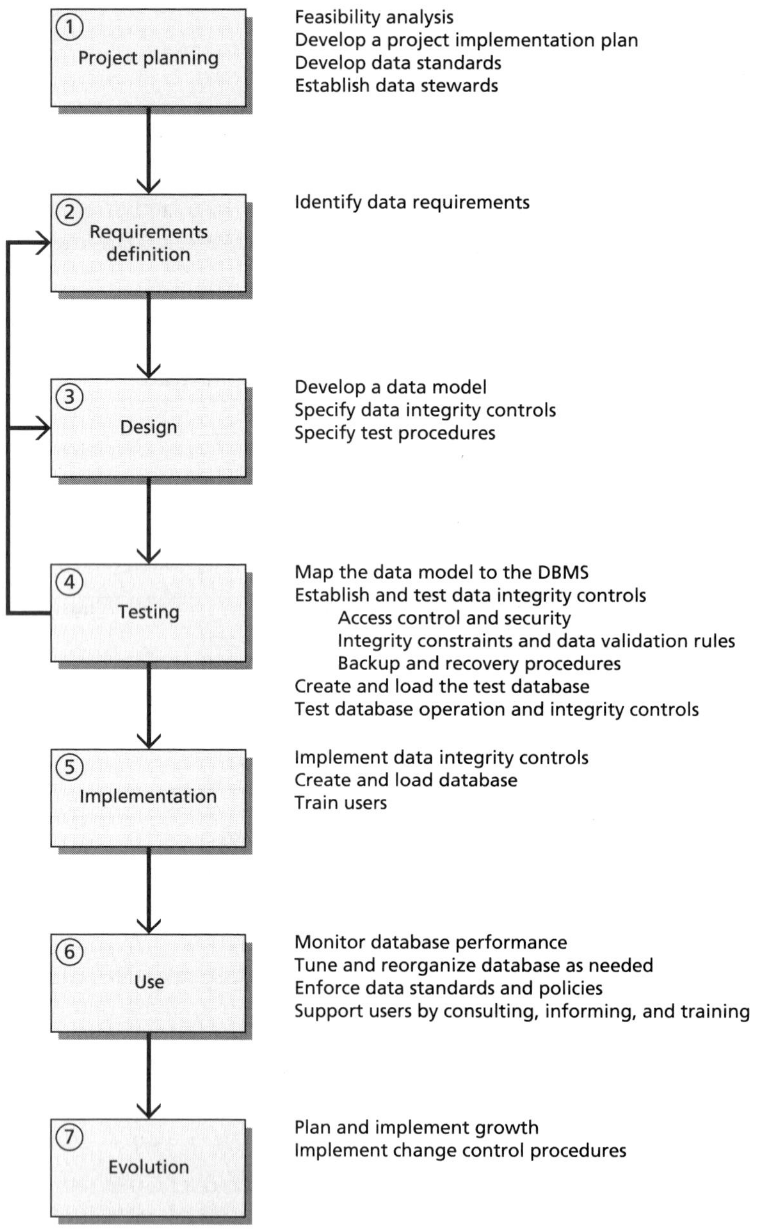

Figure 18-2. Database development life cycle

the developed database as is, in practice users' needs may actually change. Users may gain greater understanding of their requirements and business conditions may change. Consequently, the original specifications may require revision. In Figure 18-2, the arrows connecting phase 4 (testing) and phase 3 (design) to phase 2 (requirements definition) indicate that modeling and testing may identify revisions to the database specification and these amendments are then incorporated into the design.

Database design

Conceptual and internal models of the database are developed during database design. Conceptual design, or data modeling, is discussed extensively in Section 2. Database design should also include specification of procedures for testing the database. Any additional controls for ensuring data integrity are also specified. The external model should be checked and validated by the user.

Database testing

Database testing requires previously developed specifications and models to be tested using the intended DBMS. Users are often asked to provide operational data to support testing the database with realistic transactions. Testing should address a number of key questions.

- Does the DBMS support all the operational and security requirements?
- Is the system able to handle the expected number of transactions per second?
- How long does it take to process a realistic mix of queries?

Testing assists in making early decisions regarding the suitability of both the database design and the selected DBMS.

Another critical aspect of database testing is verifying data integrity controls. Testing may include checking backup and recovery procedures, access control, and data validation rules.

Database implementation

Testing is complete when the users and developers are extremely confident the system meets specified needs. Data integrity controls are implemented, operational data are loaded (including historical data, if necessary), and database documentation is finalized. Users are then trained to operate the system.

Database use

Users may need considerable support as they learn and adapt to the system. Monitoring database performance is critical to keeping users satisfied; enables the data administrator to anticipate problems even before the users begin to notice and complain about them, and tune the system to meet users' needs; and also helps to enforce data standards and policies during the initial stages of database implementation.

The terabyte backup

To research molecular structures and human health, scientists at the University of Georgia in Athens use some of the world's most advanced technologies. Each day, chemistry professor James de Haseth collects between 10 and 100 Mbytes of data, which is protected against loss by a tape backup system.

Modern science and electronic commerce has created a demand for regular, reliable data backup. The meteoric growth of multimedia enriched Web pages, e-commerce transactions, and the Web's vast and ever-changing storehouse of documents account for a large part of the anticipated 500% growth in enterprise storage needs over the next three years.

Skyrocketing storage demands can overwhelm existing backup systems. The data archiving market is predicted to grow 25 percent per year, reaching $5 billion by 2003. Tape technology vendors are continuing to develop higher-performance, higher-capacity tape systems. New tape formats are aiming for drives storing up to 1.6TB at the incredible transfer speed of 320 Mbytes/sec.

However, tapes still depend on a linear data stream, so it's time-consuming and inconvenient to restore selected, noncontiguous files. To some degree, a hierarchical storage management (HSM) system can compensate. In this three-tier architecture, software automatically moves files between the various media—RAID, DVD jukeboxes, and tape libraries. With HSM, new and frequently needed files are stored on RAID systems. Less frequently used files are moved onto near-online DVD jukeboxes. Rarely used files are archived to tape libraries, often at remote locations.

The benefits of outsourcing may encourage companies to outsource their backup operations. Lower-cost, widely available broadband will increase the adoption of off-site storage and related document management services which could eliminate the need to assign scarce resources to on-site storage systems. e-storage sites promise 99.5 percent uptime, two-hour problem resolution, and infinite scalability. In addition to eliminating infrastructure, maintenance, and reengineering expenses, e-storage offers realtime searches and retrieval as well as on-demand replays of key transactions.

Source: Millman, H. 2001. The terabyte tapes. *Computerworld*, Feb. 26.http://computerworld.com/cwi/story/0%2C1199%2CNAV47_STO58008_NLTst%2C00.html

Database evolution

Since organizations cannot afford to stand still in today's dynamic business environment, business needs are bound to change over time, perhaps even after a few months. Data administration should be prepared to meet the challenge of change. Minor changes—such as changes in display formats, or performance improvements—may be continually requested. These have to be attended to on an ongoing basis. Other evolutionary changes

may emerge from constant monitoring of database use by the data administration staff. Implementing these evolutionary changes involves repeating phases 3 to 6 of Figure 18-2. Significant business changes may merit a radical redesign of the database. Major redesign may require repeating all phases of the DDLC.

Data administration interfaces

Data administration is increasingly a key corporate function, and it requires the existence of established channels of communication with various organizational groups. The key data administration interfaces are with clients, management, development staff, and computer operations. The central position of the data administration staff in Figure 18-3 reflects the liaison role that it plays in managing databases. Each of the groups has a different focus and different terminology and jargon. Data administration should be able to communicate effectively with all participants. For instance, operations staff will tend to focus on technical, day-to-day issues to which management is likely to pay less attention. These different focuses can, and frequently do, lead to conflicting views and expectations among the different groups. Good interpersonal skills are a must for data administration staff in order to deal with a variety of conflict-laden situations. Data administration, therefore, needs a balance of people, technical, and business skills for effective execution of its tasks.

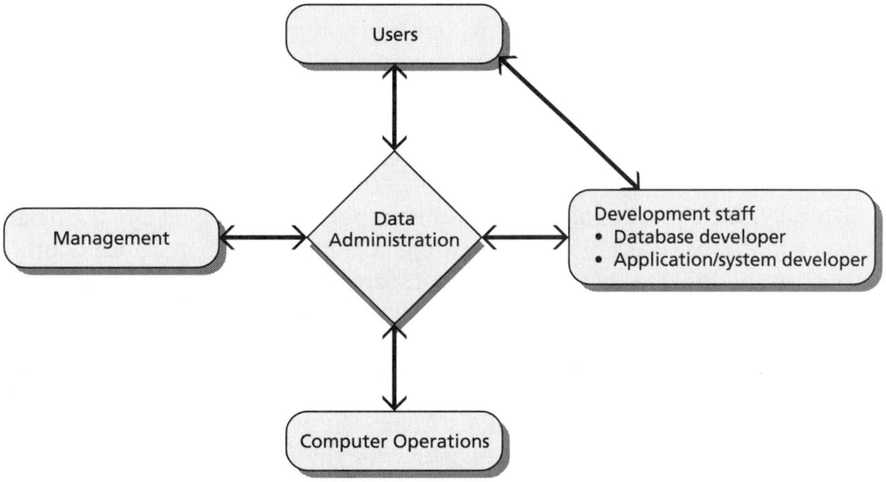

Figure 18-3. Major data administration interfaces

Data administration probably will communicate most frequently with computer operations and development staff, somewhat less frequently with users, and least frequently with management. These differences, however, have little to do with the relative importance of communicating with each group. The interactions between the data administration staff and each of the four groups are discussed next.

Management

Management sets the overall business agenda for data administration, which must ensure that its actions directly contribute to the achievement of organizational goals. In particular, management establishes overall policy guidelines, approves data administration budgets, evaluates proposals, and champions major changes. For instance, if the data administration staff is interested in introducing new technology, management may request a formal report on the anticipated benefits of the proposed expenditure.

Interactions between the data administration staff and management may focus on establishing and evolving the information architecture for the organization. In some instances, this may involve the introduction of a new technology that could fundamentally transform the organization. For example, consider the introduction of Lotus Notes into a management consulting company on an enterprise-wide basis. The introduction of Notes was a strategic technology decision that transformed the company's information architecture because it allowed consultants around the world to exchange information and gain fast access to in-house expertise. This capability became a significant source of competitive advantage. Such technological change never would have occurred without management's approval and wholehearted support.

Users

On an ongoing basis, most users will be less concerned with architectural issues and will focus on their personal needs. Data administration must determine what data should be collected and stored, how they should be validated to ensure integrity, and in what form and frequency they should be made available. For instance, the Chief Financial Officer may use the existing EIS to access financial data from external data vendors.

Typically, the data administration staff is responsible for managing the database while the data supplier is responsible for ensuring accuracy. This may cause conflict, however, if there are multiple users from separate departments. If conflict does arise, data administration has to arbitrate.

Development staff

Having received strategic directions from management, and having determined clients' needs, data administration next works with the development staff — both applications and database developers — in order to fulfill the organization's goals for the new system. On an ongoing basis, this may consist of developing specifications for implementation. Data administration works on an advisory basis with systems development, providing inputs on the database aspects. For instance, data administration is responsible for establishing standards for program/database interfaces and making developers aware of these standards. Developers may need to be told which commands may be used in their application programs and which databases they can access.

As a consultant, data administration works closely with database developers. In addition to new database projects, data administration periodically may interact with developers to make relatively minor changes to or optimize existing databases.

In many organizations, database development is part of data administration and has a very direct role in database design and implementation. In such instances, communication between data administration and database development is within the group. In other organizations, database development is not part of data administration, and communication is between groups.

Being a change agent is another important role for data administration. Data administration needs to educate development personnel on the availability of new data technologies. Such technologies may transform the systems development process and perhaps even the composition of the development team. A new database technology may improve development productivity in several ways. For instance, a decision to move to a Web-enabled DBMS with a new application development environment in a previously client/server dominated IS organization may result in significant improvements in programmer productivity. It may also result in retraining of current programmers.

Computer operations

The focus of computer operations is on the physical hardware, procedures, schedules and shifts, staff assignments, physical security of data, and execution of programs. Data administration responsibilities include establishing and monitoring procedures for operating the database. The data administration staff needs to establish and communicate database backup, recovery, and archiving procedures to computer operations. Also, the scheduling of new database and application installations needs to be coordinated with computer operations personnel.

Computer operations provides data administration with operational statistics and exception reports. These data are used by data administration to ensure that corporate database objectives are being fulfilled.

Communication

The diverse parties with which data administration communicates often see things differently. This can lead to misunderstandings and result in systems that fail to meet the needs of users. Part of the problem arises from a difference in perspective and approaches to viewing database technology.

Management is interested in understanding how implementing database technology will contribute to strategic goals. In contrast, users are interested in how the proposed database and accompanying applications will affect their daily work. Developers are concerned with translating management and clients' needs into conceptual models and converting these into physical data models and applications. Operations staff are concerned primarily with efficient daily management of database technology, computer hardware, and software.

Data models can serve as a common language for bridging the varying goals of users, developers, management, and operational staff. A data model can reduce the ambiguity inherent in verbal communications and thereby ensure that users' needs are more closely met and all parties are satisfied with the results. A data model provides a common meeting point and language for understanding the needs of each group.

As we have seen, data administration involves working closely with a variety of database stakeholders. As critical as it is to possess technical knowledge, it is equally important for data administration staff to possess excellent interpersonal skills. Data administration does not work in isolation. It must communicate successfully with all its constituents in order to be successful. The capacity to understand and correctly translate the needs of each stakeholder group is the key to competent data administration.[3]

Data administration tools

The database environment, depicted in Figure 18-1, is very complex. Even in a small organization or work unit, there may be several thousand data items. These data items may appear in hundreds of files, reports, and input transactions. It is impossible to manage this data environment without computer-based tools to support data administration activities.

Several computer-based tools have emerged to support various data administration functions. There are five major classes of tools: data dictionary, DBMS, performance monitoring, computer-aided software engineering (CASE), and groupware tools. Each of these tools is now examined and its role in supporting data administration considered. We focus on how these tools support the database development life cycle (see Figure 18-2). Note, however, that groupware is not shown in Table 18-4 because it is useful in all phases of the life cycle.

Data administration staff, users, and computer operations all require information about organizational databases. Ideally, such information should be stored in one central repository. This is the role of the data dictionary/directory system, perhaps the main data administration tool. Thus, we start our discussion with this tool.

Data dictionary/directory system

The data dictionary/directory system (DD/DS) is a database application that manages the data dictionary. It is an essential tool for data administration staff and users. In this seg-

3. For a more extensive discussion and guidance on improving your interpersonal skills in relation to IS development projects, see Bostrom (1989), Cause and Weinberg (1989), and Weinberg (1986). There are many books that discuss communication skills in a wider context and serve as useful references for self-development. Some of the most useful are Doyle and Strauss (1976) and Kayser (1990). Full details are provided at the end of the chapter.

Table 18-4: Data administration tool use during the DDLC

Database Development Phase	Data Dictionary (DD)	DBMS	Performance Monitoring	Case Tools
1. Project planning tools	Document Data map Design aid			Estimation
2. Requirements definition	Document Design aid			Document Design aid
3. Database design	Document Data map Design aid Schema generator			Document Design aid Data map
4. Database testing	Data map Design aid Schema generator	Define, create, test, data integrity	Impact analysis	Data generator Design aid
5. Database implementation	Document Change control	Data integrity Implement Design	Monitor Tune	
6. Database usage	Document Data map Schema generator Change control	Provide tools for retrieval and update Enforce integrity controls and procedures	Monitor Tune	
7. Database evolution	Document Data map Change control	Redefine	Impact analysis	

ment, we describe the DD/DS and its general and specific uses in supporting various activities during the DDLC. Our focus is on the use of the data dictionary by data administration.

The data dictionary is the repository for organizational metadata, such as data definitions, relationships, and users' privileges. The DBMS manages databases, and the DD/DS manages data about data. The DD/DS also uses the data dictionary to generate table definitions or schema required by the DBMS and application programs to access databases.

Users and data administration can utilize the DD/DS to ask questions about characteristics of data stored in organizational databases such as

- What are the names of all tables for which the user Todd has delete privileges?
- Where does the data item *customer number* appear or is used?

The report for the second query could include the names and tables, transactions, reports, display screens, user's names, and application programs.

In some systems, such as a relational DBMS, the catalog (see Chapter 10) performs some of the functions of a DD/DS although the catalog does not contain the same level of detail.

The catalog essentially contains data about tables, columns, and owners of tables, whereas the DD/DS can include data about applications, forms, transactions, and many other aspects of the system. Consequently, a DD/DS is of greater value to data administration.

Although there is no standard format for data stored in a data dictionary, several features are common across systems. For example, a data dictionary for a typical relational database environment would contain descriptions of the following

- All columns that are defined in all tables of all databases. The data dictionary stores specific data characteristics such as name, data type, display format, internal storage format, validation rules, and integrity constraints. It indicates where a column is used and by whom.
- All relationships among data elements, what elements are involved, and characteristics of relationships such as cardinality and degree.
- All defined databases, including who created each database, the date of creation, and where the database is located.
- All tables defined in all databases. The data dictionary is likely to store details of who created the table, the date of creation, primary key, and the number of columns.
- All indexes defined for each of the database tables. For each of the indexes, the DBMS stores data such as the index name, the location, specific index characteristics, and the creation date.
- All users and their access authorizations for various databases.
- All programs that access the database, including screen formats, report formats, application programs, and SQL queries.

A data dictionary may be integrated or stand alone. An integrated data dictionary is included as part of most DBMSs.

The data dictionary can be useful for both systems and project level data administration activities. The five major uses of a data dictionary are

1. Documentation support: recording, classifying, and reporting metadata.
2. Data maps: a data map of available data for data administration staff and users. A data map allows users to discover what data exist, what they mean, where they are stored, and how they are accessed.
3. Design aid: documenting the relationships between data entities and performing impact analysis.
4. Schema generation: automatic generation of data definition statements needed by software systems such as the DBMS and application programs.
5. Change control: setting and enforcing standards, evaluating the impact of proposed changes, and implementing amendments such as adding new data items.

Database management systems

The DBMS is the primary tool for maintaining database integrity and making data available to users. Availability means making data accessible to whoever needs them, when and where they need them, and in a meaningful form. Maintaining database integrity implies the implementation of control procedures to achieve the three goals discussed in Chapter 17: protecting existence, maintaining quality, and ensuring confidentiality. In terms of the DDLC life cycle (see Figure 18-2), data administration uses, or helps others to use, the DBMS to create and test new databases, define data integrity controls, modify existing database definitions, and provide tools for users to retrieve and update databases. Since much of this book has been devoted to DBMS functions, we limit our discussion to reviewing its role as a data administration tool.

Performance monitoring tools

Performance monitoring tools are often integrated into the DBMS or DD/DS. We discuss them separately, however, because in many cases they can be purchased as individual products.

Monitoring the performance of DBMS and database operations by gathering usage statistics is essential to improving performance, enhancing availability, and database evolution. As shown in Table 18-4, monitoring tools are used to collect statistics and improve database performance during the implementation and use stages of the DDLC. Monitoring tools can also be used to collect data to evaluate design choices during testing.

Many database factors can be monitored and a variety of statistics gathered. Monitoring growth in the number of rows in each table can reveal trends that are helpful in projecting future needs for physical storage space. Database access patterns can be scrutinized to record data such as

- type of function requested: query, insert, update, or delete,
- response time (elapsed time from query to response),
- number of disk accesses,
- identification of user,
- identification of error conditions.

The observed patterns help to determine performance enhancements. For example, these statistics could be used to determine which tables or files should be indexed. Since gathering statistics can result in some degradation of overall performance, it should be possible to turn the monitoring function on or off with regard to selected statistics.

CASE tools

A computer-aided software engineering (CASE) tool, as broadly defined, provides automated assistance for systems development, maintenance, and project management activities. Data administration may use project management tools to coordinate all phases within the DDLC. The dictionary provided by CASE systems can be used to supplement the DD/DS, especially where the database development effort is part of a systems development project.

One of the most important components of a CASE tool is an extensive dictionary that tracks all objects created by systems designers. Database and application developers can use the CASE dictionary to store descriptions of data elements, application processes, screens, reports, and other relevant information. Thus, during the first three phases of the life cycle (see Figure 18-2), the CASE dictionary performs functions similar to a DD/DS. During stages 4 and 5, data from the CASE dictionary would be transferred, usually automatically, to the DD/DS.

Groupware

Groupware can be applied by data administration to support any of the DDLC phases shown in Figure 18-2. Groupware supports communication between people and thus enhances access to organizational memory residing within humans. As we have pointed out, data administration interfaces with four major groups during the DDLC: management, users, developers, and computer operations. Groupware supports interactions with all of these groups.

Data administration is a complex task involving a variety of technologies and the need to interact with and satisfy the needs of a diverse range of users. Managing such a complex environment demands the use of computer-based tools. New tools are making data administration more manageable and effective. Software tools, such as CASE and groupware, can improve data administration. The emergence of such tools also signals an increasing awareness of the importance of data administration and an understanding of what it entails.

Organizing data administration

Data administration is essential to ensuring the availability and integrity of shared databases. To ensure that this function is properly performed, its importance must first be recognized. Then the necessary steps must be taken to formally integrate data administration into the organization. These steps include establishment of a data administration function, assigning data administration roles, and locating data administration in the formal organization. These steps are not necessarily carried out in sequence; indeed, there may be value in performing all three simultaneously. In most large organizations, all three steps have already been undertaken. Many smaller organizations, however, may have yet to embark on them. Even where all three steps have been completed, the second and third are continually monitored and reviewed because of rapid changes in current information technologies.

The mainframe-oriented centralized database architecture of the past is being supplanted by Web browser-based computing based on a distributed architecture. Both computing power and databases are being spread throughout the organization rather than being controlled by a central IS group. In many instances, databases are becoming locally managed by individual workgroups or departments. This transformation creates a need for data administration to be performed where workgroup or departmental databases are located rather than centrally. Where users and databases are linked by local area networks, there is a need for both local and central data administration. Central data administration is responsible for coordinating the functioning of the separate local database administrators.

Initiating data administration

Initially, the need for data administration is unlikely to be recognized by senior management; more likely, it is major data users or someone in the IS function who first recognizes the need for data administration. Establishing data administration typically involves convincing management of the importance of data administration and the need for a formal organizational function with assigned roles. A survey of data needs and practices in the organization is one approach to justifying establishment of data administration.

Data administration typically possesses very little organizational power. The power that it has derives from the extent to which senior management recognizes its importance. Management support is crucial since the function affects the generators and users of data throughout the organization.

Implementing data administration requires funds for salaries, tools, office space, and training. Management may feel that data administration can be performed without allocating separate personnel, time, or additional tools. This may be true in a small organization, but larger corporations have too much at stake to permit allocation of insufficient resources. The sponsor of data administration should emphasize the importance of providing the necessary budget to support effective performance.

Selecting data administration staff

If data administration is to be performed as an additional responsibility of existing IS or user staff, the nature and scope of duties must be detailed and clearly assigned to the nominated staff. If data administration requires full-time responsibility, either a data administrator is hired or someone from within the organization is reassigned. An internal hire may be more familiar with organizational needs but may not possess the necessary skills and thus require additional training. An external hire may have the necessary experience and skills to transform the organization but will have to learn how the organization operates.

Data administration could be undertaken by the IS department staff as well as by users, depending on the size of the organization and the nature of the databases. Furthermore, where data are distributed in various locations, connected via local or wide area networks, several persons may be assigned data administration roles and responsibilities. Depending on their managerial and technical skills, data administrators will need training for their new positions.

An effective data administrator should possess a variety of interpersonal, business, and technical skills. For system level support, there is a relatively greater emphasis on managerial and business skills. At the project level, a greater degree of technical ability is needed. In both cases, interpersonal and communication skills are essential.

Locating data administration in the organization

Throughout this chapter, we have spoken of data administration as a function or set of activities rather than as a department to emphasize that organizations can choose to locate the function in a variety of ways. The most common location for data administration is in the IS department. Where data administration is considered highly critical, there may be a separate data administration manager who reports to the CIO. The data administration staff is organized within this group (see Figure 18-4).

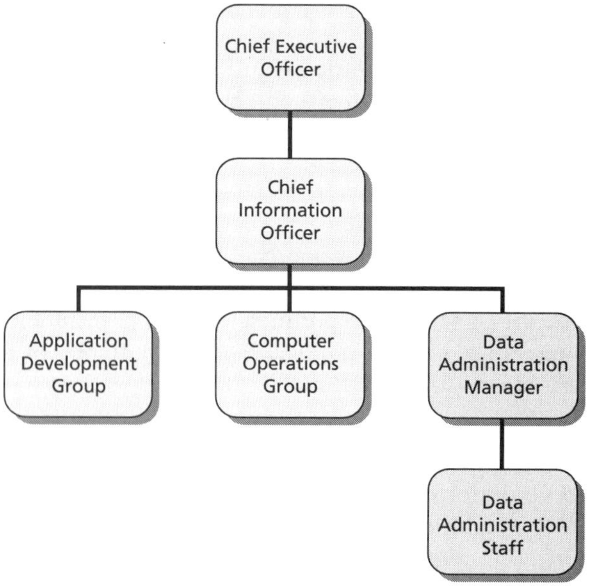

Figure 18-4. Data administration reporting to the CIO

In some organizations, data administration may be included as part of a larger group, such as support services, which may include the information center and help desk staff (see Figure 18-5). The data administration staff also could be located in application development, computer operations, or some other group reporting to the CIO.

A matrix organization, a very different approach from the structures described previously, is another choice for the location of data administration (see Figure 18-6). In a matrix organization, data administration staff belong to the data administration group in terms of the functions performed but are also members of specific project teams. Staff members are responsible to the project leader for all project specific responsibilities and deliverables. At the same time, there is a data administration manager who coordinates the performance of data administration activities across all projects and monitors and supervises data administration staff on all projects. Data administration staff report to individual

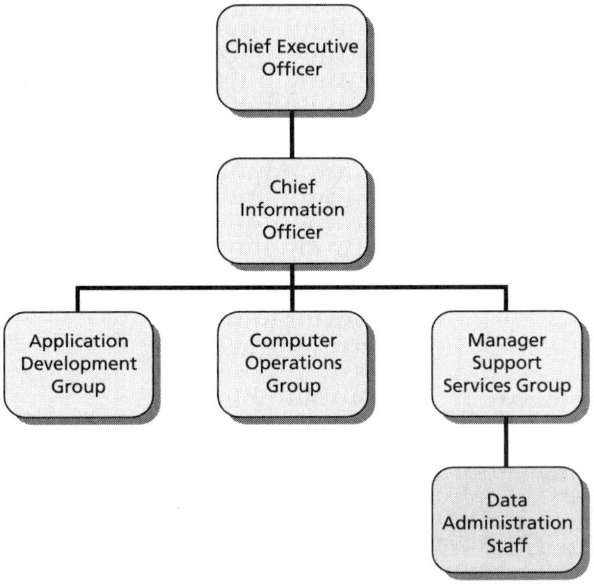

Figure 18-5. Data administration reporting to Support Services

project leaders for the duration of a specific DDLC while also being administratively supervised by the data administration manager.

A major benefit of a matrix organization is that data administration members are in close communication with other project personnel, and consequently the resulting database may be more closely integrated with the system under development and hence more effectively satisfy user needs. Furthermore, the data administration member may be able to draw on more resources when needed (from the manager and perhaps from other projects) because of the additional relationship outside of the project. Not all organizations, however, prefer to use this structure. A data administration member has, in effect, two supervisors and this potentially can result in conflicting situations and affect performance and productivity. Avoiding or resolving conflicts requires extensive communication and coordination among data administration staff, project managers, and the data administration manager. When properly managed, a matrix structure is useful in many organizational contexts.

In some instances, data administration is a staff function within the office of the CIO performed by an advisory committee drawn from within the IS function and user departments (Figure 18-7). This committee is concerned typically with system level data administration issues. Within the IS department, the advisory committee may serve to advise and coordinate the data administration activities of project database staff. If the database technology is new to the organization, the committee may undertake database architectural planning and data administration policy development. Once a DBMS is implemented, a more formal

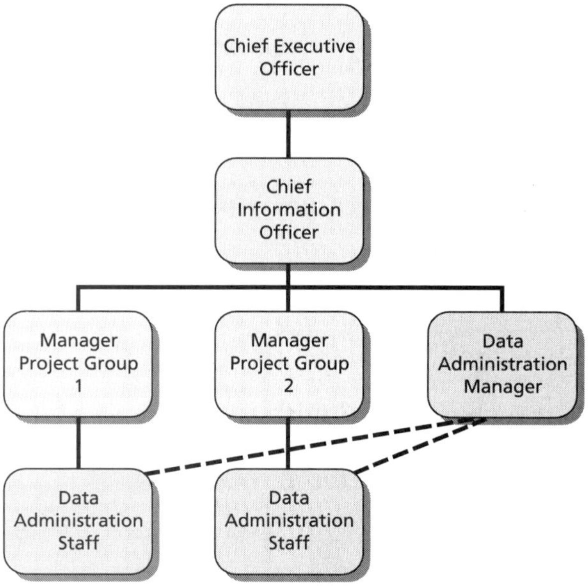

Figure 18-6. Matrix structure for data administration

and operational organizational structure is typically adopted. In workgroups or user departments, a data administration staff advisory committee helps to manage local databases in distributed database environments.

In decentralized database environments, data administration responsibilities also may be distributed among various departments, divisions, or workgroups. Local data administration reports to its respective workgroup heads while coordinating its relevant activities via a data administration manager located in the IS function (Figure 18-7). There are two different possibilities here. In one instance — perhaps in multiple, relatively independent divisions — local data administration is fully responsible for local data administration, and the staff manager is mainly a consultant who coordinates the development and enforcement of organizational standards and provides expert advice to local staff when requested. In another instance — say, multiple offices within a single campus — local data administration may actually report to the staff data administration manager who plans all local data administration activity together with local staff. In this case, the involvement and local responsibility of the data administration manager is far greater. The latter instance is an example of a true matrix organization, while in the former, the extra-departmental relationship is purely consultative.

The organizational designs described are encountered quite frequently but are not the only ways to organize data administration. Each situation demands a different way to organize, and the particular needs of the organization need to be fully considered before adopting any particular structure. In most organizations, the nature, importance, and lo-

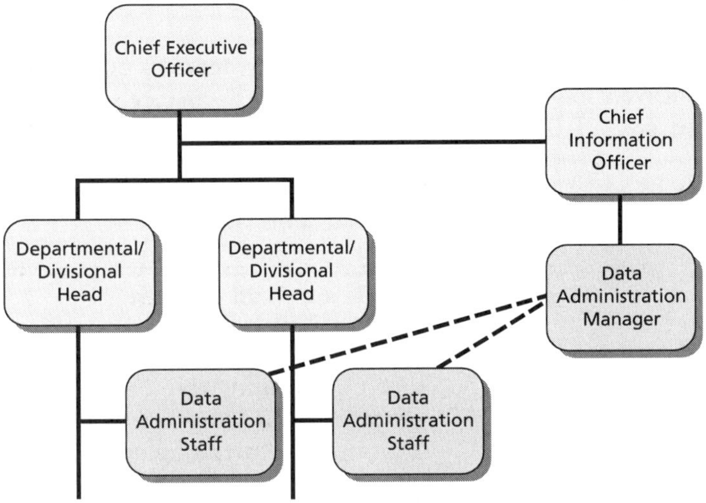

Figure 18-7. Decentralized data administration

cation of data administration change over time, and are influenced by new technologies, organizational growth, and evolving patterns of database usage. It is important to remain alert to such changes and reorganize data administration when necessary to ensure that the organization's data requirements are constantly satisfied.

Summary

Data administration is the task of managing that part of organizational memory that involves electronically available data. Managing electronic data stores is important because key organizational decisions are based on information drawn from it, and it is necessary to ensure that reliable data are available when needed. Data administration is carried out at both the system level, which involves overall policies and alignment with organizational goals, as well as the project level, where the specific details of each database are handled. Key modules in data administration are the DBMS, the Data Dictionary/Directory System, user interfaces, and external databases.

Data administration is a function performed by those with assigned organizational roles. Data administration may be carried out by a variety of persons either within the IS department or in user departments. Also, this function may occur at the personal, workgroup, or organizational level.

Data administration involves communication with management, users, developers, and computer operations staff. It needs the cooperation of all four groups to perform its functions effectively. Since each group may hold very different perspectives, which could lead to conflicts and misunderstandings, it is important for data administration staff to possess superior communication skills. Successful data administration requires a combination of interpersonal, technical, and business skills.

Data administration is complex, and its success partly depends on a range of computer-based tools. Available tools include DD/DS, DBMS, performance monitoring tools, CASE tools, and groupware.

A variety of options are available for organizing data administration, and a choice has to be made based on the prevailing organizational context.

Home Depot builds a hybrid IS team

Atlanta-based Home Depot had sales of nearly $20 billion in 1997 from its more than 600 North American outlets. Supporting IS in a firm with 25 to 30 percent annual growth is a taxing task for the 650-person IS group. In order to support technology while meeting individual needs, the IS group is restructuring under a hybrid management model.

The hybrid centralized/decentralized IS management model is becoming popular for international companies with distributed business units. This approach balances enterprise needs and the specific needs of business units. Companies that tend to centralize IS often create friction and frustration between IS and the business units. Businesses that decentralize IS let business units make their technology choices, but this leads to higher cost structures, little sharing of resources, and redundancy.

Home Depot plans to set technology standards for its business divisions, such as a common financial system, and it will customize some applications to meet individual business unit needs. The goal is to get the benefits of resource sharing without the downsides of a *one size fits all* approach.

Source: Hoffman, T. 1998. Retailer retools IS management team. *Computerworld*, February 16, 41–24.

Key terms and concepts

Application development life cycle (ADLC)
Benchmark
Change agent
Computer-aided software engineering (CASE)
Data administration
Data dictionary
Data dictionary/directory system (DD/DS)
Data integrity
Data steward
Database administrator
Database developer
Database development life cycle (DDLC)
Database management system (DBMS)
External database
Groupware
Matrix organization
Performance monitoring
Project level data administration
Request for proposal (RFP)
System level data administration
Systems development life cycle (SDLC)
Transaction Processing Council (TPC)
User interface

References and additional readings

Bostrom, R. P. 1989. Successful application of communication techniques to improve the systems development process. *Information & Management* 16:279–295.

Cause, D. E., and G. M. Weinberg. 1989. *Exploring requirements: Quality before design.* New York, NY: Dorset House.

Davenport, T. H., R. G. Eccles, and L. Prusak. 1992. Information politics. *Sloan Management Review* 34 (1):53–65.

Doyle, M., and D. Strauss. 1976. *How to make meetings work: The new interaction method.* New York, NY: Jove.

Goodhue, D. L., J. A. Quillard, and J. F. Rockart. 1988. Managing the data resource: A contingency perspective. *MIS Quarterly* 12 (3):373–391.

Goodhue, D. L., M. D. Wybo, and L. J. Kirsch. 1992. The impact of data integration on the costs and benefits of information systems. *MIS Quarterly* 16 (3):293–311.

Kayser, T. A. 1990. *Mining group gold.* El Segundo, CA: Serif.

Weinberg, G. M. 1986. *Becoming a technical leader: An organic problem solving approach.* New York, NY: Dorset House.

Exercises

1. Why do organizations need to manage data?
2. What problems can arise because of poor data administration?
3. What is the purpose of a data dictionary?
4. Do you think a data dictionary should be part of a DBMS or a separate package?
5. How does the management of external databases differ from internal databases?
6. What is the difference between system and project level data administration?
7. What is a data steward? What is the purpose of this role?
8. What is the difference between workgroups and organizational databases? What are the implications for data administration?
9. What is an information architecture?

10. Why do organizations need data standards? Give some examples of typical data items that may require standardization.
11. You have been asked to advise a firm on the capacity of its database system. Describe the procedures you would use to estimate the size of the database and the number of transactions per second it will have to handle.
12. Why would a company issue an RFP?
13. How do the roles of database developer and data administrator differ?
14. What do you think is the most critical task for the user during database development?
15. A medium-sized manufacturing company is about to establish a data administration group within the MIS department. What software tools would you recommend that group acquire?
16. What is a stakeholder? Why should stakeholders be involved in database project planning?
17. What support do CASE tools provide for the DDLC?
18. How can groupware support the DDLC?
19. A large international corporation has typically operated in a very decentralized manner with regional managers having considerable autonomy. How would you recommend the corporation establish its data administration function?
20. Describe the personality of a successful data administration manager. Compare your assessment to the personality appropriate for a database technical adviser.
21. Write a job advertisement for a data administrator for your university.
22. What types of organizations are likely to have data administration reporting directly to the CIO?
23. What do you think are the most critical phases of the DDLC? Justify your decision.
24. When might application development and database development proceed independently?
25. Why is database monitoring important? What data would you ask for in a database monitoring report?
26. Get the TPC-D Benchmark report from the TPC Web site (www.tpc.com), and answer the following questions:
    a. What are the smallest and largest databases benchmarked?
    b. How is the database populated?
    c. Why does the report specify the SQL for each query?
27. Get the TPC-C Benchmark report from the TPC Web site (www.tpc.org), and report how the SQL queries differ from those of TPC-D. Why is this so?
28. Create a benchmark for your personal computer DBMS by doing the following:
    a. Create the TPC-D database.
    b. Use Excel to generate test data and import them into your test database.
    c. Run several of the TPC-D queries.
    d. Investigate the effect of database size.

Glossary

A

Access time. The amount of time it takes for information to be read from or written to a disk. The sum of search time plus seek time.

Acronym. A word formed by taking the first letters or sounds of each word in a phrase and capitalizing them. For example, RAM (pronounced as a word) is an acronym for random-access memory.

Address. A location in memory where data are stored and can be retrieved.

Administrative strategies. Organizational policies and procedures for maintaining data integrity.

After image. A copy of a record after a change has been made. It is used for forward recovery.

Aggregate entity. An entity created from several entities having similar attributes often distinguished by a prefix or suffix.

Aggregate function. A function, such as COUNT and SUM, that operates on multiple columns.

Aggregation. A special version of an association relationship that reflects strong ties between objects.

Alphanumeric. Data represented in both alphabetic (the letters A-Z) and numeric (the numbers 0-9) form.

ALTER TABLE. An SQL command to add a column to an existing table or change the status of a referential integrity constraint.

Alternate key. A candidate primary key that was not selected as the primary key.

Anomaly. An undesirable result following update, insertion, or deletion of a record.

ANSI. American National Standards Institute.

Applet. A Java program that is downloaded into a browser and then run inside the browser's window.

Application development life cycle (ADLC). The stages of developing and maintaining an application.

Application software. A computer program or set of programs intended to perform a specific function, such as accounting, payroll, word processing, spreadsheet calculating, or database management.

Architecture. A term used by computer designers to designate the structure of complex information-processing systems. It includes the kinds of instructions and data used, the memory organization and addressing, and the methods by which the system is implemented.

Archival file. A file kept as a permanent record.

Arithmetic expression. An expression consisting of only numbers and operators, for example, 7 + 6.

Artificial intelligence (AI). The branch of computer science that attempts to understand the nature of intelligence and produces new classes of intelligent machines. Areas of study include robotics, speech recognition, image recognition, natural-language processing, and expert systems.

ASCII. An acronym for American Standard Code for Information Interchange. A seven- or eight-bit code that specifies a unique set of binary digits that represent a character set.

Association. Links or connections between object occurrences.

Associative entity. The by-product on an m:m relationship. It stores data about an m:m relationship.

Attribute. A fact about an entity that becomes a column in a table.

Authorization. Permission to take particular actions on a database (e.g., insert rows).

AVG. An SQL built-in function for determining the average of the values in a numeric column.

B

B-tree. A file in which the records are structured into an inverted tree based on a series of midpoints. For example, the root of the tree is the midpoint of a file, and more midpoints occur in each succeeding level.

Backing up. Copying program or data files in case the original is lost or destroyed.

Backup-file. A copy of a file made for safekeeping in case the original is lost or damaged.

Bandwidth. The term used as a measure of the capacity of a communication channel expressed in bits per second.

Base table. An autonomous, named table.

Before image. A copy of a record before a change has been made. It is used for backward recovery.

Benchmarking. The establishment of goals based on best industry practices.

Binary digit. The smallest unit of information capable of being represented in a computer or communication system.

Binary relationship. A relationship between exactly two entities.

Binary search. A search method in which a list of items is successively halved until the sought item is located.

Bit. Short for binary digit.

Bits per second. The number of bits of information that pass a given point in one second. A measure of the carrying capacity of a channel.

BLOB (binary large object). BLOBs contain large binary data files.

Boolean. A data type that can be true or false.

Bottom-up design. In software development, a technique that starts with the parts or most basic functional components and proceeds to build a whole or complete program.

Boyce-Codd normal form. A relation in third normal form in which every determinant is a candidate key.

Built-in function. An SQL function such as AVG, COUNT, MAX, MIN, or SUM.

Byte. A sequence of eight consecutive bits used in coding systems to represent one character of data or information.

C

C. A high-level programming language that is very popular because of its transportability between computer systems.

Candidate key. An attribute or group of attributes that is a potential primary key for a table.

Cardinality. The number of rows in a relational table.

Cartesian product. A relational operation on two tables, A and B, that produces all possible combinations of the concatenation of a row from A and a row from B.

Catalog. A database that contains details of databases.

CD-ROM. An acronym for compact disk-read-only memory. An optical disk on which data are encoded for retrieval by a laser.

Change agent. A person leading or guiding an organizational change.

Change information. Information that helps managers determine which actions might successfully close the gap between actual and desired performance.

Channel. A pathway for the transmission of data or information to and from a computer or communication system.

Child. A row on the many side of a 1:m relationship.

Class. In object-oriented programming, a generalized category that describes a group of objects that can exist within it. The class serves as the template from which specific objects are created.

Client. An end user or computer program that requests resources across a network.

Client/server computing. A combination of clients and servers that provides the framework for distributing files and databases across a network. In a database, client/server describes the situation where a client runs a database application (front end) that accesses information from a DBMS on a server (back end).

CLOB (character large object). CLOBs contain large character data files.

Clustering. Storing in the same area, or adjacent physical areas, records that are frequently accessed together.

COBOL. An acronym for COmmon Business Oriented Language. A high-level programming language that is used primarily for business-oriented applications.

CODASYL/DBTG. The task group that developed the network data model.

Code. (1) A set of symbols, such as the dots and dashes of the Morse code, that represents another set of symbols, such as the letters of the alphabet. (2) The set of rules that defines the way in which bits can be arranged to represent numbers and letters. Example: ASCII. (3) To write a computer program in a specific programming language.

Column. A vertical group of facts in a table. All values in a column have the same meaning.

Command. An instruction that tells a computer to perform an operation.

COMMIT. An SQL command to make a set of database changes permanent.

Communicability objective. The notion that a database model should facilitate effective and efficient communication between users and MIS personnel.

Communication. (1) A process by which information is exchanged between individuals through the use of a commonly agreed-on set of symbols. (2) From an engineering standpoint, the movement of electronic traffic from one point to another.

Communication server. A device that connects local-area networks (LANs) to wide-area (WANs) or telecommunication networks.

Communication software. Programs that enable a computer to connect to other computers and exchange information.

Communication system. A system that consists of senders (transmitters), physical channels, and receivers.

Compatibility. (1) The ability to connect different computer systems, devices, or software so they can work together. (2) The capability of different computer systems to process the same applications.

Compiler. A computer program (software) that reads a high-level program to (1) check it for spelling and grammatical errors and (2) translate it into lower-level language instructions.

Complete database language. A language that can be used for defining a database, creating views, specifying queries, and modifying records.

Complete programming language. A general purpose programming language that can be used to write an entire application (e.g., COBOL).

Complex service. A nonstandard service for an object.

Composite key. A key with more than one attribute or column.

Composition. A structure in which one object is composed of others. Also known as a whole/part structure.

Compression. Techniques for compacting data so that they require less storage space.

Computer address. (1) The address of a location within a computer's memory. (2) The Internet identification code of a computer (e.g., arches.uga.edu).

Computer-aided design (CAD). The use of a computer system to aid the process of design.

Computer-aided software engineering (CASE). A set of tools to automate the tasks involved in designing and developing large-scale or complex software projects. Included are data dictionaries, diagram generators, prototyping tools, and consistency-checking tools.

Conceptual schema. An abstract view of a database.

Concurrent program execution. The execution of two or more programs at the same time. They actually take turns using the computer so rapidly that they give the illusion of operating concurrently.

Concurrent update control. An error arising when one transaction's changes are overwritten by another transaction's changes. Also known as the *lost update problem*.

Consistent database. A database in which all data integrity constraints are satisfied.

Control break reporting. A method of reporting a sorted file with new headers or footers each time the sort key changes.

Correlated subquery. A subquery that cannot be evaluated once and for all before the outer query is evaluated. The inner query depends on a variable that changes in the outer query.

COUNT. An SQL built-in function for determining the number of values in a column.

CREATE INDEX. An SQL command to create an index.

CREATE TABLE. An SQL command to create a table.

CREATE VIEW. An SQL command to create a view.

Culture. The set of shared beliefs, values, attitudes, and norms that influences the behavior and expectations of each person in a group.

Cursor. A pointer indicating the row to be processed when using embedded SQL.

Cycle time. The time taken to complete an activity.

Cylinder. The imaginary surface composed of all the tracks that lie directly above and below one another on a multiple-platter disk pack.

D

Data. A general term meaning the facts, numbers, letters, and symbols processed by a computer or communication system to produce information.

Data access control. Procedures for controlling which individuals, departments, groups of people, transactions, terminals, or application programs can access data.

Data administration. The administration of an organization's data resources.

Data administrator. A person responsible for data administration.

Data communications. The transfer of data or information between computer-related devices.

Data communications manager. Software that manages communication between computers and devices.

Data definition language (DDL). A language for describing the structure of a database.

Data dictionary/directory system (DD/DS). (1) In systems design, a listing of all the data elements and data structures within a system. (2) In a database system, a file that contains descriptions of relationships among a collection of data.

Data Encryption Standard (DES). An encryption system developed by IBM and approved in 1976 by the U.S. National Bureau of Standards for governmental use.

Data independence. The ability of a database to exist independently of specific applications.

Data integrity. Techniques for protecting data from invalid alteration, destruction, or access and ensuring data are accurate and reliable.

Data item. A field or attribute in DL/I and the network model.

Data management. The management of an organization's data resources.

Data manipulation language (DML). A language for describing the processing of a database.

Data mart. A subject-specific data warehouse; often departmental or line-of-business.

Data mining. Knowledge discovery process of extracting previously unknown, actionable information from very large databases.

Data model. A graphical description of the entities, attributes, identifiers, and relationships in a database.

Data model quality. An assessment of the degree to which a data model is well-formed and its fidelity of image.

Data processing. A general term that stands for all the logical, arithmetic, and input/output operations that can be performed on data by a computer.

Data quality. The accuracy, completeness, and currency of data.

Data security. Techniques for protecting a database against access or modification without authorization.

Data steward. A person responsible for managing all corporate data for some critical business-related unit or activity.

Data structure. An organizational scheme used to structure or organize data so that they can be stored, retrieved, and manipulated by a program. Examples include records, lists, and arrays.

Data type. A data format (e.g., integer) that can be defined for a column.

Data visualization. Graphical rendering of information from a database.

Data warehouse. A subject-oriented database designed specifically for decision support.

Database. (1) A collection of different types of data organized according to a structure that minimizes redundancies and facilitates the manipulation of the data. (2) A collection of one or more files treated as a whole unit.

Database administration. (See data administration.)

Database administrator. (See data administrator.)

Database architecture. A general model for the storage of organizational data.

Database development life cy-

cle (DDLC). The stages of developing and maintaining a database.

Database integrity. Techniques for protecting a database from invalid alteration, destruction, or access and ensuring data are accurate and reliable.

Database machine. A special purpose computer designed for processing databases.

Database management system (DBMS). Software that organizes, manipulates, and retrieves data stored in a database.

Database server. Software that services requests to a database across a network.

Database system. An information system that integrates a collection of data and makes them available to a wide variety of people in an organization.

Database transaction. A group of database modifications treated as a single unit.

Dataflow diagram. A graphical method for illustrating business processes.

DBMS/server. A server that runs a DBMS and processes actions on the database at the request of client programs.

Deadlock prevention. A technique for resolving or avoiding a deadly embrace.

Deadly embrace. A condition that can occur when two transactions are competing for the same resources. Both transactions are waiting to access data the other transaction has locked. Also known as deadlock.

Decision making. The process of identifying and selecting a course of action to solve a specific problem.

Decision quality. An assessment of the decision making process.

Decision support system (DSS). An interactive, user-friendly system for supporting decision makers.

Decode. To modify information from a computer-readable form into a form that people can read or use.

Decryption. The decoding of an encrypted electronic transmission. (See also **encryption**.)

Degree. The number of columns in a relational table.

DELETE. The SQL command for deleting one or more rows.

Dependent entity. An entity that relies on another for its existence and identification. A dependent entity is indicated by a bar on its end of a relationship arc. Also known as a weak entity.

Determinant. One or more attributes that functionally determine another attribute or attributes. In the case where A $\rightarrow$ B, A is the determinant.

Difference. A relational algebra operation on two union-compatible relations A and B, where the new relation contains all rows in A that are not in B.

Digitizing. The process of translating analog data into digital data.

Direct-access file. A type of file organization scheme designed for processing records in an order other than sequential. Also called a random-access file.

Disk. A circular platter on which a magnetic or reflective coating is applied. Used for long-term storage of data.

Disk array. The combination and synchronization of multiple disk drives into one self-contained unit. A disk array features faster data access and higher data throughput than an equivalent-sized single disk drive.

Disk cartridge. Removable disks that are sealed in a container similar to a videotape cartridge.

Disk drive. A device that houses the motor to spin the disk and the read/write head for accessing and storing information on the disk.

Disk manager. A part of the operating system responsible for physical I/O.

Disk pack. A removable stack of hard disks joined together by a common spindle.

DISTINCT. The keyword used in a SELECT statement to indicate that duplicate rows should be eliminated.

Distributed computing. A type of processing that uses a number of small computers distributed throughout an organization.

Distributed database. A capability in which different parts of a database reside on physically separate computers. The goal is to access information without regard to where the data might be stored.

Distributed query processing. Query processing when a database is distributed.

Distributed transaction processing. Transaction processing when a database is distributed.

Divide. A relational algebra operation that in its simplest form creates a new relation (the quotient) from binary (the dividend) and unary (the divisor) relations. The result of dividing A (the dividend) by B (the divisor) is C (the quotient) is such that for every value of *x* in C, the pair (*x*,*y*) appears in A for all values of *y* in B.

DL/I (Data Language I). IBM's language to define and process a hierarchical database.

Document. Any text or collection of characters (letters, numbers, spaces, punctuation marks, and other symbols); usually associated with word processing and desktop-publishing applications.

Documentation. (1) The books, manuals, or tutorials that accompany a computer-related product. (2)Written specifications that are a part of the process of developing software.

Domain. The set of all possible legal values of an attribute.

DROP INDEX. The SQL command to delete an index.

DROP TABLE. The SQL command to delete a table.

DROP VIEW. The SQL command to delete a view.

Dynamic model. A representation that describes what a system actually does for any particular event.

E

EBCDIC. An acronym for Extended Binary-Coded Decimal Interchange Code. An eight-bit code designed by IBM that assigns binary digits to specific symbols. Used primarily by IBM computers.

Electronic brainstorming. The use of computer and communications technology to help a group generate ideas.

Electronic conference. A meeting that is conducted over an electronic network using terminals or personal computers.

Embedded SQL. SQL statements enclosed within the structure of a general purpose programming language.

Empowerment. The act of delegating power and authority to subordinates to further organizational goals.

Encapsulation. The concept whereby data and processes contained within an object are not visible to and cannot be changed by other objects.

Encryption. The coding of an electronic transmission for purposes of security or privacy.

End user. A person who uses a product, as opposed to a person who develops or markets the product.

Entity. Something in the real world that is represented in a data model and about which data must be stored. An entity is the basic building block of a data model.

Entity integrity. Every instance of an entity defined in a relational database is uniquely identified.

Entity-relationship (E-R) model. A data model constructed following the principles of the E-R approach to data modeling.

Equijoin. A join containing both matching columns.

Erasable optical disk. An optical disk that uses lasers to read and write information to and from the disk, but also uses a magnetic material on the surface of the disk and a magnetic write head to achieve erasability.

Exabyte (Ebyte). A unit of measure equivalent to 10^{15} bytes.

Exclusive lock. A lock on a data resource that prevents any other transaction from reading or updating the resource.

Exhaustive class. A subclass or a set of subclasses in an inheritance structure that by covering all the relevant objects results in the superclass containing no objects.

EXISTS. The SQL implementation of the *existential quantifier*. EXISTS is used in a WHERE clause to test whether a table contains at least one row satisfying a specified condition. It returns the value *true* if and only if some row satisfies the condition; otherwise, it returns *false*.

Expert system. A computer program that solves specialized problems at the level of a human expert.

External database. A database maintained by a party external to an organization.

External memory. Additional memory that is not contained within a system.

External schema. A user's view of a database.

F

Fault-tolerant computer. A computer that uses redundant hardware or software components to prevent failure from disrupting the operation of the system. The system can continue processing while the faulty component is replaced or repaired.

Field. The smallest unit of named data that has meaning in a record. A field usually describes an attribute of the record, such as a name or address.

Fifth normal form. A relation is in fifth normal form (5NF) if and only if every join dependency of the relation is a consequence of the candidate keys of the relation.

File. A collection of organized data stored as one complete unit for processing.

File manager. A single file, its indexes, and a program to handle basic tasks, such as entering, modifying, retrieving, and printing data from the file.

File server. Software that services requests to a file across a network.

First normal form. A relation is in first normal form (1NF) if and only if all columns contain atomic values only.

Flat file. A single file consisting of rows (records) and columns (fields) of data that resemble a two-dimensional spreadsheet.

Floppy disk. A flexible plastic disk coated with a magnetic recording material.

Foreign key. An attribute that is a primary key in the same table or another table. It is the method of recording relations in a relational database.

Fourth normal form. A relation is in fourth normal form (4NF) if it is in BCNF and all multivalued dependencies on the relation are functional dependencies.

Fourth-generation language. A term that encompasses (1) presentation languages, such as query languages and report generators; (2) specialty languages, such as spreadsheets and database languages; (3) application generators that define, input, modify or update, and report data to build applications; and (4) very high-level languages that are used to generate application code. Often abbreviated as 4GL.

Full-text retrieval software. Software that allows text to be indexed, edited, annotated, linked, and searched for in an electronic document.

Fully relational database. A relational database system that supports structures (domains and relations), integrity rules (primary and foreign keys), and a manipulation language (relational algebra).

Functional dependency. A relationship between attributes in which one attribute or group of attributes determines the value of another. It is shown as $A \rightarrow B$ and read as "A determines B" or "B is functionally dependent on A."

G

Gap information. Information that reveals a gap between desired and actual performance (e.g., an exception report).

Generalization/specialization. A structure in which one object generally describes more specialized objects (e.g., transportation is a generalization of car).

Geographical information system (GIS). A system that digitizes maps and images of distributions of statistical data and displays them as graphics.

Gigabyte (Gbyte). A unit of measure that is the equivalent of 10^9 bytes.

Global change. Change occurring in many different countries simultaneously.

Goal-setting information. Information that helps managers to set realistic targets for expected performance.

GRANT. An SQL command for granting privileges to a user or users.

Granularity. The level of database resources that can be locked. Locking at the database level is large granularity. Locking a column or row is low granularity.

Graphical user interface (GUI). An interface that uses pictures and graphic symbols to represent commands, choices, or actions.

Graphics. The term encompassing several elements, including color, motion, and resolution, that together result in the ability of a computer to show line drawings, pictures, or animation on a display screen or printer. Differs from an image in that it can contain embedded information.

GROUP BY. The SQL phrase for rearranging a table into groups so that all rows in a group have the same value for a specified column.

Groupware. Application software that supports collaborative work and integrates applications such as electronic mail, conferencing, calendar and scheduling software; workflow software, which automates the routing of business processes and forms over a network; document management software to handle the creation and revision of shared documents on a network; and group support software to facilitate electronic meetings.

H

Hard disk. A disk made of a rigid base, such as aluminum, and coated with a magnetic-oxide layer.

Hash function. The function for computing a *hash address* from a *hash field*.

Hashing. A mathematical technique for assigning a unique number to each record in a file.

HAVING. The SQL keyword specifying the condition the groups returned by a GROUP BY clause must satisfy. HAVING is to groups what WHERE is to rows.

Hierarchical model. A method for storing data in a database that structures data into an inverted tree in which records contain (1) a single root or master key field that identifies the type, location, or ordering of the records, and (2) a variable number of subordinate fields that defines the rest of the data within a record.

High fidelity image. A data model that faithfully describes the world it is meant to represent.

Homonym. One of a group of words pronounced or spelled the same way but having different meanings.

Host/terminal. A data processing architecture based on using terminals to access a host computer that stores and processes data.

Hybrid architecture. A relatively integrated mix of data processing and storage architectures that has developed over time.

Hybrid object relational model. A data model that combines features of the object and relational models.

Hypermedia. An extension of hypertext that includes graphics, video, sound, and music.

Hypertext. Electronic files in which an author can link information and create nonlinear paths through related material.

I

Identifier. An attribute or collection of attributes that uniquely distinguishes an entity.

Image scanner. A device that converts optically focused images, such as photographs or drawings, into digital images that can then be processed like any other digital data. A photoreceptor device is required to convert reflected light into digital images.

Images. Data in the form of pictures. Differs from a graphic in that they do not contain embedded information.

Imaging system. Information technology that converts paper documents to electronic images.

Impedance problem. The mismatch between set-at-a-time processing of a relational database and record-at-a-time processing of programming languages.

IMS. Information Management System. IBM's transaction processing system that includes a data communications monitor (IMS/DC) and an implementation of DL/I (IMS/DB).

IN. An SQL keyword preceding a set of values to be searched (e.g., FNAME IN ('Tom', 'Dick', 'Harry')).

Independent entity. An entity that is central to a data model and often prominent in the client's mind. It often has a single, arbitrary identifier.

Index. A list containing an entry for each record in a file organized in a certain way.

Index sequential. A file organization method that provides both sequential and direct-access capability.

Index set. A tree structure providing fast direct access to records in a B-tree.

Information. Data transformed into a form and content relevant for a particular situation.

Information delivery system. A system that provides information to those who need it.

Information engineering. A general approach using CASE tools to develop an enterprise-wide plan for systems development and maintenance.

Information hardness. A subjective measure of the accuracy and reliability of some information.

Information integration. The process of assembling data in many forms and from many sources to satisfy a user's needs.

Information organization. An organization that relies on information to create profitable products and services.

Information processing. The work that information systems perform, consisting of responding to input, processing that input according to instructions, and providing output.

Information requirements. A specification of the information a user or group of users needs to solve problems.

Information revolution. (1) A term used to indicate the point at which modern society shifted from being an industrial society to being an information society. No agreed-on date. (2) The reshaping of economic, social, political, and technical structures resulting from the teaming of people and computers.

Information richness. The concept that information can be rich or lean depending on the information delivery medium.

Information satisficing. The practice of decision-makers collecting enough information to make a satisfactory decision.

Information service. A business specializing in the collection and distribution of information.

Information society. A society structured around the principles of information as a commodity and as a strategic resource.

Information superhighway. The concept that every home and business will be connected electronically over a vast network of links to a wide variety of sources of information and entertainment.

Information system. A system that takes input, processes it, and produces information as output.

Information technology. A collective term for computer-and-communication hardware and system-and-application software.

Inheritance. In object-oriented programming, the passing along of certain behavior and structure from a class to its descendants. Inheritance allows new objects to be created from old ones.

INSERT. The SQL command for adding one or more rows to a table.

Instance. A particular occurrence of an entity.

Integrity constraints. Rules and procedures for maintaining data integrity.

Interfile clustering. Clustering is applied to records in several files.

Internal memory. Memory contained within a system.

Internal schema. A low-level description of a database. It specifies data types for fields and may indicate other physical details.

Internet. A worldwide network of computers and computer networks at private organizations, government institutions, and universities, over which people share files, send electronic messages, and have access to vast quantities of information.

Intersect. A relational algebra operation performed on two-union compatible tables, A and B, that results in a new table containing the rows that are in both A and B.

Intrafile clustering. Clustering is applied to records within a single file.

Inverted list. An alternative term for an index.

ISO. International Standards Organization.

Isolation. A preventive strategy that involves administrative procedures to insulate a physical database from destruction.

J

Join. A relational algebra operation on two tables, A and B, that produces a new table containing the concatenation of a row from A and a row from B where the rows in A and B satisfy a specified condition (e.g., column (a) of A 5 column (b) of B).

Journal. A file containing a record of database changes or transactions.

K

Key. A field in a file used to identify records for purposes of retrieval or sorting.

Kilobyte (kbyte). A unit of measure equal to 2^{10} or 1024 bytes.

Knowledge. The capacity to request, structure, and use information.

Knowledge base. The collection of facts, data, beliefs, assumptions, and heuristic methods about a problem area.

Knowledge work. A term used for occupations in which the primary activities involve receiving, processing, and transmitting information. Often called information work.

L

Layer. A level of detail of an OO model.

Legacy system. A system developed using prior technology that must be maintained because it still provides useful information or processes important business transactions.

Legal strategies. Externally imposed laws, rules, and regulations for maintaining data integrity.

LIKE. The SQL keyword preceding a description of characters to be searched for within a particular column (e.g., FNAME LIKE '%Fred%').

Linked list. A data storage structure that maintains relationships between records using pointers.

Local-area network (LAN). A communication channel along with interface circuitry that connects devices, such as computers or peripherals, within a limited geographical distance.

Locking. Allocating a particular database resource to a transaction or user.

Log. A file containing a record of database changes or transactions.

Logical record. A record that is defined according to its content or function.

Loop. A series of program instructions that is performed repeatedly until a specified condition is satisfied.

M

Magnetic disk. A direct access storage device that uses magnetization and demagnetization to store data on a magnetic surface.

Magnetic tape. A sequential access storage device that uses magnetization and demagnetization to store data on a magnetic surface.

Magneto-optical disk. A read-write optical disk.

Mainframe. A class of computer providing large storage capacity, high-speed processing, and complex data-handling capabilities.

Management information system (MIS). A system that gathers, condenses, and filters data until they become information, then makes them available on time and in a useful form for use in decision making at various levels of management within an organization.

Managerial work. A manager's typical behavior and activities when working.

Many-to-many recursive relationship. A relationship within a single entity in which one instance in the entity can be related to many instances in the same entity, and any instance receiving multiple relationships can itself be related to many instances in the same entity.

Many-to-many relationship. A relationship between two entities in which one instance in the first entity can be related to many instances in the second entity, and one instance in the second entity can be related to many instances in the first entity.

Mass storage. A high-capacity storage device that is typically slower than magnetic disk but less costly per megabyte.

Master file. A type of file that can be thought of as a relatively permanent collection of records.

Matrix organization. An organizational structure in which an employee reports to both a functional or divisional manager and to a project or group manager.

MAX. An SQL built-in function for determining the largest value in a column.

Megabyte (Mbyte). A unit of measure that is the equivalent of 10^6 bytes.

Member. A record type that is at the many side of a 1:m relationship in the CODASYL/DBTG model.

Memory. The component of a computer system that stores programs and data while waiting to be processed by the CPU. Also called primary storage.

Message passing. The method by which objects can communicate.

Method. A set of instructions attached to an object. Also known as a service.

Micro. (1) In precise measurement, a prefix meaning one millionth. (2) In inexact measurement, a prefix meaning small. (3) Short for microcomputer.

Microcomputer. A computer system based on a single-chip microprocessor as the central processing unit.

Microsecond. A measure of time equivalent to one-millionth (1/1,000,000) of a second.

Millisecond. A measure of time equivalent to one-thousandth (1/1,000) of a second.

MIN. An SQL built-in function for determining the smallest value in a column.

Minicomputer. A type of medium-sized computer introduced in the 1960s that provides lower-cost processing and storage capacities than the larger mainframe computers.

MIPS. An acronym for million instructions per second. Most often used as a unit of measure for comparing the processing speed of different computers.

Mirroring. The technique of writing identical copies of a record to each drive of a RAID unit.

MIS department. A department within an organization that helps people put information to work.

Multimedia. The combination of text with dynamic data types such as sound, animation, and video.

Multiprocessing. A computer system that uses two or more processors that share memory and input and output devices.

Multiprogramming. A computer system in which two or more programs are executed concurrently by one computer. In effect, the programs take turns running, usually giving the user the illusion of being the only user of the system.

Multitasking. A technique for concurrently executing tasks, or basic units of work performed by a program, on the same computer system. It is similar to multiprogramming, except the processor may be working on several portions of a program instead of several programs.

Multiuser. Systems that allow several users to share a computer's processor, memory, and mass storage simultaneously. Often characterized by systems with several terminals connected to a single central processor.

Multiuser database. A database that can be concurrently accessed by more than one person or transaction.

N

Nanosecond. A measure of time equivalent to one-billionth (1/1,000,000,000) of a second.

Natural join. A join from which one of the matching columns has been deleted.

Natural-language interface. An interface that allows the user to input simple English or other natural-language phrases in lieu of complex computer commands.

Network. An interconnected system of computers.

Network data model. A data model supporting network relationships.

Network model. A technique used in database systems to store data by combining records with a linked list of pointers.

Node. The term for a device, such as a terminal, computer, or disk drive, connected to a communication network.

Normal form. One or more rules for governing the structure of tables.

Normalization. The process of converting a table in low normal form to a higher normal form.

NOT. The SQL keyword to select the opposite of a condition (e.g., NOT EXISTS).

NOT EXISTS. The negative of EXISTS. It is used in a WHERE clause to test whether all rows in a table do not satisfy a specified condition. It returns the value *true* if there are no rows satisfying the condition; otherwise, it returns *false*.

Null. A value that may be unknown, not required, not applicable, undefined, or missing. It is *not* a blank or zero.

O

Object. A module that contains both data and instructions and can perform specific tasks. In software engineering, an object is an instance of a class or a logical grouping of objects.

Object class. A set of objects with a common structure.

Object code. Output from a compiler or an assembler that is linked with other code to produce executable machine-language code.

Object data language (ODL). A language for defining objects.

Object data model (ODM). A defined set of built-in types that is used to create and represent composite structures that mirror real-world objects.

Object identifier. An attribute used to uniquely identify an object.

Object Management Group (OMG). An industry group with the goal of creating and promulgating standards for OO technology and object interaction.

Object model. In database systems, data and instructions are combined into objects — modules that perform specific tasks when they are sent an appropriate message.

Object-orientation (OO). An approach to systems development, design, and programming based on object concepts.

Object-oriented Database Management System (ODBMS). Software that organizes, manipulates, and retrieves data stored in an object-oriented database.

Object-oriented programming. A technique in which the programmer breaks the problem into modules called objects, which contain both data and instructions and can perform specific tasks. The programmer then organizes the program around the collection of objects. An example is Smalltalk.

One-to-many (1:m) recursive relationship. A relationship within a single entity in which one instance in the entity can be related to many instances in the same entity, and any instance receiving multiple relationships is itself related to only one instance.

One-to-many (1:m) relationship. A relationship between two entities in which one instance in the first entity can be related to many instances in the second entity, and an instance in the second entity can be related to at most one instance in the first entity.

One-to-one (1:1) recursive relationship. A relationship within a single entity in which one instance in the entity can be related to at most one instance in the same entity, and an instance receiving a relationship can itself be related to at most one instance in the same entity.

One-to-one (1:1) relationship. A relationship between two entities in which one instance in the first entity can be related to at most one instance in the second entity, and an instance in the second entity is related to at most one instance in the first entity.

On-line analytical processing (OLAP). Analyzing business operations with the intention of making timely and accurate analysis-based decisions.

OO model. A graphical representation of objects in an application.

OO programming language (OOPL). A language that supports the OO concepts.

Optical disk. Disks that record and retrieve data using laser beams of light instead of magnetic methods. There are three types of optical disks: read only, also called CD-ROM; write once, which can be recorded on once by the end user; and erasable, which combines optical and magnetic techniques to record on the surface of the disk.

ORDER BY. The SQL clause for identifying columns on which to sort rows.

Organizational change. The adoption of a new idea or behavior by an organization.

Organizational memory. An organization's record of the details necessary for transacting business and making decisions.

Owner. A record that is at the one end of a 1:m relationship in CODASYL/DBTG database.

P

Page. A unit of disk storage.

Parent. A row on the one side of a 1:m relationship.

Parity. A bit, used for error checking, that is part of a binary code that indicates the number of 1's in the code.

Password. A unique, usually secret code used to identify users, which allows them to access a system. The system can be accessed by multiple users.

Performance monitoring. Collecting statistics on the performance of a system (e.g., number of transactions per minute).

Peripheral. A device that operates in conjunction with — but is not a part of — a computer, such as a printer, disk drive, or graphics tablet.

Persistent object. An object that exists between executions of a program.

Personal computer. A microcomputer usually targeted to the information processing needs of an individual, often called a microcomputer.

Petabyte (Pbyte). A unit of measure equivalent to 10^{15} bytes.

Physical file. The way in which the actual data in a database system are stored and accessed on a medium such as a disk.

Physical record. A record that is composed of one or more logical records.

Pointer. An address that specifies a storage location where data can be found.

Polymorphism. The capability to send a common message to objects of different types. Each object will respond with its own particular behavior.

Primary key. The candidate key selected as the unique identifier of a row in a table.

Product. A relational operation on two tables, A and B, that produces all possible combinations of the concatenation of a row from A and a row from B.

Project. A relational algebra operation that creates a new relation from some of the columns of an existing relation.

Project level database administration. Management and support of the development and use of a specific database system.

Protocol. A formal set of rules for specifying the format and relationships when exchanging information between communicating devices.

Prototyping. The process of building working models of a system's inputs, outputs, and files.

Public key encryption. An encryption system comprising public and private keys. The public key can be freely distributed because it is quite separate from the private key.

Q

Qualified name. The name of a column when it is prefixed by the name of the table in which it is found (e.g., STOCK.STKPRICE).

Query. A question or request for information.

Query by example (QBE). A fill-in-the-blanks approach to questioning a database. The user searches for information by filling out a query form on the display screen.

Query language. The capability to question a database or file of information without any knowledge of how or where the information is stored.

R

RAID. An acronym for a redundant array of inexpensive or independent drives. It uses a combination of mirroring and striping to give greater data protection.

RAM. An acronym for random-access memory. Its name comes from the method used to access information from the memory: random access. This means that it takes the same amount of time to access any one piece of information as it does another.

Random-access device. A device that can read and write information at any location on the device in the same amount of time, regardless of its physical location.

Random-access method. A method of accessing a file that allows a program to read or write any record in the file in the same amount of time without regard to its physical location.

Rapid application development. An approach to application development that stresses completion of a system in a short period.

Read-only optical disks. Optical disks that cannot be written on and so have the functional equivalency of read-only memory (ROM).

Record. A collection of related data treated as a unit (e.g., the payroll data about one person).

Recovery. The process of restoring a database to a consistent state.

Recursive relationship. A relationship within a single entity (e.g., a monarch is preceded by one other monarch).

Referential integrity constraint. The requirement that a foreign key cannot be defined unless its corresponding primary key exists.

Relation. A two-dimensional table in the formal terminology of relational databases.

Relational algebra. A set of high-level operators that operates on relations.

Relational database. A database consisting of relations or tables.

Relational Database Management System (RDBMS). Software that organizes, manipulates, and retrieves data stored in a relational database.

Relational model. A technique used in database systems in which one or more flat files or tables create relationships among the tables on the basis of a common field in each of the tables.

Relationally complete. A relational database management system that supports SQL but not domains or integrity rules.

Relationship. An association between entities or objects.

Relationship descriptor. A description of a relationship.

Remote job entry. The electronic submission of a program to be executed on a remote computer.

Replication. Maintaining copies of a database at several sites.

Request for proposal (RFP). A document sent to vendors seeking their response to a list of mandatory and optional capabilities and features.

Requirements planning. A broad term that includes planning for outputs, inputs, file/storage, and processing requirements. It also includes specifying any constraints and the costs and benefits associated with the system.

Resource Description Framework (RDF). A general framework for how to describe any Internet resource such as a Web site and its content.

Restrict. A relational algebra operation that creates a new relation from some of the rows of an existing relation. This operation is sometimes called select but should not be confused with the SQL SELECT statement.

REVOKE. An SQL command for removing privileges from a user or users.

ROLLBACK. An SQL command to reverse a set of temporary database changes.

Rollback. The process of recovering a database by applying before images to return the database to a consistent earlier state.

Roll forward. The process of recovering a database by applying after images to bring the database to a consistent state.

ROM. An acronym for read-only memory. A permanent memory whose contents can neither be erased nor written over—thus, the name, read-only memory.

Root. The top record or node in a tree.

Row. All columns in a table pertaining to the same instance of an entity (e.g., all the facts about a share).

S

Scalar function. A function operating on a single value (e.g., DAYS).

Scanner. A device that examines a pattern and converts it into a digital representation suitable for computer processing. Patterns then can be manipulated into a form suitable for the application.

Scenario. A typical event or sequence of events in the problem domain and the related behavior of the information system.

Search time. The time required to rotate the needed record under the read/write head of a magnetic disk.

Second normal form. A relation is in second normal form (2NF) if and only if it is in 1NF and all nonkey columns are dependent on the key.

Secondary index. In DL/I, an index on a data item other than the primary key.

Secondary storage. The component of a computer system in which programs and data are stored while not in use.

Sector. The smallest block of physical data that can be written to or read from a disk device.

Security. Precautions taken to ensure that data are protected from unauthorized use or modification.

Seek time. The time required to position the read/write head over the proper track on a magnetic disk.

Segment. In DL/I, a collection of fields that constitutes a node in a database record.

SELECT. The SQL command for retrieving rows from a database.

Sequence set. A single-index to the data in a file.

Sequential file. A file organization method that involves storing records in a predetermined sequence based on one or more key fields.

Server. A computer running software that fulfills requests from clients across a network.

Service. A set of instructions attached to an object. Also known as a method.

Servlet. A Java program that runs inside a Java-based Web server or Java applications server.

Set. A structure for representing a 1:m relationship in the CODASYL/DBTG model.

Set processing. The capability of a language to process multiple records at a time.

Shareable data. Data that can be readily accessed, not necessarily simultaneously, by more than one person.

Simple service. A standard service that most objects need to be able to perform (e.g., create).

Social memory. A society's record of the details necessary for maintaining itself.

Social network. A relationship between a group of people.

Software. Programs that control the functions of a computer system.

Sparse index. An index that does not contain an entry for every record. Also called a non-dense index.

Special register. In SQL, a built-in value (e.g., CURRENT DATE).

SQL (Structured query language). A query language that manipulates data in a relational database.

Standard operating procedures. The rules and procedures

for handling routine or common tasks.

Static model. A representation that shows what objects are capable of doing and remembering.

Storage device. A device (e.g., filing cabinet or hard disk) for storing data.

Storage medium. The material used for storing data (e.g., paper, magnetic film).

Storage structure. A formalized arrangement for storing data.

Strategy. A plan of action designed to cope with change, competition, and uncertainty.

Streaming tape. A form of magnetic tape that is specifically designed to store backup copies of disk files. Also called cartridge tape.

Striping. The technique of writing different parts of a record and parity data to different drives in a RAID unit.

Structured analysis. The examination of a complex problem by dividing it into simple functions.

Structured design. The process of designing the components of a computer program and their interrelationship in the best possible way.

Structured programming. The application of top-down design methods to programming.

Subclass. In a generalization/specialization hierarchy, an object that is a specialization of the generalization.

Subject. A cluster of objects. The subject layer reduces the overall complexity of an OO model.

Subordinate entity. An entity that stores data about an entity that varies among instances. It is used when an entity consists of mutually exclusive classes that have different descriptions.

Subquery. A query nested within another query.

Subroutine. A part of a program that can be executed repeatedly by a single statement.

SUM. An SQL built-in function for determining the sum of values in a numeric column.

Superclass. In a generalization/specialization hierarchy, the collection of objects that makes the generalization.

Supercomputers. The fastest computers made.

Synonym. A word that means the same as another word.

SYSCATALOG. In SQL, a catalog table containing a row for every base table or view in the database.

SYSCOLUMNS. In SQL, a catalog table containing a row for every column of every table in the database.

SYSINDEXES. In SQL, a catalog table containing a row for every index in the database.

System. (1) In general systems theory, a set or arrangement of parts acting together to perform a function. (2) In systems analysis, a network of interrelated procedures performed by people with the aid of tools or machines.

System level database administration. Management of issues applicable to the entire database environment and all databases managed within that environment.

System software. Programs or commands used to control the operation of the computer system.

Systems analysis. The process of understanding a user's needs and, from those needs, deriving the functional requirements of a system.

Systems development life cycle (SDLC). The stages of developing and maintaining a system.

T

Table. In relational database terminology, a table consists of rows and columns. Each row identifies a record, and each column corresponds to a field. Also called a relation.

Talk. An Internet service supporting real-time conversations. The Internet version of the telephone.

Tape drive. A device that stores data recorded on magnetic tape.

Technical strategies. Computer-based procedures designed to maintain data integrity.

Telnet. The main Internet protocol for connecting to a remote machine.

Temporary name. A name given to a table or view that remains current only for the duration of a query.

Terabyte (Tbyte). A unit of measure equivalent to 10^{12} bytes.

Terminal. A device that is used in communication systems to enter or receive data.

Text database. A collection of words such as articles in the *Wall Street Journal* or a series of legal abstracts. Text databases are stored either on-line or on CD-ROM and include the means to search through massive amounts of data to answer specific questions.

Third normal form. A relation is in third normal form (3NF) if and only if it is in second normal form and has no transitive dependencies.

Top-down approach. A technique used by systems analysts and software developers that refers to starting with the whole problem and developing more and more detail as the solution develops.

Track. A concentric circle on which data are stored on a disk.

Track density. The number of tracks per inch on a disk.

Transaction. An event about which data are recorded and processed, for example, a request for a seat on an airline flight.

Transaction file. A type of file in which records created during the input process are stored until needed for further processing.

Transaction processing. The processing of transactions.

Transitive dependency. The situation in a relation where if A determines B, and B determines C, then A determines C.

Transparent. A term used by computer designers to indicate a function of which the user is unaware.

Tree structure. A collection of records or other data structures in which the child has at most one parent.

Tuple. A row in a two-dimensional database.

U

Union. A relational algebra operation on two union-compatible relations A and B, where the new relation contains all rows that are in both A and B, with duplicate rows deleted.

Union compatible. The condition that two tables have the same number of columns and that values in corresponding columns are drawn from the same domain.

Unique key. A key that cannot have duplicate values.

UPDATE. The SQL command for updating one or more rows of a table.

Update. A term for the modification of records in a master file by replacing older information with more current information.

Use relationship. A communication relationship between objects.

User friendly. A term describing how easy a system or program is to learn and use and how gently it tolerates errors or mistakes on the part of the user.

User interface. That portion of a program that handles the human interaction with the program.

Userid. A person's user identification code.

V

Validation. The process of ensuring data quality.

Video conference. A conference held by means of one- or two-way interactive television.

View. A table constructed dynamically from operations on base tables. Also called a virtual table.

Voice data. A record of speech or sound.

Voice mail. A technology in which spoken messages are digitized, stored in computers, and later retrieved by the recipient.

Volatile file. A file in which a high percentage of records accessed are changed or records are added or deleted.

VSAM (Virtual Storage Access Method). IBM's implementation of the B-tree concept.

W

Weak entity. An entity that relies on another for its existence and identification. A dependent entity is indicated by a bar on its end of a relationship arc. Also known as a dependent entity.

Weakly typed language. A language in which the compiler or interpreter is not required to check the types of operands to ensure nonsensical operations are not performed.

Well-formed data model. A data model that clearly communicates information to the client. It obeys all the construction rules.

WHERE. The SQL keyword specifying the condition that the rows returned by a SELECT statement must satisfy.

Whole/part structure. An object structure in which one object is composed of others. Also known as a composition.

WIMP. Windows, icon, mouse, pointer.

Workflow. The manual or electronic flow of work between people.

Photo Credits

Chapter 1	page 9: Courtesy 3Com Corporation. page 20: Courtesy Environmental Systems Research, Inc. (ESRI). This map created using ESRI's ArcView GIS software.
Chapter 2	page 32: Courtesy Director General of Antiquities.
Chapter 11	page 338: Courtesy Connor Peripherals. Inc. page 339: Courtesy International Business Machines Inc. page 342: Courtesy Iomega Corp. page 343: Courtesy International Business Machines Inc.
Chapter 12	page 357: Courtesy Cray, Inc. page 358: Courtesy International Business Machines Inc.
Chapter 18	page 538: Courtesy International Business Machines Inc.

Index

J

K

L

M

S

T